The United States Literary Gazette
by Unknown

THE

·. UNITED STATES

LITERARY GAZETTE.

VOL. II.

APRIL 1, TO OCTOBER 1, 1825.

BOSTON:

CUMMINGS, HILLIARD, AND CO. NO. 134 WASHINGTON STREET.

1825.

THE UNITED STATES
LITERARY GAZETTE.

Vol. II.	APRIL 1, 1824.	No. 1.

INTRODUCTION.

WE present our readers THE UNITED STATES LITERARY GAZETTE in a new form. We think it is in many respects a more convenient form. When our Prospectus was laid before the public, it received, at once, that attention and approbation which they always bestow on a good design. Our design, as stated in that prospectus, is not changed. The success of the work is evidence, that it could not be changed with a hope of improvement. We shall, therefore, devote ourselves, zealously and perseveringly, to the attainment of the objects, which we then proposed. We shall occasionally offer our readers articles and intelligence upon some topics, which it was not in our mind to discuss when we commenced the work. But as to the future character of the Gazette, we make no promises. We shall therefore disappoint no hopes. We think it is right to merit the public approbation, and then we may with confidence expect it.　　　　EDITORS.

REVIEWS.

Greece in 1823 and 1824, being a Series of Letters and other Documents on the Greek Revolution, written during a visit to that country, by the Hon. Colonel Leicester Stanhope. To which is added, the Life of Mustapha Ali. Philadelphia. 1825. 8vo. pp. 308.

A LITTLE more than a year ago, the name of Greece was on every tongue in America. The newspapers, the magazines,

1

and the reviews echoed it from one to another.   In our cities, towns, and villages, meetings were held, and resolutions were passed; and, in some of them, (the last great proof of earnestness) money was subscribed.   Our pulpits took the alarm, and proclaimed to us the cause of Greece, as the cause of Christian liberty and truth; and, finally, on the floor of Congress, the subject was brought forward, in the most imposing form, by an individual whose name carries a sanction in it of all that he recommends; and in one of the most masterly speeches ever made, it was proved by him, that the liberation of Greece was of moment, of high moment, to the cause of political liberty in all countries.   He pointed out the dangerous language in which the crowned corporation in Europe, under the pretence of denouncing Grecian rebellion, in reality denounced the general cause of popular liberty; and he asked the representatives of the people to consider, whether, consistently with the neutral position and policy of this country, nothing could be done to encourage another free state struggling into being.

But by dint of much after speech-making, the conviction, which this most able appeal had wrought on the minds and hearts of all who heard or read it, was done away.   The question subsided in the house, and the interest taken in it subsided in the country; and had Greece herself subsided into her former quiet subjection to the Mahometan tyranny, we do not know that it could have excited much sensation here.   For the last twelve months, not to say the last twenty-four, it has been nearly impossible to get the public ear for any less dignified topic than General Jackson's traitorous recommendation of an union of parties, or Ninian Edwards' memorial.   Now that these momentous matters are awhile put to rest, the question may be said to recur upon the revolution of the Greeks.   How stands their cause ? Is there any rational probability that the Greeks will emancipate themselves ?

If there is, it is an important subject.   The Greeks, if they throw off the Turkish yoke, will become a free people.   This may seem rather a truism than a proposition of moment.   But it is not a truism.   We say, that, in all events, if the Greeks succeed in throwing off the Turkish yoke, another free state will be numbered among the nations of the earth.   Many persons think it is out of the question to establish a republican government in Greece; that the people in Greece are not ripe for it, that they are not prepared for liberty; and that if they were ripe for it, the Holy Alliance would not permit them to have a free government. We even read in the papers published by Colonel Stanhope, that many of the leading patriots in Greece, talk of a king; of a foreign king; of the son of the late crazy monarch of Sweden; of the Duke of Sussex. This may all be true, and yet it is not inconsistent with the proposition, that Greece may become a free state. We do not think monarchy so favourable to the highest degree of freedom as democracy; on the contrary, we consider monarchical institutions as totally inconsistent with the highest degree of liberty. But they are not inconsistent with some liberty,—with a good deal of liberty. There is liberty in France, in England, in Prussia; liberty worth having. Nay, though in a less degree, there is liberty in Austria and in Russia; not much political liberty, we grant, but liberty very important to private happiness. Property is secure from arbitrary and violent exaction, private justice is honestly administered, and even the growth of literature and science encouraged, when political questions are left untouched. We are now confessedly stating the bright side of things; not for the purpose of deception, but to meet the worst supposition of what would befal Greece, in the event of her throwing off the Turkish yoke. We think, in that event, even if the Turkish despotism should be succeeded by a monarchy in Greece, a monarchy upheld by the military power of the surrounding mighty states, that Greece might still be considered as a new free state, in whose appearance on the list of nations even we republicans ought to rejoice. It is certainly better that Greece should be governed by a christian king, and governed by laws, than by a lawless Mahometan tyrant. The government of Francis and Alexander, bad as it is,—and worse cannot be in a civilized christian country,—is better than the government of Ali Pacha or Sultan Mahmoud. If the Turkish government, instead of being on the verge of ruin, were as strong and menacing as in the days of the Amuraths and Mahomets,—if, instead of trembling in his seraglio, at Constantinople, the Sultan were storming the gates of Vienna, and the grand vizier landing an army in Otranto; if the Tartars were in Poland, and the Moors in Sicily and Spain, as of yore, we should all think this was much worse for the cause of liberty and humanity, than the present condition of those countries, bad as that is.

But we do not admit that it is a matter of necessity that the Greeks, if liberated from the Turkish yoke should of course come under a monarchical form of government. We have no doubt, that in 1776, the politicians of Europe speculated on the impossibility of establishing a republican form of government in America, much as they now speculate to the same purpose about Greece. We do not mean to say, that as good a foundation is laid in Greece as had been laid in America for representative and republican liberty. Nothing like it; and no zeal for the cause in foreign countries shall lead us so to disparage the character of our own. But there are, nevertheless, some circumstances in Greece highly favourable to the erection of a federal republican government. That country consists of numerous provinces, geographically separated from each other; not so remotely placed, nor so essentially disjoined, as to make it impossible to include them under a federal head: but yet marked out into states, by natural and historical peculiarities. This circumstance is in favour of a republican, and against a monarchical government. Again, nothing is more difficult than to set up a *new monarchy*. On the rock of this difficulty Bonaparte split. Prescription and antiquity are the pillars of monarchy now. Nobody talks at the present day of the divine right of kings; or, if they do, that divine right must be well made out by long rolls of parchment and ample wax seals. Of all Napoleon's new kings, not one, any more than himself, has survived the downfall of the portentous military power, by which he seated them on their thrones; with the single exception of Bernadotte, and time has not yet put the seal to his plebeian royalty. The kings of Saxony, of Wurtemburgh, of Bavaria, indeed remain; but they are the legitimate successors of the ducal and electoral houses of those countries; some of the oldest princely families in Europe. The Jeromes, and the Josephs, and the Louises, the Elizas and the Murats, the kingdoms of Westphalia and of Etruria, are vanished. Is the arm of the Holy Alliance longer and stronger than his, who set up these mushroom sovereignties? Suppose Russia and Austria were to set the son of Gustavus of Sweden on the throne of Greece? Where would he be in six months after the next war with England?—Very likely a crazed fanatic, making the pilgrimage of Jerusalem with his father. In the present state of knowledge and speculation on political subjects, when men meet together, the day before or the day after a great revolution, to renew or to erect the social compact, the idea of a monarchy is one of the last that enters their heads. There they stand, all equal, none privileged, with the physical and the political power in their hands. What shall they do with that power?—*Keep it in their own hands*, is the only answer that occurs to them. If their neighbours stand by, with overwhelming armies, and tell them they shall recall their old king, or they shall take a new one, they must, of course, for the moment, submit. But Greece presents a new case. The Spanish, the Neapolitan, the French process does not run against them. The Holy Alliance can grant no writ of *habeas corpus*, to bring up the body of an old king, and reinstate him on the Grecian throne. —No royal *mandamus* can go out, to replace the Paleologi, and Comnenas in the palace of Sparta or of Athens: there is no palace there; and a limitation of four centuries is certainly good against all the Porphyrogeniti.—Here there is a new case to be settled, not on *new* principles, but on *first* principles. If, indeed, the Duke of Brienne has a descendant; if the line of Baldwin is not extinct in France, a claim of legitimacy might be set up. But this, we suppose, will not be attempted; and the imposing of a foreign king, or the elevation of a domestic one to the throne of Greece, would be in violation of the principles of the Holy Alliance itself; which, we understand to be that the *legitimate* prince must reign; that the throne must be founded on a *historical* basis. If there is to be a king in Greece, it is much more likely that he will come in upon the original footing.

"Le premier qui fut roi, fut un soldat heureux."

It would be in the order of nature,* though not in the course of present probability, that Colocotroni or Ulysses should acquire a military *ascendancy* which might settle down into monarchical power. This, however, is not at all favoured by present appearances; and against this, there is no doubt the Holy Alliance would protest.

We think, therefore, from the best view we can take of the subject, that the probability is in favour of the erection of a free government in Greece; although, if a monarchy should be established there, we are unwilling to admit this ought to

---

* Somewhat as it was in the order of nature "*to encircle Mr Cushing's brows with a diadem*," which good Dr Johnson pronounced to be the object of the American patriots of the revolution.

cut the Greeks off from all sympathy on the part of the Americans.

In the next place, the cause of Greece is entitled to our sympathy, because, if the Turkish yoke is broken, and a government of laws is established, Greece will become a commercial state. This would be of great importance not merely to America, as a commercial nation, interested in the multiplication of markets for demand and supply, but it would be of great importance to the civilized world.

The Mediterranean sea, till the discovery of the passage about the Cape of Good Hope, was the field of the world's commerce. Hither its streams flowed from the distant tin mines of Britain, and the amber fisheries of Prussia in the west; and from the regions of silk, and pearl, and gold in the east. What countries could be better adapted to carry on this trade; to receive and distribute this commerce? The natural aptitude remains. The islands and numerous harbours of Greece and the Archipelago still exist. The face of the earth does not furnish many spots better adapted for the site of a great commercial capital, than the plain of Troy, or several of the Grecian islands near it. They do not even want that which has been mentioned as their chief defect, considered as a site for an emporium of trade, a great inland communication, by means of a navigable river. They stand at the mouth of one of the greatest river navigations in the world; in the present state of the world's population, probably the very greatest. Where do the melting glaciers, that constitute the Danube, while it can all be held in a cup, find their passage to the sea?—At the Dardanelles. Thither they flow, through Bavaria, the Tyrol, Austria, Hungary, Servia, Bulgaria, and Wallachia; and thither, if a free state were established at the mouth of the Hellespont, they would carry the productions of half the most fertile part of Germany. This alone would give to any city established there the command of a wider communication, than that which centres in New Orleans. But this is a small part only of the natural intercourse which might be opened with the Grecian Archipelago. All Poland northeast of the Carpathians, and three quarters of European Russia are drained by the rivers that flow into the Black Sea, of which the natural outlet is at the Dardanelles. We need not name the Dneister, the Bog, the Dneiper, the Don, and their tributaries; and greater than all, the Wolga, which, though it does not empty into the Black Sea, is destined by

nature to contribute a vast commerce toward that channel.
Ten years would not elapse after the establishment of a free
government in Greece, before a canal would be cut from
Sarepta on the Wolga (already an immense depot), to the
nearest point of the Don; and by this canal, not only would
a communication to the Grecian sea be opened with the commerce of the whole country drained by the Wolga, but to that
also which connects with the Caspian, and centres at Astrachan.
Pursue the circuit of the Euxine from the outlet of the Sea of
Azof, and the Kuban brings into it the produce of Georgia and
Caucasus; to this succeeds the southern shore of the Black
Sea, less known by its modern Turkish geography, than by
its ancient names of Armenia, Pontus, and Bithynia, the seat
of some of the richest states of the old world; then follow
Anatolia and Syria; Egypt, and the countries drained by the
Nile; the north of Africa, and the European coasts of the
Mediterranean, the Levant, and the Adriatic. These are the
regions, to whose commerce a free state in Greece would have
direct access; besides its proportionate share of the remoter
general commerce of the world, and the peculiar advantages
of an over-land trade with the East.

The growth of a state thus favourably situated for commerce
would be a direct benefit to every other commercial state.
Nothing is more true in commerce, than that the gain of one
is the gain of all. The advantages of commerce rest not on
the loss of the other party, but on the mutual benefit of both.
When population increases, in a free state, the customers of
all the other free states thereby increase. Where resources
multiply and develope themselves, in one country, the demand
for the commodities of every other country, and the means of
paying for them, are multiplied in equal proportion. There
is no danger of rivalry here. It is an advantage to have
rivals; for this leads to industry, frugality, and enterprise, and
these are the roads to prosperity and wealth. The English
statesmen in 1775, who were willing to foresee in America
the germ of another maritime and commercial power, fore-
boded injurious consequences to their own interests. Who
does not know that no event ever happened to England, which
has been more beneficial to her than our independence.

This, however, is a narrow view of the causes for sympa-
thizing with the Greeks, as a people destined to extend the
circuit of profitable commercial intercourse. Advanced
civilization is the first-born child of commerce. The erection

of a free state in Greece, connected with the civilized states of the earth by the bonds of a mutually beneficial trade, must be the first step towards the return of her ancient civilization to its primitive seats. Greece, Asia Minor, Syria,—are these the proper abodes of barbarity and despotism? Is it to be admitted as a fixed necessity of the political system of the modern world, that countries so well adapted by nature to be the habitation of man in the happiest condition consistent with human imperfection, should forever henceforth present the shocking spectacle which they now exhibit? And how is the change to be brought about? Gradually, no doubt; and in the application of those means which every where else have produced the desired effects,—the establishment of a government of laws, and the consequent security of property and growth of trade. Commerce is an instinct of our nature. Dr Smith would even make the *trucking* principle final and primitive in our constitutions. But there is one beyond it, from which it flows,—the love of happiness, and of the comforts enjoyments, and luxuries, which contribute, or are supposed to contribute, to our happiness. These, it is found, in the very first result of social experience, cannot be obtained without a government by laws, which shall afford security in the acquisition, possession, and transfer of the fruits of industry. Again, the acquisition of the means of supplying our wants and desires is promoted by various improvements in the arts and in knowledge: hence science is cultivated, and intellectual progress is made. Next, the opulence acquired, seeks, in the operation of other natural principles, to exhibit itself advantageously, and to win applause; and hence the patronage afforded, and the demand created, for the beautiful productions of the fine arts. Lastly, it is found that honesty, virtue, and law are the only rule, by which the immensely complicated interests that have grown up in this improved state of things, can be administered, and, therefore, moral principle is made, in all things, to be the guide and arbitress of private and public action. We state this only as the natural progress of civilization; to which partial exceptions, greater or less, exist in different civilized countries; but to which also the condition of all such countries more or less conforms.

[*To be concluded in our next.*]

Outlines of the Principal Events in the Life of General Lafayette.
                Boston.   1825.   8vo.   pp. 64.

THIS memoir was first published in the North American Review.   The author, Mr George Ticknor, one of the Professors in Harvard University, has since corrected it in some of its facts, and enlarged it by the addition of others.   It is now published in the form of a pamphlet, and it comes before the the public with a degree of authenticity, on which they may safely rely.   The memoir is peculiarly acceptable to the "American people," at the present time, and in its present form;—at the present time, because the whole nation have felt deeply, and do still feel deeply, the presence of their illustrious benefactor;—in its present form, because all wish to learn the interesting facts of his life from an authentic source; and many will now have an opportunity to learn them, who otherwise might not.   We may add, morever, that this simple narrative of the principal events in the life of General Lafayette is the more grateful to us, because it presents him in some of the most interesting and trying situations, which he has been called to sustain.   And no man has passed through more reverses of fortune, and been called, in the course of them, to sustain more important relations, in the most critical times, than General Lafayette.   Is is more grateful still, because it places his character, as connected with some of the most important events of the age, in so many attitudes, and in such strong relief,—all consistent with each other, and all conspiring to bring home the conviction and the sanction of reason, to feelings which before existed.

    These "Outlines," as the title purports, embrace only a part of the facts and events in the life of General Lafayette. But they are some of the most interesting and important.   We cannot give our readers an analysis of the pamphlet, because the subject does not admit of analysis.   It is a narrative of facts, and a description of events.   And we could not relate the one, or describe the other, in fewer words than have been used in the book.   Without attempting, therefore, to trace the same outlines which Mr Ticknor has traced, or to fill up those outlines with collateral information and reflections of our own, we shall select a few of the most striking and important events described in the pamphlet, and give them to our readers in Mr Ticknor's own words.

                2

Many yet live who remember, and all know from history, the desponding situation of the American colonies in 1777. It was at this critical time, that Lafayette first arrived in our country.

The sensation produced by his appearance in this country was, of course, much greater than that produced in Europe by his departure. It still stands forth, as one of the most prominent and important circumstances in our revolutionary contest; and, as has often been said by one who bore no small part in its trials and success, none but those who were then alive, can believe what an impulse it gave to the hopes of a population almost disheartened by a long series of disasters. And well it might; for it taught us, that in the first rank of the first nobility in Europe, men could still be found, who not only took an interest in our struggle, but were willing to share our sufferings; that our obscure and almost desperate contest for freedom in a remote quarter of the world, could yet find supporters among those, who were the most natural and powerful allies of a splendid despotism; that we were the objects of a regard and interest throughout the world, which would add to our own resources sufficient strength to carry us safely through to final success.

After the American revolution had terminated so successfully to the cause and the principles, which Lafayette had so zealously and efficiently espoused, he returned to France, and was soon called to witness the terrible paroxysms of that nation during the French revolution. But the French *people* had neither the intelligence nor the virtue of the American *people*. And the same degree of liberty, which was a blessing to the latter, would have been the greatest curse to the former. Liberty can never precede knowledge and virtue in the people, but it must and *will* follow them. The influence of Lafayette, therefore, though he was then, as he is now, considered the very Apostle of Liberty, was frequently felt on the side of the crown, bracing and strengthening it against the too violent encroachments of the people. The following extract from Mr Ticknor's memoir will show the part which he was frequently called to sustain during the French revolution, and the manner in which he sustained it. It describes the attack of the populace upon the royal family, at Versailles, on the night of the fifth of October, 1789.

He [Lafayette] arrived at Versailles at ten o'clock at night, after having been on horseback from before daylight in the morning, and and having made, during the whole interval, both at Paris and on the road, incredible exertions to control the multitude and calm the soldiers. ' The Marquis de Lafayette at last entered the château,' says Madame de Staël, ' and passing through the apartment where we were, went to the king. We all pressed round him, as if he were the master of events, and yet the popular party was already more powerful than its chief, and principles were yielding to factions, or rather were beginning to serve only as their pretexts. M. de Lafayette's manner was perfectly calm; nobody ever saw it otherwise; but his delicacy suffered from the importance of the part he was called to act. He asked for the interior posts of the château, in order that he might ensure their safety. Only the outer posts were granted to him.' This refusal was not disrespectful to him who made the request. It was given, simply because the etiquette of the court reserved the guard of the royal person and family to another body of men. Lafayette, therefore, answered for the National Guards, and for the posts committed to them; but he could answer for no more; and his pledge was faithfully and desperately redeemed.

Between two and three o'clock, the queen and the royal family went to bed. Lafayette, too, slept after the great fatigues of this fearful day. At half past four, a portion of the populace made their way into the palace by an obscure, interior passage, which had been overlooked, and which was not in that part of the château entrusted to Lafayette. They were evidently led by persons who well knew the secret avenues. Mirabeau's name was afterwards strangely compromised in it, and the form of the infamous Duke of Orleans was repeatedly recognized on the great staircase, pointing the assassins the way to the queen's chamber. They easily found it. Two of her guards were cut down in an instant; and she made her escape almost naked. Lafayette immediately rushed in with the national troops, protected the guards from the brutal populace, and saved the lives of the royal family, which had so nearly been sacrificed to the etiquette of the monarchy.

The day dawned as this fearful scene of guilt and bloodshed was passing in the magnificent palace, whose construction had exhausted the revenues of Louis Fourteenth, and which, for a century, had been the most splendid residence in Europe. As soon as it was light, the same furious multitude filled the vast space, which, from the rich materials of which it is formed, passes under the name of the court of marble. They called upon the king, in tones not to be mistaken, to go to Paris; and they called for the queen, who had but just escaped from their daggers, to come out upon the balcony. The king, after a short consultation with his ministers, announced his intention to set out for the capital; but Lafayette was afraid to trust the queen in the midst of the bloodthirsty multitude. He went to her, therefore, with respectful hesitation, and asked her if it were her purpose to accompany the king to Paris. 'Yes,' she replied, 'although I am aware of the danger.' 'Are you positively determined?' 'Yes, sir.' 'Condescend, then, to go out upon the balcony, and suffer me to attend you.' 'Without the king?' she replied, hesitating—'Have you observed the threats?' 'Yes, Madam, I have; but dare to trust me.' He led her out upon the balcony. It was a moment of great responsibility and great delicacy; but nothing, he felt assured, could be so dangerous as to permit her to set out for Paris, surrounded by that multitude, unless its feelings could be changed. The agitation, the tumult, the cries of the crowd rendered it impossible that his voice should be heard. It was necessary, therefore, to address himself to the eye, and, turning towards the queen, with that admirable presence of mind, which never yet forsook him, and with that mingled grace and dignity, which were the peculiar inheritance of the ancient court of France, he simply kissed her hand before the vast multitude. An instant of silent astonish ment followed, but the whole was immediately interpreted, and the air was rent with cries of ' Long live the queen !' ' Long live the general !' from the same fickle and cruel populace, that only two hours before had embrued their hands in the blood of the guards who defended the life of this same queen.

The attempt to rescue Lafayette from the prison at Olmütz is so interesting in itself, and so beautifully described, we can hardly forbear quoting it entire. But we have only room to say, what most of our readers probably knew before, the attempt proved unsuccessful, and both Lafayette and his romantic deliverers were soon retaken, and all confined in prison, where they suffered the more severely from the increased vigilance of their keepers. After five years' imprisonment at Olmütz, Lafayette was liberated, and returned again to France. He lived in retirement till those critical times came on, which resulted in the abdication of Bonaparte, after the battle of Waterloo. He then took part again in the public counsels. There are periods in the history of every nation, when its destinies seem to be suspended in a trembling balance. A word, a look, or a gesture, at such times, may decide the fate of nations. Of these perilous and portentous moments, France has witnessed more than any other nation for the last fifty years. We insert a description of one, in which Lafayette was conspicuous, and in which, considering the time,—the place,—the occasion,—and the consequences that were to follow from one or another decision, there is a moral sublimity hardly surpassed by any thing in history. The *time* was when Bonaparte returned from Waterloo, "a defeated and desperate man;" the *place* was the Chamber of Representatives of thirty millions of French people ; the *occasion* was a resolution offered by Lafayette, declaring the chamber to be in permanent session, and all attempts to dissolve it, high treason ; and also calling for the four principal ministers to come to the chamber, and explain the state of affairs; the *consequences* involved, were the existence of the French nation, and the happiness of the French people.

As soon, therefore, as the session was opened, Lafayette, with the same clear courage and in the same spirit of self-devotion, with which he had stood at the bar of the National Assembly in 1792, immediately ascended the Tribune for the first time for twenty years, and said these few words, which assuredly would have been his death warrant, if he had not been supported in them by the assembly he addressed : ' When, after an interval of many years, I raise a voice which the friends of free institutions will still recognise, I feel myself called upon to speak

to you only of the dangers of the country, which you alone have now
the power to save. Sinister intimations have been heard; they are
unfortunately confirmed. This, therefore, is the moment for us to gather
round the ancient tricolored standard; the standard of '89; the standard of freedom, of equal rights, and of public order. Permit then, gentlemen, a veteran in this sacred cause, one who has always been a
stranger to the spirit of faction, to offer you a few preparatory resolutions, whose absolute necessity, I trust, you will feel, as I do.'

The resolutions were adopted. Lucien Bonaparte came
to the chamber, and attempted to explain "the state of
affairs; but at length appealed to the *feelings* of the members.

'It is not Napoleon,' he cried, 'that is attacked, it is the French people. And a proposition is now made to this people, to abandon their
Emperor; to expose the French nation, before the tribunal of the
world, to a severe judgment on its levity and inconstancy. No, sir, the
honour of this nation shall never be so compromised!' On hearing
these words, Lafayette rose. He did not go to the tribune; but spoke,
contrary to rule and custom, from his place. His manner was perfectly
calm, but marked with the very spirit of rebuke; and he addressed
himself, not to the President, but directly to Lucien. 'The assertion,
which has just been uttered, is a calumny. Who shall dare to accuse
the French nation of inconstancy to the Emperor Napoleon? That nation has followed his bloody footsteps through the sands of Egypt and
through the wastes of Russia; over fifty fields of battle; in disaster as
faithful as in victory; and it is for having thus devotedly followed him,
that we now mourn the blood of three millions of Frenchmen.' These
few words made an impression on the Assembly, which could not be
mistaken or resisted; and, as Lafayette ended, Lucien himself bowed
respectfully to him, and, without resuming his speech, sat down.

The memoir of Lafayette, from which we have already
made such copious extracts, closes with a passage, in which
the principal events in his life are again alluded to, in a manner expressing the feelings of this whole people. Those
events could not have been alluded to, and the feelings of the
nation expressed in connexion with them, more happily than
in the following passage.

This is the distinguished personage, who, after an absence of eight
and thirty years, is now come to visit the nation, for whose independence and freedom he hazarded whatever is most valued in human estimation, almost half a century ago. He comes, too, at the express invitation of the entire people; he is literally the 'Guest of the Nation;'
but the guest, it should be remembered, of another generation, than the
one he originally came to serve. We rejoice at it. We rejoice, in
common with the thousands who throng his steps wherever he passes,
that we are permitted to offer this tribute of a gratitude and veneration,
which cannot be misinterpreted, to one, who suffered with our fathers
for our sake; but we rejoice yet more for the moral effect it cannot fail
to produce on us, both as individuals and as a people. For it is no com-

mon spectacle, which is now placed before *each of us* for our instruction. We are permitted to see one, who, by the mere force of principle, by plain and resolved integrity, has passed with perfect consistency, through more remarkable extremes of fortune, than any man now alive, or, perhaps any man on record. We are permitted to see one who has borne a leading and controlling part in two hemispheres, and in the two most important revolutions the world has yet seen, and has come forth from both of them without the touch of dishonour. We are permitted to see that man, who first put in jeopardy his rank and fortune at home, in order to serve as a volunteer in the cause of Free Institutions in America, and afterwards hazarded his life at the bar of the National Assembly, to arrest the same cause when it was tending to excess and violence. We are permitted to see the man, who, after three years of unbroken political triumph, stood in the midst of half a million of his countrymen, comprehending whatever was great, wise, and powerful in the nation, with the *oriflamme* of the monarchy at his feet, and the confidence of all France following his words, as he swore in their behalf to a free constitution; and yet remained undazzled and unseduced by his vast, his irresistible popularity. We are permitted to see the man, who, for the sake of the same principles to which he had thus sworn, and in less than three years afterwards, was condemned to such obscure sufferings, that his very existence became doubtful to the world, and the place of his confinement was effectually hidden from the inquiries of his friends, who sent emissaries over half Europe to discover it; and yet remained unshaken and undismayed, constantly refusing all appearance of compromise with his persecutors and oppressors. We are, in short, permitted to see a man, who has professed, amidst glory and suffering, in triumph and in disgrace, the same principles of political freedom on both sides of the Atlantic; who has maintained the same tone, the same air, the same open confidence, amidst the ruins of the Bastille, in the Champ de Mars, under the despotism of Bonaparte, and in the dungeons of Olmütz.

We rejoice, too, no less in the effect which this visit of General Lafayette is producing upon us *as a nation*. It is doing much to unite us. It has brought those together, who have been separated by long lives of political animosity. It helps to break down the great boundaries and landmarks of party. It makes a holiday of kind and generous feelings in the hearts of the multitudes that throng his way, as he moves in triumphal procession from city to city. It turns this whole people from the bustle and divisions of our wearisome elections, the contests of the senatehouse, and the troubles and bitterness of our manifold political dissensions; and instead of all this, carries us back to that great period in our history, about which opinions have long been tranquil and settled. It offers to us, as it were, with the very costume and air appropriate to the times, one of the great actors, from this most solemn passage in our national destinies; and thus enables us to transmit yet one generation further onward, a sensible impression of the times of our fathers; since we are not only permitted to witness ourselves one of their foremost leaders and champions, but can show him to our children, and thus leave in their young hearts an impression, which will grow old there with their deepest and purest feelings. It brings, in fact, our revolution nearer to us, with all the highminded patriotism and selfdenying virtues of our forefathers; and therefore naturally turns our thoughts more towards our posterity, and makes us more anxious to do for them what we are so sensibly reminded was done with such perilous sacrifices for us.

All the events in this interesting memoir, are described in a chaste and elegant style. Mr. Ticknor has told the story of the life of Lafayette with a simplicity of manner, which leaves the reader his whole mind to contemplate the character of a great man, and his whole heart to admire the virtues of a good man. And we are sure, he will always receive the thanks of his readers, for not attempting to divert their attention, or share their admiration. General Lafayette has passed a long life of trials and of sufferings. He has been tried, and has suffered the full measure which human nature can bear. But if a good man ever enjoys his reward this side of Heaven, Lafayette has now that reward in a most eminent degree, in the gratitude of a numerous, enlightened, and free people.

John Bull in America; or the New Munchausen. *New York,* 1825. 12mo. pp. 226.

In our remarks upon this work, we propose to depart from our usual custom of instructing and delighting our readers with a preliminary disquisition on the subject in general. We shall rather let the author take precedence of the critic, and without further circumlocution, allow him to speak for himself as follows.

On the fifth day of August, 1824, a rather genteel looking stranger arrived at the Mansion Hotel in the city of Washington, where he inquired for a retired room, and expressed his intention of staying some time. He was dressed in a blue frock, striped vest, and gray pantaloons; was about five feet ten, as is supposed, and had a nose like a potato. The evening of the following day there arrived in the stage from Baltimore, a little mahogany-faced foreigner, a Frenchman as it would seem, with gold rings in his ears, and a pair of dimity breeches. The little man in dimity breeches expressed great pleasure at meeting the stranger, with whom he seemed to be well acquainted; but the stranger appeared much agitated at the rencontre, and displayed nothing like satisfaction on the occasion. With the evident intention of avoiding the little dark-complexioned man, he, in a few minutes, desired the waiter to show him into his room, to which he retired without bidding the other good night.

It appears from the testimony of the waiter, that on going into his chamber, and observing a portmanteau, which had been placed there in his absence, the stranger inquired to whom it belonged.   The waiter replied : ' To the French gentleman.   As you seemed to be old acquaintance, I thought you would like to be together, sir.''   This information seemed to cause great agitation in the mind of the stranger, who exclaimed, as if unconscious of the presence of the waiter, " I am a lost man !'' which the waiter thought rather particular.   The stranger, after a few moments' apparent perplexity, ordered the waiter to bring him pen, ink, paper, and sealing-wax and then desired to be left alone. It is recollected that the dark-complexioned foreigner retired about ten, requesting to be called up at four o'clock, as he was going on in the stage to the south.   This is the last that was seen, either of the stranger, or the dark-complexioned foreigner.   On knocking at the door precisely at four o'clock the next morning, and no answer being given, the waiter made bold to enter the room, which to his surprise he found entirely empty.   Neither trunks, nor stranger, nor dark-complexioned foreigner, were to be found.   Had the stranger and his friend previously run up a long score at the Mansion Hotel, their disappearance would not have excited any extraordinary degree of surprise.   But the stranger was indebted but for two days' board and lodging, and the dark-complexioned foreigner had paid his bill over night.   A person who slept in the next room, recollected hearing a stir in that of the stranger, as he thinks, about three o'clock, but supposing it to be some one going off in the mail, it excited no particular observation.''

The reader needs no ghost to tell him, that the gentleman in the blue frock &c. left a manuscript. This turns out to be an account of travels in America, by an Englishman, whom the author, or according to the courtesy of Utopia, the editor, imagines to be one of the writers in the Quarterly. He favors the public with sundry weighty reasons for supposing him to be the reviewer of the " Memorable Days of Wiliam Faux,'' the gentleman from Somersham. From the style of this preface, we formed high expectations of the work. We expected to find in it, a lively representation of Mr. Bull, as he occasionally appears among us with his London broadcloth, *Brummagem* dignity, and talent for silence. We anticipated great amusement from a full length picture of him, as he marches through our republic, listening, with the gravity of a hogshead, to all the queer inventions, which the waggish natives are pleased to palm upon him, mentally comparing the contemptible tinkle of every village cow-bell with the sounding honours of Bow, and growling inarticulate indignation at beef-steaks which have no relish of sulphur.

The writer of this book has taken a course a little different, having contented himself with a kind of parody of the romances of Faux, Fearon, and others, who have *come over*

the good people of their native island, with an occasional
octavo volume, to the great comfort and exultation of the
gulls, and the proportional improvement of their own temporal concerns.

Though our expectations were somewhat disappointed by
this method of proceeding, we have nevertheless derived
much amusement from these Travels, and if the author be,
as we suspect, a gentleman, whose name is familiar to the
lovers of humor, he deserves to touch something more solid
than the pension of moonshine, which Mr Faux so liberally
bestowed on him, for his patriotic labours in tickling his
countrymen at the expense of Mr Bull.

We proceed to give some account of the doings and sayings of our traveller.   He sails in a British brig for Boston,
on his way to New Orleans, which would not occur to every
one as the most direct route.   But he was probably of opinion with an emigrant of whom we recollect to have heard,
that to hit somewhere upon the broadside of America, was as
much as could come within the compass of reasonable expectation.   Notwithstanding the favourable opinions, which he
entertained concerning America, he finds, in the very outset,
much that disgusts him with the state of society.   The great
proportion and cruel treatment of the slaves in Boston, excite
the most distressing feelings in his mind, as indeed they must
in that of any person, who has ever witnessed them.   He is
informed by Governor Hancock, of many instances of this
barbarity, beside what he himself has occasion to observe.
The weakness and credulity of the people, who swallow with
avidity the absurd witch-stories of their most popular living
author, the Rev. Cotton Mather, astonish him, although he
was of course prepared for much ignorance and its concomi-
tant, superstition.

From Boston our traveller crosses the Potomac to Charleston, South Carolina, where he has an opportunity of dining
with Judge D———, whom, by the way, he had lately observed in the street, " amusing himself with the *niggers*." He tells
us that

The dinner was, in the main, good enough. That is to say, there
was a plenty of things naturally good, but what was very remarkable,
it was brought up in wooden dishes, out of which they all helped themselves with their fingers, knives and forks not being in use in America, except among a few English people.   There was a very suspicious
dish on the table, which they called terrapin soup, in which I observed what had exactly the appearance of the fingers and toes of little

3

negroes. I afterwards learned that this was exactly the case, and that terrapin is the cant name for black children, as papoose is for those of the Indians. During the desert, an unlucky slave happened to let fall a knife to which he was helping his mistress, who snatched it up in a great passion and gave him a deep gash in the face. I dropped my knife and fork in astonishment, but nobody else seemed to notice this horrible incident.

We have not room to notice many of the observations on this, or indeed any other city, through which the gentleman in gray pantaloons has occasion to pass in his way to New Orleans. We shall only endeavour to give something like a general sketch of his route, with a few of its more remarkable circumstances. From Charleston, he proceeds to Portsmouth, New Hampshire, in the "stage." We suspect here either an error of the press, or of some careless transcriber. We think it must have been originally written "coach," "mail coach," or "stage coach;" since it is scarcely in character for our journalist to be guilty of a Yankee-ism so soon after his arrival. But let that pass. In the stage then, or the coach, he goes, with a driver, drunk of course, who is a member of Congress, judge, colonel, justice, deacon, constable, and jailer. During this jaunt, he is introduced to the little Frenchman, alluded to in the preface. It will be seen by the following extracts, that Monsieur himself had some notion for grumbling at the customs of the country, and truly we admit that his complaint was not without foundation.

"Diable!" exclaimed the little Frenchman in broken English; "these democrat yankees have as many offices as their citizen hogs have hind legs." "Why, how many legs have our citizen hogs, as you call them, Monsieur?" replied the communicative passenger. "Why, eight at least," said the other, "or they could never furnish the millions of hams which I see every where. Diable! I have breakfasted upon ham—dined upon ham—and supped upon ham, every day since I arrived in this country. Yes, sir, it is certain your pigs must have at least eight hams a piece;" upon which he politely offered me a pinch of snuff, which I refused with cold dignity. If I know myse Ihave no national prejudices; but I do hate Frenchmen.

He witnesses in Portsmouth the following shocking catastrophe.

It seems a fellow of the name of Ramsbottom, a man-milliner by trade, and a roaring patriot, had taken offence at a neighbour, whose name was Higginbottom, because his wife had attempted to cheapen a crimped tucker, and afterwards reported that he sold his articles much dearer than his rival man-milliner over the way, whose name was Winterbottom, and whose next door neighbour, one Oddy, was Winterbottom's particular friend. In the pure spirit of democracy, Ramsbottom determined to dirk not only Higginbottom and his wife, and Winterbottom, and Oddy, and their wives; but all the young Higginbottoms, Winterbottoms, Oddys, and little Oddities. It was some years before Ramsbottom could get them all together, so as to make one job of it. At last he collected the whole party at his own house, to spend their Christmas eve, and determined to execute his diabolical purpose. It appears, however, from what followed, that he had previously changed his mind as to the dirking, probably because it was too much trouble, (for these democrats hate trouble above all things.) Just as they were up to the eyes in a Christmas pye, the explosion took place, which I had just heard, and the whole party, Ramsbottom, Higginbottom, Winterbottom, and Oddy, together with their wives, and all the little Ramsbottoms, Winterbottoms, Higginbottoms, Oddys, and Oddities, were all blown into such small atoms, that not a vestige of them was to be found. I saw their bodies afterwards, all terribly mangled and torn to pieces. Such is the intense and never-dying spirit of vengeance, generated by the turbulent spirit of democracy, that the desperado, Ramsbottom, it appears, did not scruple, like the republican Sampson of old, to pull down destruction on himself, that he might be revenged on his enemies.

At Portsmouth our traveller accidentally discovers, that he is rather out of the direct route to New Orleans, and begins to entertain some suspicion that he has not yet reached Charleston, South Carolina. He accordingly retraces his steps, delaying his outset for one day, for the purpose of avoiding the Frenchman, whom he suspects of a design upon his purse. But fate decreed that his precaution should be vain. Being obliged to set out before daylight, for the greater convenience of highwaymen and pickpockets, he had no opportunity of reconnoitring his companions. While riding with his hands in his pockets, with the ingenious intention of baffling every furtive attempt, he tells us, that

A sudden jolt of the jarvie brought my head in full contact with the back of a passenger on the seat before me. 'Diable!' exclaimed a voice which seemed to be familiar to me, and then all was silent again. Not long after, there exploded a sneeze, which shook the whole vehicle. 'My G—d!' ejaculated I, 'I'm sure I've heard that sneeze before; it must be my little Frenchman!'—But there was no help for it now, and I determined to keep him at an awful distance.

The unusual and somewhat awkward posture already alluded to, being continued, even after daylight appeared, excited some remark among the inmates of the leathern conveniency.

'He must have his pockets full of guineas,' said the little Frenchman in a whisper, winking at the same time at the communicative traveller. I understood all this perfectly, and when we stopped to dine, managed to exhibit a neat pair of hair triggers to these two worthies, who exchanged very significant looks thereupon. 'It won't do,' observed one to the other, in a desponding tone.

The hair triggers do good service.   The following night he is near vacating half a dozen offices, civil, military, and religious, by "letting fly" at the driver abovementioned, as he is groping his way to the kitchen fire, by which our hero had undauntedly stood guard, during the whole night, over himself and baggage, with the "barkers" ready cocked and primed. Luckily coachy dodged, like a king-bird, at the flash, and the matter was hushed up by a pint of whiskey.

Having arrived again in safety at Boston, and staid three days to give the Frenchman and the banditti a fair start, he once more sets forward in the "stage," and pursues his journey through the states of Ohio, Alabama, and Connecticut. In this last state, in "the very centre," as he observes, "of steady habits," he is thus assaulted.

Although it was Sunday, (a sufficient reason for deterring any christian highwayman), we were stopped by a footpad, who demanded money with as little compunction as a be-wolf.   Upon my showing my pistols, however, he sheered off, and the driver whipping up his horses at the moment, we luckily escaped this time.   The incident of a single footpad attempting thus to rob a whole stage load of people, furnishes another proof of the fact, that stage-drivers and stage-owners, not to say a majority of stage-passengers, are accomplices of these bands of robbers. Had it not been for my pistols, we should all have been robbed to a certainty, and most probably the rest of the passengers would have shared my spoils.   What exhibits the turbulence and impious spirit of democracy in all its turpitude, is the fact, that the driver, after getting fairly out of sight, turned round to the passengers with a grin, and exclaimed, ' I guess I've distanced the deacon.'   So that this footpad was one of the pillars of the church !

"What must be the priest," might our traveller exclaim, "where a monkey is the god? What must be the congregation of a church, when the heads of it are footpads, and what must be the dissolute habits of a country, when the steady ones are Sabbath-breaking and highway robbery?"   This incident, to speak more seriously, is such a one as might easily have happened to an Englishman in Massachusetts, if not in Connecticut, a few years since, and we wonder that a similar story has never figured, with appropriate remarks, on the pages of those amusing writers, whom we mentioned, about the commencement of this article, and who are evidently much better acquainted with the nature of tithes, than of tithingmen.

But we are losing sight of our unfortunate hero, whom we shall now again permit to tell his own story, taking the liberty to omit a few sentences, which we think less interesting.

About five in the afternoon we arrivèd at Bellows Falls, at the mouth of the Ohio, where I embarked in the steam-boat for New York. These steam-boats, all the world knows, were invented by Isaac Watts, who wrote the book of psalms. Yet the spirit of democracy, as usual, has claimed the honour for one Moulton, or Fulton, I forget which; although it is a notorious fact, that Isaac Watts died before Fulton was born. This settles the question. But there is no stopping the mouth of a genuine democrat." * * *

While sitting in a state of indolent and contemptuous abstraction, with my back to as many of the company as possible, I was roused by a sneeze, that I could have sworn to in any part of the world. "It is the c——d little Frenchman! Here's Monsieur Tonson come again!" I would as soon have heard the last trumpet as this infernal explosion. In a few minutes he espied me, and coming up with the most provoking expression of old acquaintanceship, offered me a pinch of snuff—"Ah! Monsieur, I am happy! Diable!—my friend and I thought we had lost our agreeable companion. * * * You don't know how we have missed your agreeable society. Diable! we have not had a good laugh since we parted. * * *

Towards evening the boat stopped at a place called the city of Annapolis. * * * As we approached the wharf, I was standing among a coil of ropes, with my back towards the great city, when one of those sticklers for equality, in a red flannel shirt came up and desired me to move out of the way. The fellow was civil enough, for that matter, but I only answered his impertinent intrusion with a look of withering contempt.—Upon this, he gathered a part of the rope in coils, in his right hand, and when we were ten or a dozen yards from the wharf, threw it with all his force, with a design to knock a person down, who stood there. But the chap was too dexterous for him, and caught the end of the rope in his hands, which he immediately fastened to a post. The whole brunt of this Yankee joke fell upon me, for my feet being entangled in the end of the rope thus thrown, it tripped up my heels and laid me sprawling on the deck. The little Frenchman officiously helped me up, and offered me a pinch of snuff, by way of comfort; but as for the democratic gentry, they seemed rather to enjoy the thing, and if the truth was known, I dare say were at the bottom of the joke.

On the following night the grand attempt, as our author supposes, was made on his person and property by the artful Frenchman; but in vain. Neither the hair-triggers nor their master were asleep, and Monsieur narrowly escaped with his life. The man of snuff and compliments endeavours to explain the mistake which occasioned the catastrophe, but Mr Bull feels satisfied that nothing but powder and ball saved him from murder and robbery.

Having thus far accompanied our traveller, we begin to perceive, that our limits will not allow such close attendance to the time of his mysterious disappearance. We can only notice a few things, which occurred to us as most remarkable. Among these, is the following account of the Indian summer.

Such is the extent of this practice of smoking tobacco, that at a certain period of the year, during the autumn, when the people of the country have finished gathering in the products of their fields, and their leisure time comes, they commence a smoking festival, in which every man, woman, and child partakes. These festivals last five or six weeks, during which time the atmosphere throughout the whole extent of the country becomes so hazy, and obscure, that they are obliged to burn candles all day, and a perpetual drizzle prevails, owing to the unseemly habit of spitting, which all our English travellers have heretofore noticed among these immaculate republicans. This season is called the Indian summer.

It will be seen by the following quotation, that Mr Faux gives a different account of this matter.

The season called the *Indian Summer*, which here commences in October, by a dark blue, hazy atmosphere, is caused by millions of acres, for thousands of miles round, being in a wide-spreading, flaming, blazing, smoky fire, rising up through wood and prairie, hill and dale, to the tops of low shrubs and trees, which are kindled by the coarse, thick, long, prairie grass, and dying leaves at every point of the compass, and far beyond the foot of civilization, darkening the air, heavens and earth, over the whole extent of the northern and part of the southern continent, from the Atlantic to the Pacific, and in neighbourhoods contiguous to the all-devouring deflagration, filling the whole horizon with yellow, palpable, tangible smoke, ashes, and vapour, which affect the eyes of man and beast, and obscure the sun, moon, and stars for many days, or until the winter rains descend to quench the fire and purge the thick, ropy air, which is seen, tasted, handled, and felt.

Faux's Memorable Days &c.

Faucibus ingentem fumum, mirabile dictu,
Evomit ; involvitque *yankees* caligine cæcâ.

This is worse than tobacco smoke. But to proceed, our author meets again, at Philadelphia, with the diabolical Ramsbottom, who destroys, as above related, the little Oddys, &c. and at Bristol and Washington the same detestable massacre is perpetrated, in the same manner, and by the same person. It is, however, no very uncommon thing for English travellers to meet with the same circumstance in very different parts of the union, probably on account of the great similarity of manners throughout the United States. These are but a few of the extraordinary details of this eventful tour. But we close our quotations with the following, which is a part of an English emigrant's story of his disasters, as related to the author.

" I put my four acres into such order as never had been seen before. It was a perfect garden. The rows were as straight as arrows, and there was not a clod of earth above ground as large as an egg to be seen. Every body came to admire, but as yet nobody imitated me,—such is the ignorant and insolent obstinacy of the Yankee farmers. "Friend," said my neighbour, the old quaker—" friend Shortridge, what art thou going to put into thy field here ?"

" Ruta baga."

" *Ruta baga!* what is that, friend John ?"

" Turnips," replied I.

" Well, why didn't thee call them so at first ?　If thou talkest Latin here, nobody will understand thee, friend John.　But what art thou going to do with thy turnips ?"

" I shall feed my cattle, sheep, and hogs with some, and sell the rest to my neighbours."

" But thy neighbours will raise their own turnips, and will not buy."

" Then I will send them to market.'

" What, sixty miles, over a turnpike ?　That will be a bad speculation, friend John.　Thee had best put in a few acres of wheat and corn, they will pay the expense of taking to market.　Thy turnips will cost more than they will come to.'

" Not I, indeed, friend Underhill," said I.　" Sir Humphrey Davy says there is little or no nourishment in wheat and corn."

" No !" quoth the old quaker, with a sly glance at his round portly figure; " I have lived upon them all my life, and I never made the discovery, friend John."

" My ruta baga flourished to the admiration of the whole neighbourhood, and when I came to gather my crop in the fall, there was a heap as high as a hay-stack.　Some of them measured eighteen inches in diameter.　I was as proud as a peacock, for I had now done something for the honour of old England.　I determined to give my cattle, sheep, and hogs, a great feast, and invited my good neighbour, the quaker, to see how they would eat *ruta baga.*　A quantity was nicely cut up and thrown to them one morning, but to my astonishment and mortification, not one would touch a morsel.　Whether it was that they had become spoiled by a fine season of grass, I cannot tell ; but the bull turned up his nose—the cows turned their backs, and so did the sheep, while the pigs ran away screaming mightily.　'Thee should set them to reading Sir Humphrey Davy, friend John,' quoth my neighbour—'they hav'n't learning enough to relish thy Latin turnips.' "

Some of our readers may imagine, that the caricature of certain modern books of travels, which is presented by John Bull in America, is rather too extravagant, but it is not so ; the Memorable Days, above alluded to, are very little behind either this, or the original Munchausen, in the marvellous. Indeed we should have taken Faux's work for a burlesque, without the smallest hesitation, if we had not been assured to the contrary by the fifty-eighth number of the Quarterly.

We have intimated above, our good wishes for the pecuniary remuneration of the supposed inventor of the adventures, which have been the subject of this article, and we venture, before taking leave of him, to offer a piece of advice, which may conduce to this desirable end, and this is, that he publish an edition in England, omitting the preface, and substituting for the present title-page, some such popular matter as, the " Emigrant's Return from America," " Memorable Days," or the like, by Mr Mactricket, a farmer, a stocking-weaver, a pin-manufacturer, or whatever other title may best suit his ear. We have not the least doubt that half a dozen editions will be eagerly demanded by Mr Bull, who, among his other good qualities, has that of being one of the most enormous consumers of print and paper on record. We do assure the author, that the " reading public" will swallow his inventions like sack and sugar; and, in all probability, he will have the honour of a puff from the good-natured men of the Quarterly, and perhaps the pleasure to see the great *Republicomastix* himself cackling with huge exultation over his little volume, and to admire with Bartoline Saddletree, " the great muckle bird that he 'll cleck out of this wee egg."

MISCELLANY.

THE LAY MONASTERY.

The Literary Spirit of our Country.

The spirit of that day is still awake,
And spreads itself, and shall not sleep again.
Bryant.

I NEVER think of my native land without a feeling of pride in my national ancestry. Our government has passed the ordeal of time, and we have among us, neither the practical atheism of a papal hierarchy, nor that dangerous system of politics, which, in the days of Cardinal Richelieu, made France the terror of Europe. The same spirit that animated our fathers in their great struggle for freedom, still directs the popular mind to honourable enterprise, and whilst

" Westward the star of empire takes its way,"

the star of mental light still looks cheerfully upon New England. There is throughout our territories a spirit of activity, that will insure success in every honourable undertaking; and this spirit has already directed itself to literature, with an energy that increases with the exercise. What will be done, may be predicted from what has already been done; and as national talent is gradually developed in the walks of literature, and unfolds itself in greater vigor and richness day after day, a national literature will be formed. Revolutions in letters are, indeed, the most gradual of all revolutions. A single day may decide the fate of an empire, the event of an hour sweep a throne from the earth, but years must elapse, ere any sensible changes can be introduced in literature. And yet in this the mind can proceed surely with its reasonings, whilst in the science of politics it will be led into constant error, by the uncertainty of political innovations ;—for it is a principle well founded in nature, that those reasonings are most sure, whose subjects are not influenced by individual caprice, but move only with the motion of the popular mind.

Perhaps there never was a better field for the exercise of talent than our own country exhibits at the present pay. Whilst there are here but few great minds wholly devoted to letters, the exertions of genius will be far more conspicuous and effectual, than when a larger multitude has gathered around our literary altars. It is not when many have come forth into the ripened harvest, that we are to look for great individual preeminence. But it is when competition is limited to the few gifted minds, that are willing to toil in difficult and untrodden paths. Then, if ever, must appear those men, who, like Homer and Shakspeare, will have no imitators ; and who, like them, will never become models, that others would think of excelling, or hope to equal. I do not say, that this would advance to any great extent our national literature, nor even so far as it would be advanced by a more moderate, but a more universal excellence in our literary men ;—for high excellence in one individual brings with it a hopelessness of success to others, and damps for a season the ardour of competition. But I venture nothing in the assertion, that the opportunity for eminent literary success, which our country now holds out to her sons, is such as can never be given them again. The rapid changes, which are every where going on in our occupations and circumstances as a nation, render this impossible. And when we observe how boldly our country is pressing on in the march of intellect, it is not too much to prophesy,—nay, the conclusion seems almost irresistible, that the nation, whose commerce is overshadowing every ocean with its sails, will ere long enlighten with its own literature, at least, the most distant places of its own territory.

If climate and natural scenery have a powerful influence in forming the intellectual character of a nation, our country has certainly much to hope from them. And that these influences are powerful, the known principles, which regulate the phenomena of mind, render sufficiently obvious. It cannot be, that the eye should always rest upon sublime and beautiful scenery, and

4

thought be always familiar with the grand features of nature, and that we should not receive from such intercourse one deep and long continued impression.

> So mind takes colour from the cloud, the storm,
>   The ocean, and the torrent: where clear skies
> Brighten and purple o'er an earth, whose form
>   In the sweet dress of southern summer lies,
>   Man drinks the beauty with his gladdened eyes,
> And sends it out in music:—where the strand
>   Sounds with the surging waves, that proudly rise
> To meet the frowning clouds, the soul is manned
> To mingle in their wrath and be as darkly grand.
>   *Percival.*

It is upon the poetic mind, where sensibility to natural beauty is more exquiste than elsewhere, that the influence of natural scenery is most evident ; since it is through the medium of fancy and feeling, that this influence is exerted and felt.   Poetry has been correctly defined the language of the imagination and the passions ; and perhaps there is nothing which more awakens the former than the sublime in nature,—and nothing which more influences the latter, than the beautiful.   And hence, whenever national peculiarities, and the civil and religious institutions of a people have introduced peculiar and appropriate modes of thought, and given an individual character to their poetry, the influence of climate and natural scenery become eminently obvious.   Thus the sunny hills and purple vineyards of Italy and South France have given a character of delicate beauty to their poetry, and the wild scenery and severer climate of Scotland have breathed a tone of high sublimity into the writings of its bards.   In our own country nature has exhibited her works upon the most beautiful and magnificent scale.   And this vast theatre, where she has so finely mingled and varied her scenery, is the school in which the genius of our country is to be trained.   As the eye scans the open volume of nature, the lessons that it reads there, pass into the mind ; and thus we receive those gradual impressions, which go so far to form the mental character.   The sentiments with which nature inspires us—those hallowed and associated feelings— we cherish and revere through life.   And it is by this intercourse and long familiarity, that our native scenery comes to exert so strong an influence upon the mind, and that the features of intellect are moulded after those of nature.

It has been often urged against the advancement of a national literature in our country, that America is not classic ground ; and that we are not rich in those fine classic allusions, which mould the poetic mind to its most perfect beauty, and give to genius the materials for superior exertion.   But this is an objection, to which more weight is given than in reality belongs to it. Those nations that are rich in poetic associations, are not always rich in poetic minds. The Grecian monuments, ancient as they are,—whatever enthusiasm they may have awakened, have never breathed inspiration over the lyres of modern Greeks. And the wandering Improvisatori of Florence and Naples have done little for modern literature in classic Italy. But if the natural scenery of our country, where nature exhibits such various beauty and sublimity, can give strength and vigor to intellect, and with them unite poetic feeling, the lapse of another century will give to us those rich associations, which it is said are now wanting, and will make America in some degree a classic land. Time, indeed, has already hallowed those places of our territory where the people of an ancient race, that has long since ceased to be, have left " a record in the desert ;" and the tumuli, that hold their mouldering bones, are mementos of those men, who once peopled our western forests. As population advances westward, the ploughshare turns up the wasted skeleton ; and happy villages arise upon the sites of unknown burial-places. And when our native Indians, who are fast perishing from the earth, shall have left forever the borders of our wide lakes and rivers, and their villages have decayed within the bosoms of our western hills, the dim light of tradition will rest upon those places, which have seen the glory of their battles, and heard the voice of their eloquence ;—and our land will become, indeed, a classic ground.

Perhaps the chief cause which has retarded the progress of poetry in America, is the want of that exclusive cultivation, which so noble a branch of literature would seem to require. Few here think of relying upon the exertion of poetic talent for a livelihood, and of making literature the profession of life. The bar or the pulpit claims the greater part of the scholar's existence, and poetry is made its pastime. This is a defect, which the hand of honourable patronage alone can remedy. I believe it is a remark of Roscoe, that there is no intellectual occupation, which requires such high, peculiar, and exclusive qualifications as the labours of the poet. But we fail in their acquisition, through the want of a rich and abundant patronage. It is the fear of poverty that deters many gifted and poetic minds from coming forward into the arena, and wiping away all reproach from our literature. When the scholar can go on his way prosperous and rejoicing, and poetry no longer holds with us a " bootless reed ;" minds of the finest mould will be active to invigorate our literature, and to honour the country, which in its turn shall honour them. Added to this circumstance, so injurious to our literature, is the wide influence which English belles-lettres and poetry exert within our land. The delicately finished model of English taste has always been the model by which we have fashioned our writings; and perhaps it is well, that it must for a time continue to be so. But let our admiration for the excellent literary taste of England stop in the imitation;—at least, let us not cherish it to our own injury and the neglect of our own literature. Let us not esteem our native writers the less, because they are native, nor set too high a value upon those things, whose chief value is, that they came from the classic land of England. But while we admire the exertions of foreign intellect, let us cherish more tenderly that spirit of literature, which belongs to us, and entertain a cheerful and honourable pride in having already done so much as we have done. THE LAY MONK.

POETRY.

A HYMN.

The groves were God's first temples. Ere man learned
To hew the shaft, and lay the architrave,
And spread the roof above them,—ere he framed
The lofty vault, to gather and roll back
The sound of anthems; in the darkling wood,
Amidst the cool and silence, he knelt down
And offered to the Mightiest, solemn thanks
And supplication. For his simple heart
Might not resist the sacred influences,
That, from the stilly twilight of the place,
And from the gray old trunks that high in heaven
Mingled their mossy boughs, and from the sound
Of the invisible breath that swayed at once
All their green tops, stole o'er him, and bowed
His spirit with the thought of boundless power
And inaccessible majesty. Ah, why
Should we, in the world's riper years, neglect
God's ancient sanctuaries, and adore
Only among the crowd, and under roofs
That our frail hands have raised. Let me, at least,
Here, in the shadow of this aged wood,
Offer one hymn—thrice happy, if it find
Acceptance in his ear.

Father, thy hand
Hath reared these venerable columns, thou
Didst weave this verdant roof. Thou didst look down
Upon the naked earth, and, forthwith, rose
All these fair ranks of trees. They, in thy sun,

Budded, and shook their green leaves in thy breeze,
And shot towards heaven.   The century-living crow
Whose birth was in their tops, grew old and died
Among their branches, till, at last, they stood,
As now they stand, massy and tall and dark,
Fit shrine for humble worshipper to hold
Communion with his Maker.   Here are seen
No traces of man's pomp or pride ;—no silks
Rustle, no jewels shine, nor envious eyes
Encounter ; no fantastic carvings show
The boast of our vain race to change the form
Of thy fair works.   But thou art here—thou fill'st
The solitude.   Thou art in the soft winds
That run along the summits of these trees
In music ;—thou art in the cooler breath,
That, from the inmost darkness of the place,
Comes, scarcely felt ;—the barky trunks, the ground,
The fresh moist ground, are all instinct with thee.
Here is continual worship ;—nature, here,
In the tranquillity that thou dost love,
Enjoys thy presence.   Noiselessly, around,
From perch to perch, the solitary bird
Passes ; and yon clear spring, that, 'midst its herbs,
Wells softly forth and visits the strong roots
Of half the mighty forest, tells no tale
Of all the good it does.   Thou hast not left
Thyself without a witness, in these shades,
Of thy perfections.   Grandeur, strength, and grace
Are here to speak of thee.   This mighty oak—
By whose immoveable stem I stand and seem
Almost annihilated—not a prince,
In all the proud old world beyond the deep,
E'er wore his crown as loftily as he
Wears the green coronal of leaves with which
Thy hand has graced him.   Nestled at his root
Is beauty, such as blooms not in the glare
Of the broad sun.   That delicate forest flower,
With scented breath, and look so like a smile,
Seems, as it issues from the shapeless mould,
An emanation of the indwelling Life,
A visible token of the upholding Love,
That are the soul of this wide universe.

My heart is awed within me, when I think
Of the great miracle that still goes on,
In silence, round me—the perpetual work
Of thy creation, finished, yet renewed
Forever.   Written on thy works I read
The lesson of thy own eternity.
Lo ! all grow old and die—but see, again,
How on the faltering footsteps of decay
Youth presses—ever gay and beautiful youth

In all its beautiful forms.   These lofty trees
Wave not less proudly that their ancestors
Moulder beneath them.   Oh, there is not lost
One of earth's charms: upon her bosom yet,
After the flight of untold centuries,
The freshness of her far beginning lies
And yet shall lie.   Life mocks the idle hate
Of his arch enemy Death—yea—seats himself
Upon the sepulchre, and blooms and smiles,
And of the triumphs of his ghastly foe
Makes his own nourishment.   For he came forth
From thine own bosom, and shall have no end.

There have been holy men who hid themselves
Deep in the woody wilderness, and gave
Their lives to thought and prayer, till they outlived
The generation born with them, nor seemed
Less aged than the hoary trees and rocks
Around them;—and there have been holy men
Who deemed it were not well to pass life thus.
But let me often to these solitudes
Retire, and in thy presence reassure
My feeble virtue. . Here its enemies,
The passions, at thy plainer footsteps shrink
And tremble and are still.   Oh God ! when thou
Dost scare the world with tempests, sett'st on fire
The heavens with falling thunderbolts, or fill'st
With all the waters of the firmament
The swift dark whirlwind that uproots the woods
And drowns the villages ; when, at thy call,
Uprises the great deep and throws himself
Upon the continent and overwhelms
Its cities—who forgets not, at the sight
Of these tremendous tokens of thy power,
His pride, and lays his strifes and follies by ?
Oh, from these sterner aspects of thy face
Spare me and mine, nor let us need the wrath
Of the mad unchained elements to teach
Who rules them.   Be it ours to meditate
In these calm shades thy milder majesty,
And, to the beautiful order of thy works,
Learn to conform the order of our lives.

B.

SPRING.

Again the infant flowers of Spring
Call thee to sport on thy rainbow wing—
Spirit of Beauty ! the air is bright
With the boundless flow of thy mellow light ;
The woods are ready to bud and bloom,
And are weaving for Summer their quiet gloom ;

The tufted brook reflects, as it flows,
The tips of the half-unopened rose,
And the early bird, as he carols free,
Sings to his little love and thee.

See how the clouds, as they fleetly pass,
Throw their shadowy veil on the darkening grass ;
And the pattering showers and stealing dews,
With their starry gems and skyey hues,
From the oozy meadow, that drinks the tide,
To the sheltered vale on the mountain side,
Wake to a new and fresher birth
The tenderest tribes of teeming earth,
And scatter with light and dallying play
Their earliest flowers on the Zephyr's way.

He comes from the mountain's piny steep,
For the long boughs bend with a silent sweep,
And his rapid steps have hurried o'er
The grassy hills to the pebbly shore ;
And now, on the breast of the lonely lake,
The waves in silvery glances break,
Like a short and quickly rolling sea,
When the gale first feels its liberty,
And the flakes of foam, like coursers, run,
Rejoicing beneath the vertical sun.

He has crossed the lake, and the forest heaves,
To the sway of his wings, its billowy leaves,
And the downy tufts of the meadow fly
In snowy clouds, as he passes by,
And softly beneath his noiseless tread
The odorous spring-grass bends its head ;
And now he reaches the woven bower,
Where he meets his own beloved flower,
And gladly his wearied limbs repose
In the shade of the newly-opening rose.

P..

CRITICAL NOTICES.

The Edinburgh Review for October, and the Quarterly Review for December, 1824.

AN anonymous "Tour in Germany" is reviewed in both these journals, and it is no small evidence of its merit, that both unite in commend-
ing it.   It affords an opportunity to the Edinburgh Review for a *tirade*
against the Holy Alliance.   The Quarterly, with its usual servile whine,
takes the same occasion to laud the prudence, gentleness, benignity,
&c. of their allied Majesties, who, as the reviewer intimates, are gradually
preparing the minds of their subjects for the enjoyment of their natural

rights. We believe this to be true enough, but not in the sense intended by the Quarterly.

An article on "High Tory Principles," in the Edinburgh Review, is a spirited and very amusing attack upon the nauseous loyalty of the French press and pamphleteers, with the ineffable M. Chateaubriand at their head, as displayed on the occasion of the death of the old, and the accession of the new monarch.

"If," say they, "a contrast were wanted to the servile spirit displayed by the French royalists in the present day, we should look to the interesting spectacle, now exhibited by the American people, of honest and enlightened affection for their ancient benefactor and fellow-soldier in the cause of freedom. We will own, that, to us, there is something peculiarly touching in the enthusiasm which that great nation has shown upon the arrival of the truly venerable person who seeks, in their affections, a temporary refuge from the persecutions of his own government. No man can be named, who has, through a long life, acted with more undeviating integrity, and who, with more strict consistency, has pursued his course of devotion to the sacred cause of liberty, and opposed all despotism, whether exercised by the genius of Napoleon, or by those successors to his throne whose powers form so mighty a contrast with their stations. La Fayette may have fallen into errors; in flying from one danger, he did not perceive that liberty might have a double hazard to encounter, both from oppression and from conquest; but faults he has never been charged with by any whose good opinion deserves his regard; and the honours which he has received in America are as entirely due to the inflexible virtue of his riper years, and his willing sacrifice of himself on all occasions to the cause of liberty in his own country, as they are peculiarly fit to hail his reappearance in a country which the generous devotion of his younger days had helped to make a powerful state of a few dependent colonies. He must be far gone in the servile feelings of French royalism who can read, without a blush, the productions we have cited in this article; but no friend of liberal principles can feel any thing but sympathy and pride in following the progress of this great patriot through the United States, even where its details are recorded with the least reserve, and by the most ordinary chroniclers of the times."

In the last article of the Quarterly, we have the other side of the question. The subject is the Progress of Dissent in England. The article contains, among other matters of Tory sophistry, a most impudent and shameless attempt to prove the advantage and necessity of the present constitution of the hierarchy. It is asserted, for instance, that the notion of the opulence of the clergy is a *vulgar prejudice*, and that, as a body, they are poorly paid. It is argued, that the enormous incomes of the dignitaries, do not constitute wealth, because wealth is comparative; that ministers of religion must mingle with every class of individuals in the nation; that "saints in lawn" are necessary to purify the nobility; and that these are comparatively no more opulent than the "saints in crape," who perform the same wholesome service to the middling classes, or the saints in rags, who christianize the *canaille*.

A considerable portion of this number is devoted to reviews of voyages and travels, which indeed are usually better executed in this, than in the Northern journal. The reviewers of Travels in Brazil are greatly uplifted by the establishment of a government in that country, which savours of legitimacy, and mourn over the probable failure of the republican forms in South America, in a very edifying manner. They further take occasion to touch, with an air of dignified contempt, upon the quarrel of the United States with Great Britain in 1812; and close with an expression of benevolent anxiety for the future destinies of the federal union, when the population of the West shall have somewhat increased. We are happy to relieve them by the assurance, that there is no danger whatever to the Union, which is every day growing stronger. But "a confederate republic, of such vast extent, would be a phenomenon in politics!" It certainly will be so, good croaking brethren. We have told you so these many years, and are glad to perceive, that you begin to be aware of it.

A subsequent article contains a panegyric on the noble nature and pure morality and religion of the aborigines of North America, especially when compared with many of the white settlers. They had their legitimate sachems, and their panieses, or nobles, and their powows, or dignitaries, which proves, we suppose, that men are by nature subject to monarchy and hierarchy, instead of being free and equal, as our constitution ventures to assume. And these sachems, and panieses, and powows met in council, and made "long talks," and wore party-coloured dresses, and believed in scarlet and ermine. The reviewers really grow sentimental, when they enlarge upon the moral beauty and grandeur of the Indian character. And then they lament the cruel and systematic design of the American government to extirpate every Indian tribe from the Valley of the Mississippi to the Rocky Mountains, and tell how the grateful and affectionate savages, in the last war, called the king of England their *Great Father*, who protected them against the wicked plans of the Longknives. To all this we have but one word to say,—Brethren of the Quarterly, "beware of cant."

The Edinburgh Review, in an article on the "Abolition of Corn-Laws," endeavours to show, that by the repeal of these, no ruinous depression of prices would ensue; and that the average price of wheat, &c. in England is nearly as low as that, at which it could be supplied from any other country. Another, on Impresement, offers strong reasons for supposing that this practice, defended hitherto on the plea of necessity, is contrary to every sound principle of economy and policy, and that seamen could be obtained in greater abundance, and at no greater expense, if impressment was forever abolished. We are informed, in an article on Slavery, that a new and great effort is about to be made at the present session of parliament, for the emancipation of the slaves in the West India colonies. The abolitionists seem to have become tired of the slow method of parliamentary recommendation, and desire something more effectual. From an article on the Scientific Education of the People, many useful hints might be derived, for establishments in our own country.

Each of these Reviews is doubtless in a great measure, the organ of a party; but whatever may be the ultimate end of the Whigs in Britain, their journal, on most great national and political questions, speaks the language of nature and reason; while their Tory opponent is too often employed in defending the most monstrous paradoxes, by the most impudent sophistry. We have been informed, that the circulation of the latter is far before that of the former;—what does this fact, if it be a fact, say for the majority of the "reading public" of England ?

A Few Days in Athens; being the Translation of a Greek Manuscript, discovered in Herculaneum. By Frances Wright, author of "Views of Society and Manners in America." New York. 1825. 12mo. pp. 130.

This author deserves attention on the score of former merit, or we should not notice this effusion at all. The amount of it is, that a prejudiced man is not always the fairest judge ; and that he, who regulates his opinions by such a man, is very likely to have false ones. There is certainly no novelty in the text, and the commentary possesses but little interest. The history of the book is a fiction ; and, as the book itself is a mere allegory, it was hardly necessary to resort to fiction at all, especially to so hackneyed a one. The whole is an uninterrupted conversation, on a very few topics, principally doctrines of the old philosophers, and remarkably remote from any thing, that could border on an application. It fails, of course, in one of the objects of allegory. We regret that the author should not have been more fortunate in the choice of a subject. One less attractive to the mass of readers could hardly have been selected, than the whimsical and absurd doctrines of the old philosophers. Few understand the distinctions and peculiarities among them at all. Those who do, may, perhaps, be amused with a fiction, which puts them in their most agreeable form, and teaches them again. Those, who do not understand them, will hardly give themselves the trouble to learn them, for the sake of understanding and enjoying a fiction, founded upon them. Readers may well begin to be fastidious in the choice of their books, and if they are, they will certainly find enough of a much more practical and interesting character than "A Few Days in Athens." We have no more faults to find with the book, and it does not furnish any occasion for praise. It will do no good, and we are not aware, that it can do any harm. This is some praise, and it may be the author asks for no more.

American Mechanics' Magazine ; containing Selections from the most valuable Foreign Journals, as well as Useful Original Matter. Conducted by Associated Mechanics. New York. 1825. 8vo. pp. 16.

A periodical publication has lately been commenced at New York under the above title. We have seen but one number, and therefore can form no decided opinion of the ability, with which the work will be conducted. It is intended to contain statements of the principles most frequently applied in practical mechanics, and also easy and familiar illustrations of them, drawn from the experience with which every mechanic is familiar. This will induce young mechanics to refer their experience to general principles as fast as they have it; and in order to do this, they must observe more accurately what is passing before them, and think and reason more philosophically upon the phenomena which they cannot but see. The design of the work we think a laudable one ; and if intelligent mechanics are interested in its support, it cannot fail of extensive usefulness in a community like our own, where so large a proportion are devoted to mechanical pursuits.

A New Spanish Grammar, adapted to every class of learners. By Mariano Cubi y Soler. Second edition. Baltimore. 1825. 12mo. pp. 464.

About two years since Mr Sales, instructer in French and Spanish in Harvard University, translated, revised, and very much improved the Spanish and French Grammar of M. Jossé. Previously it had been a very difficult matter to procure a good grammar of the Spanish language. Those who were unacquainted with the French, were obliged to make use of the imperfect "Introductions," "Keys," and "Synopses," which were accidently found amidst the litter and lumber of our bookstores. Mr Cubi's Grammar does not differ *essentially* from that revised by Mr Sales. They are both valuable works, and both far superior to any other introduction to the Spanish language, that we have ever seen.

Mr Cubi has made many important additions and improvements in his second edition, which give evidence of much care and exertion; and we cheerfully recommend it to all, who are desirous of obtaining a thorough knowledge of the Spanish language,—a language which, from our connection with the South American nations, has already become as useful to the merchant and the statesman, as it has always been interesting and delightful to the man of letters.

INTELLIGENCE.

CHILDREN AND YOUTH IN MASSACHUSETTS.

There were in the district of Massachusetts, according to the census of 1820, five hundred and twenty-three thousand one hundred and fifty-nine souls. Of this number, *two hundred and forty-one thousand seven hundred and eleven were under the age of eighteen years.* The number is now, probably, somewhat increased. If the population has increased only as fast since the last census, as it did between the census of 1810 and that of 1820, there are now, in round numbers, about *two hundred and fifty thousand* children and youth under the age of eighteen, in Massachusetts. This number, it will be perceived, amounts to almost one half of our whole population. If we take from the older part, those between the ages of *eighteen* and *twenty-one*, and add them to the younger part of the population, we shall find at least half, and probably more than half of the whole under twenty-one years.

A few of this mass of children and youth have left the schools and all direct means of education, and entered upon the active business of life. And a portion of the younger part are yet subjects only for domestic education. But, after these deductions, it will not be extravagant to state, that one third of the whole population are of a suitable age,—have opportunity,—and do actually attend school at least some portion of the year. In Massachusetts, we have not the means of knowing accurately the number of those who attend our schools; because we have no system of returns to any authority, by which such facts can be ascertained. But we are confirmed in the belief, that the above is not an extravagant estimate, by two facts. One is, several towns have been carefully examined, and this is about the proportion of the population found in the schools. The other is, official documents and acknowledged authorities, from a neighbouring state, inform us, that *one third* of their population attend school some portion of the year. And probably the same would be true of all the New England states.

FRENCH PROJECTS.

The following Prospectus was submitted to an English gentleman, residing in Paris, with the author's hope that he would be both a contributor and subscriber: "Tomorrow in the fifteen days will be publish, one brand new work of the Litterature and the Science, the Spectacle and the Mode, to be call the Miroir of the Day; compile by a series of litterary gentlemans of France and the Grand Britain, famous for their savoir and their talents." The prospectus states that half the work is to be in French and half in English; that it is to appear three times a week, and that learned professors are to superintend the articles in each language. Terms twelve francs for three months; twenty-four for six months; and forty-eight francs a year,—to be paid in advance; the money to be returned in three months if the work does not appear.

LEHIGH RIVER AND COAL MINE.

Since the qualities and uses of the Lehigh coal have been understood, it has become a very considerable article of commerce. In a late Number we gave some account, taken from Professor J. Griscom, of the extent of this coal mine, and the purposes to which its products could be applied. When an easy communication, either by canals or otherwise, shall be opened between the Hudson, the Delaware, and the Susquehannah, there is a probability that this coal may be transported, at least to the cities on the borders of the Atlantic, with such facility, and in such quantities, as to affect materially the price of fuel. And that, in a climate like our own, must affect, materially, the condition of a large portion of the community. It may have other uses, or be converted to other purposes than that of furnishing a cheaper and more convenient fuel. In conjunction with the modern discoveries in the application of steam power, and the internal improvements by means of canals and railways, this new development of the resources of a large and already powerful state [Pennsylvania], cannot fail to become a subject of deep and increasing interest to the whole country. We are led to these remarks, by seeing, a short time since, a letter, in which the Lehigh river, the mine, and the manner of conveying off the coal, were described. From those descriptions we select such parts, as will give our readers some account of the river, and the manner by which it is made passable for the *arks*, as they are called, in which the coal is floated down. The construction of the sluice gates was to us new, extremely interesting, and ingenious.

"The Lehigh river, near its source, is a mountain torrent, having a fall of 360 feet in the distance of 46$\frac{1}{4}$ miles. The navigation is attained by the kind of improvement, called, by engineers, *flashing*. But the greatest curiosity consists in the locks or sluice gates. These locks require but little strength, and no skill for their management. A gate, which extends the whole breadth of the sluice, is fastened by hinges along its lower edge, so that it moves like the lid of a box. It is of such breadth, that when raised nearly perpendicular, it will entirely stop the opening of the sluice, and when suffered to lie flat on the bottom, leaves it entirely open. Another gate, of about double the breadth (measuring up and down the stream), and extending across the sluice, is fixed in a similar manner lower down; but the upper small gate opens down stream, and the lower large gate opens up stream, so that they resemble two folding doors, with the exception, that one overlaps the other three or four feet. Under these gates is a chamber, into which water may be introduced from the dam above by a small gate. When this is open, the hydrostatic pressure of the water above, forces the gates upwards, and the space under them forming always a close chamber, they rise until they stand like the roof of a house, and thus close the opening in the sluice. When required to be lowered, all that is necessary is, to let off the water from the chamber, and the gates sink with their own weight, one overlapping the other, to the bottom."

NEW PUBLICATIONS.

AGRICULTURE.

Address delivered before the Philadelphia Society for promoting Agriculture, at its annual meeting, on the 18th January, 1825. By Roberts Vaux. Published by order of the Society. 8vo. pp. 28. Philadelphia.

ARTS, SCIENCES, AND PHILOSOPHY.

The Boston Journal of Philosophy and the Arts, No. X.
The American Journal of Science and Arts, Vol. 9, No. 1.

ASTRONOMY.

Elements of Astronomy, illustrated by Plates, for the use of Schools and Academies, with Questions. By John H. Wilkins, A. M. Third edition. 12mo. Boston. Cummings, Hilliard, & Co.

DRAMA.

Montgomery; or, The Falls of Montmorency. A New National Drama. Written by Henry J. Finn. Boston. Wells and Lilly.

Hadad; a Dramatic Poem. By James A. Hillhouse, Author of "Percy's Masque" and "The Judgment."

EDUCATION.

An Abridgment of Murray's English Grammar, revised, enlarged, and improved; comprising rules and exercises in orthography, parsing, and punctuation; with Practical Notes; arranged in natural order, and suited to the capacities of children and youth in elementary schools. Compiled for the junior classes in Union Hall Academy. By A. M. Merchant. 18mo. pp. 216. New York.

A New Spanish Grammar, adapted to every class of learners. By Mariano Cubi y Soler. Second edition, revised, corrected, enlarged, and greatly improved. 12mo. pp. 464. Baltimore. F. Lucas, jr.

Fourth Annual School Report, made in the year 1825, to the Legislature of New York. By J. V. N. Yates, Secretary of the State, and Acting Superintendent of Common Schools. Folio. pp. 44. Albany.

GEOLOGY.

A Geological and Agricultural Survey of the District adjoining the Erie Canal, in the State of New York. Part I,—containing a Description of the Rock Formations, together with a Geological Profile, extending from the Atlantic to Lake Erie.

HISTORY.

History of Massachusetts, from July, 1775, when General Washington took Command of the American Army at Cambridge, to the year 1782, (inclusive), when the Federal Government was established under the present Constitution. By Alden Bradford. 8vo. Boston. Wells & Lilly.

History, Manners, and Customs of the North American Indians, with a Plan for their Melioration. By James Buchanan, Esq. His Majesty's Consul for the State of New York. 2 Vols. 12mo.

LAW.

An Authentic Report of a Trial before the Supreme Judicial Court of Maine, for the County of Washington, June Term, 1824. Charles Lowell vs. John Faxon and Micajah Hawks, Surgeons and Physicians, in an Action of Trespass on the Case, &c. 8vo. pp. 29. Portland.

A Treatise on the Law of Pennsylvania relating to the Estate of Decedents, the Constitution, Powers, and Practice of the Orphans' Court. By Thomas F. Gordon. Carey & Lea. Philadelphia.

A Digest of the Cases decided in the Supreme Judicial Court of the Commonwealth of Massachusetts, from March, 1816, to October, 1823, inclusive. To which is added, a Digested Index of the names of Cases in the 18 Vols. of Massachusetts Reports. By Theron Metcalf. 8vo. Boston. Richardson & Lord.

MISCELLANEOUS.

Speech delivered before the Overseers of Harvard College, February 3, 1825, in Behalf of the Resident Instructers of the College. With an Introduction. By Andrews Norton. 8vo. pp. 60. Boston. Cummings, Hilliard, & Co.

A Year in Europe, comprising a Journal of Observations in England, Scotland, Ireland, France, Switzerland, the North of Italy, and Holland. By John Griscom. Second Edition. New York. Collins and Hannay.

The Grecian Wreath of Victory. 18mo. pp. 119. New York.

An Address to the Utica Lyceum, delivered February 17, 1825. By A. B. Johnson, Prefatory to his Course of Lectures on the Philosophy of Human Knowledge. 8vo. pp. 16. Utica, N. Y.

An Address delivered in Nashville, January 12, 1825, at the Inauguration of the President of Cumberland College. By Philip Lindley, D.D. President of the College. 8vo. pp. 48. Nashville.

Remarks on Washington College, and on the " Considerations" suggested by its Establishment. 8vo. pp. 52. Hartford.

The Atlantic Magazine, No. XI.

The Town Officer's Guide, containing a Compilation of the General Laws of Massachusetts, relating to the whole Power and Duty of Towns, Districts, and Parishes, with their several Officers, &c. By John Bacon, Esq. 12mo. pp. 396. Haverhill, Mass.

Considerations suggested by the Establishment of a Second College in Connecticut. 8vo. pp. 36. Hartford.

Triumphs of Intellect, a Lecture delivered October, 1824, in the Chapel of Waterville College. By Stephen Chapin, D. D. Professor of Theology in said College. 8vo. pp. 31. Waterville, Me.

John Bull in America, or the New Munchausen, 12mo. pp. 226. New York. 1825. C. Wiley.

NOVELS.

The Refugee; A Romance. By Captain Matthew Murgatroyd, of the Ninth Continentals in the Revolutionary War. 2 Vols. 12mo. New York.

The Valley of Shenandoah; or, Memoirs of the Graysons. 2 Vols. 12mo. New York.

POLITICS.

Letter from Robert Wickliffe to his Constituents. 8vo. pp. 19. Frankfort, Ken.

Remarks upon a Pamphlet, published at Bath, Me. relating to alleged Infractions of the Laws, during the Embargo, Non-Intercourse, and War. By William King and Mark L. Hill.

THEOLOGY.

A Discourse on Christian Liberty, delivered before the First Congregational Society in Scituate, on the Lord's Day, March 6, 1825. By Samuel Deane, Pastor of the Second Church in Scituate. Published at the desire of the hearers. Cambridge. Hilliard & Metcalf.

The Unitarian's Answer; or, a Brief and Plain "Answer to any that ask a Reason" of our attachment to Unitarianism. considered as a System both of Doctrine and Instruction. 12mo. pp. 24. New Bedford.

The Doctrine of the Atonement Explained, in a Sermon delivered in the New Jerusalem Temple, in Cincinnati, on the evening of the 20th of December, 1824. By Nathaniel Holley, A. M. a Minister of the New Jerusalem Church. 8vo. pp. 22. Cincinnati. Ohio.

An Historical Discourse, delivered at West Springfield, December 2, 1824, the day of the Annual Thanksgiving. By William B. Sprague, Pastor of the First Church in West Springfield. 8vo. pp. 91. Hartford, Conn.

The Christian Spectator, Vol. VII. No. 4.

The Excellence and Influence of the Female Character; a Sermon, preached in the Presbyterian Church in Murray Street, at the request of the New York Female Missionary Society. By Gardiner Spring. 8vo. pp. 32. New York. 1825.

The Discriminating Preacher; a Sermon, preached in the North Church in the city of Hartford. December 1, 1824. At the Ordination and Installation of the Rev. Carlos Wilcox, as Pastor of said Church. By Gardiner Spring. Pastor of the Brick Presbyterian Church in the city of New York. 8vo. pp. 37. Hartford. 1825.

Biblical Repertory; a Collection of Dissertations on Biblical Literature. By Rev. Charles Hodge, Professor of Biblical and Oriental Literature, in the Theological Seminary at Princeton, N. J. No. I. 8vo. pp. 151. To be continued Quarterly.

A Sermon Delivered at the Ordination of the Rev. William Henry Furness, as Pastor of the first Congregational Unitarian Church, in Philadelphia, January 12, 1825. By Henry Ware, jun. Minister of the Second Church in Boston. 8vo. pp. 46. Philadelphia. A. Small.

A Sermon preached before the Bible Society of North Carolina, on Sunday, December 12th, 1824. By the Right Rev. John S. Ravenscroft, Bishop of the Diocess of North Carolina; with an Appendix. 8vo. pp. 32. Raleigh, N. C.

The Cabinet; or, Works of Darkness brought to Light, &c. Second Edition, Revised and Corrected. 12mo. pp. 80. Philadelphia. John Mortimer.

A Review of the Rev. Mr Colman's Sermon, delivered at the Opening of the Independent Congregational Church in Barton Square, Salem. 8vo. pp. 36. Boston.

Book of Revelation Unsealed; An Explanation of the Apocalypse, or Revelation of St John. By Alexander Smythe, Member of Congress. 16mo. pp. 59. Washington, D. C.

AMERICAN EDITIONS OF FOREIGN WORKS.

Letters and Papers of the late Rev. Thomas Scott, D. D. Author of the Commentary on the Holy Bible, never before published; with occasional Observations. By John Scott, A. M. Vicar of North Ferriby, and Minister of St Mary's Hall. First American Edition. 12mo. pp. 394 Boston.

Theological Works of Thomas Paine. 8vo. pp. 400. New York.

Rothelan; a Romance. By the Author of " Annals of the Parish," &c.

The Latin Reader, from the fifth German Edition. By Frederic Jacobs, Editor of the Greek Anthology, the Greek Reader, &c. &c. 12mo. pp. 150. Northampton.

Quarterly Review, No. LXI.

Edinburgh Review, No. LXXXI.

High Ways and By-Ways, or Tales by the Road Side; Picked up by a Walking Gentleman. Second Series. 2 Vols. Philadelphia. Carey & Lea.

Lessons for Children, in Four Parts. By Mrs. Barbauld. Second American Edition. 24mo. Boston. Wells & Lilly.

Memoirs of Goëthe. Written by himself. Collins & Hannay.

Elements of Greek Grammar. By R. Valpy, D. D. F. A S. Fifth American Edition. Arranged on an improved Plan; with extensive Additions. By Charles Anthon, Adjunct Professor of Languages in Colombia College, New York.

A New View of Society, or Essays on the Formation of Human Character, preparatory to the Development of a Plan for gradually ameliorating the Condition of Mankind. By Robert Owen. First American, from the Third London Edition. 1 vol. 18mo. Price 75 cents.

LIST OF WORKS IN PRESS.

A Grammar of the Spanish Language, with Practical Exercises. By M. Jossé. Second American, from the last Paris Edition. Revised, improved, and adapted to the English language. By F. Sales, Instructer in French and Spanish in Harvard University, Cambridge. Boston. Munroe & Francis.

The Improvisatrice and other Poems. By L. E. L. Munroe & Francis.

Hymns for Children; selected and altered. By the Author of Conversations on Common Things. Munroe & Francis.

An Inquiry into the Scriptural Import of the words, Sheol, Hades, Tartarus, and Gehenna; all translated Hell in the common English version. Second Edition. By Walter Balfour. Charlestown, Mass. George Davidson.

The Boatswain's Mate; or, Interesting Dialogues between British Seamen. In Seven Parts. Charles Whipple. Newburyport.

Thomson's Conspectus of the London, Edinburgh, and Dublin Pharmacopœiæ, with the addition of the United States Pharmacopœia, Magendie's Formulary, and the other Pharmaceutical preparations. New York. E. Bliss & E. White.

Butler's Reminiscences. Second Edition.

English Life, or Manners at Home, in Four Pictures. 2 vols. in one. New York. E. Bliss & E. White.

Decision; A Tale by Mrs Hoffland, Author of " Son of a Genius," &c. &c. New York. E. Bliss & E. White.

The Surgical and Physiological Works of John Abernethy. Complete, from a late London Edition. New York. J. & J. Harper.

WE have several articles on hand, which were intended for this Number, but the length of our reviews has obliged us to postpone them.

                EDITORS.

Erratum.—At the head of this Number, the date is, by mistake, printed 1824 instead of 1825.

Published on the first and fifteenth day of every month, by CUMMINGS, HILLIARD, & Co., No. 134 Washington-Street, Boston, for the Proprietors. Terms, $5 per annum. Cambridge: Printed at the University Press, by Hilliard & Metcalf.

THE UNITED STATES

LITERARY GAZETTE.

| VOL. II. | APRIL 15, 1825. | No. 2. |

REVIEWS.

Greece in 1823 and 1824, being a Series of Letters and other Documents on the Greek Revolution, written during a visit to that country, by the Hon. Colonel Leicester Stanhope. To which is added, the Life of Mustapha Ali. Philadelphia. 1825. 8vo. pp. 308.

[Concluded.]

On the ground, then, either of immediate commercial benefit or remote general advancement of civilization,—a common object of all wise and great statesmen,—we think the cause of the Greeks entitled to aid. We think this an object of far greater importance than the discovery of the Friendly Islands or the Marquesas; than the settlement of the problem, Whether the Niger flows into the sea, or joins the Nile, or evaporates in the desert; than effecting a perilous passage through the icebergs of the polar basin into the Pacific ocean. We do not object to the appropriation of vast sums of money to these objects; but we do sincerely believe, that half of them laid out under the patronage of the British councils, in establishing a free state in Greece, would, in one year, bring back to England a richer return, than would accrue from the discovery of the northwest passage, to the end of time. As to the consequences to the general cause of humanity, they are not to be named in the comparison.

But we must omit some further remarks, which we might have made on this subject, to speak of the cause of the Greeks in its connexion with the interests of Christianity and of the visible church. No such opportunity of doing good, in that most vital of all forms of benevolence, the extension of the pure faith of the Gospel, as now presents itself in Greece, has, within our acquaintance with history, ever offered itself. The

6

Greeks are nominally Christians, and might therefore not seem, at first, within the limits of the efforts to be now made for evangelizing the world.   But if the Greeks be Christians, it must not be forgotten that Greece is a Mahometan state ; governed by a Mahometan despotism ; and that nearly all its disposable means—as far as they are applied to the support of any kind of religion—are applied to the support of the religion of the Koran.   Here, then, is a vast Mahometan country to be brought back to the empire of the Cross ; the country where Christianity arose and was propagated, where its first churches were established, and where its first martyrs bled.   Does not this present a field for missionary exertion, more attractive and more hopeful than the distant regions of the East, or the barbarous isles of the Pacific ? Farther, in this country, which thus of itself awakens our Christian zeal, there is a germ of faith.   There is a persecuted, an oppressed, a cruelly outraged minority,—the descendants of the ancient lords of the soil,—who nominally embrace the Christian doctrine.   This furnishes a promising foothold to the teacher from the prosperous, benevolent, and civilized states of Christendom. The faithful missionary who should address the Greeks, groaning under the Turkish sway, would, in some respects, address precisely the same class of men whom Paul addressed, and who welcomed the *Gospel of the poor.*   But he would address those already professing the name of Christianity, and not, therefore, like the Mahometan, the Hindoo, the Pagan tribes of the East, prejudiced beforehand against the very name of the doctrine offered to their belief.   At the same time, we fear that the Greek Christians stand in little less need of light from abroad, than Hindoo or heathen.   It seems to be admitted, that Christianity exists among them in an exceedingly imperfect form.   The ignorance of the lower orders,—the necessary consequence of their wretched political condition,—is inconsistent with any other state of things.   But when the people are ignorant and superstitious, the priesthood must, of necessity, be divided into two classes, the ignorant who are bigoted, and the wise who are insincere.   It may be almost laid down as an axiom, that there cannot be an enlightened, pious, and sincere clergy, without an enlightened church.   Nor does the evil stop here.   The young men of talents, who, in considerable numbers, resort to the seminaries of learning in Western Europe, in consequence of the gross superstitions with which Christianity is associated at home, carry no religious impressions abroad, and, as a matter almost of course, return without any to their country.   There is too much reason to fear, that religion has no earnest friends among that class of men, who ought to be looked to as its ablest champions; those who, in consequence of distinguished talents, have been sent abroad to enjoy the advantages of schools in the West of Europe.

It is, therefore, in every view which can be taken of the subject, in the highest degree necessary to regard the Greeks as a people in need of religious aid; at the same time that we certainly regard them as the people offering the fairest scope for the efforts of religious benevolence and zeal.   Colonel Stanhope, in the work mentioned at the head of these remarks, mentions no subject more frequently, than the want of schools and teachers; and he alludes honourably to the American missionary press established at Malta.   We think it a question highly deserving of the consideration of our societies for foreign missions, Whether Greece, at this moment, is not a country where all their disposable means might be employed with the greatest hope of a rich harvest of intellectual and spiritual good.   We firmly believe, that the final expulsion of the Turks from Greece would prove the most signal extension of the empire of Christianity, which has taken place since the colonization of America.

We have not thought it necessary to offer our readers a formal analysis of Colonel Stanhope's Letters on Greece. This gentleman is the son of the Earl of Harrington, a very respectable English nobleman; and the Colonel himself, being on his half pay in the English army, repaired to Greece, under the directions of the London Greek Committee.   The work consists principally of his Letters to the Committee, which contain, of course, an account of his occupations in Greece. These were of almost every kind which zeal for the cause of liberty could prompt.   The Colonel acquired a title to the confidence of the Greeks, by the disinterestedness with which he determined to appropriate two-thirds of his income to their cause; and this pecuniary effort was but one of his claims on their gratitude.   He laboured to establish a corps of artillery and a laboratory at Missolonghi; a printing-press and news-paper there, and in two or three other places. He wrote letters, and made journies to reconcile the dissensions of the Greek chieftains, from which the most serious difficulties in the progress of their revolution have grown.   Colonel Stanhope went to Greece, furnished with propositions from Mr Bentham, whose confidence he appears to have possessed in a high degree, toward *codifying* the Greek law. The perseverance of this veteran philosopher is truly exemplary, and we do hope that the astonishing political revolutions of the age will, before long, place him in the sovereignty of some remote island, in the magistracy of some Australasian republic, where he may have it in his power to make a fair experiment of codification. As for the modern Greeks, having adopted the Code Justinian and the Code Napoleon, they are not in such a suffering state in this respect, but that they may dispense with the Code Bentham.

Colonel Stanhope was one of the Commissioners of the loan raised in London for the service of the Greeks. He informs us, in the summary of the state of the Greeks which is appended to his work, and which has been extensively copied in the public prints, " that the Greeks think they have but one want—that of money. * * The Captains (the Greek Chieftains so called) are in general averse to the loan, from a dread that it would fall into the hands of their antagonists (the popular party), and deprive them of power. The rest of the nation look forward to its arrival with feverish impatience. They think, and with truth, that, if well applied, it would not only secure their independence, but also their freedom." Some delay took place in the reception and application of the loan, in consequence of the decease of Lord Byron, who was one of the trustees appointed for those purposes. There is no doubt, that it was owing to this timely supply, that the Greeks have been enabled to meet the Turkish fleets so successfully at sea during the year. Whether supplies go from the same quarter,—the Stock Exchange of London,—to enable the exhausted treasury of the Grand Seignior to prosecute the contest, does not appear.

Meantime the late accounts from England mention that a second loan to the Greeks, of two millions of pounds sterling, has been effected in London, through the house of the Messrs Ricardo. We know not what foundation there may be for this report, but if the English capitalists are willing to keep the field with their pounds sterling, the Greeks most assuredly will keep it with their armies ; and the Turks must yield. If fair scope be given to its operation, there is no doubt that English money, backed by Greek spirit, is an overmatch for the resources of the Divan; and nothing but the direct interference of the Holy Alliance would be competent to maintain, or rather restore, the sovereignty of the Grand Seignior.

Whether public sentiment is so contemptibly weak in the civilized world, that the sovereigns of the Holy Alliance could openly take the field, to restore an atrocious Mahometan despotism over a Christian people, we will not now discuss.

We cannot suppress a remark, suggested to us by the effect which the English loans are calculated to have, in advancing the revolutionary cause in Greece. It appears to us, that English capital is acquiring a power in the political system of the world, novel in its character, astonishing in its weight, and likely to produce very momentous results. It is, at this moment, infusing life into the revolutionary cause, not only of Greece, but of four or five of the free states of this continent. It is not only creating a very strong pecuniary interest on the part of the English nation, in the emancipation of the pastures of Arcadia and the olive gardens of Attica; but it is opening the drowned mines of the Mexican mountains, sounding the pearl fisheries of the coast, and for many of the most important purposes, it is conferring on these young and scarcely organized states, all the benefits of the most powerful and best regulated governments. It is difficult to conjecture what Spain will now do toward the re-subjugation of her late Colonies, under the loss of those supplies from them, which formed the greater portion of her disposable wealth, backed by a recognition of their independence by the most powerful maritime states, and with the steam engines of Bolton and Watt pounding up the core of the Andes into dollars to pay the troops of the revolution.

But to return to Colonel Stanhope, and bring these remarks to a close,—he was an associate of Lord Byron in Greece, in the honourable efforts and sacrifices, by which that great and eccentric mind was making large atonement for his offences against the age. Some very characteristic anecdotes of Lord Byron form the most entertaining portion of the book. It sufficiently appears that his lordship was rendering great and generous services to the Greek cause; that he was profusely liberal in bestowing his funds, and as liberal with his personal exertions and labours. He appears even to have borne, with more equanimity than could have been expected, the various crosses and vexations incident to the undertaking in which he had embarked. The worth of his influence was incalculable; his presence was, we had almost said, the best hope of Greece; his death one of the greatest losses that could have befallen her.

Colonel Stanhope was finally recalled from Greece by the commander-in-chief. However much we may regret that the cause should thus be deprived of two persons like Lord Byron and Colonel Stanhope, at nearly the same time, no reasonable complaint can be made against the Colonel's recall. While the British government proposes to maintain a neutral position, it could not, of course, with consistency, allow a colonel in its army to embark in the cause. It is understood that the Turkish government remonstrated with Lord Strangford on this subject; and that this was the immediate occasion of the Colonel's being recalled. The state papers which have appeared from the Divan, in the course of this struggle, abound with remonstrances on the subject of the aid rendered to the Greeks by the various societies existing in states at peace with the Porte, particularly in England. There is no doubt that this species of aid has been of the last importance to the Greeks; and it would be a glorious triumph for humanity, if, in the result, the benevolent exertions of individuals and unofficial societies should succeed in wresting a country of Christians from a power once so formidable as Turkey.

Colonel Stanhope's book contains a good deal of information, diffused however over a larger space than was necessary. The French and Italian originals of his letters to different persons of Greece, need not have been given in addition to the English translations of them; and, for ourselves, we should have liked the book better, if it had been a little less *radical*. Sure we are, the cause of Greece is any thing rather than served, by mixing up with it the party politics of its English champions.

One word we beg leave to say, about the American edition. It omits several interesting *fac-similes* contained in the English. Of this it is useless to complain, if it is impossible for the American bookseller to sell enough of an edition to pay him reasonably, unless its price be reduced by the omission of these cheap engravings. But in this case, we think the public ought to be dealt fairly with, and informed by an advertisement or a note, that such and such articles have been omitted. If we cannot have the comfort of furnishing ourselves, in the American editions, with faithful copies of English works, we ought, at least, to be honestly told how much is left out. This omission, however, is very general. Sometimes it is so gross, that allusions and direct references are preserved in the text, to engravings that are omitted; and this in cases where the

retaining of some of the engravings authorizes a natural inference that all are given.   We could quote examples of this,
but deem it friendly to forbear.

Memoir of the Life and Character of the Right Honourable
  Edmund Burke ; with specimens of his Poetry and Letters,
  and an Estimate of his Genius and Talents, compared with
  those of his great Contemporaries.   With Autographs.   By
  James Prior, Esq.   Philadelphia.   1825.   8vo.   pp. 507.

THE life of Edmund Burke is a history of his times.   His
was an age of great men, and of great events.   Himself, one
of the greatest, he was the companion of the best.   It was
the companionship of opposition, as well as of sympathy.   It
brought him near to, and in contact with, all that was acting
upon his age, and the influence of which he could not wholly
escape.   The events, amidst which he lived and moved, were
the obvious effects of the various and strong powers, which
were in action about him.   He could not have escaped greatness, had he been ambitious of obscurity ; for there was every
thing present and acting, for all degrees of capability; and he
who possessed the greatest, was hurried into the front, by the
force of circumstances alone.

One cannot but be struck with the variety of power in that
age.   The English language had never before been put to
more various uses.   The language itself was then settled, and
received its true and permanent defences from the whole
legitimate literature of the preceding times.   A very hasty
enumeration of the great men of that age would give us, in
almost every department of human learning, one or more individuals, who remain, and will remain, at the head of their
calling; who have been exerting a vast influence upon all who
have come after them, and who will continue to do it.   It was
then necessary to know much, to be known at all.   There was
much aristocracy in the literature ; we might call it a despotism.   There was one individual, at least, in Burke's time, who
virtually declared himself perpetual dictator, and lesser minds
trembled before his.   But even with this assumption, aided by
much acquiescence, there was, perhaps, never a period, in
which real power was more surely or more truly felt.

It made but little odds what direction the mind took, so

that there were mind. Garrick's course would hardly have made him the tolerated, much less the chosen companion of the first literary men of the age. But intellectual power did for him, what it did for all who possessed it. It gave a new and high character to his calling, and made intellectual, what with ordinary men is mere mechanical parade. He was a poet in his conception of character and passion, as given by other men; and used their language, because it was as natural as his own would have been. This accounts to us for his success in the variety of character which he brought to the stage. He was at home as well in farce as in tragedy; because, though ever so much the compositions of different writers, they belong to the experience of every body.

Mr Reynolds, afterwards Sir Joshua, was the companion of Burke, and of the other great men of the time. He gave a fine and powerful mind to an art, which, like Garrick's, claims to communicate action and sentiment by a sensible representation; and his success was great. A still higher effort of Reynolds was to settle the principles of taste in regard to his own art. How successful he has been in this, we do not pretend to say. It is sufficient for our purpose to remark, that his "Lectures" have lost none of their original value by the efforts of later men.

It has been said that Burke aided his friend in this work. It is not our purpose to inquire into the truth of this, though there is abundant proof in his "Life," that he was deeply learned in the best established principles of the art. Reynolds must have possessed the power in himself; for it was a time. in which a great deal more was required than the bolstering of even the greatest men, and strongest friends, to keep one steadily at the point he might have reached, however elevated, and however it might have been attained.

We might mention Goldsmith in this connexion, the countryman and college acquaintance of Burke, who, with nothing but mind, did so much, and that so well, in his short and melancholy literary career.—And Johnson, too, were not a paragraph too short, and not a word necessary to make known one who is in the mouths of all who love his language, and who has his fame in the whole language itself.

Sheridan was one of the remarkable men of the time. He had relations with Burke which deserve notice. He was his countryman, his equal in birth, and educated in the same profession, the law. Like Burke, he sacrificed the law to

general literature, and finally, like him, became a politician.
He was with him for a long time in politics.   Here the parallel closes.

Mr Prior, after alluding to Sheridan's useful and splendid
talents, and to his neglect of them, observes :

Even as it was, indolent and dissipated, neglecting study and averse
to business, his uncommon natural powers always placed him in the
first rank.   A good poet, he would not cultivate poetry ; the first comic
dramatist of the age, and almost in our-language, he deserted the drama ; a shrewd politician, he wanted that solidity of sentiment and conduct, which, after all, form the surest passports of public men to public
favour ; a powerful orator, he would not always cultivate that degree of
knowledge which could alone render it effective and convincing ; he
was ready, shrewd, and remarkably cool in temper in debate, but like
some advocates at the bar, whose example few prudent men would desire to imitate, he seemed often to pick up his case from the statements
of the opposite side.   Power, fortune, and distinction, all the induce-
ments which usually work on the minds of men, threw out their lures
in vain to detach him from pleasure, to which alone he was a constant votary.

" With all these deductions, his exertions in parliament were frequent
and vigorous ; his wit and ingenuity never failed to amuse and interest,
if they did not persuade ; with greater preparation for parliamentary
discussion, few could be more effective.   His speech on the Begum
charge, of more than five hours' continuance, and considered one of the
finest orations ever delivered in parliament, drew from Mr Burke, Mr
Fox, and Mr Pitt, compliments of a high and unusual order ; and from
the house generally, and the galleries,—members, peers, strangers of
all sorts by common consent, vehement shouts of applause and clapping
of hands.   With such powers, who but must regret their inadequate
exercise, and unhonoured close ?   For it is melancholy to remember that
this admired man, the friend of the great, the pride of wits, the admiration of senates, the delight of theatres, the persevering apologist
of his party for so many years, should at length be permitted to ter-
minate his career in distress; adding another to the many instances too
familiar to us, of great talents destitute of the safeguard of ordinary
prudence.

Burke belonged to this age.   It is not our purpose to give
an analysis of the volume, which contains his life, nor to attempt any thing like a full character of this great man.   We
have no room to do either.   Such is the variety presented in
his history and character—he was versed in so many things,
and was profound in so many, that we should exceed our limits
by fully dwelling on any one of them.

Burke holds his preeminence among his fellows, not so
much for the extraordinary degree of intellectual power he
possessed, as for its direction.   He attained to distinction, not
among lesser minds,—but among as great, and none greater,

7

than his own. It was political distinction too, and a very cursory glance at the circumstances, will serve to show that the obstacles he encountered were neither few nor small.

These are to be found in himself, and in his native country; in his condition, and in the nature of the institutions of England. He was without connexion or wealth, and was new to the country. He took, indeed, the popular side in politics, in which the want of external distinction may, at first view, be hardly regarded as a disability. But this view is a mistaken one. The leaven of aristocracy was mixed in, and blended with, and acted upon, the whole English character; and it is a well known fact, that in his own party of whigs, it was not a pleasant matter of reflection, that a man without other distinctions, should by his inherent quality, his natural nobility alone, sweep away all that time and opinion had cooperated to preserve for many of them, and drive them back upon their intellectual resources alone, before they were allowed to think or to act with him. This is so strikingly true, that we cannot help adverting to it. It is not seen in the counter-currents, which are to be found setting in all parties, and which have their spring in merely personal views or interests. It is seen in the less obvious, but not less unequivocal bearing of the party with which he acted, and which he virtually led.

Burke was a commoner of Ireland. This single line is a volume of proof of the inherent disabilities with which he came to England. Ballitore, the scene of his infancy and earliest education, becomes St Omer's in England, and his fine English learning is but a translation from the French. The turbulence and anarchy of his native country were compendiously made to explain his pure love of freedom, and were, forsooth, the sole fountain of his equally pure and overwhelming eloquence.

How opposite to all this were the cases of his great rivals, Fox and Pitt, one of them in his own party, the other opposed to him. These were, in one sense, noblemen of England. They were at home in the country, and were allied to its best. With all this, they had the inherent distinctions of Burke, for their minds also were better than their privileges. Fox, however, loved pleasure as well as occupation, or rather, pleasure was his occupation. Hence, he was not always ready, or more correctly, was not always willing. This occasioned indolence, or habitual dissipation, kept his influence safer, by preventing its over-exertion. Pitt had the prudence of profound wisdom. He could not be committed, nor would he ever commit himself. Hence what he gained he never lost. Burke had an exhaustless zeal. He had industry, which was untired. He was always equal to, and, perhaps unfortunately for himself, sometimes greater than the occasion. When it was wanting to other men, either from interest or fear, he created the occasion. It was then, that he appeared in the fulness of his own mind, and of the minds of all others. He takes the guardianship of his country for the time into his own hands, without the formality of inquest or bond; and king and people are safe beneath his function.

This readiness to labour, in the cases from which less honest and less bold men shrink, while it was among the means of his earlier success, was also, we believe, among the causes of his faded influence at a later period.

The circumstances of his age afforded him perpetual opportunities to appear in public, as writer or speaker. The state of his party, too, furnished nutriment to his unfatigued spirit. It was divided. He ranked under the leader, whose principles accorded with his own. Hence he was forever working double tides. He was opposing the minister, a common cause with him and his party; but he was, at the same time, supporting a subdivision of the whigs, under a nominal leader. This goes far to explain his frequent, and sometimes almost fatiguing appearance in public. It helps to explain, along with his want of rank, the jealousies of friends as well as of foes, against which he had always to contend. It explains, too, his diminished influence, and the progress and political elevation of those, who had rank and connexion;— rivals who were with him, and rivals who were against him. One other cause only needs at present be named. He was for a time, at least, if not always, the greatest man of his age, and it is claiming more persistency for public opinion, however elevated, and however deserved, than belongs to it, to suppose he would always continue the most popular.

It is natural to pass, at once, from the men, to the events of Burke's time. It is necessary to do so, if we would find an explanation of his intellectual power, and especially of its uses, among the circumstances of his age. Two events stand obviously in the foreground,—the revolution in America, and the revolution in France. But there was something in the state of England itself, at that time peculiarly interesting. It may be, that the revolutions, as matters of history, have lost something of their novelty, from the frequent reference to them in all the contemporary and succeeding history.

The state of England was a continuous event, if we may so express ourselves, full of matter for surprise and admiration. England was almost alone, in the unquestioned supremacy of government, when political and moral affinities were elsewhere dissolving. It had a vast amount of evil within itself to contend with; but it had also a constitution, which successfully resisted deep-rooted diseases in its own administration. It at length shook them off. It gave its own inspiration to Burke; and if there was ever a pure and spotless priest at the political altar of a nation, it was he. He has the deepest interest to us, in his vast labours for his country. He passed between the constitution and all that would hurt it, as a father in the defence of an only child. He made sacrifices to this cause, and to his principles, neither common in amount nor degree. He rejected the prospect of advancement at one time, when he opposed the minister, because the path to promotion for him, in that direction, was dishonour; and, in his estimation, public crime. He afterwards gave up his friends, long known and long loved; not to get new ones under a worthy ministry; but because the principles he had avowed and defended for a long life, required him to do it.

It is almost a misnomer to call Burke an " oppositionist" in the course he took in regard to the American revolution. He was an Englishman defending the rights of Englishmen. He had learned these rights from a source, which to him was unerring, the constitution. "The principles and workings" of the constitution had been his earliest and favourite study; and the interest it first excited was never diminished. He knew its whole and real value; and he could not endure the thought of trifling with its privileges or abusing its authority. He was prepared to defend it for India, and he would not shrink from defending it for America. We all know what he did. We all know his failure. We all know his success. His failure was in not saving to his country its colonies. His success is the fulfilment in ourselves of his prophecies and hopes. If we would learn much, and that truly, of the history of our revolution, we should study the writings of Mr Burke. Our present business with him is as a statesman. Rockingham, his leader, is lost in Burke's own individual influence; and the minister is beaten at home, while his armies are slaughtered abroad.

Another event in this age was the French revolution. In its relations to Burke, this event has far more to interest us than has our own revolution. He might be said to have defended our rights for his party's sake; because in that way he might most successfully war upon the minister. In the other case, the part he took admits of no such explanation. It was an open, unequivocal, honest expression of his most deliberate judgment upon the whole moral and political state of France. It had its defence and explanation in the best established principles, and was confirmed, we might say dreadfully confirmed, by the immediately succeeding events. He saw that the earliest movements in France towards revolution, were not for correcting abuses of what for France was otherwise good, but the destruction of all good. It was not their object to check the waste and profligacy of a court, or the licentiousness of a people ; to bring within its proper bounds legitimate prerogative, whether royal or noble, and to make a people happier, by bestowing upon it a safe freedom. He saw, that their direct tendency and purpose was the indiscriminate ruin of distinction, and the distinguished; and that in their progress, public and private virtue were to be the surest prey.

Burke understood fully the whole character of this revolution in its earliest movements; and he lost no time, when it became necessary, in declaring his whole views. He made a public and solemn protest against all its principles in his "Reflections" on the revolution ; and warned his country in unequalled eloquence, not to fall into the snare, nor to be partaker in the sin. This conduct excited his whole party. The defender of freedom for America, they said, is its enemy for France. The cases, however, were without shadow of parallel, and the perfect consistency of Burke, in this most trying moment of his life, is no longer a matter of sober question. His party broke with him, and Sheridan and Fox went with it. We pass over the rupture with Sheridan, to give some account of that with Fox. It places these two men in strong contrast, and brings out some of their peculiarities.

A bill for providing a constitution for Canada, was brought forward, when Burke was not in the house. When it came up again, Burke, in reply to Fox, alluded to the French constitution, by name ; and to the scenes, to which it had given rise. Violent calls to order were immediately made from all quarters, and at length an express vote of censure for noticing these affairs, was moved against him by Lord Sheffield, and

seconded by Fox.   Mr Pitt defended Burke, and urged that
he was in order.

Mr Fox [observes Mr Prior] followed in a vehement address, alternately
rebuking and complimenting Mr Burke, in a high strain, vindicating his
own opinions, questioning the truth and consistency of those of his right
honourable friend, whom he must ever esteem his master, but who nevertheless seemed to have forgotten the lessons he had taught him, and
quoting in support of the charge of inconsistency several sarcastic and
ludicrous remarks, of little moment at any time, and scarcely worth
repeating then, but which, as they had been expressed fourteen and
fifteen years before, seemed to have been raked up purposely for the
occasion.

There was an appearance of premeditation and want of generosity in
this, which hurt Burke, as he afterwards expressed to a friend, more than
any public occurrence of his life, and he rose to reply under the influence
of very painful but very strong feelings.   He complained, after debating
the main question, of being treated with harshness and malignity for
which the motive seemed unaccountable—of being personally attacked
from a quarter where he least expected it, after an intimacy of more than
twenty-two years,—of his public sentiments and writings being garbled,
and his confidential communications violated, to give colour to an unjust
charge ; and that, though at his time of life it was obviously indiscreet to
provoke enemies or to lose friends, as he could not hope to acquire others,
yet if his steady adherence to the British constitution placed him in such
a dilemma, he would risk all, and as public duty and public prudence
taught him, with his last breath exclaim, ' Fly from the French constitution !' Mr Fox here whispered, 'There is no loss of friendship.' ' I
regret to say, there is,' was the reply—'I know the value of my line
of conduct ; I have, indeed, made a great sacrifice ; I have done my duty
though I have lost my friend, for there is something in the detested French
constitution that envenoms every thing it touches ;' and, after a variety
of comments on the question, previous and subsequent to this avowal,
concluded with an eloquent apostrophe to the two great heads of their
respective parties, steadfastly to guard against innovation and new theories, whatever might be their other differences, the sacred edifice of the
British constitution.

Unusually agitated by this public and pointed renunciation of long
intimacy, Mr Fox found relief in tears.—Some moments elapsed before
he could find utterance, when, besides touching on the bill and on French
affairs, an eloquent appeal burst forth to his old and revered friend—to
the remembrance of their past attachment—their unalienable friendship—their reciprocal affection, as dear and almost as binding as the
ties of nature between father and son.   Seldom had there been heard
in the House of Commons an appeal so pathetic and personal.   Yet, at
this moment, when seemingly dissolved in tenderness, the pertinacity of
the professed, thoroughbred disputant prevailed over the feelings of the
man ; he gave utterance to unusually bitter sarcasms, reiterated his
objectionable remarks, adding others not of the most conciliatory tendency, and of course rather aggravating than extenuating the original
offence.

There is much that is remarkable in the character of Fox.

The good and evil in him seem hardly to have blended with and modified each other. They were rather separate principles, and, in the present instance, at bay. He weeps for the loss of a long tried friend, and before the tears are dry, he insults and abuses him.

One cannot but be struck at the decline of Burke's influence, after Mr Pitt came into the administration. We have incidentally alluded to this before. We are the last to explain this, either by accidental advantages possessed by Mr Pitt, or by a momentary admission, that Burke's powers had declined, or were less actively employed. The cause is to be looked for, and it can be found, in the character and administration of Mr Pitt. There were strong points of resemblance between these great men; not so much in their power, modes of thinking, speaking, or even acting, as in the deeper principles of their minds, their ultimate convictions respecting moral and political truth, as well as duty. Pitt had indeed paid the French revolution, at first, his tribute of admiration. This Burke never did. But it was not long before their minds met on the essential character of that revolution, and equally so on the measures to be adopted on the part of the English government and nation. They were thus wholly agreed upon a war with France. They differed about the probable duration of the war, the mode of conducting it, and the amount of means to be used in its prosecution. Pitt thought it would be a short war, and that it might be best waged at a distance, on the skirts of France. Burke said, it would be long in duration, and that it must be carried on in the heart of the enemy's country; and Burke was right. In an earlier period of their history, when Pitt did not see as Burke did the things around them, he nevertheless regarded him at his whole worth; and instead of a vulgar patronage, which might have bought a man poorer in principle than Burke, he awarded to him all that his character and conduct claimed. When Pitt came into power, and when the coalition took place, who in his senses ever believed that Burke was bought, or his principles sold?

Burke's private history is a short one. He had no time to be a private man. The recesses of parliament were spent in laborious study, in writing for the press, or in preparation for the succeeding meeting. He had a power of application, which may well be called intense. The amount of knowledge he could thus acquire on any or all subjects of interest with him, has perhaps never been equalled, and excited the surprise and admiration of his contemporaries. His early history offers but little of peculiar interest. The *memorabilia* of boyhood are often not worth remembering. They consist for the most part of unusual dulness, as contrasted with much distinction in after life ;—in great precocity, which fulfils none of its own promises; or in tolerable attentiveness and acquisition, followed for the most part by mediocrity, or sometimes by a reach of intellect and extent of influence, which neither occasion nor circumstance fully accounts for. This last class comprehends the mass of men, and Burke has his place among the most remarkable of its last division. He was fortunate in his earliest domestic friends. He learned early to value moral purity, and this lost no value to him in after life. He was a singular instance in his time and in his order of singleness and honesty of purpose. His morality no man impeached, and his piety was habitual, unostentatious, and sincere. We were delighted with many of his characteristics, and with the manner in which he displayed them. He loved children with a freshness of interest, which seems hardly possible, when we recollect his rough encounters with men. Sometimes he expressed this interest after a manner almost ludicrous from its circumstances.

Burke never forgot his early friends, if they continued worthy of his memory. His abiding affection for Ballitore appears perpetually. He could show it indeed but rarely, but visits there occupied much of his short leisure. Active benevolence accompanied this feeling whenever the association was necessary. Barry, the painter, experienced largely the benefits of their union. Burke felt a deep interest in the progress and success of this artist. He felt a strong hope and belief that his efforts would be successful in this instance. Many of his letters to Barry appear in this volume, full of wise maxims for the conduct, and showing a true knowledge of the principles of his art. Barry hardly seems to have fulfilled any of the promise; and his failure occurred just where Burke had predicted, and against which he had laboured so much to guard his friend.

Burke's great characteristics were excessive ardour and unequalled zeal. Their direct operations were discovered in an unrestrained and strong expression of his convictions. These were not merely qualities of temperament, whether intellectual or physical. They were also, and we believe mainly, the products of his foresight, which in some cases

seems prophecy.   He was before and far ahead of the men
of his time, because he saw before and beyond them.   This
troubled his contemporaries.   He failed to gain all he might
have gained by the fulfilment of his predictions, because they
left him still in advance.   Men are not always convinced of
their errors, or pleased with the proof, however useful both
might be for their own minds, and for the wider interests in
which they acknowledge the most concern.   These characteristics were the external marks, the obvious growth of his
mind.   These with some other things have been mentioned
as causes of his diminished influence, or were offered as an
explanation of its not having been greater.   But there was
another cause in his mind itself.   This was either never apprehended in its fulness or depth, or if apprehended, it was not
acknowledged.   Burke was a philosopher in politics.   He did
not require expediency in his system, if what was so universally applicable, so wholly practical, could be called a system.
He saw things as they were ; knew what they had been ; and
wisely gathered what they would be.   This was his philosophy ; and all he proposed and did, had a direct correspondence
with this.   Lesser minds, or less accurate thinkers, his contemporaries, did not, or would not know and admit this ; but
made occasion of the more obvious and external, for their
judgments and value of him.

Burke had an only child, a son.   This son was a single
object, to which was drawn as if to a point, and by the strongest
affinity, his whole moral and intellectual being.   He loved this
child with a power, which, directed elsewhere, had been the
instrument of his wide influence over a whole empire.   He
was his son's friend ; and this son was the friend of his father.
In this short sentence we have expressed a relation, which if
not at once understood by the reader, we could not make
intelligible by any explanation we might offer.   He had arrived at full manhood ; had appeared in public life as a statesman, and was fulfilling the promise which his own powers had
given, and the imagination and deep love of his father had
added to.   At this moment he died.

We have said nothing of the literary execution of this
volume.   It is very unequal.   It would almost seem the work
of more than one writer.   There are some excellent sketches
of character in it, with much good remark by the author, but
with much that is commonplace.   It wants continuousness, an
essential quality to a perfect work in its class.

8

Burke would have been created peer had his son lived. We confess, that to us, the loss of the peerage adds but little to the amount of the calamity. We cannot sympathize here at all with Mr Prior. *Lord* Burke would have sounded no better to us, than *Lord* Pitt or *Lord* Fox. Mr Burke belonged to us all. He only asked to be buried near his beloved son, in the simple church of Baconsfield. His mind is with us; and his memory is safe, and his fame secured, in this his own legacy.

The Album.   New York.   1825.   12mo.   pp. 156.

WE do not approve of works of this kind.   Little use, and many inconveniences result from them.   They give the purchaser scraps selected from perhaps fifty different writers, oftentimes not the best specimens of the authors from whom they are taken.   If the selections are made from the *best* authors, they are of course from the most common ones. Those who could or would buy an " Album," are generally in possession of the complete works of the originals.   To such persons, an " Album" can be of no value, unless they buy books on the same recommendation upon which a certain tailor attempted to sell the library of his literary friend, to wit, because they are *well proportioned* books.   Judging by this criterion, the present publication is valuable.   In its externals, it is truly a charming volume.   We do not remember, that we ever before saw so beautiful a title-page.   The picture is admirably designed, and exquisitely engraved.   The paper and the typographical execution are in a correspondent style of elegance.   We suppose that the price, too, must correspond with the appearance, and really it would be too great a tax upon us poor reviewers, to fill our shelves with books of this kind.   We should have to pay twice, and in some instances three times, for the same matter.   Thus, there are in this Album several poems of Bryant, which were originally published in our Gazette, and which we hope yet to see in one or other of sundry goodly octavo volumes, lettered " Bryant's Poetical Works."

Lord Coke says of abridgments, that " they are most useful to those who make them," and a proper Album may be a convenient book as a receptacle for those solitary essays and short poems, which we sometimes meet, the authors of which have written nothing else worthy of preservation.

This volume contains twelve original poems, and fifty-two selected from American and English poets. Of the original poetry, there is none which falls below mediocrity, and but one which rises above it. That one we quote with pleasure, hoping that the author will write more, and renew our pleasure.

LINES TO A LADY.

BY MR N. P. WILLIS.

The leaf floats by upon the stream,
　Unheeded in its silent path;
The vision of the shadowy dream
　A similar remembrance hath.

The cloud that steals across the moon
　Scarce brightens ere its hues are gone;
The mist that shrouds the lake—as soon
　Must vanish, when the night hath flown.

The dove hath cleft the pure blue sky,
　No traces of his wing are there;
The light hath dwelt in beauty's eye;
　It was but now—and now is—where?

The winds of night have passed the flower—
　Hath morning found its gay leaf dim?
The bird hath sung by lady's bower,
　To-morrow—will she think of him?

Thus, lady, have I crossed thy path,
　Like bird, or mist, or leaf, or cloud—
My name a like remembrance hath;
　Deep shall its sleep be—in my shroud.

But still, the clouds may not forget
　The moon's serene, but fleeting light—
The bird, the leaf, remember yet,
　All that hath made their pathway bright.

And I—though cold neglect be mine,
　My name to deep oblivion given,
Will, while on earth, remember thine,
　And breathe it to my lyre in Heaven.

We regret that the publishers did not make all their selections from the works of American poets. If they had not found poems equal in beauty to those which they have borrowed; they would at least have spared their fair readers one or two yawns over the vapid verses of Prior and Shenstone, and one blush at the indelicate lines of Waller, which they have printed. Some of the English poems here republished, are very beautiful, but we will not extract, as specimens of this part of the work, any of the selections from those rare books, the poetical works of John Milton and of Lord Byron. Neither do we think it proper to reprint within the year, some of the beautiful poems of Bryant, which, as the proprietors of The United States Literary Gazette purchased them of the author, might, we think, without any impropriety have been acknowledged to be taken from our columns. We were glad to see here the poem of Washington Allston, first printed, we believe, in Coleridge's *Sybilline Leaves*, and without the author's name. They are verses which do honour to the man and the poet, to his native country and the country of his ancestors; it is a "strain that will not die." We are happy in the opportunity of adorning our Gazette with such poetry as this; and, though many of our readers have doubtless seen it, we trust, that none will complain of the space which it occupies.

LINES

BY WASHINGTON ALLSTON.

Though ages long have past,
　　Since our fathers left their home,
Their pilot in the blast,
　　O'er untravelled seas to roam,
Yet lives the blood of England in our veins;
　　And shall we not proclaim
　　That blood of honest fame
　　Which no tyranny can tame
　　　　By its chains?

While the language free and bold
　　Which the bard of Avon sung,
In which our Milton told,
　　How the vault of Heaven rung,
When Satan, blasted, fell with all his host;
　　While these, with reverence meet,
　　Ten thousand echoes greet,
　　And from rock to rock repeat,
　　　　Round our coast;

While the manners, while the arts,
　　That mould a nation's soul,
Still cling around our hearts,
　　Between, let ocean roll,
Our joint communion breaking with the sun;
　　Yet still from either beach
　　The voice of blood shall reach
　　More audible than speech,
　　　　WE ARE ONE!

Among the extracts from English writers, we were most pleased with "The Mourner," by Miss Roscoe; and the rather because there is in it nothing about *beauty* and a *rose*, budding or full-blown, a comparison which occurs much too frequently in the other selections. The whole is true to nature, and the best feelings of our nature.

THE MOURNER.

BY MISS ROSCOE, OF LIVERPOOL.

She flung her white arm round him—Thou art all
That this poor heart can cling to ; yet I feel
That I am rich in blessings : and the tear
Of this most bitter moment still is mingled
With a strange joy. Reposing on thy heart,
I hear the blasts of fortune sweeping by,
As a babe lists to music—wondering,
But not affrighted. In the darkest hour
Thy smile is brightest : and when I am wretched,
Then am I most beloved. In hours like this
The soul's resources rise, and all its strength
Bounds into being. I would rather live
With all my faculties thus wakened round me,
Of hopes, and fears, and joys, and sympathies,
A few short moments, even with every feeling
Smarting from fate's deep lash—than a long age,
However calm and free from turbulence,
Bereft of these most high capacities.
Not vainly have I nursed them ; for there is
An impulse even in suffering ; and so pure
Rise the eternal hopes, called by the anguish
Of a world-wearied spirit ; with such light
They rush before me like a sunny ray,
Piercing the dark shades of my clouded thoughts,
That for such high and holy consolations,
I welcome misery ; and I know thy heart
Hath the same blessed anchor. In heaven-ward hopes,
We drank the cup of youthful happiness ;
And now, when sorrow shades our early promise,
In heaven-ward trust, we comfort one another.

MISCELLANY.

ROBERT OWEN'S NEW VIEWS OF SOCIETY.

Had I plantation of this isle, my lord,
And were the king of it, what would I do?
I would with such perfection govern, sir,
To excel the golden age. *Tempest.*

THOUGH it is now about fourteen years since Mr Owen first began publicly to support his system of education and government ; its peculiar features would probably have been matter of little interest in this country, but for his late arrival from England, and his public addresses in the Capitol. These have excited considerable attention, and it may not be amiss to take some notice of his theory.

From his various, diffuse, and declamatory productions, we gather the following principles.

1st. Any general character, from the best to the worst, from the most ignorant to the most enlightened, may be given to any community, even to the world at large, by the application of proper means, which means are to a great extent at the command, and under the control of those who have influence in the affairs of men.

2d. That the will of man has no power over his opinions ; he must, and ever did, and ever will believe what has been, is, or may be impressed on his mind by his predecessors, and the circumstances which surround him. That the character of man is, without a single exception, always formed for him ; that it may be, and is, chiefly created by his predecessors ; that they give him, or may give him, his ideas and habits, which are the powers that govern and direct his conduct; that man therefore never did, nor is it possible he ever can, form his own character ; and that children can be trained to acquire any language, sentiments, belief, or any bodily habits, and manners, not contrary to human nature.

3d. That the only principle of action, that ought to be recognised, is the happiness of self clearly understood and uniformly practised ; which can only be attained by conduct, that must promote the happiness of the community.

These principles he considers undeniable, and proceeds to infer from them, that the character of the present generation of mankind may be much improved, if not wholly altered by placing them in favourable circumstances ; and that succeeding generations may be trained so as to possess a perfect character.

In order to bring mankind within the control of these favourable circumstances, Mr Owen proposes to divide them into separate communities, each consisting of from five hundred to two thousand individuals, possessing as many acres of land and occupying a village, arranged in the form of a parallelogram. In these societies there is to be a full community of interest, and an equality, in the first instance as great as possible, and finally full and complete.

It is unnecessary to enter further into the details of this philanthropic imagination. A community of goods is no new scheme. It has been repeatedly tried, but never with success, except where it has made a part of peculiar religious systems, which Mr Owen altogether disclaims. Our ancestors, both in Virginia and New England, made the experiment, but were soon compelled to relinquish it, and it is obvious to every one who has attended to the history and character of man, that while the latter remains unchanged, arrangements of this sort will ultimately lead to any thing rather than industry and prosperity.

But Mr Owen proposes to change this character entirely, by a course of instruction and government founded upon the prinples which we have quoted above. In regard to these, he seems to have fallen into two important errors. He supposes them to be both original and true, while unfortunately some of them are in one only of these predicaments, and the remainder in neither.

The first, for instance, taken in its widest acceptation, though most undeniably true, is as old as the world, and has afforded argument for moral essays and sermons without number.

The second involves a question, about which so much ink has been poured out and to so little purpose, that it would argue small discretion to engage here in the discussion of it; the question, to wit, of free-will and necessity, which has been bandied from school to school, and from philosopher to philosopher, and " deil ony thing the wisest o' them could make it," as Mackitchinson says, but just to throw it back again. Like many similar questions, however, this was long ago settled by the common sense of mankind, and the learned of modern days seem disposed to accept the solution. A modern lecturer has arrived, in a great book and in due form, to the conclusion which a great moralist of the last century bluntly and satisfactorily announced in the following terms—" We know we 're free, and there 's an end of it."

Seriously, it is idle to talk, in the face of all experience, of man's being the mere creature of circumstances, or, in other words, the subject of irresistible necessity in any other sense, than that philosophical and abstract one, which can have no possible bearing on practical systems of reform.

That circumstances have a powerful influence on character, no one ever gravely doubted; but Mr Owen's proposition is, that characters are created by circumstances, over which the individual has no control ;—a proposition, which, if correct, would lead to consequences rather unfavourable to the success of his designs. For if circumstances have caused in all the rest of the world those opinions and characters which now exist, and which are exceedingly hostile to his plans of reform, his arguments alone cannot, by his own theory, be expected to effect any sensible alteration.   In the conflict of influences he is likely to have the worst of it, and possibly to fare like the philosopher of a lunatic asylum, who was persuaded that his friends had confined him because he would not go mad like the rest of the family.   Assuming that he alone has a character formed by proper influences, the burden of gradually creating the new state of mankind falls on his individual shoulders, and he must mollify humanity, as Captain Bobadil proposed to conquer an army, by detachment.   Now this process will require time, and what is worse, will be affected by circumstances which our theorist cannot control, and which may chance to alter his own opinions and throw cold water on his enthusiasm.

But Mr Owen brings the testimony of experience to back his theory.   He has put his plans in operation at his cotton manufactory at New Lanark, and changed a company of indolent, dishonest, corrupt, and miserable workmen, to one that is comparatively industrious, virtuous, and happy.   There is nothing miraculous in this.   He has been scrupulously just, liberal, and kind to persons whose situations placed them in a great measure in his power.   Men are not stocks and stones.   Impartial justice will forever command respect, and undeviating kindness ensure affection. It was an arduous, but not an impracticable undertaking to convince them that industry in his service was the best policy.   It was an easier task for one so amiable as he is represented, to make them love him.   And this is the whole secret of the improvements at New Lanark.

But what are the circumstances, to use his own language, which will surround Mr Owen in the United States, and the materials on which he is to operate.   Can he find here a population, crowded to suffocation, starving for want of employment, or depending for their happiness, or misery, on the personal character of a lord of the soil, or a master manufacturer.   No such thing.   He will find a self-willed generation, who will judge for themselves of the circumstances by which they are to be surrounded.   He will learn that independent " shingle palaces" will possess more charms than parallelogrammatic villages ; that a system, which places him, or any one, perpetually at the head of an establishment, will never agree with the doctrine of rotation in office ; and that it is absurd to think of surrounding with any particular circumstances a people who can and will have their own way.

But " the happiness of self, clearly understood and uniformly practised, is the only principle of action that ought to be recognised."   There is no occasion for Mr Owen to press this point, since in one form or another a regard for the happiness of self is the only principle on which mankind have ever deliberately acted.

More modest philanthropists have doubted whether it was possible for short-sighted humanity to discover, without assistance, the true method of promoting its best interests, and effecting its highest happiness, on the whole, or in any particular case; and have concluded that the only certain course lay in obedience to the revealed will of that Being, whose omniscience alone beholds the extended chain of effects and causes. We say the only principle from which mankind deliberately act; for most of our actions are the effects of impulses. But why should we not always deliberate? Why should we ever act from impulse? is the language of Mr Owen. Why, indeed, but because we cannot always help it. He tells us that he has devoted much time to the study of books relating to the history, constitution, and necessities of human nature;—but in what language have the books been written, which do not teach that man never was nor ever will be governed by reason alone; that a knowledge of the right way is not always a sufficient inducement to pursue it; that the affections and passions are the master springs of human actions; and that a system which does not touch these, is useless and worse than useless? One book, at least, he cannot have studied, and that is—the Bible.

He tells us, that he has "read the Christian Scriptures," and that he finds in them "more valuable truths than in any others;" but "that all known religions contain too much error to be of any use in the present advanced state of the human mind;" by which we are to understand that the natural religion of Plato, Seneca, and Mr Owen, is a more perfect one, than that which is adapted, not to the tenants of the academy, the porch, or the parallelogram, but to man as it finds him, in all situations and under any circumstances; which proposes not to root out those affections which are inseparably united with his constitution, but to direct them to objects, grand, comprehensive, and ennobling; not to confine the intellectual and moral nature within the control of accidental circumstances, but to raise it above them.

It must be admitted that Mr Owen is an amiable, though mistaken enthusiast, who has done much good and may do more, and that he deserves the praise which is due to a benevolent disposition and zealous philanthropy; but it must also be admitted, that a theory of moral discipline, which leaves out of the question one, at least, of the great principles of the christian religion, neither can nor ought to be encouraged.

G.

9

CHAPEL IN WHITEHALL PALACE.

A LEAF FROM THE JOURNAL OF A TRAVELLER IN ENGLAND.

I went to day to the chapel in Whitehall Palace, from which Charles, " the Martyr," was conducted to the scaffold erected in front of this edifice. In the porch I was met by a doorkeeper, and informed that no person was permitted to enter that chapel, unless he intended to stay through the service. I made no difficulty in agreeing to this condition, and was admitted. The preacher was dull, as those of the establishment here are apt to be, and my attention was soon diverted from his soporific sermon to the architecture and decorations of the building. It was erected in 1619 according to a design of Inigo Jones. The ceiling was painted by Rubens, for which he received £3000; and it has been retouched at an additional expense of £2000. The subject is the Apotheosis of James I. The old monarch is represented in the different stages of his metamorphosis from a mortal to a demigod. His shrivelled and antiquated person appears dropping piecemeal its earthly exuviæ, and gradually assuming a fair and youthful form.

This chapel, like St Paul's, is adorned with trophies taken from the French and other nations. On the right and left of the altar are twelve of Napoleon's eagles and two standards—the latter taken at Waterloo, and the former at Albuera, Madrid, and Salamanca. The eagles, which differ considerably from ours, being modelled after the brown eagle of Africa, are perched upon staves about six feet in length. The standards bear, on one side, the names of

ELBING.

JENA.

WAGRAM, &c.

and on the reverse

L'EMPEREUR
AU REGIMENT 105me.
DE LA LIGNE.

———

AU 45me REGIMENT
DE LA LIGNE.

On a brass plate, at the foot of each staff, are recorded the time and place of taking these trophies. One of the eagles, for what purpose I know not, is stated to have been thrown into the Ceira during the retreat of the French army from Portugal. Perhaps the fact was considered as indicative of disaffection to the Napoleon dynasty.

Above the galleries, and entirely round the walls, are suspended the standards of various nations—among others, some of the United States, taken at Queenstown, Niagara, Detroit, and, mirabile dictu, at New Orleans. Four standards were of the kingdom of Candia, two of them richly emblazoned and embroidered; others were from Egypt, India, Badajos, and Martinique. The galleries were occupied in a very orderly manner by companies of soldiers perfectly clean and well dressed. Although a little attached to " the pride, pomp, and circumstance of glorious war," I cannot look upon a European soldier without a degree of indignation; for they seem to me to be designed rather to enslave the people at home, than to combat their enemies abroad. The British soldiery certainly have a very martial air—appear to feed well, and feel their own importance. Apparently they have less connexion and sympathy with the citizens than the soldiers of Portugal or Spain. The reason I presume is, that they are made more independent of society than in those countries where they are poorly fed, clothed, and paid.

NO HANDS.

Unhand me, gentlemen. *Hamlet.*

An ingenious essay lately appeared in the New Monthly Magazine, proving to the world the decided advantages of "having no head." And I did entertain sanguine expectations, that some one more able than myself would have employed his pen earlier in setting forth the manifold advantages of "having no hands." Disappointed in this respect, I take upon myself the arduous task; conceiving it to be my bounden duty to convince mankind how unfortunate is the situation of every one possessing two, live, naked hands!—although I cannot but regret my inability to handle this feeling subject in a manner more worthy of its merits.

The principal design of those uncouth appendages to the human figure, is, to perform all the duties and offices, which we are apt to suppose cannot be done, at least in so handy a manner, by the toes, the ankles, the elbows, or any of the other members, with which man is provided. But, however paradoxical it may appear—and however opposed to the vulgar adage, which says " many hands make light work"—I venture to affirm that no hands make work still lighter. For if one is so happy as to be without those awkward and ungainly limbs, is it not a fair inference that he will have none of their peculiar duties to perform? Thus, at once, a world of trouble is shaken off his hands. He may then enjoy dignity and ease without the pains—to use a sailor's phrase—of

" lending a hand" to obtain them.   Never will he undertake any ignominious handicraft—be seen toiling at a handcart—labouring at a handsaw—or confined between the degrading poles of a hand-barrow.

In military affairs he will never know the use of the manual, and war will have for him no danger.   Hard indeed must be the heart of the " orderly," who could command him to take up arms, or handle a musket.   And then, in pecuniary matters, what advantages will he not possess !   No one will ever think of borrowing from one who can never have money on hand.   His credit, too, would be unbounded, for it would be barbarous to require of him a note of hand ;   unless he could sign it with his feet, with which, indeed, a man may sometimes make a pretty good running-hand.

Another advantage, Mr Editor, deserves particular consideration.   He never will be obliged, as we double-handed wretches too often are, to shake hands with a disagreeable acquaintance ; and can never injure his reputation by being hand and glove with an exceptionable character.   Those disgusting articles, called handkerchiefs, will form no item in his wardrobe or his washing bill.   And then, how many seven-and-sixpences will he not save in the single article of gloves !   They, and the want of them, will be equally unknown.   And yet he will never complain of cold hands or warm hands, of damp hands or dirty hands.   'Tis true, he can never attain the fair fame of possessing " a hand open as day to melting charity."   But he will be equally free from the opprobrious appellation of a close-fisted fellow.   What a guaranty for honesty !   he will never lay his hands upon the property of another.   And of perjury he can never be guilty, till oaths are very differently administered.   He will live in peace with all his neighbours ; at least, no one will ever receive an injury at his hands.   He will never be liable to reproach himself with having fingered a bribe, or with having held up his hand to vote against the people and his country.

On the other hand, it cannot be denied that there are some privations, to which this improved specimen of the human animal will be subject.   They are so trifling, however, in comparison with his advantages, that I cannot suppose any will hesitate to adopt the improvement.   It is undoubtedly true, and I mention these things to show my candour, and do justice to the old-fashioned form of men, that there are many little pleasures—tending, perhaps, to make life agreeable—which he would be entirely obliged to forego.   At card-parties, for example, he could only be a spectator, for no one would think of inviting him to take a hand.   He could never take a lady's hand—or hand her to her coach—or, what is worse than all, Mr Editor, offer her his hand.

Is he desirous of pursuing the study of medicine ? Alas ! it would be a melancholy consideration, that he could never hope to have a single patient under his hands. In the law, too, who would plod through its rubbish of black-letter folios, unless he were cheered by the anticipation of one day being able to grasp the rich reward of some grateful and feeling client ? As a divine, however powerful and persuasive the appeals he might pour forth, few at least of his fair auditors would be convinced of the purity of his motives or the soundness of his doctrines, unless his arguments were enforced in a more handsome and striking manner than they could be by this fingerless, ringless being.

But, notwithstanding these minor considerations, I trust enough has been said to convince all of the expediency of immediately relieving themselves of these appendages. And though some may be " up in arms" at the suggestion, they must be few who will not go hand-in-hand with me, in my benevolent plan for meliorating the condition of the human race.

POETRY.

AN APRIL DAY.

When the warm sun, that brings
Seed-time and harvest, has returned again,
'T is sweet to visit the still wood, where springs
The first flower of the plain.

I love the season well
When forest glades are teeming with bright forms,
Nor dark and many-folded clouds foretell
The coming-in of storms.

From the earth's loosened mould
The sapling draws its sustenance, and thrives :
Though stricken to the heart with winter's cold,
The drooping tree revives.

The softly-warbled song
Comes through the pleasant woods, and coloured wings
Glance quick in the bright sun, that moves along
The forest openings.

And when bright sunset fills
The silver woods with light, the green slope throws
Its shadows in the hollows of the hills,
And wide the upland glows.

And when the day is gone,
In the blue lake the sky o'erreaching far
Is hollowed out, and the moon dips her horn,
And twinkles many a star.

Inverted in the tide
Stand the gray rocks, and trembling shadows throw,
And the fair trees look over, side by side,
And see themselves below.

Sweet April!—many a thought
Is wedded unto thee, as hearts are wed ;
Nor shall they fail, till to its autumn brought
Life's golden fruit is shed.

H. W. L.

GEN. FRASER—SLAIN AT SARATOGA.

In the pride of his daring, Fraser fell,
And while slowly away we bore him,
The warriors rude whom he loved so well
Shed burning and stern tears o'er him.

I die—he cried to his heart-struck chief,—
Life flows away like a fountain—
Let my funeral rites be few and brief,
And my tomb, the peak of the mountain.

There was not a heart but heaved with wo,
As the hero's hearse ascended,
And the vengeful shot of the watchful foe
With our farewell volley blended.

The pilgrim of honour secks his grave,
Where the bright clouds rest in glory—
His memory lives in the hearts of the brave,
And his fame in his country's story.

S. H.

THE FOUR AGES.

FROM SCHILLER.

The dark purple wine in the goblet now foams,
Now sparkle the eyes of each guest ;
The bard too appears,—to the banquet he comes,
And to good things he adds far the best.
For joy without song is but common and low,
Though in halls of the gods the rich nectar should flow.

His heaven-gifted spirit is pure and serene,
And the world as a mirror reveals ;
All things, that on earth have been done, he hath seen,
And all that futurity seals.
When the gods met in council, he sat in their ring,
And watched the first causes whence worlds were to spring.

He unfolds in its cheerful and glittering hues
    Life's varied and intricate folds ;
The earth as a temple he decks ; from the Muse
    Such powers of enchantment he holds.
No roof is so low, and no hut is so small,
But heaven and its gods enter in at his call.

As the sculptor of old, to whose far-seeing eye
    Invention called beauty at will,
Could carve earth and sea, and all stars in the sky,
    On a shield's narrow orb with his skill ;
The image of worlds, which are held by no bound,
He stamps on the moment's most fugitive sound.

The infantile age of the world he hath seen,
    When the nations were happy and young ; .
As a light-hearted pilgrim hath socially been
    All times and all races among.
His eye hath beheld the four ages pass o'er,
And now to the fifth he describes all the four.

First, Saturn was king, kind and just ; all the while
    As to-day, so to-morrow was fair ;
The nations were shepherds, and lived without guile,
    And needed for nothing to care.
They lived, and they loved, and they did nothing more,
For fruits in profusion the earth freely bore.

Then labour succeeded ; then fought each brave man
    With the monsters and dragons of old,
And the heroes appeared, and the kingdoms began,
    And the weak flew for help to the bold ;
On the fields of Scamander the lances were hurled,
But Beauty was still the one queen of the world.

But victory followed at last on the storms,
    From energy gentleness sprung ;
Then rose in perfection of gods the bright forms,
    Then the Muses in harmony sung !
The age of sweet Fancy, the maiden divine,
Is past ; ne'er again will so fair an one shine.

Then sank all the gods from the heavenly throne,
    The columns, the temple's beam ;
And born for mankind was the Virgin's son,
    The trespass of earth to redeem.
The transient delights of the senses were past,
Man's thoughts on himself were contemplative cast.

And the vain and the brilliant attraction was gone,
    Which made the young world seem so bright ;
In cloistered recesses hard penance was done ;
    And tilted the iron-clad knight.
But if life was then sombre and fearfully wild,
Yet love did not cease to be lovely and mild.

And still for the Muses there tranquilly stood
    The holiest altar apart ;
And all that was noble, and moral, and good,
    Was sheltered in woman's pure heart.
The flame of affection was kindled anew
By her tenderest feelings and love ever true.

And hence an eternal, a delicate band,
    The bards and the fair shall unite ;
They weave and adorn, with hand joined to hand,
    The girdle of Beauty and Right.
When Love and the Muses in union are seen,
The world wears anew of its youth the fresh mien.

CRITICAL NOTICES.

A Greek Grammar of the New Testament. Translated from the German of George Benedict Winer, Professor of Theology at Erlangen. By Moses Stuart, Professor of Sacred Literature in the Theological Seminary, Andover, and Edward Robinson, Assistant Instructer in the same Department. Andover. 1825. 8vo. pp. 176.

WE regard with high satisfaction the recent indications of an increasing attention to philological and classical studies in our community. We have among us a few scholars, who would be ornaments to any institution in any country ; and they, with a zeal the most praiseworthy, have been and are exerting themselves to excite an interest in these studies, to convince the public of their importance, and to furnish the best elementary works to facilitate the prosecution of them. We hope, and we believe, that they will, ere long, have their reward in the flourishing state of these studies in our community.

One consideration that gives importance to philological inquiries, and which ought to save them from the contempt in which they have been held by some, is their connexion with the just interpretation of that volume which contains the revelations of God. For this reason, we receive with welcome, not only as scholars but as Christians, the many excellent works—principally translations from the German,—which have within a few years been presented to the community, as helps to the study of the Bible.

The character of the language of the New Testament, as distinguished from that of classical Greek authors, has for some time been pretty well understood by scholars. It has been known that, though the New Testament is said to have been written in Greek, much more than a knowledge of the Greek language, as it exists in the classics, is necessary in order to understand it. A knowledge of the Hebrew has been allowed to be essential to the right understanding of very many words and forms of expression. Lexicons have been formed, explanatory of the peculiar language of the New Testament, so that very little remains to be done in that department. But to the peculiarities in the forms, the use, and the construction of the language of the New Testament, very few have directed their attention.   It is true the New Testament Greek departs from that of the classics, more in the department of the lexicon than in that of the grammar, more in the meaning of words than in their forms.   Still there are important peculiarities in the forms of words and their uses, in the use of the modes and tenses of verbs, and of several other of the parts of speech, and in the syntax, which perplex the student of the New Testament, and on which the common Greek Grammars throw no light whatever. An elementary work was evidently wanted, in which all these pecu- liarities, all the facts relating to the forms of words and their uses should be classified under proper heads, so as to form some rules for the direction of one entering upon the study of the New Testament.

The author of this work does not, however, confine himself merely to the *peculiarities* of the New Testament diction, but introduces the nicer and more uncommon phenomena of the language generally, and particularly such as are regarded as exceptions to the common rules. The advantage of this course is great in giving a systematic form to the work.

The design of this work then is manifestly excellent.   The next ques- tion is, how has it been executed?   We have already intimated, that the author has correct notions of what constitutes a good grammar, viz. a convenient classification of the actual phenomena of a language, and not *a priori* rules for its explanation.   The qualities of a good grammar are convenient arrangement, correctness or freedom from error, and com- pleteness.   In regard to the first, the arrangement of the work is not liable to exception.   It is natural, distinct, and convenient.   In regard to correctness, or freedom from error, we think the work entitled to great praise.   It is evidently the production of a thorough scholar.   His rules he justifies and illustrates by numerous examples.   He differs from some of his predecessors in important particulars; for instance, in the chap- ter on the use of the article.   Many remarks which are scattered over the best and latest commentaries, are here to be found in methodical ar- rangement.   The author, in general, seems more solicitous to be correct, so far as he goes, than to be comprehensive and complete.   But it is so far complete as to be a most valuable work for those entering upon the study of the New Testament.   There can be no doubt, how- ever, that much remains to be done in reference to this subject.   It is new; and perfection is not to be expected in a first attempt.   In course of time, considerable additions will undoubtedly be made to it, particularly in the chapter on the Preposition, which seems to us more defective than any other.

We were a little surprised at seeing a work from this source, hav- ing the Greek without the accents.   We supposed that of late there had been no doubts among our scholars, as to their convenience and advan- tages; since there are so many who would like to have them, and as they can do no harm to those who do not want them.

———

Address delivered before the Massachusetts Peace Society, at their Ninth Anniver- sary, December 25, 1824. By John Ware, M. D. Boston. 1825. 8vo. pp. 24.

We look upon the efforts of Peace Societies, as part of that succession of droppings, which is able to wear away stones, and upon the spread of

10

these societies as both an effect and cause of the progressive amelioration of
society. To one who should ask, What advantage shall I obtain, or what
good can I do, by uniting myself with a peace society, we should say,
As a member of such a body, you will be in the way of reading its various
publications. Your mind will acquire a habit of regarding war in its
true light, that is, as a great evil, and one that is rarely necessary at
present, and that may one day cease altogether to be so. The influences
which spread from your mind as a centre, like the circles from an impulse on the water, over those of numbers around you, will be kindly,
and you will have added your mite to the treasury of universal charity.

The interest of the various publications of these societies is, of course,
various. Some are calculated to produce little more effect than the
common consequence of repetition. This is something, since one cannot long read or meditate on a momentous truth, without being influenced by it. But many of these pamphlets do more than barely tell the
truth. They tell it agreeably; they present it in a dress which gratifies
the taste and excites the interest of the hearer.

Of this last class is the Address which gave occasion to this notice.
We took it up without any great expectation, and laid it down with a
resolution to recommend it to the perusal of our readers. We honestly
assure every one of them, that it will afford him much pleasure, and do
him some good, at the expense of very little money and very little time.
Whoever does not read it, after this recommendation, must be wanting
in good sense, faith in our sincerity, or confidence in our judgment; and
as we would not willingly believe this of any of them, we shall rest
satisfied, that we have been the means of doing them all a service.

The writer of this Address offers a very encouraging view of the
probable effect of the diffusion of just and liberal principles of government in restraining war. Wherever these prevail, the people, and not
kings, are the real rulers; and the proverbial sport of the latter is too
often death to the former to be engaged in without powerful reasons of
expediency, and such as are not often likely to occur between well
ordered communities. Republics may, therefore, be expected to be
pacific. If it be said, that those of Greece were far otherwise, it may be
replied, that universal and genuine liberty and equality of rights were
as little or even less known under those governments, than they are in
some of the monarchical establishments of Europe,—that force was there
paramount to law, as much as it now is in Austria or Russia, and that
instead of one tyrant, a man had to fear a thousand.

"The ancient republics," says Dr Ware, "were any thing rather than
what we call liberal. Of equal, well regulated liberty—of the proper rights
of mankind, they had no true conception. The freedom of which they
boasted so much, and of which we are told so much, amounted only to a
licentiousness for themselves, founded upon the subjection and slavery of
others. There is scarcely a government in existence at the present day,
which does not in reality make a nearer approach to an acknowledgment of the proper liberty of mankind, than the Athenian republic.
Even in the community of Athens itself, where was the security for personal rights! To be truly free is not merely to be delivered from foreign
bondage, or the yoke of a tyrannical monarch. Kings and conquerors
are not the only source from which our liberties may be infringed. We
require to be protected from one another, and I know not whether a just

men has not more to fear from the jealousy of a despotic mob, than from that of a despotic monarch."

Another view, here presented, gave us much pleasure, inasmuch as it agreed closely with notions, which we have always entertained.

" All nations," says Dr Ware, " seem to vie with each other, which, when the work of blood is concluded, shall treat the wounded or imprisoned enemy with the greatest consideration and humanity. Inconsistent as this is—this preposterous alliance between barbarity and humanity—it yet furnishes us with ground for expectation, that the principles which have already produced so great a change, will produce one which is complete and consistent."

Now there are in the world, who are loud in their indignation at the practice of licensing privateers—w do nevertheless defend the necessity, propriety, and even advantage, of wars, not merely defensive; and bestow upon the mention of a peace society a compassionate smile, and the name of a " devout imagination." Far be it from us, either in jest or earnest, or by any possible implication, to defend the practice of privateering—but we think that those who denounce it, ought in common consistency to be ready to go a step further. They should be ready to add the weight of their influence, whatever it may be, to that of the peace party, and to push melioration to the point when war shall be nothing worse than a contest of diplomacy.

Of the style of this Address, it is only necessary to observe, that it is the style of a practised writer, and that it did not occur to us, to think of it once during the perusal.

———————

Tales for Mothers. Translated from the French of J. N. Bouilly, Member of several Learned and Literary Societies, and Author of " Contes à Ma Fille," " Conseils à Ma Fille," and "Les Jeunes Femmes." New York. 1824. pp. 184.

These Tales are pretty, and nothing more. As far as their style and manner are concerned, they are rather adapted to children than mothers. The stories are commonplace, and possess very little interest for the mothers in this country,—who can find so many better ones in their own language. Probably, too, they have lost much of their spirit by translation. One circumstance only gives them a certain interest. It is the description contained in them of domestic life among the French. The tale-teller of course lays his scene in the interior of families. He is constantly speaking of circumstances simple in themselves, and familiar to his native readers. Many of them, however, are new to us, and probably to every one, who has not resided for some length of time, among the the class of people who are the subjects of them. As a means of adding to our knowledge of national manners and customs, therefore, the work is doubtless useful. We observe, that religious motives are not often brought forward. Religion seems to be a subject, which is not so much avoided, as disregarded. In the last tale, the moral turns upon the punishment of a wife's infidelity, which is termed an irreparable *misfortune*. The punishment is that of sentiment entirely. Her husband falls in a duel, indeed, but he bequeaths to her a sufficient estate. Her children, except one, as they grow up to maturity, decline meeting her, but treat her with respect; and the one who remains with her, though she does not wish her to " lean her hand on her shoulder, when she speaks of her father," does nevertheless express strong filial affection. The grief, remorse, &c. is all sentimental; there is no intimation of repentance of the crime, as a breach of the law of God. In fact a story of horrid ingratitude and wickedness is told in that gentle and well-bred manner, which "never mentions hell to ears polite." We were strongly impressed with the contrast, when it occurred to us to imagine how the same story would have been told by such writers as the author of Adam Blair, or the Human Heart.

An Explanation of the Apocalypse or Revelation of St John.   By Alexander Smyth.   Washington. 1824.   12mo.   pp. 59.

The question which the author of this pamphlet intends to settle is, whether the Revelation of St John the Divine, is a prophetical vision of future events, or *an enigmatical relation of past events*, under the form of prophecy.   General Smyth thinks the latter its true character.   And he solves the enigma, by applying in some detail the different chapters and texts of the book of Revelation to persons who lived, and events which happened near the Christian era.   He concludes, and gives his reasons for the conclusion, that the book was written by Irenæus, a disciple of Polycarp, and afterwards bishop of Lyons, A. D. 177.   The author has shown much learning and historical research.   He calls his work the solution of an enigma, and surely he has proved himself a very Œdipus.

INTELLIGENCE.

PRESIDENT MUNROE.

The London Magazine and Review, for February, comments with great freedom and candour upon the Message of President Monroe at the opening of the last session of Congress.   A cordial approbation of our political system is expressed; and the lucid exposition of the state of the country by the President seems to excite great admiration. "No American," say they, "can rise from the perusal of this address without feeling that there has been a fair and full disclosure made to him, by the head of the government, as to the actual state of his country;—there is in it neither reservation nor mystery; and whatever may be his sentiments as to the subject matter, he is, at all events, certain, that nothing has been withheld from him."

LIGHT PRODUCED BY CRYSTALLIZATION.

M. Buchner, having mixed some impure benzoic acid, perfectly dry, with the sixth part of its weight of vegetable charcoal, placed it on a soup plate, which was covered with a cylinder, luted to it by almond paste, in such a manner, that what took place in the interior could be distinctly seen through an aperture disposed for this purpose.   After the whole had been exposed several days to a moderate heat, and some beautiful crys-

tals formed, it was removed to a hotter furnace, and half an hour afterwards M. Buchner observed a brilliant flash of light in the interior of
the cylinder. A succession of flashes ensued, which completely filled
the cylinder, and continued half an hour, when it was taken off the furnace and examined. A great quantity of crystals of benzoic acid were
deposited. They resembled the crystals of the same substance obtained in the usual way by a more moderate heat and without light, except
that they were less regular. M. Buchner attributed this phenomenon
to a neutralization of electricity, as it took place at a moment when
the crystal was deposited on the inner surface the cylinder. The same
effect has been noticed on crystallizing acetate of potassa, and in preparing oxygen by means of chlorate of potassa and manganese.

MOTION OF THE ELECTRIC FLUID.

It has long been received as a fact, that an electrical discharge was
capable of being transmitted through a considerable distance (say three
or four miles) instantaneously, and without any sensible diminution of its
intensity. Mr Barlow, however, by employing wires, of various lengths
up to 840 feet, and measuring the energy of the electric action by the
deflection produced in a magnetic needle, has found that the intensity
diminishes very rapidly, and very nearly as the inverse square of the
distance. Hence the idea of constructing electrical telegraphs is quite
chimerical. He found also, that the effect was greater with a wire of a
certain size than with one smaller, yet that nothing was gained by increasing the diameter of the wire beyond a given limit.

DISCOVERY OF A FOSSIL BAT.

About the middle of last October, the workmen employed in the
quarries of Montmartre discovered the fossil remains of a bat. This
most interesting specimen was almost immediately presented to Baron
Cuvier by the gentleman into whose possession it had come. Permission to examine this hitherto unique production was readily granted to
the author of this notice, who was then in Paris. The portion of stone
in which the fossil remains are imbedded, had been subdivided during
the operation of quarrying, so as to leave the exact impression of the
animal equally well marked on each surface. The specimen altogether
seemed to be exceedingly perfect, and to resemble in size, proportion
of the pectoral members, head, &c. the ordinary species of bats now
existing. Nothing positive, however, can be said as to any exact resemblance between the antediluvian bat and those of the present day,
until the anatomy of the head and teeth be made out, by removing
from them the incrustation of solid stone, at present entirely conceal-
ing the structure of these parts.
The discovery of a fossil bat must be considered as a sort of era in
the history of the organic remains of a former world; hitherto, so far
as we know, no animal so highly organized has been unequivocally
shown to exist in a fossil state. Between the bat and Man, naturalists
have interposed but a single species, the Quadrumana: may we not
hope that future research may at last add to the list of antediluvian remains, the so much sought for Anthropolite?

NEW PUBLICATIONS.

BIOGRAPHY.

Lempriere's Universal Biography, containing a Critical and Historical Account of the Lives, Characters, and Labours of Eminent Persons of all Ages and Countries. With original articles of American Biography. By Eleazer Lord. 2 vols. 8vo. New York. F. Lockwood.

EDUCATION.

Essay on Language, as connected with the Faculty of the Mind, and as applied to Things in Nature and Art.' By William S. Cardell. New York. C. Wiley.

Story of Jack Halyard, the Sailor Boy, or the Virtuous Family; designed for American Children in Families and in Schools. By William S. Cardell. Third edition, corrected and enlarged. New York.

GEOGRAPHY.

Universal Geography. By M. Malte-Brun. No. 4. 8vo. Boston. Wells & Lilly.

HISTORY.

History of Boston. 8vo. No. 8. Price 25 cents per Number. Boston. A. Bowen.

LAW.

A Digest of the Laws of Pennsylvania, from the year 1700 to the 30th day of March, 1824, &c. By John Purdon. 1 vol. 8vo. Philadelphia.

Proceedings in the Courts Martial in the Cases of Lts. Weaver and Conner of the United States Navy. 8vo. pp. 84.

. The Laws passed at the Second Session of the Eighteenth Congress, 8vo. pp. 120. Washington. Gales & Seaton.

MINERALOGY.

A Catalogue of American Minerals, with their Localities; including all which are known to exist in the United States and British Provinces, having the Towns, Countries, and Districts in each State and Province arranged Alphabetically. With an Appendix, containing Additional Localities and a Tabular View. By Samuel Robinson, M. D. Member of the American Geological Society. 8vo. pp. 320. Boston. Cummings & Hilliard.

MEDICINE.

The Medical Recorder. No. XXX. Philadelphia.

MISCELLANEOUS.

A Selection of Hymns and Psalms, for Social and Private Worship. Third edition, corrected. 12mo. pp. 463. Cambridge. Hilliard & Metcalf.

The North American Review, No. XLVII. for April, 1825. Boston. Cummings, Hilliard, & Co.

First Annual Report of the Proceedings of the Franklin Institute of the State of Pennsylvania, for the Promotion of the Mechanic Arts. To which are prefixed the Charter, Constitution, and By-Laws of the Institute, with a List of the Members, &c. 8vo. pp. 107. Philadelphia.

New Edition of Spring's Essays. New York. F. Lockwood.

An Address, delivered March 8th, 1825, in the Hall of the Medical Faculty of Jefferson College, located in Philadelphia. By B. Rush Rhees, M. D. Professor of Materia Medica in Jefferson College. Philadelphia.

Lafayette, or Disinterested Benevolence; A Moral Tale for Youth. 18mo. pp. 36. Boston.

Philadelphier Magazine für Freunde der Deutchen Literatur in America. No. II. Philadelphia.

Private Correspondence of Lord Byron, including his Letters to his Mother, written from Portugal, Spain, Greece, and other parts of the Mediterranean. Published from the Original, with Notes and Observations. By R. C. Dallas, Esq. (This is the work for which an Injunction was granted by the Lord Chancellor, preventing its publication in England.) Philadelphia. Carey & Lea.

An Examination of the " Remarks" on " Considerations suggested by the Establishment of a Second College in Connecticut." 8vo. pp. 26. Hartford. Peter B. Gleason & Co.

The Grecian Wreath of Victory. 16mo. pp. 119. New York. W. E. Dean. Price 50 cents.

NOVELS AND ROMANCES.

Goslington Shadow; A Romance of the Nineteenth Century. By Mungo Coultershoggle, Esq. 2 vols. 12mo. New York. J. & J. Harper.

POETRY.

Mengwe; a Tale of the Frontier. A Poem. 18mo. pp. 76. Philadelphia. Carey & Lea.

Occasional Pieces of Poetry. By John G. Brainerd. 12mo. pp. 111. Price 75 cents. New York. E. Bliss & E. White.

Hymns for Children, selected and altered. By the author of " Conversations on Common Things." 24mo. pp. 143. Price 25 cents. Boston. Munroe & Francis.

THEOLOGY.

A Sermon delivered at the Old South Church, in Boston, before the Auxiliary Foreign Mission Society of Boston and the Vicinity, at their Annual Meeting, January 3, 1825. By Warren Fay, Pastor of the First Church in Charlestown, Mass. Boston. S. T. Armstrong.

The American Baptist Magazine, No. 100, for April, 1825.

Biblical Repertory, a Collection of Tracts in Biblical Literature. By Charles Hodge. Vol. I. No. 2, for April, 1825. Princeton, N. J.

An Interpretation of the Rev. Ezra Stiles Ely's Dream, or a few cursory Remarks upon his Retrospective Theology, or the Opinions of the World of Spirits; published for the benefit of dreamers. Philadelphia.

A Vindication of the Doctrine contained in a Sermon, entitled the Universality of the Atonement, with its undeniable Consequences, simply and plainly stated, in a consistent manner, agreeably to Scripture and Reason. By Joshua Randell. 12mo. pp. 32. Haverhill.

The Missionary Herald. Vol. XXI, No. 4, for April, 1825. Boston.

Gospel Advocate. Vol. V, No. 4. Boston.

TOPOGRAPHY.

A Report of the Board of Engineers of the Examination which has been made with a View of Internal Improvement. 8vo. pp. 112.

Report of the Canal Commissioners to the General Assembly of Ohio. Published by authority. 8vo. pp. 66. Columbus, Ohio.

AMERICAN EDITIONS OF FOREIGN WORKS.

New Monthly Magazine. No. XLIX. Boston. Cummings, Hilliard, & Co.

The Private Journal of Madame Campan, comprising Original Anecdotes of the French Court; Selections from her Correspondence; Thoughts on Education, &c. Edited by M. Maigne. 1 vol. 12mo. Philadelphia. A. Small.

Paley's Natural Theology. 1 vol. 8vo. Trenton, N. J. D. Fenton.

A Treatise on the Parties to Actions, the Forms of Action and on Pleading. By J. Chitty, Esq. Barrister at Law. Fourth American, from the Second London Edition. With Corrections and Additions, by John A. Dunlap, Esq. and Notes and References to late Decisions, by E. D. Ingraham, Esq. In 3 vols. Philadelphia. Philip H. Nicklin.

LIST OF WORKS IN PRESS.

The Boston Journal of Philosophy and the Arts. Vol. II. No. V. Cambridge. Hilliard & Metcalf.

The Northern Traveller, containing the Routes to Niagara, Quebec, and the Springs, with Descriptions of the Principal Scenes, and Useful Hints to Strangers; with Maps and Copperplates. The work will be handsomely executed, forming a neat pocket volume. New York. Wilder & Campbell.

The Journal of "Madam Knight" from Boston to New York, in the year 1704; and of the Rev. Mr Buckingham, Chaplain in the Army, in some of the Northern Campaigns, in the year 1709; both from Original Manuscripts, making a small 12mo volume.

Wyandance, an Indian Tale of Long Island. 1 vol. 12mo. New York. Wilder & Campbell.

A Register of Debates in Congress. Vol. I. Comprising the leading Debates and Incidents of the Second Session of the Eighteenth Congress, with an Appendix. Washington. Gales & Seaton.

Resignation; An American Novel. By A Lady. In 2 vols. 12mo. Boston.

A Reply to Mr James Sabine's Lectures on Balfour's Inquiry. In Two Parts. 1st. A Defence of the Inquiry. 2d. His Proofs of a Future Retribution Considered. Second edition, with Corrections by the Author. New York. C. Wiley.

John Bull in America, or the New Munchausen. Second Edition, with Corrections by the Author. New York. C. Wiley.

Scougal's Life of God in the Soul of Man, or the Nature and Excellency of the Christian Religion. Trenton, N. J. D. Fenton.

The New Jersey Preacher. Vol. II. Trenton, N. J. D. Fenton.

Published on the first and fifteenth day of every month, by CUMMINGS, HILLIARD, & Co., No. 134 Washington-Street, Boston, for the Proprietors. Terms, $5 per annum. Cambridge: Printed at the University Press, by Hilliard & Metcalf.

THE UNITED STATES

LITERARY GAZETTE.

| VOL. II. | MAY 1, 1825. | No. 3. |

REVIEWS.

Memoirs of Göthe: Written by Himself. New York. 1824.
8vo. pp. 360.

We wish it suited the taste of bookmakers and the convenience
of publishers to be a little more explicit in their title-pages. It
is impossible to find out, from that which we have just quoted,
some things, which the purchaser has a right to know, without
the risk of buying or the labour of reading the work. In the
present case, there is the less reason for the conciseness of
which we complain, because nothing is suppressed, which
could be injurious to the circulation of the work. It is a
translation, as we are partly informed in the Preface, from a
German work written by Göthe, with a title which may be
rendered " Poetry and Truth, or Passages from My Life." The
present translation, we presume, was made and published in
England, although no notice to that effect appears on the title-
page of the American edition.

This is, therefore, a translation of a work written some ten
or eleven years since in Germany, and two or three times
reviewed in the English and American journals at the time of
its publication. Our readers will no doubt call to mind one
or two rather clever and very bitter articles upon it, in the
Edinburgh Review; in which the venerable patriarch of German letters is handled with an unkindness and even a rancour,
which seem out of place and unaccountable in a British journal, even on the principles upon which the modern British
journals are conducted. The old poet, one of the first geniuses
and first writers of this or of any other day, is scoffed at with

11

a relish, and baited with an open-mouthed zeal, which leave the
reader to suppose, that there is some secret about it, which he
does not understand.   This secret is, that the articles were
written by a German, naturalized in England.   None but a
countryman hates with such genuine *gout ;* and expresses his
hate with such heartfelt and venomous eloquence.   The particular circumstances, which inspired the worthy critic, we
never learned.   It was very likely some little slight, which
he had received or fancied he had received in Germany from
the poet ; an unfavourable judgment, perhaps, dropped by the
patriarch of the German Parnassus, relative to some lucubra-
tion of the critic ; in short, some one or other of those causes
of offence, which an individual like Göthe can never avoid,
toward the minor wits :

> If foes, they write, if friends, they read him dead ;

and if he will not submit to the latter, he must to the former.

But the outrageous ridicule and abuse lavished by the Edinburgh reviewer on the work before us, and on Göthe, its author, would of itself have been an imperfect gratification of the
critic's ill temper.   Another step was wanting to give him full
content.   It happened, at the very time that the articles alluded to were appearing in English, that a literary journal
was published at Jena, within a few miles of Göthe's residence
at Weimar, conducted by a non-descript in the literary kingdom, of the name of Oken, at that time a professor in the
university at Jena.   His eye was also evil because Göthe's
was good ; and he immediately began to issue in numbers a
very spirited translation of the first of the articles in the Edinburgh Review ; by which means it was not only republished
to the world, beneath the eye of Göthe himself, but secured
an extensive circulation in Germany, where not twenty copies
of the original would ever have arrived.   The effect was, that
Göthe's work, on its original plan, was arrested.   Three small
volumes only had appeared at the time the first of these articles was translated by Oken ; in which three volumes, the
Life of Göthe was brought down only to his twenty sixth or
seventh year, and to the composition of his first works.   A
fourth volume has since appeared, devoted to his observations
on a journey in Italy ; but the tone is evidently changed.   Instead of the unreserved freedom with which, in the three
other volumes, Göthe indulged in the ease of garrulous, but
not doting old age ; this fourth volume is cold, stately, critical,
and consequently dull.

We do not know, upon the whole, that this is to be regretted, however much we may disapprove the way in which it was brought about. There was a good deal to censure in the three first volumes, considered as a matter for the eye of the world. The taste of the community for which the work was written,—the German,—is indeed very different from that of ours. Much, not only tolerable but acceptable there, would be wholly out of place, offensive, and ridiculous here. It is a certain fact, that these three first volumes,—of which the single volume now before us purports to be a translation,—are considered by the Germans as a classical work, both as to style and matter. But they are not a work, which can do Göthe full honor in the great republic of letters, and in after times.

A part of the evil resides in the very nature of this species of composition, self-biography. A man by genius and industry acquires a great name. By his actions or his writings, he attracts the notice of his contemporaries in his own and in other countries. They take an interest in him, as the performer of great actions, political or military; or as the conceiver of sublime thoughts, uttered in the most powerful language. It is *for* these performances and *in* these performances, that he is known; and for and in these alone, that he has any right to be known, or that it can often be his interest to be known. It is true, he is not only a general, a statesman, a poet, but he is also a man—a son, a husband, a father, a neighbour. It is possible that in all these personal and private capacities, he may be as amiable and respectable, as he is eminent as a public character; and much no doubt will be added by this circumstance, where it exists, to the value and interest of his life in the hands of a judicious biographer. But in his own hands—in the account of his character, written by himself—how rarely does it happen, that the private life of distinguished men furnishes materials, that can conveniently and wisely be spread out before the public. It is not for their private life, that the public admires them; that is to say, however gratifying it may be to read the private biographies of men like D'Aguesseau, Sir Matthew Hale, Washington, and others, whose private and public characters are in beautiful harmony; yet it is as public characters, that they are known to the world; and as public characters alone that it is generally desirable to know them. At any rate, whatever else is told; whatever anecdotes, family adventures, and personal traits the intelligent biographer may think it safe to preserve, as he has obtained knowledge of them from authentic sources; no one can think, without pain, of a memoir, in which these or any similar great men should have brought to light the forgotten trifles of their boyhood, or the small gossip of their thoughtless days.

There is something like an exception to the justice of this remark in one class of society, in the older world. By the peculiar structure of their institutions, in consequence of which men are born to rank, wealth, and power, and from the days even of infancy are invested with a species of social importance, there are some men so placed in the world, that they seem to have no private life; they are always before the public. Like the kings and queens of France, they even take their meals before the world. They are never out of full costume; they are made up even for those occasions, when common men are not only glad to be let alone, but necessarily are let alone. In the case of these individuals, personal and private anecdote acquires an importance. We love to read how Queen Elizabeth patted Lord Bacon on the head, when he was four years old, and called him her little lord-keeper. But Lord Bacon's father was lord-keeper too, and from the moment of the chancellor's birth he was surrounded by whatever was great, dignified, and honourable. But who could wish to read a self-biography of Sir Peter King (a man, who may perhaps be compared with Lord Bacon, at least as having like him sat in the chancellor's seat), in which he should tell us all about the times, when he stood behind his father's counter and sold groceries. There is nothing dishonourable in selling grocery; Heaven forbid; but we suppose one man weighs out a pound of Muscovado or breaks up a drum of figs, much as another; and whether it be Sir Peter King, or Neighbour Smallspice, there is no dignity in the action,—nor is it worth being recorded.

Now it so happens that Göthe was born in respectable, but rather humble life. His youth was passed among companions not equal even to himself; among associates, few of whom had, at the time, any name, we will not say in the world, but even in the good city of Frankfort on the Main. Some of them, in fact, were exceeding sorry fellows; and were so esteemed by Göthe himself; and yet he takes us into their circle, and tells us all about them, and relates all the pranks that he and they played together. This is a gratuitous sacrifice of dignity. If it were necessary to make a literary use of the knowledge of low life thus obtained, it could have been abundantly done in the form of a work of fiction, a German Gil Blas. But to make one's self the hero of his own Gil Blas is rather a hazardous experiment on the good nature of the world. Many of the most respectable English writers,— Goldsmith and Johnson at least we may name, and Shakspeare unquestionably beyond all others,—owed the truth and accuracy of their sketches of low life to their having mingled in it themselves. In their moral essays or fictitious pictures, the display of this knowledge does not impair their dignity; but who wishes to know more,—who is not sorry that he knows so much,—of Johnson rioting at midnight with Savage, in the streets of London ?

We shall not enter into an analysis of this work, which has been done repeatedly in the literary journals of the day. In what we have said of it, we have hinted at the worst. It is a very entertaining and not uninstructive work. It contains a great deal of literary anecdote, criticism, and speculation. It will make the reader feel more at home with the great German writers, than any other book of the size which we could name to him. He will here see Klopstock, Wieland, Herder, and men like these, in a light, which, if he be not deep in the literary history of Germany for the last generation, will be new to him. As the commencement of Göthe's literary career, the only part of it comprehended in this work, was precisely at the period of the great literary fermentation in Germany, at which her peculiar literature was springing into being, the work will form in many respects, an important accession to the literary history of Europe.

The account given of those of Göthe's own productions which were composed in his youth, is particularly attractive. His *Sorrows of Werter* is the production, by which he was first, and is still chiefly known in England; though only through the medium of a miserable English translation of a more miserable French one; unless a second has since appeared. The incidents of this sentimental romance were borrowed, to a considerable extent, from occurrences in real life, at the time that Göthe was a youthful practitioner of law at the imperial chamber of Wetzlar. He did not, however, confine himself to the train of events which actually took place; for while he furnished from himself several of the traits of Werter, various others, and the fatal catastrophe of the whole, were borrowed from the history of one of his youthful

co-practitioners at the court.   The following is the description
of the prominent personages of this far-famed romance, of which
the exact title is " The Sufferings of the Young Werther."*

Among the young men attached to the court, as a school of preparation for their official career, was one, whom we used to call, without
ceremony, the *Betrothed*. He was distinguished for a quiet, steady deportment, clearness of views, precision of word and deed. His ever cheerful
activity and unrelaxing diligence recommended him so effectually to his
superiors, that they promised him early promotion ; and this reasonable
ground of hope had induced him to plight his faith to a young lady whose
character afforded him the fairest hopes of a happy union.   After her
mother's death, this lady had undertaken the management of the family,
and had consoled her father by the zeal and intelligence which she had
displayed in her care of his numerous infant children—a happy omen for
him on whom her hand was to be bestowed. He might fairly expect her
to prove a good wife and mother.   Nor was it necessary to be so particularly interested, in order to perceive that she was a person worthy of the
affections of a man of merit.   She was one of those who may not, perhaps, excite violent passions, but who please generally. A graceful
form, a pleasing countenance, a pure heart, a sweet temper, a cheerful
activity resulting from this happy disposition, an easy and exemplary
method of performing the daily duties requisite in the care of a family—
all these gifts were her portion.   I had always observed such qualities
with peculiar pleasure, and been fond of the society of women endowed
with them. If I could find no opportunity of being useful to them, I at
least shared with them, more willingly than with others of their sex, the
innocent joys of youth, which every moment renews, and which may be
procured without trouble and with so little expense.   It is allowed that
women indulge in dress only for the purpose of exciting envy in each
other ; and that in this rivalship, which frequently destroys their best
qualities, they are indefatigable.   Those, accordingly, appeared to me
the most amiable, whose simple and modest toilette aims only at decency,
and satisfies the lover—the intended husband—that they think of him
alone, and that they can pass their lives happily without splendour or
luxury.
Ladies who resemble her whose portrait I have sketched, are not the
slaves of their occupations.   They can find time for company, and can
disengage their minds sufficiently to enjoy it. A suitable propriety of
behaviour costs them no effort, and a little reading suffices to form their
minds.   Such was this amiable bride elect.   Her intended husband, with
the confidence natural to men of an honourble character, introduced to
her, without hesitation, all whom he loved or esteemed. Entirely occupied in business during the greater part of the day, he was glad to see
his mistress amuse herself with a walk or a little excursion into the
country, with her friends of both sexes, after having completed her daily
round of household cares.   Charlotte—for this was she—was, in every
respect, unpretending. She was rather inclined by her disposition to

---

*The name Werther is significant, and not unlike in import to St
Preux.

general benevolence than any determined preference; she considered herself, moreover, as consecrated to a man worthy to possess her, whose fate might, at any moment, be eternally united with hers. The air that surrounded her might be said to breathe serenity. It is a delightful sight to behold fathers and mothers devoting themselves wholly to their children; but it is something still more interesting to see a sister display a maternal affection towards her brothers and sisters. The former sentiment seems to be inspired by nature and habit; the latter has more the appearance of free will and generous sensibility.

As a new comer, free from all engagements, I felt myself in full security in the presence of a young lady whose hand was engaged. She could not interpret the marks of the most perfect devotion as attempts to attach her to me; and she was therefore free to accept them as disinterested proofs of affection and esteem. I neither wished to be, nor could be more than her friend, and hence I was the more easily enthralled. The youthful couple showed a sincere friendship for me, and treated me with perfect confidence. I, who had hitherto been idle and absent, like a man dissatisfied with his condition, now found all I wanted in a female friend, who, although her thoughts were constantly fixed on the future, knew how to abandon herself to the present moment. She took pleasure in my company; and it was not long before I found it impossible to exist out of hers. I had daily opportunities of seeing her: we might all be said to live together, and we became almost inseparable, at home and abroad. As soon as business left the lover at liberty, he flew to the presence of his mistress. Thus, without thinking of it, we all three accustomed ourselves to each other, and always found ourselves together, without having formed any plan for meeting. We lived together in this manner a whole summer, like the characters of a true German Idyl, the foundation of which was a fertile country, while a pure, lively, and sincere attachment formed its poetry. We took walks amidst rich harvests, moistened by the copious dew of the morning; we listened to the cheerful song of the lark, and the quail's shrill cry. If the heat became oppressive, or a storm overtook us, we never thought of separating; and the charm of an affection, equally constant and tender, easily dispelled any little domestic anxieties. Thus one day succeeded another, and all were holydays to us. Our whole calendar might have been printed in red letters. Whoever remembers the expressions of the happy and ill-fated lover of Julia will easily understand me. "Seated at the feet of my beloved, I shall peel hemp, and desire nothing further, this day, to-morrow, the day after—all my life."

I must now introduce a person whose name will hereafter appear but too often; I mean Jerusalem, the son of the celebrated theologian. He held a place under the deputation. He was a middle-sized young man, but elegant, and of prepossessing appearance. His face was almost a perfect oval; his features delicate and mild, as we usually see them in a handsome fair-haired man: his blue eyes were rather beautiful than expressive. His dress was that of Lower Germany, and imitative of the English costume. He wore a blue frock, a yellow leather waistcoat, and boots with brown tops. We never visited each other, but I often met him in company. His manners were reserved, but amiable. He took an interest in the productions of the arts, and was fond of drawings or sketches representing the calm character of profound solitude. He

praised Gessner's engravings, and recommended the study of them.   He
seldom joined in social amusements, and was fond of living to himself
and his own ideas.   His attachment to the wife of one of his friends was
talked of; but he was never seen in public with the object of his love.
On the whole, people knew very little of his affairs, except that he
devoted much time to the study of English literature.   His father being
rich, he did not take a very active part in business, or exert himself
much to obtain an appointment.

Such, with a few verbal corrections of some errors in the
translation, is the account of three of the personages from
whom the leading characters in Werter were taken.   A few
years since Charlotte was living at Hanover, the mother of
nine children.   We ought perhaps to say one of the Char-
lottes; for Göthe informs us, in the present work, that he
made a business to combine in the description of her person
and character, traits which had fixed his admiration in various
fair ladies of the day; and that as these were respectively
recognised by their common friends, he was not a little annoyed by inquiries, which the real Charlotte was.

This work, as far as it can be called a biography, terminates,
in the original, somewhat abruptly, with the third volume.   A
fourth has been published, as we observed, containing an account of the travels of Göthe in Italy, and possibly the series
has been still farther continued.   The work before us contains
a translation only of the three first volumes.   It is a translation apparently done by the job; and is not only full of errors
in the meaning of words and construction of sentences, but is
entirely destitute of the style and spirit of the original.   With
these great defects, however, it is valuable; and will be read
with interest by all who feel a curiosity either in German
literature in general, or the life of its Nestor.   The volume
is rendered considerably more useful by an Appendix, containing biographical notices of the principal persons named
in it.   This appendix appears to have been abstracted from a
German Dictionary of authors of good authority, and though
not very ample, either as to the number of articles it contains,
or the amount of what is said of each, it will generally reward
the English reader who may consult it.   We close this article
with an abstract of the life of Göthe, from the time when his
own Memoirs stop, as it appears in the Postscript to the present
volume.

From Joerden's Lexicon of German Authors, it appears that our
author spent in Frankfort the year 1775 as well as 1774, towards the
end of which he has chosen to take leave of his readers.   Except the

accounts of his travels, there are no farther biographical materials from his own pen; and the supply from other sources is very scanty, and may consequently be stated within a small compass. But before the few facts which have been collected are detailed, the following description of the personal and mental qualities given of a man who holds so distinguished a rank in the literary world, by one of his contemporaries in early life, will perhaps be acceptable. It occurs in a letter written by Heinse to Gleim while Göthe was at Dusseldorff, which place he frequently visited during the years 1774 and 1775:—' We have Göthe here at present. He is a handsome young man of twenty-five; all genius from top to toe, power, and vigour;—with a heart full of feeling, a spirit of fire eagle-winged, *qui ruit immensus ore profundo.*" What is here said of the mind of Göthe appears still to be the general opinion of his countrymen. The author of the Lexicon above referred to, observes, that the account given by Heinse of his external appearance is confirmed by the testimony of all who knew him in his youth. "Indeed," adds Joerden, " if we judge of him by what he now is, he must have been a remarkably fine-looking man. Old age has not impaired the dignity and grace of his deportment; and his truly Grecian head, large penetrating eyes, and elevated forehead, continue to rivet the attention of all who look on him."

Charles Augustus, Duke of Saxe-Weimar, while hereditary prince, visited Frankfort: where Göthe, as has already been stated, was introduced to him. The result of the impression made by this meeting on the young prince, was the invitation of Göthe to Weimar; whither he went in the year 1776, and where he has since, with the exception of the time occupied by his journeys in France, Switzerland, and Italy, continued almost constantly to reside. Immediately on his arrival he was appointed a member of the Legislative Council, with a seat and vote in the Privy Council. In 1779, he became actually a member of the Privy Council, and in company with his patron undertook a second journey to Switzerland, where he had previously travelled in the year 1773 with the Counts Christian and Frederick Leopold Von Stolberg. On his return from his last Swiss tour, Goëthe devoted much of his attention to the business of the dutchy of Weimar. In 1782, letters patent of nobility were granted to him, and he was made President of the Council of State. Between the year 1774 and this period, however, several of the author's works were published; for the Duke was very far from wishing, by the appointments which have been enumerated, to divert the exercise of talents he so highly esteemed, from literary to political labour.

In 1786, Göthe undertook a journey to Italy; in visiting various parts of which, the island of Sicily included, he spent nearly three years. His stay at Rome occupied a considerable portion of his time; and with a mind stored with classical reminiscences and associations, he returned to Weimar in 1789. In 1792, the Duke of Weimar having joined the Prussian army which entered Champagne, Göthe accompanied him, and was a spectator of the events of that extraordinary campaign, in which the Prussian veterans, led by the Duke of Brunswick, were compelled to fly before the raw levies of Republican France. It is said, that since that period, our author has constantly lived at Weimar. In 1808, he received the cross of the Legion of Honour from the Emperor Napoleon; and in the same year the Emperor of Russia conferred on him the order of St Alexander Newsky.

12

Weimar has been called the German Athens; a distinction which it in some measure merits, on account of the number of learned men there gathered together by the government, the liberality and enlightened views of which are worthy the imitation of the rulers of larger states. This little town is surrounded by elegant houses and delightful gardens. Ettersburgh, the Belvedere, Wilhelmsthal and Ilmenau, are to the Germans what the Portico, the Academic Groves, and the banks of the Cephisus and the Ilissus, were to the Greeks. Before the arrival of Göthe, Wieland, Bode, Musæus, and Bertuch had shed a lustre over this retreat of the German Muse. Herder and Schiller more recently joined the author of Werther. Weimar became the capital of a literary republic, which Knebel, Emsiedel, Segesmund Von Seckondorff, Bœttiger, Bahrdt, the brothers Schlegel, Madame Wollzogen, and Amelia Imhoff, contributed, with the great characters already mentioned, to render illustrious. All whose names were distinguished in art or literature, obtained a flattering reception at Weimar, and were detained, at least for a time, as welcome guests in that temple of the muses. Göthe was ever the soul of these assemblages; but less occupied with his own personal fame and superiority, than with the ardent desire of establishing the glory of his country, he devoted his whole life to promote the advancement of German literature, and the interests of those who seconded his efforts. He was constantly the warm friend of Herder and Schiller; whom, had his heart been less generous, he might have regarded as his rivals. His memoirs have shown how much Herder tried his patience; and to Schiller, whose melancholy and often peevish disposition may be attributed to impaired health and excessive occupation, he constantly manifested the indulgence and attention of an affectionate brother. His merit in these particulars is universally acknowledged by his countrymen; and it is a merit which is not always due to superior geniuses. One individual alone attempted to interrupt the harmony that prevailed at Weimar. He wished to gain admittance to this sanctuary of literature; but his character excited distrust, and his proposals were declined. His wounded vanity avenged itself by a libel, which occasioned an individual, whose name he had assumed, to forfeit his situation. This agent of discord was the unfortunate Kotzebue.

It must indeed be admitted that Göthe seems to have always regarded his varied powers of mind, and his rank in society, merely as means by which he might be enabled to accelerate the advancement of science, literature, and art in Germany. He has been constantly engaged in stimulating and encouraging talent of every kind, and in publishing works which have exercised a powerful influence over the public mind of his country. He has left no path of literature untrodden. The dramatic art in all its branches, epic poetry, detached poems of every description, novels, travels, the analysis and theory of the polite arts and literature, criticism, epistolary correspondence, translation, memoirs, and works of science;—in short, Göthe's genius has embraced every thing. He appears to have neglected no task by which he conceived he might open a road to improvement, or hold out new lights to guide the steps of adepts in the pursuits of human knowledge; and there is no work, however trivial, of this Colossus of German literature, in which the extravagant admiration of his countrymen does not recognise the impress of originality and genius.

History of Massachusetts, from 1764, to July, 1775: when General Washington took Command of the American Army. By Alden Bradford, Secretary of the Commonwealth. Boston. 1822. 8vo. pp. 414.

History of Massachusetts, from July, 1775, when General Washington took Command of the American Army at Cambridge, to the year 1782, (inclusive), when the Federal Government was established under the present Constitution. By Alden Bradford. Boston. 1825. 8vo. pp. 376.

THE history of Massachusetts, from its first settlement by the pilgrims in 1620 to the year 1750, by Hutchinson, and continued by Minot to 1765, is in these volumes brought down to 1782, the period of the settlement of the federal government on its present basis. Few commonwealths of equal extent and duration can boast so complete an account of their origin and progress, and we have an honest pride in believing, that few have so well deserved it. The little party on board the Mayflower, who, in December, 1620, did " solemnly and mutually, in the presence of God and one another, covenant and combine themselves together into a civil body politic," gave a pledge to the world, that the territory of which they were about to take possession, should be the abode of civil liberty and equal rights ; a pledge which their posterity have amply redeemed. With sure and steady steps the sons of the pilgrims have marched in the van of the army of freedom, bearing down, or turning aside every obstacle to its progress. If the world delights to honour in individuals that firmness of purpose, that unconquerable will, which, steadily directed to the accomplishment of one great object, pursues it through every difficulty and at every hazard, we may well be permitted to glory in belonging to a community, which, for two centuries, has been distinguished by a similar character. The history of this community does not show us the occasional struggles of a people infuriated by oppression, and wielding the weapons of ignorant and savage despair, alternating with abject submission to debasing tyranny. It does not tell us of a degraded populace, now crouching under the lash of a driver, and now seizing a favourable opportunity to fly at his throat. We are not told of the varying fortunes and alternate predominance of a cruel aristocracy, and a factious and fierce democracy. These things belong to the history of the nations beyond the Atlantic. Our annals recount the deliberate commencement, persevering defence, and glorious establishment of a system of government founded on principles, which nature and reason approve,—a system with which oppression and insurrection, thrones and mobs are alike incompatible, and under which, power can seldom be abused, or resisted. Philosophers have supported the liberties of mankind with the pen, and heroes have defended them with the sword. Our fathers wielded both weapons with equal readiness and power. While the question was a peaceful one of right, they wrote down their antagonists; and when it came to be a question of might, they demonstrated, that the *ultima ratio* of the British ministry was as feeble as their former arguments.

Some of our readers may possibly be surprised, that we should thus dwell on a subject so trite, and tell over a tale so often told, as that of the wisdom, foresight, and valour of our ancestors. They may think that we are labouring to deserve the reproaches, which have been lavished upon American vanity, and regret that the periodical presses of this country should thus continue to furnish occasion for foreign sarcasm. We shall be sorry if any should entertain sentiments of this kind, but are unable to agree with them. We might have some doubts about the policy of defending the claims of the Columbiad to immortality, or contending for the euphony of our New England christian names, but we have none with respect to the expediency of sounding the praise of those whose efforts and sacrifices have procured for us the blessings we now enjoy. We believe that a portion of the time of the public of these states could not be better employed, than in contemplating the actions of those exalted characters, which have shed such lustre on our country. We think it the duty of every individual in this republic to study its annals, and that the performance of this duty will be its own reward. We are, therefore, ready to welcome any trustworthy publication on this subject, and shall think these remarks were made to good purpose, if they have the effect of inducing a single individual to peruse the works which stand at the head of this article, who would otherwise have been ignorant of much that they contain.

The official situation held by the author of these volumes during ten years, enabled him to draw his materials from the best sources. He had the best opportunity of becoming acquainted with the authentic documents relating to his subject. To these qualifications were added an intimacy with the traditions of the country, which is possessed by few, and an extensive acquaintance with distinguished individuals, who had taken an active part in the proceedings of the state, during the revolutionary war. The first volume is the more interesting of the two. Soon after the commencement of the proceedings, which are the subject of the second, the history of Massachusetts becomes subordinate to that of the United Colonies generally. The theatre of warlike operations was removed to another portion of the union, and the detail of the exertions of this particular state have a less animating interest. They ought, however, to be generally understood. Her contributions of men and money, far beyond her just proportion—the immense burdens upon her citizens—and the industry and energy of her government, are related with great minuteness and accuracy. The first volume has been long before the public, and we shall not notice it further. Upon the second, as the proper object of this article, we offer a few remarks.

We sometimes, in the course of the work, meet with expressions, which belong rather to the spirit of the times, than to the impartial historian. Thus, on the first page, we read of the " attack by a detachment of the British army upon the *defenceless* citizens of the province at Lexington and Concord." The citizens had no regular army, it is true, but they were in possession of military stores, which it was the object of the British expedition to destroy, and those actually attacked were in arms. The epithet *defenceless*, must be, moreover, received with exception, since they did defend themselves, and that to good purpose. The spirit with which the troops, on this and another occasion, were resisted, produced a powerful effect upon the British officers. The salutary dread, inspired by the result of these attempts, had a great share in producing their subsequent inactivity, during the siege of Boston. In this siege, if it can be so called, ten thousand regular soldiers were, for eight or nine months, cooped up in that city, suffering extreme privations, from which they made few or no efforts to relieve themselves; and that by a body of ill-armed, undisciplined militia, with a very inadequate supply of ammunition, and four brass field-pieces. The real situation of affairs in the American army, in all probability was pretty well known to the British commandant, through the treacherous communications of Dr Church. But the army had suffered too severely from resistance, made under still greater disadvantages, to venture another excursion, and probably it was suspected by their officers, that the courage of the men was too completely cowed by the rough handling of the provincials on former occasions, to be much depended on.

On page 345, we find the following paragraph:

In appointing to office under the federal government, General Washington selected those who had been distinguished by their zeal and patriotism during the war of the revolution. And his appointments were bestowed on none but men of integrity and talents, which fully qualified them for the stations in which they were placed. This policy was approved by all impartial men; and yet Mr Jefferson, who succeeded to the presidency, some years after General Washington declined it, removed some of the revolutionary characters from the offices they held, merely for difference of political opinions, on subjects or measures of minor consideration, which did not implicate their patriotism or their republican principles.

The latter part of this, we think, had better been omitted. The history of Mr Jefferson's administration belongs to a period beyond the limits of this volume. Posterity will decide upon its merits; and admitting both the fact and the implied consequence to be correct, it seems to us, as if the writer had gone out of his way to give utterance to an expression of disapprobation of a political measure, with which he had, in that place at least, nothing to do.

We noticed a few typographical errors, perhaps not more than were to be expected in a work of this length, but some are important, as, for instance, the wrong spelling of names; thus, "Howe" is three times spelled "How," and in the only instance in which the name of "Pulaski" is mentioned, it is printed "Polaski." In another place we find "Goreham," instead of "Gorham."

We remarked also the following errors in construction and the use of words:

'His decision and zeal *equal to those* distinguished men,' &c. P. 37.

'The legislative assembly of Massachusetts, which met and *organized* on the 19th of July,' &c. P. 65.

'They had some belief that administration would retract *of* its despotic purposes,' &c. P. 68.

'That the governor of Canada would *avail of* the occasion,' &c. P. 89.

'Some of the paper was of so little value, *as* that thirty,' &c. P. 181.

'A singular *phenomena* occurred,' &c. P. 192.

'Avowed the most *disorganizing* sentiments,' &c. P. 267.

They are neither very numerous nor important, and though a more careful examination may possibly detect a few more, we think the number cannot be considerable.

One fact related here, which we do not recollect to have met with in any other place, is a singular proof of the poverty and simplicity of the times ; on the occasion of the brilliant affair at Bennington, a present was ordered by the legislature to General Stark, of *a suit of clothes, and a piece of linen.*

The following anecdote of Washington was also new to us.

Hon. Mr Partridge, one of the committee, [appointed by the Legislature of Massachusetts to go to the head-quarters of General Washington to consult him on the subject of enlistment] related afterwards, that he never saw Washington discover any thing but perfect self-command, except on that occasion. When a year was mentioned for the time of service, he started from his chair, and exclaimed, ' Good God, gentlemen, our cause is ruined, if you engage men only for a year. You must not think of it. If we ever hope for success, we must have men enlisted for the whole term of the war.'

The exertions of the Massachusetts government at every period of the war, were very great. A singular instance of this appeared on one occasion, when we are told, that

Lead and flints to a considerable amount, were again furnished the state of Connecticut, for the supply of their troops. Nor was this done because of a great quantity in Massachusetts ; for at this time the people were requested to take *the weights from their windows for the public use.*

It is well known that opinions were various respecting the federal constitution, of which the results have been so glorious. Many of the states, and among the number, New York and Rhode Island, resisted obstinately and for a long time its adoption, and if the public opinion had not been powerfully influenced by the writings of some of the greatest politicians of the age, the constitution would probably not have been adopted. The example of Massachusetts had a great share in effecting this beneficial result, though its acceptance in this state was carried by the small majority of nineteen in an assembly of three hundred and sixty persons, and this after a discussion of several weeks, and the unwearied exertions of its eloquent advocates. Washington, we are told, " expressed great satisfaction when informed that Massachusetts had adopted it."

We conclude our remarks upon this work by again recommending it to the notice of our readers, as a work from which they may derive both profit and amusement.

Hadad, a Dramatic Poem.   By James A. Hillhouse, Author of
   "Percy's Masque," and " The Judgment."   New York. 1825.
   8vo.   pp. 208.

THIS is a highly finished and beautiful poem.   It is worthy
the former works of the author, and fulfils whatever promise
of excellence they may have given.   It is written with great
care, perfectly free from all imitation of that off-hand and
flippant style so characteristic of the modern school, and at
once richly and chastely ornamented; vigorous in its diction,
elegant and expressive in versification, though sometimes wanting in the easy flow of syllables; and with great purity and
frequent sublimity of thought.   In the general structure of the
plot, selection and arrangement of incidents, and portraying of
character, there seem to us eminent felicity and judgment.
In a word, we consider this as the offspring of superior genius,
under the direction of the truest taste; and as deserving to
be numbered with the memorable works of the day, and to
meet with a hearty and grateful reception from the reading
public.

   We do not apprehend that any, who shall read this little
volume with attention, will think our expressions of admiration
too strong, though we may not be able fully to justify them to
our readers in the remarks and extracts we may now offer.
The effect of all narrative and dramatic writings depends
much on their being read in course; and scenes or passages
which are striking and affecting to him who has become interested in the circumstances of the story and the fortunes of the
persons, may be cold and unattractive to him who reads them
only as disjointed paragraphs, in critical specimens.   Yet at
the same time, the merit of the poetical diction will not be lost
from the most insulated extract; and we think it would be
difficult to select a passage of any length from the present
work, which could be considered as the production of an ordinary or unskilful mind.

   Mr Hillhouse has laid his scene in Jerusalem, at the time
of Absalom's rebellion.   The prominent features of the Scripture history of that event are adhered to with fidelity, and
most of the principal actors are historical personages.   As it
is thus a drama founded on sacred history, a comparison is
involuntarily suggested with the sacred dramas of Mr Milman;
a comparison which our author might fearlessly invite.   The

present poem has not indeed the gorgeous and elaborate splendor, which characterizes the works of the other writer; but it has, if we mistake not, more of the soul of poetry, and, in point of language, evinces a juster taste. We think, too, there is better discrimination of character, and far greater success in the difficult union of fine poetry with seemingly real conversation; not to say that there is a true tenderness and pathos occasionally displayed, which we never perceived in Milman. In a word, the one is more the work of the artificer, the other of the poet; the one is more scholastic, the other is more natural.

In the selection of an event on which to build his plot, we think our author has been fortunate. But we are not certain that we should not have been better pleased if the plot had been conducted without the intervention of supernatural machinery. This, however, appears to have been the favourite object of the writer, is defended in the preface, and is executed with such singular skill, that we will not suffer ourselves to censure it. It does not seem so shocking to us in reading the poem, where the fact is made gradually, and, as it were, by glimpses to betray itself, and is not fully stated till we are fully prepared for it, and reconciled to it;—in this case, it is not so great a shock to discover that Hadad is the spirit of evil, in human form, as it is to be told of it plainly before we begin to read. The author adopts the ancient notion, that good and evil spirits are active in human affairs, and uses it in various ways to promote the purposes of his plot. The evil " Peer of Angels" being enamoured of Tamar, the beautiful daughter of Absalom, takes the form of Hadad, her lover, who had, unknown to her, been slain in hunting. He attaches himself to Absalom, encourages his pride, stimulates him to rebellion, and hopes to possess his daughter. His character is well conceived and well supported. Not a trace of human sympathy or feeling is to be discovered. He is wholly the demon, pursuing his selfish ends without the slightest regard to the interests of others, and coldly unconcerned amidst the tumult and perils of their affairs. The scenes between him and Tamar are particularly fine. They are more like the real communings of a spirit with a mortal, than any thing of the kind we have seen; and when we say this, we remember Moore and Byron. One of these scenes closes in a manner, which appears to us in the highest degree touching and sublime. We shall quote it hereafter.

13

The action opens with an interview of Hadad with the lame
son of Jonathan, Mephibosheth, and with Absalom, which is
well contrived to bring before us the state of the kingdom, to
introduce the feelings and jealousies on which the plot is to
turn, and prepare the way for the intrigues which are to follow.   The next scene finds David and the prophet Nathan in
council on the question of granting the suit of Hadad for
Absalom's daughter; in the course of which the seer expresses
his dislike of Absalom's conduct, and the father defends him.

The next is a powerful scene between Hadad and Tamar,
which opens beautifully.

> *Tam.* How aromatic evening grows! The flowers
> And spicy shrubs exhale like onycha;
> Spikenard and henna emulate in sweets.
> Blest hour! which He, who fashioned it so fair,
> So softly glowing, so contemplative,
> Hath set, and sanctified to look on man.
> And lo! the smoke of evening sacrifice
> Ascends from out the tabernacle.   Heaven
> Accept the expiation, and forgive
> This day's offences!—Ha! the wonted strain,
> Precursor of his coming!—Whence can this—
> It seems to flow from some unearthly hand—

> *Enter* HADAD.

> *Had.* Does beauteous Tamar view, in this clear fount,
> Herself, or heaven?
> *Tam.* Nay, Hadad, tell me whence
> Those sad, mysterious sounds.
> *Had.* What sounds, dear Princess?
> *Tam.* Surely, thou know'st; and now I almost think
> Some spiritual creature waits on thee.
> *Had.* I heard no sounds, but such as evening sends
> Up from the city to these quiet shades;
> A blended murmur sweetly harmonizing
> With flowing fountains, feathered minstrelsy,
> And voices from the hills.
> *Tam.* The sounds I mean,
> Floated like mournful music round my head,
> From unseen fingers.
> *Had.* When?
> *Tam.* Now, as thou camest.
> *Had.* 'T is but thy fancy, wrought
> To ecstacy; or else thy grandsire's harp
> Resounding from his tower at eventide.
> I 've lingered to enjoy its solemn tones,
> Till the broad moon, that rose o'er Olivet,
> Stood listening in the zenith; yea, have deemed
> Viols and heavenly voices answered him.

The second act still further discloses the machinations of Hadad, who stirs the ambitious jealousy of Absalom, by repeating the rumor that young Solomon has been appointed to the royal succession, and throws himself in the way of that young prince, for the purpose of corrupting his mind, and learning the truth of the report. His purpose is defeated by the sudden appearance of Nathan, which affords another opportunity of some obscure and mysterious intimations of Hadad's true character. This plan having failed, he persuades Absalom to make inquiry of an eastern magician. They accordingly meet him in the sepulchre of David, and there, in obedience to his incantations, a spirit rises in the vapour, and utters ambiguous prophecies, which inflame the prince's ambition, and precipitate him into immediate rebellion.

In the third act, the plot advances, and we are introduced into a meeting of the conspirators, who prepare for sudden action, and the crowning of Absalom the next day. The hurry, consternation, and tumult, which attend the out-breaking of the rebellion, are excellently pictured in the various following scenes, which, with several of a similar character in the remaining acts, have great dramatic power. They are living, moving, real representations. The calm and dignified demeanour of the king, the distraction of the attendants, the severity and impatience of Joab, whose character, little as he appears, is most admirably sketched;—indeed all that attends the flight of the royal party, is depicted with great spirit and truth.

Tamar, in the mean time, half distracted by the shock she had received from the news of the rebellion, wanders forth for the purpose of joining David, and after a long search amidst the confusion of a tumultuous night, is restored to her father. On the approach of the battle, he gives her in charge to Hadad, who retires with her to a tent of Ishmaelites in the vicinity, where they remain during the heat and violence of the contest. The progress of the battle, and its issue, are known from the reports of Ishmaelites arriving from time to time at the tent; by which mode, most agreeably to truth and probability, the author has avoided the difficulty, not to say the impossibility, of presenting the details of battle on the stage, and has escaped the necessity of exhibiting David after the death of his son. The pathetic account in the Scriptures is too familiar to all, to allow of its being successfully introduced into a work like this. What remains, therefore, after the tidings of Absalom's discomfiture and death, is only the *dénouement* of the action, as it relates to Hadad and Tamar. They retire from the tent, and he attempts to persuade her, by the most magnificent promises, to share his fortunes; but she resists all solicitation. He reveals his true character and power, and she spurns him. He seizes her by force, and drags her away. She is rescued by some superior spirit, who destroys Hadad; and one of David's generals approaching, conducts her to Jerusalem.

Different opinions will be entertained of this introduction of supernatural, demoniacal, and angelic agency into events so strictly historical. For ourselves, we could say much against it; especially the fiction of the demon dromedary, which is not only unnecessary, but an absolute blemish. And on the whole, we should have been better pleased, were the historical drama exclusively such, and had our author interwoven these spiritual appearances into some fable of his own invention. A certain feeling of dissatisfaction now intrudes upon the reader's pleasure, which would then have been avoided. But there can be no difference of opinion, we think, respecting the skill with which this very difficult matter is managed in all its parts. We do not think it, upon the whole, inferior, and, in some particulars, we conceive it to be superior, as we have before said, to that of any writer whom we remember to have made a similar attempt. It has a greater appearance of reality or possibility; and it is enveloped in the choicest graces of poetry; and, as the author seems to have written the whole for the sake of this part, we will quote a passage, which may enable our readers to judge of it. We refer particularly to the character of Hadad.

> *Tam.* I shudder,
> Lest some dark Minister be near us now.
> *Had.* You wrong them. They are bright Intelligences,
> Robbed of some native splendour, and cast down,
> 'T is true, from Heaven; but not deformed, and foul,
> Revengeful, malice-working Fiends, as fools
> Suppose. They dwell, like Princes, in the clouds:
> Sun their bright pinions in the middle sky;
> Or arch their palaces beneath the hills,
> With stones inestimable studded so,
> That sun or stars were useless there.
> *Tam.* Good heavens!
> *Had.* He bade me look on rugged Caucasus,
> Crag piled on crag beyond the utmost ken,
> Naked, and wild, as if creation's ruins
> Were heaped in one immeasurable chain

Of barren mountains, beaten by the storms
Of everlasting winter.   But, within
Are glorious palaces, and domes of light,
Irradiate halls, and crystal colonnades,
Vaults set with gems the purchase of a crown,
Blazing with lustre past the noon-tide beam,
Or, with a milder beauty, mimicking
The mystic signs of changeful Mazzaroth.
   Tam. Unheard-of splendour!
   Had. There they dwell, and muse,
And wander; Beings beautiful, immortal,
Minds vast as heaven, capacious as the sky,
Whose thoughts connect past, present, and to come,
And glow with light intense, imperishable.
Thus, in the sparry chambers of the Sea
And Air-Pavilions, rainbow Tabernacles,
They study Nature's secrets, and enjoy
No poor dominion.
   Tam. Are they beautiful,
And powerful far beyond the human race?
   Had. Man's feeble heart cannot conceive it.   When
The sage described them, fiery eloquence
Flowed from his lips, his bosom heaved, his eyes
Grew bright and mystical; moved by the theme,
Like one who feels a deity within.
   Tam. Wondrous!—What intercourse have they with men?
   Had. Sometimes they deign to intermix with man,
But oft with woman.
   Tam. Ha! with woman?
   Had. She
Attracts them with her gentler virtues, soft,
And beautiful, and heavenly, like themselves.
They have been known to love her with a passion
Stronger than human.
   Tam. That surpasses all
You yet have told me.
   Had. This the Sage affirms;
And Moses, darkly.
   Tam. How do they appear?
How manifest their love?
   Had. Sometimes 't is spiritual, signified
By beatific dreams, or more distinct
And glorious apparition.—They have stooped
To animate a human form, and love
Like mortals.
   Tam. Frightful to be so beloved!
Who could endure the horrid thought!—What makes
Thy cold hand tremble? or is 't mine
That feels so deathy?
   Had. Dark imaginations haunt me
When I recall the dreadful interview.
   Tam. O, tell them not—I would not hear them.

Had. But why contemn a Spirit's love? so high,
So glorious, if he haply deigned?—
   Tam. Forswear
My Maker! love a Demon!
   Had. No—O, no—
My thoughts but wandered—Oft, alas! they wander.
   Tam. Why dost thou speak so sadly now?—And lo!
Thine eyes are fixed again upon Arcturus.
Thus ever, when thy drooping spirits ebb,
Thou gazest on that star. Hath it the power
To cause or cure thy melancholy mood?——
                    [*He appears lost in thought.*]
Tell me, ascrib'st thou influence to the stars?
   Had. (*starting.*) The stars! What know'st thou of the stars?
   Tam. I know that they were made to rule the night.
   Had. Like palace lamps! Thou echoest well thy grandsire.
Woman! the stars are living, glorious,
Amazing, infinite!
   Tam. Speak not so wildly.—
I know them numberless, resplendent, set
As symbols of the countless, countless years
That make eternity.
   Had. Eternity!—
Oh! mighty, glorious, miserable thought!—
Had ye endured like those great sufferers,
Like them, seen ages, myriad ages roll;
Could ye but look into the void abyss
With eyes experienced, unobscured by torments,—
Then mightst thou name it, name it feelingly.
   Tam. What ails thee, Hadad?—Draw me not so close.
   Had. Tamar! I need thy love—more than thy love—
   Tam. Thy cheek is wet with tears—Nay, let us part—
'T is late—I cannot, must not linger.—
              [*Breaks from him, and exit.*]
   Had. Loved and abhorred!—Still, still accursed!—
     [*He paces, twice or thrice, up and down, with passionate
       gestures; then turns his face to the sky, and stands a
       moment in silence.*]
                    —Oh! where,
In the illimitable space, in what
Profound of untried misery, when all
His worlds, his rolling orbs of light, that fill
With life and beauty yonder infinite,
Their radiant journey run, for ever set,
Where, where, in what abyss shall I be groaning?   [*Exit.*]

We have unavoidably passed without notice several characters and scenes not less deserving approbation than those,
which we have mentioned. We refer the reader to the poem
itself. Our opinion of it has been sufficiently expressed. We
might point out some faults, but we have neither disposition
nor room. We will only mark one or two blemishes of lan-

guage, which we should be glad to see removed from a work deserving so high praise for its carefulness and purity in the use of words.   It might easily be made almost immaculate.

> ' O pause, my Lord, ere such a covenant ;
> Heaven frowns on *them*, our Law allows *them* not.'   p. 27.

> ' All my hopes *are so ingraft to yours*.'   p. 44.

> ' Assents he to the alliance, which would rest
> The pledge of amity ? '   p. 49.

This is obscure, and not made clear by the connexion.

In one instance *thou* and *you* are intermixed in the same sentence.   p. 51.

> ' But such designs
> Require immediate action, cannot *linger*
> An old man's ebbing sands.'   p. 90.

This is unusual, if not unauthorized.

We object to " *bosom-free*," p. 151 ; and to the expression " Never saw I wrath so fell and *followed ;*" and " fought *from out* a chariot."   p. 183.

This is a small list, after all.   We had designed to extract a few passages merely for their poetical beauties, but are now straitened for room.   We the less regret this, as we hope to see the work itself in the hands of every lover of poetry and of our country.   The only obstacle to this will be its costly form ; and we trust that this will be removed, by its immediate publication in a less expensive and more accessible shape.

MISCELLANY.

THE STUDY OF BOTANY.

The return of this charming season invites our attention to a study which has peculiar attractions at such a period.   I allude to the study of Botany.   The science of natural history partakes largely of the extraordinary advancement, to which every intellectual pursuit has been carried in the present age.   Botany, beyond all its kindred branches of knowledge, deserves to be considered one of the popular and fashionable studies of the times. It has been the case in our own country, especially, where the rich abundance of the indigenous vegetable productions affords so many facilities to the gratification of a taste for the study of plants. The great number of botanical works composed and published among us, in the lapse of a very few years past, are infallible signs of the popularity of botany, both as an object of scientific inquiry and of elegant recreation.

As a science, I will not affirm that botany is entitled to a very elevated rank, even when regarded in the most comprehensive points of view in which it is capable of being presented to us. Indeed it ranges, I am ready to admit, within a peculiarly limited scope, and treads in an humble path. Natural history, as a whole department of knowledge, must yield preeminence to nobler kinds of learning ; and the history of the inanimate productions of the earth will not challenge equality with that of things instinct with feeling, motion, and intelligence. The physiology of vegetables abounds in curious subjects of investigation, interesting to such as love the contemplation of nature in all the varying forms which she assumes. Their economical uses, also their medicinal properties, deserve an ample share of the philosophical observer's attention. But he must be unduly partial to the object of his own individual taste, who can compare in dignity the study of botany, especially descriptive botany, to the study of the heavenly bodies, for instance, and of the stupendous powers of nature, by which the stars and planets, each in itself a world for the mere naturalist, are wheeled along their orbits. Who would think of ranking botany with any of those physical sciences which teach all the properties of matter, whether organized or unorganized, and which embrace the entire vegetable kingdom within their comprehensive laws ; governing not more the motions of the massive globe, than the budding of the frailest flower that springs from its surface ? Botany, indeed, is but the study of a single one of the numerous forms of organized matter, and therefore it can at most only exhibit examples of the application of the great laws of universal nature. Again,—surely animated nature is a far higher study than inanimate. The hand of the Creator is less visibly stretched forth in the creation of a vegetable, even of the noblest tree which shoots upward its tall trunk and spreads abroad its ample foliage, the pride of a tropical forest, than it is in the formation of the eagle which soars high above it,—the bird of beautiful plumage or harmonious voice, which seeks shelter in its branches,—the lordly lion, who couches at its foot,—or man himself, whose finely compacted frame, nice organization, and erect shape, would mark him as the master of all other created beings, of whom earth is the common mother, did not the wonderful powers of his intellect still more decisively indicate his supremacy. And in the same degree, that the study of intel-

lectual man himself, of his passions, duties, actions, and the infi-
nitely diversified subjects of examination which his social relations unfold, is, above all, most interesting to us,—in the same
degree that mind is more attractive to the philosopher than matter—must the moral sciences ever assert their superior importance
over botany, as well as over the other physical sciences.

I speak not thus in disparagement of botany ; but only for the
purpose of assigning its true value to it, and to avoid being misunderstood as over-rating its importance, in expressing a great,
and, I think, a well-grounded partiality, for this delightful and
fascinating study.   Its influence on the mind is altogether beneficial.   It may not be so powerful an instrument of mental discipline as the exact sciences.   It may not liberalize and expand
the comprehension of the understanding, or enlarge our faculties,
like the pursuits which have given to the Platos and Aristotles,
the Bacons and Newtons, a glorious name to endure through the
ages of time.   But nothing is better calculated to indue the mind
with useful habits of analysis and arrangement than botany, so
rigidly are all its parts reduced to order by the modern systems of
classification.   This effect is not produced, as some undistinguish-
ing admirers of botany have seemed to imagine, by the influence
of the regularity of nature in the structure and distribution of
plants ; because, strikingly as she makes this quality manifest in
them, it is one which is alike common to all her works.   There
is not less of curious regularity in the crystallization of a gem,
than in the development of the loveliest lily's petals.   The tiniest
insect, that whirs upon the midnight air, has an anatomy as exact
and systematic as the structure of the majestic palm.   The same
beautiful order pervades all created things.   The hand of nature
operates according to unchangeable laws.   Her very vagaries are
systematic.   In her most fantastic moments, when she seems to
scatter abroad her productions in wild prodigality of confusion,
there is a never failing regularity of plan discernible beneath all
her apparent caprice.   The study of botany, therefore, does not
unfold to the careful observer any stronger proofs of order than
the rest of the material universe ; and the same spirit of classification, which it imparts, might be acquired, and is daily acquired,
in the study of other branches of natural history.

Still, botany, in my estimation, holds forth attractive allurements, which well account for its popularity in comparison with
its sister sciences.   The subjects of it, in the first place, are much
more accessible, and more within our control, than any other
natural productions, except minerals.   The flowers of the field
are spread open beneath our feet.   They do not dive into the
recesses of the deep, nor wing their path through the trackless

14

realms of air, to elude our search. They are fixed to their localities on the earth, and there we are sure to find them in their appointed seasons. Again, the short periodical growth of the larger portion of plants enables us, with little labour, to study their regularly returning development through all its stages. In mineralogy, we may amuse ourselves, it is true, with the process of crystallizing a few salts ; but the great mass of things in the mineral kingdom are of slow production, and the meanest stone in our cabinets probably might have seen generation after generation of men arise and depart in the course of its own tardy progress to maturity. We may sow the seed, on the contrary, and watch the speedier increase of the vegetable, as it issues from the earth, sends out its leaves, blooms into the gay tints of summer, yields its fruit, and having thus performed the great act appointed of nature for all living things, the reproduction of its species, decays and perishes beneath our eye. We may do the same in some sort with animals ; but far less easily than with vegetables. A *ménagerie* of wild beasts is not quite so manageable an establishment as a green-house ; nor even a quiet collection of anatomical preparations so handy as a *hortus siccus*. Besides, it is impossible to study the history of sentient beings without some degree of cruelty, which, however justifiable, nay laudable, when exercised by philosophers in scientific investigations, is undoubtedly to be counted among the repulsive circumstances in the study of a great part of natural history. You cannot enter upon the first elements of zoology or ornithology, without destroying, or at least imprisoning, the free tenants of the woods. Nay, the very classification of most animals in the systems of natural history, presupposes some knowledge of their anatomy. And although I profess not to feel any of that morbid sensibility, which shudders at the empalement of an unoffending bug by the prudent entomologist ; and although I cannot grant, with the poet, that

> —— the poor beetle, which we tread upon,
> In corporal sufferance finds a pang as great
> As when a giant dies;

yet, *cæteris paribus*, I must think the study of plants more agreeable, certainly more suitable to delicate and youthful minds, than a study where the constant sacrifice of life is indispensable. And there is something of grossness, of ungrateful toil, involved in the most moderate attention to all other branches of natural history, which deserves to be had in consideration in estimating their relative claims to general popularity.

For the sedentary student, there is nothing so admirably adapted to the purposes of recreation as botany. It requires just so much attention of the mind as to occupy without fatiguing it,—to furnish it with a gentle stimulus to activity, without agitating or straining its faculties by too powerful an impulse. Addressing the senses not less than the understanding, acting on the mind through the medium of external perception, and exciting the memory more strongly than the judgment, it is precisely the kind of study needed as a relief in the intervals of severer intellectual labour. Nor is this the least of its excellencies in the present relation. The votary of botany is called forth by it from the solitude and confinement of his study, he is torn from that sedentary life, which, combined with constant exercise of the mind in abstract speculations, weighs so heavily on the health and spirits. Exercise ought to enter into every scholar's religion. And yet all students, I apprehend, experience the greatest repugnance to taking regular exercise from a mere sense of duty as a bodily regimen. We need an additional motive to stimulate us. There is something in the practices of the ancients, in the oral instructions given by their philosophers in the perambulations of the Porch, in the wisdom gained by their youth, not in the debilitating vigils of nocturnal research in the student's cell, but under the face of heaven, and drunk in with the living eloquence of the orator's lips, amid Athenian groves, or under the cool shades of the Tusculan plane-tree,—there is something in all this, which, to me, seems not more delightful to the imagination, than consonant to the dictates of nature. Modern learning is most generally drawn from the pages of books. The lectures of our universities constitute but a small portion of the intellectual aliment, which the modern scholar, the modern advocate, the modern gentleman, nay, the modern man of business, requires. Day after day, and year after year, he must pore over the printed records of human knowledge, condemned to a mode of life, which, however necessary in refined existence, and however capable nature may have made our bodies of recovering from its deleterious effects, certainly is not a state which she designed as the properest one for the human constitution. She did not make man sedentary; she made him, says the great Roman, to stand erect towards heaven. "Primum eos humo excitatos, celsos et erectos constituit, ut deorum cognitionem, cœlum intuentes, capere possent." Now the study of botany is to be pursued with advantage only in the wild woods and fertile meadows, where the vegetable world flourishes in the luxuriance of unstinted nature; and it therefore impels the naturalist to active, invigorating exercise in the open air, and exercise of a kind the most useful to the body and the most useful to the mind.

For myself, I shall never cease to be grateful to botany, were it only for many a delightful ramble, into which it has led me, amid rural scenes of tranquillity, beauty, and peace ; where, dropping the burdens of life, and throwing off the oppression which sedentary occupation loads upon the spirits, I have passed from green valley to green valley, exultingly hailing, at every step, the discovery of some lovelier and rarer floweret, whose acquisition imparted a temporary triumph, I do no say greater, but how much more innocent, than the triumphs gained in prouder conquests. And how revivifying it is, in the heat of summer, when the whole sky seems to swim in a sea of dazzling light, to quit the world of brick and mortar in our cities, for the cool, refreshing shades of the country, whither the botanist is summoned. Art may present you with the spectacle of riches and power springing out of her persevering efforts. She may point to the curious fabrics wrought by her fingers, and the wonderful machinery set in motion by her skill. She may tell you how the enterprise of her children has prompted them to descend into the bowels of the earth for jewels and precious metals, and plough the faithless seas for the spice of eastern climes. She may show you the busy haunts of men enlivened by her activity, and place before you the marble palace and the city thronged with the gorgeous specimens of human genius, to illustrate the splendor of her success. But, notwithstanding all this, there is a lavish and careless profusion of beauty and grandeur in the productions of Nature, which the narrow art of man strives in vain to emulate. We shall leave the sublimest exercise of human power, the most faultless exhibitions of human genius, to find all its sublimity shrink into littleness, and all its beauty seem lifeless and tame, when compared with the works of nature. And amid these it is, that the ardent lover of botany seeks the gratification of his taste. His favourite haunts are the mountain-side clothed in its everlasting forests, the margin of the sun-bright lake spotted with islets and embosomed in picturesque hills, or the banks of the stream winding along amid gay fields fertilized by its waters, where his imagination and his heart are equally elevated and improved by the contemplation of God's magnificent creations.

These are among the considerations, which recommend this charming science to the studious lover of nature, to the female sex, who are in a manner debarred the study of all other branches of natural history, and to persons of whatever class or condition of life, who seek relaxation from more arduous pursuits in the examination of the beauties of the vegetable world. It is foreign to my present purpose to inquire how largely a knowledge of the properties and uses of plants contributes to the solid comforts of life. I leave this to the pen of professional writers, and to the pages of works devoted to medicine or the useful arts.

                                                  C. C.

THE ENGLISH HOUSE OF COMMONS.

A LEAF FROM THE JOURNAL OF A TRAVELLER IN ENGLAND.

London, February 24, 18—.

I ATTENDED to-day, for the first time, in the House of Commons. The debate was on a proposition of Mr Williams, member for Lincoln, to raise a committee to inquire into the delays, expenses, and vexations of the Court of Chancery. Mr Williams spoke with great wit, eloquence, and effect. He was abundantly provided with facts. He gave the history of cases, that had gone on fifteen, twenty, thirty, and more years, and every one of them with a great annual expense, and in many of them the parties, in final despair of a decision, had compromised the cause. Among others, was one, the subject of which was a windmill, which went to decay and fell down before a decree was obtained!

Mr Secretary Peel (who is a small man with red hair and a youthful look, thirty-eight or forty years old) replied, and accounted for the delay, which he did not deny to exist, by saying, that the business had increased so as to be above any human power to perform. Lunatic, bankrupt, accomptant general, and appealed cases were enumerated as having increased beyond all example. He stated that the lawyers in chancery occupied a great deal of time. In one instance, a lawyer occupied "eighteen—*minutes*, you will say,—*hours*, those who are most extravagant; but both would be wrong—he had occupied *eighteen whole days!!*" Mr Peel, however, admitted the necessity of inquiring: and said, that his Majesty's government were engaged upon the subject, and would shortly appoint a committee, composed of the Lord Chancellor and several other distinguished gentlemen, chiefly, as it appeared, from the ministerial ranks.

Mr Abercrombie, a Scotch member, and a chancery lawyer, animadverted with great force on the absurdity of setting such men to inquire into this matter, and declared that it would be a mockery.

Mr Brougham (five feet nine inches high, spare form, nose turned up, head thin and high, brown hair, and about forty-seven years old) spoke to the same effect. He was utterly astonished, that the Lord Chancellor should hesitate upon every thing else; but should not hesitate a moment to head and to designate the committee, which was to inquire into his own conduct!

Mr Canning (five feet eight or nine inches high, rather retreating forehead, nose long and slightly Roman, brown hair, and about fifty years old) assured the house, that the inquiry was intended to be sincere and beneficial. He would not, however, consent to have the political and judicial functions of the Lord Chancellor separated (which was to be one of the points of the inquiry). It was one of the most beautiful prerogatives of the crown, that it could take the meanest man—the meanest, not in talents and endowments, but in birth and fortune—from the walks of Westminster, and place him at the head of the peerage. He saw in this transition from the court *piepowder* to the woolsack and the peerage, the most beautiful illustration of the mixed monarchical and democratical principles of the British constitution. There was an eloquent fervour in this part of his remarks, which I found very poorly preserved in the reports of the London journals on the following day. The truth is, that these journals report very badly, notwithstanding the great perfection to which *we* suppose them to have brought the art.

I have seen one or two speeches of Mr Randolph, reported by the senior editor of the National Intelligencer, better than any that I have met with in the journals of this country; but those were on occasions, when that expert tachygraphist made exertions, which he is seldom induced to make, and which no unassisted individual would often make if he could help it. Accurate reporting is a desideratum in literature. How little has been preserved of the many eloquent speeches which have been made in the United States, at the bar and in deliberative and popular assemblies. If any are preserved, or are pretended to be, they are not genuine; but are so mutilated, and so disfigured, that the reputed authors would not know nor acknowledge them. Under the present system (in England as well as with us) the reporter reduces or raises every thing to the standard of his own mind. If he happens to be intelligent and quick, and to have a good memory, he may give a tolerable abstract of a speech, catching occasionally, and preserving a striking or characteristic expression; but more than this none of them do—few do so much. I doubt very much whether any of the *ex tempore* speeches on record, attributed to first-rate orators, do them any thing like justice. The most perfect are those, which have been corrected or subsequently written by themselves; but who does not know, that a truly eloquent man speaks at times better than he can write, or than any man can write. There is occasionally, in *ex tempore* debate, and under the excitement produced by opposition and sympathy, a pathos, an inspiration, a swelling of the soul, an intensity of feeling, and power of language, an *aliquid immensum*, that no closet composition can ever—I will not say reach—but approach. Pinkney is not only dead, but his well earned fame as *an orator* has died with him, and is gone forever. The same may be said of Hamilton, of R. H. Lee, and indeed is more or less true of all our orators.

The remedy, as it regards the *future*, is obvious. We have only to *educate* men for this art, as we do for other arts much less laborious and difficult. Boys must be early initiated into the mysteries of *cryptography*, commence practice in childhood, and go through a regular apprenticeship. No learning that they might acquire would come amiss. The art, having been thus learned, ought to yield them a genteel support, and be esteemed a liberal calling, for it is obviously more important than that of portrait-painting; inasmuch as the peculiar features of the minds of illustrious men are more interesting to us than those of their faces. By contemplating a distinct and vivid representation of the former, we may draw instructive lessons for the improvement of our own minds; but we shall hardly be able to assume the features of a fine face, though we may look upon a picture of it forever.

POETRY.

TRUE GREATNESS.

There is a fire, that has its birth
Above the proudest hills of earth;
And higher than the eternal snows,
    The fountain whence it rose.

It came to man in ancient days,
And fell upon his ardent gaze,
A god descending in his car,
    The Spirit of a star.

And as the glorious vision broke
Full on his eye, at once he woke,
And with the rush of battling steeds
    He sprang to generous deeds.

Then first he stood erect and free,
And in the might of destiny
A stern, unconquerable fate
    Compelled him to be great.

He strove not for the wreath of fame;
From heaven, the power that moved him, came,
And welcome, as the mountain air,
    The voice that bade him dare.

Onward he bore, and battled still
With a most firm, enduring will,
His only hope, to win and rise,
    His only aim—the skies.

He saw their glories blaze afar;
A soul looked down from every star,
And from its eye of lightning flew
    A glance, that thrilled him through.

Full in the front of war he stood ;
His home, his country, claimed his blood :
Without one sigh that blood was given ;
   He only thought — of Heaven.

                   P.

THE REIGN OF MAY.

I feel a newer life in every gale ;
   The winds, that fan the flowers,
And with their welcome breathings fill the sail,
   Tell of serener hours, —
     Of hours that glide unfelt away
     Beneath the sky of May.

The Spirit of the gentle south-wind calls
   From his blue throne of air,
And where his whispering voice in music falls,
   Beauty is budding there ;
     The bright ones of the valley break
     Their slumbers and awake.

The waving verdure rolls along the plain,
   And the wide forest weaves,
To welcome back its playful mates again,
   A canopy of leaves ;
     And from its darkening shadow floats
     A gush of trembling notes.

Fairer and brighter spreads the reign of May ;
   The tresses of the woods,
With the light dallying of the west-wind play,
   And the full-brimming floods,
     As gladly to their goal they run,
     Hail the returning sun.

                   P.

TO A FRIEND AT SEA.

I bless the bright moon, as in heaven she rides
   All pure and serene in her maiden splendor,
That, while thou art cleaving the pathless tides,
   Her silvery lustre is thy defender.

I listen by night to the rushing wind,
   As through the blue skies it is coldly sweeping,
And hope the wild breezes may never find
   Their way to the pillow where thou art sleeping.

Whenever I look on the dark green sea,
   Or think of the fathomless depths of ocean,
Oh ! sadly my spirit then turns to thee,
   And prays thou art safe from the wave's commotion.

But joyfully swelleth my gladdened heart,
   When favouring gales, in their balmy sweetness,
As lightly they glide o'er the deep, impart
   Their freshness to thee, to thy keel their fleetness.

                                                        C.

CRITICAL NOTICES.

Blackwood's Edinburgh Magazine for February and March, 1825.

THIS journal has greatly degenerated within a year or two, and is now remarkable for nothing but ultra-toryism and scurrility. About six months since, there appeared in it a sort of chronicle of American writers, arranged alphabetically. This has been continued through five numbers, and is now concluded. When we first observed this, we were surprised at the acquaintance with the personal character and history of many of our writers, which was displayed in it, and at the number of names collected. We were astonished to perceive such a formidable list; and though the notices were generally abusive, we were rather flattered that our friends over the water should have taken the trouble to notice so many of our writers at all. There seemed to be something enigmatical about the whole affair; for though there were many mistakes, they did not appear to be such as a stranger would be likely to fall into; the writer seemed to have too much knowledge of many things, to be so ignorant of some others; and often appeared to be telling a lie rather than making a blunder. He has not had the wit, however, to keep his own secret. In the fifth and last number, he lets " the cat out of the bag," and completely nullifies every effect of his strictures, whether good or evil, by discovering himself to be a Mr John Neal, of Baltimore. This person is the author of several novels; one of which, called Randolph, we had occasion to notice in an early number of this Gazette. For this work Mr Neal is said to have received in a most unfortunately literal sense, "more kicks than coppers." / This sort of *honorarium*, indeed, to do him justice, he strenuously denies the receipt of, and certainly he is as likely as any one to know. If we erred in publishing an intimation of this kind, we now make the *amende honorable* to Mr Neal, by giving equal publicity to his denial, and admitting, that at the worst, the thing was rather his misfortune, than his fault. Mr Neal was seen by several persons in this vicinity, some years since. We gather from their account of him, as well as from his writings, that he possessed some natural talent, and had he been " caught young," might have made something; but that he has been left to himself so long, that he can scarcely be expected ever to be fit for any thing better than a contributor to the Edinburgh Magazine. There are several other articles in these numbers, of which we intended to give some account, but as we can say nothing good of them, we shall perhaps do more wisely to say nothing at all.

Adsonville, or Marrying Out; A Narrative Tale. Albany. 1824. 12mo. pp. 285.

THIS is a very ordinary book, printed in a very ordinary manner. The author promises, " if this shall pass with impunity, to sin no more." It

15

is an American novel in the strongest sense of the term. It abounds in *Americanisms*, and the scenes and characters are copied from American nature, whenever they are copied from any. Few will probably understand the meaning of the secondary designation, "Marrying Out." The hero is a Quaker, who *marries out* of the society. We are told, that "the tale was mostly written whilst the author had extreme youth to plead in extenuation of its faults," and that it was published at the request of "particular friends." We are sorry to be severe upon a book, that makes so little pretension, but we must needs tell the truth. It is not a sufficient excuse for publishing such a work, that it is not "considered of sufficient consequence to affect American literature." A cheap novel is likely to fall into the hands, and to have its effect upon the minds, of the very class of people, whose language most needs improvement, and will, of course, have more or less effect in perpetuating bad language and bad construction. We believe that the following specimen of the book will be sufficient for most readers, who have any curiosity respecting it.

"Edgar had now so far recovered, as to discover their confusion, and that Caroline was missing, or that something bad befallen her. He inquired where she was; but not receiving any answer, he *pitched off* the bed, and made for the door, whilst, to prevent it, they all surrounded him. Caroline, who had inadvertently shut the door after her, having recovered, and hearing them entreating Edgar to be pacified, now entered, and coming up behind him, took hold of his arm. 'Here,' said Penelope, 'here, cousin Edgar, is Caroline.' He turned, and falling towards her, clasped her in his arms, whilst she, from her recent misfortune, scarcely able to sustain her own weight, sunk under the addition of his, and the carpet, by receiving them both, fortunately kept them from coming to the floor."

———

An Address to the Utica Lyceum, delivered February 17, 1825. By A. B. Johnson, prefatory to his course of Lectures on the Philosophy of Human Knowledge. Utica. 1825. 8vo. pp. 16.

We have received a pamphlet with this title, from which we learn two facts: that there is a Lyceum at Utica,—and that they are about to have a course of lectures on the "Philosophy of Human Knowledge." We rejoice in the organization and establishment of every institution for the promotion and diffusion of useful knowledge; and have no doubt the Lyceum at Utica is one of those institutions, though we know little of its particular objects, or its means and resources for obtaining them. "The philosophy of human knowledge" is rather a vague subject for a course of lectures; and it would be difficult to predict how a lecturer would manage such a subject. Unfortunately the "prefatory" lecture does not aid us in forming a conjecture. Mr Johnson, on this point, only tells us "it is his misfortune to possess a strong inclination for abstruse studies." But his Address shows a discriminating mind. A remark upon the imperfections of language as an organ of communication between different minds, is worthy of attention. "Words," he says, "may be compared to music. When a Briton listens to a certain tune of Handel, the notes articulate distinctly, 'God save great George the King;' but when an American hears it, the notes articulate 'God save great Washington.' Hence the difficulty of understanding a new idea. The words will constantly excite old ones, though the speaker intends new."

—

INTELLIGENCE.

RECOVERED EDITION OF SHAKSPEARE.

A literary treasure of no common value, and of most singular rarity, which is likely to excite a strong interest in the minds of all well-read lovers of the ancient English drama, and will awaken the hopes and fears of every ambitious and zealous collector of scarce books, has, within a short time, been brought to light.

This exhumated curiosity is a book in small quarto, said to have been once possessed by Sir Thomas Hanmer, but not alluded to by him; and containing scarce editions of eleven of Shakspeare's plays, among which is Hamlet of an edition printed in 1603. Of this edition not the slightest mention has ever been made; it is therefore fair to conclude, that to the various able and learned commentators of Shakspeare it was utterly unknown, the earliest which has ever obtained notice being that of 1604, of which Mr Malone gives the title, though it is quite clear be had no other knowledge of it.

Hamlet first appeared, according to Malone's calculation, in 1600, the newly discovered edition, therefore, was published only three years after the tragedy was produced. Hence it may be, in many respects, a more exact copy of the original than any subsequently printed. The following notice is taken from the London Literary Gazette. It is proper to remark, that the copy shows abundance of typographical errors, and a great want of skill in the copyist. The errors, however, are retained in the quotations which are made.

Hamlet—Edition of 1603.

" We will rather express our gratification that an edition of Hamlet, anterior to any hitherto known to the world, has just been brought to light, than our surprise that it should have been so long hidden. Yet it is a strange thing that such a volume as that in which it has been found, and in the possession of the parties to whom it belonged, should have been suffered to be undiscovered or unnoticed among the lumber of any library. Every person of literary taste must wonder, and every enthusiastic admirer of Shakspeare be inclined to utter an exclamation of dismay, when we lay before them the contents of this precious book. They are as follow—

1. The Merchant of Venice. Printed by J. R. for Thomas Heyes. 1600. First edition. [*Perfect.*]
2. The Merry Wives of Windsor. Printed by T. C. for Arthur Johnson. 1602. First edition. [*Wanting last leaf but one.*]
3. Much Adoe about Nothing. Printed by V. S. for Andrew Wise and William Aspley. 1600. First edition. [*Perfect.*]
4. A Midsommer Nights Dreame. Printed for Thomas Fisher. 1600. First edition. [*Wanting four leaves in the middle.*]
5. Troylus & Cresseida. One of the two first editions, both printed in 1609. [*Wants title.*]
6. Romeo & Juliet. Printed by Thomas Creede for Cuthbert Burby. 1599. First edition of the enlarged Play. [*Perfect.*]
7. Hamlet. Printed by N. L. and John Trundell, 1603. First known edition. Last leaf wanting; but contains Hamlet's Death, and very few lines are wanting, probably not half so many as occur after the hero's death, in the received text of the play.

8. Henry IV. Part II.   Printed by V. S. for Andrew Wise and William Aspley,
1600. First edition. Signature E has six leaves. [*Perfect.*]
9. ———— Part I. Printed by P. S. for Andrew Wise. 1598. First edition.
[*Perfect.*]
10. Henry V. Printed by Thomas Creede, for Thomas Pauier. 1602. Second
edition. [*Perfect.*]
11. Richard III. Printed by Thomas Creede, for Andrew Wise. 1602. Third
edition. [*Perfect.*]
12. The Two Noble Kinsmen, by John Fletcher and William Shakspeare. 1634.
First edition. [*Perfect.*]

The size of this important and curious volume is the ancient small
quarto, and, with the exceptions specified above, it is in excellent order. It was the property of Sir T. Hanmer, but must have been purchased by him after he had published his Shakspeare; otherwise he
would have made use of it in that publication. From Sir T. Hanmer, it
passed into the possession of the Bunbury family; and it was from one
of its branches that it came into the hands of its present owners, Messrs
Payne & Foss.

[*To be continued.*]

HARRIS' NATURAL HISTORY OF THE BIBLE.

We are happy to learn, that this valuable work has been reprinted in
London, and very favourably reviewed in the Philosophical Magazine
and Journal for January, 1825. We quote a few sentences from that
review with the greater pleasure, because they will serve the double
purpose of furnishing a notice of the work, and of showing the estimation
in which it is held where it has been reprinted.

" Among the valuable contributions to science and literature, with
which our American brethren are now enriching our language, we are
happy to notice this useful volume. The want of such a work has been
much felt in this country. * * * It is of essential service to the public
to possess works on subjects of common interest, comprising in a small
compass, what before could not be found without access to voluminous
authors and extensive libraries.

" In order fully to understand the Sacred Writings, a knowledge of
whatever is local and peculiar becomes important. Not the least important, as contributing to the illustration of Scripture, is Natural History. The poetical books of the Hebrews, in particular, abound in
lively comparisons, local allusions, and strong metaphors, drawn from
material objects, whose most powerful charms arise from their individu-
ality. The real import of the sentiment, expressed by such allusions
and metaphors, must be gathered from a knowledge of the objects on
which they are founded. Much of the poetry of the Hebrews, like that
of every people of a remote age, partakes largely of the pastoral kind,
resulting from the personal occupation of the authors, or the common
condition of mankind. To enjoy the beauty of the pastoral scenery,
which is so often alluded to in the Hebrew Scriptures, one should have
some knowledge of the climate and natural productions of the country
which furnishes it; and every thing which tends to make the Sacred
Scriptures more engaging to the mass of readers, by illustrating what is
obscure, is a great good.

" In the use he has made of his various authorities, Dr Harris manifests a due discrimination, and puts it in the reader's power, generally,

in cases of doubt, to weigh the evidence for himself; and we consider him to be entitled to the thanks of the public for having brought within a reasonable compass the most valuable materials on the subjects of which he treats;—for having arranged them in a convenient method;—and, in general, for having arrived at his own conclusions, on the best evidence which the subjects admit."

AMERICAN NATURAL HISTORY.

Mr Robert Wright, of Philadelphia, has undertaken to publish by subscription an extensive work, entitled American Natural History, which is to be edited by Dr John D. Godman. It will be illustrated by numerous engravings from drawings by that eminent naturalist and artist, Mr Lesueur, which have been made, in every practicable instance, from the living animal or preserved specimen in the American Museum. The first part, in three volumes octavo, will be ready for delivery in September next.

LADAHK SHEEP.

Mr Moorcroft, in a letter from Tartary, says, "The novelties which have already met my view in natural history, are so great as to invite the introduction of details that would swell this letter to a volume." One example is the Ladahk sheep. "This animal, at full growth, is scarcely so large as a South Down lamb of five or six months; yet in the fineness and weight of its fleece, the flavour of its flesh, and the peculiarities of its constitution, it is inferior to no race. It is as completely domiciliated as a British dog. In the night it shelters in a walled yard, or under its master's roof; in the day it feeds often on a surface of granite rock, where cursory observation can scarcely discover a speck of vegetation. If permitted, it will pick up crumbs, drink salted and buttered tea or broth, or nibble a cleanly picked bone. It gives two lambs within twelve months, and is twice shorn within that period. A British cottager might keep three of these sheep with more ease than he now supports a cur-dog, as they would live luxuriantly in the day on the strips of grass which border the roads, and by keeping clean hedge bottoms." Mr Moorcroft has procured some of them with a view to import them into Britain. The letter contains, likewise, a notice of a non-descript wild variety of horse, which he thinks might be domesticated for the use of the small farmer and poor in Britain. It is about fourteen hands high, of a round muscular form, with remarkably clean limbs.

ANTEDILUVIAN REMAINS.

Professor Buckland has published a letter relative to the cave lately discovered at Banwell, Somerset. He states the thickness of the mass of sand, mud, and limestone, through which the bones, horns, and teeth are disposed, to be in one place nearly forty feet. He adds, " Many large baskets-full of bones have already been extracted, belonging to the ox and deer tribes : of the latter there are several varieties, including the elk. There are also a few portions of the skeleton of the wolf, and of a gigantic bear. The bones are mostly in a state of preservation equal to that of common grave bones; but it is clear, from the fact of some of them belonging to the great extinct species of the bear, that they are of an antediluvian origin."

THEOLOGY.

A Critical History of the Projects formed within the last three hundred years for the Union of the Christian Communions.

Seven Letters to Elias Hicks, on the tendency of his Doctrines and Opinions; with an Introductory Address to the Society of Friends. By a Demi-Quaker. Philadelphia.

Four Sermons on the Doctrine of the Atonement. By Nathan S. S. Beman, Pastor of the Presbyterian Church in Troy. 12mo. Troy, N. Y. W. S. Parker.

TRAVELS.

Schoolcraft's Travels in the Central Portions of the Mississippi Valley. With Maps and Plates. 8vo. pp. 460. Price $3 50. New York. Collins & Hannay.

AMERICAN EDITIONS OF FOREIGN WORKS.

The Young Artist's Companion, containing Plain and Easy Directions for the acquirement of the art of Drawing, &c. To which are added, General Rules of Perspective. By T. Barnes. From the Fourth London Edition, considerably enlarged and improved. 8vo. Baltimore. J. Roach.

A Treatise on Derangements of the Liver, Internal Organs, and Nervous System. Pathological and Therapeutical. By James Johnson, M. D.

Joyce's Scientific Dialogues. A New Edition. 3 Vols. 18mo. With numerous Plates. Philadelphia. A. Finley.

A Narrative of the Voyages Round the World, performed by Captain Cook. With an account of his Life, during the previous and intervening periods. By A. Kippis, D. D. F. R. S. In 2 Vols. 18mo. New York. D. Mallory.

Immediate, not Gradual Abolition; or, an Inquiry into the shortest, safest, and most effectual means of getting rid of West India Slavery. 8vo. New York. J. V. Seaman.

A Translation of Horace. By Sir Philip Francis. 2 Vols. 18mo. New York. S. King.

Falconer's Shipwreck; with Plates. New York. S. King.

An Inquiry into the Human Mind, on the principles of Common Sense. By Thomas Reid, D. D. Professor of Moral Philosophy in the University of Glasgow. 18mo. New York. S. King.

English Life; or, Manners at Home. In Four Pictures. 2 Vols. 12mo. New York. E. Bliss & E. White.

Living Plays. Vol XIII. New York. D. Mallory.

Decision; a Tale. By Mrs Hofland, Author of Integrity, a Tale, &c.

Sergeant & Lowber's Common Law Reports, condensed. Vol. III. Carey & Lea.

Sayings and Doings; a Series of Sketches from Real Life. Second Series. Philadelphia. Carey & Lea.

A Review of the Efforts and Progress of Nations, during the last twenty-five years. By J. C. L. De Sismondi. Translated from the French. By Peter S. Duponceau. 8vo. pp. 36. Philadelphia. H. Hall.

Reminiscences of Charles Butler, Esq. of Lincoln's Inn, with a Letter to a Lady, on Ancient and Modern Music. Second American from the Fourth London Edition. 12mo. pp. 350. Price $1 50. New York. E. Bliss & E. White.

NEW PUBLICATIONS.

EDUCATION.

Lessons in Elocution; or, a Selection of Pieces in Prose and Verse, for the Improvement of Youth in Reading and Speaking. By William Scott. Also, an Appendix, containing Lessons on a New Plan; to which is added, an Abridgment of Walker's Rules for the Pronunciation of Greek and Latin Proper Names, &c. Plymouth. E. Collier.

Reading Lessons for Primary Schools. 18mo. pp. 126. Boston. Richardson & Lord.

HISTORY.

Notes, Geographical and Historical, relating to the town of Brooklyn, in King's County, on Long Island. By Gabriel Furman. 1 Vol. 12mo. Brooklyn. A. Spooner.

LAW.

Remarks on the Projected Revision of the Laws of New York. First published in the Atlantic Magazine for April, 1825. 8vo. pp. 19. New York.

MEDICINE.

The Monthly Chronicle of Medicine and Surgery. No. VIII. New York. E. Bliss & E. White.

An Address, delivered at the Annual Commencement of the Berkshire Medical Institution, Pittsfield, December 23, 1824. By Rufus William Bailey, A. M. 8vo. pp. 24. Pittsfield, Mass.

The New England Journal of Medicine and Surgery. Vol. XIV. No. II.

Medico-Chirurgical Review and Journal of Medical Science. No. XVI. New York. J. V. Seaman.

MISCELLANEOUS.

Pierre and his Family; or, a Story of the Waldenses. By the Author of Lilly Douglas. 1 Vol. 18mo. Philadelphia.

An Essay on the Study and Pronunciation of the Greek and Latin Languages. By William White, A. M. Philadelphia. A. Finley.

Auxiliar Vocabulario de Bolsillo Español e Ingles, Par J. Jose L. Barry. 18mo. New York. J. Desnoues.

The Virginia Housewife. A Second Edition, with Amendments and Additions. 12mo.

POETRY.

The Minstrel's Cabinet; a new Collection of the most popular Sentimental, Comic, Patriotic, and Moral Songs. In 2 Vols. 18mo. New York. D. Mallory.

POLITICS.

Suggestions on Presidential Elections, with particular reference to a Letter of William C. Somerville, Esq. 8vo. pp. 32. Boston. Cummings, Hilliard, & Co.

An Address, delivered at Watertown, March 4th, 1825, at a Dinner in Honour of the Inauguration of President John Quincy Adams. By David Lee Child. 8vo. pp. 10. Price 25 cents. Boston. Cummings, Hilliard, & Co.

THEOLOGY.

A Critical History of the Projects formed within the last three hundred years for the Union of the Christian Communions.

Seven Letters to Elias Hicks, on the tendency of his Doctrines and Opinions; with an Introductory Address to the Society of Friends. By a Demi-Quaker. Philadelphia.

Four Sermons on the Doctrine of the Atonement. By Nathan S. S. Beman, Pastor of the Presbyterian Church in Troy. 12mo. Troy, N. Y. W. S. Parker.

TRAVELS.

Schoolcraft's Travels in the Central Portions of the Mississippi Valley. With Maps and Plates. 8vo. pp. 460. Price $3 50. New York. Collins & Hannay.

AMERICAN EDITIONS OF FOREIGN WORKS.

The Young Artist's Companion, containing Plain and Easy Directions for the acquirement of the art of Drawing, &c. To which are added, General Rules of Perspective. By T. Barnes. From the Fourth London Edition, considerably enlarged and improved. 8vo. Baltimore. J. Roach.

A Treatise on Derangements of the Liver, Internal Organs, and Nervous System. Pathological and Therapeutical. By James Johnson, M. D.

Joyce's Scientific Dialogues. A New Edition. 3 Vols. 18mo. With numerous Plates. Philadelphia. A. Finley.

A Narrative of the Voyages Round the World, performed by Captain Cook. With an account of his Life, during the previous and intervening periods. By A. Kippis, D. D. F. R. S. In 2 Vols. 18mo. New York. D. Mallory.

Immediate, not Gradual Abolition; or, an Inquiry into the shortest, safest, and most effectual means of getting rid of West India Slavery. 8vo. New York. J. V. Seaman.

A Translation of Horace. By Sir Philip Francis. 2 Vols. 18mo. New York. S. King.

Falconer's Shipwreck; with Plates. New York. S. King.

An Inquiry into the Human Mind, on the principles of Common Sense. By Thomas Reid, D. D. Professor of Moral Philosophy in the University of Glasgow. 18mo. New York. S. King.

English Life; or, Manners at Home. In Four Pictures. 2 Vols. 12mo. New York. E. Bliss & E. White.

Living Plays. Vol XIII. New York. D. Mallory.

Decision; a Tale. By Mrs Hoffland, Author of Integrity, a Tale, &c.

Sergeant & Lowber's Common Law Reports, condensed. Vol. III. Carey & Lea.

Sayings and Doings; a Series of Sketches from Real Life. Second Series. Philadelphia. Carey & Lea.

A Review of the Efforts and Progress of Nations, during the last twenty-five years. By J. C. L. De Sismondi. Translated from the French. By Peter S. Duponceau. 8vo. pp. 36. Philadelphia. H. Hall.

Reminiscences of Charles Butler, Esq. of Lincoln's Inn, with a Letter to a Lady, on Ancient and Modern Music. Second American from the Fourth London Edition. 12mo. pp. 350. Price $1 50. New York. E. Bliss & E. White.

LIST OF WORKS IN PRESS.

A New Edition of Blackstone's Commentaries. 4 Vols. 8vo. With the Notes of Archbold and Christian united. Philadelphia. R. H. Small.

Boaden's Life of Kemble. 8vo. A Small. Philadelphia.

The fifth volume of the Memoirs of the Philadelphia Agricultural Society. Philadelphia. A. Small.

The Travellers; or, some Extracts from Juvenile Journals. Designed for young people, 1 Vol. 18mo. New York. E. Bliss & E. White.

A New Edition of Thomas' Practice, from the Eighth London Edition. With Notes by David Hosack, M. D. F. R. S. 1. Vol. 8vo. New York. Collins & Co.

A New Novel, by the Author of "The Spy," "Lionel Lincoln." &c. &c. New York. Charles Wiley.

Richerand's Physiology. From the last London Edition. 8vo. New York. Collins & Co.

The History of the United States, for the Use of Schools. By the Rev. Charles A. Goodrich. Fourth Edition. 1 Vol. 18mo. New York. Collins & Co.

Redfield; A Long-Island Tale. 12mo. New York. Wilder & Campbell.

"Biographia Americana;" or, a Historical and Critical Account of the Lives and Writings of the Most Distinguished Persons in North America; from its first settlement to the present time, with numerous Portraits. By a Gentleman of Philadelphia. New York. D. Mallory.

Tales of the Genii. 2 Vols. With Engravings. New York. D. Mallory.

Telemachus. 2 Vols.

Life of Benjamin Franklin. Written by Himself. With Engravings.

Goldsmith's Poems and Essays.

Living Plays. 14th and 15th Vols. New York. D. Mallory.

A Synopsis of the Diseases of the Eye, and their treatment, &c. By Benjamin Travers, F. R. S. Surgeon to St Thomas' Hospital. From the Third London Edition. With Notes and Illustrations, by Edward Delafield, M. D. 8vo. New York. E. Bliss & E. White.

The Lady of the Manor; a Novel. By Mrs Sherwood. New York. E. Bliss & E. White.

The Works of William Cowper. New Edition. 3 Vols. 18mo. New York. S. King.

Moore's Melodies. A New Selection. New York. W. B. Gilley.

An Epitome of Paley's Principles of Moral and Political Philosophy. By a Member of the University of Cambridge, Author of the "Epitome of the Evidences of Christianity." New York. E. Bliss & E. White.

C. Cornelii Taciti Historiarum Libri Quinque : cum libro de Germania, et vita Agricolæ. Ad Fidem optimarum editionum expressi, cum notis Barbon. New York. Solomon King.

Bayley on Bills, with Notes of American Decisions. Boston. Harrison Gray.

Published on the first and fifteenth day of every month, by CUMMINGS, HILLIARD, & Co., No. 134 Washington-Street, Boston, for the Proprietors. Terms, $5 per annum. Cambridge: Printed at the University Press, by Hilliard & Metcalf.

THE UNITED STATES

LITERARY GAZETTE.

| VOL. II. | MAY 15, 1825. | No. 4. |

REVIEWS.

High-Ways and By-Ways ; or, Tales of the Road-side, Picked up in the French Provinces. By A Walking Gentleman. Second Series. Philadelphia. 1825. 2 vols. 12mo.

It has been announced in the London papers, that a Mr Grattan is the author of these tales. When we closed the two small volumes, which were re-published here about a year since, embracing the first series, we felt confident from the popularity of the work, that at no very distant period there would be a renewal of intercourse between this author and the public. But we hardly wished—we certainly did not expect to meet him again after so short an interval. It was well and truly said by a favourite author of the last century, "Little writers compose books apace : for naturalists observe, that the less the insect is, the oftener it lays, and the faster it propagates ; but then their brood is very short-lived." We would not be understood to apply these remarks critically to Mr Grattan, though we confess, that we felt a little regret on seeing a second series of his Tales of the Road-side, announced so soon after the publication of the first. We did not then know what these volumes were—we knew what the former had been ;— they promised well of those which were to follow them ; and we are glad, that our author has done even so well, what he has done so hastily.

We have not room here to give a full description of the style of these writings ; but by our extracts, we shall exhibit it, as far as we are able, in its various lights and shades. There is a freshness and vigour in his thoughts, which always please

16

the reader.   We can see them, as it were, springing up within his mind, and coming forth naturally and beautifully; but the great fault is, that he does not use care enough in selecting them.   We should not, however, call Mr Grattan an original writer.   There is in his works not a little imitation of those of Washington Irving.   In this we wish to be clearly understood. We do not mean, that the author of High-Ways and By-Ways is a servile imitator of the style and sentiments of Irving; but that there is something in the general character of his writings, and the peculiar vein of thought which he seems fond of pursuing, that frequently reminds us of our countryman.   Indeed, were we to judge of the feelings of writers from what they have written, we should say, that those of Irving and Mr Grattan, and we may add, their minds too, were of the same complexion; though, with regard to style, the freedom and familiarity of the latter bear no resemblance to the highly-finished manner of the former.   This elegance of the one, and careless freedom of the other mark one great distinction between them.

The author of these tales has exhibited great power in his descriptions of natural scenery; and particularly in those of his first series.   His scenes are marked out with a vivid colouring and a distinct outline, and it is left to the reader's own imagination to finish the picture.   After all, then, it depends upon the temperament of our own minds, whether we are pleased or offended; since the pleasure which we derive from mere descriptions of nature, belongs, and, in its degree, bears an intimate relation to the energy and beauty, with which our own fancy fills up the outline.   We observed, that Mr Grattan had succeeded well in his descriptions of natural scenery;—he has succeeded well, too, in his characters—in unveiling the deep workings of human feelings—in laying open the secret springs of human action.   If we would paint nature well, we must frequent her still and solitary places; if characters, we must go out into the high-ways of the world, and make the living history of mankind our study.   The author of the tales before us possesses the power of description, both of character and natural scenery; and though he has not reached the highest excellence in either, he has done well in both.   And here we are led to notice one evident difference between the first and second series of his tales.   In the first, he has indulged to the full his natural predilections for rural life, and that "in-door quiet, and out-of-door stillness," which hang over secluded places;—in the second, those predilections themselves seem to be stealing away from him, and he keeps us longer in the crowds and tumults of the town, than before,—though we can still detect a fondness in him for breaking away from the precincts of populous cities.

From these desultory remarks upon Mr Grattan's merits and peculiarities as a writer, we now come to speak with more particular reference to his Tales, and the sources from which he has drawn his materials. These volumes were written from the personal observations of a wayfaring man, who, on foot, to use a phrase from his former series, has "traversed France from frontier to frontier; cut across the highways, and struck into the open country; passed by where curiosity is generally arrested; loitered in spots unknown to fame or fashion; always yielding to the impulse of feeling or the whim of fancy." France is a fine field for a genius such as our author's. It has been at times the scene of oppression and bloody deeds;—at times, the home of a happy people. A pleasant or a painful association is connected with the very names of its cities, its public places, and royal dwellings. They were splendid in the Augustan age of France, and have since felt the convulsions of that disastrous revolution, which shook Europe to its centre. With the events of this revolution, the greater part of Mr Grattan's tales have been in some way connected. Two of them—"La Vilaine Tête," of the first series, and "The Priest, and the Garde-du-corps," of the second, are particular descriptions of some of its desperate struggles. Upon the political tendency of these, we have no comments to make; we are to deal with the author as a writer, not as a politician. And as we turn over the pages of his volumes, we find there sketches of French manners, that are highly characteristic of national feeling,—sketches of French scenery, that exhibit the touches of an artist's pencil,—and a beautiful light thrown out upon the romantic vales of the French provinces, which have hitherto slept in the shadows of their own mountains. Our author has evidently the mind and feelings of a poet; but unfortunately the specimens of his versification, interspersed here and there through his writings, do little credit to either. He has an eye that sees nature, and a heart that feels nature; but there is something wanting when he would give utterance to those feelings in their proper language. He seems to be at a loss to express in poetry, what he feels in reality, and can express so well in prose.

It was our intention when we commenced these remarks, to give a full view of these Tales by a separate analysis of each; but the limits within which our reviews of works of this kind must be embraced, and the length to which these introductory remarks, have already run out, render this impossible. We shall, therefore, confine ourselves to an extract from each tale.

The first of this series is "Caribert the Bear-Hunter." From this we extract the description of a bear-hunt and the death of Caribert's father.

Soon after Caribert and his father had quitted their home, the morning, which had only just broke, began to be more than commonly overcast. A snow shower, mixed with rain, assailed them ere they reached the Pic du Midi; and the piercing cold of the air, added to the sleet beating cuttingly into his face, brought on, with Caribert, repeated attacks of violent and alternate fever and shivering. When they arrived at the den of the bear, which was formed of a cavity in the western side of the mountain, close to that terrific precipice which I have already endeavoured to describe, they were both benumbed, and scarcely capable of exertion; but the old man, rousing up all his wrath and courage for the onset, approached the cave, and with loud shouts of defiance, endeavoured to stir up the savage animal's rage. The summons was no sooner heard than answered. A horrible growl sent out from the recess, was followed by the appearance of the bear, which rushed forth as if in conscious recollection of yesterday's triumph. At the appalling sound and sight, Pero, the faithful and courageous dog, unsupported by his former ally, and having his share of brute remembrance too, of the late rencontre, hung down his head, dropped his tail, and fled yelping down the mountain. Old Lareole grasped his pike firmly, and advanced. The hideous monster reared itself up on its hind legs, stretched out its fore paws, and as, with its jaws yawning wide, its fearful tusks displayed, and growling with horrid energy, it was in the very act of springing forward, the veteran hunter stepped close up, and aimed a thrust, with no flinching strength, right at his enemy's heart. He was not far wide of that vital spot. His pike pierced the left breast, and went out clearly at the shoulder. Rendered frantic by the pain, the bear bounded up, flung itself full upon its undaunted assailant, and fell upon him to the earth. The old man, burying his head under the body of his foe, received on the back and shoulders of his doublet its unavailing efforts to penetrate the thick folds of armour with tusks and nails. He tugged at the pike to extricate it from the body, but his position was such that he could not succeed, and every new effort only tended to give issue to the thick stream of blood which flowed from the wound. During this frightful struggle, the yells of the bear were mixed with and smothered by the loud execrations of the old man. The latter, at length, gave up the hope of recovering his pike, but strove fairly next to get rid of his terrific burden. He succeeded so far as to get one leg clear, and with his nervous grasp, entwined round the body of the brute; he was rising on his knee, and called out, 'Now, Caribert, now! To his heart—to his heart the death blow, now! strike, strike!'—but Caribert struck not! He stood gazing on the scene—panic-struck—fixed to the spot with emotions not fathomable to man,—a terrible but not solitary instance of the perilous risks run by mental courage, as well as by human virtue. I do not inquire into the mystery—but there he stood, its horrible and shuddering illustration!

The old man was now getting clear, but the bear had his hold in turn. His huge paws were fastened with a dreadful force round one of his victim's thighs; and recovering from his sprawling posture, he began to draw him backwards, evidently in the design of regaining his den. The old man's courage rose with his danger, for he alertly drew his knife from his belt, opened the blade, and plunged it repeatedly into the body of the bear. The latter leaped and bounded with agony; and Lareole, recovering his feet once more, succeeded in grasping the savage in his arms. But the trial could not be prolonged. He was drooping under the dreadful gripe.—Breathless and faint, he could only utter some terrific curses against the recreant who had abandoned him; and while Caribert gazed, his brain on fire, his hands outstretched, his tongue cleaving to his mouth, but his limbs trembling, his heart sunk, and his feet rooted to the earth, he saw the white locks of his aged father floating over the neck of his destroyer; while the dying animal, in his blindness, not knowing what he did, had retreated to the very edge of the precipice, slipping at every backward plunge in the slough formed by the snow and his own heart's blood, by which it was dissolved. The old man, seeing his terrible fate, seemed to acquire for an instant the gigantic energy of despair. Throwing one glance across the horrid space on the border of which he stood, he screamed in a voice of thunder, ' Caribert! Caribert!' The terrible expression conveyed in this hoarse scream, struck on the mind of his son with an electrical shock. Suddenly roused from his stupor, he recovered for an instant all his recollection and his courage. He uttered a cry of corresponding fierceness,—swung his brandished pike—rushed forwards, with open arms to seize his father, and snatch him from his destiny,—but it was too late! The monster touched on the extreme edge—lost his footing—plunged instinctively forward—took another backward step,—and just as Caribert believed he had grasped his father in his outstretched arms, both man and bear were lost to his sight, and their groans came mingling in the air, as they went crashing down below.

The second tale, "The Priest, and the Garde-du-Corps," is one of uncommon interest, and decidedly the best of the three. The principal hero of the piece is a garde-du-corps of the sixteenth Louis—a young Irishman, who had attached himself most devotedly to the person and declining fortunes of Marie Antoinette, every particular of whose conduct in the troubled and trying times of the revolution, is deeply interesting. But our author has not exhibited her in public life alone. He has allowed us to see her in the rich and virtuous enjoyment of that seclusion, which she found in the Trianon with the circle of her royal and chosen friends around her. And it is from this happy retirement, that we see her coming to perform her part in the bloody tragedy.   The following is a part of our author's description of the assault of the populace upon the splendid palace of Versailles, and the catastrophe of the eventful night of the fifth of October.

While this was passing at the hospital, the palace presented a scene of indescribable terror and confusion ; the splendid halls and tapestried apartments being the theatre of bloody and protracted outrage.   As soon as the queen fled from her sleeping-room, and the doors of the ante-chamber were forced open, some of the Garde-du-corps had dexterously thrown themselves between the mob and the room where they supposed she was still in her bed.   They there renewed the contest with the as-sailants, who were at last persuaded by the assurances of the household servants that the queen had escaped.   Quitting the point of immediate attack, they then rushed by another passage towards the gallery called *l'œil de Boeuf*, hoping there to intercept her flight; but she was safely sheltered in the apartment of the king, where with her children in her arms and her husband beside her, she was firmly prepared to meet what-ever might happen.   The small but devoted band of the Garde-du-Corps, on being assured of the queen having left her bed-room, passed through it into the *œil de Boeuf*, and by barricadoing the doors, were able for a while to resist the efforts of the grenadiers of the Parisian National Guard to burst them open.   But as the resistance must have been in the end unavailing, one of the guardsmen, named De Chevanne, resolved to devote himself a victim to the chance of saving his comrades; and he threw himself into the ante-chamber alone—in the midst of his foes. Struck by this act of isolated intrepidity, the assailants paused, and he in a few moments of earnest eloquence made one of those effective ap-peals to the turbulent passions of men, which are oftener successful in France than in all other countries of the globe.   In a few minutes the National Guard and the Garde-du-Corps were seen like brothers, ex-changing cockades and caps, embracing and shouting together, " *Vive le Roi! Vive la Nation! Vivent les Gardes-du-Corps.*

From this moment all was safe.   The impulsion spread like wild fire through the troops, and from them was caught by the people.   The palace was cleared, and instead of the atrocious threats and murderous vociferations, mixed with the clash of arms and tramp of a furious multi-tude, the profaned but now uncrowded corridors and halls echoed the joyous embracings of the household, the boisterous gratulation of men, and the hysteric laugh of women, all nearly as frantic with delight as they had so lately been with fear.

For some hours after this, a boisterous incertitude prevailed through-out.   The struggling elements of the mob power, which had been decom-posed during the night, were now rapidly massing once more, under the effect of the stimulus which the attack on the palace had given to all. The *Place d'Armes*, the court-yards, and the terraces were thickly thronged with the armed multitude, who insisted with imperative de-mands that the king and his family should abandon Versailles, and accompany them to Paris.   Resistance was at this crisis vain, and it is useless to record the names of those who advised an impotent refusal.

The king gave his consent to the measure. 'I confide myself to the people,' said he, 'let them do with me as they please;' and the preparations for departure were hurried on.   But the outrageous impatience of the rabble would not be satisfied without the visible testimony of obedience to their commands, and the actual presence of their victims. They vociferated in angry tones for the queen's appearance at the balcony which opens from the room where Louis XIV. expired, upon the marble-paved court called *la Cour de Marbre*. Imprecations and threats accompanied the call, and those who surrounded the queen and who heard the tone, tremblingly intreated her not to appear, as they little doubted their intention to fire at her as she stood, and thus complete their diabolical design against her life.   She alone stood calm and courageous at this awful moment.   She took her children one in each hand, and stepped out upon the balcony with a confident mien.   'No children; no children! send them back—stand out *alone!*' shouted by a thousand voices, were the horrid orders which assailed her.   She did not hesitate a moment, but putting the children in at the window-door behind her, she turned round again towards the crowd, and raising her eyes and her clasped hands to heaven, she stood a while in the undismayed conviction that each successive moment was her last. A murmur of astonished approbation rolled hoarsely through the throng, and of all the sinewy arms that bore a weapon among it, but one was raised to take her life, thus offered as it were to their assault.   One ruffian, flushed with fury and covered with clotted blood from the morning's conflict, stood at the corner on the left of the *Cour de Marbre*, on the very spot where the assassin Damiens had placed himself to strike at the heart of Louis XV.   Seeing the queen thus exposed, within thirty paces of his design, and while the rushing tide of popular inconstancy was on the point of turning in her favour, he levelled a musquet at her breast, and snapped the trigger.   The piece went off; but the bullet flew high in the air, almost perpendicularly over the roof of the palace; for an arm beside the murderer had struck the weapon up at the very instant of its being discharged.   The wretch looked round on him who had frustrated his aim, but did not recognise Cornelius in the pale and wounded being who leaned against the corner of the wall beside him.   Our hero, who, devoured by agitation, had insisted on crawling from the hospital, weak as he was, and had placed himself in this position, supported by Father O'Collogan, thus saved the life of her, for whose service he lived, and instantly knew in the would-be-murderer, that very soldier of the Regiment of Flanders, who a short month before had in an explosion of unprincipled loyalty climbed up the palace walls to shout blessings on the king! Prompt as the voice of the storm, which answers the lightning's flash, the voice of Cornelius followed the flash of this inebriate madman's weapon.   'Long live the queen!' once more burst from his pallid lips, and the words were repeated in a shout from the tumultuous assemblage which rung from the fifty niches in the surrounding walls, filled with the busts and statues of emperors and kings.

The author would have succeeded better in this exhibition of the deserted but undaunted queen coming before her persecuting people, had he deviated less from history, and introduced the patriot Lafayette; who, despairing of being heard in the tumult around him, turned, and with an eloquence more impressive than words, kissed the hand of the royal sufferer.

The third and last tale is "The Vouée au Blanc." Its date is that eventful epoch in the history of France and of the world,—the fall of Napoleon. One extract will afford a specimen of our author's humour.

Monsieur Hippolite Emmanuel Narcisse de Choufleur was an offshot from one of those ancient and noble families, which, had I at hand a blood-bound of heraldry, I might perhaps succeed in tracing back to the most dismal depths of the dark ages. This gentleman was an hereditary royalist, a prating, busy, and empty-pated fellow, who had owed the good luck of keeping his head on his shoulders in the stormy seas of the revolution, merely to the lightness of the freight it carried. He floated on the waters like the buoy of an anchor, and just served to denote the grounds where his family had fixed, and where the privateers that were then abroad might find safe harbourage and shelter. Persecution and confiscation had driven all the other individuals of his race far from their native land, and left him pennyless. His whole possessions on the establishment of the republic, consisted in some half-dozen sky-blue, pea-green, and rose-coloured coats; about twenty pair of nankeen breeches; a large quantity of ruffles, with shirts and frills in the proportion of one of the first to every dozen of the latter; some silk stockings, snuff boxes, pastebuckles, rings, and brooches; and a satin-wood casket, containing sundry patents of nobility, marriage articles, grants of estates, and other proofs of gentle blood, legitimacy, and feudal rights. With this stock of merchandize, Monsieur de Choufleur, or, as he was more familiarly called, Monsieur Hippolite, commenced his trade of emigrant, knight-errant, fortune-hunter, and *soi-disant* marquis. After buzzing and bustling about his native Normandy for some years following the annihilation of such pretensions as were his only inheritance, he determined to expatriate himself to the hospitable shores of Great Britain; and as his stay in his own country had attracted no attention, so did his departure meet with no difficulty. He landed from a fishing boat at Brighton, in a miserable plight; told a long lying story of misfortunes, imprisonment, and escape; was warmly received by some honest John Bull; remained two years or more in our island, acquiring a marvellously insufficient knowledge of the language, and a perfect taste for roast beef; and having supported himself by his skill in dancing, which no native teacher could compete with, and upheld his claims to the title of marquis by appeals to his satin-wood casket, which no one would take the trouble to examine, he availed himself of the first amnesty granted by Napoleon, and returned to look after the remnants of his family inheritance, which he protested most solemnly were buried somewhere adjacent to the site of the three villages.   *   *   *

He was in the first place precisely five feet and an inch in height, and, being then somewhat turned of forty, it was commonly believed that he had acquired his complete growth. There was no proportion between the length and thickness, either of the whole person or its component parts, and, geographically described, it would not offer a favourable specimen of man's fair proportion. The head leaning forward like a promontory, was large and long, the body showed like a great continent long and thick, the isthmus neck was at once short and slender, the arms reached nearly to the knees, and the thighs and legs were appallingly stout and muscular. An elevation and protuberance of his right shoulder gave to what nature meant for its fellow, the air of a very distant correspondence, and caused him when in action to proceed with that movement best defined by the military phrase *en échelon.* The only good parts were the well turned ancles and the diminutive and prettily formed feet, and they were surmounted by a pair of calves, whose Herculean dimensions seemed to threaten on the least exertion to burst their searments, that is to say, the seams of the old darned silk stockings, whose natural white was blended with the yellow leaf of time, and the powder blue of the washerwoman. The face was of a peculiar nature. It was not actually ugly, but particularly droll. The forehead slanted back directly from the eye-brows, the nose advanced beyond the utmost verge of the aquiline. The eyes, of light blue, followed the nose with dreadful strainings, and stood far out of their sockets; white eye-brows, and lids unlashed, offered no relief to this unnatural projection; and the small mouth and chin sloping inwards, precisely in the same ratio with the forehead, gave a grey-hound sort of look to the whole physiognomy. The hair, naturally flaxen, was short and curled, and filled with powder and pomatum; the cheeks were ruddy, and covered in part with an amber-coloured down, that formed a perfect caricature of whiskers on each.

A reverential regard for the antiquity of family relics, and a natural love of finery, made M. Hippolite not only preserve those which remained to him, but carry them on his person on all occasions. He wore rings, and brooches, and buckles, in enormous profusion, and he had through all the changes of his latter life contrived to keep one dress suit formed out of the remains of his ancient wardrobe. On the present occasion, he had all his treasures on his back and other appropriate parts. His one last pair of silk stockings have been already mentioned. The garments next in order, formed of what once looked nankeen, now wore the semblance of very ill-washed white calico, and his waistcoat was silk that had been originally a bright violet, but was now washed into the hue of the outer edge of an expiring rainbow; and, saying nothing of the cravat or frill, and less than nothing of the mysterious garment to which they formed appendages, I may notice the ancient rose-coloured coat, which had long since been dyed, first a brilliant purple, and afterwards the most sombre shade of black. Monsieur Hippolite's former profession of dancing master had had a much more bracing effect on the muscular expansion of his preposterous calves, than on the nervous system of his thread-bare coat. It was reduced to the very shadow of a shade; and the many hues imprinted upon it during its various changes, gave to it a chameleon-coloured mixture that had a most extraordinary effect, as its flimsy texture was sported with by the various accidents of light and shade.

17

*A Year in Europe ; comprising a Journal of Observations in
England, Scotland, Ireland, France, Switzerland, the North
of Italy, and Holland. In* 1818 *and* 1819.   By JOHN
GRISCOM, Professor of Chemistry and Natural Philosophy
in the New York Institution, Member of the Literary and
Philosophical Society of New York, &c. New York. 1824.
Second edition.   2 vols.   12mo.

OF the many Americans, who have within a few years made
the "tour of Europe," few have published the result of their
observations, either for the amusement or the instruction of their
less favoured countrymen.   We are not disposed to complain
too loudly of this; for some of the few books of this description, that have been offered to the public, had better never
extended beyond the circle of the private friends of the
author.   But, on the other hand, we believe there have been
some who have visited Europe, whose modesty has persuaded
them to withhold more than was meet from the public eye.
   A fairer specimen of the "multum in parvo," than is exhibited in the volumes before us, we have seldom seen.   In
the short space of one year, Professor Griscom visited, as
stated on the title-page of his work, England, Scotland, Ireland, France, Switzerland, the North of Italy, and Holland ;
and he has given us much valuable information from them
all.   His attention in all these countries was directed to the
useful, often to the neglect of what might be merely agreeable ; hence, in preference to other objects, we find him visiting schools and hospitals, and literary, scientific, and benevolent institutions, wherever they were to be found ; and he has
collected a mass of information on all these subjects, which
may be, and in some instances has already been applied to
the improvement of similar institutions in our country.   In
grace and elegance of style, our author has been surpassed by
some writers, whose labours in practical utility fall far short
of his.   We have even noticed some inaccuracies in expression,
and in the construction of his sentences ; but these are so far
atoned for by the intrinsic excellencies of the work, that we
refrain from any more than this passing notice of their existence.   We have heard this called a dull book.   But we consider the remark an unfortunate one, rather impeaching the
judgment of those who made it, than bringing discredit on the
book which was the subject of it.   He, who as a traveller

would depend for his amusement principally upon visiting operas and masquerades, might be expected, as a reader, to find fault with a book like the one before us; but he who can make the performance of his duty contribute to his highest pleasure, and whose heart expands with feelings of benevolence toward his fellow-creatures, will not find these volumes tedious or uninteresting.

There is another point of view, in which the writings of such travellers as Professor Griscom may be eminently useful to their countrymen. By introducing to their notice much that is excellent and praiseworthy in the character and institutions of the nations of Europe, they remove asperity of feeling, and do away those national jealousies and antipathies, in which too many among us are prone to indulge. The more an intercourse of this kind is encouraged—the more we become acquainted with one another through the interposition of those who are disposed to look around them with a friendly eye, the more will those barriers which separate and make enemies of nations, be broken down; and those kindlier feelings, which have been too long restricted within the narrow limits of a single nation, will assume the character of that enlarged philanthropy, which can hold fellowship even with those who speak an unknown language and inhabit a distant land. Had the Europeans who have travelled in this country and published their accounts of us afterwards, been influenced by that desire to produce a mutual good understanding, which appears to have had such place in the mind of Professor Griscom,—had they been desirous that their countrymen should think more justly of us than they had thought before, much more might have been done than yet has been done, for the accomplishment of an object so desirable. Nor need it be feared, that in thus inculcating feelings of respect and good will toward the people of other nations, we shall weaken the attachment which binds us to our own; for we cannot doubt, that when all that is excellent in the institutions of Europe, and in the character of her people, shall be rightly appreciated, there will still be found enough to cheer and encourage us in the prospect at home, and make us cling closely to the land of our nativity. Neither do we suppose, though willing to acknowledge the superiority of many of the institutions of Europe over our own of a similar character, that the advantages of improvement are to be all on our side. For, apart from the advances we have made in the science of government and from the excellence of our political institutions, there must surely be some of our establishments for purposes more purely benevolent,—our hospitals and penitentiaries, for instance,—in which we have something to impart, and not every thing to learn.

In saying that the subjects to which our traveller's attention was mainly directed, were such as most travellers might have neglected, it is not to be inferred, that his pages are exclusively devoted to these topics.   Many descriptions of towns, public buildings, and occasionally of some curious phenomenon of nature, contribute their measure to enhance the interest of the work.   Entertaining, as we do, these favourable sentiments of the work, it is with much satisfaction we find, that a second edition has been demanded at the hands of the author. It speaks well for the good sense of the community ; it shows a prevailing disposition not merely to be amused, but to be instructed—a willingness to cherish the feelings, which are here strongly inculcated, of respect and good will for the intelligent and the worthy, though they dwell among a strange people and in a foreign land.

Much as we are disposed to commend the disposition, which our traveller has so uniformly manifested, to devote his time to subjects of practical utility, we should have found it difficult to repress our curiosity so far, when within seven miles of Stonehenge, as to pass on without visiting it.   The excellent description of it, given by Professor Silliman, to which our author refers, instead of satisfying, would have excited curiosity the more.   But it is not on the reader's account, that we complain of this omission, for as long as we must remain content with knowing it from description only, that of the author referred to, leaves us nothing further to require.

No part of these volumes has afforded us more satisfaction than the description of the respective schools of Fellenberg and of Pestalozzi in Switzerland.   For the account of Fellenberg's institution at Hofwyl, occupying thirteen closely printed pages of this edition, we must refer our readers to the work itself, as the article is too long to be extracted entire, and too interesting to be mutilated.   The description of the school of Pestalozzi at Yverdun occupies a much smaller space, but we can give only a part of that.   We select that part which relates particularly to his principles of government and instruction.

The two great instruments with which he works are faith and love. He discards the motives of ambition and emulation, as unnecessary, and as tending to counteract the sentiment of good will toward others. He thinks there is enough in the intuitive understanding of every child to accomplish the complete growth and maturity of its faculties, if its reason be properly trained and nourished, and not warped by injudicious treatment. The common plans of education he regards as too artificial, too wide a departure from nature. Too much stress is laid upon the memory, while the imagination is too much neglected. If the native feelings of the heart are allowed to operate, under the dominion of the native powers of the mind, drawn out and expanded by faith and love, the child is competent of itself to arrive gradually at the most correct and important conclusions in religion and science. There is a native and inherent life, which only requires to be cherished by genial treatment, to bring it into the full attainment of truth, and to the utmost perfection of its being. He therefore insists upon the greatest pains being taken to draw out this native life and to preserve it in full vigour. There is a constant danger of urging the child forward beyond its natural strength, of anticipating its conclusions, and thus weakening its confidence in its own powers. In the plans he adopts nothing is to be got by heart. The understanding is to be thoroughly reached, and then the memory will take care of itself. 　　*　　　*　　　*

Very few books are used, as it is expected the children can read well before they come there. But to describe the modes of teaching, so as to render them clearly intelligible, would require much more time and space than I can possibly allot to it, were I ever so competent to make it known. We saw the exercises of arithmetic, writing, drawing, mathematics, lessons in music and gymnastics, something of geography, French, Latin, and German. To teach a school, in the way practised here, without book, and almost entirely by verbal instruction, is extremely laborious. The teacher must be constantly with the child, always talking, questioning, explaining, and repeating. The pupils, however, by this process, are brought into very close intimacy with the instructer. Their capacities, all their faculties and propensities, become laid open to his observation. This gives him an advantage, which cannot possibly be gained in the ordinary way in which schools are generally taught. The children look well, appear very contented, and apparently live in great harmony one with another; which, considering the diversity of national character and temper here collected, can be attributed only to the spirit of love and affection which sways the breast of the principal of the institution, and extends its benign influence throughout all the departments. 　　*　　　*　　　*

The success of this mode of instruction greatly depends on the personal qualifications of those who undertake to conduct it. There is nothing of mechanism in it, as in the Lancasterian plan; no laying down of precise rules for managing classes, &c. It is all mind and feeling. Its arrangements must always depend on the ages, talents, and tempers of the scholars, and require, on the part of the teachers, the most diligent and faithful attention. Above all, it requires that the teacher should consider himself as the father and bosom friend of his pupils, and to be animated with the most affectionate desires for their good. Pestalozzi himself is all this. His heart glows with such a spirit, that the good old man can hardly refrain from bestowing kisses on all with whom he is concerned. He holds out his hand to his pupils on every occasion, and they love him as a child loves its mother. His plan of teaching is just fit for the domestic fireside, with a father or mother in the centre, and a circle of happy children around them. He is aware of this, and wishes to extend the knowledge of his plan to every parent. Pestalozzi is seventy-two years of age. It has been quite unfortunate for the progress of his system on the continent, that he pays so little attention to exteriors, regarding dress, furniture, &c. as of no moment whatever, provided the mind and heart be right.

The attention of many of our benevolent and intelligent fellow-citizens has been turned of late to the improvement of the mode and means of education in this country. Many causes have, no doubt, conspired to give this direction to their exertions, and we are disposed to attribute to the publication of " A Year in Europe" its due share. The school established at Northampton, of which an account was given in a late number of this Gazette, resembles in some respects the institutions of both Fellenberg and Pestalozzi. A few months since an advertisement appeared in the public papers, proposing to establish an institution at Windsor in the state of Connecticut, on the model of that at Hofwyl. Whether this has gone into operation, or with what success, we have not the means at hand to determine. A school has been established at Gardiner, in Maine, upon the same model, and is now in successful operation. Of this school we hope soon to give a more detailed account. Others, conforming very nearly to the plan of Pestalozzi, have been established at Philadelphia and in its neighbourhood.

Since our author's return from Europe, his efforts have been directed to the establishment of a school of a very different description from those of which we have been treating. Some benevolent and influential citizens of New York, where he now resides, have been induced, principally, we believe, by his representations, to establish a " High School " in that city, upon the plan of the High School at Edinburgh, of which he gives the following account.

With an American acquaintance, I went to the high school, of Edinburgh, and was introduced to the rector, J. Pillans. This grammar school is of ancient standing, and like the university, it is under the direction of the magistrates of the city. It dates an existence of nearly 300 years, but the present building was erected in 1777, and is 120 feet long. The number of scholars is at present between 8 and 900. Four teachers are employed, in addition to the rector. This gentleman, by the effort of a particular genius, and indefatigable activity, has completely succeeded in introducing into this large school, the system of monitorial instruction, and applying it to classical learning. He has under his exclusive charge, twenty-three classes, each containing nine boys. Every class has its monitor, who hears the rest recite. The rector superintends the whole, and decides all questions of dispute, when appeals are made to him against the decision of the monitors. In each room is a *custos morum*, who watches the behaviour of the scholars and notes every instance of remissness. Almost the only punishment resorted to, is the imposing of additional tasks on offenders; and obliging them to attend the school, during the hours and half days of ordinary vacation. The twenty-three classes all recite the same lesson at the same time. The noise they make is unavoidably great, but it is the sound of useful activity. We were highly gratified with the evidences of intelligence and attainment which the boys displayed when collected into one room, and examined before us by the rector. The superiority of their instruction appeared not only in the facility of their translations, but in the readiness with which they recited parallel passages, and referred to the illustrations of different classical authors, and in their acquaintance with the geography, chronology, &c. of the historical passages, which were given them as extemporaneous exercises. Great merit is obviously due to the rector, for bringing this method of teaching so perfectly to bear upon the higher parts of education, and showing its adaptation to subjects which have generally been thought beyond its reach. The high school contains a good library for the benefit of the teachers, and boys of the upper class. The whole cost of tuition in this excellent school, is but three pounds per annum, including the use of the library. There are few boys in the school above sixteen years of age, a period which leaves them sufficient time for apprenticeship to almost any kind of business. With such advantages of intellectual and moral instruction, is it surprising that Scotland should have taken such an elevated stand among the nations, for the intelligence, industry, and sobriety of her people?

This, it will be seen, is an application of the monitorial system to the higher branches of education, which, he informs us, has been practised with great success in that literary capital of the North. The New York High School has just commenced its operations, under the superintendance of Professor Griscom and another eminent teacher of New York; and in the facilities, which it will afford for the acquisition of the higher branches of education to the children of the middling and poorer classes in that city, and in all others where it may be introduced, it may do much toward securing the permanence and stability of a government, whose very existence depends upon the virtue and intelligence of the people.

MISCELLANY.

ITALIAN LYRICAL POETRY.

THE mighty fame of a few great Italian poets, of Dante, Petrarch, Ariosto, Tasso, Alfieri, has overshadowed and obscured the reputation of the less gifted of their imitators and competitors. English readers, I imagine, possess a very imperfect knowledge of the number and of the merit of numerous lesser Italian poets, who form a distinct and remarkable class of literature, well deserving the attention of the enlightened and liberal scholar. I will not say their school is entitled to pre-eminence over that of the Spanish, the German, or the English lyrical and fugitive poetry ; but certainly it is not destitute of characteristic excellencies, and exhibits many beautiful features of no mean order. These beauties are accompanied, I admit, by several striking defects ; but the Italian poets have, like the poets of other countries, a national character, and by that character they should be judged.

I propose to introduce into the Gazette brief notices of the most eminent among them, with translations, which may serve to give an idea of their peculiar manner, and of the general style of the minor Italian poetry. I shall not attempt any systematic order in the series of the poets whom I describe ; but shall call them up in the succession, and at the intervals, which circumstances may render most convenient. I begin with

SAVIOLI.

The Count Ludovico Savioli was a Bolognese of noble family, whose light and melodious canzonets gained for him, among his countrymen, the name of the Anacreon of the eighteenth century. Both the Italian and the Greek poet are distinguished by the same graceful fancy, the same sweetness of versification, and the same luxurious abandonment of soul to the emotions of love and pleasure. Savioli has left behind him none but fugitive pieces of this description, all conceived in a similar spirit, and written in precisely the same measure. They are filled with allusions to the pagan mythology, and with imagery drawn from its ancient stores. Indeed, he seems to have completely imbibed the feeling and assumed the tone of a genuine Greek. Instances of the use of the classical mythology in allegorical senses abound in modern Italian poetry, and are apt to offend a pure taste by their triteness and by their incongruity. But we read Savioli as we would a Roman or a Greek. Classical associations are so wrought into the whole texture of his mind and writings, that we cease to judge of him as a modern, and are no longer sensible of any falseness of taste in the poet.

The short stanzas of Savioli's canzonets each compose a distinct and independent idea. They are full of picturesque conceptions, without any depth of sentiment, or elevation of thought, which glide smoothly through the mind, exciting, it is true, an agreeable emotion as they pass, but leaving no permanent impression behind them.

In the specimens, which I subjoin, of the manner of Savioli, I have carefully preserved the structure of his verse, as necessary to the full apprehension of his qualities. The first is his favourite ode

TO VENUS.

Bright queen of smiles and joy,
    Ægiochus' fair daughter,
    Who first, in naked loveliness,
    Rose from the foaming water.
Soft goddess, erst with jealous rage
    The hoary Vulcan firing;
    But oh! the son of Cinyras
    With blissful love inspiring.
Thine is the laughing quivered boy,
    Who wears the golden pinion,
    To whom in sweet succession fall
    Obedience and dominion.
To thee the blooming maiden's hand
    Is vainly lifted never;
    And gray-haired matrons only find
    Thy face averted ever.
The strings of silver Sappho rang
    To soft Æolian numbers,
    When from her couch victorious Love
    Was chasing tranquil slumbers.
Thy course, kind Venus, at her prayer,
    To earth was oft directed;
    The ambrosial feasts of heaven forgot,
    Its golden halls neglected.
Before thy bright Idalian car
    Now buoyant doves are driven;
    But then, by dark-winged sparrows drawn,
    It fleetly wheeled o'er heaven.
And whilst thine ear propitious heard
    Her strains of love-sick madness,
    Thy rosy fingers dried her tears
    Of broken-hearted sadness.
And in my bosom glow the fires
    Of more than wonted pleasure,
    As bolder yet I strike the lyre,
    To sound love's dulcet measure.
I care not for the ire of gods,
    By thee, dear Venus, shielded,
    To whom the Dardan shepherd's voice
    The palm of beauty yielded.

A VENERE.

O figlia alma d' Egioco,
    Leggiadro onor dell' acque,
    Per cui le Grazie apparvero,
    E 'l riso al mondo nacque.
O molle dea, di ruvido
    Fabbro gelosa cura,
    O del figliuol di Cinira
    Beata un dì ventura.
Teco il Garzon, cui temono
    Per la gran face eterna,
    Ubbidienza e imperio
    Soavemente alterna.
Accese a te le tenere
    Fanciulle alzan la mano:
    Sol te ritrosa invocano
    Le antiche madri invano.
Te sulle corde Eolie
    Saffo invitar solea,
    Quando a quiete i languidi
    Begli occhi Amor togliea.
E tu richiesta, O Venere,
    Sovente a lei scendesti,
    Posta in obblio l' ambrosia,
    E i tetti aurei celesti.
Il gentil carro Idalio,
    Ch' or le colombe addoppia,
    Lieve traea di passeri
    Nera amorosa coppia.
E mentre udir propizia
    Solevi il flebil canto,
    Tergean le dita rosee
    Della fanciulla il pianto.
E a noi pur anco insolito
    Ricerca il petto ardore,
    E a noi l' esperta cetera
    Dolce risuona amore.
Se tu m' assisti, io Pallade
    Abbia, se vuol, nimica:
    Teco ella innanzi a Paride
    Perdè la lite antica.

18

I ask not Pallas for defence —
  One shaft of Cupid's quiver,
  Against the immortal Ægis driven,
  Its glittering orb would shiver.
Let altars only rise to thee,
  Sole object of devotion ;
  Thine own Cythera then will be
  The realms of earth and ocean !

A che valer può l' Egida,
  Se 'l figlio tuo percote ?
  Quel che i suoi dardi possono
  L' asta immortal non puote.
Meco i mortali innalzino
  Solo al tuo nome altari ;
  Citera tua divengano
  Il ciel, la terra, i mari.

The Ode to Venus illustrates all the marked peculiarities of Savioli's manner, and carries us back to the scenes and associations of classical times. I give one other specimen of this poet, which strongly expresses his admiration of antiquity, and is eminently distinguished by his characteristic qualities.

SOLITUDE.

Away with fabled names, that shine
  In modern knightly story;
  I tune my lyre to sing the deeds
  Of nobler ancient glory.
Old Sparta, sternly virtuous, made
  The pure and spotless maiden
  To join the wrestler's ring, by nought
  But nature's vesture laden.
No crimson hues along the cheek
  Arose to mar her beauty ;
  Why feel dishonest shame, if true
  To honour and to duty?
Nor word nor look betrays the fire,
  Which in the bosom gathers
  Of Lacedæmon's youths, who sit
  Beside their warlike fathers.
But Beauty yielded not the palm
  To gold or false devices ;
  Arm in your country's cause, they cried ;
  And Hope each heart entices.
How boldly fought the Spartan host,
  When Love the victor cherished,
  And tears of secret grief were shed
  O'er the brave men who perished !
Oh, wherefore have ye fled, ye days
  Pure, holy, ever-glorious?
  While avarice, luxury, and fraud
  Now reign o'er all victorious.
Then haste away, O dearest one,
  To scenes where peace abideth ;
  Far from the haunts of haughty men,
  The day in calmness glideth.
Lo there, 'mid lovely verdant slopes,
  On high the mountain towers ;
  Penelope, in all her pride,
  Dwelt in less regal bowers.
The cypress there, pale Hecate's tree,
  Its sacred leaves uncloses ;
  And, o'er each rocky dell, the fir
  Dark shade to shade opposes.
There, too, the tree, which, as it sighed
  Above the lonely fountain,
  The Berecynthian goddess loved
  To hear on Phrygia's mountain.

LA SOLITUDINE.

Lascia i sognati Demoni
  Di Falerina, e Armida ;
  Porgi l' orecchio a storia
  Più antica, e meno infida.
Sparta, severo ospizio
  Di rigida virtude,
  Trasse a lottar le vergini
  In sull' arena ignude.
Non di rossor si videro
  Contaminar la gota :
  E' la vergogna inutile,
  Dove la colpa è ignota.
Fra padri austeri immobile
  La gioventù sedea,
  E sconosciuto incendio
  Per gli occhi il cor bevea.
Ma d' oro, o d' arti indebite
  Preda beltà non era :
  Sacre alla patria, dissero :
  Per lei combatti, e spera.
Grecia tremò : vittoria
  De' chiesti amor fu lieta ;
  Premio gli estinti ottennero
  Di lagrima segreta.
Chi v' ha rapito, o secoli
  Degni d' eterna lode?
  Tutto svani ; trionfano
  Fasto, avarizia, e frode.
Fuggiamo, o cara, involati
  Dalla città fallace :
  Meco ne' boschi annidati,
  Che sol ne' boschi è pace.
Remoto albergo spazia
  Su i colli, e al ciel torreggia :
  Certo invecchiò Penelope
  In men superba reggia.
Là ciparisso all' Ecate
  Sacro le cime innalza :
  Là densi abeti crescono
  Ombre d' opposta balza.
L' arbore ond' arse in Frigia
  La Berecintia Diva,
  Contrasta al vento : ei mormora,
  E i crin parlanti avviva.

Erst a lone grot, with native marks
　Of rudeness on it clinging.
　Was opened by the living stream,
　Fresh from the soil up-springing.
'T was found by art, who emulous
　With nature joined her treasure ;
　And Thetis drew from all her stores
　To deck the abode of pleasure.
In tranquil grace, beside the cave,
　Its guardian Naiad standing,
　Pours from her mossy shell a fount
　To silvery streams expanding.

Un antro solitario
　Nel tufo apriron l' acque,
　Forse, che a di più semplici
　Fu rezzo, e rozzo piacque.
Il vide arte, e sollecita
　Vi secondò natura ;
　Teti di sua dovizia
　Vesti le opache mura.
Onde argentine in copia
　Dalla muscosa conca
　Versa tranquilla Najade
　Custode alla spelonca.

C. C.

THE BACHELOR.

He shows me where the bachelors sit, and there live we as merry as the day is
long.　　　　　*Much Ado About Nothing.*

Mr Editor—My father was blessed with a large property, and,
what is much more common in New England, a large family.　His
estate, when divided at his decease, afforded each of his children a
moderate income, sufficient, so long as we remained single, to maintain
a decent style of living, but altogether inadequate to the necessities
of a wife and children.　Most young persons in my situation would
have sought to increase their means, with a view to the attainment
of these blessings, as well as some others, which are equally incompatible with a short purse.　For several months, I did myself
meditate upon the best means of effecting this desirable object ;
but was unable to find any profession or calling, which was without its objections.　After some ineffectual attempts to get myself
fairly engaged in some useful pursuit, I came to the conclusion,
that I was unfit for any, and determined to settle myself in some
retired village, in which my small means would enable me to plod
through life with comfort and independence.　I accordingly set
up my rest in B——, where I have resided ever since, doing
neither harm nor good, except so far as I have afforded a subject
of speculation to my worthy neighbours.　Indeed my life and
conversation have been, and will probably continue to be, a
problem of difficult solution to them.　They can neither understand how a man can be without business of his own, nor how he
can avoid meddling with that of others.

At first, when I refused to attend a subscription ball, and declined becoming a candidate for the fire society, they were disposed to set me down as an unsociable fellow.　This opinion was
relinquished, when it was perceived, that I returned the various
calls with which I was favoured, that I appeared well pleased
when a neighbour dropped in to sit an hour in the evening, and

was always ready for a little chat in the road. Some of the ladies suspected that I had met with a disappointment in an affair of the heart, till they found out, that I told a good story, and enjoyed a good dinner and a good joke. Others took me for a poet, and Miss Lydia Lovesong actually went the length of requesting a few lines for her album. But it would be tedious to detail all the opinions, which have at various times prevailed respecting my character and motives. My good townsmen have never yet hit upon the truth, that I am a thoroughly lazy fellow, at which I am the less surprised, as it was some time before I discovered it myself. In the mean time, I have gradually risen in the good graces of those around me. I tilt with no man's hobby, and am willing to listen to any man's story; and as I have rarely any thing to do, which may not as well be left undone, a visit can hardly be unseasonable. My advice is frequently desired by those who have already made up their minds, and as it always confirms their resolutions, it is always agreeable. In short, the bachelor's room has become a favourite evening resort with most of the gentry of our village, and would probably be more frequented than it is, if the practice was as agreeable to the matrons of the community as it is to their husbands. But, from some cause or other, these ladies entertain but a slender opinion of the advantage to be derived from the frequent visits of their spouses to my establishment, which they look upon with about as much favour as they do upon a lodge of freemasons. This aversion does not seem to extend to myself; on the contrary, they are well pleased to see me at their own houses, and occasionally make considerable exertion to drag me out from my retreat. I am, therefore, at some loss to understand the motive of their opposition to their husbands in this matter. But such is the fact, and I pass it by, as one of those *bizarreries* of the sex, which it is useless for a bachelor to attempt to comprehend.

My most regular visiters at present are the minister, the doctor, the two lawyers, and the cashier of the bank, for we have a bank in the village, of which more hereafter. These gentlemen, with the exception of the younger attorney, have been long resident here, and have gradually come to a sort of tacit convention with their better halves to abstain from my parlour for six evenings in the week, provided they are suffered to assemble there on that of Saturday, without let or molestation by word, deed, or look. Habit has rendered this arrangement so agreeable to all parties, that I am of opinion, that the good ladies would find their husbands as much in the way, should any accident detain them at home on that evening, as if the same thing had happened on a Monday morning; whilst the gentlemen on their part, in such an event, would feel as if the week was turned wrong end foremost.

Among these periodical visiters I mentioned the cashier of our bank, Mr Richard Allbright, or as he is often nicknamed, Dick Moonshine. This gentleman is one of those over-ingenious persons, whose brains are eternally disturbed with some new project, and who spend, in seeking short cuts to an object, double the time necessary to arrive at it by the usual route. He inherited a tolerable estate, but he had so many schemes for becoming opulent, that he became poor, before he could bring any one to perfection. The only one which met with any success, was that of a bank. When Dick first started this project, it was received with ridicule. His neighbours told him it was nonsense ; that as there was little or no trade in the village, there could be little demand for discount, and as little circulation of its notes. Dick, however, argued, that if there was no trade in B——, there was enough elsewhere ; that whoever was willing to lend money, would always find borrowers, and that as to the circulation of notes, it was easily effected by means of agents, in the larger towns of the state ; and that, though they might now and then be returned upon their hands, they would run some risk of being lost or destroyed on the passage. By dint of perseverance, Dick got his bank, and the office of cashier, with a small salary—for himself—and here he was wise enough to stop. Though a schemer, he was not without a portion of mother wit, and he began to be sensible, that he was generally unlucky in his projects. He has, therefore, attended diligently to his business, during those hours of the day which are usually devoted to it, and made up for the stupefaction of his faculties, as he terms it, by indulging at all other times in plans and castles, without number. These, however, are generally of a kind, unlikely to do any harm to himself or any one else, and as he is too much used to ridicule to be annoyed by it, he affords us a good deal of amusement. Of the bank, it is only necessary to observe, that it succeeds as well as was to be expected. Now and then an express arrives, armed with a bundle of bills, and followed at a distance by a wagon, for the purpose of carting off a few kegs of specie. These occasional apparitions, however, serve only to put the directors in a bustle, and keep them awake. In the ordinary course of things, people are too busy to inquire whether the bank is in *rerum natura* or not. The bills pass from hand to hand, till a large portion of them are thumbed to pieces, lost, or burned. The yearly loss to any individual is small, but the sum total is a very handsome item to the credit side of the account of the concern. But, to return to Mr Allbright; last Saturday evening, he came in, full of a new scheme, which was neither more nor less than that we should club our wits to produce an occasional article for your Gazette. This met with as much favour with the rest of the company as Dick's notions

usually do; but some how or other, it made a deeper impression
upon my mind.   I could not help thinking of it the next day, and
lost a part of the sermon in the afternoon by unconsciously allowing my ideas to wander from the subject in hand, to that of a
page of neat type and fair margin.   To make a long tale short, I
could not rest till I had written this epistle, to inform you, that
you may consider me as a subscriber, if you are willing to look
for no other remuneration, than an occasional essay ; and as I
am aware, that readers are always more interested in an article,
when they know something of the author, I think you had better
print this as a sort of introduction.   It being understood, that I
shall not be pledged to write any more unless it shall please me.
I send a title and motto, which I believe to be as good as if they
were new.

BENEDICTUS.

POETRY.

THE GRECIAN PARTIZAN.

Our free flag is dancing
  In the free mountain air,
And burnished arms are glancing,
  And warriors mustering there ;
And true and brave, though passing few,
  Are they whose bosoms shield it ;—
Their life-blood shall its folds bedew
  Ere to the foe they yield it.
Each dark eye is fixed on earth,
  And brief each solemn greeting ;—
There is no look or sound of mirth
  Where those stern men are meeting.

They go to the slaughter,
  To strike the sudden blow,
And pour on earth, like water,
  The best blood of the foe ;
To rush on them from rock and height,
  And clear the narrow valley,
Or fire their camp, at dead of night,
  And fly before they rally.
Chains are round our country prest,
  And cowards have betrayed her,
And we must make her bleeding breast
  The grave of the invader.

Not till from her fetters
  We raise up Greece again,
And write, in bloody letters,
  That tyranny is slain,—
Oh, not till then the smile shall steal
  Across those darkened faces,
Nor one of all those warriors feel
  His children's dear embraces.
Leave unreaped the ripened wheat,
  Till yonder hosts are flying,
And all their bravest, at our feet,
  Like autumn sheaves are lying.

                                    B.

THE INDIAN HUNTER.

When the summer harvest was gathered in,
And the sheaf of the gleaner grew white and thin,
And the ploughshare was in its furrow left,
Where the stubble land had been lately cleft,
An Indian hunter, with unstrung bow,
Looked down where the valley lay stretched below.

He was a stranger there, and all that day
Had been out on the hills, a perilous way,
But the foot of the deer was far and fleet,
And the wolf kept aloof from the hunter's feet,
And bitter feelings passed o'er him then,
As he stood by the populous haunts of men.

The winds of autumn came over the woods
As the sun stole out from their solitudes,
The moss was white on the maple's trunk,
And dead from its arms the pale vine shrunk,
And ripened the mellow fruit hung, and red
Were the tree's withered leaves round it shed.

The foot of the reaper moved slow on the lawn,
And the sickle cut down the yellow corn,—
The mower sung loud by the meadow side,
Where the mists of evening were spreading wide,
And the voice of the herdsman came up the lea,
And the dance went round by the greenwood tree.

Then the hunter turned away from that scene,
Where the home of his fathers once had been,
And heard by the distant and measured stroke,
That the woodman hewed down the giant oak,
And burning thoughts flashed over his mind
Of the white man's faith, and love unkind.

The moon of the harvest grew high and bright,
As her golden horn pierced the cloud of white,—
A footstep was heard in the rustling brake,
Where the beech overshadowed the misty lake,
And a mourning voice, and a plunge from shore ;—
And the hunter was seen on the hills no more.

When years had passed on, by that still lake-side
The fisher looked down through the silver tide,
And there, on the smooth yellow sand displayed,
A skeleton wasted and white was laid,
And 't was seen, as the waters moved deep and slow,
That the hand was still grasping a hunter's bow.

H. W. L.

VENETIAN MOONLIGHT.

The midnight chime had tolled from Marco's towers,
  O'er Adria's wave the trembling echo swept ;
The gondolieri paused upon their oars,
  Mutt'ring their prayers as through the night it crept.

Far on the wave the knell of time sped on,
  Till the sound died upon its tranquil breast ;
The sea-boy startled as the peal rolled on ;
  Gazed at his star, and turned himself to rest.

The throbbing heart, that late had said farewell,
  Still lingering on the wave that bore it home,
At that bright hour wept o'er the dying swell,
  And thought on years of absence yet to come.

      'T was moonlight on Venetia's sea,
      And every fragrant bower and tree
          Smiled in the golden light ;
      The thousand eyes that clustered there
      Ne'er in their life looked half so fair
          As on that happy night.

      A thousand sparkling lights were set
      On every dome and minaret ;
          While through the marble halls,
      The gush of cooling fountains came,
      And crystal lamps sent far their flame
          Upon the high arched walls.

      But sweeter far on Adria's sea,
      The gondolier's wild minstrelsy
          In accents low began ;
      While sounding harp and martial zel
      Their music joined, until the swell
          Seemed heaven's broad arch to span.

Then faintly ceasing—one by one,
That plaintive voice sung on alone
  Its wild, heart-soothing lay ;
And then again that moonlight band
Started, as if by magic wand,
  In one bold burst away.

The joyous laugh came on the breeze,
And, 'mid the bright o'erhanging trees,
  The mazy dance went round ;
And as in joyous ring they flew,
The smiling nymphs the wild flowers threw,
  That clustered on the ground.

Soft as a summer evening's sigh,
From each o'erhanging balcony
  Low fervent whisperings fell ;
And many a heart upon that night
On fancy's pinion sped its flight,
  Where holier beings dwell.

Each lovely form the eye might see,
The dark-browed maid of Italy
  With love's own sparkling eyes ;
The fairy Swiss—all, all that night,
Smiled in the moonbeam's silvery light,
  Fair as their native skies.

The moon went down, and o'er that glowing sea,
 With darkness, Silence spread abroad her wing ;
Nor dash of oars, nor harp's wild minstrelsy
 Came o'er the waters in that mighty ring.
All nature slept—and, save the far-off moan
Of ocean surges, Silence reigned alone.

         F. M.

CRITICAL NOTICES.

Edinburgh Review for January, 1825.

It seems to be conceded on all hands that Mr Campbell's last poem
will not add to his reputation. But the poem and its author are treated with unusual gentleness and respect in the first article of the Edinburgh Review. The review briefly states the plan of the poet, and
quotes the poem as an illustration. It is, on the whole, a very satisfactory apology for Mr Campbell's laziness in writing so little poetry, and
that at such long intervals. The reviewers even thank the poet for con-
descending to write so well, or to write at all ; because, forsooth, he is
not the Laureate. We entertain a profound respect for Mr Campbell's
poetical talents, and are great admirers of his poetry ; but we doubt if
he ever published a poem to oblige the public. And if he has, we do

not think that circumstance ought to disarm the critic, and prevent the application of those wholesome rules of criticism, which are applied with such keen relish on other occasions. It is matter of very little consequence to the public, how a work comes before them—whether the author is retained by the patronage of the crown or the public—whether the work is paid for before it is written, or afterwards, or not paid for at all. If it is published, it becomes a part of the literature of the language, and as such is public property; and ought to be dealt with justly, but in the usual style of that review, without favour, hope, or fear.

The second article is a sketch of the " Manners and Morals of Absolute Princes," with particular reference, by way of example, to the court of Louis XIV.—the most polished court at the most polished period of modern times—the Augustan age of France. The reviewers are at home here; for they have an opportunity, which they never fail to improve, to abuse *legitimacy* and every thing thereunto pertaining. They sketch the corruption and profligacy of the French court above alluded to, as far as it may be sketched, with their usual spirit and power. They then proceed to draw some general conclusions in regard to the manners and morals of the privileged classes of society. We suppose these general conclusions of the reviewers serve the double purpose of checking the profligacy and licentiousness of the higher orders, and of making the lower more contented with being the most refined, the most virtuous, and the most happy part of the community. After copious quotations from the book under review, and accompanying remarks of their own, the reviewers observe—

" It is at least abundantly evident, that, in grossness of idea, in coarseness of expression, in a familiarity with thoughts which are impure, and a proneness to make those thoughts the subjects of conversation, in language alike degrading to the speaker and the hearer—the very highest class of all approaches most closely to the lowest of the vulgar. *   *

" That what is properly termed refinement, the utmost delicacy of sentiment and feeling, may exist in very humble life, is a truth which every day's experience will tend more and more to inculcate. In proportion as even the lowest classes of society learn to withdraw their affections from the vulgar enjoyments of the senses and to fix them upon intellectual gratification, their thoughts will be more exalted, and their words and actions become more pure. Whoever has read one of the most delightful pieces of biography that exists, the early life of Marmontel, written by himself, must long ago have come to the important conclusion that a delicacy of mind, and an elegance of taste almost romantic, are perfectly compatible with a state of poverty hardly to be envied by the poorest of our peasantry; and there is not a cottage in the whole kingdom where equal refinement and equal happiness might not be naturalized, by banishing ardent spirits, infusing a taste for books, and teaching children from their youth upwards to place half their enjoyment on the prosperity and the affection of those around them. This is the point at which society may arrive, and to which it is tending—in spite of the interested efforts of its deceivers and oppressors: But we have digressed from our purpose, which was to show how much better the middle classes now are, even in their unimproved state, than the highest of all, in the very delicacies which these have been wont to claim as peculiarly their own. We are not thoughtless enough, or prejudiced enough, or ignorant enough, to institute any such comparison with the ranks immediately above them, and below the highest; because in these, until corruption has destroyed it, refinement must always be expected to prevail in its purest state. But these too would swiftly feel the debasing effects of exaltation, if the wholesome checks under which they lived were removed."

The review of a work entitled " Plans for the Government and Liberal Instruction of Boys in large numbers, drawn from experience," was to us interesting. But the chief interest was derived from the extracts from the book; and as we have the same book, and propose soon to do as the Edinburgh Review has done,—lay it before our readers,—we at present forbear further remarks upon it.

The fourth article details at some length, and remarks with some severity upon the policy pursued by the British government, or rather the agents of the British government, in regard to the different powers of Western Africa.

" The many small conflicting powers between whom the Gold Coast was formerly divided, have, by recent events, been condensed into two great interests. One is that of the interior kingdom of Ashantee, whose armies, within the last fifteen years, have repeatedly overrun, and reduced to a tributary and dependent state, all the nations of the coast. The opposite interest is that of those nations now rallied under the leading standard of Fantee, and eagerly seeking the opportunity to shake off the yoke. Britain, in plunging into the vortex of African politics, has attached herself to this last confederacy, and is now following its fortunes."

The reviewers then attempt to show that this policy is a mistaken one; that the Fantees and their native allies are the most barbarous, most cowardly, and least faithful of the tribes of Western Africa; and that the Ashantees are more powerful, more civilized, and offer far greater advantages to British commerce than those tribes to which they have allied their interests.

The State and Prospects of Ireland form the subject of the fifth article. The reviewers inquire into the causes of those violent political and religious contentions, which have so long disgraced and agitated the country; and into those of the extreme poverty and wretchedness of the people. Under the first of these heads they enumerate *Catholic Disabilities—Government and Magistracy—and Church Establishment and Tithes.* It is contended, that full and entire emancipation—emancipation in *law* and and in *fact*—is an essential preliminary measure, before attempting, by other means, to calm the fury and sooth the desperation of their crowded and starving population. It is shown that the magistracy, and the administration of the laws, are in a deplorably defective state; that there are two kinds of justice, one for the rich and another for the poor, both equally ill administered; that the highest class, from the difficulty and danger of discharging the duties of the magistracy faithfully, decline it; and it falls into the hands of those who are poorly educated, and who prostitute it to the worst of purposes. But the church establishment is the greatest source of the discontent and disaffection, and of the poverty and misery of Ireland. Of the seven millions of Irish population, six millions are Catholics; and, of the remaining million, not more than half are of the established church. Yet, small as this fraction is, the *establishment* for Ireland costs little less than that for the whole of England. This evil alone, if the spirit of the nation is not broken by long oppression, is sufficient to make them frantic, and prevent their being patted with affectionate condescension and soothed to quietness, till the cause of it is removed. Among the causes of the extreme wretchedness and squalid poverty of the Irish peasantry, besides those above enumerated, is to be reckoned the great increase of population for the last century, compared with the capital of the country.

"If the amount of capital be increased without a corresponding increase taking place in the population, a larger share of such capital will necessarily fall to each individual, or, which is the same thing, the rate of wages will be proportionally increased; and if, on the other hand, population is increased faster than capital, a less share will be apportioned to each individual, or the rate of wages will be proportionally reduced. The well-being and comfort of the labouring classes are, therefore, especially dependent on the proportion which their increase bears to the increase of the capital that is to support and employ them. If they increase faster than capital, their wages will be progressively reduced; and if they increase slower than capital, they will be progressively augmented. In fact, there are no means whatever by which the command of the labouring class over the necessaries and conveniences of life can be really augmented, other than by accelerating the increase of capital, or by retarding the increase of population; and every scheme for improving the condition of the poor, not founded on this principle, or which has not for its object to increase the ratio of capital to population, must be wholly and completely ineffectual.

"The principle we have now stated, goes very far indeed to explain the cause of the misery of the Irish peasantry. It is certainly true that there has been a considerable increase in the capital of Ireland during the last hundred years; though no one in the least acquainted with the progress of the different parts of the empire, has ever presumed to say that this increase has been either a *third* or even a *fourth*, so great as the increase of capital in England and Scotland during the same period. But the increase of *population* in Ireland as compared with its increase in Britain, has been widely different from the increase in the *capital* of the two countries, or in their means of maintaining and supporting population. According to the tables given in the Parliamentary Reports, the population of Britain amounted, in 1720, to 6,955,000, and in 1821, it amounted to 14,391,000, having a little more than doubled in the course of the century. But from the same Reports it appears, that the population of Ireland, whose capital had increased in so very inferior a proportion to that of Britain, amounted to a very little more than *two* millions in 1731, and to very near *seven* millions in 1821; having nearly *quadrupled* in less time than the population of Britain took to *double!* "

And facts and data are brought forward to show, that Ireland, sunk as she is in beggary and destitution, *is the most densely peopled country in the world.* The reviewers investigate, at some length, the causes which have occasioned this extraordinary increase of population, compared with capital, and point out the means by which they may be counteracted. But we are obliged to pass over all these, as well as the sixth article of the Review, on the "Court of Chancery," and the seventh, on "Letters illustrative of English History."

The eighth article is on a subject frequently discussed in the Edinburgh Review,—"The Criminal Law of Scotland,"—and calls again for a revision of the system, states the evils of its present organization, and answers objections to improvements which have been before proposed. The ninth is a frightful picture of the Slavery of the British West India colonies, as it exists, both in law and practice. The reviewers, as they have often and with some effect done before, make their eloquent and powerful appeals to the British nation to interfere and spare humanity the enormities practised by the colonists upon their slaves.

" We believe that, on this subject, the hearts of the English People burn within them. They hate slavery. They have hated it for ages. It has, indeed, hidden itself for a time in a remote nook of their dominions : but it is now discovered and dragged to light. That is sufficient. Its sentence is pronounced ; and it never can escape ; never, though all the efforts of its supporters should be redoubled,—never, though sophistry, and falsehood, and slander, and the jests of the pothouse, the ribaldry of the brothel, and the slang of the ring or fives' court, should do their utmost in its defence,—never, though fresh insurrections should be got up to frighten the people out of their judgment, and fresh companies to bubble them out of their money,—never, though it should find in the highest ranks of the peerage, or on the steps of the throne itself, the purveyors of its slander, and the mercenaries of its defence ! "

In the tenth article facts are stated to show that the less the duty on Coffee is, within certain limits, the greater the consumption ; and that the increase of consumption, when the duties are low, is so rapid as to yield the greatest revenue to government when the duties are least. They believe, that by reducing the duties on coffee to a *third* or *fourth* of their present amount, the government may increase the wealth, comforts, and enjoyments of a large class of the community, and effectually check that adulteration of coffee which is now practised to a very great extent; and that they may do all this not only without any sacrifice of revenue, but even with a considerable addition to its amount.

The next article is a very interesting one on the state of Hayti. It shows, conclusively, by authentic facts, that the natural increase of population, even under the disadvantages of a long and sanguinary struggle for the attainment and maintenance of independence, is far greater than in the slave colonies ; and that the enemies of abolition must waive their objection, " that the numbers could never be kept up without importation." Hayti is represented not only in a flourishing condition in regard to population, military force, commerce, and revenue ; but as improving in civilization and the arts and refinements of civilized life.

" The following is part of a letter from General Inginal, Secretary-general to the President ; and it will be seen from its tenor how much attention is paid there to the greatest of all subjects which can occupy the attention of rulers, that in which all others are indeed compressed, the Education of the people. It also marks that the improvement of agriculture and commerce is rapidly increasing—and it displays the good spirit which prevails with respect to foreign aggression.

' I can assure you, sir, that being perfectly convinced that education and agriculture are the chief sources of the strength of states, the Government of the Republic does not neglect any thing which can promote these two objects; and I can announce to you with great satisfaction, that both in their progress answer fully to the care bestowed on them. The number of youth of both sexes who study in the elementary schools and in the upper classes, is prodigious. In all our towns, the schools kept by private people, and the national schools, are much increased, and they are found in all the large villages of the interior. I am myself astonished at the happy change which has taken place in public education, and which is daily taking place in the improvement of morals—all which is effected tranquilly and with satisfaction, under the mild influence of a truly paternal government.'

The last article is a short notice of Mr Brougham's pamphlet on the Education of the People. The Edinburgh Review has taken up the subject of education, for the last year or two, with a zeal and a power which cannot fail of their results upon the condition of the systems of public instruction in England. The truth of the maxims, that " knowledge is power," and that " knowledge is essential to freedom," has long had a speculative assent. We are glad to perceive that the *belief* begins to affect the *practice;* and that knowledge is beginning to be diffused with a zeal which shows men in earnest.

North American Review for April, 1825.

BESIDES reviews and notices of several popular works, as Redwood, Butler's Reminiscences, Professor Everett's Orations, &c. this number contains an account of the Insurrection of Tupac Amaru in Peru, in 1780 and 1781. This person was a descendant of the ancient Incas, and well qualified for the undertaking. The contest was fierce and bloody, and threatened the downfall of the Spanish power in Peru; but though of so much importance, was scarcely heard of in Europe till mentioned by Humboldt.

Another article relates to the vindication of Count Pulaski from a charge of gross neglect of military duty, on a certain occasion, during our revolutionary war. This charge appeared in Judge Johnson's Biography of General Greene, and was repelled with great indignation, by a brother officer of the count, in a pamphlet, which is the subject of the review. There can be no doubt that the charge was entirely groundless. The reviewer takes the opportunity of doing that honour to the memory of this gallant officer, which it so well deserves from every American writer.

A very elaborate article, occupying more than fifty pages, is devoted to the History of Modern Astronomy, and the advancement of the science during the last half century, by various astronomers in England and France. We have not space to enter into any analysis of this, which we recommend to our readers, as the most learned and comprehensive article which has ever appeared in any American periodical publication within our knowledge.

An article on Napoleon's Codes of Law, gives an account of their character, and the mode in which they were drawn up. It appears that the emperor did much more than merely to command the services of learned men for this purpose. The articles were separately discussed before the Council of State, at which he was almost always present, and participated in the discussion, and that with ability apparently not inferior to that of any of the counsellors.

In general, we are disposed to agree with the sentiments advanced in the several articles of this number. We think, however, that in one instance, the impression likely to be given to the public to be erroneous; we refer to the notice of Garnett's Lectures on Female Education. We omit particulars at present, as we intend to make this book the subject of a particular notice.

The Westminster Review for January, 1825.

THIS Review is conducted with less talent than either the Edinburgh or Quarterly. The present number contains an article on the works of Dallas and Medwin, respecting Lord Byron. From some internal evidence, we suspect it to be the work of Mr Hobhouse. The writer stigmatizes Mr Dallas, sen. as ungrateful and greedy; not content with spunging Lord Byron during his life, but eager to make the most of his remains. He contradicts Mr Dallas' statements in many instances; but we have not room to go into the details of this squabble, which is rather disgusting. Medwin's work is handled with still greater severity. The reviewer prints many of Medwin's assertions with an opposite column containing the fact. We find no reason to alter materially the opinion which we gave in our own review of this work; except, perhaps, that we incline to think Medwin a greater blackguard, than before.

A work on the French Monarchy, Dibdin's Library Companion, and Letters from an Absent Brother, are reviewed in that style of severity, which is so popular with the British journalists. A new number of Moore's Melodies is treated with great favour. A notice of the Penal Code of Louisiana, we shall take occasion to treat of at greater length than our limits, in this place, will permit.

An article on Contagion and Sanitary Laws is interesting, as any thing tolerably written on that subject must always be. Though we agree in general with the writer, we think him rather too confident, and not sufficiently aware of the uncertainty and difficulty of reasoning on medical subjects. His doctrines are in the main the same with those of Dr Smith's Etiology and Philosophy of Epidemics, which we had occasion to notice in our number for November 1st, 1824.

The most entertaining articles are an attack on Mr Southey and his Book of the Church, and a severe criticism of an article on Panegyrical Oratory, published in the Quarterly Review. We cannot but be somewhat amused, when we see our old enemies, the British periodicals, turning and rending each other with such zeal and execution.

Triumphs of Intellect; a Lecture delivered October, 1824, in the Chapel of Waterville College. By Stephen Chapin, D. D. Professor of Theology in said College. Waterville. 1824. 8vo. pp. 31.

UNDER this captivating title, we expected to find sketched some of the great achievements of mind in modern times, in extending its empire more widely both over itself and over the material word. Or, we thought we might find described some of the practical arts, to which the improvements in science have given rise, and the influence of these same arts upon the condition and prospects of our country, or of mankind. But Professor Chapin has disappointed us in our reasonable expectation. By "triumphs of intellect," he only means "the distinguished success attending well directed and persevering applications of the mental powers." And he takes occasion to stimulate the students to whom he addresses himself, to make such "persevering applications of their mental powers," in order to ensure the "triumphs of intellect" as described. He gives many instances of eminent men, who have attained their distinction by persevering industry, without having given in early life any indications of their future greatness.

The discourse is desultory, and sometimes declamatory. The author, in point of time, passes from age to age, rather more rapidly, than we can conveniently follow him ; and in point of place, he bounds from mountain to valley, from continent to continent, with the utmost facility. He seems acquainted with *all history*, at least, those remarkable facts and events, which are convenient for learned allusions. He alludes to them happily, and with facility ; and seems to take it for granted, that his young auditors understand his allusions as well as himself. But when the force and beauty of a sentence is made to depend upon an allusion to a fact in history, there is some danger, especially when we address young people, that the fact may not be known ; and then an eloquent sentence is wasted, by being misunderstood or not understood at all. Those who address young men, that cannot fairly be supposed to have the same knowledge of what *has been* as themselves, would do well to take this into consideration. Or they will find at the close of a discourse, that they have amused rather than instructed their hearers, and made them, perhaps, admire what they could not understand. The style of Dr Chapin is energetic, though sometimes bombastic. He evidently possesses great interest in his pupils, and ardour in his pursuits, and will without doubt inspire them with some of his own feelings.

INTELLIGENCE.

RECOVERED EDITION OF SHAKSPEARE.

[*Concluded.*]

Before we proceed to give a more particular account of the chief ornament of this tome, it may be agreeable to state certain data from Commentators on and editions of Shakspeare's Plays.

Mr Malone had seen the Hamlet 1604, for he preserved its title ; and indeed we are assured that he had that copy, now the Duke of Devonshire's, (from the late J. Kemble's library), for many months in his possession. Its title is,

The Tragicall Historie of Hamlet, Prince of Denmark. By William Shakespeare. Newly imprinted and enlarged to almost as much again as it was, according to the true and perfect Coppie. Printed by J. R. for N. Landre.

Succeeding editions were—

	The same, ... 1605.
Smethwicke by assignment	John Smethwicke, ... 1607.
from Ling.	Ditto, ... 1609.
	Ditto, ... 1611.*
	Ditto, ... 1637.
	- Ditto, ... no date.

Hamlet was first registered in the books of the Stationer's Company, 26 July, 1602. Malone thinks it was then published. He thought the earliest extant of that of 1604. N. V. The entry was to James Roberts.

The title-page of the play in Messrs Payne and Foss's book is as under—

THE

TRAGICALL HISTORIE OF

HAMLET,

Prince of Denmarke,

By William Shake-speare.

As it hath beene diuerse times acted by his Highnesse Seruants in the Citfie of London—as also in the two Vniuersities of Cambridge and Oxford, and else-where.

Ⓝ   Ⓛ

At London printed for N. L. † and Iohn Trundell.
1603.

The Play consists of thirty-one leaves, and on an average about thirty-five lines on a page, making in all about 2200 lines; while the edition of 1604 (the quarto edition reprinted in Steevens' four volumes) consists of sixty leaves, with an average of thirty-two lines *per* page, or total of above 3800 lines. This shows that the newly-discovered drama does not contain much more than half the text of the earliest edition previously known.

But it is very singular also in other respects. There are various new readings, of infinite interest; sentiments expressed, which greatly alter several of the characters; differences in the names; and many minor points which are extremely curious. For example, every alternate page is headed Tragedie and Tragedy; Laertes is Leartes, throughout; Polonius is Corambis; Gildenstern is Gilderstone; Osrick has no name, but is styled a Braggart Gentleman of the Court; and in the Closet-scene *" the Ghost enters in his nightgown."*

From these variations, and the absence of so much of what appeared in the edition of the ensuing year, 1604, we hardly know what to infer. It has been said that Shakspeare founded his play, as was often his custom, on a preceding drama; but this has too much of Shakspeare in it to be *that* drama.‡ It may be surmised, that in the course of its immense popularity, some piratical bookseller obtained a garbled copy of Hamlet, and published it; for at this period copyrights were not sold by authors as in our days, and Shakspeare seems never to have paid much attention to literary profit, or to any fame beyond the walls of the theatre where

---

* This is the ed. in Steevens' 4 vols. with the same account as above.
† N. L. is evidently N. Landure, who published the known edition of 1604.
‡ Kidd's, if we remember rightly.

his productions were performed. But we will leave the discussion of this point to others, and proceed to make our readers acquainted with some of the most striking features in the Play, as it is given.

It opens as in later editions.

Enter two Centinels.

1. Stand : who is that ?
2. Tis I.
1. O you come most carefully vpon your watch,
2. And if you meete Marcellus and Horatio
The partners of my watch, bid them make haste.
1. I will: See who goes there.

Enter Horatio and Marcellus.

Hor. Friends to this ground.
Mar. And leegemen to the Dane, &c.

The omissions here, as well as throughout, which will readily be discovered by looking at a modern edition, tend strongly to confirm the suspicion, that the play was picked out by hearing it performed, and getting speeches and parts from some of the actors. From where our quotation ends, the text is nearly the same as in the quarto of 1611, The first appearance of the Ghost is at the line, " The bell then *towling* (not ' beating') one." The dialogue continues nearly the same, except that the omissions are considerable ; as, for instance, the Ghost re-enters at the cue, " ground of this our watch," after which, in the latter editions, there is much matter. But the difference of text is also observable ; for example, when the Ghost vanishes the first time, Horatio says—

In what perticular *thought*, to worke I know not,
But in the grosse & scope of my opinion,
This bodes, &c.   [4to. of 1611.]

Whereas the newly-found Play reads—

In what particular to worke I know not
But in the thought and scope of our opinion
This bodes some strange eruption to the state.

In the next scene the King, Queen, &c. enter ; and it is chiefly remarkable for the name of Corambis being introduced instead of Polonius and Leartes. *Two Ambassadors* are also mentioned, and is an improvement, as their presence gives occasion for the King's speech, otherwise uncalled for, to his own court. It begins, " Lordes we have writ," omitting all the foregoing parts ; and the whole is greatly amplified in the later copies. We will not occupy our page by quoting Hamlet's Soliloquy, when these *exeunt*, as it can be seen by turning to the common play ; but we imagine that readers will be pleased to have it as it stands in this original.

Ex. all but Hamlet.

Ham. O that this too much grieu'd and sallied flesh
Would melt to nothing, or that the vniuersall
Globe of heauen would turne al to a Chaos !
O God within two moneths ; no not two : married,
Mine vncle ; O let me not thinke of it,
My fathers brother : but no more like
My father, then I to *Hercules*.
Within two months, ere yet the salt of most

Vnrigteous teares had left their flushing
In her galled eyes : she married, o God, a beast
Deuoyd of reason would not have made
Such speede : Frailtie, thy name is Woman,
Why she would hang on him, as if increase
Of appetite had growne by what it looked ou.
O wicked wicked speede, to make such
Dexteritie to incestuous sheetes,
Ere yet the shooes were olde,
The which she followed my dead fathers corse
Like *Nyobe*, all tears : married, well it is not,
Nor it cannot come to good :
But breake my heart, for I must hold my tongue.

We cannot go through the minutes of the new (old) Play, and point out where it differs and coincides with the later copies. After the above Soliloquy, Horatio enters with " Health (not *hail*) to your lordship;" and the dialogue continues to, " For Godsake let me heare it."

A fine Shaksperian expression occurs here in the line usually printed, " In the dead *waste* (or even *waist*) and middle of the night," which is—

In the dead *Vast* and middle of the night.

Opelia appears as usual. The Ghost appears to Hamlet at the line,

More honoured in the breach than in observance.

Hamlet's Soliloquy, on his entrance after Opelia's correspondence is shown, runs thus :

To be, or not to be, I there's the point.
To die, to sleepe, is that all ? I, all :
No, to sleepe, to dreame, I marry there it goes,
For in that dreame of death, when wee awake
And borne before an euerlasting Iudge,
From whence no passenger euer return'd
The vndiscouered country, at whose sight
The happy smile, and the accursed damnd.
But for this, the ioyful hope of this
Whol'd beare the scornes and flattery of the world,
Scorned by the rich, the rich curssed by the poore ?
The widow being oppressed, the orphan wrong'd
The taste of hunger, or a tirants raigne,
And thousand more calamities besides,
To grunt and sweate vnder this weary life,
When that he may his full *quietus* make
With a bare bodkin, who would this indure,
But for a hope of something after death ?
Which pulses the braine, and doth confound the sence,
Which makes vs rather beare those euilles we haue,
Than flie to others that we know not of.
I that, O this conscience makes cowardes of vs all.
Lady in thy orizons, be all my sinnes remembred.

This is a poor version; but, passing over the intervening scenes which follow the common course, we come to the most remarkable difference in the whole—the famous Closet Scene ; though in doing so we omit the beginning (here)

Why what a dunghil idiote slaue ame I,

and that in the advice to the players, where " town criar" reads " a towne bull bellow." There is one striking word in the Play Scene, which removes a phrase that has been much objected to—

> *Ham.* Lady will you give me leave, and so forth:
> To lay my head in your lappe.
> *Oph.* No my Lord.
> *Ham.* Vpon your lap, why do you thinke I meant
> *contrary* matters.

But we are brought to a conclusion, and can only add some remarkable passages of the Closet Scene :

> Looke you nowe here is your husband
> With a face like *Vulcan,*
> A looke fit for a murder and a rape,
> A dull dead hanging looke, and a hell-bred eie
> To affright children and amaze the world :
> And this same have you left to change with death
> What divell has thus cosoned you at hobman-blinde ?
>
> *Enter the Ghost in his Night Gowne.*

Hamlet exclaims—

> Saue me, saue you gratious
> Powers above, &c.

At the exit of the Ghost the Queen says,

> Alas it is the weakeness of thy braine
> Which makes thy tongue to blazon thy hearts griefe ;
> *But as I have a soule, I sweare by Heauen,*
> *I never knew of this most horride murder :*
> *But Hamlet, this is onlie fantasie,*
> *And for my love forget these idle fits.*
> *Ham.* Idle, no mother my pulse doth beate like yours
> It is not madnesse that possesseth Hamlet.
> O mother, if euer you did my deare father loue
> Forbeare the adulterous bed to-night
> And win yourself by little as you may
> In time it may be you will lothe him quite.
> *And mother, but assist me in revenge*
> *And in his death your infamy shall die.*
> *Queene.* Hamlet, *I vow by that Majesty*
> *That knowes our thoughts, and lookes into our hearts*
> *I will conceale, consent, and doe my best,*
> *What stratagem soe're you shall denise.*
> *Ham.* It is enough, mother good night.

These are very striking, and would have tempted us to go farther in this analysis, but we trust we have done enough to satisfy, in a sufficient measure, the intense curiosity which this book has raised in every literary circle—and the more so, as we have learnt, with much gratification, that Messrs Payne and Foss are about to commit the Hamlet to the press, for a *literatim* impression. They will greatly oblige the public by this judicious conduct, and every lover of Shakspeare, *i. e.* every lover of literature, will thank them for it. The work may be looked for in about a fortnight.

The original volume is valued at from 200*l.* to 300*l.* by the *Philobiblion.*"

APPLICATION OF A PRINCIPLE IN HYDROSTATICS.

The acquisition of knowledge and the application of it to the practical business of life are very different things. The former engages our almost exclusive attention, while its results are valuable to us chiefly as they are possessed in connexion with the latter. Philosophers spend their lives in the investigation of abstract principles, while they are often taught all that is useful by the practical mechanic, who could not state his knowledge in the form of a principle at all. These two things, so distinct in all our systems of instruction, yet so inseparable for all practical purposes, ought to be learned more in connexion with each other. They would then lend mutual aid. The philosophical investigation of principles would be much facilitated, and would proceed with much surer steps, by a constant reference to the facts and phenomena from which they are derived. And the observer of facts would be much aided by knowing how to class them, as they present themselves, and where to look for those suitable to verify, restrict, or extend the application of a doubtful, vague, or limited principle. The abstract principles of science, as learned by philosophers, are generally much in advance of their practical applications in the common pursuits and business of life. Most of the splendid discoveries which characterize our age, are but combinations and applications of principles, which have long been understood. We are much more indebted to those, who reduce to practice and promulgate a useful discovery, than to those who rest satisfied with having made it. Because, however the individual may enjoy in private his own inventions, the world of mankind are not made glad by them, till they are turned to some practical account, which affects their condition and happiness.

It would be of incalculable utility both to the philosopher and the artisan in their different pursuits, to bring science and the arts together —to learn theory and practice at the same time—and to observe phenomena, and trace the laws, which govern them, as parts of the same process in acquiring knowledge. It is well, therefore, occasionally to apply to phenomena the principles by which they are explained; and as locks and canals are so much the order of the day, a principle in hydrostatics is here applied to explain the great pressure upon the gate of a canal lock, when the water is high upon it, but when there is little difference in the height on each side.

Let us suppose the gate to be ten feet long and the water to be *ten* feet deep on the upper side, and *nine* on the lower side. At first thought it would seem that the pressure of the nine feet on one side, would exactly counteract the pressure of nine feet on the other; and that the gate would be pressed with only one foot, in the same manner as if there were water of but one foot deep pressing the gate on one side, and none on the other. But this is not the fact. In this case, each foot of the top of the gate would be pressed by the weight of one half of a cubic foot of water, or $31\frac{1}{4}$ lbs, which, on ten feet in length, would amount to $312\frac{1}{2}$ lbs. This pressure might be easily overcome, and the gate opened with a lever of small power and with but little strength. But this one foot of water on the top acts on all the water below, and causes a pressure on each foot twice as great as it exerts itself on the upper foot of the gate.

The pressure on the upper side of the gate, then, by the principles of hydrostatics, is

$$\frac{10 \times 10 \times 62\frac{1}{2}}{2} = 3125 \text{ lbs.}$$

for each foot in length; and for the whole ten feet

$$10 \times 3125 = 31250 \text{ lbs};$$

the pressure on the lower side, by the same principles, is

$$\frac{9 \times 9 \times 62\frac{1}{2}}{2} \times 10 = 25312\frac{1}{2} \text{ lbs.}$$

The difference is 5937½ lbs. which is the actual pressure upon the upper side of the gate under the supposed circumstances. As the gate is turned towards the upper lock with a lever of but small power, we may suppose one man to be able to move about 200 lbs. At this rate it would require the strength of 30 men to move it.

NEW PUBLICATIONS.

HISTORY.

A History of the Lexington Battle, 19th of April, 1775. By Elias Phinney. Price 31 cents. Boston. Lincoln and Edmands.

LAW.

Town Officer; or, Laws of Massachusetts relative to the Duty of Municipal Officers; together with a Digest of the Decisions of the Supreme Judicial Court upon those subjects. By Isaac Goodwin, Counsellor at Law. 12mo. Worcester. Dorr & Howland.

A Digest of the Probate Laws of Massachusetts, relative to the Power and Duty of Executors, Administrators, Guardians, Heirs, Legatees, and Creditors. To which is subjoined an Appendix of Forms. By Joshua Prescott, Esq. Consellor at Law. Boston. Richardson & Lord.

The Virginia Justice, comprising the Office and Authority of a Justice of the Peace in the Commonwealth of Virginia, &c. To which is added, an Appendix, containing all the most approved forms in Conveyancing. Also, the Duties of a Justice of the Peace, arising under the Laws of the United States. By William Waller Hening, Counsellor at Law. The Fourth Edition, revised, corrected, and greatly enlarged. Richmond, Va.

MATHEMATICS.

The Mathematical Diary. No. II. For April, 1825. Conducted by Robert Adrain, LL. D. F. A. P. S. F. A. A. S. &c. and Professor of Mathematics in Columbia College. New York. James Ryan.

MEDICINE.

Memoir on the Discovery of a Specific Medicine for the Cure and Prevention of the Yellow Fever, Plague, Malignant and Pestilential Fevers, with Documents, &c. By John James Giraud, M. D. of Baltimore. 8vo. pp. 23. Baltimore. William Woody.

MISCELLANEOUS.

John Bull in America; or, the New Munchausen. Second Edition, with Corrections by the Author. 12mo. New York. C. Wiley.

Nature Displayed in her mode of Teaching the French Language, &c. By N. G. Dufief. Sixth Edition. 2 vols. 8vo. Price $7. New York. Collins & Co. and others.

The African Repository and Colonial Journal. Vol. I. No. I. Price $2 per annum. Washington. Way & Gideon.

Later from Hell; or, Philotheologiastronomos' Eulogium of Rev. Ezra Stiles Ely's Dream, with Illustrations. 8vo. pp. 30. Philadelphia. Printed for the Purchaser.

The Philadelphia Directory and Strangers' Guide for 1825. Philadelphia. John Bioren.

Philadelphier Magazin. No. IV. For April, 1825.

The Eighth Annual Report of the American Society for Colonizing the Free People of Colour of the United States, with an Appendix. 8vo. pp. 71. Washington, D. C.

NOVELS.

The Travellers; a Novel. By the Author of "Redwood." New York. E. Bliss & E. White.

Redfield; A Long-Island Tale. 12mo. New York. Wilder & Campbell.

POETRY.

Poems. By John Turvill Adams. Price 50 cents. 12mo. pp. 47. New Haven. A. H. Maltby & Co.

POLITICS.

Orangeism Exposed, with a Refutation of the Charges, &c. brought against the Irish Nation, by Lawyer David Graham, of New York, in his Defence of the Orangemen, tried in that city, on the 13th and 14th days of September, 1824, for an Assault and Battery on a poor Irishman, on the 12th day of July, 1824. By an Unbiassed Irishman.

THEOLOGY.

Views in Theology. No. III. President Edwards' Doctrine of Original Sin, the Doctrine of Physical Depravity. 12mo. pp. 104. New York. F. & R. Lockwood.

The Literary and Evangelical Magazine. Vol. VIII. No. IV. For April. 1825. $3 per annum. Richmond, Va.

The Christian Repository. By Samuel C. Loveland. Vol. V. No. VI. For April, 1825. Woodstock, Vt.

Remarks on the Rise, Use, and Unlawfulness of Creeds and Confessions of Faith, in the Church of God. In two Parts. By John M. Duncan, Pastor of the Presbyterian Church, Tammany street, Baltimore.

A Sermon on the Death of Rev. John H. Livingston, D. D. S. T. P. Preached before the General Synod at Albany, and at Poughkepsie. By the Rev. C. C. Cuyler, A. M. With a short Memoir of his Life. 8vo. Price 25 cents. New York.

Lincoln's Scripture Questions, stereotyped, being the Fifth Edition to which are now annexed the Answers from Scripture. 18mo. pp. 126. Lincoln & Edmands.

Prospective Theology; or, a Peep into Hell. By the Rev. Ephraim Spooney, A. U. S. 8vo. pp. 30. Philadelphia. J. Mortimer.

AMERICAN EDITIONS OF FOREIGN WORKS.

The Improvisatrice, and other Poems. By L. E. L. Price $1 25; 18mo. pp. 287. Boston. Munroe & Francis.

Volume VII. of the Works of Maria Edgeworth, containing "Patronage." 8vo. Price $1 50 cents per Vol. Boston. S. H. Parker.

The Edinburgh Review; or, Critical Journal. No. LXXXII. Boston. Wells & Lilly.

The Letters of Mrs Elizabeth Montagu, with some of the Letters of her Correspondents. Published by Matthew Montagu, Esq. her Nephew and Executor. 3 vols. 12mo. Boston. Wells & Lilly.

Mosheim's Ecclesiastical History. In 4 vols. 8vo. New York. J. & J. Harper.

Female Quixotism; exhibited in the Romantic Opinions and Extravagant Adventures of Dorcasina Sheldon. A New Edition. 2 Vols. 18mo. Boston. J. P. Peaslee.

LIST OF WORKS IN PRESS.

Two Volumes of the Works of Maria Edgeworth, containing " Early Lessons." 8vo. Boston. S. H. Parker.

A Treatise on the Law of Property, arising from the Relation between Husband and Wife. By R. D. Roper, Esq. 8vo. 2 vols. Philadelphia. P. H. Nicklin.

The Elements of Medical Chemistry, embracing only those branches of Chemical Science, which are calculated to illustrate and explain the different objects of Medicine, and to furnish a Chemical Grammar to the Authors' Pharmacologia. Illustrated by numerous Engravings. By John Ayrton Paris, M. D. F. R. S. &c. New York. J. & J. Harper.

The Evidence of Christianity, derived from its Nature and Reception. By J. B. Sumner, M. A. Prebendary of Durham, &c. Philadelphia. A. Finley.

The Difficulties of Infidelity. By Rev. G. S. Faber, B. D. &c. Philadelphia. A. Finley.

The Duties of an American Citizen. Two Sermons, delivered on Fast Day, April 7th, 1825. By Francis Wayland Jr., Pastor of the First Baptist Church and Society in Boston. James Loring.

A Series of Orations for Missionaries after the Apostolical School. In 4 Parts. By the Rev. Edward Erving, A. M. New York. E. Bliss & E. White.

A Northern Tour; being a Guide to Saratoga, Niagara, and Canada, through the States of Pennsylvania, New Jersey, New York, Vermont, New Hampshire, Massachusetts, Rhode Island, and Connecticut, with an Account of the Grand Western and Northern Canals, &c. With a Map of the State of New York. Philadelphia. Carey & Lea.

Memoirs of the Countess de Genlis, illustrative of the History of the Eighteenth and Nineteenth Centuries. Written by Herself. New York. Wilder & Campbell.

Published on the first and fifteenth day of every month, by CUMMINGS, HILLIARD, & Co., No. 134 Washington-Street, Boston, for the Proprietors. Terms, $5 per annum. Cambridge: Printed at the University Press, by Hilliard & Metcalf.

THE UNITED STATES
LITERARY GAZETTE.

| VOL. II. | JUNE 1, 1825. | No. 5. |

REVIEWS.

Goslington Shadow: A Romance of the Nineteenth Century. By
Mungo Coultershoggle, Esq. In 2 volumes. New York.
1825. 12mo.

THE scene of this Romance is laid in Scotland, its characters
are nearly all Scottish, and many of them express themselves in
the dialect of that country; it purports to have been written
there, and yet it is printed and published in America. The
editor informs us, that he received it from the author, an old
friend living on the other side of the water, for publication
in the Western Hemisphere; for what particular reason, does
not appear. Now according to all the common principles by
which we judge of these matters, this would be deemed one
of those affairs, which are of every day occurrence to novel
writers; and we very naturally concluded, that Mungo Coultershoggle was one of those benevolent persons who travel
about the world in various disguises, for the purpose, it would
seem, of aiding authors in distress, by leaving, or putting in
their way, some precious manuscript, which is to make their
fame and fortune. We expected also to find, that like many
other American novels, it was simply *located* in America or
Scotland, but capable of being adapted, by a suitable change
of names, to any other country or latitude under the sun. But
we were certainly mistaken;—we can hardly conceive, that it
should have been written by any other than a native of the
country, to which it relates; for it evinces a familiarity with
customs, manners, characters, and language, which we do not
believe a foreigner could ever acquire. We do not pretend,

21

of course, to be very profoundly skilled in these points, from personal observation, yet to a certain extent, we may deem ourselves capable of forming a tolerable judgment with regard to the representations of an author, from the materials that are furnished by the writings of those who are acknowledged to have described accurately and faithfully. We were reminded frequently, in reading Goslington Shadow, of the author of " Annals of the Parish," and sometimes of Hogg. The resemblance exists, not so much in the powers and genius of the authors themselves, as in the intimacy which they exhibit with the characters, domestic habits, and manners of their countrymen, and the apparent accuracy with which they delineate them.

It would be useless and uninteresting to attempt any detail of the plot of this Romance, if indeed it can be said to have any. It consists merely of a series of incidents, not forming a continued and unbroken chain of events tending to forward the business of the story, but, on the contrary, possessing only this circumstance to unite them, that they relate to the same person, and occur around the same spot. It is enough to say, with regard to the story, that it relates to the family and fortunes of Goslington Shadow, the hero, whose father, Matthew, is a plain, honest, and shrewd farmer, averse to the plan of educating his son at college, to which he is urged by his wife and family. To this plan, however, he is persuaded to accede, by his son's teacher ; whose anxiety on this point is finally explained by the fact, that he is possessed of the secret, that the Shadow family are in reality of noble descent, and legal heirs to an earldom. Goslington goes, then, to college, makes a distinguished figure, becomes a fine gentleman, gets the friendship and protection of an earl, falls in love with the earl's daughter, turns out to be his near relation and heir apparent, and is of course successful in his suit to the young lady. His father, in the meantime, by the death of an old uncle in the East Indies, comes into possession of a princely fortune;—his mother dies, and his sister marries a hopeful young specimen of Yankee blood, from New York, who, in the end, also proves to be descended from a Scotch noble family, and is endowed with the honours of his race.

The chief merit of the writer of this work consists in a clear and distinct conception of character, and a happy talent of developing it in conduct and conversation. It is very common for a novelist to tell us, of his personages, that they possess such and such qualities and traits of character, which, however, one would never have inferred from the conduct he attributes to them, or from the language he puts into their mouths.   The talent of manifesting character in this way is somewhat rare.   It is a point in which most writers are deficient.   But our author has rather an unusual degree of it. His characters speak and act for themselves.   Their conduct and conversation show what they are, and show them always the same.   And this remark is true, not only of the prominent individuals, upon whose delineation more pains are usually bestowed, but is applicable also to others of secondary importance. Will Waddell, the house servant of Matthew Shadow,— O'Halloran, whether appearing as a hypocritical Methodist priest, a swindler, a gamester, or a fine gentleman,—the spend-thrift Sir Belfry Battledore, Jock Baird, &c. &c. are all as distinctly and definitely drawn, and sketched with as much fidelity, as if they had been principal performers.

The chief fault, which we have to point out, arises from the desultory and unconnected manner, in which the work of the piece is carried on.   A vast deal of matter is introduced, which has no relation to the business in hand,—contributes nothing towards the consummation of the plot,—and has nothing witty, wise, or sentimental about it to redeem it.   There is a want of sufficient interest and excitement.   There is no regular train of events, no well maintained action tending to bring about some important end.   The work is written in a loose, rambling manner, as if the author had brought his *dramatis personæ* together, without knowing what to do with them, and had gone on at random with only a very general idea of the track he was to follow.   A great deal of time is occupied by desultory conversations, unnecessary digressions, and uninteresting prosing, which retard the story, weaken the interest, and contribute to render many parts dull and tedious.

Matthew Shadow, the father of the hero, is, we think, sketched with a good deal of success.   He is plain, blunt, shrewd, sarcastic, and sometimes humorous, with much honesty, independence, and benevolent feeling.   It is true, we detect him often saying very foolish things, and in talking too too much, and too little to the purpose ; but on the whole he is very entertaining.

The following is his account of a trick played off upon a congregation at a field preaching.

'Some o' our neighbours,' said Matthew, 'an' amang others, my ain wife, wanted to hear the doctor preach, an' so the cleverest o' them managed to erect a tent, wi' twa carts, a close ane an' open ane. The close cart was the pu'pit, an' the open ane was ta'en aff the wheels, an' was set up on en wi' the trams stannen up like the masts o' a boat, an' o'er a' they flang the winnow claith, makin' a decent sort of a tent o't, a' things consider't. Weel,' continued Matthew, 'the weemen bodies a' about, an' the young chiels, some o' them, mair for fun than preachin', like a flock o' doos an' daws, (and may be auld nick to the bargain), ware a' set doon on a brae side—auld Willy Muckle was rulin' elder: so the doctor began his sermon, an' just i' the middle o' his discourse, some o' them took awa' the cogs from ahint the wheels, an' as the tent stood on the tap o' a knowe, aff it set screeven down the hill side, wi' the puir doctor, an' afore he could get time to loup out, o'er tumbl't him, and tent, an' a', wi' an awfu' slounge, into a deep well o' the Kype. The jaups flew about, I ne'er saw the like o't—my very een blin't i' my head. Guid sauf me, I thought the body was kill't; doon cam' the winnow claith i' the tap o' him, like to smoor him, an' they had to jump in to help out aneth't, or he maun hae been droon't. It makes me laugh yet, as he was na' hurt, when I think I see him, stannen like a scoort fleece, drippin', spreadin' out his legs, an' hawden out his arms, as wat as water could mak' him. The preachin' was a' sticket o' course, so we cam' our ways hame. But the young laird o' Frearhill, by way o' keepin' the doctor frae catchin' cauld, gied him that muckle whiskey, that he filled him as fou's a warlock; and he got out and danc't chantruse i' the loan, half naket!'

His opinion of the ancients.

'Am tell't, the ancients didna' even ken how to bigg a lum to their hooses, but the reek cam' spuing out o' the hole in the roof, or at the door—an' for glass windows they had nane—just like our moorlan' bodies—and they sat doon on their hunkers, like a wheen tinklers. As for a drap o' whiskey, ne'er ane o' them e'er pree't it, or dream't that sic a thing could be made o' John Barleycorn. But,' continued Matthew, 'I hae seen wi' my ain een, the de'ils causey, or the auld Roman road, running past within a few gunshot o' my ain door; why its just a rickle o' muckle stanes, no braid eneugh to drive a hurl-barrow on, an' sae fu' o' lumps an' jumps, that it wad break ane o' my carts a bits. Tell nae me about the Romans—we Scots soon sent them hame again, like a dog wi' a shangay on his tail.'

Of Milton.

'Hold!' cried the Laird; 'I will neither hear the speech which he puts into the mouth of the Father, nor the Son—I will hear no such impious speeches, fabricated by man, repeated in my presence. In this description, which you have just praised as beautiful, he first tells us that the omniscient Father is about to take a survey of all things at once; then the poet forgets himself, and speaks of him first beholding our first parents, and then discovering Satan, who had forsaken Hell, and was on the very borders of the world, before he is descried. Milton's idea of Deity may be more elevated than the ideas of Homer were respecting Jupiter, and they may be so very truly, and yet be low enough after all

I will spare you the trouble,' continued the Laird, ' of reading about St Peter and his keys at the wicket gate; of the paradise of fools; and Satan's disguising himself so as to cheat Uriel, after having made him steal a march on God himself, for that the arch-deceiver should bamboozle an angel, is only what is to be expected. Come to some of those fine battles, where he places the contending hosts of Heaven and Hell, front to front, in direful combat.'

The following is an extract from a letter to his son.

' *Dear Son*—The neist time that ye are in want o' siller, as I carry the purse mysell, dinna come whully-whaen e'er your mother as I ware for stenten you to a saxpence or a shilling; therefore, send na mair o' wishy-washy letters, but speak out mensfu' like, and tell me frank and furthy what ye want. An' dinna think that when ye're alang wi' decent company, and I houp ye draw up wi' nane that are otherwise, and they, whan they meet, want to tak a crack and weet their whitters, that I wad hae you sit, like a whistle-binkie at a penny-waddin', for want o' pocket-money to pay your score; the feint a bit o' me; I wad like to see you, whan occasion ser's, be as campy as ony o' them. And I dinna mean that ye should set the won' abried aneth a' the gear that I hae gather't thegither, neither; be just as canny as possible, and tak gude tent o' what I send you. Am no for you to spend o'er muckle time, scrapin' on the fiddle, or blawin' the whistle, for its uncoo like to lead you into wauff company; fiddling and flinging may do weel aneugh for a dancin' master, but they're no soncey ava in a minister.'

We should imagine, that, in describing the practice of a quack doctor, who makes his appearance in the course of these volumes, the author must have had in his eye, the method of treatment lately recommended among us, by a benevolent, but enthusiastic physician; although there seems no reason for connecting the allusion with a low and infamous character; since, whatever may be the value of the mode of practice, we know of no reason to doubt the sincerity and disinterested zeal of the physician who proposes it.

His mode of treatment was exceedingly simple; his remedies were applied directly through the organs of respiration to the seat of the disease; while all medicines.exhibited according to the established practice, could only act indirectly through the medium of the whole system, and could never reach the parts affected. His success, it is true, had not quite answered their expectations; the cures had not been so rapid as they had been led to expect, but they could not expect miracles;—he had as yet been but a short time among them, and they must have a little patience.

The Whult, as he is called, a lazy, shiftless neighbour of Matthew, is well contrasted with him.

'The lazy hallion!' continued the Laird; 'after he had been at the expense to get it cut, and the wife and the dochter were at the trouble to make it into hay, and rake it together, left it there in the condition ye see it. But every thing's of a piece; a' the yets are wide open, and so mony slaps in the dykes, that ware it no for the colley dog, the kye wad ne'er be out o' the corn; but the poor dumb beast has mair care than its master; for the Whult wad no loup o'er the dyke to drive them out if they ware a' in the kailyard. If I ware the wife, I wad be for serving the Whult as her auld mither did her auld gudeman, when she wanted to get quit of him; but I maun tell you this story. "The feckless auld body was ill abed, and, as the wife thought, asleep; so she gat a halter round his neck, and flinging the cord o'er a bauk, gat the end out at the window. But if the gudeman choosed to pretend to be asleep till she got round the halter, when she slippet quietly out for fear of wakening him, he took it off his neck, and put the bouster in the noose. As soon as she could, she got hold of the rope, and drew a' her pith, thinking to hang him. But he was o'er auld farren for her, and as she drew, he held the bouster doon wi' a' his weight; as soon as she slacket, he took out the bouster, and put his neck again into the halter. The vile rudden came into the room to take off the halter, thinking she had finished her job; 'that charr is charr'd,' said she; but whan she came to look into the bed, the auld fallow was lying laughing; 'Losh me,' quoth she, 'my dear, do ye ken me?' 'Better than e'er I did,' said he, as he took the halter aff his neck and flang it at her. Frae that day to this she gat the name o' hang the bouster." * * *

'See, see!' said Mr Rifleman to the Laird, 'the dog is chasing the cat in and out at the window.'

The Whult had been at some pains to teach them this pastime, for the gudewife and daughter not liking to see the crown of an old hat, or some old article of wearing apparel supplying the place of a pane of glass, when so many suitors were coming about the house, had the windows all mended. The Whult hated all innovations of this sort, and in a violent passion, he stood before the window, and shaking his coat tail, called 'Halloo, halloo,' to the dog that was lying before the fire, who, jumping up in haste, took his usual route through the window, and in a few days, old hats, and breeches, and petticoats, were seen sticking in the windows as usual, and the dog passing and repassing in full chase after the cat.

There are many passages we should like to extract, for the purpose of illustrating the character we have given of this work, but they would exceed our limits. It will be perceived, that, upon the whole, our opinion of it is favourable. If read with moderate expectations, we are persuaded, that it must afford entertainment, though no strong interest or excitement. There are some offences against delicacy, and many against good writing. If it be an American novel, we think it superior, in point of talent, to most of those, which have issued from the press on this side of the Atlantic.

Occasional Pieces of Poetry.   By JOHN G. C. BRAINARD.   New York.   1825.   12mo.   pp. 111.

WE are sorry that Mr Brainard should have published his poems at this time. If his principal object, indeed, was " to make a little something by it," we should regret the circumstance still more; without repeating what has been a thousand times said of Milton and Bacon, who wrote as no other men ever wrote, and who wrote, not for money, but for fame, we may, we think, be allowed to say, without incurring the imputation of canting, that a man of Mr Brainard's unquestionable genius, ought not to be actuated by so sordid a motive. We cannot, however, believe, that this was his real object; we doubt not that he was mainly influenced by " the request of friends," prompted withal by a secret consciousness that he needed not deprecate criticisms. This knowledge of an author, that he has done pretty well, and can do better than most others when he pleases, has consigned more than one individual to oblivion, who might otherwise have marked his age by his own name.

Nil sine magno
Vita labore dedit mortalibus,

is a maxim as true in literature as in physics. No truly valuable work,—nothing that could safely be committed to " time, truth, and posterity," was ever thrown off at a single heat. The advice of Quintilius is even more necessary at the present day, than it was two thousand years ago :

.... ' Corrige, sodes,
Hoc,' aiebat, ' et hoc ;' melius te posse negares,
Bis terque expertum frustra,—delere jubebat,
Et male tornatos incudi reddere versus.

We have been led to these remarks, from the great power displayed in some of these poems, and the manifest want of care in the construction of almost all of them. We are satisfied, that had the author's labour in their composition been commensurate with his energy of conception, his volume might have placed him, at once, on a level with Bryant and Percival. There are two distinct and independent essentials of poetry, that the thoughts of the poet should be well conceived, and well expressed. Mr Brainard thinks well; he is a bold, vigorous, and original thinker ; and we are not afraid to give him advice, that to a poet of an inferior order might be dangerous, that he should study to express clearly, and vividly, and attractively to others, what he has distinctly and strongly thought.   We have no fear that he will ever "lose a *thought* in snapping at a *rhyme*." But he has evidently been too easily satisfied with his own performances.   He must have been aware of his own originality, and he appears to have trusted to that too exclusively.   But we can assure him, that his thoughts are like diamonds, which, while they gain in splendour, increase also in value, by the labour of polishing.   The following lines are a good example both of the beauty of the author's thoughts, and his carelessness of execution.

TO MY FRIEND G———.

THE LOST PLEIAD.*

Oh ! how calm and how beautiful—look at the night !
The planets are wheeling in pathways of light ;
And the lover, or poet, with heart, or with eye,
Sends his gaze with a tear, or his soul with a sigh.

But from Fesole's summit the Tuscan looked forth,
To eastward and westward, to south and to north ;
Neither planet nor star could his vision delight,
'Till his own bright Pleiades should rise to his sight.

They rose, and he numbered their glistering train—
They shone bright as he counted them over again ;
But the star of his love, the bright gem of the cluster,
Arose not to lend the Pleiades its lustre.

And thus, when the splendour of *beauty* has blazed,
On light and on loveliness, how have we gazed !
And how sad have we turned from the sight, when we found
That the fairest and sweetest was "*not on the ground.*"

The good taste, which dictated the first two of the foregoing stanzas, must, we think, have revolted at the not merely prosaic, but low and vulgar metaphor, with which the poem concludes. The editor of the Connecticut Mirror had found a rhyme, however, and business at the time may have prevented him from searching for a better.   This would, we admit, have been an available excuse, had the poem never been transferred from the corner of a newspaper ; but when Mr Brainard collected his poems, and published them with his name, he should have thought more of his reputation, than to commence a poem with the planets' "pathway of light," and end it by an allusion to

—————————————————————————————

" * 'T is said by the ancient poets, that there used to be one more star in the constellation of the Pleiades."

a *horse-race.* We do not love to dwell on trifling blemishes, and, therefore, did not mark the frequent occurrence of bad rhymes and harsh metres, which again and again offended our ears.

The lines, "To the Dead," which, by the way, should have been entitled, "Of the Dead," we quote as highly beautiful, and as strikingly characteristic of the author's chief excellence—of thinking genuine poetry, which is unlike any other man's poetry.

TO THE DEAD.

How many now are dead to me
  That live to others yet!
How many are alive to me
Who crumble in their graves, nor see
That sick'ning, sinking look which we
  Till dead can ne'er forget.

Beyond the blue seas, far away,
  Most wretchedly alone,
One died in prison—far away,
Where stone on stone shut out the day,
And never hope, or comfort's ray
  In his lone dungeon shone.

Dead to the world, alive to me;
  Though months and years have passed,
In a lone hour, his sigh to me
Comes like the hum of some wild bee,
And then his form and face I see
  As when I saw him last.

And one with a bright lip, and cheek,
  And eye, is dead to me.
How pale the bloom of his smooth cheek!
His lip was cold—it would not speak;
His heart was dead, for it did not break;
  And his eye, for it did not see.

Then for the living be the tomb,
  And for the dead the smile;
Engrave oblivion on the tomb
Of pulseless life and deadly bloom—
Dim is such glare: but bright the gloom
  Around the funeral pile.

With this extract we must take our leave of Mr Brainard for the present; but with hopes soon to receive another volume from his hands, which shall amply fulfil the high promise, which this work makes us, that we have poets of an exalted order among us, and whom untoward circumstances, " the hopes of making a little something," have alone hitherto repressed.

22

Plans for the Government and Liberal Instruction of Boys in large numbers; drawn from experience. London. 1822. 8vo. pp. 238.

THIS book contains so much practical good sense as well as sound philosophy upon the subject of education, that we are resolved to lose no time in laying it, at some length, before our readers. If the book itself were in their hands, we should proceed at once to make our remarks upon its peculiarities and its merits, alluding to it only, as occasions might require, as to a subject with which they are already familiar. But as few copies have probably reached this side of the Atlantic, we shall first give a pretty full analysis of it, reserving our remarks for the close of this or perhaps for some future article. The " Hazelwood School," of which this book contains the plan, has attracted considerable attention in England for the last few years, and is destined, if we mistake not, to attract much more; and to be made in many respects, the model of other schools there, as well as in our own country. But the plan is not such as can be generally adopted for the efficient instruction of the whole people, either in England or in the United States. The complicated machinery of its government would require pupils of an age, when the most interesting, and perhaps the most important period of their education, as it respects both the moral and intellectual character, would be passed. Habits are contracted—principles are in some degree fixed—and traits in character are strongly marked, by instructions received, and examples observed long before a pupil would be capable of sustaining many of the relations, which would devolve upon him as a member of a school like the one here described. This consideration limits the application of the Hazelwood system of government to pupils of an age, when much must have already been done. Another will limit it still more. A full development of the plan, and such, according to our author, it must have, in order to ensure its success, would involve expenses, which must place it at once beyond the reach of a great proportion of the people in this country, and of at least as great a proportion of them in England. This limitation confines the application of the system to a certain class; and could only be removed by the benevolent exertions and appropriations of individuals, for establishing institutions of a similar character, free, or partially free, to the whole population of the country; or by the government's assuming the whole responsibility and expense of organizing and supporting the elementary schools, and throwing the burden of it upon property.

The former is not likely to be the case to any considerable extent; and the latter policy we fear will not be adopted till the question is more definitely settled, whether the government ought to interfere at all in the education of the people farther than to *allow* them to educate themselves, and perhaps to offer some few facilities to encourage them to do it. One other plan, perhaps, may suggest itself, by which the system will become more generally applicable to our higher schools, viz. by connecting more of agricultural or mechanical pursuits with it, by which they may wholly or in great part defray their own expenses.

With these restrictions, the Hazelwood School promises to be an interesting and instructive model. Its system of government will afford hints, which, with some modifications, may be advantageously adopted in those schools and academies, which have a large number of pupils, and those attending constantly and for a long time. On failure of any of these conditions, the system will be found inapplicable to any class of schools in this country; however it may have succeeded under other and more favourable circumstances. The principles of government, though familiar to us on a somewhat larger scale, were new as applied to schools. And the projectors of the Hazelwood establishment certainly must have the credit of ingenuity, as well as originality. The government of schools has generally been a monarchy, and so administered as to become the very essence of tyranny. By this plan it is made essentially democratic, by vesting most of the power in the body of pupils, who form the community of the school. They make and execute all the laws for its regulation, except those which " determine the hours of attendance, and the regular amount of exercises to be performed." The master and teachers have only a negative authority in these matters, if all their powers are fairly stated in the following constitution. How far their personal influence may extend in swaying *public opinion,* we are not informed. But we hasten, without further preliminary remarks, to quote the plan of government at length, in the hope thus to gratify those, who are more particularly interested in the subject; and, perhaps, at the expense of being thought particularly dull by most of our readers.

The government of the school is lodged in the hands of the master, the teachers, and a committee of boys elected by their companions.

The committee is chosen on the first Monday in each month, at a general meeting of the school, over which one of the boys is called upon to preside as chairman.   The boy who is then highest in rank, the means of obtaining which are hereafter described, appoints a member of the committee; the two next in elevation jointly nominate a second; the three next choose a third, and so on to the bottom of the list; the last section, if incomplete, being incorporated with the previous division.

The committee at present consists of eleven boys; but its number must evidently vary with any considerable increase or diminution in the school.   Each of the assistant teachers is a member *ex officio*; but, as we think it desirable to leave the management of affairs as much as possible in the hands of the boys themselves, only one teacher has been in the habit of attending the committee's meetings.

The committee meets once a week; it has the formation of all the laws and regulations of the school, excepting such as determine the hours of attendance and the regular amount of exercises to be performed; but when the committee has resolved upon any law, a copy is presented by the secretary to the head master, whose sanction is necessary before it can be put in force.*   The law is afterwards read aloud in the presence of the school, when its operation immediately commences, and a copy is hung in a conspicuous part of the school-room, for at least three days.

The regulations of the committee require, that previously to the discussion of any new law, a week's notice shall be given.   This necessary arrangement having sometimes occasioned inconvenient delay, a sub-committee, consisting of the judge and magistrate for the time being, has been empowered to make regulations, liable as usual to the *veto* of the master; which, unless annulled in the mean time by the general committee, continue in operation for a fortnight.   A great advantage of this arrangement is, that it affords opportunity of trying as an experiment the effect of any regulation, and modifying it, if necessary, before it forms a part of the code of written laws.

Immediately after its election, the new committee assembles, and proceeds to appoint the officers for the ensuing month.   A chairman and secretary are first chosen; then the judge, the magistrate, the sheriff, and the keeper of the records, are elected.   At the same time also, the master appoints the attorney-general, the judge nominates the clerk and the crier of the court, and the magistrate his two constables.

Of the duties of the judge we shall speak hereafter.   The magistrate has the power of enforcing all penalties below a certain amount.   When an offence is committed which is beyond his jurisdiction, he directs the attorney-general to draw an indictment against the offending party, who takes his trial in a manner which will be hereafter described.   The magistrate also decides petty cases of dispute between the boys; and is

---

* The first committee was appointed on the 3d of February, 1817; and although from that time to the present (October, 1821), the committees have been constantly employed in repealing, revising, and correcting the old laws, and in forming new ones, the master's assent has never, in a single instance, been withheld, or even delayed.

expected, with the assistance of his constables, to detect all offences committed in the school. At the end of the month the boy who has officiated as magistrate is rewarded with a half holiday, and, in order to secure to him the good-will and active co-operation of the other boys, he has the privilege of choosing a certain number of them to enjoy the holiday with him. This number is estimated by the master, according to the success of the police in preserving order. The magistrate has also the power to reward the constables with half a day's holiday at the same time, and to permit each of them to confer the same favour on either one or two other boys, according as he shall think his constables have performed their duty.

The sheriff has to enforce all penalties levied by the court of justice; and in case of the inability of the defaulter to pay the fine, it is his duty to imprison him. The rate at which penalties of marks shall be discharged by imprisonment has been determined by the committee. The sheriff has also some other duties, which will be mentioned hereafter.

The keeper of the records has the care of the indictments and other papers belonging to the court of justice.

The attorney-general is the officer who conducts the proceedings against those boys who are tried by order of the magistrate. In cases of appeal, which will be hereafter explained, it is the duty of the attorney-general to draw up the necessary documents, if required by the appellant; for this he receives a fee of a certain number of marks from the unsuccessful party.

The court of justice assembles on Wednesday afternoon, whenever there is business which requires its attention. At this time every teacher and every pupil is expected to be in attendance. All boys, except the officers of the court, those who are in certain lower classes, and such as have been convicted by the court within the last month, are competent to serve upon the jury.

The jury consists of six, who are chosen by lot from among the whole body of qualified boys. The lots are drawn in open court, the first by the judge, and the remaining five by the first juryman drawn. The jury choose their own foreman.

The attorney-general and the accused party, if the case be penal, and each disputant, if civil, have a peremptory challenge of three, and a challenge for cause, *ad infinitum*. The judge decides upon the validity of objections.

The officers of the court and the jury having taken their seats, the defendant (when the case is penal) is called to the bar by the crier of the court, and is placed between the constables. The clerk of the court then reads the indictment, at the close of which the defendant is asked if he object to any of the jury, when he may make his challenges, as before stated. The same question is put to the attorney-general. A short time is then allowed the defendant to plead guilty, if he be so disposed; he is asked no question, however, that he may not be induced to tell a falsehood: but in order to encourage an acknowledgment of the fault, when he pleads guilty a small deduction is made from the penalty appointed by the law for the offence. The consequence is, that at least five out of six of those who are justly accused acknowledge the offence in the first instance. If the defendant be determined to stand his trial, the attorney-general opens the case, and the trial proceeds. The defendant may either plead his own cause, or employ a schoolfellow as counsel, which he sometimes does.

The judge takes notes of the evidence, to assist him in delivering his charge to the jury; in determining the sentence he is guided by the regulations enacted by the committee; which affix punishments varying with the magnitude of the offence and the age of the defendant, but invest the judge with the power of increasing or diminishing the penalty, to the extent of one-fourth.

The penalties appointed by the judge are entered in a book by the sheriff, and a copy of the sentence is laid before the master for his signature, when he can, if he please, exercise his power of mitigation or pardon.

The fines are paid in open court immediately after the ratification of the sentence; otherwise the defendant is imprisoned.

Any one who has committed an offence may, with the permission of a teacher, escape the shame of a public trial, by undergoing the greatest possible punishment that he could suffer from the sentence of the judge.

A register is kept of all who have been convicted before the court of justice, and of those who have paid the increased fines in order to escape trial. Some boys are acutely sensible of the disgrace of appearing in this book; and in order to make this very proper feeling a spur to moral improvement, it has been thought advisable to allow any one, whose name, at the last arrangement according to good behaviour (on a system to be explained hereafter), shall have stood above a certain number, to move the court to order the erasure of his name from the criminal register. The boy in this case is obliged to give notice of his intention to the attorney-general, and, to succeed, he must prove to the satisfaction of a jury, that his conduct for a long time past has been exemplary. This has been done in some instances.

The offences which come before the court of justice are, principally, leaving the school before the appointed exercises are completed and examined, going beyond the school boundaries, and falsehood. Petty acts of dishonesty have sometimes been the subjects of legal investigation; but these, we are happy to state, occur very rarely indeed. When a case of prevarication comes before the court, the offender is likely to be severely dealt with, for the juries have hitherto shown a decided aversion to every kind of deception; and a quibble is, perhaps, punished more rigorously than a direct falsehood.

Any one who shall think himself aggrieved by a decision of the magistrate, a teacher, or of the court of justice, may appeal to the committee. Two instances only have occurred of appeals from the court of justice, both of which were brought by the attorney-general, against verdicts of acquittal; and upon each occasion the committee reversed the decision of the inferior court. Neither of these cases was of that clear and undoubted nature which would authorize a charge of partiality against the jury; moreover, in each instance, evidence was brought before the committee which had not been heard below. Appeals against the decisions of the teachers and magistrate have been frequently made. The committees have generally ratified the former decisions; and when they have not, (with a few exceptions only), they have acted in conformity with the opinions of the teachers as a body. We can remember only two instances in which that has not been the case; even here all that was done was to reduce the penalties, not to remit them altogether; and though it was the opinion of the teachers that in these instances the committees were actuated in some measure by party feeling, we cannot be certain that such was the fact, because it is not impossible that the teachers themselves might be influenced by a sentiment of *esprit du corps* in favour of the acts of an individual of their own body.

· It has lately been the etiquette, when any case of appeal concerning a teacher comes before the committee, to leave the decision entirely with the boys; the only teacher who is in the habit of attending the meetings declining to vote on the question.

When any boy above the age of thirteen leaves the school, his character becomes the subject of judicial consideration; a report thereon is drawn up, and laid before the general committee by a sub-committee appointed for the purpose. In this report, the boy's merits and demerits are impartially stated; his improvement while at school, his rank and general character, and the offices of trust he may have served, are here recorded. On the other hand, the criminal register is consulted, and should his name be found therein, the fact is now brought forward against him. Offences committed long ago, however, are not unkindly dwelt upon; and moral improvement is always recorded with pleasure.

These reports are entered in a book, and read to the whole school. If any boy desire a copy of his character, he is furnished with one by the secretary.

Such is the organization of the system of government in detail. It struck us at first as exceedingly complicated, farcical, and boyish. And if we had not been before assured on high authority,* that " it works admirably in practice," we should have said without hesitation, that it could never be executed at all, or at best, at an expense of most of the time and attention of the scholars. But the operation of the system cannot be fully understood in the abstract; and we deem one successful experiment better evidence of its practicability than all the speculations which could be bestowed upon it. Such experiment has been made; and our scepticism is so far overcome by the favourable result as to leave a belief, that some modification of the system, by which the older pupils may be admitted to a share in the details of government, would be an improvement in the plans of our larger and higher schools;—because such an arrangement would relieve the governors and teachers of by far the most difficult and perplexing part of their duty; and because it would remove the impression, which always exists in a community of pupils, that they are the subjects of an arbitrary power,—a tyranny *to* which they must either quietly submit, or *from* which they must escape by violence or intrigue.

* See Edinburgh Review, No. LXXXII.

Wherever a large number of pupils are brought together, there we may always expect an *esprit du corps*, which, unless it be very diverted, will naturally be arrayed against the power which restrains or controls it.   This impatience of control, and this spirit of opposition, are peculiarly strong in youth; and they are imparted by sympathy from one to another with electrical rapidity.   A leading and essential point, therefore, in any plan for the government of boys in large numbers, must be to remove, as far as possible, the causes which excite, and the occasions which bring out, this spirit of opposition; and if this point be not by some means and in some good degree gained, opposition will always exist, and concert and combination will give it energy and direction. Vigilance and power may restrain it, but it still exists.   It is a force too elastic to be broken or crushed, and every increase of weight causes a double reaction.   The system just quoted has for its object, to relieve the masters and instructers from the trouble of imposing these odious restraints, and the pupils from the trouble of feeling them; and at the same time to secure all the order necessary for the attainment of the objects of the institution.   Restraints imposed by the constitution of the school, and punishments inflicted by an executive from their own body, will be felt as a much less evil, than when imposed by superiors, who have fewer sympathies with them, and who take the whole government into their own hands, and make, interpret, and execute their laws; wisely, perhaps, for every purpose but that for which they are designed— viz. to produce good dispositions, and promote the greatest moral and intellectual improvement of the community of pupils.

Rank, we are assured by our author, is an object of great ambition in the school, and it is conferred according to moral and intellectual merit.

As we have before stated, it is an object with us to make rank as important in the eyes of the boys as possible.   The weekly arrangement determines for a time the precedence of the boys.   With a few exceptions, which will be stated shortly, they sit according to it at their meals: when presenting their exercises to a teacher for examination, superiority in rank gives them a prior claim to his attention; and it has been seen, that the higher a boy ranks, the more influence he acquires in the election of the committee, and, consequently, the greater is his control in the affairs of the school.   There are other motives which render this rank desirable, but is not necessary to enumerate all.

They have two species of circulating media in the establishment, one called *penal marks*, and another *premial marks*.

These, somewhat unlike our vulgar circulating medium, represent this same moral and mental merit; and not what the pupils possess of the good things of this world. The whole system of rewards and punishments consists almost exclusively in giving or withholding these two species of marks or " *counters.*" The following is our author's description of one of them.

Our rewards are chiefly conferred by the distribution of certain counters, which the boys obtain by superiority in the classes, by filling certain offices,—and by various kinds of voluntary labour. In the forfeiture of these counters our punishments chiefly consist; hence the pieces are called penal marks.

Every boy in the school devotes such part of his play-hours as he may think proper to the obtaining of these marks. The product of almost any kind of labour or study is received, provided it is presented in a complete state, and is tolerably well executed. As each boy, for this purpose, is at liberty to employ himself in the way he shall think proper, he of course engages in those pursuits which are most consonant with his taste. * * *

The penalties are entered at the time they are incurred in a book which is kept for the purpose; and at an appointed hour in each day the boys are expected to pay certain teachers, who are in readiness to receive them, all the penalties which may have been registered against them on the preceding day: those, however, of the younger boys are lessened by subtracting a sixth for every year which the age is under eleven. At the same time other teachers are occupied in giving the rewards for voluntary labour. The names of those boys who cannot pay their fines are entered on a list (called the defaulters' list), which is kept by the sheriff, the penalties being doubled. Those who remain on this list are confined to the school-room, except at meal-times, and during one half hour in each day which is allowed for exercise: they are also obliged to rise at an hour earlier than the other boys in the morning; and at the next holiday, should they be still upon this list, provided their names have not been entered within the preceding twenty-four hours, *the sheriff has the power of confining them separately in the dark, for a time proportionate to the amount of their debts.*

The other species of counters differs from the one just described, both in the kind of merit which it represents, and the purposes to which it may be applied.

Besides the counters already mentioned, rewards of another description are given, which we call premial marks: these can only be obtained by productions of the very best quality, and, unlike the penal marks, are strictly personal; that is, they cannot be transferred from one boy to another: with a certain number of them, a boy may purchase for himself an additional holiday, which can be obtained by no other means; and in the payment of penalties, they may be commuted at an established rate for penal marks. To prevent unnecessary interference in the arrangements of the school, the purchase of holiday with premial marks is confined to a certain afternoon in each week, when any one who is able may obtain his liberty. But an inducement to save their

23

premial marks is offered to the boys by making them the means of procuring rank. Thus once and sometimes twice in every half year, (according to the number of weeks from vacation to vacation), the first place is put up to auction, and given to the boy who is willing to sacrifice for it the greatest number of premial marks : the second place is then sold in the same manner, and so on. By these means the possession of premial marks is made to bear upon the determination of the prizes; and so powerful is the motive thus created, that we find, on an examination of the accounts, that a boy of fourteen, now in the school, although constantly in the possession of marks amply sufficient to obtain a holiday per week, has bought but three quarters of a day's relaxation during the whole of the last year. The same boy, at a late arrangement, purchased his place on the list by a sacrifice of marks, sufficient to have obtained for him twenty-six half days' exemption from the labour and confinement of the school.

These are the essential principles of all that is peculiar to the government of the Hazelwood School. The division of the scholars into classes, and the minor regulations for the preservation of order, present nothing new. There is considerable mechanical ceremony in going through the manœuvres of a day; but all this is common in principle, if not in form, with the system of Mr Lancaster; and we shall not go into a more particular account of it. The volume contains our author's defence of his own system of government, and a sketch of the principles of instruction he has adopted. These make more than half the volume, and constitute by far the most valuable part of it; although they are less peculiar than the part we have already examined. These, as well as the moral influence of the education received at school, we must reserve for some future number.

MISCELLANY.

HYDE PARK—STATUE IN HONOUR OF WELLINGTON—KENSINGTON GARDENS—CHELSEA HOSPITAL.

A LEAF FROM THE JOURNAL OF A TRAVELLER IN ENGLAND.

April 18th, 18—.

OF all the crowds of London, the most numerous and various is that which is poured forth from this great metropolis into Hyde Park, between one and four o'clock of a pleasant Sunday. We may learn the numerical population of London in our closets, but no one can have a full and just conception of its immensity without taking the view, which a few minutes walk procured me to-day. The principal north entrance (about four yards wide) at Hyde Park Place was about as much crowded as the doors of that worthy edifice, Cambridge meetinghouse, on a Commencement morning, and that not for a few minutes, but for successive hours. For one mile on the city side of the Park, the wheel-way was occupied by two lines of coaches and other vehicles, moving in opposite directions; but unable to exceed, in any instance, a moderate walk, and often obliged to halt, as they sometimes do in our most extended and solemn processions. The walkers occupied a footway within that for carriages, and separated from it by a slight fence; and they formed, for the same distance, viz. a mile, a solid column from two to four rods wide. Besides these, there were numerous riders, drivers, and pedestrians scattered around and over the Park. I committed myself to the stream, which bore me down towards Hyde Park Corner, the principal south entrance, near which, and in full view of Wellington's house, is the statue of Achilles, erected (saith the superscription) by the ladies in honour of Wellington and his associates! This statue has been the subject of much ridicule, as well as of grave censure; and, in my opinion, it deserves both, and would not be tolerated a single day in a place of public resort in the United States; not, perhaps, that we are more virtuous, but that we have less temptation. The statue was cast from twelve twenty-four pounders, and weighs upwards of thirty tons. On the pedestal I read as follows :

> To Arthur, Duke of Wellington,
> And his brave companions in arms,
> This statue of Achilles, cast from cannon taken
> In the battles of Salamanca, Vittoria, Toulouse, and Waterloo,
> Is inscribed by their countrywomen.
> Placed on this spot the 8th day of June, 1822,
> By command of His Majesty
> George IV.

I doubt exceedingly if the country-*women* of those heroes had any concern in putting up this statue, though it may be difficult for them to avoid taking some interest in it, now that it is up, so peculiarly does it offer itself to their notice. I cannot but think that their name has been usurped to sanction what themselves would never sanction; and to supply the place of the drapery or the brick walls, which ought to hide this figure from the public view,—a figure fit only for an artist's workshop. I am willing to presume, for the honour of English dames and from some particular circumstances of the case, that the part of the inscription which relates to them, is a fiction. But perhaps some one will start up, and begin to discourse to me of prudery—of classical models—and of the old proverb about purity. He shall be welcome; and when he is done, I will reply,—that we have a purer and more intellectual religion than the Greeks had; that moral aberrations, which in them might be excused, or at least would not imply a radical and irreclaimable wickedness of heart,—would in our stage of improvement be wholly unpardonable, and would argue an utter and hopeless abandonment to vice. Ought we not, and do we not, profess to aim at a higher standard of morality and of public decorum than existed at Athens, where a favourite of the city caused himself to be drawn in a car through the principal streets and in open day, in a manner too indecent and disgusting to admit of description? I have a great respect for proverbs, and think, that rightly understood, they always contain much that is true and useful; but this one, " 'To the pure all things are pure," if literally understood, would not more justify the statue of Achilles, than it would the *four*-in-hand driving of Themistocles, or the huge nakedness of the women of Timmana. I am disposed to believe, that his Grace the Duke of Wellington ought to bear all or a greater part of the blame of this statue; for his taste it was (reinforced perhaps by that of certain privy counsellors) that directed the making and the placing of it.

After this *reconnoisance* of Achilles, and after contemplating for some time the innumerable multitudes passing in review before me, and seeing some quit and others come, I continued my perambulation to the western extremity of the Park, or rather of Kensington Gardens, about three miles. There is situated Kensington palace, the residence of the Duke of Sussex (a great friend to America); of the princess Sophia, the king's sister; and of the Dutchess of Kent, whose young daughter is heir presumptive to the throne. It being Sunday, I did not apply for admission, but understood that on week days, the chaplain of the establishment would show it to all visiters for a shilling, the usual price for such gratifications in England. Near the palace is an extensive green-house, suitably filled. What interested me most about it, was the inscriptions scratched on the large glass windows; which, whether done last year or sixty years ago, were equally bright and legible. On a first glance, several of the mottos, names, and dates appeared, by the freshness of the lines, to have been just written, but on examination I found them from fifty to seventy years old. The following are specimens.

Wilkes is a rogue;

and under it,

The writer is a liar.

May the present contest between the American congress and their mother country be unanimously settled to the satisfaction of every true British subject.

These show the spirit and opinions of particular times. The following belong to all times.

> Cupid shall never pierce my heart,
> Though he strike it with his fiercest dart.

To which was subjoined by another hand,

> This lady all her resolution spoke,
> But wrote on glass, in hopes it might be broke.

This Park, or rather that part of it called Kensington Gardens, which may be considered a continuation of it, is covered with shrubs, beech, hemlock, lime, and other trees, in some places thinly scattered, and in others thick and nearly impervious. Not far from the palace there is a large and beautiful artificial lake, with swans and canoes gliding over its surface. Summer-houses, rustic seats and lodges invite to rest at suitable intervals. The Serpentine river, so called, I know not why (its form being an *oblong square*), is in Hyde Park, not above half a mile from the city.

Chelsea lies nearly south of Hyde Park, and about three miles from Soho square, so that I was not carried any farther from my lodgings by making a visit to the Hospital in that place. The buildings have an air of perfect neatness and great comfort ; the architecture is in good taste (it was finished by Wren), and the material brick, with stone columns and pilasters. The grounds are finely laid out, and well enclosed with iron railing. In the centre court, which is open on the south or Thames side, is a bronze statue of Charles II., the founder. The scene and the walks on this side are charming beyond description. What an enormous tribute this nation pays to the spirit of war and of conquest ! It is well, perhaps, that the mutilated remains of these blind instruments of pride and selfish ambition are not cast off when their services are done ;—that nourishment and rest are afforded to the surviving men and limbs, which have lost their fellows in distant lands. When the old and invalid soldiers arrive from abroad, and are paid off, and put upon this establishment, they throw off their campaigning caps, knapsacks, and coats, and strew them over the grounds ; they get intoxicated, the place is filled, and their money obtained by merry friends, or rather fair enemies, from London, and thus, *le fin couronne les œuvres.*

The pensioners are dressed in coarse blue surtouts, with military buttons, and generally a cocked hat. The dining hall is spacious, handsome, and perfectly clean. They breakfast on bread and cheese, and porter; and dine on meat five days in the week ; pease-soup is substituted for meat the remaining two days. They receive from sixpence to one shilling and sixpence per day, according to their rank. One monoped pensioner told me, that his absent leg was at New Orleans ;—that he saw General Packenham wounded and borne from the field, having his own leg carried away at the same moment by a cannon ball. I concealed the fact of my being an American, and endeavoured to obtain from him some opinion of American courage ; but all that I could get from him, was, " Why shoul'nt they be brave—they are the same as we." The English, he said, stood no chance at New Orleans ; they were cut down by scores without being able to strike a blow. Besides the cannon shot which deprived him of his leg, he received four musket balls in his body. The Americans had breast-works seven feet high, with loop-holes. I asked, why they attacked in that manner. He replied, that it was the fault of a Colonel M——, who was to have been on the ground a quarter of an hour first, and placed ladders across the fosse, and planks on them, so as to have formed foot-bridges. Instead of this, the main body arrived on the ground, and had to stand a dreadful fire, while the means of attack were being procured. This soldier belonged to the fourth or " King's own." Lord Chatham was colonel of it, but the acting commandant at New Orleans was Colonel Brooks.

If an intelligent person would take pains to visit the pensioners, and converse with them, he might obtain a great many interesting details respecting the military events of the last fifty or sixty years.—details, which would be useful to history, and which will probably die with the veterans, who alone possess them. It appears to me, that a careful inquirer might collect among them materials for an amusing and valuable book.

In passing through St James' Park, on my return to London, I observed one of the sentinels (for they are posted all round this Park) calling very vehemently after an old lady, who was scrambling off as vehemently in an opposite direction. Finding that vociferation would not arrest her, the sentinel pursued, and overtook her, just as I encountered them both. The old lady's offence was that of walking with *pattens*, a practice prohibited in these parks. Being ordered by the soldier to take them off, she complied, and was permitted to go her way.

THE LAY MONASTERY.

Poets and Common-sense Men.

THERE is something of mystery in the poetical character. We may talk as we will of gifted minds, and inspired thoughts, and holy feelings,—and may see in each other the strong light of some intellectual feature throwing a deep shadow over the rest of the mind,—and yet we are not a step nearer the solution than before. We may say, that poets hold secret communion with nature,—that they enter within the veil of her temple, and come out to reveal what other eyes have not seen nor other ears heard; aye, that poets themselves have their altars, their worshippers, their devotees,—and yet there is a mystery. We may say, that the same temperament, which prompts a man to be a poet, prompts him to love,—that the same enthusiasm in thought and sensibility in feeling are working out their different ends in each;—but the silent miracle is still going on within those thoughts and feelings, we know not how. Many poets have said, that they had seasons of inspiration and "thick-coming fancies"—and intervals of mental rest—relapses into life's actuality and commonplace; Milton could not write until the sun had passed down the autumnal equinox, nor after it had come up from the vernal; and poor Chatterton was idle save when the moon was near her full; but all this, so far from giving light upon the subject, makes us wonder still more at the anomaly.

The generality of mankind have little romance in their characters. But poets can create a fairy land in their own imaginations; and, looking abroad upon their own creation, they can enjoy a bright day even amid the storms of the world. This is a great and peculiar privilege,—one that nature alone gives, and withholds, and with which we usually find united a high and exquisite tone of feeling,—often too high for the tone of ordinary life. I am, however, far from thinking, that this excess of feelings is what sometimes renders the poetical temperament an unhappy one; it is rather a want of harmony between these feelings themselves, and between them and the feelings of other men. There seem to be certain unseen, but powerful sympathies existing between the hearts of our great human brotherhood; so that an emotion awakened in one should find its echo in all others;—as the sound of a flute finds a corresponding one on the strings of a harpsichord. A want of unison, arising from hearts and minds too highly strung, is the fountain of the poet's proverbial unhappiness—full even to overflowing. And thus it is, that the poetical temperament unfits men in some degree for life's ordinary scenes and duties,—that it lays them open to embarrassments,—and gives many a one occasion to say of the dead son of song, as a forgotten French poet once sung over the grave of the unfortunate Malherbe,—

> Il est mort pauvre.—et moi,
> Je vis comme il est mort.

In reference to the poetical faculty, as distinguished from its peculiar exercise, poets may be divided into two great classes,—those who have within them the light of original genius, and those who borrow their lustre and draw their inspiration from the full urns of others. From the strong minds of the first, spring up vigorous conceptions, which have not been nurtured with a careful, overweening prudence. These are men who hold, and who dare to exercise, the mighty prerogative of genius. They have minds full of energy and high aspirings,—trying hazardous flights, and sustaining themselves long and gloriously. The poetical vein grows excellent by use; and these have shown, from an early and first beginning, the germs of that power, which, by exercise, gave them in its maturity a wide sway in the intellectual world. These are the suns of their spheres,—stars of the first magnitude,—fixed, and shining with a steady brightness; others are but satellites, changing and vacillating in their orbits, with a pale and borrowed light. These last are poets of the second class,—poets who are afraid to follow the waywardness of fancy, but, in the spirit of weighing and measuring, give all diligence to suit their writings to the spirit of the age they live in, and bring down every thing to an unambitious level. They grow old in aping the ways of better writers,—the faults and follies of genius. We see in them a constant effort to familiarize the mind to a preciseness of thought and a nicety of style,—a constant fashioning of all things by favourite models,—which we call the *good breeding* of poetry. True poets embody and give form to the fine thoughts which are passing through their minds; but these men, like mere painters, only animate those forms, which have long existed in every one's fancy. They die in imitating, and they are forgotten by imitating!

These are poets; and common-sense men differ widely from them. It has lately been my good fortune to meet with one of these plain, on-going men in the affairs of life,—a man of good desert,—a studious observer of the world and its changes,—who, from a well saved experience has gained something of a prophetic foresight into the things of the world. "Although," said he, "it is idle for men to speculate much concerning futurity, yet there is in the history of every nation a kind of prophecy of what its history will be hereafter. Each age, indeed, has its peculiar and distinguishing character; but the spirit of the times may be traced back to the gradual operation of causes in former times, and will hereafter be found to have exerted its influence in giving character to succeeding periods. The spirit of the present age, in our own country, is a spirit of intelligence and activity; and is such as our fathers predicted would arise from their firmness and sufferings. What the character of the succeeding age will be, may be foretold from the many causes, which we see in operation for the gradual increase of mental power in our country; and the thorough removal of ancient errors, that are fast wearing out of the world." There was an energy in the speaker's manner, that gave force to what he uttered; and I found, that, although a thorough-going, matter-of-fact man, he still entertained that high respect for the ornamental arts of life, which originates in a well ordered taste and a due degree of natural sensibility. From him I shall trace in its outlines the character of the common-sense man.

It is a position laid down by many writers on education, that nothing but nature can fit a man for "learning ;" and that without a peculiar temperament for the pursuits he engages in, application, however close and long continued, is to no purpose. But this is an opinion, which bears too closely upon human happiness to be embraced without some limitation. It seems to give countenance to the idea, that we should cherish some one mental power to the neglect of all the rest,—an idea harmonizing well with our inclinations and our indolence ; when, at the same time we know that system of education to be alone perfect, which develops and cherishes equally every faculty of the mind, giving light, and life, and vigor to all. And it is here that we may mark the first characteristic of the common-sense man. Though he has not the superiority of one intellectual faculty, which we call genius, yet there is within his mind, that beautiful proportion and exact balance of its powers, which, from their several relations, produce a harmonious whole. This fits him for the business of life, and for its enjoyment; for keeping up that just equipoise of his passive impressions and active principles, which will keep his sympathies from ending in feeling.

The common-sense man is a deliberate, thinking man ; grown cautious from his treasured wisdom in human affairs,—always consistent with himself, and true to his own character. The world is full of those who are precipitate in forming their opinions, and equally precipitate in changing them. So emphatically are they the creatures of circumstances, that we have no evidence of their being to-morrow what we have found them to be to-day. But the common-sense man forms his opinions with a cool, discriminating judgment, and when once embraced, keeps them with a saving faith. He has directed his mind to those practical pursuits, which have so wide a bearing upon the state of society, and with a cautious prudence has treasured up facts for his future benefit. He has done good to society both from speculation and from action. His theories rest upon facts, and their truth is known by their practical application. This constitutes the useful virtue of human prudence. When a man speculates upon the future circumstances of the world, and gives us tidings of what will be from what has already been, he must have closely studied human affairs, lest future realities should contradict his prophecy. And if he has turned faithfully over the volumes of nature, and has grown wise from the study of what he there found, we have a well grounded assurance, that whatever he shall say concerning things to be hereafter, in reasoning from present circumstances, will be at least an approximation to the truth.

24

It is an objection to the exclusive and devoted study of a favourite profession, that it limits those wide and liberal views of mankind and of worldly doings, which the mind should be led to embrace; and brings men to think that every thing of public utility may be traced to their own pursuits. But the experience of the common-sense man is continually widening the field of his views, and giving liberality to his opinions.

The common-sense man, then, is one who is really experienced in human ways, and who knows how to apply his knowledge to the increase of human happiness. Nor is this all. He is active in the right exercise of that power, which one individual has over the happiness of many,—going out into the busy world,—engaging cheerfully in the cares and enjoyments of life,—mingling with society,—speaking in good faith the thoughts of a good mind. Few of us have time and opportunity to form our own opinions of men and things. We take them, and we must take them, from others; and we reverence the character of the common-sense man in so readily embracing his, and in doing as he has done. Thus in the credit of his opinions, and the imitation of his actions, we see his influence upon society. The virtue of a good name has given reputation to his thoughts and actions,—the excellence of a good character has led men to honour and to imitate them. Has he enjoyed life well? He has shown us the means of that enjoyment existing in well regulated feelings and affections. Has he prospered in the world? He has shown us, in his honourable precepts and honest dealings, the way of that prosperity.

THE LAY MONK.

POETRY.

HYMN OF THE MORAVIAN NUNS
AT THE CONSECRATION OF PULASKI'S BANNER.

The standard of Count Pulaski, the noble Pole who fell in the attack upon Savannah, during the American Revolution, was of crimson silk, embroidered by the Moravian Nuns of Bethlehem in Pennsylvania. See N. A. Review, New Series, vol. XI. p. 390.

When the dying flame of day
Through the chancel shot its ray,
Far the glimmering tapers shed
Faint light on the cowled head,
And the censer burning swung,
Where before the altar hung

The proud banner, that with prayer
Had been consecrated there.
And the nuns' sweet hymn was heard the while,
Sung low in the dim mysterious aisle.

Take thy banner!—may it wave
Proudly o'er the good and brave,
When the battle's distant wail
Breaks the sabbath of our vale,—
When the clarion's music thrills
To the hearts of these lone hills,—
When the spear in conflict shakes,
And the strong lance shivering breaks.

Take thy banner!—and beneath
The war-cloud's encircling wreath,
Guard it—till our homes are free—
Guard it—God will prosper thee!
In the dark and trying hour,
In the breaking forth of power,
In the rush of steeds and men,
His right hand will shield thee then.

Take thy banner! But when night
Closes round the ghastly fight,
If the vanquished warrior bow,
Spare him!—by our holy vow,
By our prayers and many tears,
By the mercy that endears,
Spare him—he our love hath shared—
Spare him—as thou wouldst be spared!

Take thy banner!—and if e'er
Thou shouldst press the soldier's bier,
And the muffled drum should beat
To the tread of mournful feet,
Then this crimson flag shall be
Martial cloak and shroud for thee!

And the warrior took that banner proud,
And it was his martial cloak and shroud.

                                        H. W. L.

LOVE ASLEEP.

Wake him not, he dreams of bliss;
His little lips put forth to kiss;
His arms, entwined in virgin grace,
Seem linked in beautiful embrace.

He smiles,—and on his opening lip
Might saints refresh and angels sip;
He blushes,—'t is the rosy light
That morning wears on leaving night.

He sighs,—'t is not the sigh of wo;
He only sighs that he may know
If kindred sighs another move;
For mutual sighs are signs of love.

He speaks,—it is his dear one's name;
He whispers,—still it is the same;
The imprisoned accents strive in vain,
They murmur through his lips again.

He wakes! the silly little boy,
To break the mirror thus of joy;
He wakes to sorrow, and in pain;
Oh! Love, renew thy dreams again.

C.

SONG.

'T is the season of joy and delight,
   The season of fresh-springing flowers;
Young Spring in her innocent beauty is bright,
   And leads on the rapturous hours;
Fair Nature is loud in her transport of pleasure,
   The woods and the vallies re-echo her lay;
The robin now warbles his love-breathing measure,
   And scatters the blossoms while tilting the spray;
One impulse of tenderness thrills through the groves,
While the birds carol sweetly their innocent loves.

How mild is the Zephyr that blows!
   What fragrance his balmy wings bear—
He breathes as if fearful to brush from the rose
   The dew-drops so tremulous there!
The stream flowing gently beside the green cresses
   So lightsomely dashes their tendrils away—
She seems some fond mother, who, while she caresses,
   Would sportfully chide her young children at play.
Hear the minstrel-bee lulling the blossoms to rest,
For the nectar he sips as the wild-flowers' guest!

Look out then on Nature awhile,
   Observe her inviting thee now,—
Benevolence beams in her sun-shiny smile,
   And blandishment sits on her brow:
Come stray with me, love, where the fountains are flowing,
   And wild flowers cluster to drink of the stream;
While watching the lily and daffodil blowing,
   No moment of bliss shall so exquisite seem;
While Nature invites thee, oh! why then delay;
While Joy is still waking, away! love, away!

D.

CRITICAL NOTICES.

Quarterly Review for March, 1825.

Mr Gifford, who, as our readers probably know, has been rather unsparing of his abuse of this country, closed his labours as editor of this work with the last number. It will hereafter be conducted by Mr J. Coleridge, brother of the poet. Assurances have been given and circulated pretty freely in our public papers, that the work will henceforth assume a different tone towards the United States; and we hope they have been given by those who are authorized to pledge the character of the most popular and extensively circulated journal of the kind printed in Great Britain. There is certainly nothing in this number to contradict the report; and a few sentences may be found, which seem to confirm it. It contains, besides several lighter and interesting reviews of popular books recently published, a long article on the " Funding System;" and another on the comparative advantages of " Canals and Rail-roads." It is shown conclusively, that the advantages are decidedly in favour of the latter, and on the following grounds:

" The disadvantages of a canal are numerous. The frost at one season of the year entirely puts a stop to all conveyance of goods; and the drought at another renders it necessary to proceed with half cargoes. A rail-road is exempt from both these serious drawbacks; and even if snow-blocked, nothing can be so easy as to send forward a scraper at the front of the steam-carriage to clear it as it proceeds.

" The speed, by which goods can be conveyed on a rail-road, can be so regulated as to be certain and constant, while boats are frequently delayed for hours at the lockages of a canal. This speed besides is limited on canals, as we shall presently show, but unlimited, as far as the power of steam can be made to exceed the power of friction, on rail-roads. To what extent, with safety and convenience, this advantage is capable of being carried, nothing but experience can determine. Rail-roads may be made to branch out in *every direction* to accommodate the traffic of the country, whatever be the nature of the surface;* the possibility of carrying branches from a canal in *any direction* must depend entirely on the surface, and a supply of water.

" In every case, with regard to speed and the weight to be moved, the rail-road has the advantage, except when that speed is less than 2.82 miles an hour, when it is in favour of the canal,—but even this small advantage is lost by the circuitous windings of the one, and the direct line of the other."

A horse will draw, at the rate of two miles an hour, about three times as much upon a canal as upon a rail-road; but the expense of constructing the canal will also be three times as great; so that neither, in this point of view and under these circumstances, seems to have an advantage over the other. But when the speed is increased, the power of the horse is rapidly diminished, and, at thirteen miles per hour, he can exert no power at all.

---

* " A stationary engine will pass the wagons up and down any hill that may occur in the line."

" But this diminution of strength in proportion to the speed of the animal is not the only disadvantage; the resistance of any body floating in the water increases as the square of the velocity; thus whatever power is required to move a floating body with any given velocity, it will require four times that power to give it twice that velocity, and nine times that power to give it three times that velocity. Nor is this all. The horse, when put to the speed of four miles an hour, can exert only a force of eighty-one pounds, a loss equal to that of two horses at that speed. It would therefore require no less than six horses to draw along a canal, at the rate of four miles an hour, the same load that one horse would draw at the rate of two miles an hour.

" The application of steam to canal navigation, if practicable, would, to a certain degree, supply the irremediable defect of that of horses; that is to say, an engine of 16 horse power would drag the same load at the rate of eight miles an hour, that one horse would do at the rate of two miles an hour; but the result would be destructive to the canal. The rapid motion of the wheels would cause such an agitation of the water, as to wash down its banks. Several attempts have been made to move the barges in canals without disturbing the water; and Mr Perkins has succeeded in this to a certain extent, by a sort of perpetu-. al sculler at the stern, in the shape of the four arms of a windmill's sails, moving in pairs, in a contrary direction; but as increased speed must cause an accumulation of the water, which, on falling from the vessel against the banks of a narrow canal, would create the mischief complained of, it would seem that all improvement, as to speed on canals, is nearly, if not altogether, hopeless."

The writer of an article on "Artizans and Machinery," though he acknowledges the correctness of the policy, which encourages an unrestricted system of trade, contends that the exportation of machinery is one of the cases wisely to be excepted from the wisest rule.

" That considerable injury would accrue to the English manufacturer, by extending this system of free trade to machinery, seems almost universally admitted; and the principal reason hitherto assigned for the repeal is, that by withholding these machines from the French, we compel them to make them for themselves, and that ultimately they will equal ours in excellence. In the first place, they have as yet only made a small quantity, and those of a very inferior quality. In the next place, supposing that in process of time they will gain skill and experience, that seems scarcely a reason for giving them *now*, what it must cost them much time to acquire, nor for enabling them at once to profit by the numerous experiments, and the many years' labour of Great Britain, and by furnishing them with all our machinery, place them, in a single day, on that very elevation, to attain which has cost our manufacturers such an expense both of money and of time."

The review of " Daru's Venice" is a rapid sketch of the origin, progress, decline, and final extinction of that interesting republic.

In the article on " The Church in Ireland," we have a defence of the tithe system. It is contended, that the church have a right to their tenth prior to and stronger, than the landholders have to the remaining nine parts. Because, amidst the revolutions in the history of the country, the nine parts of the land have been repeatedly forfeited to the crown, and have *changed owners* by its authority; while the tenth has been steadily appropriated to the church. So on this ground the government itself could not abolish tithes in Ireland, without a more flagrant act of injustice to the church, than they would be guilty of by taking the other nine parts from the landholders, and appropriating them to other owners. And, although the country is indirectly admitted to be miserable in the last degree, it is contended, that its miseries are, and ever have been, to be attributed to other causes than the church, and principally to the landholders. The facts cited in this article differ widely, in some instances, from those cited in the article on the same subject in the last number of the Edinburgh Review, of which we gave a notice in our last. And the reasoning and conclusions differ still more widely from those of that article; but our limits forbid us to go into the same extended analysis, which we then indulged.

The review of "Washington Irving's Tales" is interesting to us, as all foreign notices of American writers are interesting to Americans. We suspect, however, it would have been quite as agreeable to Mr Irving, as well as to his friends on this side of the water, if the reviewers had not seemed to take so much credit to themselves for their kindness and candour in admitting him to the "English guild of authorship." We quote a few sentences, which express as unqualified praise as any thing in the article. Of Knickerbocker's humourous History of New York, they say :

" To us it is a tantalizing book, of which all that we understand is so good, and affords us so much pleasure, even through an imperfect acquaintance with it, that we cannot but conclude that a thorough knowledge of the whole point in every part would be a treat indeed. We may compare it now to a book of grotesque hieroglyphics, in a great measure unintelligible, but intrinsically diverting from the humour and imagination which their fantastical combinations display."

The following is their estimate of Mr Irving's talents, and their very graceful and friendly leave of him.

" It may be doubted, perhaps, whether Mr Irving would succeed in novels of a serious and romantic cast, requiring, as they do, heightening touches of the savage and gloomy passions. Every thing in his style and conceptions is of a happy and riant nature, except when saddened for a moment by those touches of pathos which come and pass like April clouds; and the darker shades of revenge, remorse, and ominous presage, which hang over the Bride of Lammermoor, like the thunder-cloud over Wolf's crag, appear never to gather over his mental horizon. But there is a class of novel for which he possesses every requisite, and which is at once popular and capable of great improvement : the art of blending the gay, the pensive, and the whimsical, without jarring and abrupt transitions, so as to take by surprise the stubborn reader, who resists the avowed design of making him wretched, is so rare a gift, as to have compensated in the case of Sterne, for want of plot, and digressions which often degenerate into stark nonsense ; and combining, as Mr Irving does, so large a share of the indescribable humour of Sterne with a manly tone of moral feeling, of which the latter was incapable, we are convinced that moderate labour and perseverance might enable him to make material additions to our literature in the style to which we allude.

" Whether or not however we are likely to see our wishes realized, we may congratulate him on the rank, which he has already gained, of which the momentary caprice of the public cannot long deprive him; and with hearty good will, playfully, but we hope not profanely, we exclaim as we part with him, ' Very pleasant hast thou been to me, my brother Jonathan !'"

Correspondence of Lord Byron, with a Friend, including his Letters to his Mother, written from Portugal, Spain, Greece, and the Shores of the Mediterranean, in 1809, 1810, and 1811. Philadelphia. 1825. 12mo. pp. 200.

THIS book contains those letters of Lord Byron, which were intended to form a part of Mr Dallas' " Recollections," and which were prevented from being inserted in the English edition of that work. This objection, however, as we observed in our review of the " Recollections," did not apply to the American edition, and they should accordingly have made a part of it. This course, it seems, did not suit the views of the publishers, so that we have first a volume of " Recollections" garbled, by being deprived of Byron's letters, and then another, of which about one half is a mere reprint of the first. If the booksellers would publish the letters separately, why not publish them, by themselves, in a form calculated to be bound with the Recollections, to which they belong. We do not wish to pay twice for the same nonsense. The truth is, that the volume before us contains as much of Mr Dallas' production as is worth having; the volume of " Recollections" is altogether unnecessary; and, in fine, the whole affair is a specimen of impudent book-making, only to be paralleled by the publication of the Giaour by peacemeal,— a circumstance, which probably most of our readers recollect. We hope the public will show their indignation at this method of proceeding, by treating it with the contempt it merits. And what, after all, are these letters, about which Mr Dallas has made such a disturbance, and which required the interposition of the court of chancery to prevent their promulgation? Why, next to nothing; a few commonplace epistles to his mother, such as any young man of tolerable education and smartness might have written, and such as are written, we presume, by hundreds, every day, from travellers to their friends in England and America. Besides these, we have a number of such notes as are constantly passing between writers and the publishers or editors of their works. Why, we would engage to furnish the public with a dozen such volumes yearly, from the scraps which are lying upon, beneath, and around our study table; and right glad should we be to turn them to some account other than that of lighting our candles. Lord Byron wrote directions for correcting errors of the press, striking out and amending lines, sentences, and passages, just as any body else does. The following are specimens.

TO R. C. DALLAS, ESQ.

Cambridge, October 25th, 1811.

Dear Sir—I send you the conclusion to the *whole.* In a stanza towards the end of canto 1st, in the line,

Oh, known the earliest and *beloved* the most,

I shall alter the epithet to " *esteemed* the most." The present stanzas are for the end of canto 2d. In the beginning of the week I shall be at

No. 8, my old lodgings, in St James' street, where I hope to have the pleasure of seeing you. Yours ever,

B.

TO R. C. DALLAS, ESQ.

8, *St James' street, 29th October*, 1811.

Dear Sir—I arrived in town last night, and shall be very glad to see you when convenient. Yours very truly,

BYRON.

TO R. C. DALLAS, ESQ.

December 17th, 1811.

We will have the MSS. and extracts printed in an appendix. I leave to you to determine whether the lighter pieces in rhyme had better be printed before, or after the Romaic. Yours ever,

BYRON.

The letters to his mother are the only things in the book which have the slightest claim to the attention of the public; and these occupy by the assistance of spaces and margin, just fifty-four duodecimo pages. Printed in the same form with the "Recollections," they would have made a thin pamphlet, easily inserted by the binder in their proper place in that work,—if any one should think them worth buying,—the rest of the book being a mere saddle upon these. In short, we are utterly disgusted with the whole matter, and desire to waste no more words upon it.

A Catalogue of American Minerals, with their Localities; including all which are known to exist in the United States and British Provinces, and having the Towns, Counties, and Districts in each State and Province arranged Alphabetically. With an Appendix, containing additional Localities and a Tabular View. By SAMUEL ROBINSON. M. D. Member of the American Geological Society. Boston. 1825. 8vo. pp. 320.

THE rapid progress which the science of mineralogy has made in the United States within the last few years, may be fairly attributed to the industry and talent of Professor Cleaveland, whose Mineralogical Manual has not yet been equalled in any part of Europe; other works of the kind are either too brief, too technical, or too learned for general use. The second edition of this work appeared in 1822, with some improvements, and a great deal of additional knowledge of the minerals which have been discovered in the United States. Notwithstanding the recent appearance of this edition, so much information has since been added to the common stock, by several periodical publications and essays by different individuals, that for localities, at least, a new edition is almost requisite for the convenience of the active collector. This deficiency is in a great degree obviated by the present publication, which presents a geographical view, alphabetically arranged, of all the known localities of mineral substances discovered in the United States down to the date of the publication. Localities will, of course, continue to increase by the unparalleled industry of the American youth, who are searching every bill and brook to add to the knowledge of the mineral productions of their country; but many additional species to the present extensive number can hardly be expected. And such additions alone would call for a new manual in the science. The present publication, therefore, drawn up with great fidelity and industry, may justly be considered as a very necessary and useful addition to our mineral knowledge; and an accompaniment of practical utility to the last edition of Professor Cleaveland's Manual. But, besides the extension of our geographical knowledge, which this Catalogue embraces, there are no less than seventy substances added to the American list of minerals, which are not found in Cleaveland's last edition. The sources of information employed by the author have been also more numerous than could have been well imagined, for a science of such recent origin as that of mineralogy in the United States. It was, therefore, necessary for the collector at least to employ no inconsiderable number of expensive publications to acquire the necessary knowledge of the subject. The work is not merely an empty catalogue, as may be seen by its containing 320 octavo pages, but includes useful notes added or compiled by the author, on the uses and characteristic or remarkable traits of the substance.

A Practical Treatise on the Law of Partnership. By NIEL Gow, Esq. of Lincoln's Inn, Barrister at Law. First American from the last London edition. With Notes and References to American Decisions, by Edward D. Ingraham, Esq. Philadelphia. 1825. 8vo. pp. 518.

THIS Treatise on the Law of Partnership is valuable principally because it contains most of the recent decisions on the subject, and brings the law down to the present time. There were two excellent ones in use before,—those of Watson and of Montagu. The volume before us, however, differs very materially from both of these. It is much more elaborate, and perhaps more scientific in its form. The chapters and sections are in the nature of dissertations. The author writes as if he had thoroughly investigated all that has been said or decided on the Law of Partnership; but he gives us the result of his inquiries in his own language, without much quoting, and, indeed, with seldom more than a general reference to the authorities, on which his positions rest. The other two treatises we alluded to, have more the character of digests; or rather they are collections of legal decisions classified judiciously. This is particularly the case with the very popular one of Mr Montagu. After laying out his work generally, he states briefly, under each division, the principles belonging to it, and then inserts the decided cases, from which he has deduced those principles, either at full length, or at least so much of them as were material for the decision of the question before the court.

And we think this last is, on the whole, decisively the best way. The other, it is true, may exhibit more talent, and appear in a much more imposing form at first. There seems to be some play of original thinking about it. But a law-treatise is the last place for genius to shine in,—indeed originality may here be a great defect. Gentlemen of the bar want to know how questions have already been argued and settled. It is fact—it is what has actually been said, done, and decided by those superior tribunals, who preside over the law,—that they hunt among musty folios for; and a practical lawyer will never repose full confidence in the most satisfactory treatise that ever was written, without recurring likewise to the original cases, on which that treatise was built. Able essays or disquisitions are of little authority in our courts of judicature. It is not always safe to cite even the best digests or commentaries.   The decisions, or the adjudged cases themselves, out of which the digested principles are drawn, ought to be first examined and produced, if they are in existence; and it is only when these were never properly repeated, or when they have been lost by lapse of time, that the digest or the commentary is resorted to, as the next best evidence of the reality of those decisions, that the nature of the case admits of. These things have been applied to even the great work of Sir William Blackstone, one of the ablest judges who ever sat on the English bench. It was lately said of that work by an eminent jurist in delivering a judicial opinion: " I am always sorry to hear Mr Justice Blackstone's Commentaries cited as authority; he would have been sorry himself to hear the book so cited; he did not consider it such."

  · For these reasons, we think Mr Gow's treatise will not supersede the use of Watson and Montagu. It is certainly, however, a very able work. The editor, too, has added much to its value by the copious supply of American decisions, which he has introduced into it.   And perhaps as an elementary book for the student at law, or for the general reader, who wishes merely for a broad view of the subject, and has no occasion to look into the original cases themselves, in order to see the exact application of them,—it is the most interesting of the three; but to the accurate practical lawyer, the other two are in their manner decidedly preferable.

Memoirs of the Life of John Philip Kemble. Esq., including a History of the Stage from the time of Garrick to the present period.   By JAMES BOADEN, Esq.   Philadelphia. 1825. Two vols in one. 8vo. pp. 607.

The history of the English Stage for the last fifty years, with memoirs and anecdotes of the *principal* actors, affords a subject for a moderate-sized book, which might be interesting and valuable, not only to those more immediately connected with the stage, but to the general reader. But the size of this book is out of all proportion to the intrinsic interest of the subject of it, especially to readers in this country; and the ability with which the author has treated it, is not such as will atone for this inherent and appalling difficulty.   Seven eighths of the huge volume is taken up in stating facts of no consequence to any one at the present time—in relating stupid anecdotes of more stupid people—and in detailing with a tedious and provoking minuteness the bickerings and petty squabbles of a host of actors totally insignificant in the history of the stage.   We do intreat our respectable and enterprizing publishers to spare the public from more such books as this.   It can have but little interest, even with English readers, and much less with us. The mention of a few distinguished names in it may attract some notice, but that will make but slender atonement for the mass of nonsense in which they are involved.   We do not profess to have read the book through,—we would sooner give up our review than attempt such a thing.   But we have read enough to acquire a thorough disgust for it, and to convince ourselves that the folly of the plan is only equalled by the feebleness with which it is executed.   If others have patience and good nature enough to worry themselves through it, and can honestly arrive at a different conclusion, we shall be very happy to have our impressions corrected; but till that is done, we shall most conscientiously believe it is one of the most stupid books with which we have ever been afflicted.

INTELLIGENCE.

ACADEMY OF NATURAL SCIENCES AT PHILADELPHIA.

This is, perhaps, the most useful and active scientific association which at present exists in the United States. It combines a considerable number of individuals of talent, industry, and great zeal, and they promise to labour extensively in that almost untrodden field, the Natural History of America. It has been in existence several years, and its transactions have been submitted to the public; but the present year the first annual report of the Secretary of the Society, containing an account of its transactions for 1824, has been published. The view which it gives of its activity and zeal is highly honourable to the Society, and encourages us to look to this source for many important additions to the natural history of our country.

The meetings of the Society are, we believe, frequent, and are occupied by the reading of scientific communications or the delivery of lectures upon scientific subjects. The number of communications read before the Academy during the year 1824, was thirty-seven; of these some account is given by the Secretary under three heads, 1. Zoology; 2. Geology and Organic Remains; 3. Mineralogy; with a brief abstract of their contents. The number of lectures delivered was twenty-five. Of these, fourteen related to the physiology or the natural history of animals, two to botany, four to mineralogy and geology, and the remainder to subjects of mathematical or general science.

The Academy, during the year, published two half volumes of the Journal of their Transactions, containing the greater part of the communications which have been alluded to; and several remained on hand, which were to be put to press early in the present year. The report contains a most flattering view of the condition and prospects of the Society.

"Whether we estimate," says the Secretary, "the progress of this institution by the number of scientific communications submitted to it—by the number or merit of the memoirs deemed worthy of insertion in your journal—by the interest taken in your proceedings by the members themselves, as evinced in their more regular attendance at the meetings, and in the increased number of lectures delivered this year—by the accession to our list of associates,—or, finally, by the improved state of our finances, we shall, in each of these bearings, discover great cause for rejoicing, and an assurance that our institution is daily increasing in importance, in respectability, and, what is still more desirable, in usefulness."

LIVINGSTON'S PENAL CODE OF LOUISIANA.

In the number of the Westminster Review for January, 1825, is an article on the Penal Code of Louisiana, as drawn up by our distinguished countryman, Edward Livingston, Esq. The Code is examined in detail, and treated in a style of commendation very unusual in foreign reviews. The greatest praise is given to the principles advanced by

Mr Livingston, and the processes recommended by him. It is objected, however, to the Code, that its punishments are, in many instances, defective, since they do not extend to the compensation of the sufferers by the crime, which, in the opinion of the reviewer, ought to form a fundamental part of every penal infliction. Very large extracts are made in the course of the article, which concludes with the following tribute to Mr Livingston.

" We cannot conclude this notice of his labours, without joining our feeble voice to that of the legislative assembly for which he is preparing this code, and ' earnestly soliciting Mr Livingston to prosecute his work ' in the spirit of this Report. In England the eyes of its most enlightened philosophers, of its best statesmen, and of its most devoted philanthropists, will be fixed upon him; and in his own country, his name must be had ' in everlasting remembrance,' venerated and loved. He is one of those extraordinary individuals whom nature has gifted with the power, and whom circumstances have afforded the opportunity, of shedding true glory and conferring lasting happiness on his country ; and of identifying his own name with its freest, and most noble and most perfect institutions."

SIR WALTER SCOTT.

The students of the University of St Andrews have unanimously elected Sir Walter Scott Rector of that University. But the *Senatus Academicus* have declared the election void, by the statutes of the University, which, they contend, restrict the choice to persons holding certain situations within its precincts. This construction, they assert, has the sanction of four hundred years' usage, and cannot now be modified by the University itself. This subject is under investigation before a committee, in order to settle the principle of the eligibility of persons *not* holding said " certain situations within its precincts." In the mean time Sir Walter has declined the honor intended him, on the score of increasing years and aversion to business.

GERMAN UNIVERSITIES.

A great sensation has been produced throughout Germany by the appearance of a work entitled, " The Disgraceful Proceedings of the Universities, Lyceums, and Gymnasia of Germany ; or, History of the Conspiracies of the Schools against Royalty, Christianity, and Virtue, by K. M. E. Fabricius." This work, of about 200 pages, is dedicated to the German members of the Holy Alliance, and to their ministers and ambassadors at the Diet, and it denounces and vituperates the most enlightened and estimable of the German literati and men of science. It proposes to abolish all universities, or to put them under a more severe *surveillance.*

ANCIENT CHRONICLES OF THE NORTH.

There exists, in manuscript, in the Royal Library, and in several other collections in Copenhagen, a great number of *Sagas,* or chronicles, written in the Icelandic language, the publication of which is the more desirable, as they would throw a powerful light on the ancient history of the North, and as there is reason to fear that they will perish by decay, if they are not soon withdrawn from the dust of the libraries. These considerations have induced three learned Icelanders to associate themselves, in the task of publishing these precious relics of antiquity, with M. Rafu, who has just edited a tract called "The Chronicle of the Warriors of Ioonsburg." The intended publication will be in three different languages—in the original Icelandic, accompanied by two translations, the one in Danish and the other in Latin. The work just mentioned, which was copied from a manuscript of the 12th century, collated with two others of the 14th century, has been published only in Danish, as a specimen, in order to give the public an idea of the utility, as well as of the nature of the projected work, which is to be commenced in 1825.

STATISTICS OF HAYTI.

The population of Hayti, in 1824, amounted to 935,335. The whole number of inhabitants in the island, before the revolution, did not exceed 660,000. The regular army, for the same year, is stated at 45,520 men, and the national guards at 113,328.

DISCOVERY OF AN ANCIENT WELL AT ATHENS.

Pausanias, in his "Attics," chap. xxvi. mentions a well in the citadel in the temple of Erechtheus, cut in the rock, said to contain salt water, and to yield the sound of waves when the south wind blows. This well, after remaining closed up and unknown for perhaps a thousand years, was discovered in 1823. Want of provisions, and, still more, want of water, had compelled the Turks to surrender. The Greeks, after they got the fortress in their hands, foresaw that similar privations might operate against themselves, and having observed, while engaged in the scige, some water filtering through the soil at the foot of the rock, they dug down from above towards the spot whence it seemed to proceed, and soon came to a subterraneous stair of 150 steps, conducting to a small square chamber, in which was a well yielding a copious supply of fine water.

NEW PUBLICATIONS.

ARTS AND SCIENCES.

Five Hundred Questions, selected from a full course of Illustrations and Experiments upon Chemistry. Applied to the Useful Arts, given at the Agricultural Seminary at Derby, Connecticut; with a short statement of the Course of Instruction pursued at that Institution. 12mo. New Haven.

BIOGRAPHY.

Memoir of the Life of Josiah Quincy, Jun. of Massachusetts : by his son, Josiah Quincy. 8vo. Boston. Cummings, Hilliard, & Co.

COMMERCE AND MANUFACTURES.

An Essay on the Manufacture of Straw Bonnets, containing an Historical Account of the Introduction of the Manufacture, &c.: with Moral, Political, and Miscellaneous Remarks. 18mo. pp. 69. Providence. Barnum, Field, & Co.

EDUCATION.

A Polyglot Grammar of the Hebrew, Chaldee, Syriac, Greek, Latin, English, French, Italian, Spanish, and German Languages, reduced to one Common Rule of Syntax, &c. with an extensive Index, intended to simplify the Study of the Languages. By Samuel Barnard. 8vo. pp. 312. New York. Wilder & Campbell.

HISTORY.

The History of New England, from 1630 to 1649. By John Winthrop, first Governor of Massachusetts, with Notes by James Savage, with an elegant Engraving of the Author. Vol. I. 8vo. Price $3. Boston.

A Particular Account of the Battle of Bunker, or Breed's Hill, on the 17th of June, 1775. By a Citizen of Boston. 8vo. Boston. Cummings, Hilliard, and Co.

MEDICINE.

The Carolina Journal of Medicine, Science, and Agriculture, conducted by Thomas Y. Simons, M. D. and William Michel, M. D. Vol. I. No. I. for January, 1825.

The Philadelphia Journal of the Medical and Physical Sciences. No. XIX. Philadelphia. Carey & Lea.

MISCELLANEOUS.

An Oration delivered at Concord, April the Nineteenth, 1825. By Edward Everett. 8vo. Boston. Cummings, Hilliard, & Co.

The African Repository and Colonial Journal. Vol. I. No. II, for April, 1825.

A Dissertation on the Nature, Obligations, and Form of a Civil Oath. By William Craig Brownlee, D. D. 8vo. pp. 44.

POETRY.

The Pleasures of Friendship, and other Poems. By Dr James M'Henry. 12mo. Philadelphia. A. R. Poole.

THEOLOGY.

The Christian Spectator: conducted by an Association of Gentlemen. Vol. VII. No 5, for May, 1825.

Redeeming the Time; a Sermon by the Rev. Samuel M. Emerson, Pastor of a Church in Manchester.

The American Baptist Magazine. Vol. V. No. 5, for May, 1825.

Discussion of Universalism; or, a Defence of Orthodoxy against the Heresy of Universalism, as advocated by Mr Abner Kneeland, in the Debate in the Universalist Church, Lombard-street, July, 1824, and in his various Publications, as also in those of Mr Ballou and others. By W. L. McCalla. Philadelphia.

The Christian Journal and Literary Register, for May, 1825. New York. T. & J. Swords.

The Christian Examiner and Theological Review, No. VIII. for March and April. Boston. Cummings, Hilliard, & Co.

The Literary and Evangelical Magazine, Vol. VIII. No. V, for May, 1825. Richmond, Va.

Cunningham's Morning Thoughts on St Matthew. Philadelphia. A. Finley.

TRAVELS.

The Journal of Madame Knight and the Rev. Mr Buckingham, from the original Manuscript. Written in 1704 and 1710. 12mo. pp. 129. New York. Wilder & Campbell.

AMERICAN EDITIONS OF FOREIGN WORKS.

The Quarterly Review, No. LXII. Boston. Wells & Lilly.

The Lady of the Manor, being a Series of Conversations on the subject of Confirmation, intended for the Use of the Middle and Higher Ranks of Young Females. By Mrs Sherwood, author of Little Henry and his Bearer. 2 vols. 12mo. New York. E. Bliss & E. White.

On the Importance of the Study of Anatomy ; from the Westminster Review, with some Additional Remarks. 8vo. pp. 12. Boston. Wells & Lilly.

Quotations from the British Poets, being a Pocket Dictionary of their most admired passages ; the whole being Alphabetically Arranged according to their subjects. Philadelphia. Carey & Lea.

Lempriere's Universal Biography ; with Selections from Watkins, and American additions. 2 vols. 8vo. $8,25.

New Monthly Magazine. No. LI.

LIST OF WORKS IN PRESS.

A Treatise on the Law of Husband and Wife. By R. S. Donnison Roper, Esq. of Gray's Inn, Barrister at Law. New York. E. B. Gould.

Magee on the Atonement. From the last London edition. In 2 vols. 8vo. Philadelphia. S. Potter & Co.

Commentaries on the Laws of England, by Sir William Blackstone ; a new edition, with the last corrections of the author ; and with Notes and Additions by Edward Christian, Esq. Also containing Analyses and an Epitome of the whole work, with Notes, by John Frederick Archbold, Esq. In 4 vols. 8vo. Philadelphia. R. H. Small.

An Address to the Members of the Suffolk Bar, Boston, Mass. at their stated Meeting, on the first Tuesday of March, 1824. By William Sullivan. Boston.

Discourses on the Offices and Character of Jesus Christ. By Henry Ware, Jun. Minister of the Second Church in Boston.

Tadeuskund, the Last King of the Lenape. An Historical Tale. 12mo. Boston. Cummings, Hilliard, & Co.

Published on the first and fifteenth day of every month, by CUMMINGS, HILLIARD, & Co., No. 134 Washington-Street, Boston, for the Proprietors. Terms, $5 per annum. Cambridge: Printed at the University Press, by Hilliard & Metcalf.

THE UNITED STATES

LITERARY GAZETTE.

| Vol. II. | JUNE 15, 1825. | No. 6. |

REVIEWS.

Travels in the Central Portions of the Mississippi Valley: comprising observations on the Mineral Geography, Internal Resources, and Aboriginal Population. Performed under the sanction of Government, in the Year 1821. By HENRY R. SCHOOLCRAFT, U. S. I. A., &c. &c. New York. 1825. 8vo. pp. 459.

BY the treaties concluded between the United States and the Indians, at Spring Wells, St Mary's, and Saginaw, we acquired the larger and better part of the Michigan peninsula. But we had not yet gotten the whole—and as the Indian tribes had melted away until they were too few to hunt through the land reserved by them, and the game was getting very scarce, our national rulers, who, in their purchases of territory, illustrate the " nil actum credens, dum quid superesset agendum" admirably, thought it might be well to " extinguish the Indian title " to so much of the territory between the Lakes and the northern boundary of Indiana, as it still embraced. Accordingly, Governor Cass and Solomon Sibley were appointed, in 1821, commissioners to meet the Indians at Chicago, and make the contemplated purchase ; Mr Schoolcraft was secretary of the commission, and this volume is the record of his journey from Detroit to Chicago. The commissioners chose rather a circuitous route ;—the Indian trail, from the sources of the Raisin to Chicago, is computed to be about three hundred miles, but they saw fit to go down the Wabash to Shawnee-town, thence across Illinois to

26

St Louis, and thence up the Illinois to Chicago,—which, as
we should judge from the map, about quadrupled their journey.   But Mr Schoolcraft has made so pleasant a book out
of his experiences, that we should not have found fault had
his travels, and this record of them, been much longer.   The
country through which his course lay, is interesting on many
accounts ; he appears to be an excellent observer, and tells
well what he sees.   There is no affectation about him—unless
it be in an occasional preference of scientific terms over common words, which mean precisely the same thing,—and in its
literary character, the volume is highly respectable, and
creditable to its author.   In the Introduction Mr Schoolcraft
describes his work so accurately, that we will use his own
words.

This work does not aspire to the graver character of elementary
compositions, either in geography or statistics, in natural science, or in
moral research, while its details will occasionally partake of each.   A
narrative of daily events, will be interspersed with historical, descriptive,
and practical observations, with accounts of what the country has been,
and speculations respecting what it will be, and with such " appliances to
boot " as the time or the subject may suggest.   With these we shall
blend notices of the physical resources of the country ; more especially
in reference to the sciences of mineralogy and geology, and such passing remarks on the still imperfectly described manners and customs of
the Indian tribes, as we can feel a confidence in presenting.   To be faithful
in what we advance, will be to compass our highest aim.   Thoughts
committed to paper in the hurry of voyaging, often by the light of a
camp-fire at night, and literally revised " in the depths of the wilderness," will not be expected to bring to the classical scholar, either the
charms of diction, or the exactness of literary ease.   With these remarks
the reader will be enabled to follow us in the description of the voyage
more understandingly ; and we shall only entreat that he will not take
it ill, if the narration becomes tedious, when the journey is so.

The voyagers, having provided themselves with a light
travelling canoe, sailed along the southern shore of Erie, and
after a gale, which exposed them to some danger, they reached Maumee bay.   The first and second chapters contain
long accounts of the Indian wars of that vicinity.   Perhaps
Mr Schoolcraft tells nothing, or very little, that is absolutely
new, but his relations are interesting.   The following paragraph may serve to show how well the human character
adapts itself to all kinds of circumstances and exigencies.
If this heroic wife and mother had lived where the war-
hoop was never heard and the dangers and horrors of Indian warfare never reached, the strongest traits of her character might have never been developed and known.

On the 24th, the dwelling-house of a Mr John Merril, in Nelson County, Kentucky, was attacked by a party of eight Indians. Mr Merril was first alarmed by the barking of his dog. On going to the door he received the fire of the assailants, which broke his right leg and arm. They now attempted to enter the house, but were anticipated in their movement by Mrs Merril and her daughter, who closed the door in so effectual a manner as to keep them at bay. They next began to hew a passage through the door, and one of the warriors attempted to enter through the aperture: but the resolute mother seizing an axe, gave him a fatal blow upon the head, and then with the assistance of her daughter drew his body in. His companions without, not apprized of his fate, but supposing him successful, followed through the same aperture, and four of the number were thus killed before their mistake was discovered. They now retired a few moments, but soon returned, and renewed their exertions to force the house. Despairing of entering by the door, they climbed upon the roof, and made an effort to descend by the chimney. Mr Merril now directed his little son to empty the contents of a feather-bed upon the fire, which soon caused so dense and pungent a smoke, as nearly to suffocate those who had made this desperate attempt, and two of them fell into the fire-place. The moment was critical; the mother and daughter could not quit their stations at the door; and the husband, though groaning with his broken leg and arm, rousing every exertion, seized a billet of wood, and with repeated blows despatched the two half-smothered Indians. In the meantime the mother had repelled a fresh assault upon the door, and severely wounded one of the persons who attempted simultaneously to enter there, while the others descended the chimney.

These things occurred in 1793. It is interesting to contrast with such passages those which tell how the theatre of these horrors appears now.

The road is carried along the immediate banks of the stream, seldom deviating so far as completely to exclude it from the eye. We were pleased to see, where recent openings had been made in the forest, that the farmers had evinced the good taste to leave a number of the tallest and finest oaks, elms, and honey-locusts, as shade trees. Wherever the trees had been indiscriminately felled, the marly character of the soil, covered with a coat of impalpable dust, united to the great heat of the weather, rendered our progress slow and oppressive.

A short distance above Presque Isle, we turned from our way to inspect the construction of a newly finished grist-mill, driven by horse-power, and built on the principle of the inclined plane;—a method which is daily coming in vogue, in those level parts of the western country, where waterfalls are rarely to be found. It is recommended by the simplicity of its mechanism, and great cheapness; two important considerations in a district of country, in which neither money nor mechanics can be said to be superabundant. Here, the gentlemen from Fort Meigs took leave of us, and left us to reflect how much we stood in need of their remarks and experience in the subsequent parts of our journey.

A series of well-enclosed and well-cultivated farms, characterizes this part of the valley for a number of miles ; and we have seldom observed in any part of the Western States, such luxuriant and extensive fields of Indian corn. Although it was but the beginning of July, many of the stalks of this grain were above six feet in height, and had already put forth the silky tassel, which indicates the formation of the grain. Potatoes, cucumbers, and pumpkins were here in blossom ; and the mature growth of various pot herbs gave promise of an early and plenteous reward of horticultural labour.

The party proceed up the Maumee, cross the portage at Fort Wayne, and go down the Wabash. All this is travelled country, and there are many accounts of it ; but Mr Schoolcraft goes on, describing the most striking scenes which his voyage presents, and telling various anecdotes and stories, which the spots he passes by suggest to him,—and the reader accompanies him always without weariness and generally with pleasure.

A frequent mistake of their Canadian boatmen, in this part of the voyage, suggests to Mr Schoolcraft the following remarks.

We here had occasion to observe the repetition of an amusing mistake of our canoemen, who are Canadian Frenchmen, and of course Roman Catholics, with respect to the public buildings erected for county purposes, at the numerous towns we have passed ;—which they never fail to admire as being most commodious chapels.*

It is a little remarkable that the emigrants from New England should so easily lose the habit of religious exercises, and, if we may so speak, the taste for these customs, which one would expect to have become fixed by the constant usage of many generations ; but so it seems to be. At home, scarcely one of the many emigrants who go to people the Western Wilderness, was without his own seat in his meeting-

---

" * But does not this trifling incident prove more than the mere visual aberrance of unlettered peasants ? Does it not indicate one of those traits in the character of a people which may be seized upon to mark a predominance of national customs or manners—to distinguish an American from a striking French custom ? When the latter plant a colony, or found a settlement, one of the earliest and most important preliminaries regards the means of ensuring the speedy erection of a house of worship. The chapel of the cross, like the tabernacle of Judah, is first set up. Happy would it be if we were always equally attentive to this subject, in the foundation of our infant towns and settlements—we allude, more particularly, to those west of the Alleghanies. Our first public edifice is a court-house, a jail, then a school-house, perhaps an academy, where religious exercises may be occasionally held ; but a house of public worship is the result of a more mature state of the settlement. If we have sometimes been branded as litigious, it is not altogether without foundation : and, notwithstanding the very humble estimate which foreign reviewers have been pleased to make of our literary character and attainments, we are inclined to think there is still more likelihood of our obtaining the reputation of a learned, than of a pious people."

house, and scarcely one was unaccustomed to the religious usages of our land. Yet many respectable families of our yeomanry seek a new home, and gather themselves into villages and till their farms, and have their court-houses and school-houses, without any house devoted to religious meetings, and without any regular administration of religious ordinances.

There is, on page 158, an anecdote illustrative of another trait in the Yankee character.

The conversation now led to the various traits of character displayed by emigrants; whose *locus natalis* was thus clearly to be ascertained. Several jocose remarks on New England manners had been indulged. Some years ago, said General Taylor, Henry Clay and myself made an excursion upon the Wabash, above Fort Harrison. On descending the river, one evening, about the time we began to think of stopping for the night, we met a soldier who had killed a fine goose with his rifle, and, demanding his price, readily paid it. We stopped, a short distance below, at the house of a Yankee emigrant, to whom we presented our game. We took tea, rather at his solicitation than from any inclination of hunger, and lodged there. On getting up very early the following morning, we were just on the point of embarking, before it occurred to us, that our entertainer might expect payment for the tea, although, as is customary with us, we presumed he would accept nothing. On inquiry, he promptly stated his charges, which were as promptly paid; but the incident afterward afforded us a subject for laughter, when reflecting how narrowly we had escaped going off without paying our bill. We supposed, in the evening, the goose would have satisfied him for the tea. "But is it possible, General Taylor," replied Governor Cass, "that Henry Clay, the Speaker of the House of Representatives of the United States, and yourself, should think of travelling through the western country, and expect to pay your bills in *geese!*" And this was the best defence we could make for Yankee parsimony; for it must be acknowledged, the anecdote is quite illustrative of eastern providence.

The account of the lead mines of Missouri is minute and interesting. It places within reach of all, important information respecting this source of national wealth, and—so long as wars are fashionable and are carried on as they now are— this instrument of national security. The mines have been worked for a long period, but rather by farmers than miners; and hence there has not only been a great waste of effort and of material, but a very defective system of operations has become established. Certain rules and practices are fixed and universally recognised, and they have become as obligatory as the Stannary laws of Cornwall. In smelting the ore, no fuel but wood can be used, as coal has not been discovered in the country. At no very distant period the ore must be carried down to the Mississippi, and smelted with the coal upon its banks, as it will cost less to carry the dross of the ore to the river than coal to the mines, and the metal must go to the river at all events.   These mines are national property, having been reserved in the sales of public lands; they are leased by the executive authority at a rent of one tenth of the produce, payable in lead.   It is said that the leases are very eagerly sought.   The country where the mines are situated is less barren than mining countries usually are; most of it is well suited to the cultivation of the *cerealia*.   The following passage compares the produce of these mines with those of other countries.

The greatest lead mines on the globe, according to Professor Jameson, are those of Great Britain, which produce an annual quantity of 250,000 quintals.   The next in point of importance are those of the several kingdoms and states of Germany.   France yields 60,000 quintals; Spain 32,000; and Russia 10,000.   Although we have estimated, from imperfect data, the quantity of lead raised from the earth in Missouri, at about 25,000 quintals per annum, yet it must appear evident, that the mineral capacities of the country are adequate to employ profitably almost any amount of labour that can be applied to them.

On the 17th of August the Commissioners met the Indian Council at Chicago, and although the Indians at first peremptorily refused to sell their lands, they were, after a negotiation of some days, induced to accede to the terms offered. The debates are recorded with great minuteness, but such readers as are interested in observing the character and habits of Indians, will not find this part of the work tedious.   It is a little amusing to observe how assured the governor was throughout the negotiation, of its successful termination.   He says to the Indian orators, " I know we shall in the end conclude a bargain for the lands, and have therefore listened to what has been said without any apprehension about the result."   And it was in this spirit that he seems to have talked and acted throughout the controversy.   Some severe things have been said about the management of the American commissioners in conducting this affair, but Mr Schoolcraft declares,—indeed we may say, shows,—that they have little foundation.   The following remarks upon some observations which certain English journalists made upon this treaty, are true, sensible, and patriotic.

The result of this treaty was hardly announced in our public journals, before it was published in England, with some severe animadversions. " The United States," observes the editor of the London Times, " have driven another bargain, and a hard bargain it is, with the miserable Indians. For thirty-five thousand dollars in merchandise, a little more than five thousand pounds in money, as valued by those who furnished it, and an annuity of less than two thousand pounds per annum, Governor Cass, whose diplomatic talents appear on this occasion to have been highly applauded by his countrymen, has prevailed upon the helpless aborigines to surrender five millions of fertile acres, to the westward of the lakes, and equal in surface to about one fourth of Ireland. Verily, Governor Cass may be said to understand his business."

This long-enduring prejudice, and habitual propensity to vilify our country and our institutions, seems to be confined to no particular political sect in Great Britain, nor to exempt from its operation any particular measure, which, by the power of association, is calculated to call up our original sin, of thinking, and acting, and judging for ourselves. With a power to expel the Indians from a territory, which, during all our wars with Great Britain, they have only occupied as a convenient avenue to make inroads upon our frontiers, we draw them into amicable treaty on the restoration of peace, and pay them what they acknowledge an ample equivalent for their title. We introduce into all our treaties provisions for bettering their condition, and enlightening and improving their minds. We furnish them blacksmiths and teachers, implements of husbandry and stock. We pay them large annuities; we pass laws to protect them from the cupidity of traders; and we employ agents to reside among them, to ensure the punctual payment of these annuities, and the faithful observance of these laws; and attend to their numerous wants, and complaints, and distresses. If it be asked what amount of moneys we pay them, what laws we have enacted to protect their territorial rights and to preserve their morals, let our statute books furnish the reply. If it be asked what injuries we have redressed, what distresses we have relieved, let the monthly, and quarterly, and annual returns of our Indian, and our subsistence department be examined. And yet, because we have not done all that an enlightened, virtuous, humane, and opulent nation could, might, or perhaps ought to do, all this is to pass for nothing, or, if we would believe the vituperative prints of England, to be put down to the score of ingratitude, neglect, and national depravity.

Our English neighbours, in the Canadas, manage these matters in a different way. When they covet a piece of Indian territory, they boldly take possession of it, in the name of the king. There is no consulting with the chiefs and head men of the tribe, no long and expensive treaty, no recognition of their title to the soil which is so unceremoniously taken away, and no annuities paid out with punctilious formality. The thing is cut short " by His Majesty's command." This single line has cancelled more Indian title in America, than the government of the United States ever have, or probably ever will purchase, with all their accumulated and accumulating wants and means. But let us, for a moment, cast our eyes upon Hindostan, and behold the unholy wars, the murders, and abominations, which, like a burning sirocco, have swept away the native institutions of that devoted country, and drenched it with the blood of its simple, unoffending inhabitants. It is truly becoming, in those who have despoiled the rich inheritance of about ninety millions of Hindoos, to reproach us for paying a few scattered bands of hunters for portions of territory which they do not want, cannot improve, and are willing to part with.

We wish this volume contained more information respecting the Michigan Territory; this portion of our country is becoming more interesting every day, and we know less of it than we should, whether we consider its importance or the facility with which it may be, and, indeed, perpetually is explored.

It is rather remarkable, that the tide of emigration, which set so strongly from the east to the west, should have rolled by the southern boundary of this peninsula without leaving scarcely a solitary deposite within its borders. Perhaps one reason for this was, that the New-Englanders, who were induced to desert the homes and graves of their fathers, were prompted by the love of change, or the hope of improving their condition, to go where the soil and climate might vary as far as possible from that they had left. There can be little doubt that, in these respects, Michigan is more like New England than any other portion of our yet unsubdued wilderness. In temperature, in the changes and general character of the seasons, and in the nature of the soil, there is a great resemblance. In parts of the territory epidemic disease occasionally prevails; but it is probably as salubrious, taken as a whole, as any unreclaimed, well watered, and heavily wooded country can be. In process of time it must give sustenance to a very large population. If one half the area of the peninsula be considered unproductive, and this is certainly a large allowance, there will remain nearly twelve millions of acres capable of cultivation; and it must not be forgotten, that those parts of this territory which are too low and flat for cultivation, are almost universally thickly wooded with forests of the most useful and necessary timber. Should any circumstances occur to throw forward upon the western country another wave of emigration, the advantages offered by this fine territory will not be again neglected. Indeed, it is now rapidly filling up, and in the common course of things, will doubtless soon support a population as dense as that of some more southern districts, which, within the memory of young men, were, as this is now, an untamed and almost unvisited wilderness.

1. [*Report of a Committee of the Overseers of Harvard College.*]
Boston. 1824. 8vo. pp. 11.
2. *Remarks on a Report of a Committee of the Overseers of Harvard College, proposing certain Changes, relating to the Instruction and Discipline of the College; read May 4, 1824, and to be taken into consideration June 1, 1824.* By One, lately a Member of the Immediate Government of the College.
Cambridge. 1824. 8vo. pp. 12.
3. *Report of a Committee of the Overseers of Harvard College, January 6, 1825.* Cambridge. 1825. 8vo. pp. 179.
4. *Speech of John Pickering, Esq. before the Board of Overseers, on the question of the acceptance of the Report of a Committee recommending some Alterations in the Discipline and Mode of Instruction in the University.* Published in the American Statesman, February 1, 1825.
5. [*Memorial of the Resident Instructers of Harvard College to the Corporation of that Institution.*] 1824. 8vo. pp. 31.
6. *Remarks on a Pamphlet printed by the Professors and Tutors of Harvard University, touching their Right to the Exclusive Government of that Seminary.* By an Alumnus of that College. Boston. 1824. 8vo. pp. 58.
7. *A Letter to John Lowell, Esq. in Reply to a Publication entitled "Remarks on a Pamphlet, printed by the Professors and Tutors of Harvard University, touching their Right to the Exclusive Government of that Seminary."* Boston. 1824. 8vo. pp. 102.
8. *Further Remarks on the Memorial of the Officers of Harvard College.* By an Alumnus of that College. Boston. 1824. 8vo. pp. 36.
9. *Report of a Committee of the Overseers of Harvard College, on the Memorial of the Resident Instructers. January 6, 1825.* 8vo. pp. 23.
10. *Speech delivered before the Overseers of Harvard College, February 3, 1825, in behalf of the Resident Instructers of the College. With an Introduction.* By ANDREWS NORTON. Boston. 1825. 8vo. pp. 59.

THE University at Cambridge, like every other important establishment, has at all times found many in the community who were ready to discredit its management and censure its officers. The vulgar, whether great or small, who are unable to appreciate intellectual endowments or to conceive of intellectual labour, have been inclined to look with an

27

evil eye upon those who seem to thrive without exertion. The friends of those who may have missed the honours or suffered the punishments of the institution, have occasionally permitted partial affection to get the better of their love of discipline in the abstract. Those who were unable to govern their children at all, have been disappointed that they could not be governed at College with a milder sway. And of those who were without children, some have wondered that severity should be necessary in the government of the young, while others have been astonished that it was so seldom exercised. The literary *outs*, again, have looked coldly on the literary *ins* ; and the parties, whether religious or political, which have at different times divided the state, have not been more ready to agree on the subject of the management of the University, than on any other considerable point. Difficulties and clamours from such sources were to be expected ; and the governors of the College have submitted to bear what human wisdom could neither prevent nor avoid.

Within a few years, however, the complaints and objections have assumed a shape, and proceeded from quarters, which seemed to demand more attention. Not the careless and inimical only, but the well-wishers of the institution have lately thought they could perceive evils which required remedy, and incongruities which demanded explanation. It appeared to them that the number of pupils and their improvement was not in proportion to the increasing wealth and endowments of the College. They heard of frequent and large bequests to the funds, while they perceived no diminution of the expenses of education. They were told of the increasing apparatus and advantages of the institution, and were surprised that its classes did not greatly outnumber, and that in some instances they did not even equal, those of other institutions much less richly endowed. The reproach of these matters, when uttered by those unacquainted with the nature of the government, fell principally upon the resident instructers, who, of course, felt somewhat uneasy under the blame of a system over which they had no control, and for the errors of which, if any existed, they were not responsible. This uneasiness has been manifested in various ways, as will appear in the sequel of this article. In the mean time, as the real nature and organization of the government of Harvard University may not be known to the majority our readers, we shall quote the following account of it from one of the pamphlets at the head of this review.

The institution has been almost entirely under the control of the Corporation, a body, which has been composed of the President of the College, and six non-resident members; and which perpetuates itself, by filling its own vacancies. The Corporation originate all laws, appoint to all offices, confer degrees, and have the disposal of the funds of the College. Their more important measures are subject to the approval or rejection of the Overseers. But the power of the latter body has lain, till within a short period, almost dormant, and its proceedings have been little more than matters of form. * * *

The Overseers consist of the Governor of the State, the Lieutenant Governor, the Speaker of the House of Representatives, the President of the College, the members of the Council and of the Senate, all *ex officiis*, and of twenty permanent members, namely, ten laymen and ten clergymen, chosen from the community at large. Beside the Corporation and Overseers, there is a third body, called the Immediate Government, composed of the President of the College, of most of the resident instructers, and of the librarian. Four resident instructers, on account of the character of their offices, or from some other particular considerations, are not members. The duties of the members of this body, collectively and individually, are simply to carry into effect the laws of the Corporation respecting instruction and discipline.

Professor Norton's Speech, p. iv.

We quote from the same pamphlet the account of the first steps towards the correction of the abuses and evils which were supposed to exist in the system of instruction and discipline.

It is well known to many, that for a considerable number of years past, great dissatisfaction with the condition of the College has existed in the minds of the resident officers, and others who have had an opportunity for a near view of its real state. In the summer of 1821, that is, about four years and a half since, a paper was drawn up by a highly respectable officer of the institution in the form of a letter to a member of the Corporation, containing a statement of some of the evils which existed, accompanied with proposals of remedy and reform. This communication, taken in connexion with the prevailing dissatisfaction with the state of the College, led the Corporation to direct their attention to the subject. A circular letter addressed to the resident instructers, and to one instructer not resident (I am uncertain whether to any others), was accordingly issued by them, dated in September, 1821. It filled seven closely written folio pages, and contained a great variety of questions, respecting the discipline, instruction, and morals of the students, to which answers were requested. Replies were given by most of the gentlemen addressed, as soon as practicable, some of them entering into the subject much at length. These replies were referred to a committee of the Corporation; and, that body having apparently by its proceedings pledged itself to undertake a reform, it was confidently expected by some that important changes would be introduced. Nothing, however, was done except promulgating some regulations respecting the expenses and dress of the students. With this exception, the whole business was suffered to sleep. In the summer of 1823, two years after the subject had been first agitated; when it had become apparent that no effectual measures were to be expected from the Corporation, the only body, which, according to the usages of the College, exercised the power of originating any measure, the feeling of discontent with the existing state of things, which had been in some degree suspended by the hope of improvement, again recovered strength. It was determined by some gentlemen, with the full consent and approbation of those resident officers, who were acquainted with the design, to endeavour to bring the subject before your Honourable Body. p. 3.

So far matters seem to have been conducted with sufficient prudence and caution. The following proceedings seem more remarkable for zeal than good judgment. We continue the quotation from Professor Norton.

In July, 1823, several gentlemen were accordingly requested to meet in Boston at the house of a distinguished officer of the College. The gentlemen, thus called together, met, to the number of nine; but, unfortunately, there was no resident officer of the College among the number invited. The gentlemen, however, who composed this meeting, discussed the nature of the improvements and changes, which the institution was thought by them to require, and determined to use proper measures to procure the appointment of a committee of your Honourable Body, for the purpose of recommending to the Overseers the plan which had been agreed upon. p. 4.

If evils existed which the Corporation could not or would not remedy, it was expedient to procure an investigation by the board of Overseers—to prove to this board the existence of these evils; and when the facts were ascertained, to use means, if necessary, to excite them to call on the Corporation for the amendment of the abuses. To the Corporation, as Professor Norton intimates above, it belongs to " originate laws ;"—the business of the Overseers is to confirm or annul the doings of the Corporation. To call on the board of Overseers for an investigation of the actual state of the College is one thing; it was a very different one, we apprehend, to take measures for recommending to them " a plan which had been agreed upon," by a number of gentlemen, who supposed themselves to be better acquainted with the evils and wants of the College than its appointed governors. A plan, too, which, " unfortunately," very unfortunately, we think, had been drawn up without the advice and concurrence of the resident officers. Certainly, if the Corporation are thrown out of the question, as they evidently were by the proposers of this reform, the resident officers must be the only body who have adequate knowledge of the true state and deficiencies of the institution. What were the Overseers expected to do with the plan recommended? What could they do with it? They could send it to the Corporation to be acted upon if it pleased the gentlemen of that body, or to sleep with the statement which was addressed to them in the first instance. The Overseers could demand of the Corporation a reform of existing evils or the supply of existing wants; and when they were satisfied of either, they would doubtless make such demand. The thing necessary, therefore, as we before observed, was to demonstrate to them that the present state of the College needed improvement in the whole system of government and instruction, or in certain parts of it. The proper questions for the consideration of the Overseers would seem to be—What is the state of the College? Do any evils or wants exist, and what are they? What circumstances displease us, and what shall we call upon the Corporation to amend? These points were to be ascertained carefully and deliberately by a committee or otherwise, and the necessity of reform demonstrated—and that by public investigation, before any notice could be taken of a plan framed upon the presumption of evils, the existence of which was inferred from private, unofficial, and therefore, inadequate information; and, in some instances, from data which were exceedingly erroneous. The gentlemen in this instance, therefore, it must be acknowledged, were somewhat more hasty in their views than the magnitude and importance of the work which they assigned themselves would seem to justify. We extract from Professor Norton the account of the doings of the committee, which, in consequence of these measures, was appointed " to inquire into the state of the University, and to report at the next meeting, or as soon thereafter as may be, whether any, and if any, what changes it would be expedient to recommend to the Corporation for its adoption relating either to instruction or discipline."

Immediately after the appointment of this committee, I took the liberty of addressing a letter to the chairman, in which I strongly urged the importance of consulting the resident instructers respecting those changes which would most conduce to the good of the College; of cooperating with them; and of taking advantage of their knowledge and judgment respecting the institution, and their deep concern in its prosperity. His answer was satisfactory. But there was, notwithstanding, no communication whatever between your committee and the resident instructers, on the subject of their report. It was not seen, nor were its features known by any one of them, before it appeared in print. I have, during the present session of the General Court, received a message from the chairman of that committee, stating, that before offering the report in question, he had believed that it had been seen by the resident instructers and had met their approbation; and that particularly he had expected my support. My opinion of the report has already been publicly expressed;[*] and the character of the proposals it contains is of such a nature, that I feel confident, that every one, having any practical acquaintance with the concerns of the College—any one who is, or who has been, a resident officer of the institution, will concur with me generally in that opinion. I must regret that the Hon. Chairman of your committee, after finding that he had been misinformed upon so very material a point, as the approbation or acquiescence of the resident instructers, did not mistrust his information upon other subjects, concerning which it was not so easy to ascertain the truth. p. 4.

Let us now hear the committee's own account of the matter. They respectfully beg leave to report,

That they have had several meetings on the subjects referred to them, and have been greatly assisted in their inquires and deliberations by a Committee of the Corporation appointed at the suggestion of the Board of Overseers. At these meetings the most free and unreserved interchange of opinion has taken place between the gentlemen of both Committees, and every topic has been discussed in a spirit of the most liberal candour. The result is now to be communicated.

In examining subjects of such importance and difficulty, affecting the character and destiny of the University, it did not escape the Committee of this Board, that every proposal for an alteration in the existing mode of instruction and discipline in the University ought to be received with caution, and adopted only upon the fullest deliberation. The present state of the University affords just cause of congratulation among its friends. At no period, perhaps, has it been more flourishing, or possessed more reputation. On examining the history of its past state, there will be found a steady progress in useful knowledge, in the means of instruction and in the adaptation of those means to the public wants, constantly advancing with the public patronage. It may be safely affirmed, that at this moment the University stands the first in rank and honour in the nation; and it ought not to be forgotten, that its present elevation is, in a great measure, owing to the disinterested services of some of our most enlightened citizens.

It is not therefore with any notion of detecting faults in the past management of the concerns of the University, that the Committee have entered upon their laborious duties. On the other hand, their present inquiries have led to the belief, that as much has been hitherto accomplished at the University, for philosophy, science, and classical learning, by the President, Professors, and Tutors, as the means placed within their power could reasonably enable them to accomplish. In point of fact, the University has undergone very great changes by the increase and subdivision of Professorships, and in the modes of instruction, within the last twenty years. These changes have not perhaps ac-

" [*] In 'Remarks on a Report of a Committee of the Overseers of Harvard College: By One, lately a Member of the Immediate Government of the College.' "

complished all that was expected, because they were engrafted upon
the existing system, from time to time, without that system itself having undergone a general and correspondent modification.

In a society, like ours, which is continually expanding and embracing
more elevated objects of research, the nature and extent of an University education, and the methods of instruction, must be, in some degree,
liable to change, so as to be adapted to the spirit of the age. A course
of studies, fully adequate, at one period, to all the wants and wishes of
the community, may be ill fitted for another of higher cultivation. A
moderate knowledge of classical literature, of philosophy, and the sciences, may satisfy all that the ordinary business of life requires, at an
early period of national existence; and yet it may fall far short of the
demands, even of humble education, in a more aspiring age. The same
thing may be affirmed as to the discipline and economical arrangements
for the internal government of an University. A system is not therefore necessarily good for the future, because it has accomplished much
good in the past. The great question must always be, what modes of
instruction are best adapted to the present exigencies of our society, so
as to give the most finished education in the shortest period that our
pursuits require. It is as unwise to resist improvements called for by
the spirit of the age, as it is to court innovations merely to gratify a
restless love for new experiments.

This seems a remarkable result. " A dissatisfaction with
the condition of the College exists in the minds of the resident officers, and others who have an opportunity of a near
view of its present state." An application is made to the
Corporation for redress and reform. The application is supposed to have been ineffectual. Resort is then had to the
Overseers; and their committee, assisted by a committee of
the Corporation, find " that the present state of the University affords just cause of congratulation among its friends;"
" that at no period perhaps has it been more flourishing, or
possessed more reputation," &c. &c.—and that " it is not with
any notion of detecting faults in the past management of the
concerns of the University, that the committee have entered
upon their laborious duties. On the other hand, their present inquiries have led to the belief, that as much has been hitherto
accomplished at the University, for philosophy, science, and
classical learning, by the President, Professors and Tutors, as
the means placed within their power could reasonably enable
them to accomplish." The resident officers are the friends
of the University or they are not. If they are not they
should be turned out; and the College cannot be considered
in a good condition, while they remain. If they are friends,
they should, by this report, have " just cause of congratulation," on account of its present state. But they are said to

be dissatisfied with its present state, and surely if they are reasonable men, they can render a reason for their disapprobation. Were their objections altogether groundless, or were the committee, which was appointed, it would appear, in consequence of this dissatisfaction, ignorant of its existence? Or was there no real and general dissatisfaction among the resident officers? It seems an " intricate impeach," and we cannot understand why a dissatisfaction, which was clearly something more than " the spirit of the age," and which was sufficient to call the attention of the superior boards of the College, should not have been examined into and censured if it were groundless, or explained if it were well founded. The preamble of this report is obscure and wanting in that distinctness which is necessary to make any thing intelligible to common understandings. It seems to be implied, that the present mode of instruction and government is not " the best adapted to the exigencies of society, so as to give the most finished education in the shortest period that our pursuits require." Why not? What are its particular defects? are natural questions, to which no answer is given in the Report, except what is to be inferred from scattered passages in it. We do not find in it any clear distinction between the faults of the system, and those of the governors of the College.. Thus in one part of the Report we are informed, that the expenses of the students are too great, and such as require a system of sumptuary laws; but sumptuary laws are a part of the present system, and if they are not well constructed or well administered, there is surely mismanagement somewhere—either on the part of the Corporation, who frame—of the Overseers, who sanction or reject—or of the Immediate Government, who execute.

We intended to present to our readers a full analysis of the new system proposed by this committee, but shall omit this as likely to occupy much more room than we can well afford. Some of the propositions certainly appear to be judicious, as the shortening of vacations and the discountenancing of servants. But on these points opinions differ much among those acquainted with the subject. The committee propose, among other plans for lessening the expense, that " all the students shall be required to board in commons," and they seem to take it for granted, that this will lessen the expenses of College on the whole. But this is by no means evident. In foreign universities, where no commons exist, a larger proportion of the students subsist at a rate considerably lower than they could in any common establishment, which could well be constructed. For the price and arrangement of commons, after all,'must be established according to some average. The poorer students must pay more than they otherwise would, while the rich will pay less, and all will be dissatisfied. Relinquish commons altogether, and the College will at once be freed from the trouble and expense of managing this part of the establishment. But commons, it is said, are a necessary check upon private boarding-houses, which, without this, would be extravagant; which is to suppose that boarding-houses in Cambridge will be conducted upon principles different from those in any other town, where competition always reduces the rate of profits to the lowest possible point; not to mention that in many instances the students could procure their own provisions at a still cheaper rate than they could be furnished either in commons or in a boarding-house. Besides, it is obvious that the boarding-houses might then, as in point of fact they are now, be under the control of the government, which will always have the power to deprive them of their boarders. We said the trouble as well as the expense of commons, and this is a point of great importance, since it is well known that by far the greater number, as well as the most serious, of the disturbances in Harvard College have been more or less connected with the establishment for commons. We do not, however, intend to recommend the relinquishment of this establishment, or any other measure. We are sensible of the objections and difficulties that beset any project for reform, however plausible in appearance. We mean merely to show that the advantages of the positions, taken with such decision by this committee, are not quite so evident as they seem to have imagined.

The Report, to which we have alluded, was taken into consideration at the meeting of the Overseers on the first day of June, 1824. From the vote passed on that day we should suppose that the majority of that board were of opinion that they were not sufficiently enlightened by it, respecting the actual state of the College, which, as we have been contending, was the proper object of investigation. They appointed another committee, " with instructions to make a report setting forth in detail the finances of the University and its ways and means; an estimate of its expenses for the present year, and an account of the compensation, obligations, and duties of the instructers; of the course of study and progress of

28

the students, and of the practical inconveniences, if any, arising from the present organization of the Immediate Government; and to propose such specific regulations as they should deem conducive to the prosperity of the Institution; and to revise the College Laws, and reduce them to a simple and brief form." To this committee was also referred a Memorial of certain of the resident officers. Of this Memorial, and the discussions to which it led, we shall speak in another part of this article, endeavouring thereby to keep distinct two several series of proceedings and arguments, which we believe have been frequently confounded by the public.

[*To be continued.*]

The Travellers. A Tale. Designed for Young People. By the author of Redwood. New York. 1825. 18mo. pp. 172.

A work from the pure and instructive pen of the author of Redwood cannot fail to be welcome; and as we eagerly seized on this little volume, so we read it with pleasure, and assure our readers that they will do the same. It has much of the same sweetness and beauty of style and sentiment which characterized the former work; though it seems somewhat hasty and unfinished. We might make objections to a few particulars; but as it would neither show our ingenuity nor profit our readers, we prefer to express in general terms our approbation.

The idea on which the story is built is very happily conceived, easily uniting the interest of a fictitious narrative with the description of real places and the memory of actual events. A family is represented as making " the grand tour of Niagara, the lakes, Montreal, Quebec, &c." This affords an opportunity for describing places and local habits, which has been just sufficiently used. Some beautiful though short descriptions of natural scenery occur, and a few romantic events; and a great many moral reflections drop from the mouth of the mother for the instruction of her children. Upon the whole it is a pleasant book, as may be guessed from the few *morceaux* which we are able to serve up on our pages. We will just remark, in passing, that the author has sometimes forgotten to keep herself down to the level of young people, and writes in an elevated and poetical strain, which it belongs to the mature to appreciate.

The scene at Niagara may give a good idea of the general tone of the book.

"The vehement dashing of the rapids—the sublime falls—the various hues of the mass of waters—the snowy whiteness, and the deep bright green—the billowy spray that veils in deep obscurity the depths below—the verdant island that interposes between the two falls, half veiled in a misty mantle, and placed there, it would seem, that the eye and the spirit may repose on it—the little island on the brink of the American fall, that looks amidst the commotion of the waters like the sylvan vessel of a woodland nymph gaily sailing onward; or as if the wish of the Persian girl were realized, and the 'little isle *had* wings;'—a thing of life and motion that the spirit of the waters had inspired.

"The profound caverns with their overarching rocks—the quiet habitations along the margin of the river—peaceful amid all the uproar, as if the voice of the Creator had been heard, saying, 'It is I, be not afraid.'—The green hill, with its graceful projections, that skirts and overlooks Table-rock—the deep and bright verdure of the foliage—every spear of grass that penetrates the crevices of the rocks, gemmed by the humid atmosphere, and sparkling in the sun-beams—the rainbow that rests on the mighty torrent—a symbol of the smile of God upon his wondrous work.

"'What is it, mother?' asked Edward, as he stood with his friends on Table-rock, where they had remained gazing on the magnificent scene for fifteen minutes without uttering a syllable, 'what is it, mother, that makes us all so silent?'

"'It is the spirit of God moving on the face of the waters—it is this new revelation to our senses of his power and majesty which ushers us, as it were, into his visible presence, and exalts our affections above language.

"'What, my dear children should we be, without the religious sentiment that is to us as a second sight, by which we see in all this beauty the hand of the Creator; by which we are permitted to join in this hymn of nature; by which, I may say, we are permitted to enter into the joy of our Lord? Without it we should be like those sheep, who are at this moment grazing on the verge of this sublime precipice, alike unconscious of all these wonders, and of their divine Original. This religious sentiment is in truth, Edward, that Promethean fire that kindles nature with a living spirit, infuses life and expression into inert matter, and invests the mortal with immortality.' Mrs Sackville's eye was upraised, and her countenance illumined with a glow of devotion that harmonized with the scene. 'It is, my dear children,' she continued, ' this religious sentiment, enlightened and directed by reason, that allies you to external nature, that should govern your affections, direct your pursuits, exalt and purify your pleasures, and make you feel, by its celestial influence, that the kingdom is within you; but,' she added smiling, after a momentary pause, ' this temple does not need a preacher.' "

The episode of Marguerite and Louis may afford another specimen.

"A commandant of this fort (which was built by the French to protect their traders against the savages,) married a young Iroquois who was before or after the marriage converted to the Catholic faith. She was the daughter of a chieftain of her tribe, and great efforts were made by her people to induce her to return to them. Her brother lurked in this neighbourhood, and procured interviews with her, and attempted to win her back by all the motives of national pride and family affection; but all in vain. The young Garanga, or, to call her by her baptismal name, Marguerite, was bound by a threefold cord—her love to her husband, to her son, and to her religion. Mecumeh, finding persuasion ineffectual, had recourse to stratagem. The commandant was in the habit of going down the river often on fishing excursions, and when he returned, he would fire his signal gun, and Marguerite and her boy would hasten to the shore to greet him.

"On one occasion he had been gone longer than usual. Marguerite was filled with apprehensions natural enough at a time when imminent dangers and hairbreadth escapes were of every day occurrence. She had sat in the tower and watched for the returning canoe till the last beam of day had faded from the waters;—the deepening shadows of twilight played tricks with her imagination. Once she was startled by the water-fowl, which, as it skimmed along the surface of the water, imaged to her fancy the light canoe impelled by her husband's vigorous arm—again she heard the leap of the heavy muskalongi, and the splashing waters sounded to her fancy like the first dash of the oar. That passed away, and disappointment and tears followed. Her boy was beside her; the young Louis, who, though scarcely twelve years old, already had his imagination filled with daring deeds. Born and bred in a fort, he was an adept in the use of the bow and the musket; courage seemed to be his instinct, and danger his element, and battles and wounds were 'household words' with him. He laughed at his mother's fears; but, in spite of his boyish ridicule, they strengthened, till apprehension seemed reality. Suddenly the sound of the signal gun broke on the stillness of the night. Both mother and son sprang on their feet with a cry of joy, and were pressing hand in hand towards the outer gate, when a sentinel stopped them to remind Marguerite it was her husband's order that no one should venture without the walls after sunset. She, however, insisted on passing, and telling the soldier that she would answer to the commandant for his breach of orders—she passed the outer barrier. Young Louis held up his bow and arrow before the sentinel, saying gaily, "I am my mother's body-guard you know." Tradition has preserved these trifling circumstances, as the events that followed rendered them memorable.

"The distance," continued the stranger, "from the fort to the place where the commandant moored his canoe was trifling, and quickly passed. Marguerite and Louis flew along the narrow foot path, reached the shore, and were in the arms of———Mecumeh and his fierce companions. Entreaties and resistance were alike vain. Resistance was made, with a manly spirit, by young Louis, who drew a knife from the girdle of one of the Indians, and attempted to plunge it in the bosom of Mecumeh, who was roughly binding his wampum belt over Marguerite's mouth, to deaden the sound of her screams. The uncle wrested the knife from him, and smiled proudly on him as if he recognised in the brave boy, a scion from his own stock.

" The indians had two canoes; Marguerite was conveyed to one, Louis to the other—and both canoes were rowed into the Oswegatchie, and up the stream as fast as it was possible to impel them against the current of the river.

" Not a word nor cry escaped the boy : he seemed intent on some purpose, and when the canoe approached near the shore, he took off a military cap he wore, and threw it so skilfully that it lodged, where he meant it should, on the branch of a tree which projected over the water. There was a long white feather in the cap.   The Indians had observed the boy's movement—they held up their oars for a moment, and seemed to consult whether they should return and remove the cap; but after a moment, they again dashed their oars in the water and proceeded forward.   They continued rowing for a few miles, and then landed ; hid their canoes behind some trees on the river's bank, and plunged into the woods with their prisoners.   It seems to have been their intention to have returned to their canoes in the morning, and they had not proceeded far from the shore, when they kindled a fire and prepared some food, and offered a share of it to Marguerite and Louis.   Poor Marguerite, as you may suppose, had no mind to eat ; but Louis, saith tradition, ate as heartily as if he had been safe within the walls of the fort.   After the supper, the Indians stretched themselves before the fire, but not till they had taken the precaution to bind Marguerite to a tree, and to compel Louis to lie down in the arms of his uncle Mecumeh.   Neither of the prisoners, as you may imagine, closed their eyes.   Louis kept his fixed on his mother.   She sat upright beside an oak tree ; the cord was fastened around her waist, and bound around the tree, which had been blasted by lighting ; the moon poured its beams through the naked branches upon her face convulsed with the agony of despair and fear. With one hand she held a crucifix to her lips, the other was on her rosary.   The sight of his mother in such a situation, stirred up daring thoughts in the bosom of the heroic boy—but he lay powerless in his uncle's naked brawny arms.   He tried to disengage himself, but at the slightest movement, Mecumeh, though still sleeping, seemed conscious, and strained him closer to him.   At last the strong sleep, that in the depth of the night steeps the senses in utter forgetfulness, overpowered him—his arms relaxed their hold, and dropped beside him and left Louis free.

He rose cautiously, looked for one instant on the Indians, and assured himself they all slept profoundly.   He then possessed himself of Mecumeh's knife, which lay at his feet, and severed the cord that bound his mother to the tree.   Neither of them spoke a word—but with the least possible sound they resumed the way by which they had come from the shore ;   Louis in the confidence, and Marguerite with the faint hope of reaching it before they were overtaken.

" You may imagine how often the poor mother, timid as a fawn, was startled by the evening breeze stirring the leaves, but the boy bounded forward as if there was neither fear nor danger in the world.

" They had nearly attained the margin of the river, where Louis meant to launch one of the canoes and drop down the current, when the Indian yell resounding through the woods, struck on their ears.   They were missed, pursued, and escape was impossible.   Marguerite panic-struck, sunk to the ground.   Nothing could check the career of Louis. " On—on, mother," he cried, " to the shore—to the shore."   She rose

and instinctively followed her boy.   The sound of pursuit came nearer
and nearer.   They reached the shore, and there beheld three canoes
coming swiftly up the river.   Animated with hope, Louis screamed the
watch-word of the garrison, and was answered by his father's voice.
"The possibility of escape, and the certain approach of her husband,
infused new life into Marguerite.   "Your father cannot see us," she said
"as we stand here in the shade of the trees; hide yourself in that thicket,
I will plunge into the water."   Louis crouched under the bushes, and
was completely hidden by an overhanging grape-vine, while his mother
advanced a few steps into the water and stood erect, where she could
be distinctly seen.   A shout from the canoes apprized her that she was
recognised, and at the same moment, the Indians who had now reached
the shore, rent the air with their cries of rage and defiance.   They
stood for a moment, as if deliberating what next to do; Mecumeh maintained an undaunted and resolved air—but with his followers the aspect
of armed men, and a force thrice their number, had its usual effect.
They fled.   He looked after them, cried, 'shame!' and then with a
desperate yell, leaped into the water and stood beside Marguerite.   The
canoes were now within a few yards—He put his knife to her bosom
—"The daughter of Tecumseh," he said, "should have died by the judgment of our warriors, but now by her brother's hand must she perish:"
and he drew back his arm to give vigour to the fatal stroke, when an
arrow pierced his own breast, and he fell insensible at his sister's side.
A moment after Marguerite was in the arms of her husband, and Louis,
with his bow unstrung, bounded from the shore, and was received in his
father's canoe; and the wild shores rung with the acclamations of the
soldiers, while his father's tears of pride and joy were poured like rain
upon his cheek."

MISCELLANY.

A RESIDENCE IN GLASGOW.

DR. CHALMERS AND MR IRVINE.

MY DEAR FRIEND,
          I have at last found leisure to redeem my promise
of giving you an account of my visit to the "commercial metropolis" of Scotland.   On the thirtieth morning after leaving
New York, we caught a glimpse of the blue hills of Ireland,
and inhaled the strong fumes of her turf fires.   The odour was
not quite so grateful as that you are regaled with from the young
pine-trees, as you approach our own Southern coasts; but it came
fresh from the land; and that was enough to give it a zest to
those who had not seen the green earth for a whole month.   The
day was fine, but calm.   Towards evening, however, a breeze
sprung up; and, before we went to sleep, we could discern the
rocky and naked hills of the Western Isles.

To the American traveller approaching the western coasts of Scotland, the most striking feature of the country, is the bare and desolate aspect of the surface. As he sails up the Clyde, he sees here and there a romantic spot which city opulence has appropriated for the site of a villa, and the enjoyment of health or of indolence. On drawing near to the "quays" of Greenock he is struck with a few of the pecularities of auld Scotland :— draught-horses of hideous, disproportioned make, with legs thick enough to be split up into a double set for any American quadruped of the same kind ; a profuse display of bare feet and ankles, on the part of the women and children on the wharf, the ankles of the former remarkable for their doric air of massiveness, strength, and durability ; and "though last, not least," the harsh accents of the national dialect, growling along the line of idlers, inquirers, and porters, that forms an animated margin to the quay.

A steam-boat passage succeeded, and brought me to Glasgow in a few hours. It was Saturday afternoon, when I arrived. I had barely time to enjoy one noble view, as I hurried along to my boarding-house, or "lodgings," as the Scotch call it. The view I have mentioned, is that which, all at once, presents itself to you, on entering the principal street of the city, after you came up from the river. I have been you know in many a "farre countrie," and have seen many a fine city ; but the view from the west end of Argyll street eastward to Trongate street of this city, if taken on a summer afternoon, whilst a little shade yet falls on the south side, is one of the most striking I have ever seen. The street is very wide ; and to the terminating point of your view, about a mile long. If you stand in the western part of the street you have before you a history of the architectural taste of successive ages. Near you are the neat, but comparatively slight, fabrics of modern days, farther eastward, the air of the buildings becomes more and more ancient and venerable, till your eye rests on the spire of the Tron church, on the one hand, and that of the old Tolbooth on the other. The mass of stone of every shape and hue, and the grotesque aspect of some of the time-worn edifices in the eastern end of the street, are new and striking objects to the eye of an American.

My first sally into the street was on Sunday morning, to St John's church, a non-descript piece of architecture in the eastern part of the city, but the centre of attraction for the many passengers who throng the pavement of the Gallowgate, as they move onward "to hear Dr Chalmers." I went in company with the son of my landlady, who occupied a pew in that church. The steps were thronged by a crowd of rejected applicants for admission ; the desire of hearing so distinguished a preacher, inducing many struggles to attempt forcing their way in, to the no slight inconvenience of the legitimate pew-holders.

We got in just as the preacher rose to read out the first psalm. The reading was excessively awkward, his voice wretched, and his pronunciation so disfigured by national accent as to be sometimes unintelligible. Still there was a vein of deep and earnest emotion pervading the whole exercise, which made it, to say the least, impressive. His opening prayer I shall remember whilst I live. It was begun in the low husky utterance, which he has entailed on himself by that excessive exertion of the voice which is inseparable from the vehemence of his emotions, and the climax fashion of his interminable sentences. At first he was barely audible ; but he seemed to gather strength as he proceeded. There was still, however, a kind of hesitancy in his manner: he seemed to labour with gigantic conceptions, for which even his own lofty expressions were utterly insufficient. His countenance bespoke a solemnized fervency of feeling, such as I had never before seen on human features. The vehemence of his manner startled me at first ; but I soon lost sight of this, and of his accent, and of all that was disagreeably peculiar in his manner. A more sublime address to the throne of eternal majesty I have never heard from the lips of man. The force of the preacher's mind seemed to burst through the veil that hides the spiritual world from ordinary minds, and to be holding intercourse with living and present realities. Every thing that he wished you to perceive, became as it were palpable to the very sense. In the conceptions of his grand, but somewhat rude mind, the grotesque I found often mingled with the sublime. What do you think, for instance, of the following idea in a prayer? Alluding to the commercial distress then prevailing, and interceding for the victims of a glutted market, his expressions were, " And now that the surfeited and overlain world is rolling back on the heads of its children, the fruits of their frantic speculations," &c.

But it was in the sermon that the preacher seemed to make his deepest impression. He began in the same manner as in the psalm and the prayer, and went through the introduction in a sort of conversational undertone which almost bordered on the ludicrous. As his ideas expanded, and his feelings began to play, he became more and more animated in his delivery, from animation he rose to vehemence, and from vehemence I had almost said to phrenzy ; he literaliy screamed till his voice broke. His one and only gesture was repeated with fiercer and yet fiercer energy till he seemed about to fling himself from the pulpit. Then his corporeal powers would fail ; he would make a long pause, and wipe off the copious perspiration which actually gushed from his head and face. Here a roar of coughing &c. &c. from all parts of the church, reminded you of the breathless stillness, which had hitherto reigned over the audience. Silence once more resumed its sway, and the preacher began again in his low broken utterance. Again he rose, and again he sunk under fatigue; till at last, he was fairly compelled to take refuge in the expedient of breaking off and giving out a psalm to be sung, whilst he was recovering his jaded energies.

The succession of effort and respite in the speaker, drew away my attention, sometimes even from the magnificent succession of images which the eloquence of the composition raised before me; and more than once, I could not help thinking of an account of an English boxing-match, which I had read in an old newspaper; the pugilists had so many rounds of athletic effort and so many minutes respite, in succession, till the struggle was closed. However, to speak the sober truth, there is a moral sublimity in the spectacle of a man sacrificing his health and his life to a sacred enthusiasm; and this must be the sum total of the eloquence of Dr Chalmers' delivery; for in every other point of view it has no power whatever.

In force and sublimity of thought, Dr Chalmers has surpassed the whole generation of preachers among whom he lives. For my own part, I never had so many new and stupendous thoughts brought before me in one hour, as in the discourse I heard that morning. They say that people of every, and of no character, crowd to hear this preacher. I do not wonder at the fact. Mental excitement is, more or less, the happiness of all men; and certainly it can nowhere be had to a higher pitch, than in a sermon of Dr Chalmers.

[*To be continued.*]

ITALIAN LYRICAL POETRY.

DE ROSSI.

Giovanni Gherardo de Rossi, a gentleman of Rome, was distinguished, among the Italian poets of the last century, as the author of comedies and of small poems. To the former are assigned a very high rank by Sismondi, and they are praised for their vigorous and exact painting of manners, their elegance of language, their liveliness, wit, and ingenuity; although, in consequence of the bitterness of their satire and their too vivid representation of low and vicious characters, they have enjoyed little popular success. My present business is with his poems only, which consist of epigrams, fables, short amatory pieces, and all the varieties of light, fugitive poems. They are lively, animated, and pretty, but of a

29

very slight texture, and destitute of all genuine sentiment; being, in short, good examples of the cheap, easy, *extemporaneous* verses, with which the modern Italian Parnassus abounds. As illustrating national taste, therefore, and as specimens of a popular poet, rather than for any uncommon merit of the original pieces themselves, I proceed to my translations from this author, in which I scarcely attempt to imitate their versification with much care.

THE WOLF AND THE SHEPHERD.

A wolf, who, grown infirm and old,
  Could rob and rend the flock no more,
Kneeled to the shepherd of the fold
  For pardon, and devoutly swore
His hand from rapine to withhold,
If he might share the food in store : —
You should have come, our shepherd said,
To beg before your teeth decayed.

IL LUPO E IL PASTORE.

Un Lupo che già vecchio non potea
Sul gregge esercitar lo strazio usato,
Fe' sapere al pastor ch' egli volea
Far penitenza d' ogni suo peccato,
Dalle stragi cessar, da ogni opra rea,
Purché parco alimento gli sia dato :
Disse il Pastor : si umani sentimenti
Dovea spiegarmi quando aveva i denti.

LOVE'S ANTECHAMBER.

A solemn audience Love proclaims
  And gives Caprice the usher's rod,
Who, deaf to merit's idle claims,
  Admits his minions to the god.

Frolic and Laughter first appeared,
  Yet neither made a long delay ;
But Youth was much caressed and cheered,
  And Grace and Beauty urged to stay.

With Folly, Love held large discourse,
  Nor gave less time to Jealousy,
Since wont to both to have recourse
  For many a potent remedy.
And Treachery came with troubled eye,
  Yet seemed, when passing out, to smile ;

Then Scorn addressed the Deity,
  Who, though they'd lived averse awhile,
Yet sent his guest well pleased away ;

Fidelity and Innocence,
Who came their best respect to pay,
  Slighted, in anger hurried thence.

And now bad Love, in guise polite,
  Received and welcomed all the rout,
Save Reason, whom Caprice in spite
  Had left to stay uncalled without.
At last Caprice, who joyed to view
  His ancient foe thus stand apart.

L' ANTICAMERA D' AMORE.

Udienza solenne
  Amore un giorno tenne ;
  Il regolar l' ingresso
  Fu al Capriccio commesso,
  Che senza aver rispetti
  A chi più merto avea
  Gli amici prediletti
  Al Nume introducea.
Entraro il Riso e il Gioco,
  Ma si trattener poco.
Con Amore assai più
  Parlò la Gioventù.
Fu la bellezza udita,
  Ma colle Grazie unita.
Dopo la Gelosia
  Ascoltò la Follia,
  E momenti non brevi
  Ad ambedue concesse,
  Perchè affari non lievi
  Suole affidare ad esse.
Torbido in viso e tetro
  Passò poi il Tradimento ;
  Ma nel tornare indietro
  Parve lieto e contento.
Entrò lo Sdegno ancora
  A favellar col Nume ;
  E benchè ad esso ognora
  Avverso di costume,
  Pur gli si lesse in volto
  Che avealo bene accolto.
Fu ammessa la Costanza
  Coll' Innocenza a lato ;
  Ma usciron dalla stanza
  In aspetto turbato.
Avea già udito Amore
  Tutto l' accorso stuolo,
  E la Ragione solo
  Aspettava al di fuore ;
  Che a lei per odio antico
  Il Capriccio nemico

Said,—Here is madam Reason too,
　And smiled with triumph in his heart.

Love, when he heard the ungrateful name,
　Pensive, abashed, his head let fall,
And said,—Too late the lady came ;
　'T is best she make another call.

BEAUTY FREE.

Unthinking Beauty loud complains,
　That love has loaded her with chains ;
Old Time, who sees her twist and writhe,
　Soon cuts her fetters with his scythe ;
Proud of her liberty and grace,
　The nymph Love meets and quick accosts ;
Holding a mirror to her face,
　Behold, he cries, what freedom costs.

LOVE TURNED PAINTER.

One day, dear Sarah, with surprise,
　I marked young love in busy mood ;
His bandage stripped from off his eyes,
　Before a frame he painting stood :—
But when I came a step more near
　To view the youthful limner's art,
Judge of my wonder and my fear;
　His pencil was a pointed dart,
　The canvass my poor naked heart ;—
Where, lo ! thy lovely traits appear !

Aveva per dispetto
　D' annunciarla negletto ;
　E allor che il Nume vide
Dal lungo udire stanco ;
　V' è la Region par anco,
　Dice ; e fra sè poi ride.
Quando quel nome ascolta
　Pensoso abbassa i guardi,
　Poi dice Amore : è tardi;
　Che passi un' altra volta.

LA BELLEZZA IN LIBERTA'.

Gemeva la Bellezza
　D'Amor fra le catene avvinta e op-
　　pressa ;
Il Tempo le si appressa,
　E colla falce le divide e spezza ;
A lei, ch' esulta allor lieta e felice,
　Di nuovo Amor si accosta ;
　Le presenta uno specchio, e poi le
　　dice :
Guarda la libertà quanto ti costa.

AMORE PITTORE.

Un dì sorpreso, o Fille,
　Vidi Amor fanciulletto,
　Che, squarciata la benda alle pupille,
Pingeva attento innanzi al cavalletto :
　Ma quando mi appressai
Al Pittore novello,
　Doppiamente sorpreso rimirai,
　Che un dardo era il pennello,
　La tela era il mio core,
　E la tua imago dipingeva Amore.
　　　　　　　　　　　C. C.

ORIGINAL POETRY.

THE SOUL OF SONG.

Where lives the Soul of song ?
Dwells it amid the city's festive halls ?
Where crowd the eager throng,
Or where the wanderer's silent footstep falls ?

Loves it the gay saloon,
Where wine and dances steal away the night,
And bright as summer noon
Burns round the pictured walls a blaze of light ?

Seeks it the public square,
When victory hails the people's chosen son,
And loud applauses there
From lip to lip in emulous greetings run ?

Dwells it amid the host,
Who bear their crimson banners waving high ;
Whose first and only boast
Draws tears of anguish from the patriot's eye ?

Follows it on the path,
Where the proud conqueror marches to his home,
And wearied of his wrath
Smiles as he steps beneath the imperial dome ?

No—not in festive halls,
In crowded marts, nor in the gay saloon ;
Not in the forum falls,
Nor on the conquering host, the gracious boon :

But where blue mountains rise
Silent and calm amid the upper air,
And pure and cloudless skies
Bend o'er a world, that lies below as fair ;

But where uncultured plains
Spread far and wide their beds of grass and flowers,
And heaven's bright pencil stains
Clear gems that roll away in silent showers ;

But in the depth of woods,
Where the slant sunbeam gilds the hoary trees,
And the soft voice of floods
Glides on the pinions of the evening breeze ;

But in the broken dell,
Where the crispsed ivy curls its tangled vines,
And the wild blossom's bell
Drops with the dew, that in its hollow shines ;

But in the gulfy cave,
Where pours the cascade from the glacier's height,
And all its waters wave,
Like rainbows, in their luxury of light ;

There dwells the Soul of song,—
It flies not to the city's festive halls
But loves to steal along,
Where the lone wanderer's silent footstep falls.

P.

THE PROCLAMATION OF SALADINE.

Fui et nihil amplius.

The wars of Saladine are ended ;
Half Asia's sons in bondage sleep ;
And few are left that e'er offended,
And fewer still that do not weep.
No foe is left his sword to try on ;
O'er the wide East he reigns alone,
For Guy is dead, and Cœur de Lion
Re-occupies his British throne.

Now tired of war, with havock sated,
And rich with battle's glorious spoil ;
The ship of state with daggers freighted,
Its chief unfit for further toil.
He, knowing that his reign is over,
That death's cold hand is o'er him flung,
Calls to his tent the desert-rover,
And bids these warning words be sung.

" I Saladine, long Asia's wonder,
Lord of the land where Nilus flows ;
Whose word went forth arrayed in thunder,
Who fed his crocodiles on foes ;
Now being aged, my sinews failing,
And weakness creeping through my bones,
Leave these few words to conquerors sailing
O'er seas of blood to short-lived thrones.

" Of birth and parentage most lowly,
I came Noureddin's troops to lead ;
And ere I warred against the unholy,
I grasped the sceptre of his seed.
Ye know my deeds, by fame recorded,
My power and valour stand confessed,
But know, the realms o'er which I lorded
Like mountains lie upon my breast.

" Why came, ye 'll ask, regret unto him ?
Mourn hunters when they win the game ?
Why crept the chill of horror through him ?
What grieved, since he had won him fame ?
Ye 'll not talk thus, when ye are jaded
With toils of war, and youth has flown ;
Ye 'll not ask why, when ye have waded
Through blood and carnage to a throne.

" But ye will ask why the red torrent
At all rushed from the battle field ;
And ye shall seek but find no warrant
For the stained cimiter and shield.
Nought shall the fame on which ye prided
Avail you in the dying hour ;
Then could ye see your realms divided,
So ye were free from Eblis' power.

" Now wherefore does the soldier cherish
His thirst, unsated and uncloyed ?
Reckless he sees whole nations perish,
And none repeopling the void.
What gains he by his deeds of violence ?
By blossoms cropt like flowers by frost ?
A rood of land :—a little while hence
He goes to count its awful cost.

" Now here I lie ;—o'er Asih's master
A worthless leech dominion holds ;
No Kurd that roves o'er Dewen's pasture
A heart so sore as mine enfolds.
What though my actions are recorded,
My power and valour stand confessed ?
Yet know the realms o'er which I lorded
Like mountains lie upon my breast."

         J.

It was stated in a New York Paper a short time since that the Moon was nearer
the Earth at the present time than it has been for 500 years previous. The following lines were suggested by the fact.

Mild Queen of light and loveliness,
I hail thy nearer smile ; for thou
Dost love with thy chaste look to bless
The stricken heart ;—and even now
While I am gazing on thy face,
I feel the cooling tears come stealing,
As if they knew thy light should chase
Away the shades of tearless feeling.
Why comest thou, with that sweet smile
Of eloquence, so near us now,
Gazing with thy calm look the while,
As if our world were pure as thou,
And thou did'st love to gaze and dwell
Upon our path, as we on thee ?
Perhaps thou 'rt sad, and there 's a spell
Of soothing in our sympathy ;
Or haply thou art come to bring
The weary ones of earth away,
And I should be with thee a-wing,
Unshrouded from these robes of clay.
Canst thou not send some minister
Of thy pavilion down, to lead
My spirit where thy chariots are,
When from its earthiness 't is freed ?
I long to stretch my flight away—
My pinion's plumage fades beneath
The dampness of this weight of clay—
'T would brighten at the touch of death ;
And with the flood of hope and feeling
Which mingles in thy silver light
Pour'd on my soul, and thy revealing
To make my aery vesture bright,
Oh I would wing it up with thee
To the pure source of light and love,
And sweep my lyre eternally
To the sweet airs they sing above.

         ROY.

CRITICAL NOTICES.

Westminster Review for April, 1825.

The first article in this number treats of the "Law of Libel and Liberty of the Press." It contains much ingenious reasoning which our limits will not permit us to analyze, in support of the following positions, which the reviewers, in conclusion, consider as fully established :

" That the law of England, as delivered by its authorized interpreters, the judges, however earnestly the same judges may occasionally disavow this doctrine, prohibits all unfavourable representation with respect to institutions, and with respect to the government and its acts: and, consequently, that if any freedom of discussion is permitted to exist, it is only because it cannot be repressed; the reason why it cannot be repressed, being, the dread of public opinion."

The greater part of the reasoning of course relates to public libels. The following extract exhibits the opinion of the reviewers concerning private libels.

" In most law books, if we look for a definition of libel, we find nothing but a fiction. Libel is punishable, we are there told, because it tends to provoke a breach of the peace. The person libelled, may, out of resentment, commit the crime of assault against his accuser; it is fit, therefore, that the law should extend its protecting shield over the libeller, and save him from the chance of a broken head, by inflicting upon him a year's imprisonment. A tweak by the nose, according to this doctrine, should be more criminal than any libel, for it is certainly far more likely to provoke the species of retaliation alluded to. Miserable as this fiction is, it has served as a foundation to lawyers for building up the excellent law maxim, ' the greater the truth, the greater the libel.' A bad man, it is alleged, is more easily provoked than a good man! and a true accusation, being usually more cutting than a false one, exposes the accuser to a greater hazard of being knocked down !

" ' One might almost as reasonably contend,' says Mr Mence, ' that it ought to be criminal in point of law for any person to carry money about him, lest it should tempt some scoundrel to pick his pocket or knock his brains out. The punishment in such a case, as the law now stands, would fall upon the thief, instead of the tempter. And the peace would be at least as well secured, and the interests of morality much better consulted, in cases of alleged libel, by punishing not the man who exposes vice and holds it up to deserved infamy; but the man whose vicious conduct is exposed, and who to his crimes has added the farther crime of braving the disgrace, and committing violence upon the person who may justly and meritoriously have exposed him.'

" The reader may be curious to learn for what purpose this ludicrous fiction was invented. The purpose was to render libel a penal offence, instead of being merely a civil injury. Had it been classed among private offences, under the head of injuries to reputation, it would have been necessary to prove, in the first place, that an injury had really been sustained ; and then the damages awarded would not have exceeded a fair compensation for the actual injury which had been proved. To make it a public offence, it was erected into a sort of virtual breach of the peace, which, again, by another equally contemptible fiction, is the king's peace ; and thus, a libel against an individual became an offence against the king.   Englishmen, who have been accustomed to hear, and to believe, that the law is the perfection of human reason, will be astonished to learn, that there is scarcely one, even of its good principles, which has any thing better than such fictions as the above for its basis.   *In fictione juris semper æquitas*, say the lawyers.   It is an assertion which they would not venture to put forth, were not the apathy of the public a sufficient security for its being believed without inquiry. Yet here is, at any rate, one instance (and every one who has examined the law without a resolution to find every thing as it should be, can supply many more), in which such fictions have been devised for the most mischievous of all purposes."

The next article is devoted to " Schlegel's Lectures on Literature." The reviewer gives Schlegel the credit of learning and ingenuity, but accuses him of endeavouring to pervert the public mind ; his opinion of the work is thus summed up.

" We close our remarks on a book, which, possessing many excellencies, and teaching many truths, aims principally at introducing into the mind, under cover of an artful eloquence, the principles of slavery ; and at perpetuating the dominion of bigotry and despotism undisguised and unashamed.   Mr. Schlegel stands forward, the unblushing advocate of the debasing principles of the Austrian government; and makes even his literary discussions the means of perverting the minds of the rising generation."

The third article gives a detailed account of the discoveries in " Magnetism," by M. Poisson in France, and Professor Barlow in England. It is an exceedingly elaborate as well as curious and interesting article. That part, which relates to M. Poisson's researches into the general laws of magnetism, we have not space to analyze, but must confine ourselves to a brief account of Professor Barlow's invention, which we noticed slightly in a former number of this Gazette.   It has been observed of late years, that besides that variation of the compass needle, which takes place to a degree more or less considerable in different parts of the globe, and which is independent of any known external circumstances, except geographical position, there is another depending upon the local attraction of the iron, contained in ships.   This has become more remarkable since the introduction of iron cables, ballast, capstans, water tanks, &c.   Now it is obvious that the greater part of this mass of iron being between the compass, in its usual situation, and the head of the ship, it will have a powerful tendency to keep the needle in a direction parallel to the keel, or length of the vessel.   It will therefore be of no consequence only when the ship is sailing on the magnetic meridian, or for the sake of clearness, throwing the natural variation out of the question, when she is steering north or south.   On the contrary when she is steering east or west the local attraction will be exactly opposed to the natural direction of the compass, and not being known may lead to fatal accidents, as it undoubtedly has done in many instances of otherwise unaccountable shipwrecks. This variation amounted in the Griper, swung for the purpose in the river Thames, to 14°, at east and west, making an extreme difference of 28°, or about two points and a half, and this increased so rapidly in high latitudes, that in some of the late northern expeditions, the compass was actually stowed away as an useless article. We are unable to detail the various experiments of Professor Barlow, with a view to the correction of this evil. It is sufficient to state generally, that he found that when the compass was placed over a large iron ball, the north end of the needle was attracted; when it was placed beneath it, the south end was attracted in like manner. By moving the ball vertically it was found to pass through a point which had no effect on the needle; and the same result was obtained, whether the ball was solid, or hollow with any thickness greater than one twentieth of an inch; or whether a ball, bar, or plate, was used. The result is, that he has been enabled to construct a plate, which, without being inconvenient from its size or weight, is sufficient when placed in a certain position abaft and near the compass, to counteract and neutralize the disturbing forces already mentioned. This nautical guide is thus restored to its former credit and usefulness; and the merit of its restorer is certainly akin to that of its first discoverer.

An article on Italy praises a work entitled " Rome in the Nineteenth Century, with a zeal and heartiness rather unusual among critics, and this praise is so well supported by the extracts from the book, that we cannot but hope it will be republished in this country. On the subject of the exportation of machinery, the reviewers are in opposition to the Quarterly. The reasoning is on the general principles of the advantages of free trade. Enable your neighbours, say they, to make silk, cotton, woollen, or any other goods, cheaper than they now do, and you will be able to buy them cheaper, your imports will be greater, and you will grow richer. You cannot sell without buying, and the cheaper your neighbours can manufacture, the better will be your bargain. In fact the policy of nations should be to sell any overplus that their neighbours will buy: and if they, say the reviewers, can make every thing else, why, sell them machinery, which it appears they cannot make. It seems to us that this reasoning is correct. If the maxims upon which the removal of restrictions and prohibitions are founded, are good for any thing, they are applicable to every article, and if restrictions upon the cotton, the woollen, or the silk trade are absurd and impolitic, they are just as much so, when extended to the exportation of machinery. The maxim, that it is best to let the natural course of commerce alone, appears to be the one which governments, whether despotic, limited, or popular, are least willing to learn. The British government are leading the way in this department of improvement, with decided steps, and it is among the deepest mortifications, which an intelligent American is called on to suffer, that his government, whose very key-stone is the abolition of absurd prejudices, should still cling to the miserable dogmas of the theory of restriction and protection.

[*To be continued.*]

30

Redfield ; a Long-Island Tale, of the Seventeenth Century. New York, 1825. pp. 214.

There is very little to be said about this novel.   There is nothing in it to praise very highly, and nothing that calls for very severe censure. It moves, for the most part, on a dead unvaried level of mediocrity, seldom sinking below, and as seldom rising above.   The hero, Redfield, is a young gentlemen, who has left England, in the troublesome persecutions of the reign of Charles II. to take refuge in the colonies, and the volume is occupied with the narrative of his shipwreck,—his rescue by the Indians,—his introduction to an English gentleman-farmer on Long Island, with whose daughter he falls in love,—his doubts and misgivings on the propriety of this passion.   Then follows a history of his trading voyage among the Indians for furs, occupying some fifty or sixty pages, which we would recommend to the especial consideration of the North West Company, and of all persons engaged in a similar traffic;—his sagacity and prudence as displayed in the negotiation or rather the purchase of a treaty for the tribe of Indians, by whom he had been saved from drowning, which we believe might have been got for half the money ;—and finally, his own marriage and that of a couple of his aboriginal friends ; which with some circumstances of minor importance, close the book.

It will be perceived that, except to an author of very powerful genius, the subject affords no opportunity for the excitement of strong feeling, and accordingly there are few striking scenes and little development of interesting individual character.   The principal faults to be remarked, besides those which must be apparent from what has been said, are a looseness in the use of language, a carelessness in the construction of sentences, and occasionally some considerable defects of grammar.   A few instances of such inaccuracies we subjoin.

" Here the rude sons of nature became expert *whalers*, the fat *of which* they tried down to oil."

" There are few perhaps who have not heard the *term, Indian file*, made use of, *which* is this: the elder chief took the lead," &c.

" Tamane saw without a tear the conflagration of her *nativity*."

There is a want of relish and spirit in the dialogue among some of the lower characters ;—this is not so remarkable ; but among the gentlemen and ladies there is certainly a great want of colloquial powers.   The following is a specimen ; though, perhaps, not a very favourable one.

" ' What sail is that ? ' says he, as he looked upon the Sound. ' Certainly 'tis a vessel.   It cannot be a waterfowl! '   Miss Norwood now rose from her seat, saying, ' I will get the spy-glass,' and in an instant she handed the instrument into his hands.

" He looked steadfastly upon the magnified object, saying, ' It seems a sloop, and is standing this way.   Her sails are hanging loosely, for want of wind.   The tide is, however, in her favour, and waits her along with the help of sweeps, I perceive.   Possibly it is the trader, returned already.   I think the vessel compares.' "

We suspect no gentleman in the reign of Charles the First or Second could have invented so outrageous an Americanism, as is put into the mouth of such an individual, p. 53.

" ' And before I left the place, *located upon this site* for the erection of my buildings.' "

Poems by John Turvil Adams. New Haven. 1825. 12mo. pp. 47.

Who John Turvil Adams is, we do not know, and we are glad that we do not. We set ourselves to réad his poems through, but, while reading the first page, were surprised by a shadowy consciousness, that we had seen something *like* it before; as we read on, the mist began to clear away, till at length we took up our copy of Bryant's " Ages;" and exclaimed, in the words of Wordsworth, " Like ! but oh how different ! " If any one will have patience to do as we have done, compare Mr Adams' " Our Country " with Bryant's " Ages," he will see a curious process of transmutation; and learn that, though no alchymist may have succeeded in changing lead into gold, Mr Adams is a proficient in the art of transmuting gold into lead. The first half or three fourths of " Our Country," may be tolerable poetry to those, who have not read the " Ages;" but after that, where Mr Adams has been either thrown upon his own powers, or has poached upon a less luxuriant manor, the drivelling is insupportable. As to the smaller pieces annexed, they are, if possible, worse. Truly, if there were not two or three such men, as Percival, Bryant, and Hillhouse, we should give up the poetical department of our review in hopeless disgust. We trust, however, there are more such men yet to make their appearance; and we consider it our duty to the young whose minds may be tainted by trash like these poems, before they have learned to discriminate, occasionally, to brush such insects as their author away from the fields of our springing literature. It is never our wish to depress hope, where there is any ground for hope; and if we could have found one good line, or hemistich even, in this volume, which we believed to be original, we would gladly have quoted and praised it; but we have travelled from the Dan to the Beersheba thereof, and it is all barren.

INTELLIGENCE.

SUBSIDENCE OF THE BALTIC.

A very singular and interesting fact has been ascertained respecting the level of the Baltic. It had been long suspected that the waters of this sea were gradually sinking; but a memoir, published in the Swedish Transactions for 1823, has put the change beyond a doubt. Mr Buncrona, assisted by some officers of the Swedish piloting establishment, has examined the Swedish coast with great care from latitude 56° to 62°, and Mr Halstrom has examined those of the Gulf of Bothnia. The results of both inquiries are given in the form of a table; and though, as might have been expected, they are not completely uniform, they correspond sufficiently to place the subsidence of the waters beyond dispute. The Baltic, it is to be observed, has no tides, and is therefore favourably situated for making observations on its level; but with regard to the periods within which the changes observed have taken place, it was of course necessary to rely on records or oral testimony. At the latitude of 55°, where the Baltic unites with the German ocean through the Categat, no change seems to be perceptible. But from latitude 56°

to 63°, the observations show a mean fall, of one foot and a half in forty years, or four tenths of an inch annually, or 3 feet ten inches in a century. In the Gulf of Bothnia, the results are more uniform and indicate a mean fall of four feet four inches in a century, or rather more than half an inch annually. The Baltic is very shallow at present, and if its waters continue to sink as they have done, Revel, Abo, Narva, and a hundred other ports, will by and by become inland towns ; the gulf of Bothnia and Finland, and ultimately the Baltic itself will be changed into dry land.

SAY'S AMERICAN ENTOMOLOGY.

The first volume of this work has been published, and so far as mechanical execution is concerned, it fully answers the most sanguine expectations which had been formed respecting it. Of its merits in a scientific point of view we do not pretend to be competent judges ; but there can be little doubt, from the well known talents, science, and industry of its author, that it is deserving of equal commendation in this respect. As a work of American art it fully keeps up the character established by Wilson's American Ornithology ; and the engravings of some of the most beautiful insects are executed in a style not inferior to that of the most celebrated foreign productions of the same kind. In its plan, however, we fear that this book is essentially defective. As a book to be read, it is fit only for the mere scientific entomologist ; it consists almost wholly of the dry details of technical description, with very little notice of the manners, habits, physiology, &c. of insects, which are the only interesting parts of this subject to the general reader, and ought to be the most so even to the entomologist. The charm which the excellent work of Wilson possessed to all readers was derived from this source, and the subject of entomology is capable of being made almost as interesting as that of ornithology. At present the work of Mr Say is not exactly what is wanted, by either the man of science or the general reader. It is too costly and ornamental in proportion to its quantity of matter, to suit the purposes of the former, and too dry and technical to be relished by the latter, except as a book of fine engravings. We hope however, notwithstanding this, which we consider a mistake in the plan, that it will receive the ample encouragement which it deserves as a specimen of art and a monument of the talents and science of its author.

ITALIAN NOVELISTS.

Mr Thomas Roscoe has translated selections from the Italian novelists, in four volumes 12mo, and added notes, critical and biographical. "It is interesting to observe," says a reviewer of the work, "the progress of that mental alchymy, by which metal, base, soiled, or shapeless, becomes delicate in its polish, and graceful in its proportions. Into no worthier hands could the task of selection and translation have fallen than into those of Mr Roscoe ; he has both the industry for research and the taste for appreciation. The character of these Italian novels is well known ;—partly historical facts dressed up romance fashion ;—odd hoaxes ;—love tales, purely imaginative, and others of a humorous and satirical turn. They reflect the whole spirit of the age in which they had birth." The collection contains selected tales so far back as the *Cento Novelle Antiche*, or Hundred Ancient Tales, down to Robustiano Girono; and it is to the last degree curious to remark in how many forms these fictions have become familiar to us.

RUSSIAN WINES.

Dr Lyall, in his travels in Russia, describing his visit to the Imperial vineyards in the vale of Sudák, says, they are of considerable extent, and, besides the native vines of the climate, they contain many species which have been introduced at different times. The kinds of wine now made here, chiefly from foreign vines, are (as literally translated) red and white wine of Zante,—red and white wine of Corfu,—red French wine,—white Hungarian wine,—and red claret! besides different kinds of red and white Krimean wine. The whole quantity of wine produced by these vineyards in 1821, amounted to 60,000 védros (each of fifteen small-sized bottles). According to their quantity they were sold at from two and a half to four roubles *per* védro; so that the whole revenue, perhaps, amounted to above 200,000 roubles.

TRAVELS IN GREECE.

Dr P. O. Bröndsted has issued a prospectus of an extensive work to be published in London, called "Travels in Greece," accompanied with critical and archæological researches, and illustrated by maps and numerous engravings of ancient monuments recently discovered. A society of artists and travellers, of whom the author was one, undertook and executed a series of journies in European and Asiatic Greece, in the course of which they discovered, chiefly by means of excavations, several monuments of Greek art of the highest interest, as well as many other remains very important to Grecian archæology, and to the elucidation of the manners and institutions of this illustrious people. These researches were made in the years 1811, 1812, 1813, and 1820; and the proposed work will contain their principal results.

"His great object has been to collect, from his journals and portfolios, all that appears to him new, remarkable, or important, whether it has reference to science, to art, or to the proper understanding of the present state of Greece; to place these chosen materials before the reader with a rigorous regard to historical truth, and to explain them, as well as he is able, by the assistance of modern erudition.

"The large plates will contain works of Greek sculpture never before published, together with figures, bas-reliefs and bronzes recently discovered, views of remarkable places, geographical and topographical plans, fac-similes of unpublished inscriptions, and outlines of many other objects, which will be regularly classed."

The work is divided into eight parts or numbers, the last of which will be concluded by a critical review of all the travels or rather of all the scientific inquiries undertaken in Greece from Pausanias to the present time. Four of the numbers will be published during the present year, a part in Royal and a part in Imperial 4to, and the remaining four in the course of the next.

NEW PUBLICATIONS.

ARTS AND PHILOSOPHY.

The Boston Journal of Philosophy and the Arts. No. XI. Boston. Cummings, Hilliard, & Co.

COMMERCE.

A Report of the Secretary of the Treasury, on the Commerce and Navigation of the United States during the year ending on the 30th of September, 1824. 8vo. pp. 300. Washington, D. C. Gales & Seaton. Price $2.

EDUCATION.

A Complete Key to Smiley's Arithmetic, entitled, The New Federal Calculator, or Scholar's Assistant, &c. By T. T. Smiley, Teacher, author of School Geography, &c. Philadelphia. I. Grigg.

GEOLOGY.

Lectures on Geology; being Outlines of the Science; delivered in the New York Athenæum in the year 1825. By Jer. Van Rensselaer, M. D. Associate, and Lecturer on Geology to the Athenæum, &c. 8vo. pp. 358. New York. E. Bliss & E. White.

HISTORY.

The History of Boston. No. XI. Boston. A. Bowen.

LAW.

Trial of Amos Furnald for the Murder of Alfred Furnald, before the Superior Court of Judicature, holden at Dover, within and for the County of Strafford and State of New Hampshire, on the first Tuesday of February, A. D. 1825. Reported by Richard Ela. 8vo. pp. 127. Concord, N. H. Jacob B. Moore.

MISCELLANEOUS.

An Address to the Members of the Bar of Suffolk, Mass. at their Stated Meeting, on the first Tuesday of March, 1824. By William Sullivan. 8vo. pp. 63. Boston.

Review of a Pamphlet entitled " A Report of the Evidence in the Case, John Atkins, Appellant, vs. Calvin Sanger & al. Executors, relative to the Will of the late Mrs Badger, of Natick, &c. By Thomas Noyes. 8vo. pp. 71. Dedham, Mass.

An Oration in Honor of General Lafayette, delivered in his presence, at Nashville, May 4, 1825, at the request of the Grand Lodge of Tennessee. By William Gibbes Hunt. 8vo. pp. 12. Nashville, Tenn.

Address delivered before the Alumni of Columbia College, on the 4th of May, 1825, in the Chapel of the College. By Clement C. Moore, A. M. 8vo. pp. 37. New York. E. Bliss & E. White.

New York Review and Athenæum Magazine. No. I. June, 1825.

The Duties of an American Citizen. Two Discourses, delivered in the First Baptist Meetinghouse in Boston, on Thursday, April 7th, 1825, the Day of Public Fast. By Francis Wayland, jun. 8vo. pp. 52. Boston. James Loring.

These are able political discourses. The author takes broad and comprehensive views of the state and organization of society in the old as well as in the new world. He sketches with discrimination and power the causes which are in operation to carry forward the work of improvement in the condition of mankind. As the result of the wide and earnest diffusion of knowledge, which characterizes our age, he confidently anticipates more rational forms of religion, and more popular forms of government among the older nations of the earth. He shows a patriotic and laudable attachment to the institutions of our own country; and thinks they are destined to have no small influence on those of other countries. Hence spring our duties, as American citizens, to preserve them pure, as examples to the world of the ability of a nation to govern themselves by their own laws. We confidently recommend these Discourses to our readers; and regret that our limits do not allow us to give a more full analysis of them.

The Leper of Aost. Translated from the French of Lemaistre. 12mo. pp. 37. Boston. Cummings, Hilliard, & Co.

NOVEL.

Resignation; an American Novel, by a Lady. In 2 vols. 12mo. pp. 408 & 444.

PYROTECHNY.

A System of Pyrotechny, comprehending the Theory and Practice, with the Application of Chemistry, designed for Exhibition and for War. In four parts. Containing an Account of the Substances used in Fireworks—the Instruments, Utensils, and Manipulations—Fireworks for Exhibition—and Military Pyrotechny, adapted to the military and naval officer, the man of science, and the artificer. By James Cutbush, A. S. U. S. A. &c. 8vo. pp. 600. Philadelphia. Clara Cutbush. Price $4,50.

TOPOGRAPHY.

The Northern Traveller, containing the Routes to Niagara, Quebec, and the Springs, with descriptions of the Principal Scenes, and Useful Hints to Strangers, with Maps and Copperplates. New York. 18mo. pp. 222. Wilder & Campbell.

This work will be found highly interesting and useful to those who are making the tour and visiting the places which it describes.

The Traveller's Directory through the United States, with an Appendix, &c.; the whole illustrated by appropriate Maps. By John Melish. A new edition, revised and enlarged. Philadelphia.

THEOLOGY.

A Brief Outline of the Evidences of the Christian Religion. By Archibald Alexander, D. D. Professor of Didactic Theology in the Theological Seminary, Princeton, N. J. Price 87 cents. Princeton.

A Mirror, in which is shown the Likeness of Professing Christians, who place no confidence in the Light Within, or Spirit of Truth, as being the Gift of God. New York.

Essays on some of the First Principles of Metaphysics, Ethics, and Theology. By Asa Burton, D. D. Pastor of the Church of Christ in Thetford, Vt. 8vo. pp. 411. Portland. Arthur Shirley.

The Christian Spectator. Vol. VII. No. VI. June, 1825. New Haven.

Discourses on the Offices and Character of Jesus Christ. By Henry Ware, jun. Minister of the Second Church in Boston. 12mo. pp. 217. Boston.

A Sermon on the Art of Preaching, delivered before the Pastoral Association of Massachusetts, in Boston, May 25, 1825. By Edward D. Griffin, D. D. President of Williams College. 8vo. pp. 35. Boston.

The Gospel Advocate, No. LIV. for June, 1825.

The Claims of Past and Future Generations on Civil Rulers. A Sermon preached at the Annual Election, May 25, 1825, before His Honor Marcus Morton, Esq. Lieutenant Governor, the Honourable Council' and the Legislature of Massachusetts. By William B. Sprague, Pastor of the First Church in West Springfield. 8vo. pp. 36. Boston. True & Green.

A Collection of Essays and Tracts in Theology. By Jared Sparks. No. X. Boston.

AMERICAN EDITIONS OF FOREIGN WORKS.

The Museum of Foreign Literature and Science. No. XXXV. for May, 1825.

The Elements of Natural and Experimental Philosophy. By Tiberius Cavallo, F. R. S. &c. Third American edition, with Additional Notes, selected from various authors. By F. X. Brosius. 2 vols. 8vo. Philadelphia. Towar & Hogan.

Precepts for the Improvement and Preservation of the Sight. Plain Rules, which will enable all to judge exactly when and what Spectacles are best calculated for their Eyes, &c. By William Kitchiner, M. D. author of the Cook's Oracle, &c. 1 vol. 18mo.

Morning Thoughts, in Prose and Verse, on the Gospel of St Matthew. By J. W. Cunningham, author of the Velvet Cushion. First American from the third London edition. New York. Wilder & Campbell.

A Treatise on the Law of Mercantile Guarantee, and of Principal and Surety in General. By Walter W. Fell, Esq. Barrister at Law. With Notes and References to American Decisions, by Charles Walker, Esq. of the New York Bar. Philadelphia. P. H. Nicklin.

Helon's Pilgrimage to Jerusalem, a Picture of Judaism in the century which preceded the Advent of our Saviour. Translated from the German of Frederick Strauss. 2 vols. 12mo. Boston. Wells & Lilly.

Universal Geography. By M. Malte-Brun. 8vo. Boston. Wells & Lilly.

New Monthly Magazine, No. LII.

LIST OF WORKS IN PRESS.

Memoirs and Recollections of Count Segur, Ambassador from France to the Courts of Russia and Prussia. New York. Wilder & Campbell.

Lectures on Female Education. By James M. Garnett. To which is annexed the Gossip's Manual. Third edition, with corrections and additions by the author. Richmond, Va. Thomas W. White.

The Christian Father's Present to his Children. By Rev. S. A. James, author of "Sunday School Teacher's Guide." Boston. Crocker & Brewster.

Juliana Oakley. A Tale. By Mrs Sherwood. Boston. Crocker & Brewster.

The Life of the Chevalier John Paul Jones. Washington, D. C.

Published on the first and fifteenth day of every month, by CUMMINGS, HILLIARD, & Co., No. 134 Washington-Street, Boston, for the Proprietors. Terms, $5 per annum. Cambridge: Printed at the University Press, by Hilliard & Metcalf.

THE UNITED STATES
LITERARY GAZETTE.

| VOL. II. | JULY 1, 1825. | No. 7. |

REVIEWS.

Memoir of the Life of Josiah Quincy, Jun. of Massachusetts : By
his son, JOSIAH QUINCY. Boston. 8vo. pp. 498.

THEY, whose toils, and pains, and perils established for all
nations and all time a principle in political philosophy of
vast importance, have not all gone from among us. A few yet
live to see that great principle in practice. They held an un-
doubting belief in the capacity of men to govern themselves,
—in the utter uselessness of that cumbersome machinery,
which held nations together in all other climes,—and in the
injurious influence upon human character, of institutions,
which all preceding generations had thought demanded by
its essential needs ; and they have lived to see the wisdom of
their belief justified. But although that generation has not
wholly passed away, yet the lapse of time has made their
deeds matter of history ; the tale of their efforts and sacrifices falls upon ears which never heard the sound of their
voices ; their children and their children's children are men,
filling all the offices and relations, and active in all the employments of society ; and asking of the historian to tell them
what things their fathers did. This call should be answered ; it is an imperious duty of all who are acquainted with
facts and possessed of documents which throw any light upon
the causes or conduct of our revolution, or upon the character of those who brought it forward or were brought out by
it, to give these facts and documents to the public. There
must be many alive, who have it in their power to communi-

31

cate valuable information ; and although we cannot hope for
many volumes filled with papers so important as those which
form the bulk of this, yet there are doubtless many letters
and journals and notes extant, which, were they within the
reach of the historian, would materially assist him. One man,
mighty among the mightiest of those who led our fathers on their
way to independence, was permitted,—perhaps unavoidably,—
to destroy a mass of papers, the loss of which can never be fully
supplied.   We rejoice that those which Josiah Quincy Jun.
left, have met with better fortune ; his son has performed an
acceptable service to more than his fellow-citizens and his
own age, by placing them upon an imperishable record, and
thus building, of materials over which time can have no power, the best monument to his father's memory.

Before we proceed to make an abstract of the life of Mr
Quincy, or to give extracts from his papers, we would stop to
acknowledge the good taste and sound discretion which the
author of this memoir has manifested. The family history of
Mr Quincy and the principal facts of his life, are stated with
brevity and simplicity ; and little more is added to them than
is requisite for the right understanding of the various papers
now, for the first time, published.

Mr Quincy was descended from one of the earliest pilgrims ;
and his ancestors, in all their generations, filled important offices in the government of the province.   He was born in Boston, February 23, 1744 ;—and in his childhood and youth
those qualities were indicated, which characterized him
through life, and enabled him to earn, in his short career, a
fame, which will never die.   He was educated at Cambridge,
and as soon as he left the University, entered upon the study
of the law.   By good fortune, which his abilities and efforts
improved to the utmost, he succeeded to an extensive practice immediately after the expiration of the student's term ;
and during the remainder of his life he held a high rank
as a lawyer.   About a year after he commenced the practice
of his profession, he turned his attention to public affairs, and
published in the Boston Gazette two pieces signed " Hyperi-
on."   Their character is sufficiently obvious from the following extracts.

" Be not deceived, my countrymen.   Believe not these venal hirelings
when they would cajole you by their subtleties into submission, or
frighten you by their vapourings into compliance.   When they strive to
flatter you by the terms ' moderation and prudence,' tell them, that

calmness and deliberation are to guide the judgment, courage and intrepidity command the action. When they endeavour to make us ' perceive our inability to oppose our mother country,' let us boldly answer: In defence of our civil and religious rights, we dare oppose the world; with the God of armies on our side, even the God who fought our fathers' battles, we fear not the hour of trial, though the hosts of our enemies should cover the field like locusts. If this be enthusiasm, we will live and die enthusiasts.

" Blandishments will not fascinate us, nor will threats of a ' halter' intimidate. For under God, we are determined, that wheresoever, whensoever, or howsoever. we shall be called to make our exit, we will die freemen. Well do we know that all the regalia of this world cannot dignify the death of a villain, nor diminish the ignominy, with which a slave shall quit his existence. Neither can it taint the unblemished honour of a son of freedom, though he should make his departure on the already prepared gibbet, or be dragged to the newly erected scaffold for execution. With the plaudits of his conscience he will go off the stage. A crown of joy and immortality shall be his reward. The history of his life his children shall venerate. The virtues of their sire shall excite their emulation." * * * *

" By the sweat of our brow, we earn the little we possess; from nature we derive the common rights of man;—and by charter we claim the liberties of Britons ! Shall we,—dare we,—pusillanimously surrender our birthright? Is the obligation to our fathers discharged, is the debt we owe posterity paid? Answer me, thou coward! who hidest thyself in the hour of trial ! If there is no reward in this life,—no prize of glory in the next, capable of animating thy dastard soul; think and tremble, thou miscreant ! at the whips and stripes thy master shall lash thee with on earth,—and the flames, and scorpions, thy second master shall torment thee with hereafter !

" Oh, my countrymen ! what will our children say, when they read the history of these times, should they find we tamely gave away, without one noble struggle, the most invaluable of earthly blessings? As they drag the galling chain, will they not execrate us? If we have any respect for things sacred ; any regard to the dearest treasure on earth ; —if we have one tender. sentiment. for posterity ; if we would not be despised by the whole world ;—let us, in the most open, solemn manner, and with determined fortitude, swear,—we will die,—if we cannot live freemen ! "

Although he continued to express these sentiments unreservedly, in 1770 he was solicited by the British officers and soldiers under trial for " the Boston Massacre," to undertake their defence in conjunction with John Adams ; and after mature consideration he complied with their request. This resolution, before the motives which had led to it were known, produced the greatest consternation among the people, who were at this time under a high degree of excitement at the outrage which they believed had been committed upon them. Mr Quincy was now considered one of the master spirits who were to lead the opposition to government; and he seemed all at once to have deserted the cause, and gone over to the enemy. The following letter, addressed to his father, will show the state of the public mind, and the importance which was attached to Mr Quincy's decision.

> "*Braintree, March* 22, 1770.
>
> "My Dear Son,—I am under great affliction, at hearing the bitterest reproaches uttered against you, for having become an advocate for those criminals who are charged with the murder of their fellow-citizens. Good God! Is it possible? I will not believe it.
>
> "Just before I returned home from Boston, I knew, indeed, that on the day those criminals were committed to prison, a sergeant had inquired for you at your brother's house,—but I had no apprehension that it was possible an application would be made to you to undertake their defence. Since then I have been told that you have actually engaged for Captain Preston;—and I have heard the severest reflections made upon the occasion, by men who had just before manifested the highest esteem for you, as one destined to be a saviour of your country.
>
> "I must own to you, it has filled the bosom of your aged and infirm parent with anxiety and distress, lest it should not only prove true, but destructive of your reputation and interest! and I repeat, I will not believe it, unless it be confirmed by your own mouth, or under your own hand.
>
> "Your anxious and distressed parent,
>
> "Josiah Quincy."

His reply to his father is eminently characteristic of his intrepidity in the discharge of what he considered his duty.

> *Boston, March* 26, 1770.
>
> "Honoured Sir,—I have little leisure, and less inclination either to know, or to take notice, of those ignorant slanderers, who have dared to utter their "bitter reproaches" in your hearing against me, for having become an advocate for criminals charged with murder. But the sting of reproach, when envenomed only by envy and falsehood, will never prove mortal. Before pouring their reproaches into the ear of the aged and infirm, if they had been friends, they would have surely spared a little reflection on the nature of an attorney's oath and duty;—some trifling scrutiny into the business and discharge of his office; and some small portion of patience in viewing my past and future conduct.
>
> "Let such be told, Sir, that these criminals, charged with murder, are *not yet legally proved guilty*, and therefore, however criminal, are entitled, by the laws of God and man, to all legal counsel and aid; that my duty as a man obliged me to undertake; that my duty as a lawyer strengthened the obligation; that from abundant caution, I at first declined being engaged; that after the best advice, and most mature deliberation had determined my judgment, I waited on Captain Preston, and told him that I would afford him my assistance; but, prior to this, in presence of two of his friends, I made the most explicit declaration to him, of my real opinion, on the contests (as I expressed it to him) of the times, and that my heart and hand were indissolubly attached to the

cause of my country ; and finally, that I refused all engagement, until
advised and urged to undertake it, by an Adams, a Hancock, a Molineux,
a Cushing, a Henshaw, a Pemberton, a Warren, a Cooper, and a Phillips. This and much more might be told with great truth, and I dare
affirm, that you, and this whole people will one day REJOICE, that I became an advocate for the aforesaid "criminals," *charged* with the murder of our fellow-citizens.

"I never harboured the expectation, nor any great desire, that all
men should speak well of me. To inquire my duty, and to do it, is my
aim. Being mortal, I am subject to error ; and conscious of this, I wish
to be diffident. Being a rational creature, I judge for myself, according
to the light afforded me. When a plan of conduct is formed with an
honest deliberation, neither murmuring, slander, nor reproaches move.
For my single self, I consider, judge, and with reason hope to be immu-
table.

"There are honest men in all sects,—I wish their approbation ;—there
are wicked bigots in all parties.—I abhor them."

I am, truly and affectionately, your son,
"JOSIAH QUINCY JUN."

These gentlemen have been perhaps duly honoured for
this remarkable sacrifice of the strongest personal and party
passions to principle and a sense of duty ; but we have thought
that the vast good which they did to their country, and the
immense advantage, which the cause they loved, derived from
their courage and success, has hardly been rightly estimated.
The condition, to which the troubles of those times should
lead, depended almost wholly upon the course which public
opinion should finally take. All eyes, in all parts of the continent, were fixed upon Boston, and although the principles of
Mr Quincy and his compatriots spread 'rapidly and widely,
and seized upon men's minds with a power, which might well
be deemed miraculous, still their success was protracted and
difficult. What would it have been, if these patriots had not
profited by this opportunity, not merely to protect their cause
from an indelible stigma, but to give it a most dignified and
imposing character, and win for it the approbation and zealous good will of the noble-minded every where?

In 1773, his health had so much declined, that it was
thought a change of climate afforded the only hope of his
recovery. Accordingly, in February of that year he sailed
for Charleston, South Carolina, whence he returned by land
to Massachusetts. He visited, of course, the most prominent
individuals wherever he went, and his interesting letters and
journal show that his thoughts seldom wandered from that object, which he had most at heart. He immediately resumed
his professional practice, but testified his interest in the public

affairs of the day and the strength of his intellect, by various efforts in the public service, and particularly by his celebrated " Observations on the Boston Port-Bill," and essays on the Hutchinson papers, under the signature of " Marchmont Nedham." In 1774 he determined to abandon his profession and embark for England. In that country he remained some months, exerting himself with unremitted assiduity to advance that cause upon which all his thoughts and cares were concentrated. His health again failed him ; but he determined to return home, although his London physicians were very confident that a residence in Bristol for a season would be eminently useful. When at sea, he grew rapidly worse, and, on the 26th of April, died in sight of his native shore.

_ We cannot do justice to the motives, which induced him to encounter the risk of this voyage, without giving to our readers some extracts from a letter, which he dictated to a sailor on board, after he became incapable of writing.

" At Sea, April 21, 1775.

" Foreseeing that there will be many inexplicable circumstances in the way of my friends, to account for many things relating to my conduct, I should have been glad, if God had spared my life, to converse with them once more. But this, his holy Providence seems fully settled to deny. Some few matters I have prevailed with a friend on board to minute for their information.

My going to America at this time was very considerably against my inclinations, especially as Doctor Fothergill was of opinion that Bristol waters would be of great advantage to me. But he did not dissuade me from going to America, but advised it very strongly in preference to my staying in London, or its environs.

" The most weighty motive of all that determined my conduct, was the extreme urgency of about fifteen or twenty most stanch friends to America, and many of them the most learned and respectable characters in the kingdom, for my immediately proceeding to Boston. Their sentiments what ought to be the conduct of Boston, and of the continent, at this, and the approaching season, I had heard very often in the social circle; and in what things they differed I perfectly knew. It appeared of high importance that the sentiments of such persons should be known in America. To commit their sentiments to writing was neither practicable nor prudent at this time. To the bosom of a friend they could intrust what might be of great advantage to my country. To me that trust was committed, and I was, immediately upon my arrival, to assemble certain persons, to whom I was to communicate my trust, and had God spared my life, it seems it would have been of great service to my country. * * * * * * * * * * * *
* * * Ever since I have been out, almost every thing has been different from what I expected. Instead of pleasant weather, the most inclement and damp, which removes me entirely from the deck, and when I was flattered with the hope of getting into port six days ago, I

am yet here, as distant from it as when the encouragement was given me. Had Providence been pleased that I should have reached America six days ago, I should have been able to converse with my friends. I am persuaded that this voyage and passage are the instruments to put an end to my being. His holy will be done ! "

"Mr Quincy is so low, that he probably will not be able to read a word ∉ the foregoing, but it is to be hoped it will be intelligible with a little pains."

We had marked for quotation many passages of his Journal while in England, and of his letters thence ; but, upon the whole, we think it unnecessary to insert them, as we cannot doubt that the peculiar merits of this volume will ensure a thorough perusal of it, by all who are interested in the history of our Revolution.

Reform of Harvard College.   (For the Titles, see last Gazette.)

[CONTINUED.]

THIS second committee, it must be admitted, performed their duty faithfully.   The result of their labours was the pamphlet marked No. 3, in the list at the head of this article. It contains the most complete account of the actual state of the University which we have ever met with ; we may add, the most complete which could well be given in any reasonable compass.   It consists of four several documents, and the manner in which they were obtained is thus briefly, clearly, and satisfactorily stated.

The Committee have invited and received communications from the President and Treasurer of the University, from the Immediate Government as a body, and from each of the Instructers ; and the documents herewith submitted exhibit the statements received from them, comprising all the information which the Committee were instructed to procure.

The nature of these documents is thus described.

No. I. is the Statement received from the Treasurer, setting forth the Finances of the University, comprising a particular account of its ways and means, the expenses necessary during the present College year, the salaries of all the officers, and the funds from which the same are paid.

No. II. contains the Foundations, Statutes, and Regulations of the several Professorships and Tutorships, showing the duties which are required of each Instructer, or may be required of him consistently with the terms of the original foundation, or with the contract made between him and the University.

No. III. contains the Answers of the Immediate Government to a series of questions proposed by the Committee with the view of ascertaining and exhibiting the present organization of the Government and the practical effects of that organization, the course of instruction and modes of discipline, the duties performed by the College officers, the conduct and proficiency of the Students, the necessary expenses of education, the changes which have taken place in these respects during the last twenty years, and such further particulars in relation to the condition of the University in all its departments, as would enable the overseers to form a satisfactory opinion of the application and probable effect of the various alterations which had been, or might be suggested.

With a view to the performance of the further duties assigned them, that of recommending such specific regulations as they should deem expedient, and that of preparing a code of College Laws in a simple and brief form, including those regulations; the Committee communicated to each of the instructers their intention of asking a personal interview with him after receiving his answer to their letter. Their object was to enter into a free discussion of the measures to be proposed, with those, whose situation and experience enabled them to ascertain with the most accuracy the nature and extent of existing evils, and to suggest the most appropriate and effectual remedies. On learning afterwards, however, that the Immediate Government had been for some time engaged, at the request of the Corporation, in preparing a new code of laws, as a manual for the use of the Students, intended to embrace all the specific regulations, which they should think it expedient to adopt at present, the Committee determined to postpone any further proceedings in relation to this subject, until the Report of the Government should be completed. This is now done, and the contemplated code has been laid before the Corporation, by whom it has been recently transmitted to this Committee with the information, that it is substantially approved by that body, though it has not yet been acted upon definitively.

No. IV. exhibits this Code.

The publication of this collection brings the actual state of the University distinctly before the public, an important and highly valuable result of the discussions, if they had produced no other. We are thus enabled to form our own opinions from the facts of the case, instead of depending upon vague and general representations. We shall avail ourselves of the opportunity, which is thus afforded us, to make some remarks which are suggested by portions of this report.

It is well known to many of our readers, that it has been objected to Harvard College, that an education in that seminary is too expensive—and it is admitted directly or indirectly by both committees, that this is the fact. We believe this objection has had much greater weight than any single one, perhaps than all others together, in deterring parents in moderate circumstances from sending their children to Cambridge.

We are naturally inclined to inquire, in the first place, into the causes of this increased expenditure. And the first question would seem to be, Are the necessary expenses of this University much greater than in many other colleges of reputation in the United States. Let us examine the expense of boarding. The report informs us that the charge for Steward and Commons for thirty-eight weeks of term time is $76.50 or $2 per week,—that those who board at private houses, pay (including the charge for steward and a general assessment for the commons establishment) from $2.67 to $3.42 per week. But the commons-hall being sufficient to accommodate all the students, it is clear that boarding out must be a matter of taste with the students, sanctioned by their parents or guardians; the real and necessary expense, therefore, cannot fairly be considered greater than the first charge, or $2 per week. If we compare this with the rate of board at the colleges in our own and the five neighbouring States, we shall see no reason to object to the expense at Cambridge in this particular. The following table is collected from Worcester's Gazetteer of the United States.

Harvard	per week				$2.00
Williams	"	usually			2.00
Brown	"	about			2.00
Union	"	about			2.00
Princeton	"				2.75
Burlington	"	from			1.50 to 1.75
Dartmouth	"	from			1.25 to 1.50
Yale	"	about			2.25
Bowdoin	"	from			2.00 to 2.50

From this table it appears that of eight institutions of this character, the price of board in two only is less than it is at Cambridge, while in three it is greater. And considering the situation of this University, and its neighbourhood to a populous city, it will appear that this part of the establishment is conducted with remarkable economy. This is an expense, moreover, that cannot well be affected by the superior endowments of this College, since no part of its funds could be expected to be appropriated to the diminution of the expense of subsistence till all that of instruction was wholly extinguished. This remark of course is not intended to apply to the beneficiaries of the institution, whose expenses of every kind are diminished by the application of the income of specific bequests.

The next in order of the necessary expenses is thus stated.

32

"Instruction for the two first years $46, for the third and fourth $64. Average $55."

Let us compare this, as in a former instance, with the same expense in other colleges.

Harvard	$55.00
Yale	32.00
Bowdoin	20.00
Dartmouth	20.00
Middlebury average	18.00
Brown, including room rent,	25.00
Princeton, N. J. "	62.34
Burlington, including rent and library,	16.00
Columbia, all College charges,	80.00
Williams, all charges exclusive of board,	40.00
William and Mary's, instruction,	60.00

It will be perceived from this statement that the expense of instruction in this college is, with one or two exceptions, greater than in any in the neighbourhood, and in most instances exceedingly so;—that it is nearly double that of Yale, and more than double that of Dartmouth. It may be observed in regard to this subject, that the instructers of Harvard are more numerous, and the opportunities for a complete e lucation or improvement in many particular branches are more complete. But, on the other hand, it must be considered, that Harvard College is far more richly endowed; and sufficiently so, it has been supposed, to balance this circumstance, and to furnish a more complete education at a less expense, so far as mere instruction is concerned, than any of its neighbours. We are not in possession of documents which would enable us to institute a comparison between the income of the funds of this and any other College, but we are enabled by this report to ascertain what the income is in this particular instance, and to form an opinion concerning the economy with which it has been managed.

From the first document of this report we learn, that the income of the College for the year 1824, arising from various permanent sources, as stock, rents, annuities, &c. was

	$22244 74
That there was received for admission to advanced standing	1000 00
From fees of certain degrees (probably medicine and law)	280 00
	23524 74

That there was assessed on the students exclusive
   of charges for board ·   ·   ·   ·   ·   21431 41
                                                  44956 15

    To this amount ought to be added the value of the rent of
the President's house, as it forms a part of the income of his
office, and stands in the place of an amount which must have
been assessed upon students, provided he had the same income that he now enjoys, $300 00
    A similar remark may be made concerning half the fees for
the degree of A. M. amounting, according to the treasurer's,
average, to about 35, at $5,   · $175 00
    Also the fees for the degree of A. B. which are in fact paid
by the students, and of which the average, if we judge from
the Triennial Catalogue, is about 60, at $5, $300 00

The whole amount of income then will be $45731 15

    The expenditure during the same year, including, as above,
the addition for the President, was $44841 36
Of this expenditure, there was devoted to the officers concerned in the instruction or discipline
   of Undergraduates   ·   ·   ·   ·   24556 16
The funds, other than the amount levied upon undergraduates for the payment of this sum,
   amounted to   ·   ·   ·   ·   ·   9328 09

Balance to be assessed upon undergraduates, including fees for degrees of A. B.   ·   ·   ·   15228 07
The actual amount assessed upon undergraduates,
   according to the treasurer's account, was   15710 00
Add fees for degrees not included by the treasurer   475 00

                                        $16185 00
Deduct balance in treasury   ·   ·   ·   ·   894 79

                                        $15290 21
which differs from our calculation by $62, which is probably
an error in our account. The exact amount, however, is not
material in this investigation.
    Whether so large an expenditure, and its consequence, so
large an assessment, is necessary, may be estimated by a
more particular consideration of the salary of each individual of the instructers.

The President's income is thus stated.

Salary $2250—grant 300—income of Cotton legacy 8 40	2558	40
Rent of house and appurtenances, not valued in report, but estimated at	300	00
Half the fees for degrees of A. M. which average 35, at $5	175	00
The fee for degrees of A. B. of which the average for the last ten years is 60, at $5 . .	300	00
	3333	40

That part of this sum, which goes to increase the assessments on the students, is about one-sixth of the whole amount of these assessments, and that exclusive of the fee for degrees of A. B. which is in reality also assessed upon them.

In the next place, we observe that there are seven resident Professors concerned in the instruction of undergraduates, each of whom has an income, under the names of salary and grant, of $1700, amounting to $11900. One of these Professors has an addition of $325 to the above salary and grant, for other services. And another has an addition of $150. The whole amount, therefore, is $12373. The regular funds for the payment of these salaries will furnish only $3546.68, leaving a balance of $8826.32, which is to be furnished by assessments.

[*To be continued.*]

An Address to the Members of the Bar of Suffolk, Mass. at their Stated Meeting on the First Tuesday of March, 1824. By WILLIAM SULLIVAN. Boston. 1825. 8vo. pp. 63.

In this address Mr Sullivan " proposes to offer such facts as he has been able in a short time, and amidst many avocations, to collect, on the origin and history of the profession " of law in Massachusetts. In pursuance of which design, he gives numerous memorabilia of the history and practice of the law, with biographical notices of its professors ; taking a cursory view of the rank of the profession and mode of practice in other countries in one of the notes, and in others touching concisely upon the subjects of chancery jurisdiction and codification.

Mr Sullivan cites Hutchinson for a fact, which shows both the simplicity of the early times, and the thoroughly popular spirit of our institutions. It was enacted by the colony laws, that " whensoever any juror or jurors are not clear in their judgment or conscience concerning any case wherein they are to give their verdict, they shall have liberty in open court (but not otherwise) to advise with any man they shall think fit to resolve or direct them, before they give their verdict."*

The first lawyer noticed in our history was one Lechford, who came over about ten years after the settlement of the colony. But he did not merit, or at least he did not find, much encouragement; for in consequence, as is supposed, of some offence committed by him, he was debarred from pleading any man's cause except his own. He accordingly returned *home* very little satisfied with the colony; and published a pamphlet under the title of *Plain Dealing*, in which he said, that in New England he found that every church member was a bishop, and not being inclined to become one himself, he could not be admitted a freeman among them—that the general court and quarter-sessions exercised all the powers of parliament, king's bench, common pleas, chancery, high commission, star chamber, and all the other courts of England. But a law of 1654 prohibited any common attorney in any inferior court from sitting as a deputy in the general court.

In Rhode Island, at the present day, as every body knows, the judges are not usually selected from among practising lawyers. So it was formerly in Massachusetts, and Mr Sullivan says, that since 1776 three judges have been appointed to the supreme bench, who were not lawyers; two of whom accepted the appointment. In a subsequent part of the discourse Mr Sullivan, while he acknowledges that the profession is held in some respect, seems to think that the prospect of emoluments is somewhat discouraging. The modern practice of selecting the ablest lawyers for judges is doubtless one of the causes of blighting the prospects of the rest; for it is obvious that where the judges are least competent, and the lawyers are most railed at, litigation, especially of the most vexatious sort, is the most flourishing.

Mr Sullivan (though he does not mention this himself) took an active part in 1804 in introducing a very important improve-

---

* General Laws and Liberties of the Massachusetts Colony, Ed. 1672, p. 87.

ment in the judicial administration of this state.   Before that
time the full court was present at jury trials, and the law and
facts of the case were settled at once by the verdict.   At that
time it was provided that jury trials in civil actions might be
had before one judge, and that questions of law might be reserved for the consideration of the full court.   This seemed
to be a necessary step towards the establishment of any
thing like a regular system of adjudication ; and this practice,
extended, by an act passed the next year, to allow one judge
to try all criminal causes, except where the offence was capital, has continued ever since.   Those laws, together with the
provision made about the same time for reporting and publishing the adjudged cases involving questions of law, have
contributed greatly to the rapid progress that has been made
in forming a uniform system of legal administration.

In a short note relating to the chancery jurisdiction, Mr
Sullivan notices the groundless prejudice existing in the state
against this species of judicial administration—a prejudice
which every friend to an adequate administration of the laws
ought to omit no opportunity of combating.   For the imperfection and inadequacy of the remedies afforded by the laws,
without this kind of jurisdiction, are daily becoming more apparent, as the forms of property, the modes of business, and
the species of contracts become more complicated and various.   Great progress has been made, it is true, in providing
equitable remedies for particular cases, but there are numerous instances of the loss of rights on the one part, and the
evasion of obligations on the other, for the want of sufficient
provisions of law in this respect.

In naming the commissioners appointed a few years since,
under a resolve of the legislature, to make a compilation from
the records of Plymouth colony, a mistake occurs in the
christian name of one of them.   The commissioners appointed for this purpose were the Rev. Dr James Freeman, Samuel
Davis, Esq. and Benjamin R. Nichols, Esq. ; under this commission the entire public records of Plymouth Colony were
transcribed, and a copy has been placed in the archives of
the Commonwealth.

Speaking of an article in the North American Review for
July, 1823, on the history of the laws of Massachusetts, Mr
Sullivan says, " the writer has omitted some traits of the
[early] times, which prove our forefathers to have been more
polished than has been commonly supposed ;" and he instan-

ces the solemn protest of Governor Endicott, Deputy Governor Dudley, and seven others, against the wearing of *long hair*, as a thing " detestable, uncivil, and unmanly, whereby men doe deform themselves and offend sober and modest men, and doe corrupt good manners ;" and also the Colony law providing as follows—" Nor shall any take *tobacco* in any inne or common victual house, except in a private room there, so as the master of said house, nor any guest there shall take offence thereat ; which if any do, then such person shall forthwith forbear upon penalty of two shillings and sixpence." In addition to those two instances, we have a law of 1663, in which our forefathers agree with Lord Chesterfield in one of his doctrines of politeness, proscribing the drinking of healths ; viz.——Be it enacted, " that no masters of ships or seamen having their vessels riding within any of our harbours in this jurisdiction, shall presume to drink healths, or suffer any healths to be drunk within their vessels by day or by night, or to shoot off any gun after daylight is passed or on the sabbath day, on penalty for every health twenty shillings, and for every gun so shot twenty shillings. And the Captain of the Castle is hereby enjoined to give notice of this order to all ships that pass by the Castle."

It is hardly necessary to add, that this Address and the notes make an interesting pamphlet. Every one who reads it, whether he belong to the profession of law or not, will regret that there is no more of it ; and we hope that Mr Sullivan will find leisure to pursue his inquiries farther, and present the public with a larger work upon the plan adopted in his discourse.

MISCELLANY.

A RESIDENCE IN GLASGOW.

DR CHALMERS AND MR IRVINE.

[*Concluded.*]

In the afternoon, I repaired again to St John's, but was somewhat surprised to find, in a city proverbial for church-going, that comparatively so few people seemed to attend the afternoon service. When the preacher rose up, I was surprised and disappointed to observe that it was not Dr Chalmers. You may wonder at my not discovering who the preacher was before he stood up; but your wonder will cease when I tell you, that in Scotland the good old custom continues of having the minister speak out of a deep box misnamed a pulpit. Well, uprose the tall, gaunt figure of the now celebrated Mr Irvine. My disappointment I could plainly see was participated by many of the audience. But I can plead no excuse for the ill breeding of those who deliberately rose up, and left the church, on perceiving that the speaker was not Dr Chalmers. Your inquiries about Mr Irvine indicate an uncommon interest in him; I shall therefore endeavour to give you a full and fair statement of the effect he produced on my own feelings.

The introductory prayer was stiff, lifeless, and uninteresting; and an awkward imitation of the manner of Dr Chalmers, only made the bareness of the speaker's ideas more conspicuous. The national accent was not so observable on his tongue; but the gesture, and the general attitude he assumed, were a close imitation of Dr Chalmers. I am told that, after going to London, "he reformed it altogether," and had the good sense to make gesture a study; so that his majestic figure, and his bold, commanding action, now harmonize finely in producing much of the peculiar effect of his eloquence.

The ideas and the composition of the discourse, were somewhat peculiar. In the first part of the sermon, there was nothing to distinguish Mr Irvine's mind from that of the common class of preachers in Scotland. The matter was sufficiently abstract, argumentative, and formal; and the style had the due degree of stiff and bookish phraseology. After dragging through a few sentences of this kind, he flung me back, all at once, into the days of Spenser, by a sudden and fantastic attempt at an imitation of the style of the "olden time." After an awkward caracole or two, he descended from his borrowed Pegasus; and, for a while, was content to tread the vulgar earth once more. Again the spirit of affectation assaulted him; in a moment "black Surrey was saddled for the field;" and once more we were favoured with a display of the gallant and antiquated horsemanship of the rider.

I returned to my "lodgings" in that perplexed and perplexing mood of mind, in which we cannot tell whether we are pleased or dissatisfied, delighted or vexed, or why we should either be the one or the other. Since Mr Irvine's "transportation" (as the Scotch call it) to London, he is become an adept in this business of imitation; so that his discourses are now not unlike the immortal Baron of Braidwardin's castle : an odd, picturesque, combination of ancient and semi-modern art.

During my stay in Glasgow I exercised a truly American inquisitiveness with regard to Dr Chalmers. I had the happiness of becoming somewhat acquainted with him ; and I found that my countrymen have almost universally fallen into a mistake with respect to his genius and character. From vague report, and from a perusal of his sermons, many people have imagined Dr Chalmers' peculiar cast of thought and expression to be all a thing got up on purpose to produce a certain effect. There never was a greater mistake. I never in my life saw a man who had more downright, native simplicity of character. He is as incapable of doing any thing for effect, as of achieving a metempsychosis. His broad dialect, his blunt manners, his homebred honesty of heart, legible in all his looks and actions, are so many guaranties of his godly sincerity. Dr Chalmers composes and preaches just as he talks to a friend, if the subject of conversation is interesting to his own feelings. Touch any department of the cause of christian benevolence or of common philanthropy, one, especially, on which he has been contradicted or opposed, and immediately you kindle him up to the same sublimity of thought and vehemence of emotion, which characterize him as a speaker. It is true that Dr Chalmers is a mannerist, and his manner is wretchedly bad ; that he ought, long ago, to have cast off all this, together with his provincial accent ; that he ought to reduce his ideas to a less unwieldy form ; that his enormous, overgrown sentences should be pruned, and that he should change his action from the style of Vulcan to that of Apollo. But to require a change now, would be unreasonable. The man's physical and intellectual habits are unalterably fixed by early neglect and subsequent inattention. Suppose a person of his age willing to submit to the school-boy drudgery of mending his utterance and his action ; the attempt would, in all probability, be fruitless. Habit is proverbially powerful in New England ; but in Scotland it has the merciless sway of a tyrant. To appreciate or to relish Dr Chalmers, you must give up all the externals of oratory, and take, in exchange, the majestic sweep of his mind ; and if you are willing to accept of fervor and vehemence, instead of correctness and grace, you may even come to think of him as a powerful orator.

A mistake of an opposite kind to that made about Dr Chalmers, prevails in the estimation of Mr Irvine. Whilst the former is supposed to be one who artificially works himself up to a certain strain of sublimity, the latter gets the credit of being a man of wonderful originality of genius. The truth of the matter, as nearly as I could learn, is this. Mr Irvine began the career which has issued in his present popularity, by patching his composition with here and there an imitation of the older writers. Practice makes perfect. The transition from a sentence to a paragraph of imitation gradually became easy ; till, at last, there was found to be no difficulty in writing a whole discourse in the antique style. Here you have the whole secret of the matter. I do not mean to deny Mr Irvine's native talent for grand and elevated conceptions; but I think I have given you a fair history of his progress.

As for the weekly crowd and bustle about his chapel in London, I would not give a rush for it. The inhabitants of that city are always in that state of jaded, yet craving appetite for novelty, which induced the ancient monarch to advertise a reward for the discovery of a new pleasure. It is true that men of distinguished intellectual rank resort to the Caledonian chapel; but it is only because the imitative style of the preacher has now attained its finish. Had Mr Canning seen the dove-tailed piece of work that came under my notice, he would, I suspect, have sided with those of the preacher's Glasgow hearers, who did not care to be favored with a repetition of such matter; but rose and went out as soon as they observed he was about to officiate.

I admit that Mr Irvine's imitations are sometimes very fine; but what then?—imitation is but a very ordinary attainment, at its best. The most that we can say about Mr Irvine, is, that he throws a romantic garb over the subject of religion. In this age the world runs mad after romance; and Mr Irvine perhaps thinks it lawful to put on the tragedian's robe, for the sake of attracting notice to his subject.

Adieu.

ITALIAN LYRICAL POETRY.

BEMBO.

THE Italians pride themselves on ranking among their poets, and among those of the highest class, many of their first nobles, ecclesiastics, philosophers, and statesmen, who sought relief from severer studies or from the cares of life, in the cultivation of elegant literature. Of this number, and an illustrious name in the list of the restorers of Italian poetry, was the Cardinal Pietro Bembo.

His father was a patrician of Venice, honoured in his time with many high offices, and still more honored by posterity for his patronage of learned men, and his having renovated the tomb of Dante in Ravenna. Pietro was born at Venice in 1470; and from the earliest age he zealously improved the advantages which the taste and condition of his father afforded him for the study of literature, philosophy, and the arts. After his arrival at manhood he was occasionally employed in the public service of his native country, but more in the indulgence of his fondness for study, and in the pursuit of knowledge in the most refined cities of Italy. The reputation which he there acquired, caused Leo X., on his accession to the pontifical dignity, to make Bembo his first secretary. In the luxurious court of this epicurean pontiff, Bembo lived in the enjoyment of all the pleasures of taste, wealth, and rank ; and even yielded so far to the example of the age as to assume a degree of license in his manners wholly unsuited to his profession and station. In his official character, however, he is without reproach, and his letters are remarkable for their pure and elegant latinity, his style being exactly modelled upon that of Cicero, whom he copied with scrupulous exactness amounting to affectation.

In 1520 Bembo retired from Rome to Padua for the benefit of his health, and his patron, Leo X., dying about that time, he determined not to return to Rome. He continued at Padua, therefore, attracted by the splendid collections of books and monuments of art in that polished city. Whilst here, he entirely reformed his morals ; and here he conceived the plan and wrote a great part of his History of Venice. In 1539 he was honoured with the purple by Pope Paul III., when he transferred his residence to Rome. He remained there until he died, in 1547, at the advanced age of seventy-seven years, a patriarch in letters as he was in the church, the friend of all the distinguished literary men of the age, and loaded with public distinctions.

His literary reputation depends chiefly, perhaps, upon his prose writings ; but his rank as an Italian poet, nevertheless, is such as to entitle him to this extended notice here. He was one of the earliest to discriminate, by his example and his precepts, purer principles of taste than had generally prevailed among his immediate predecessors. He took Petrarca for his guide, and by the diligent study of his writings acquired a comparatively correct and pure style of composition, though he was unable to divest himself altogether of a certain stiffness of manner, incompatible with the highest poetic excellence. In fact, his poetical reputation was derived rather from the polished elegance of his style, than from any depth of sentiment or thought which he displayed ; for though always chaste, he is often cold and insipid ; and therefore his character has never stood so high with posterity as it did with his contemporaries.

His poems consist of *Rime,* from which the following sonnets are selected.

TO ITALY.

Fair land, once loved of heaven o'er all beside,
　Which blue waves gird and lofty mountains screen ;
　Thou clime of fertile fields and sky serene,
　Whose gay expanse the Appennines divide ;

What boots it now, that Rome's old warlike pride
  Left thee of humbled earth and sea the queen?
  Nations, that served thee then, now fierce convene
  To tear thy locks and strew them o'er the tide.
And lives there son of thine so base at core,
  Who, luring foreign friends to thine embrace,
  Stabs to the heart thy beauteous, bleeding frame?
Are these the noble deeds of ancient fame?
  Thus do ye God's almighty name adore?
  Oh hardened age! oh false and recreant race!

TURNING TO GOD.

If, gracious God, in life's green, ardent year
  A thousand times thy patient love I tried;
  With reckless heart, with conscience hard and sear,
  Thy gifts perverted, and thy power defied:
Oh grant me, now that wintry snows appear
  Around my brow, and youth's bright promise hide,—
  Grant me with reverential awe to hear
  Thy holy voice, and in thy word confide;
Blot from my book of life its early stain;
  Since days misspent will never more return,
  My future path do thou in mercy trace;
So cause my soul with pious zeal to burn,
  That all the trust, which in thy name I place,
  Frail as I am, may not prove wholly vain.

GUIDICCIONI.

Giovanni Guidiccioni was born at Lucca in the year 1500. He was educated at the best Italian universities by his uncle, the Cardinal Bartolommeo Guidiccioni, who finally carried him to Rome and placed him in the service of Cardinal Alessandro Farnese, afterwards Pope Paul III.; in which situation he had access to the society of the first literary men of the city, and contracted a very close friendship with the poet Annibal Caro. In 1534 his patron was raised to the pontificate, and afterwards constantly employed him in the highest offices of the papal see, both at home and abroad, until his premature death in 1541, which alone prevented his receiving the purple. As a literary man, he is most eminent for his poems. His style is particularly adapted to grave and heroic subjects; and on these, in the opinion of the Italian critics, it is impossible for any style to be more select in diction or to possess greater nobleness and sustained dignity. His chief blemish is an occasional obscurity, arising from his aiming too sedulously at compressed strength. The two following are among the most admired of his sonnets.

TO ROME.

Thou noble nurse of many a warlike chief,
  Who in more brilliant times the world subdued;
  Of old, the shrines of gods in beauty stood
  Within thy walls, where now are shame and grief;.
I hear thy broken voice demand relief,
  And sadly o'er thy faded fame I brood,—
  Thy pomps no more,—thy temples fallen and rude,—
  Thine empire shrunk within a petty fief.
Slave as thou art, if such thy majesty
  Of bearing seems, thy name so holy now,
  That even thy scattered fragments I adore ;—
How did they feel, who saw thee throned on high
  In pristine splendor, while thy glorious brow
  The golden diadem of nations bore ?

TO ITALY.

From ignominious sleep, where age on age
  Thy torpid faculties have slumbering lain,
  Mine Italy, enslaved, ay more, insane,—
  Wake, and behold thy wounds with noble rage.
Rouse, and with generous energy engage
  Once more thy long-lost freedom to obtain ;
  The path of honour yet once more regain,
  And leave no blot upon my country's page.
Thy haughty lords, who trample o'er thee now,
  Have worn the yoke, which bows to earth thy neck,
  And graced thy triumphs in thy days of fame.
Alas ! thine own most deadly foe art thou,
  Unhappy land ; thy spoils the invader deck,
  While self-wrought chains thine infamy proclaim !

                                   C. C.

ORIGINAL POETRY.

THE GRAVES OF THE PATRIOTS.

Here rest the great and good—here they repose
After their generous toil. A sacred band,
They take their sleep together, while the year
Comes with its early flowers to deck their graves,
And gathers them again, as Winter frowns.
Theirs is no vulgar sepulchre—green sods
Are all their monument, and yet it tells
A nobler history, than pillared piles,
Or the eternal pyramids. They need
No statue nor inscription to reveal
Their greatness. It is round them, and the joy

With which their children tread the hallowed ground
That holds their venerated bones, the peace
That smiles on all they fought for, and the wealth
That clothes the land they rescued,—these, though mute,
As feeling ever is when deepest,—these
Are monuments more lasting, than the fanes
Reared to the kings and demigods of old.

Touch not the ancient elms, that bend their shade
Over their lowly graves ; beneath their boughs
There is a solemn darkness, even at noon,
Suited to such as visit at the shrine
Of serious liberty.   No factious voice
Called them unto the field of generous fame,
But the pure consecrated love of home.
No deeper feeling sways us, when it wakes
In all its greatness.   It has told itself
To the astonished gaze of awe-struck kings,
At Marathon, at Bannockburn, and here,
Where first our patriots sent the invader back
Broken and cowed.   Let these green elms be all
To tell us where they fought, and where they lie.
Their feelings were all nature, and they need
No art to make them known.   They live in us,
While we are like them, simple, hardy, bold,
Worshipping nothing but our own pure hearts,
And the one universal Lord.   They need
No column pointing to the heaven they sought,
To tell us of their home.   The heart itself,
Left to its own free purpose, hastens there,
And there alone reposes.   Let these elms
Bend their protecting shadow o'er their graves,
And build with their green roof the only fane,
Where we may gather on the hallowed day,
That rose to them in blood, and set in glory.
Here let us meet, and while our motionless lips
Give not a sound, and all around is mute
In the deep sabbath of a heart too full
For words or tears—here let us strew the sod
With the first flowers of spring, and make to them
An offering of the plenty, Nature gives,
And they have rendered ours—perpetually.

                                        P.

SUNRISE ON THE HILLS.

I stood upon the hills, when heaven's wide arch
Was glorious with the sun's returning march,
    And woods were brightened, and soft gales
    Went forth to kiss the sun-clad vales.
The clouds were far beneath me :—bathed in light
They gathered mid-way round the wooded height,

And in their fading glory shone
Like hosts in battle overthrown,
As many a pinnacle, with shifting glance,
Through the grey mist thrust up its shattered lance,
And rocking on the cliff was left
The dark pine blasted, bare, and cleft.
The veil of cloud was lifted,—and below
Glowed the rich valley, and the river's flow
Was darkened by the forest's shade,
Or glistened in the white cascade,
Where upward in the mellow blush of day
The noisy bittern wheeled his spiral way.

I heard the distant waters dash—
I saw the current whirl and flash—
And richly by the blue lake's silver beach
The woods were bending with a silent reach.
Then o'er the vale with gentle swell
The music of the village bell
Came sweetly to the echo-giving hills,
And the wild horn, whose voice the woodland fills,
Was ringing to the merry shout
That faint and far the glen sent out,
Where, answering to the sudden shot, thin smoke
Through thick-leaved branches from the dingle broke.

If thou art worn and hard beset
With sorrows that thou wouldst forget,—
If thou wouldst read a lesson that will keep
Thy heart from fainting and thy soul from sleep,
Go to the woods and hills!—no tears
Dim the sweet look that nature wears.

                                        H. W. L.

THE SPIRIT OF BEAUTY.

The Spirit of Beauty unfurls her light,
And wheels her course in a joyous flight:
I know her track through the balmy air,
By the blossoms that cluster and whiten there;
She leaves the tops of the mountains green,
And gems the valley with crystal sheen.

At morn, I know where she rested at night,
For the roses are gushing with dewy delight;
Then she mounts again, and around her flings
A shower of light from her purple wings,
Till the spirit is drunk with the music on high,
That silently fills it with ecstacy!

At noon, she hies to a cool retreat,
Where bowering elms over waters meet;

She dimples the wave where the green leaves dip,
And smiles, as it curls, like a maiden's lip,
When her tremulous bosom would hide, in vain,
From her lover, the hope that she loves again.

At eve, she hangs o'er the western sky
Dark clouds for a glorious canopy ;
And round the skirts of each sweeping fold,
She paints a border of crimson and gold,
Where the lingering sunbeams love to stay,
When their god in his glory has passed away.

She hovers around us at twilight hour,
When her presence is felt with the deepest power ;
She mellows the landscape, and crowds the stream
With shadows that flit like a fairy dream :
Still wheeling her flight through the gladsome air.
The Spirit of Beauty is every where !

D.

EPITAPHS FROM THE ITALIAN.

ON AN HONEST MAN.

The memory of Aristus must
Be trusted to this stone obscure ;
Know, reader, he was wise and just,
You may imagine he was poor.

ON A BANKRUPT.

Here Alcon lies, who fearing none
Upon his grave would drop a tear,
Gave all his creditors good cause
To show a grief the most sincere.

ON NIGELLA.

Gentle shepherds, lightly tread
On the flowers of this mead,
Underneath its turf were laid
The ashes of a beauteous maid.
And Love perhaps has given the fair
The semblance of some flowret rare.

ON A MAGISTRATE.

Alceus here lies buried,
And let each malefactor
Come pay the last sad tribute
Unto his benefactor.

ON A PLOUGHMAN.

Here lies, with years and toil borne down,
A swain, his labours done.
With sheaves his monument we 'll crown,
The trophies that he won.

CRITICAL NOTICES.

CRITICAL NOTICES.

Westminster Review for April, 1825.

[Concluded.]

An article on the " Corn Laws " is opposed to a late opinion of the Edinburgh reviewers, that the price of corn would not be much lowered by the removal of the prohibitory regulations. The Westminster reviewers contend that it would be so, and we think reasonably. Neither party appears to us to be aware of the increasing quantity which is likely to be exported from New York, as the back part of that state becomes settled.

A writer on " Prison Discipline" joins in the general cry, which seems to prevail throughout Great Britain, against the use of the tread-wheel, as a means of employment in penitentiaries.

There is a long article on " Emigration," of which the interest is principally of a local nature. It contains some erroneous opinions respecting the treatment of the coloured population in our northern states, which we intended to notice at length, but are prevented by the limits assigned to this article.

The remaining articles are on " Boaden's Memoirs of Kemble," which is treated with great contempt; on " Contagion and Quarantine," which is interesting, without containing any thing very novel to those familiar with the various reviews, which have been published on this subject for the last ten years.

In perusing the various political articles in this volume, we were led to remark, what has occurred to us before, namely, the apparent popularity and enlightened character of the present ministry of Great Britain. This seems to be admitted, with little exception, by all parties in the state; and if they go on long as they have begun, the opposition will have no " thunder " left.

There is nothing particularly interesting among the Critical Notices of this number.

Sayings and Doings, or Sketches from Life. Second Series. Philadelphia, 1825. 2 vols. 12mo.

The first of these volumes contains three tales, the latter only one. Like those of the former series they are intended to illustrate certain proverbs, of which the reader never hears till the end of the story. They are of unequal merit, but are all interesting; and indeed we consider the work as among the most entertaining of any of those ephemeral matters, which one reads but to forget.

The principal merit of the tales consists in the liveliness of the dialogue and spirited sketching of common characters. The writer does not attempt to paint the workings of remarkable minds, from strong motives, or on great occasions. His characters are every-day people, placed now and then in picturesque or strange situations, and acting from ordinary motives, and generally, as he himself expresses it, from those eight-and

34

sixpenny ones, which lie at the bottom of so much of human conduct. The writer seems to have seen much of the world, and to have regarded mankind with some shrewdness, without penetrating far beneath the surface.   He has a kind of easy philosophy, which leads one to laugh goodnaturedly at the follies and vices of one's fellow-creatures, without being much disgusted with the one or offended with the other.   He is evidently of the Democritus school, and considers ridicule better than preaching ; and if he does not always paint vice in colours sufficiently revolting, he certainly does not attempt to make it agreeable.   It is a fault of many good books, that they paint both virtue and vice in colours so much stronger, than commonly exist in nature, that they defeat their own purpose. The pictures are evidently caricatures, and the characters monstrous. In these tales the aim is to make the virtuous respectable, and the evil not so much hateful as contemptible.

In this attempt he has succeeded indifferently well ; and the effect, though not considerable, we think likely to be advantageous, since it is not difficult to identify the characters of such a work with many that we see around us in nature, and it leads us to associate the ideas of contempt with their evil and of respect with their good qualities.   We shall not attempt an analysis of either tale. The following is a specimen of the dialogue.   Colonel Arden, the principal personage of the second story, on setting up an establishment in London, is presented, among others, with a French cook.

"The particular profession of this person, the Colonel, who understood very little French, was for sometime puzzled to find out; he heard a vocabulary of dishes enumerated with grace and fluency, he saw a remarkably gentlemanly looking man, his well-tied neckcloth, his well-trimmed whiskers, his white kid gloves, his glossy hat, his massive chain encircling his neck, and protecting a repeating Breguer, all pronouncing the man of ton ; and when he came really to comprehend that the sweet-scented, ring-fingered gentleman before him, was willing to dress a dinner on trial, for the purpose of displaying his skill, he was thunderstruck.

'Do I mistake?' said the Colonel : 'I really beg pardon—it is fifty-eight years since I learned French—am I speaking to—a—(and he hardly dared to pronounce the word)—cook?'

'Oui, Monsieur,' said M. Rissolle; 'I believe I have de first reputation in de profession : I live four years wiz de Marqui de Chester, and je me flatte dat, if I had not turn him off last months, I should have superintend his cuisine at dis moment.'

'Oh, you have discharged the Marquis, Sir?' said the Colonel.

'Yes, mon Colonel, I discharge him ; because he cast affront upon me, insupportabic to an artist of sentiment.'

'Artist!' *mentally ejaculated* the Colonel.

'Mon Colonel, de Marqui had de mauvais gout one day, when he had large partie to dine, to put salt into his soup, before all his compagnie.'

'Indeed,' said Arden ; 'and, may I ask, is that considered a crime, Sir, in your code?'

'I don't know code,' said the man, 'Morue ?—dat is salt enough without.'

'I don't mean *that*, Sir,' said the Colonel ; 'I ask, is it a crime for a gentleman to put salt into his soup?'

'Not a crime, mon Colonel,' said Rissolle, 'but it would be de ruin of me, as cook, should it be known to the world,—so I told his Lordship I must leave him; dat de butler had said, dat he saw his Lordship put de salt into de soup, which was to proclaim to the universe dat I did not know de proper quantité of salt required to season my soup.'

An Address pronounced at the Opening of the New York Athenæum, December 14, 1824. By HENRY WHEATON. New York. 1824. 8vo. pp. 44.

IT is not unknown to our readers that, in emulation of the liberal endowment and patronage of the Boston Athenæum, a similar association was recently formed among the opulent and enlightened citizens of New York. Mr Wheaton's Address, at the opening of this institution, is very properly devoted to considering the intellectual progress of America thus far, and inquiring what is to be anticipated from the genius of our countrymen in future times. In the pursuit of this investigation, he casts a rapid but penetrating glance over a wide and fruitful field.

He hastily alludes to the embarrassments of our colonial condition, and the peculiar difficulties with which our country's young strength was forced to grapple, as being fully adequate to account for the tardy development of an elegant literature in the land. Our faculties were tasked in the hard duty of reclaiming a wilderness to the uses of civilized man; in ascertaining, defending, and enforcing free principles of civil polity; in achieving an independence not dearly bought with their blood; in laying deeply and broadly the foundations of a great republican government. Strangers in the crowded family of nations, enough was it for us, newly emerged from European guardianship, to make good our place in that mighty contention for wealth and power, in which empires, not men, are the competitors. But that period, he conceives, is now quickly passing away, and our country is beginning to afford allurements to something beside active, professional, and business talents.

Mr Wheaton refers to the want of a peculiar national language and literature, and the consequent servitude to foreign models and the habit of self-depreciation—the absence of patronage and of the aid of extensive libraries, as being serious obstacles to our advancement in the cultivation of objects of refined taste. But the injurious operation of all these circumstances, in his opinion, is counteracted by the advantages derived from the geographical features of the country—its federal constitution—its division into states, which will be emulous to excel as much in liberal arts and science as in affairs of government—and, above all, by the free spirit, which is the moving, animating, and sustaining power of all our institutions. The consideration of this last point leads him into remarks upon the question, whether there is any sympathy between civil freedom and the polite arts,—which occupy most of the residue of the Address.

Mr Wheaton is entitled to great praise for his persevering attention to literature, amid the cares of professional and public duties; and every thing, which comes from him, evinces the liberal taste of a scholar, and is stamped with the marks of a vigorous and accomplished mind. The piece before us bespeaks a ready, practised, and skilful writer, alike familiar with the classic lore of ancient and modern ages, and versed in the living wisdom of our own busy days. His subject led him, in some portions of it, over the same paths which Mr Everett trod in his Phi Beta Kappa Oration; and this last is so rich in pregnant matter, so profusely stored with admirable allusions in support of his opinions, that, in subsequently handling a kindred topic, Mr Wheaton sometimes inevitably falls into trains of thought, and adopts illustrations, which had been preoccupied by Mr Everett. But Mr Everett is an *unfair* writer, in the sense in which King Charles accused Dr Barrow of being an *unfair* preacher. His acute and comprehensive mind instantly seizes upon the strong points of a subject, and works up its best parts, so as to leave little for the diligence of aftercomers to glean, where his sickle had entered;—and to such a man neither Mr Wheaton, nor any other American, need be unwilling to own acknowledgments.

The Refugee, a Romance. By Captain Matthew Murgatroyd, of the Ninth Continentals in the Revolutionary War. In two vols. New York. 1825. 12mo. pp. 325 and 328.

WE suppose it has happened to most persons, at some time in their lives, to be placed in situations which they felt to be awkward, and to conceal their own consciousness by a display of ease and vivacity, which, instead of imposing upon the bystanders, served only to make themselves more ridiculous. This seems to us to be precisely the case with the author of the work before us. Now when a person is so unfortunate as to get into such a predicament, without any fault of his own, it is the height of rudeness to attempt to aggravate his mortification by ridiculing, or even noticing it. Our novel-writer, however, being under no compulsion, and having put himself in this situation with his eyes open, cannot fairly shelter himself under any law of politeness, which is acknowledged by reviewers; and we have therefore the less hesitation in noticing the combination of restraint and counterfeit ease which seems to us to distinguish this work.

The hero of this story is Gilbert Greaves, of Welsh descent, and the son of an ex-officer in the British service, who resided on the banks of the Hudson at the commencement of the Revolutionary War. On that occasion, the father joins the British army in New York, and is followed by the son; the latter soon sees cause to repent, revolts to the American army, is taken prisoner, and hardly escapes execution as a deserter.

The scene is principally in New York and its vicinity. The characters are numerous; so much so, indeed, that it is difficult to keep them all in mind, whilst one is perusing the work. We find some returning, at the close of the second volume, whom we had utterly forgotten our introduction to, in the first. Like too many of our novelists, the author spreads himself over too great a surface, apparently finding it easier to say a little of many persons and things, than to give an accurate, full, and lively description of any individual. There are many strange anachronisms in the course of the work, and occasionally a degree of levity in treating serious things, which we consider reprehensible. But the most serious objection to it, as we have already intimated, is the laborious affectation of the style. There is a continual effort to be witty or sententious pervading the whole. We are obliged to think of the author instead of his persons; and whenever he does achieve wisdom or wit, we are naturally inclined to give him the less credit for his success, as he has so often tried in vain. He who shoots perpetually at the same mark, will sometimes hit it, but his success is more likely to be attributed to chance than skill. This air of pretension naturally prejudices the reader against the book, and leads him to set down much as indifferent, which, perhaps, if it came in humbler guise, might be regarded as respectable.

Seven Lectures on Female Education; inscribed to Mrs. Garnett's Pupils, at Elm-Wood, Essex County, Virginia. By James M. Garnett. Richmond. 1824. 12mo. pp. 261.

THE importance of the subject which this book professes to treat—the unqualified recommendations of the friends of the author,—and the echo of these same recommendations, with faint and equivocal censure from the tribunals qualified to decide upon its character, have given it a reputation, which it never deserved, and which its own merits never could have gained. We are not about to be severe upon an innocent little book; for it is the result no doubt of the best intentions, and as such is entitled to respect. But we wished merely to account upon the true principles for the facts, that two editions have been published in as many years, and that the public are now threatened with a third.

We have as high an opinion of the importance of female education as Mr Garnett, or any of the gentlemen whose names adorn and recommend his book; but we doubt if its best interests will be much subserved by his exertions as an author. And it is much to be regretted, that the influence of such distinguished names as John Marshall Esq. Chief Justice of the U. S., and the Right Rev. Richard Moore, Bishop of the Diocess of Virginia, and others which it is unnecessary to mention, should not be directed to some object more worthy of them, than giving currency to a book of such slender merit. We have read the work with considerable attention, and the more, because we were desirous of resisting the conclusion, which seemed to be forcing itself upon us, that the respectable names of friends, and the good motives of the author, were its chief recommendations. But such conclusion is settled, and we will give our reasons for it.

The preface, " in which a summary view is taken of the principal obstacles to the progress of Education in general, but particularly to that of Females," occupies thirty-seven pages, and is much the best part of the book. Then follows what the author calls the "Gossip's Manual," filling thirty-one pages. These are ironical maxims, intended to satyrize some of the most common faults " in people of both sexes beyond the age of childhood." They are generally very silly, and therefore must fail of their intended effect. The Lectures make up the book. These are upon the following topics. 1. The Moral and Religious Obligations to the Improvement of Time. 2. The best Means of Improvement. 3. Temper and Deportment. 4. Foibles, Faults, and Vices. 5. Manners, Accomplishments, Fashions, and Conversations. 6. Associates, Friends, and Connexions. These several topics are discussed with some zeal and spirit; but we have not been able to discover one principle in education, which has not long since been much better stated and inculcated by almost all the most popular authors upon the subject. Fenelon, Archbishop of Cambray, although he wrote somewhat more than a century since, will afford more instruction upon the subject, than the volume before us. We recommend Miss Hamilton's Letters on the Elementary Principles of Education; and her Letters addressed to the Daughter of a Nobleman, on the formation of religious and moral principle, as much more complete and satisfactory upon the subject than any thing Mr Garnett has written. Miss Edgeworth's works are worth Mr Garnett's consideration before he makes another edition of his book; although we must always express regret, that she has not added to the motives she addresses to the young, " In the name of the Lord Jesus." These authors wrote for purposes more general, than those of Mr Garnett, but their works will nevertheless accomplish all his objects much better than his own. We might name various other authors who are decidedly preferable on every account to Mr Garnett, but it is, at present, unnecessary.

The work before us, therefore, offers nothing new upon the subject, and repeats what is old, in exceedingly coarse, vulgar, and disgusting language. This last remark we shall proceed to illustrate and justify by a few specimens.

" If husbands and wives *will live* in that sort of amity which generally prevails between cats and dogs, they must expect that their daughters will *play the cat* too, whenever they have opportunities. If mothers and nurses will scold, and *hector*, and *storm*, and *rave*, and fall into fits of ' the sullens,' (a very malignant disease, by the way) either *with* or *without* any colour of excuse, the children under their management will certainly imitate their example."

We have not the reputation of being remarkable for cant, but we think when the inspired writings are quoted with such levity as in the following passage, they must, at least, fail of their intended effect.

" Yet thus it is, (in thousands of instances,) by incalculating ' envy, and hatred, and malice, and all uncharitableness,' in the compendious form of ' emulation' *a priori*; and by the administration of *birching without form*, and often without *measure*, *a posteriori*, that the youth of our country are to be imbued with all those amiable qualities of the heart, and useful endowments of the understanding, which are to fit them for this world, and prepare them for the next."

Mr Garnett discourses to his audience of " young ladies " of being " *Tygresses*," " *Tartars*," " *Spitfires*," " *She-Dragons*," and " *She-Devils* "; and of becoming as loathsome as " *hogs dressed in women's apparel*." If this is appropriate language to be addressed to young ladies in Virginia, we hope the unqualified recommendations of the book which contains it, will not introduce it here. We could multiply instances of similar offences against decency, but are unwilling to disfigure our pages with any more.

The Grecian Wreath of Victory. New York. 1824. 24to. pp. 120.

In the course of the last year, an association of ladies in the city of New York caused a " Grecian Cross," forty feet high, to be prepared, and placed at the disposal of General Swift, who had presided at a meeting, held at Brooklyn, in 1822, at which meeting were passed " various resolutions expressive of the sympathy of Americans in the struggle now carrying on by the Greeks."

It was afterwards decided to plant the Cross on the Brooklyn Heights, and to surmount it with a wreath of victory, to be composed of the same material with the " victorious wreaths" of ancient Greece. What was this material, then became a question, for the solution of which the " Grecian ladies" offered a gold medal of considerable value. This procured them various communications from gentlemen of high literary standing, and these communications compose the work before us. The profits of it are to be devoted to the purpose of procuring some memorial of American sympathy, to be presented to the Grecian senate.

When we consider the various respectable names connected with this little work, and remember that the whole matter of the cross and wreath is an affair of the ladies, we dare not say, that it sounds very silly to us. We can only venture to acknowledge, that we are so obtuse as not to see the point of this erecting of crosses, surmounted with pagan wreaths; and to hint, that if such a thing had been elevated on any of the heights in the neighbourhood of Boston, we should have shrugged our shoulders at the " notion."

But leaving the origin of the book, for its contents, we observe in the first place, that among those who took part in this discussion, and whose lucubrations are here published, are the names of Professors Moore and Anthon of Columbia College, Drs Hosack and King, Colonel Trumbull, Mr Genet, and Mr Bancroft of Round Hill. The principal arguments adduced are in favour of the palm, the laurel, the myrtle, and the olive. The claims of the latter are defended by Professor Anthon, in four several communications, which are decidedly the best in every point of view. The volume is closed by the decision of Professor Everett, in favour of the olive, a short essay by Governor Clinton, in which he comes to the same conclusion, and a translation of a Roman war song, by Professor Doane of Washington College. Professor Anthon seems, therefore, to have obtained the prize.

Considerable industry and learning are displayed in many of these essays, accompanied often with a very unnecessary display of exultation. Surely our professors ought to be able to quote Pliny, Plutarch, Potter's Antiquities, Lempriere's Classical Dictionary, Moore's Anacreon, and, if need be, even Pindar, Dion Cassius, or Tertullian, without glorification. There are also some pitiable juvenilities about the fair hands of the Grecian ladies, &c. ; and, lastly, there is a metrical translation of the song of Callistratus, which is very bad indeed.

Now we wish well to the cause of the Greeks, and to every rational exertion in their behalf; but we think money might be applied to better purpose, and one quite as advantageous to the Greeks as that of setting up crosses, and dragging grave professors from their elbow chairs, to execute unskilful gambols before them, for the amusement of the public.

Decision, a Tale ;   By Mrs Hofland, author of Integrity, a Tale ;   Patience, a Tale ; The Son of a Genius ; Tales of the Priory ; Tales of the Manor, &c. &c.   New York. 1825. 18mo. pp. 264.

Mrs Hofland is known to the public as the author of several small vol-

umes, by one of which, " The Son of a Genius," she has attained some celebrity.   This Tale, as its title purports, is intended to illustrate and
encourage the truly estimable and valuable trait of character, *Decision* ;
and so far as the work has any tendency, it undoubtedly has the desired
one.   The story, although it is said to be founded on fact, seems in some
respects to be rather improbable ; and is told with no very absorbing
interest.   Mr Falconer, a gentleman in easy circumstances, is suddenly
reduced to poverty, by an unfortunate speculation in *iron*.   His only
child and daughter, Maria Falconer, *resolves* to retrieve the affairs of
the family.   In order to this, she becomes a dealer in *iron* also.   She
travels about, establishes foreign correspondences—and by great hard-
ships and perseverance in business, succeeds in making her own fortune,
which, with filial piety, she appropriates to the support of her parents
and the assistance of her friends.   This outline, filled up with minor incidents and interspersed with a proper relish of " love affairs," constitutes the story.   Maria Falconer becomes initiated in all the mysteries
of waste-book, journal, and ledger.   She weighs out her *iron* to her dusty
customers, with scrupulous exactness ; and nothing can divert her from
her purpose till her object is achieved.   But when the business of the day
is over, she changes her identity, and appears the delicate and beautiful
young lady, such as would grace a fashionable drawing-room.   These
two characters never interfere with each other ; except that in a few
instances, a little colour flashes in her face, and her hands wander at random over her files of papers without finding what she is not looking for,
when a certain gentleman comes into her *store* on business.   With this
very brief notice, we must dismiss Mrs Hofland's " Decision " with the
recommendation which we are obliged frequently to give, and which
usually attends domestic prescriptions in medicine, " If they can do no
good, they can certainly do no harm, and therefore may be safely
taken."

The Town Officer's Guide, containing a Compilation of the General Laws of Massa-
    chusetts, relating to the whole Power and Duty of Towns, Districts, and Parishes,
    with their several Officers ; with a Digest of the Decisions in the Supreme Judicial
    Court of Massachusetts, relating to the several Subjects.   To which is subjoined
    an extensive Appendix of Forms, for the use of Town Officers and Individuals.
    By JOHN BACON, Esq.   Haverhill, Mass.   1825.   12mo.   pp. 396.

THIS is a labour-saving age ; we can make our clothes, sweep our chim-
nies, mend our pens or our morals, and educate our children, at a great
profit, compared with the prices, which our ancestors paid for these useful purposes.   Steam-engines, railways, digests, compends, reviews, and
every sort of invention in every department of improvement, of industry,
of literature, and of science, obtrude themselves upon the community, to
the great delight of the lazy scholar and the rich manufacturer, and the
great grievance of all plodding students and poor labourers.   Literary
turnpikes can be travelled at a less expense than the old roads ; and,
although we lose some of the pleasant views and delightful associations,
which the latter afford, we are transported to the desired point, with less
labour and more expedition.   A *M'Adamizing* system is applied to our
learning as well as our roads; the rocks in literature and science, which
formerly obstructed our paths, are now broken up, and made subservient

to our purposes, in the reduced and compacted form of abridgments, digested indexes, &c. &c.   A man, in these days, who should undertake to read any work consisting of more than one volume (novels always excepted), would be looked upon as demented, and as wilfully disregarding and neglecting the means put into his hands to save his time and his labour.

Town officers have ever been especially favoured of the gifted few, who understand the science of compressing knowledge; and any selectman, overseer of the poor, culler of hoops and staves, hog-reeve, or weigher of beef, who does not understand his duty, and conduct on all occasions " according to the law in such cases made and provided," must, from his stupidity, be "unworthy the suffrages of a free and enlightened people."

Mr Bacon, in the work before us, has contributed his full share to enlighten our municipalities; and has faithfully made the last condensation and refinement, of which his medley of a subject is susceptible.

His abridgments of the statutes are generally correct; his practical forms very good, and some of them very useful.   His dedication is of a character, which proves that he is more at home when compiling laws "for the use of town officers and individuals," than when he attempts politics or original composition.   President Adams, to whom the work is pompously dedicated, will undoubtedly be delighted with the offering; though he must be somewhat surprised to learn, that to him, " we owe the defence of those immunities and privileges, and the preservation of those rights and possessions, with which our laws have invested us"!!

Upon the whole, and seriously, we recommend this work to town officers, as a valuable and safe guide in the discharge of their duties, and as an improvement upon any former publication of its kind among us.

To the author, we especially recommend, that he abstain, for the future, from all prefaces, notes, and " epistles dedicatory;" and take our leave of him, hoping that he will be rewarded for compiling, and his patrons for reading his book.

The New-York Review, and Atheneum Magazine.   No. I. June 1825.

This is the first number of the third volume of the Atlantic magazine which appears under a new name, and with the addition to the editorial department of a gentleman well known to the lovers of poetry.

This number contains eight reviews, and among others one of the Journal of Madam Knight.   This singular performance, which has been generally considered as an imposture, the reviewer declares to be authentic.   He asserts, that he has seen the manuscript, and that it is " of unquestionable yellowness, of most manifest fragility, and withal, of a very ancient and fish-like smell."   On this whole matter we desire for the present to suspend our opinions, and the rather as the reviewer's manner savours so much of irony, that we are not quite sure of his meaning in some instances.

The reviewer of Lionel Lincoln agrees with us in expressing a more favourable opinion of that work, than it has received from the public in general, we should rather say perhaps in our neighbourhood.

We think the magazine department in this number not so interesting

35

as the reviews, and remarked, as somewhat singular, an editorial note in praise of a poetical article contained in it. It seemed to us like an indirect way of complimenting one's own work.

The articles in this number are of various merit, but on the whole we read it with interest. We think the editors are not always sufficiently impressed with the importance of preserving the purity of the language, nor sufficiently careful to exclude slight errors in construction, or unauthorized words; we could select a few trivial instances of this sort, but it would probably seem to some of our readers hypercritical, and we wish only to hint at the importance of vigilance in this particular. The typographical execution of the work, is very good. The price, 6 dollars per annum, seems to us too high, when compared with those of our New England periodical Journals.

A Particular Account of the Battle of Bunker or Breed's Hill, on the 17th of June, 1775. By a Citizen of Boston. Boston. 1825. 8vo. pp. 26.

This pamphlet is rather a continuation of the controversy, which took place a few years since, upon the same subject, than a correct narrative of that important event. And it appears remarkably deficient in the two properties, to which it pretends, and which alone could give an additional work on the subject any value, viz. great research and perfect impartiality.

INTELLIGENCE.

NEW WORK RELATING TO LORD BYRON.

The most intense curiosity seems still to exist, in regard to every thing, that relates to this remarkable man. And this new work is announced to the public in a manner exceedingly well calculated to excite and keep it alive. The London Courier of May 14th, says, " We smell a work in the press, which will create a great fermentation among the fashionable and literary world. Endless conjectures are already abroad respecting its author. Some have imagined it to be a distinguished nobleman, others a *chère amie* of Lord Byron's ; at any rate it contains what cannot fail to be eagerly sought after—Recollections of a perusal of his Lordship's self-written memoirs, and will, we understand, be given to the world this week, splendidly embellished, under the title of The Life, Writings, Opinions, and Times of the Right Hon. Lord Byron, in three interesting volumes, including anecdotes and sketches of all the public and noble characters and courtiers of the present polished age, and court of His Majesty George the Fourth, dedicated to the Right Hon. George Canning, M. P." This, as we observed before, is exceedingly well calculated to provoke curiosity upon the subject ; and we doubt not that in due time we shall be favoured with the forthcoming volumes. We hope we may have them all at once, without any garbling or reservations, for we are quite discouraged in buying and noticing books about Lord Byron. He was a great genius, no doubt, and we need not withhold our admiration of his splendid talents; but his infidelity and recklessness of moral principle made him a curse to his own age, and will make his writings one to posterity. It is in connexion only with such splendid talents as Lord Byron's, that depravity so deep has the power to taint the moral atmosphere of more than one age. And the fewer *recollections* the world have of his private life and history, the better it will be both for his character and their condition.

A PEEP AT THE PILGRIMS IN 1636.

This novel, which was seasonably noticed in the first volume of the United States Literary Gazette, has been lately reprinted in London; and is thus noticed in the Literary Gazette.

" The moderns have certainly added another muse to the nine maiden ladies of the ancients, viz. the muse of novel-writing; and were the works of her votaries to be heaped up in a pile to her honor, they would, like the tower of Babel, reach even unto the clouds. Novels seem to be also quite the national literature of America. The present one is no discredit to the land of its birth. Without exciting any very overwhelming emotion, it yet attracts and keeps up a pleased attention, and presents an interesting, and we doubt not, true account of the time and country it describes—New England, about the middle of the seventeenth century."

NUMBER OF AMERICAN WORKS PUBLISHED DURING THE LAST QUARTER.

In the last six numbers of this Gazette, embracing a period of three months, we have collected and published the titles of one hundred and eighty-five new American works, including pamphlets and periodicals, which have issued from the different presses in the United States during that time. Nine of them are works of two volumes each, making, in all, one hundred and ninety-four volumes. A goodly portion of them, however, are *twelve and a half cent pamphlets*, of which our authors and presses seem abundantly prolific. In the same numbers, we have published the titles of fifty foreign works, making sixty-nine volumes, which have been reprinted in this country during the same time. The whole number of volumes, therefore, foreign and domestic, which have issued from our presses, during the last three months, is two hundred and sixty-three. Probably many works have been published, which have not reached us, but we think this is as complete a list as can be found in any journal in the country for the same time.

STATISTICS OF PARIS.

The number of births in Paris was, in 1820, 24858: in 1821, 25156: in 1822, 26880: in 1823, 27070. The number of deaths was, in 1820, 22464: in 1821, 22917: in 1822, 23882: in 1823, 24500. The consequent increase of which amounts, in 1820, to 2394: in 1821, to 2239: in 1822, to 2998: in 1823, to 2570: making a total increase of population, during the four years, of 10201. The number of natural children in 1820 was 8870 ;

in 1821, 9176; in 1822, 9751; and in 1823, 9806; the proportion of the latter year being rather less than $\frac{2}{3}$, or rather one third, of the total of births. There are generally more boys than girls born; the difference in 1820 was 448; in 1821, 564; in 1822, 264; 1823, 434. The number of deaths in 1823 was as follows, 15273 at their residences; 8227 in the hospitals; 661 military, 72 in prison; and 267 deposited at Morgue. There were also 1509 still-born children in 1823, of which 847 were boys. There has also been a tremendous increase in the deaths occasioned by the small pox: in 1820 they were only 105; in 1821, 272; in 1822, 1084; and in 1823, 649, of which 365 were boys. In 1823, there were 6280 marriages between bachelors and spinsters; 332 between bachelors and widows; 680 between widowers and spinsters; and 212 between widowers and widows, making a total of 7504. There were consumed in the same year 915958 hectolitres of wine; 51416 of brandy; 11465 of cider and perry; 16860 of vinegar; 150069 of beer.

JOHN BULL IN AMERICA.

This burlesque upon English travellers in America, a work which we noticed in a late number of our Gazette, has been reprinted and published in London by John Miller, who seems among the London publishers to take the deepest *interest* in American literature. The work has been reviewed of course in the Literary Gazette, and openly attributed to Mr Paulding of New York. A review in the London Literary Gazette, however, means no more, than that the work has been again reprinted in that journal. For the conductors of it seldom do more than pirate the best parts of a book and connect them by a few sentences of their own.

SCHOOL UPON THE PLAN OF FELLENBERG.

We learn from the New Monthly Magazine for April, that another school has been lately established in Switzerland under the care of M. Eberhardt upon the plan of the one at Hofwyl, conducted by M Fellenberg, by whom young Eberhardt was instructed. The experiment began with two pupils; the number is now increased to twenty-four. The aim of the institution is to form honest and religious men, and make them good practical agriculturists. The expense of the two first was, at the utmost, 200 francs per head. Since the number has increased, this sum is diminished; and it is expected, that by the fifth year there will not only be no loss, but a surplus remaining to the establishment.

WOODEN WATCHMAN.

A curious piece of mechanism has been invented and exhibited in Great Britain. It is called the Alarm Statue, and is intended for presentation to the king. It is designed for the protection of dwelling-houses &c. from midnight depredators. This automaton represents a soldier in full regimentals, six feet in height; its position is erect, in the manner of a sentinel on duty, having a blunderbuss in his hand. Upon touching a wire, it immediately turns round in that direction, drops its head, and fires the piece, at the same time ringing two alarm-bells, and pronouncing the word " fire " in a distinct and audible voice.

MORTALITY OF THE RICH AND POOR.

A memoir was lately read by Dr Villerone before the Academy of Sciences at Paris, " on the mortality in France in the class in easy circumstances, compared with what takes place among the indigent." In two arrondissements of Paris, the first and the twelfth, he makes it appear, that the former, which is inhabited by rich persons, has a mortality of one in 50; and the latter, which is inhabited by poor, has a mortality of one in 24, and there being no other assignable cause for this enormous difference than wealth and poverty. He found the deaths in Rue de la Mortellerie, where poor people are crowded together in unhealthy lodgings, four times and a half as numerous as in the quays of the Isle St Louis, where rich people live in large and well ventilated apartments. He also shows that the mortality in the hospitals rises or falls with the rate of wages of those who enter them.

Of Jewellers, Compositors, &c. there die in the Hospitals 1 in 11
" Milliners - - - - - - - - - - 1 in 8
" Shoemakers - - - - - - - - 1 in 7
" Masons - - - - - - - - - - - 1 in 6
" Labourers - - - - - - - - - - 1 in 5
" The poorest of them all, Rag-gatherers &c. - - 1 in 5
" Soldiers, who are the best off, - - - - - 1 in 20

NEWLY DISCOVERED QUADRUPED.

Dr T. William Harris of Milton, a very intelligent and promising naturalist, has lately received from Machias in the state of Maine, a specimen of an animal of the genus *Condylura*, which he believes, after an investigation, to belong to a species hitherto unknown. This genus, we believe, has hitherto embraced but one species, the "radiated mole," which was included by Linnæus under the genus *Sorex*, and by Cuvier under that of *Talpa*. Other naturalists have, however, thought it presented differences sufficient to authorize its establishment as a separate genus, and we have now a new species added to it, to which Dr Harris has proposed to give the name *prasinata*. The fur of this animal is of a green colour, and it nearly corresponds in size to the species previously known. We understand that Dr Harris has prepared a full account of this animal, which will appear in the Number of the Boston Journal of Philosophy and the Arts, which is now in press.

NEW UNIVERSITY IN ENGLAND.

Such is the number of students accustomed to resort to the Universities now in operation, that it is proposed to establish a third, somewhere in the vicinity of York. To this institution Earl Fitzwilliam has promised to subscribe fifty thousand pounds.

NEW ROUTE.

An English journal announces, among other American projects, that it is in contemplation " to cut a canal between the Delaware and Rariton and Barnstaple rivers and Buzzard's bay."

NEW PUBLICATIONS.

HISTORY.

Annals of Portsmouth, comprising a Period of Two Hundred Years, from the First Settlement of the Town; with Biographical Sketches of a few of the most respectable Inhabitants. By Nathaniel Adams. Portsmouth. Published by the Author.

MATHEMATICS.

Elements of Geometry, by A. M. Legendre, Member of the Institute and the Legion of Honour, of the Royal Society of London, &c. Translated from the French for the use of the Students of the University at Cambridge, New England, by John Farrar, Professor of Mathematics and Natural Philosophy. Second edition, corrected and enlarged. 8vo. pp. 224. Boston. Cummings, Hilliard, & Co.

An Introduction to Algebra, upon the Inductive Method of Instruction. By Warren Colburn, Author of "First Lessons in Arithmetic," &c. 12mo. pp. 372. Boston. Cummings, Hilliard, & Co.

MISCELLANEOUS.

An Address delivered at the Laying of the Corner Stone of the Bunker Hill Monument. By Daniel Webster. 8vo. Boston. Cummings, Hilliard, & Co. pp. 40.

Address delivered before the Alumni of Columbia College, on the 4th of May, 1825, in the Chapel of the College. By Clement C. Moore, A. M. 8vo. pp. 37. New York.

The author has given a brief sketch of the history of Columbia College from the date of its first charter in 1754, to the present time. "As the institution now stands," says he, "its Faculty consists of a President and five Professors, all of whom the students are required to attend, and a Professor of Law, the attendance on whose lectures is voluntary." The address closes with a statement of the advantages of the association, and the annual meetings of the alumni of the college; and a few judicious remarks upon the purposes and means of education.

The Order of Exercises in the Chapel of Transylvania University, A Collection of Original Pieces in Honour of the Arrival of General Lafayette. 12mo. pp. 16. Lexington, Ky.

This pamphlet contains an Address to General Lafayette in French—three Odes in English—an Eclogue and two Odes in Latin. The Ode by Samuel Wilson, A. M. in Sapphic and Adonian measure, is highly poetical in its conceptions and classical in its language. We hope to see it published in some form which will meet the public eye in this part of our country.

Philadelphia Magazine, No. V. Philadelphia.

An Exposition of the Facts and Circumstances which justified the Expedition to Foxardo, and the Consequences thereof; together with the Proceedings of the Court of Inquiry thereon, held by Order of the Honourable the Secretary of the Navy. By D. Porter. 8vo. pp. 107. Washington. Davis & Force.

This pamphlet was published after the Court of Inquiry upon the conduct of Commodore Porter at Foxardo had closed its examination; and was transmitted to the Secretary of the Navy by Commodore Porter, after he had been apprised by the navy department, that further proceedings would be had, and that he would be arrested and tried by a Court Martial. Commodore Porter, it seems, hoped to obviate the necessity of further proceedings, by making this seasonable defence. But the Secretary of the Navy has expressed his surprise that Commodore Porter should have thought it proper to make a publication relative to his case, while it was still under the consideration of the Executive, " and especially a publication in so many respects deficient and inaccurate."

Memoir read before the Historical Society of the State of New York, December 31, 1816. By E. Benton. Second edition, with Notes. New York. Wilder & Campbell.

Remarks on the Proceedings at Concord, N. H. on the Subject of Internal Improvement. 8vo. Price 20 cents. Boston.

An Essay on the Study and Promotion of the Greek and Latin Languages. By William White, A. M.

Notes on Virginia. By Thomas Jefferson. A new edition. 1 vol. 12mo. Philadelphia. Carey & Lea.

An Address delivered at the Opening of the Eleventh Exhibition of the Academy of the Fine Arts, May 10th, 1825. By William Beach Lawrence. 8vo. pp. 44. New York.

An Address delivered to the American Friendly Association, on their Third Anniversary, being the 22d of February, 1825. By Faneuil Hunt. Published by request. 12mo. pp. 14. Charleston, S. C.

This is a very clever address ; and we are glad we happened to lay our hands upon it. It is short, much to the point, and abundantly patriotic. The blessings of free institutions, and the sufferings of nations in their progress towards the attainment of them, are subjects not wholly new to us, but we like to be reminded of them occasionally, and especially when it can be done so well as it is in this little pamphlet. The following passage notices two striking peculiarities in our institutions, and is all we can subjoin. " Education disseminated through every class ; and *the possession and habitual use of arms*, constitute Americans a peculiar people. It is a coincidence without a parallel in history. When learning was the attribute of a select few ; when information was extended only by oral repetition, corruption and ignorance were powerful instruments in the hands of reckless ambition ; but ours is an age, which is to give direction to the future destinies of the world. The light, which general education, disseminated through the instrumentality of the press, is capable of diffusing, will penetrate the inmost recesses of ignorance and superstition, and exhibit in their native hideousness the atrocities of arbitrary power.' If men are convinced that a general diffusion of knowledge is the only safe foundation for free and happy institutions, we think they had better set themselves zealously to the work of laying that foundation, and let alone prophesying about the future destinies of the world, and the downfall of arbitrary governments. We have enough to do to purify, improve, and perpetuate our own institutions, without meddling with "the atrocities of arbitrary power" beyond the natural influence of our example.

NATURAL HISTORY.

Fauna Americana, being a Description of the Mammiferous Animals inhabiting North America. By Richard Harlem, M. D. Professor of Comparative Anatomy, &c. 1 vol. 8vo. Price $2.

NOVELS.

Stranger of the Valley; or Louisa and Adelaide. An American Tale. By a Lady. 2 vols. 12mo. pp. 241 and 218. New York.

POETRY.

Ode for the Celebration of the Battle of Bunker Hill, at the Laying of the Monumental Stone, June 17, 1825. By Grenville Mellen. 8vo. pp. 16. Boston. Cummings, Hilliard, & Co.

This is an appropriate and beautiful Ode. It evinces poetical talents of a high order; though in some instances fancy has prompted the author to the use of words, not sanctioned by the canons of taste. "Jewelry" (p. 10) is a bad word, and we noticed a few others, which struck us in a similar light. The stanza on the death of WARREN is a bold and poetical conception beautifully expressed ; and the allusion to Lafayette is happy, and worthy of the occasion. We shall be much gratified if

the high opinion we here express of this Ode, should have any influence to induce
Mr Mellen to favour the public with more lyrics. The age has produced but little
worth perusing in that difficult department of writing.

THEOLOGY.

A Dissertation on the Divinity of Christ.   By William Fowler.

The Design and the Importance of the Education Society of the Protestant Episcopal Church, in the Diocess of Pennsylvania :   A Sermon
preached on the Evening of Sunday, the 8th May, in St Stephen's
Church, Philadelphia.   By William H. De Lancey, an Assistant Minister of Christ's Church, St Peter's, and St James, Philadelphia.

AMERICAN EDITIONS OF FOREIGN WORKS.

The Itinerary of a Traveller in the Wilderness, addressed to those
who are performing the same Journey.   By Mrs Taylor of Ongar,
author of " Maternal Solicitude," &c. &c.   18mo. pp. 224.   New York.
Bliss & White and Wilder & Campbell.

This little allegory is designed for a moral effect upon the young.   Mrs Taylor
quotes many passages of Scripture, and of course gives many good lessons ; but the
work inspires no great interest, and therefore will fail of affording the most instruction and the deepest impression which might have been given in the same space.
There is some cant in the style, but it is written with a good spirit, and every youthful reader will rise from the perusal of it with solemn feelings, and more sober views
of life and its duties.

Lights and Shadows of Scottish Life.   A new and cheap edition.

The Difficulties of Infidelity.   By George Stanley Faber, D. D. Rector of Long Newton, New York.   Wilder & Campbell.

New Moral Tales ; Selected and Translated from the French of
Madame De Genlis.   By an American.   New York.   Wilder & Campbell.

New Monthly Magazine, No. LII.

LIST OF WORKS IN PRESS.

A Tour in Germany, and some of the Southern Provinces of the
Austrian Empire, in the years 1820, 1821, 1822.   1 vol. 8vo.   Philadelphia.   E. Littell.

Starkie on Evidence.   3 vols. 8vo.   Philadelphia.   P. H. Nicklin.

Roper on Property.   2 vols. 8vo.   Philadelphia.   P. H. Nicklin.

Wharton on Corporations.   Philadelphia.   P. H. Nicklin.

Medwin's Conversations of Lord Byron, from the latest London edition.   Baltimore.   E. Mickle.

An Abridgment of all the Acts of Congress now in force, except
those of a Private or Local Application ; with Notes of all the Decisions of the Supreme Court on Questions of Construction, &c.   By
Edward Ingersoll, of the Philadelphia Bar.   Philadelphia.

NOTE.—Since the article on " Harvard University" was printed off, we have
learned that the price of board at Williams and Bowdoin Colleges is $1,75 per week
instead of $2, as there stated. This, however, will not materially affect our inference
concerning the economy of commons

In some copies of this number, p. 249, for " last edition of Worcester's Gazetteer,"
read " Worcester's Gazetteer of the United States."

Published on the first and fifteenth day of every month, by CUMMINGS, HILLIARD,
   & Co., No. 134 Washington-Street, Boston, for the Proprietors.   Terms, $5 per
   annum.   Cambridge : Printed at the University Press, by Hilliard & Metcalf.

THE UNITED STATES

LITERARY GAZETTE.

| Vol. II. | JULY 15, 1825. | No. 8. |

REVIEWS.

Reform of Harvard College.
(For the Titles see No. 6 of this Gazette.)

[CONTINUED.]

It appears, from the statement in our last Number, and from other circumstances in the Report, from which we derive our facts, that some of the foundations in this College are of very dubious advantage. It is naturally expected by the public, that whenever a foundation for a professorship exists, it should be filled by some capable person ; but it may happen that foundations shall be more numerous than are required by the number of pupils, or the state of the country. This would be no evil, indeed, if the income of the foundation sufficed for the salary of the incumbent. But this is not the case with a single foundation among those of the resident professors ;— in three of them, indeed, the income is so small, that all united would not pay half of the present salary of a single professor. Professorships of this sort, therefore, are a cause of increased expense, and so far an unnecessary one, that if the foundations did not exist, their places might be supplied by tutorships, or College professorships, as they are termed, with a much smaller salary. This evil may be in some degree remedied by allowing the capital of the foundations to accumulate, as opportunities occur, by the vacation of the offices. But even this resort is, in some instances, precluded by the will of the donor, which compels the Corporation of the University to fill the office within a limited period. The poli-

36

cy of accepting foundations, in the present state of the country, so inadequate to the support of a professor; and thus allowing the donor, by giving a limited sum, to appropriate to a specific object of his own choice a large amount of the unappropriated College funds, has been a mistaken one from the beginning.   And it has led to most of the evils of which the public have loudest complained, and the cause of which they have least understood, viz.—While bequests were repeatedly made by benevolent individuals, there was no diminution of the expense of instruction,—but the reverse.   And the evil of this policy has been unnecessarily increased, by making the salaries too high.   They are higher than is necessary, considering the permanency, the respectability, the hitherto slight responsibility, and the easy and agreeable nature of their offices.

These offices are, in the first place, of a permanent character,—more so than almost any other situation can be in a republican government.   The destruction or abolition of Harvard University is a more improbable event, if possible, than that of the government of the United States.   Whatever occasional uneasiness or complaint may arise against the Institution and its management, there can be no reasonable doubt of its final continuance, and increasing resources and dignity.

The offices are highly respectable.   They have a rank, which does not depend upon show and parade.   It is intrinsic, and cannot be taken away by any thing short of a course of gross mismanagement on the part of the higher branches of the government of the College, or gross misbehaviour on the part of the officers themselves.   They have a rank, in short, which does not depend upon a large income, which does not require a large income for its support, and which is, therefore, to be desired unaccompanied by a large income,—and which, we may add, is desired, and would be desired, by many, well qualified for the duties, with a much smaller salary than is now attached to it.   In this particular the situation resembles that of the New England clergy, whose salaries are low in accordance with this very principle, that their rank and respectability do not depend upon their income.   Like the clergy, they are respected not merely on account of individual merit, but also in consideration of their offices,—and, like them, they are exempted from taxes and many other burdens more or less vexatious to their fellow-citizens.

The offices, again, are, in our opinion, without any anxious

or disagreeable responsibility.   It is true that the interest of all
the professors is more or less connected with the flourishing
state of the Institution ; but they have not the sense of direct individual responsibility, which is annexed in most instances to
the professions, to civil offices, and most other stations of trust
and profit in our country.   In a former paragraph we compared their situations to those of our clergy.   In this particular they have the advantage over them ; as there is but little
heresy in literature, and no angry sects are to be reconciled by
their doctrines.   A Professor may be a Wernerian or a Huttonian, a Nominalist or a Realist, a believer in one electric
fluid or two, without risking either his peace or his salary.

These offices, in the last place, are comparatively easy and
agreeable.   We are not now about to join in the vulgar slang,
which associates the idea of luxury and ease with every situation which does not compel its occupant to swing a sledge, brand-
ish a flail, or exert his physical force in some obvious manner.
The literal sweat of the brow is neither the most uncomfortable effect, nor the only evidence of toil.   But we do believe,
that the situation of a Resident Professor in most Universities,
and especially in a great and wealthy institution, like that at
Cambridge, is neither very toilsome nor disagreeable.   There
are evils, there are vexations, no doubt, which none can appreciate so justly as those who suffer them.   But we are persuaded that there is less of that occasional and utter weariness of flesh and spirit, which is more or less incident to every employment of which we have any knowledge.   A Professor is, or at least ought to be, appointed to his office on
account of some strong predilection and consequent excellence in a particular department of literature or science.   His
pleasure consequently becomes his business, and he is paid
for following those pursuits, to which most other literary men
in society are glad to devote the moments which can be cut
off from the stock which is claimed by their necessary duties.   He must communicate his knowledge, it is true, but he
is not bound down to an eternal round of the merest elementary instruction, whose dull monotony is only varied by the
petty vexations which beset the " little tyrant " of a school.
More than this, he is placed in a society of literary and congenial spirits, and in the midst of a scientific and literary apparatus, which removes the necessity of private expense, that
too often bears hard upon the scanty funds of the scholar in
any other situation.

It does appears to us, therefore, that the Professors to whom we have been alluding, are, in almost every particular, on a level with the clergy of New England, and that in some they have the advantage of them. If then, as we believe is the case, a salary of a thousand dollars is the highest, with very few exceptions, received by any clergyman out of the metropolis, certainly it would appear that seventeen hundred ought to be regarded as too great for a Professor.

On the other hand, we are ready to admit, that great difficulties present themselves in the way of any alteration of these salaries. "One false step," says the proverb, "costs many;" and some false steps were taken a good while since, the consequences of which it may be found difficult to repair. In the first place, with regard to the present incumbents. These gentlemen have enjoyed their incomes for a considerable period. They have learned to consider them necessary. They have, in fact, become necessary to their comfort. There is no doubt that they would have discharged their duties as well, have been as rich, and as happy with smaller salaries, as they have been with the present ones; but there is a great difference between always conforming to a small income and being reduced to it after enjoying a larger. It was not their fault, that they have at times desired an increase of salary. Such desires are incident alike to the drudge and the philosopher. It is not their fault that they have received it. They have no control over the funds. If our principle be correct, that the salaries are too large, it was an error of the superior boards of the College to make them so.

There is another and we think a weighty reason against any diminution of the salaries of actual incumbents. We spoke above of the permanent character of these salaries. And this character ought to belong to them. Devotion to literature is of all things most apt to render a man helpless in regard to the cares and competition of society. Fluctuations of incomes, therefore, are likely to be highly injurious to them, and any principle, which recognises the propriety of fluctuations, ought to be discountenanced. And though it may seem at first sight paradoxical, it is obvious, upon reflection, that one of the strongest reasons for considering the present salaries too high, is equally strong against diminishing them in the case of actual incumbents.

But the College lives forever, it may be said, and the evil may be repaired in the case of future incumbents. But another false step has thrown impediments in the way of this measure. From the notion of the necessity of a certain amount of salary, the capital in some of the professorships has been allowed to accumulate till the income amounts nearly to the present full salary of a Professor. This salary, therefore, can never be diminished, but, on the contrary, must increase with every vacancy. Further,—it has long been recognised as a general principle, that all the salaries should be equal, and this principle appears plausible, since there seems an injustice in bringing together gentlemen of equal or nearly equal standing in society, with labours not excessively different in amount, compelling them to a similar style of living, which follows almost necessarily from their situation, and furnishing them with incomes so utterly different as those of the several foundations. But if you go out of the limits marked by these incomes, it is clearly a matter of great difficulty to draw any line which will be just and satisfactory.

The principle, however, of equal salaries, although plausible, we think, on the whole, erroneous, and that this will appear by carrying it out to its consequences. Suppose, for instance, that by frequent vacancies or other delays, in process of time the income of a foundation should become an extravagant one, and that to a great degree,—it is surely a possible case,— would it be expedient to raise the others to the same amount? We think not; and that the principle, therefore, is not well founded. Again,—the fair question respecting the amount of salary is not what may be thought just and sufficient for any present incumbent accustomed to a situation, and unwilling to break old habits and associations, and relinquish a place which time and circumstances have endeared. The fair amount is that, which will induce gentlemen well qualified for the place, and fully apprised of its advantages and disadvantages, to accept it. A man may have other sources of income ; he may perceive that the situation will enable him to obtain additions to his regular salary. A Professorship that does not offer much value, may offer much time, and this may, in his views, be an equivalent. Or he may have few wants, or be an habitual economist ; in short, many reasons may induce some to accept a lower salary, with a full view and complete knowledge of the duties which it will require. There would be no injustice nor hardship, therefore, in confining him to this salary, provided no remarkable and unforeseen changes in the circumstances of the country or the College should render it

20.   It is obvious that reasoning in many respects similar will apply to the Presidential salary.

To return to the amount of the several salaries of the Resident Professors.   No considerable saving in this particular appears easy by a reduction of individual incomes, except a small one, of the sum paid for the duties of Registrar and Inspector of public buildings.   These duties, from the Report, do not seem to be considerable, and might be imposed upon some of the officers without any increase of their income.   It further appears, that the amount of duty is not the same in every Professorship.   If $1700, therefore, be sufficient for those who perform the greatest amount of duty, it is clearly unequal to give the same to those who perform less; and though objections would arise, as we have already stated, to diminishing their income, there can be none to giving them additional duties, especially when they are not great.   On the other hand, those who are deprived of the small addition of salary, are in some degree recompensed by the addition to their leisure.   This, however, is not very important in fact, as the whole income of both offices is but $300.   Another change is much more important, while it affects the income of none.   One Professorship is now and another will be vacant in a few months.   These are both well endowed, though neither of them is adequate to the support of a Professor without the additional appropriation of large sums from those monies which are at the free disposal of the Corporation.   By promoting, therefore, if we may use the word without offence, two College Professors * in the same branches to these vacant Professorships, there will be a clear saving to the College of a very large proportion of the salaries now enjoyed by these gentlemen, which amount together to $3400; and a consequent diminution of the yearly amount assessed upon the scholars.

[*To be continued.*]

---

* By a "College Professor," we mean one who is supported exclusively by appropriations from the income of those donations, which have been made to the College, without conditions restricting the discretion of the Corporation as to their expenditure.

Lectures on Geology, being Outlines of the Science, delivered in the New York Atheneum, in the year 1825. By Jer. Van Rensselaer, M. D. &c.   New York. 1825. 1 vol. 8vo. pp. 358.

Popular lectures, as they have been styled, have been viewed as well calculated to excite a taste in the community for scientific acquirements, and as one of the best means of imparting instruction to those, whose professional, commercial, or other occupations leave them but few and limited portions of time to devote to such pursuits.   But we have often thought that the beneficial effects of most lectures of this kind have been overrated—that they have had in some instances an opposite effect, arising from the manner in which they have been got up, or in which they have been conducted and attended.

A large proportion of those who attend a course of instructions of this kind, cannot apply themselves to close investigations, or follow up the various subjects at their leisure.   The impressions, with which they leave the lecture room, are in general the strongest, and sometimes the only ones they receive. Under these circumstances it becomes doubly incumbent on the governors or founders of institutions for the promotion of literature and science, to be influenced in their selection of teachers, by a spirit of impartiality, and a full conviction of the capability of those who are to make these first and strongest impressions.   A spirit of candour and sincerity,—a deep love of his subject,—an ardour and zeal that shall never tire,—a thorough acquaintance with all that has been done by others,—a facility in selecting and compressing all that constitutes the foundations of his science,—a sound and impartial judgment of what is to be rejected or deemed irrelevant or uncertain,—a simple, intelligible, familiar, yet accurate method of conveying his knowledge to others ;—all will acknowledge these to have a greater influence than the most perfect facility of copying from others,—of quoting from the poets,—or of talking about " the glorious orb of day."   Far be from us to decide which of the qualifications we have hinted at influenced the choice of the author of this book, as lecturer on an important branch of science in the New York Atheneum.

Although some of the objections, which have been made to " popular lectures," are well founded, we are not disposed to concede that the imperfect views, which they give, and the superficial knowledge which they often impart, are obstacles to the progress of science and general improvement. If the larger proportion of an audience repair to the lecture room, some to pass away an hour which would otherwise hang heavy on their hands; some for the mere gratification of curiosity, by the sight of brilliant experiments, beautiful minerals, or ingenious models of machinery;—while a few, perhaps, are led thither in compliance with the reigning fashion; still we believe that much real benefit may result to society at large from the patronage and countenance of even this class of auditors. It may happen that by some happy illustration the slumbering spark of genius is unexpectedly kindled; some future Watt, or Arkwright, or Davy starts in his career; and who can estimate the new sources of power, the great mechanical improvements, or the unknown means of individual and national wealth, which may result.

But it is unnecessary to enlarge on these points; it is sufficiently obvious, that the value and usefulness of popular lectures must depend on the ability and zeal of the teacher. When these are directed by the wisdom and sustained by the countenance and patronage of a great public institution, their results come to us with superior claims to attention and respect. It was, therefore, with high expectations that we took up the Lectures on Geology delivered at the New York Atheneum.

It has been fashionable to speak of geology as a new science; and every writer has endeavoured to convince his readers that he has contributed something to its development and progress, though not always with success. Professor Cleaveland has given, at the end of his most excellent treatise on Mineralogy, an epitome of Geology, a science the object of which he there informs us, is "to ascertain the arrangement and mutual actions of the *solid*, *fluid*, and *aeriform* materials of the earth." The first edition of this work was published in the year 1816. It was immediately introduced into very general use; and from it, probably, most of our now numerous geologists derived their first notions of the science. Prior to this time, however, we find in Europe many treatises on Geology, and the third volume of Professor Jameson's Mineralogy, published in 1808, is wholly devoted to this subject. But this, as well as the various French treatises upon the subject which had been published, were before almost unknown among us. Within a few years, however, they have

evidently been very carefully read and studied. It is somewhat strange that it did not occur to the lecturer on geology
at the New York Atheneum, that his readers might have
met with some of these publications; that he did not "catch
the idea" (as he tells us Whiston did that of Halley) is evident from the modest manner in which he informs us that
" geology is generally considered as embracing a knowledge of
rocks merely," and that there is no work published, " that even
hints at the many important points properly treated of under
the head of geology." Had Professor Jameson's " Manual "
the " Classification of Rocks," by Dr Macculloch, and Messrs
Conybeare and Phillips' "Outlines" not appeared, we are
somewhat suspicious that the present publication would never
have come to light. The fact is, we are sorry to say it, that
nine-tenths of these lectures are copied almost verbatim from
these works——all that part in particular which relates to highland and lowland, mountain chains, mountains, the bottom of
the sea, &c. is from Jameson. The notices of Guettard, on
page 27, and of Lehman, on page 28, are from page 42 of Conybeare and Phillips' " Outlines of the Geology of England and
Wales." The learned authors of that work in their introductory sketch of the progress of geological science have the following very appropriate figure, " As we approach the middle
of the 18th century, we find the scattered rays of information,
which alone can be discerned previously, converging into a
more condensed and steady light; the disjoined atoms falling, as it were, into a regular system." How much more
beautiful the language of the lecturer to the Atheneum, on
page 34. "The few rays of light were scattered, until an
unexpected nucleus attracted the wandering atoms and drew
them together." The notice of Saussure, on page 37, is from
the 45th of the same work.

In the first lecture we have outlines of the various fanciful
and exploded theories of the earth, commencing with that of
Burnet. These are very nearly in the language of Professor
Brande. The same may be said of our author's account of
the theories of Leibnitz, Woodward, Buffon, and others, all
of which may be found in Brande's Lectures or in Cuvier's
Essay. The theory of Dr Hutton, we are told, is in unison
with many geological facts as seen in Scotland. Unfortunately, it is well known to all who have made themselves acquainted with the writings of both Scotch and English geologists,
since the publication of the Huttonian theory, that nearly all

37

the geological appearances relied upon by the learned author of the theory, and its eloquent advocate, the late Professor Playfair, can be explained quite as satisfactorily by other hypotheses. The granite' veins of Arran, the porphyry of the same island, the slate at Tarbet and Luss, the quartz rock of Tyndrum, the magnificent granite veins of Garviemore, and innumerable other geological phenomena, have been examined and described again and again, and made to accord with the previously adopted theory of each observer.

We were somewhat surprised at the bold assertion that Dr Hutton's book continues to be the text book of the best English geologists! There is something indeed approaching to the Huttonian hypothesis in some of their works, but had Dr Van Rensselaer studied these with attention, he would have found innumerable points of difference. Almost the only writer, who may be considered as taking Dr Hutton's work as a " text book," is Prof. Brande, and although Dr Van Rensselaer has apparently made this same work his own text book, he should have known, that however deservedly eminent as a chemist Prof. Brande may be, he has no pretensions to a high rank as a geologist.

In the second lecture our author proceeds to point out the advantages to be derived from the study of geology, in which he shows himself familiar with some of the papers of Mr Maclure, and has given nothing new. He follows up the system of Mr Brande, and like him tells us, that we do not select the most permanent materials for architectural purposes. This affords 'a good opportunity of letting us know he has been abroad, and seen the chapel of Henry VII. undergoing repairs.

The third lecture commences with an account of the changes produced on the earth's surface by the formation of peat &c. Although we are fully aware how very compressible this substance is, we should hardly have conceived that the thirty-five pages of Dr Macculloch's Essay upon it in the second volume of the Edinburgh Philosophical Journal could have been condensed into about four ; but by some unfortunate accident all that peculiar essence on which the value of the original depended escaped during the process, and we have nothing left but the dry stalks. Thus we have a string of eighty or more hard names, being the list given by Dr Macculloch of the plants from which the different kinds of peat are derived, while the important details and facts are omitted ;

the recital of this list must have been listened to with deep interest. Before leaving this chapter, we must not omit the recipe at the close of it for making a volcano; which we presume was furnished by the worthy proprietor of Vauxhall garden.

If any of you wish for a volcano on a small scale in your garden, take twenty-five pounds of *powered* sulphur, and as much iron filings, mix them into a paste with water, and place the whole in a large iron pot, covered with a cloth, some little distance under ground. In a few hours, from nine to twelve, the earth swells, heats, and cracks—hot sulphureous vapours arise, and the cracks enlarging, a brilliant flame bursts up, thus forming a volcano in miniature," &c.

The " opportunities for the study of geological phenomena in Europe &c." enjoyed by our author have unquestionably been " numerous and extensive ;" he has therefore an un-doubted " right to form his own opinions," as he remarks in his preface. That " these have generally coincided with the ideas of others" we have the most abundant proof, as will be evident from a few quotations. The following is his " opin-ion " of what have been termed irregular masses of rocks.

Irregular Masses may be of any size ; and often constitute mountains, as is the case with granite, serpentine, porphyry, and the overlying rocks, as trap, &c.

Dr Macculloch in page 99 of his " Classification of Rocks" says,

Irregular Masses. These may be of any size, even of mountainous bulk. Examples of them are afforded by granite, and by the overlying rocks, as the traps and porphyries.

At page 129 we have Dr Rensselaer's " opinion " in regard to nodules.

Nodules or *imbedded irregular masses* is a term lately adopted to in-clude rocks which are not stratafied nor disposed in pseudo-strata (beds) and which do not resemble in their connections other large irregular masses. The forms of the nodules are various, and they are usually im-bedded in the stratafied rocks; but occasionally in granite. The size varies from a foot to a mile.

What says Dr Macculloch ?

NODULES. Or imbedded irregular masses. This term is adopted for want of one more appropriate, to include rocks which are not stratified, nor disposed in pseudo-strata (beds) and which do not resemble in their connexions the large irregular masses. The form of nodules is very various. Nodules are frequently imbedded in stratified rocks, but they are also found in granite. The size of these masses varies from a foot to a mile or more.

The fourth lecture we should be half inclined to say was copied from the 7th, 8th, 9th, and 10th chapters of Dr Macculloch's work—but as we learn from the preface that these lectures were " addressed to a large and enlightened audience," and with " no small degree of reluctance and timidity," and as we find no inverted commas, or references to other writers, they must be received as remarkable coincidences " with the ideas of others." Messrs Humboldt, Macculloch, Conybeare, and Phillips are under great obligations to one whose " numerous and extensive opportunities " have thus enabled him to confirm and place their opinions beyond the reach of doubt.

The account of Werner, on page 38, is familiar to every one who has read the scientific journals, or even the newspapers of the day. The repetition may have relieved the ennui of the attendants on these lectures, but adds little to the usefulness of the book. It is asserted that Werner never published. This is not the fact. His " Kurze Classification " appeared in 1787, and his work on Veins in 1791.

Some of the attempts at fine writing, and the occasional displays of learning in the first lecture, are highly amusing. We cannot omit to notice here the account of Lord Bacon, which the Dr has rendered doubly damning, by his annotations to the old, hackneyed quotation, seasoned by a truly scientific attempt at a pun. " Bacon," he exclaims, " unhappy name in the annals of science," " the wisest, brightest, meanest of mankind,"—" a blazing *beacon* to show us the fallacy of man." We are continually meeting, too, with expressions, which are ambiguous, and sentences so constructed as to mean almost any thing, but what was probably intended. The whole work bears marks of having been got up in haste, with more attention to inflated diction and personal narrative, than to scientific accuracy. We might quote many examples of want of accuracy and precision in language. Thus, on page 36, " In this theory [the Huttonian] there is a happy union of the agency of both fire and water ; the one [fire] collecting and depositing, the other [water] consolidating and elevating."—" Quartz is the purest variety of siliceous earth, containing about 69, and some even 96 per cent. of pure silex. Rock crystal is quartz. It [quartz] forms a large proportion in the composition of chalcedony, agates, flints, jaspers, &c. It [quartz] is also a constituent in many gems ; opal and cairngoram are nearly pure quartz. Topaz, hyacinth, schorl, and torumaline, aventurine, emerald, beryl, and garnet all contain large portions of this earth " [quartz].

Felspar, " Persia, Arabia, and Ceylon furnish the green variety." We are not informed whether Dr Van Rensselaer visited these countries ; if so, he may have discovered localities of green felspar heretofore unknown to mineralogists.

In conclusion, we will merely remark, that those who are in possession of Cleaveland's Mineralogy or Jameson's Manual will add nothing to the value of their libraries by adding this volume to the number of their books.

An Oration, delivered at Concord, April the Nineteenth, 1825. By EDWARD EVERETT. Boston. 8vo. pp. 59.

THIS Oration, delivered in commemoration of the first shedding of blood at the opening of the Revolution, and containing a clear, animated narrative of that leading scene in the great drama, intermixed with most eloquent and patriotic reflections arising naturally out of the occasion, is too fresh in the minds of our readers to leave room for any elaborate commendation of it on our part. We design here simply to offer a few remarks, which the perusal of it suggests, and to make one or two extracts in illustration of its style and spirit.

We cannot sympathize with the feelings of those among us who deprecate an occasional reference to the sorrows and triumphs of the revolutionary war. Such men, in complaining of the tone assumed, of the language uttered, and of the sentiments professed by public orators on our great national festivals, exhibit a morbid attachment to the cause of peace and goodfellowship, and an exuberant sensibility, which are very closely allied with coldness and indifference to the interests of home and country. When Mr Adams, in his address delivered at Washington in 1821, Mr Webster on occasion of laying the corner stone of the Bunker Hill Monument, Mr Everett in the piece before us, and numerous obscurer men in like situations, recur to the memorable era in which our Independence was established, they do it with no desire to rekindle animosities, which are now slumbering in the dust of time. They do it with no unfriendly wish, no hostile feeling towards the country which gave our progenitors birth, and from which we derive our language, our literature, and some of our dearest and most valued institutions. England was the birthplace and home of our forefathers ; and though she did persecute them, though she did endeavour to reduce them to a state of degrading servitude,—she is England still,—the freest of the great nations of Europe,—the mistress of the ocean, disputed in her empire over it only by ourselves,—the country of the Alfreds, the Henrys, and the Edwards, whose names shine brightly in the darkness of the middle ages, like solitary stars in the distant sky,—the conqueror of Crecy, of Agincourt, of Trafalgar, of Waterloo,—endeared to us by the ties of a common origin, a common language, and a common spirit,—and only alienated in sentiment from Americans for a time by her temporary lust of dominion over America. Our anniversary orators, therefore, allude to and dwell upon the emigration of the pilgrims, the subsequent history of the colonies, and the revolutionary struggle, with no disposition to tear open wounds which are healed, but only so far as it is necessary to keep alive those hallowed recollections, which are part and parcel of the common patrimony of every American. We ourselves require to be reminded, and our children to be informed, why it was, and with what intent, that our ancestors abandoned the comforts of their father-land, planted their household gods in the wilderness, and engaged in the stormy contests of war and revolution.

Mr Everett touches upon this topic in the introductory part of his oration; and his views of it will be not inopportune at this time.

A pacific and friendly feeling towards England is the duty of this nation; but it is not our only duty, it is not our first duty. America owes an earlier and a higher duty to the great and good men, who caused her to be a nation; who at an expense of treasure, a contempt of peril, a prodigality of blood—the purest and noblest that ever flowed—of which we can now hardly conceive. vindicated to this continent a place among the nations of the earth. I cannot consent, out of tenderness to the memory of the Gages, the Hutchinsons, the Grenvilles and Norths, the Dartmouths and Hillsboroughs, to cast a veil over the labours and sacrifices of the Quincys, the Adamses, the Hancocks, and the Warrens. I am not willing to give up to the ploughshare the soil wet with our fathers' blood; no! not even to plant the olive of peace in the furrow.

There is not a people on earth so abject, as to think that national courtesy requires them to hush up the tale of the glorious exploits of their fathers and countrymen. France is at peace with Austria and Prussia; but she does not demolish her beautiful bridges, baptized with the names of the battle fields, where Napoleon annihilated their armies; nor tear down the columns, moulten out of the accumulated heaps of their captive artillery. England is at peace with France and Spain, but does she suppress the names of Trafalgar and the Nile; does she overthrow the towers of Blenheim castle, eternal monuments of the disasters of France; does she tear down from the rafters of her chapels, where they have for ages waved in triumph, consecrated to the God of battles, the banners of Cressy and Agincourt?—No; she is wiser; wiser, did I say? she is truer, juster to the memory of her fathers and the spirit of her children.

Nothing seems more remarkable to the superficial observer of the early days of our national history, than the seeming unpreparedness of the country for the war upon which it was about to enter, and out of which it issued so gloriously. As the sun of our liberty arose to pour the light of his beams over the land, he shone luridly out from the clouds of doubt and confusion and discord, which obscured the nation's destiny.

> Sad was the year, by proud oppression driven,
> When transatlantic liberty arose,
> Not in the sunshine and the smile of heaven,
> But wrapt in whirlwinds and begirt with woes.

Sad, indeed, was the year, and mournfully indeed, to the fallible eye of man, unskilled to pierce through the hidden mysteries of futurity, did our Independence begin. The power, which was aiming to enslave us, was mighty, beyond all which it seemed within our ability to bring against it; and we had dared provoked the extremity of its wrath. We had dared England to the combat,—England, out of whose womb we sprang, whose inhabitants were not less brave and resolute than ourselves,—who had at her command all the treasures of the east and the west, who possessed disciplined armies, and whose navies crowded every sea. ` What had we to oppose to all this tremendous array of strength? Whence were we to gather the riches and summon the armies and collect the fleets, which could withstand the potent armaments of Britain? We had a Washington to lead on our embattled hosts to the fight; but his followers were only the raw and undisciplined yeomanry of the country; and could they hope to vanquish the vanquishers of France and India? We had a Franklin, a Jefferson, and an Adams to guide our public councils and wield our national resources; but those resources consisted in nothing but the native energies of a people resolved to be free; and could they be deemed adequate to prevail over the most opulent and most powerful kingdom of Europe?

It is necessary that we should enter into these considerations, if we would realize the strength of resolution, the moral sublimity of character, which actuated the heroes and sages of the revolution. We must recollect that the colonists had petitioned, they had remonstrated, they had had recourse to all pacific means that were honourable, to avert the impending

storm.   Their petitions were disregarded, and their remonstrances were "·spurned with contempt from the foot of the
throne."   Their prayer for peace received its answer at the
cannon's mouth.   Their enemies appeared determined to
spare no exertions to rivet on them the chains which they
had forged.   Navies and armies had been equipped for our
subjugation, and the hostile fleets were riding in defiance upon
our waters, and the hostile armies were swarming upon our
shores.   Our ancestors were, to all outward appearance,
weak and powerless in competition with their invaders.   But,
to copy the vigorous expressions of one of the great men of
that period, whose language we have already imitated, the
contemporary sages and heroes felt, that if they were weak,
they would not gather strength by delay, and they must either
resolve to gird up their loins manfully and draw their swords
boldly and promptly in the cause of freedom, or to lie down
supinely on their backs until they were bound hand and foot
and made slaves forever.   Nor were they in reality so weak.
They felt that " three millions of people, armed in the sacred cause of freedom, were invincible by any force which
our enemy could send against us ; and that we should not
fight our battles alone, because there was a righteous God, who
presided over the destinies of nations, and who would raise
up friends to fight with us in the cause of humanity."

We will introduce one more quotation from Mr Everett's
Oration, as beautiful as it is apposite.

It was the people, in their first capacity, as citizens and as freemen,
starting from their beds at midnight, from their firesides, and from their
fields, to take their own cause into their own hands.   Such a spectacle
is the height of the moral sublime ; when the want of every thing is
fully made up by the spirit of the cause ; and the soul within stands in
place of discipline, organization, resources.   In the prodigious efforts of
a veteran army, beneath the dazzling splendor of their array, there is
something revolting to the reflective mind.   The ranks are filled with
the desperate, the mercenary, the depraved ; an iron slavery, by the
name of subordination, merges the free will of one hundred thousand
men, in the unqualified despotism of one ; the humanity, mercy, and remorse, which scarce ever desert the individual bosom, are sounds without a meaning to that fearful, ravenous, irrational monster of prey, a
mercenary army.   It is hard to say who are most to be commiserated,
the wretched people on whom it is let loose, or the still more wretched
people whose substance has been sucked out, to nourish it into strength
and fury.   But in the efforts of the people, of the people struggling for
their rights, moving not in organized, disciplined masses, but in their
spontaneous action, man for man, and heart for heart,—though I like
not war nor any of its works,—there is something glorious.   They can

then move forward without orders, act together without combination, and brave the flaming lines of battle, without entrenchments to cover, or walls to shield them. No dissolute camp has worn off from the feelings of the youthful soldier the freshness of that home, where his mother and his sisters sit waiting, with tearful eyes and aching hearts, to hear good news from the wars; no long service in the ranks of a conqueror has turned the veteran's heart into marble; their valor springs not from recklessness, from habit, from indifference to the preservation of life, knit by no pledges to the life of others. But in the strength and spirit of the cause alone they act, they contend, they bleed. In this, they conquer. The people always conquer. They always must conquer. Armies may be defeated; kings may be overthrown, and new dynasties imposed by foreign arms on an ignorant and slavish race, that care not in what language the covenant of their subjection runs, nor in whose name the deed of their barter and sale is made out. But the people never invade; and when they rise against the invader, are never subdued.

Before quitting the subject, we are tempted to pause a moment and advert to the consequences to ourselves, and the consequences to the world, of the noble and manly stand taken by our free-spirited fathers in those trying days. As to the effects of it on ourselves, we have only to cast our eyes over the green fields stretched out around us, which are waving with the rich and verdant abundance of the promised harvest, under the tillage of a hardy yeomanry, protected by a system of equal laws, and flourishing in union with all the blessings which free institutions can impart to a happy people; and ask ourselves how much of all this would have been, had not our fathers drawn the sword in vindication of their insulted rights. Or look forth upon the broad and fathomless ocean, and as you behold the canvass of our ships whitening every sea, and the striped flag of our country floating in triumph over the remotest waters, and the thunder of her cannon resounding on every shore, do you not feel persuaded that none of this glorious display of naval strength would ever have met the eye, if our ancestors had not declared, as they saw the contest approaching, Give us freedom or give us death? Enter the populous cities, which are now scattered abroad over the country, and as you hear the busy hum of active life, and see the stately palaces which arise on all sides, and note all the marks of splendor, opulence, and power, which abound in them, consider what portion of this would exist, had we continued to bow the neck to the yoke of transatlantic taskmasters. In fine, our ancestors were then feeble and oppressed colonists, they were, comparatively speaking, few in number, and they were only sprinkled along the shores of

38

the Atlantic or on the banks of our majestic rivers on this side of the Alleghany; but since then, and under heaven, because our sires resisted when they did, we are now wealthy, numerous, and powerful; we have taken our rank with the nations of the earth, as among the first in arts and arms,— among the first in social improvement,—and promising to continue among the first for ages yet to come. And we have now spread the empire of our civilization far into the interior regions of our country, where but a few years ago was nothing but a wide and waste wilderness, and where are now the busy haunts of men, who, the same at the mouth of the Mississippi or the Merrimac, on the far-off waters of the princely Missouri or on the sea-girt rocks of Massachusetts, are every where free-born Americans.

And unless we greatly deceive ourselves, the consequences have not been less distinctly marked upon other nations. The inhabitants of Europe and of Spanish America had for centuries been groaning under the tyranny of the feudal institutions,—obliged to cower beneath the sceptre of military despots, or to kiss the foot of haughty temporal priests. The people had no rights,—no liberties,—no privileges, but such as the condescension of their kings saw fit, out of their most princely pleasure, to grant. But the example of our revolution went forth, and taught them that there was no mystic charm in royalty which brave men could not break. The name, the fame, and the achievements of our heroes and statesmen were sounded abroad, and served as a watchword to the lovers of liberty all over the world. Our country was the birthplace of modern freedom; but no sooner had her pinions acquired strength and maturity, than she flew forth into other climes, to establish her temples on the ruins of baronial castles and feudal prison-houses.

> The prophets of young freedom, summoned far,
> From climes of Washington and Bolivar;
> Henry, the forest-born Demosthenes,
> Whose thunder shook the Philip of the seas;
> The stoic Franklin's energetic shade,
> Robed in the lightnings which his hand allayed;
> And Washington, the tyrant-tamer:—

these are the names, which have imparted inspiration to all who spurn at slavery, wheresoever they wander, on the banks of the Po or Tagus, the Amazon or La Plata, and which will continue to impart it, until Truth and Freedom and Justice shall cease to have a name among men.

MISCELLANY.

THE IMPROVEMEMT OF COMMON ROADS.

THE spirit of improvement is abroad in our country. Canals are intersecting it in various directions, and Bridges, which, next to ships, exhibit the proudest evidence of skill in architecture, are spanning our mighty rivers to enable us to pass from shore to shore ; while Steamboats, which of themselves will be sufficient to constitute an epoch in the history of man's inventions, are penetrating our territories by every navigable river which can afford them access. Thus every succeeding year is furnishing new testimonials of the march of improvement.

Canals are of vast benefit to the community, wherever the amount of transportation, and the resources and wealth of the population, will enable us to avail ourselves of the natural facilities afforded for constructing them. Railways too, we are willing to concede to our brethren of the Quarterly Review, under equally favourable circumstances are of even greater utility. But we entertain an opinion that the latter are adapted only to a country of dense population and great internal resources ; and could yet be applied in very few places to advantage, in a country so extensive and thinly peopled as our own. Our common roads, or, in the language of the statutes, our public highways, must continue, for a long time to come, to afford the principal means of transportation to the greater part of the community ; and to the improvement of these roads, we should think, a portion of that public spirit, which now prevails in the land, might be profitably directed.

In their contributions to support the public burthens, no tax is apparently paid with more cheerfulness by our yeomanry, than that which is assessed for the repairs of the roads. But the funds appropriated to this object, though barely sufficient in most parts of the country to make the roads tolerable under the best management, are often sadly misapplied. No regular system of repairs has been pursued. Surveyors in many towns are changed at every annual appointment. The duty is an arduous one, the compensation trifling, and the doctrine of rotation in office appears in this case to have been effectually reduced to practice. Every supervisor has a plan of his own, which, without more than an ordinary share of confidence in his individual judgment, he thinks at least as good as that of his neighbour ; and too often the chief purpose of the new surveyor seems to be to undo the labours of his predecessor. A temporary repair, such as may last till the next wintry deluge shall sweep it away, seems frequently the farthest bound, to which the common notions of road-making have extended ; as if the annual appropriation was designed for the benefit of the present year, and that alone.

But it is an ungrateful office to find fault, if we are not prepared to suggest some remedy ; and, in the present case, a remedy has been devised, which needs only to be known, that it may be brought more extensively into practice. The defects of the common method of constructing roads must be attributed to a want of experience. Nor have we, who inhabit a country comparatively new, been the only sufferers. The long-travelled countries of Europe have almost equally with ourselves endured the inconveniences incident to the want of a settled system on this subject. The science of road-making (and in practical importance it more justly claims the rank of a science, than many pursuits which have been dignified with that title) is just beginning to be understood in Great Britain. For about ten years the new method of constructing roads, first adopted and practised by Mr McAdam, has been pursued there ; and such has been the success which has attended it, so complete has been the conviction of its superiority over all former methods, wherever it has been introduced, the conflicting interest and prejudice, which in common with every important improvement, it has had to encounter, have in this short time been so completely removed, that its excellence can no longer be questioned ; and there can be no doubt that it will henceforth be adopted in preference to all other modes of making and repairing roads in that kingdom. Travellers of all descriptions, mail contractors, and civil engineers, parliament and people, unite in the most ample testimonials in its favour, and liberal grants have been made to Mr McAdam in remuneration for his service in this department as a public benefactor.

A concise description of the plan on which these roads are constructed is all that our limits will admit. For a more particular and satisfactory account we must refer to the Essay of Mr McAdam himself, the eighth edition of which was published in London the last year, and which we hope soon to see republished in this country. His method mainly consists, after preparing the bed of the road for the purpose (in doing which all the stones near the surface must be removed), in covering it with a flooring of broken stone of eight or ten inches in thickness, the largest stone not to exceed six ounces in weight. These fragments of stone are soon worn smooth by the travelling, and unite by their angles into a solid, impenetrable mass, over which the wheels of the heaviest carriages will pass without making any sensible impression. Another important part of the system is to have the side gutters or watercourses so constructed as effectually to drain the water from the earthy bed of the road, that it may not be injuriously affected by the winter frost ; and for this purpose it is desirable, that the bed of the road should not be below the level of the adjacent fields, but when practicable raised a little above that level. The impervious covering or roofing of stone will prevent any inconvenience from the rain, which falls upon it, and, thus protected, the road is subject to no other injury than the necessary but gradual wear of the stone materials of which it is constructed. Under such circumstances an earthy bed is even preferred to a rocky one, as it yields more beneath the weight of the load carried over it, and the wear of the road is less on that account. It is particularly insisted on by Mr McAdam that no stones exceeding six ounces in weight be admitted in any part of the road. If larger stones be placed at bottom, according to the method which has been long pursued by many road-makers, while those of a smaller size are placed on the surface, the larger stones will in a short time rise to the top, thus making the surface rough and uneven, and at the same time penetrable by the rain-water, which will gradually undermine and destroy the foundation or bed of the road.

Such is a brief outline of the manner of making roads, which we hope ere long to see extensively introduced into our country. It is doubtful whether any portion of the globe is more favourably situated to reap the benefit of this improvement, than is our own New England. Our seaboard districts are abundantly supplied with granite, which is said to be the very best material for this purpose ; while the greenstone of our western counties resembles very nearly the whinstone of Scotland, which is represented by Mr McAdam as second only to granite in the good qualities by which it is recommended. With such facilities to encourage us in the race of improvement, what but a more general acquaintance with the system can be wanting to ensure its application to the important public roads in this section of the union ? The first expenditure will no doubt be somewhat greater than is incurred by pursuing the old method, but in every instance it cannot fail to prove excellent economy in the end ; and in very many cases it will be found, that the annual expense now necessary to keep the roads in tolerable repair falls little short of what would, upon the new principle, construct a good road, which would last several years with scarce any additional expense.

The experiment has been tried and with the best success in this country. Two of the streets in the town of New Bedford were constructed last year upon this plan, and we believe a few other attempts have been made on a small scale, sufficient to satisfy all, who have had an opportunity of witnessing them, of the excellence of the system. In the cities of London and Bristol, the pavements of several entire streets have been taken up, and the broken-stone roads of Mr McAdam substituted in their place. This has been done from a conviction of the superiority of the stoned road for smoothness and ease of draught; while in cases where pavements are not already laid, it will be found to afford not only a much better road, but a much more economical one, than the old method of paving.

Before we close this article, we must take occasion to reprobate one practice in connexion with our system of repairing highways, which prevails more or less in every section of the country,—it is the custom of permitting every person either to pay his tax or *work it out* (to use the common phraseology), at his option. This custom derives its origin from the feudal system, and is a remnant of the personal service which the lord of the manor exacted of his vassals,—one of the few relics of a barbarous age, which the spirit of our free institutions has not yet shaken off. At a time when rents were paid in kind; and when the convenience of having a circulating medium was comparatively unknown, there might be some necessity for resorting to this expedient; but now when the product of every man's labour can be so readily converted into money, we see no valid reason for retaining it. Men, unaccustomed to the kind of labour required in repairing a road, however industrious their habits may be, cannot be employed upon it to the public advantage. Those who are suitable might, in all cases, we presume, obtain the employment of the surveyor, if they desired it, without placing him under an obligation to employ them, whether competent or not. The most competent men would be employed to do the work, if the surveyors were furnished with the means and left at liberty to use them to the best advantage; and as far as an inferior class of labourers are admitted, whether they are indolent or unskilful, the public are certainly the sufferers.

The adoption of Mr McAdam's system would of itself go far towards correcting these abuses. A man's labour would here be estimated, not by the time he is employed, but by actual measurement of the quantity of stone which he has prepared, for the purpose of the road; so that if he is idle, or if he is awkward and unskilful at his task, it will be his own loss; and the obvious result will follow, that those only, who can work most advantageously at this employment, or who from youth or imbecility cannot be profitably engaged in a more laborious occupation, will offer their services; and in either case the community will be the gainer; for it will be a public benefit, that persons of the latter description be employed to the extent of their abilities, while their reward is justly proportioned to the services which they perform.

MOLSEY HYRST—GAME OF CRICKET PLAYED BY LADIES—A BOXING MATCH—SPECULATIONS UPON THE CAUSE OF THIS TRAIT IN THE ENGLISH CHARACTER—HAMPTON CHURCH-YARD—HAMPTON COURT—THE CARTOONS OF RAFAELLE.

A LEAF FROM THE JOURNAL OF A TRAVELLER IN ENGLAND.

February 14th, 18—.

The day before yesterday I walked down to Molsey Hyrst, 12 miles from London, to see a fight. I was not induced to visit the scene by any particular fondness for such exhibitions, but simply from a desire to observe for myself a trait, rather a *striking* one, of national character. Certainly the pugilists of England deserve the attention of a stranger as much, at least, as the \pancratiastæ of Greece or the gladiators of Rome do that of the liberal scholar.

This Hyrst is an extensive plain apparently used for mowing, and lies on the south side of the Thames. It seems to have been the theatre of games and combats from time immemorial. It is mentioned in the Gentleman's Magazine, about fifty years back, as the scene of a famous game of cricket played for a considerable wager between six married women on one side and six maidens on the other. The game is represented to have been played with extraordinary dexterity and spirit in the presence of a vast concourse of spectators. The young women, if I recollect right, were the challengers ; at any rate they were the winners, for the same reason perhaps, that young officers, who have their fortunes to make, are observed to fight better than old ones, whose fortunes are already made.

I crossed the Thames from Hampton church-yard in a wherry, a boat rather larger than an ordinary canoe. The parties and spectators were assembled in the middle of the plain, the former attended by their *seconds*, certain veteran fighters, their bottle-holders, and a referee, mutually chosen to decide all disputes which might arise in the course of the combat. The lists, within which I found the fighters and their *suites*, enclosed about a square rod ; and were formed by stakes driven firmly into the ground, three on a side, with two ropes passing round them, one near the top and the other about the middle of them. At the distance of three or four rods from the lists was a circle formed of various vehicles, such as gigs, coaches, Stanhopes, tilburies, and market carts, the latter the most numerous, and designed to be let to pedestrian spectators for stands. Between the circle of carts and the lists was another entire circle of spectators, who did not choose to pay 2d. or 6d. for a stand. The parties prepared themselves for the combat in the following manner ; they exchanged their shoes for light, laced boots or buskins, they threw off their heavy fearnoughts, and all their upper garments, leaving only their white kerseymere small-clothes, confined by a handkerchief about the waist, their white cotton stockings and red buskins. They then resumed their great coats to wait the signal to engage. They walked about in a hurried and anxious manner; particularly the one who was the pet, and on whom the bets were two to one. When the moment came to begin, they again threw off their great coats, and put themselves in the fighting attitude, which shows a muscular form to some advantage. They fought nearly an hour before either party gave up, and then it was his second, not himself, that yielded. One of them, the pet, could not stand alone when the fight was over, and the other was but little better. The face of the first bled at all points, and became frightfully black and swollen; although between the rounds, of which there were about forty, he was bathed and sprinkled with spirit and every method was employed to cherish and refresh him. When they were leading him off, he observed, as well as he could, for he could scarcely speak, " that he hoped Mr Whittle would not grumble." This Mr Whittle was his backer, and this remark was made in allusion to the practice of " selling fights," which is when one of the parties betrays the person or persons who have bet in his favour, and allows himself, after a show of resistance, to be beaten, being induced thereto by a valuable consideration received from the backers of his antagonist. I am told that almost all the great pugilists do at some time or other sell their fights, but the consequence is, that it is difficult for them to find backers again. There have been instances of selling fights for £1000 sterling. The mode of challenging, when the challenge is given on the ground, is by throwing up hats. The practice of selling fights has done more to diminish the number of these combats than the labours of magistrates or moral societies, and I should hope that this with other causes might ultimately put an end to a custom so disgraceful to England and to human nature. There were but few people present on this occasion, perhaps eight hundred in all. They were of various characters and conditions, many of them of the lowest class, some of them respectable-looking yeoman, and a still greater number of jockey-looking gentleman, ycleped " of the fancy." This fight was bloody; the vanquished party was dreadfully mauled, and his white small-clothes were all red with with blood, which fell from his nose and face. The backs of both were terribly excoriated by falling and struggling upon the ropes. As the interest gradually increased, the spectators began to press towards the centre, till at last they rushed in and crowded it just as the fight was over. The sight of this combat seemed to put others in a fighting humour, for several hats ascended in quick succession, but no backers appeared. When the affair was ended, a hat was carried round to collect contributions " for the losing man," whom the person, a jockey-looking gentleman, who bore the hat, called "a very game fellow." I saw but two females present, though I believe it is common for them to attend in considerable numbers, as happened at the great fight which took place lately at Worcester between the respective champions of England and Ireland.

Many Americans as well as other foreigners wonder how a nation so civilized as the British can tolerate so barbarous a custom. The truth is, that a considerable portion of the dense population of England is in a state of comparative barbarism at the very moment, when as a nation they have arrived at the highest pitch of refinement and grandeur. Unless Malthus' preventive checks are applied with more skill and success than they have ever yet been, an epoch must arrive in the history of all nations, not excepting our own happy republic, when a large portion of the population will be as exclusively occupied in providing for their physical wants, as the savages who roam in the wilderness, and much more than the beasts, which those savages pursue. This is that second barbarism, which happens to nations, as much as second childhood to men ; and those Americans are much more patriotic than philosophic, who think that we shall be exempt from it. This is precisely that stage of the national existence of England, in which barbarous and cruel sports take place, and in which there is the same disregard of human life and human suffering, that is observed among the negro tribes of Africa or the Indians of America. The luxury, the listlessness, and the *ennui* of the higher classes demand extraordinary excitements ; and the necessities and vices of the lower impel them to minister, at the hazard of life and limb, to the gratification of these unnatural and vicious inclinations. In most nations, however, mortal combats for the amusement of the people (not those for the amusement of kings and ministers !) have been confined to wild and ferocious animals. It has been only in the most populous, wealthy, and corrupt nations,—among whom, as among individuals, it has always been observed, that luxury, wantonness, and cruelty increase just in proportion as they become wealthy and powerful,—in such or in savage nations only is it, that men have consented to assume the place and imitate the actions of wild beasts in the games of the circus. It was at Rome, that great centre of the population, wealth, and corruption of the world, that the combats of gladiators were invented and carried to such a shocking extent. It was in a city containing three or four millions of people, that ten thousand men engaged successively in mortal combat in the space of four months in honour of a military triumph and for the gratification of the Emperor's court. It is now only in England, whose capital is the greatest centre with which we are acquainted in modern times, of commerce, wealth, luxury, and vice, that the amusement, which often produces the death of a human creature, is practised. This progressive disregard of human life and human suffering is observable also in the different frequency of capital and other severe punishments in different countries or at different epochs in the same country. Where the population is scarce, and especially if it have hostile and dangerous neighbours, the government are always very tender of the lives of the subjects and citizens. Our pious ancestors, the pilgrims, spared and protected a certain most desperate Dutchman, who had committed numerous and enormous crimes, because he could be useful in fighting the savages. In the United States, the comparative infrequency of capital punishments is matter of surprise to many foreigners. However, I believe that in Russia they are still more infrequent, certainly they were so some years ago, and in Spain and Portugal and Scotland, they are equally rare. In England, France, Germany, and Italy, which have a much denser population than either of the above countries, they are much more frequent and more or less frequent, nearly in the ratio of their respective populations; though doubtless the difference of their penal codes may vary in some degree the results in these respects.

If then I am right in my view of the causes of this custom, it is idle and absurd to quarrel with it, any more at least than we should with every vice, which results from a crowded population, great wealth and luxury in one class, and extreme poverty and debasement in another. Our institutions, the general diffusion of knowledge, and the ambition to be respectable, may retard the approach of this epoch with us; but that these or any other causes hitherto known, will prevent its ultimate arrival is what I rather hope than expect. Barbarous this custom certainly is—more barbarous than the bull-fights of Spain, or the bear-baiting and badger-baiting of England herself; but it is quite amusing to hear some of our orators and writers, who flatter the national vanity for selfish and base purposes, pretend that it is because we are highly and intrinsically virtuous, and England a very vicious nation, that this and like customs exist among them and not among us. We are what great circumstances have made us;—so is England, so will all nations ever be.*

---

* It would seem from a recent pugilistic combat in New York, which we are sorry to say has been very amply described in the newspapers, that some of the travelled and tasteful gentry of that city are quite impatient at our tardy progress in the march of refinement, and are resolved to accelerate it. We regret exceedingly, that the names and the brutal deeds of those degraded beings, who have consented to beat and bruise one another for the amusement of the idle and worthless men who encourage it and enjoy it, should have found a place in the column of any respectable journal, or indeed of any journal; for the notoriety so injudiciously given to these combats and to the persons who engage in them, through the public press, is the greatest fermenter of the evil. If there were no Pierce Egans, there would be fewer pugilists.

After refreshing myself with some excellent ale, I recrossed the Thames to Hampton church-yard, which is finely situated on a rising bank of the river, and contains a most ancient Gothic church and a great number of marble monuments. It serves as a thorough-fare for those, who go to the church or the ferry. The church, like most others of its antiquity and architecture, stands in the midst of the church-yard or burying-ground, and is surrounded up to its very walls and doors by monuments great and small. The grave-yard appears cheerful instead of gloomy, being much frequented by the villagers, and intersected by well-worn footpaths, which cross it in every direction. It was at this time almost as much crowded by the living as the dead. A high wooden settee placed nearly in the centre of the church-yard, and looking across and up the Thames, afforded me a resting-place, while I was contemplating the multitude around and beneath me. From Hampton I proceeded along a beautiful road with a smooth, clear sidewalk to Hampton Court, where there is a fine old palace built by Cárdinal Wolsey, and presented by him to Henry VIII. It is very extensive, a quadrangle having been added in the reign of William III. under the superintendence of Sir Christopher Wren. The interior is very royal and very interesting. The first room, or guard chamber, so called, contains arms for a thousand men, arranged with great taste and kept in the best order. The most remarkable among them were some Dutch bonnets of steel used in William's time, and some Dutch knives. After this, followed the presence-chambers, audience-chambers, drawing-rooms, bed-chambers, dinning-rooms, beauty-room, closets, &c. there being in general one of each for the king, and one for his queen. Many valuable paintings are distributed among them. A picture of Charles I. by Vandyck and the Cartoons of Raffaelle are the most celebrated. These represent, 1. The miraculous draft of fishes ; 2. The charge to Peter ; 3. Peter and John healing the lame at the gate of the temple ; 4. Death of Ananias ; 5 Elymas the sorcerer struck with blindness ; 6. The sacrifice to Paul and Barnabas by the people of Lystra ; 7. Paul preaching at Athens. The Gallery which contains these pictures is much frequented by artists for the purpose of studying and copying these celebrated models. Engravings of them are also offered for sale, with the condition of sending them to any part of the world. The wings of this palace are occupied by several noble ladies, who enjoy this privilege either by hereditary right or by the special favour of the king. Its situation on the north bank of the Thames, though not commanding, is extremely agreeable ; and the pleasure gardens contain beautiful sculptures, and some natural objects of great curiosity and interest. Among these are " the maze," and " the vine," the most fruitful in Europe. It has in one season produced 2272 bunches, weighing eighteen hundred pounds. It was planted in 1769, and the trunk is about thirteen inches in circumference.

ORIGINAL POETRY.

THE DESOLATE CITY.

I had a vision.—
A city lay before me, desolate,
And yet not all decayed. A summer sun
Shone on it from a most etherial sky,
And the soft winds threw o'er it such a balm,
One would have thought it was a sepulchre,
And this the incense offered to the manes
Of the departed.

In the light it lay
Peacefully, as if all its thousands took
Their afternoon's repose, and soon would wake
To the loud joy of evening. There it lay,
A city of magnificent palaces,
And churches, towering more like things of Heaven,
The glorious fabrics, fancy builds in clouds,
And shapes on loftiest mountains—bright their domes
Threw back the living ray, and proudly stood
Many a statue, looking like the forms
Of spirits hovering in mid air. Tall trees,
Cypress and plane, waved over many a hill
Cumbered with ancient ruins—broken arches,
And tottering columns—vaults, where never came
The blessed beam of day, but only lamps
Shedding a funeral light, were kindled there,
And gave to the bright frescoes on the walls,
And the pale statues in their far recesses,
A dim religious awe. Rudely they lay,
Scarce marking out to the inquisitive eye
Their earliest outline. But as desolate
Slumbered the newer city, though its walls
Were yet unbroken, and its towering domes
Had never stooped to ruin. All was still ;
Hardly the faintest sound of living thing
Moved through the mighty solitude—and yet
All wore the face of beauty. Not a cloud
Hung in the lofty sky, that seemed to rise
In twofold majesty, so bright and pure,
It seemed indeed a crystalline sphere—and there
The sun rode onward in his conquering march
Serenely glorious. From the mountain heights

Tinged with the blue of heaven, to the wide sea
Glassed with as pure a blue, one desolate plain
Spread out, and over it the fairest sky
Bent round and blessed it. Life was teeming there
In all its lower forms, a wilderness
Of rank luxuriance; flowers, and purpling vines
Matted with deepest foliage, hid the ruins,
And gave the semblance of a tangled wood
To piles, that once were loudly eloquent
With the glad cry of thousands. There were gardens
Round stateliest villas, full of graceful statues,
And temples reared to woodland deities;
And they were overcrowded with the excess
Of beauty. All that most is coveted
Beneath a colder sky, grew wantonly
And richly there. Myrtles and citrons filled
The air with fragrance. From the tufted elm,
Bent with its own too massy foliage, hung
Clusters of sunny grapes in frosted purple,
Drinking in spirit from the glowing air,
And dropping generous dews. The very wind
Seemed there a lover, and his easy wings
Fanned the gay bowers, as if in fond delay
He bent o'er loveliest things, too beautiful
Ever to know decay. The silent air
Floating as softly as a cloud of roses,
Dropped from Idalia in a dewy shower,—
The air itself seemed like the breath of Heaven
Filling the groves of Eden. Yet these walls
Are desolate—not a trace of living man
Is found amid these glorious works of man,
And nature's fairer glories. Why should he
Be absent from the festival of life,
The holiday of nature? Why not come.
To add to the sweet sounds of winds and waters—
Of winds uttering Æolian melodies
To the bright, listening flowers, and waters falling
Most musical from marble fountains wreathed
With clustering ivy, like a poet's brow—
Why comes he not to add his higher strains,
And be the interpreter of lower things,
In intellectual worship, at the throne
Of the Beneficent Power, that gave to them
Their pride and beauty?—" In these palaces,
These awful temples, these religious caves,
These hoary ruins, and these twilight groves
Teeming with life and love,—a secret plague
Dwells, and the unwary foot, that ventures here,
Returns not.——Fly! To linger here is death."

]

TO GENEVIEVE.

I' ll rob the hyacinth and rose,
I' ll search the cowslip's fragrant cell,
Nor spare the breath that daily blows
Her incense from the asphodel.

And these shall breathe thy gentle name,
Sweet Naiad of the sacred stream,
Where, musing, first I caught the flame,
That Passion kindles in his dream.

Thy soul of Music broke the spell,
That bound my lyre's neglected strings ;
Attuned its silent echo's shell,
And loosed again his airy wings.

Ah ! long had beauty's eyes in vain
Diffused their radiant light divine ;
Alas, it never woke a strain,
Till inspiration beamed from thine.

Thus vainly did the stars at night
O'er Memnon's lyre their watch prolong,
When nought but bright Aurora's light
Could wake its silence into song !

                        D.

TO THE ARNO.

Bright stream ! how calm upon thy waters rest
The hues of evening, when th' empurpled West
    Droops its soft wing upon thy floods ;
    And the dark waving of thy woods
Deepens the shadows on thy tranquil breast.

And when the mountains catch, upon their heights,
The last faint blush of glory, and the lights
    Of heaven twinkle in the sky ;
    How sweet the cicăda's lone cry
Mourns through thy woods in Autumn's mellow nights.

How lovely are thy shores when on the air,
O'er the rich vineyards stealing from afar,
    The vintner's careless cheering soars,
    Lingering amid thy olive bowers ;
And bright in heaven burns the evening star !

Flow on, thou classic stream, thy verdant shore ;
Will live within our hearts till life is o'er !
    Still will fond memory think of thee,
    Thou pride of blooming Tuscany,
And sigh to look upon thy stream once more !

                        F. M.

CRITICAL NOTICES.

Rothelan; a Romance of the English Histories. By the author of "Annals of the Parish," "Ringan Gilhaize," "The Spaewife," &c. New-York. 1825. 2. vols. 12mo.

THE author of this book is pretty well known to the reading community, by his works at least, if not by his name, and he has acquired a certain degree of currency among novel readers, which, when the number and merits of his competitors are considered, is indicative of some share of merit. One or two of his works have acquired a considerable popularity; others have been received with some cordiality for relations' sake, and a few have been barely tolerated. Rothelan, we apprehend, will come into the second class, possibly into the third, certainly not into the first. The story is not put together in a manner to command an interest; the characters, although in situations to demand sympathy, do not seem to have the faculty of exciting it; in short, a languid air prevails over the whole production, and although this is sometimes relieved by touches of vivacity and spirit, the impression left upon the whole is not very favourable. It is but justice to say, that its general merits are much obscured by a quantity of miserable trash, which the author introduces about the "book of beauty," as he is pleased to style it, recovered from the "gorgeous hermitage of Fonthill," a book which, as he says, is bound up with a back of opal, covers of lapis lazuli, invisible hinges of adamant, and nine clasps of gold representing the nine muses; with a deal more of such affected stuff. This occurring at the very outset of the work, and repeated in regular doses through the whole, has perhaps rendered us a little fastidious and captious, and less disposed to do justice to that which really deserves commendation. It was very unwise in this writer to attempt a new history of the surrender of Calais, which he has succeeded in making so eminently dull and uninteresting, that one would hardly suppose it the same event, in the account of which we have been accustomed to be so much interested.

The most striking and efficient part of the work is that, which gives a description of the plague in London. We quote the account of the arrival of the ship in which it was imported.

" 'She hath had a hard voyage,' rejoined Rothelan : 'look how dishevelled she is in the cordage. Some of her top-sails too hanging in rags; and I can see, as it were, strips of green moss down the seams of the others. They have surely been long unhanded.'

"Adonijah continued looking towards the ship, and appeared thoughtful and touched with care, as he said—

" ' Her voyage hath been very long—all the way from the land of Egypt,—but she was in Italy as she came, and her course hath been in the sunny days and with the gracious gales of the summer; yet is she like a thing of antiquity, for those signs of waste and decay are as if Oblivion were on board. They have not come of the winds nor of the waves.'

" ' The crowd on the shores,' added the lady, 'grows silent as she passes.'

" ' There are many persons abroad,' said Rothelan.

" ' Yea,' replied Adonijah, ' but only the man at the helm hath for some time moved ; all the others are in idleness—still, still.—A cold fear is crawling on my bones, to see so many persons and every one monumental.'

" ' Some of those who are looking over the side,' said Rothelan, partaking in some degree of the Jew's dread, ' droop their heads upon their breasts, and take no heed of any object. Look at those on the deck ; they sit as if they were indeed marble, resting on their elbows like effigies on a tomb.'

" ' Merciful Heaven ! ' cried the Lady Albertina, ' what horror does she bring ? '

" At that moment the boats assembled round the ship suddenly made rapidly for the shore—many of the watermen stayed not till they reached the landings, but leaped into the river ; then a universal cry arose, and the people were seen scattering themselves in all directions. Rothelan darted from his mother's side, and ran towards the spot to which, instead of holding onward to the moorings, it was evident the vessel was steering to take the ground.

" In his way thither, he met his old friends, Sir Gabriel de Glowr, and his lady, who, at his request, were remaining in London. They, too, had been among the spectators, and were hurrying from the scene. The lady was breathless with haste and fear, her mantle was torn, and she had lost a shoe in her flight.

" The Baron of Falaside, before Rothelan could inquire the cause of so singular a panic, looked at him wildly, and shook his head, dragging his lady away by the arm.

" ' Stop ! ' exclaimed Rothelan, ' and tell me what is the cause of all this ! '   But they would not stop.   He also addressed himself to others with no better success.   ' Turn back, come back,' every one said to him, as he rushed against the stream of the crowd.

" The pressure and tide of the multitude slackened as he advanced ; and when he was within a short distance of the place where the ship had in the mean time taken the ground, he found himself alone.   He paused for a moment ; as he saw nothing to alarm, but only the man at the helm, who, the instant that the ship touched the ground, had leaped on shore, and was coming towards him.

" Rothelan ran forward to meet him, in order to inquire how it was that all on board appeared so motionless ; but scarcely had he advanced ten paces, when, casting his eyes forward, he saw that each of those who were leaning over the vessel's side, and resting on the deck, were dead men, from whose hideous anatomy the skin had peeled, and the flesh had fallen.   They had all died of the plague."

North American Review for July, 1825.

This Number of the North American Review is much more national and popular than the general character of the work.   The first article is an interesting sketch of the history of our Navy, from its first commencement down to the peace with Tripoli, in June, 1805.   The facts are principally derived from Clarke's " Naval History," and Goldsborough's " Naval Chronicle." The history of the brilliant achievements of our navy from 1805 to the present time would make another interesting volume, which we hope soon to receive from some one capable of doing justice to the subject. And when we have a complete history of the *achievements* of the navy, we hope we may be favoured with one more volume, which shall penetrate a little deeper into some transactions connected with it, for the last ten or fifteen years.

The second is a continuation of an articles in a preceding Number of the North American, on " Brown's Philosophy of the Mind." To this last article is annexed some account of the character of Dr Brown, taken from the Edinburgh Magazine, and from information derived from private sources, together with some strictures upon his writings. These articles are beautifully written,—too beautifully, we think, for a metaphysical subject. We should be glad to see it stated, by some one capable of the undertaking (and no one is more capable than the writer of these articles), in distinct and definite propositions, which may be taken in at one view, precisely how far Dr Brown has advanced the science of metaphysics beyond the points where its different branches were left by his predecessors. This we have not yet seen.

The review of " Recollections of the Peninsula " is exceedingly interesting. To us, however, who reviewed the same book, in the same manner, viz. by quoting its best parts, about six months since, it has not the charm of novelty. But such beautiful descriptions as the " Recollections " contain will bear to be read many times. We think this is the correct course in reviewing books of this class. It is quite as instructive to readers; and much more just to authors, if they have any thing worth saying, to let them say it in their own way, rather than to catch their ideas from them—invert their sentences, and call them our own. To this review, thus made, is annexed twenty pages on the Popular Amusements in Spain. Here is an elaborate, classical, and etymological history of the origin, progress, decline, and subsequent revivals of *bull-fights.* It is one of the most beautiful and finished pieces of description which has ever come under our notice. The execution of the piece, we are sorry to add, is worthy of a better subject, than those brutal amusements of the Spaniards. It produces in the reader an intense interest, and will probably be read by many with greater avidity than any article in the present Number of the North American; but this is not a good reason why the public taste should be depraved, and, so far as its influence goes, the national character corrupted. These, we contend, will be the results of such descriptions; and we will omit no fair opportunity of protesting against them, in whatever form they appear. The more attractive the descriptions are, the more certain will be their influence, and the more to be deprecated the practice of making them. When we closed this article, we had become so interested by its elegance and the vividness of its descriptions, that we should have had no objection to witnessing such a scene without delay, although we were provoked with ourselves for yielding to the feeling a moment. No doubt many a chivalrous youth will feel not only no reluctance to witnessing such a scene, but perhaps even a desire to take a tilt at a mad bull, if it could be done so genteelly as is here described.

Upon the article on " Recent American Novels " and the bravery of the writer of it, in venturing to insinuate at this late period, that they are not all of them perfect, we have not much at this time to say, having given nearly the same opinions, without apology, upon all of them which we deemed worthy of notice, in former numbers of this Gazette. The public opinion has long since settled down upon most of these subjects. The fortunate authors are enjoying their fame, and the sale of large editions of their books, and have no need to be cumbered with praise at this late period ; and the unfortunate ones have become reconciled to their fate, and have no need to be told what the public have long since virtually told them. The booksellers too have cleared off the dusty remains of the editions from their counters, and placed them in their cellars or their garrets, and are ready to begin upon some new work. So that none will be likely to be very much affected or disturbed by any anathemas now bestowed. It really requires no great boldness or independence to say what has before been said, and what every body is known to believe.

Upon the principle involved in the concluding paragraph, we beg leave to observe, that it is perfectly useless to attempt to sooth and pat into good nature, an author who has just been tortured by what he deems perversions of his meaning, or who is yet writhing under the lash of satire for his folly. It is an insult to his feelings and his common sense to make overtures for peace at such a moment. The authors of wicked or silly books, and reviewers in their official capacity, are natural enemies ; though they may be at the same time personal friends. It is the ambition and the interest of the former to extend their fame and the circulation of their works ; and it is the duty of the latter to limit their fame, if it be undeserved, and to prevent the circulation of their books ; because they corrupt the public taste, and cumber the ground which would be otherwise occupied by those of a higher and a better order. Upon the subject of "sweeping denunciations," and the efficacy of "flippancy," and "bitterness," we observe, that we have always thought the greatest refinement and the boldest exercise of "flippancy" was to bestow the epithet upon others.

[*To be continued.*]

English Life, or Manners at Home, in four Pictures. London,—reprinted at New-York. 2 vols. 12mo. pp. 234 and 243.

This book has been some time under our hands for a character, but the difficulty of explaining in what its signal want of merit more particularly consists, and a reluctance to read enough to give a fair account of it, have prevented our noticing it before. There are so many good novels now, that a bad one is a heavy task ; but as it comes within our plan to notice all republications of foreign books as well as native American productions, we must say something of this. For that purpose we have honestly read it through ; and if we are not the last who do so, it shall not be our fault. The most remarkable thing about it is, that any one who can write so tolerable English, and can quote so much that others have written well, one who commits so few faults, should have made two volumes so utterly worthless as to defy all criticism. The worst and the best that can be said of them is, that they are good for nothing. They contain four tales, professing to be pictures of English Life. If they be really so, the whole business of life in England is love, and matrimony its only object ; for these tales tell of absolutely nothing else. And what is most remarkable, and must produce great confusion and distress in that singular country, every body at first falls in love with the wrong person.　Life there goes always to the same dull tune of perfect beings captivated by showy qualities in the unworthy,—discovering their mistake, and then marrying their own shadows. The only thing which we notice as a positive fault in these stories is, that they contain a large portion of religious cant.　We should judge them to have been written on contract by some poor young clergyman, who put in just as much religion as would excuse him to his conscience for writing novels. If such books sell here, we are sorry for the public ; if they do not sell, we are not sorry for the publishers.

INTELLIGENCE.

DON ESTABAN, OR MEMOIRS OF A SPANIARD.

We have long thought that a work describing Spanish manners, and sketching the changes which have taken place in the Spanish Government for the last twenty years, would be peculiarly acceptable to all, who have taken any interest in the struggles of that devoted nation. And if the title of the following work is any indication of what we may expect it to contain, it will be eagerly sought for here as well as in England.　All we have seen upon the late Spanish revolutions amounts to little more than newspaper paragraphs, or books written by those who, from their situations, could take but partial views of the important events which they have attempted to describe.　"Don Estaban, or Memoirs of a Spaniard," has lately been published in England, and is said by the London papers to contain, not only a picture of the Spanish manners in the various classes of society, and at the court of Spain, anecdotes of the king and the royal family, and of public and private individuals ; but also sketches of the Guerilla Partisans and their mode of warfare, descriptions of scenes in various parts of the Peninsula, and an account of the most remarkable public events from 1808 to 1823,—the whole blended with the author's own interesting adventures.　We cannot but hope this work, which we expect soon to receive, will give us what we have hitherto sought for in vain.

RECORDS OF SCOTLAND.

The Public Records of Scotland have lately been reprinted by the king's command under the direction of Thomas Thompson, Deputy Clerk and Register. They now amount to fourteen large folio volumes, a full copy of which has been sent as a present to the Library of the Northern Scientific and Literary Institution.　The work contains the Acts of the Parliament of Scotland from 1424 to the Union in 1707 in ten volumes, the Returns of Services in three volumes ; and the Register of the Great Seal during the Reign of Robert I., David II., Robert II., and Robert III.

BARTON'S POEMS.

The poems of the Quaker, Bernard Barton, have reached the fourth edition, to which he has added several pieces.

NEW ROMANCE FOUNDED ON IRISH HISTORY AND SCENERY.

The London Courier states, that a Romance founded on the celebrated Geraldine Rebellion, in the reign of Henry VIII., and headed by Thomas Fitzgerald, has made its appearance ; that the writer is thoroughly conversant with the manners and customs of that period ; and that the language is very good, and the story possesses great interest.

CHRONOMETERS.

The prize of £300, assigned by the LORDS OF THE ADMIRALTY for the best chronometer, after one year's trial at the Royal Observatory, Greenwich, has just been awarded to Mr R. Widenham of East street, Red Lion square, a very young and ingenious artist. His chronometer, which was an elegant piece of mechanism, only suffered within the year an extreme variation of one second and 84 hundredths of time, according to the tables of mean rates computed by the Astronomer Royal, from actual daily observation. There are generally thirty chronometers sent to the Royal Observatory for competition. Mr Widenham's, having varied the least, has been purchased at the prize value by the Lords of the Admiralty.

LONDON EDITIONS OF MR WAYLAND'S SERMON.

Four editions of the sermon of the Rev. Mr Wayland of this city " on the Moral Dignity of the Missionary Enterprise," have been published in London.

THE ROYAL INSTITUTION.

Great differences are said to exist among those, who have taken an active part in the management of this institution ; and it is feared, that the consequences will be a dissolution of the institution.

NEWLY DISCOVERED FRESCOES.

We learn from the London Literary Gazette, that two new *frescoes* have just been discovered at Pompeii, which are most remarkable for the perfect correctness of their design and for the excellence of their colouring. They represent *Briseis taken from Achilles*, and the *Nuptials of Thetis and Peleus*. These pictures still remain in the place where they were found, and are considered as the finest that have ever been discovered belonging to ancient times.

REMAINS OF THE OBELISKS AT ROME.

The same paper informs us, that M. Champolion Jr. is pursuing with great zeal his archæological researches at Naples and in the surrounding country. He has visited Pozzuoli, Baia, Pompeii, and Pæstum, and has been present at the searches made at Nola. The Bourbon Museum at Naples has furnished him with new subjects of Egyptian investigation ; he has ascertained that three large engraved fragments of red granite, which are there preserved, are remains of three of the obelisks at Rome. He has discovered also for the first time the case of a mummy, the legends drawn on which are in *hieratic* characters ;

they are followed by another inscription in writing, which is neither
Egyptian nor Grecian, and respecting which the enlightened traveller
promises to give further details.

NEW ZOOLOGICAL PROJECT.

Sir Humphrey Davy has started a project for organizing a zoological
society and establishing a *ménagerie*, which are designed to answer the
same purposes and afford the same facilities for the study of the science
of zoology as the Horticultural society and establishment do for Botany.
" The great objects," he says in his prospectus, " should be the introduction of new varieties, breeds, and races of animals for the purpose of
domestication, or for stocking our farm-yards, woods, pleasure-grounds,
and wastes ; with the establishment of a general zoological collection,
consisting of prepared specimens in different classes and orders, so as to
afford a correct view of the animal kingdom at large, in as complete a
series as may be practicable, and at the same time to point out the
analogies between the animals already domesticated, and those which are
similar in character, upon which the first experiments may be made."

THE PLEASURE OF LOVE QUARRELS.

The following aphorism, taken from a work recently published, called
" To-day in Ireland," though it may not come very appropriately under
the head of literary and scientific intelligence, will, we think, revive a
consciousness of its truth in the minds of many literary and scientific
people. " There is a pleasure in quarrelling, which none but a piqued
lover knows, and which it would be idle to attempt to explain. Fancy
has generally ere then exhausted the store of hope, and hath run
over the fair side of the question, till not one new source is left to imagine :—it then, perforce, turns the canvass, and having spent all its gay
colours on one side, it delights to employ its untouched stock of lugubri-
ous ones upon the reverse. If a lover's hope be supreme bliss, a lover's
despair is not without its soothing and flattering accompaniments, so that,
on the whole, perhaps he is not vastly to be pitied ! "

DR. BIGELOW'S AMERICAN MEDICAL BOTANY.

This valuable work, published a few years since, has been noticed and
highly complimented in a late number of the *Revue Encyclopédique*,
published in Paris. The reviewers think we ought to live forever, if we
have *medicinal* plants, in such numbers, that the description of them fills
three quarto volumes.

WRITING ON BOARDS COVERED WITH SAND.

We learn, on the authority of the London Literary Gazette, that
the Counsellor Slootsoff, in a tour of inspection, which he recently made
in the countries beyond the lake Baikal in Siberia, having occasion to
explain to the elders of the tribes of Bouriaates on the banks of the
Salenga the most simple mode of teaching the children to write, was
much surprised to learn from them, that their Lamas were in the habit
of using boards covered with sand in teaching arithmetic to their pu-

pils, and that this method had been borrowed from Thibet. Bell and Lancaster have hitherto claimed and received the honor of being the first to use these means for teaching writing.

LOUIS XVIII. AND NAPOLEON IN THE ELYSIAN FIELDS.

A book has lately been published in Paris with the above title. We think they must have some interesting conversation, and hope the volume will reach us, that we may hear what they have to say to each other.

STEAM ENGINES IN ENGLAND.

The steam engines in England represent the power of 320,000 horses, equal to 1,920,000 men; which, being in fact managed by 36,000 men only, add actually to the power of the population 1,884,000 men.

NEW PUBLICATIONS.

ARTS AND SCIENCE.

The American Journal of Science and Arts. Conducted by Benjamin Silliman. Vol. IX. No II. June 1825. New-Haven.

This work is published in quarterly numbers, making two volumes each year of at least 320 octavo pages each. The plan of the work was projected by Professor Silliman four or five years since; and by his talents and industry it has been in a great degree sustained. He has now, however, the assistance of many able and intelligent correspondents in different parts of Europe, as well as in our own country. These together with the industry of the editor, bring into his journal a greater mass of intelligence upon those subjects to which it is more particularly devoted, than is collected in any other work of the kind published in this country. The present number contains many interesting and original articles, on Geology, Mineralogy, and Topography; Botany, Entomology, and Ichthyology. And under the department of Mathematics, Mechanics, Physics, and Chemistry, we notice a communication on *crank motion*, from Mr A. B. Quinby, a distinguished mathematician in New-York, which shows a great deal of research. It seems there has been some controversy on the subject before, as this article is called a "Reply to the remarks of the author of an article in the North American Review." We have not now the leisure necessary to trace the controversy to its origin, but we think Mr Quinby in the present article worries his antagonist of the North American with some zeal and effect.

MEDICINE.

The Carolina Journal of Medicine, Science, and Agriculture. Vol. I. No II. Charleston. Gray & Ellis.

MISCELLANEOUS.

Boston Monthly Magazine. No I. June 1825. Boston.

Views on the subject of Internal Improvement, Steam Boats on the Susquehanna, &c. By William Hollins. Nos. I. & II. Baltimore. Etting Mickle.

A Lecture, being the second of a Series of Lectures, introductory to a Course of Lectures, now delivering in the University of Maryland. By David Hoffman. Published at the Request of the Faculty of Law. 8vo. pp. 50. Baltimore. John D. Toy.

North American Review. No. 48. July 1825.

The Inquisition, examined by an Impartial Reviewer. No. I. New-York. Thomas O. Conner.

The New Jersey Monthly Magazine for April, 1825. Edited by Thomas S. Wiggins. Vol. 1. No. I. 8vo. pp. 32. Belvidere.

A new periodical work, to be published on the first day of every month. We have no yet received our number for May or June. We hope no accident has befallen the work in this early stage of it.

The Long Island Journal of Philosophy and Cabinet of Variety. Conducted by Samuel Fleet, assisted by a number of Literary Gentlemen. Vol. I. No. II. June, 1825. 8vo. pp. 50. Huntington, L. I.

A new periodical work under this title has lately been established at Huntington, L. I. to be published monthly. The second appellation indicates its character rather the more accurately. We welcome the conductors of it to a place among us, but fear they will find the labourers quite equal to the harvest. Truly the population of this part of our country must increase, at least as *the square of the time*, to afford readers for us all.

NOVELS.

The Christian Indian ; or, Times of the First Settlers. First of a Series of American Tales. 1 vol. 12mo. pp. 251. New-York. Collins & Hannay.

We have glanced at this book ; and are persuaded, that the author is a little presumptuous to threaten the public with *a series* of American Tales, on the strength of any talents manifested in this one. It is the height of folly, merely because a few authors of superior talents, have been able to interest the public in a series of books upon kindred topics, for young or inexperienced writers to announce on the title page of their first attempt at making a book, their intention to make a series. We think they had better try the success of the first, before they enter into any very extensive arrangements for the publication of more. We intend to give a little more extended notice of this book on the first page we can spare, from those occupied by subjects of more importance ; but we were anxious to improve the first opportunity, which presented itself to us, for intimating to the author the imminent danger he is in of feeling extremely silly, when the public have manifested the indifference which they generally do, to a *series* of such books. Should he prosecute his design, however, we promise him candour in our remarks, and assure him, that we are honest and zealous inquirers after truth, and violently patriotic advocates and admirers of the literature of our own country. But when we think we have discovered the truth, we have a propensity to state it, which we cannot resist. Our consciences too are extremely tender on points of literary justice, and it may prove, that this *justice* is the very thing which our author has most to fear.

POLITICS.

The General Convention of Peace, Amity, Navigation, and Commerce, between the United States of America, and the Republic of Colombia, concluded and signed at Bogota October 3, 1824, and ratified at Washington May 31, 1825. Philadelphia. J. Mortimer.

THEOLOGY.

The Literary and Evangelical Magazine. Vol. VII. No. VI. for June 1825. Richmond, Va.

The American Baptist Magazine. Vol. V. No. VII.

The Christian Examiner and Theological Review. No. IX. for July 1825.

TOPOGRAPHY.

A Northern Tour : being a Guide to Saratoga, Lake George, Niagara, Canada, Boston, &c. &c. Embracing an Account of the Canals, Colleges, Public Institutions, Natural Curiosities, and Interesting Objects therein. 18mo. pp. 279. Philadelphia. Carey & Lea.

AMERICAN EDITIONS OF FOREIGN WORKS.

The Memoirs of Madame De Genlis, illustrative of the History of the 18th and 19th Centuries, written by Herself. New-York. Wilder & Campbell.

This is a very interesting book, and we have prepared a review of it; but are obliged for want of room to postpone its insertion till some future number.

Gaieties and Gravities, by one of the Authors of "Rejected Addresses," 2 vols. Philadelphia. Carey & Lea.

The Old Fashioned Farmer's Motives for leaving the Church of England, and embracing the Roman Catholic Faith, and his Reasons for adhering to the same : together with an Explanation of some particular Points, misrepresented by those of a different Persuasion. With an Appendix, by way of Antidote against all upstart new Faiths, concluded with asking thirty plain Questions. Price 50 cents. Washington. D. C.

Paley's View of the Evidences of Christanity. A New Edition. 1 vol. 12mo. Philadelphia. Towar & Hogan.

LIST OF WORKS IN PRESS.

An Elementary Treatise on Electricity and Magnetism, being the Second Part of a Course of Natural Philosophy, compiled for the use of the Students of the University at Cambridge, N. E. By John Farrar, Professor of Mathematics and Natural Philosophy. Cambridge. Hilliard & Metcalf.

The Foresters, ; by the author of "Lights and Shadows." 1 vol. 12mo. New-York. Wilder & Campbell.

Remarkable Events in the History of Man. By the Rev. L Watts, D. D. New-York.

The Novice, or Man of Integrity, from the French of L. B. Picard, Author of "Gil Blas of the Revolution." 2 vols. New-York.

Political Economy, from the Supplement to the Encyclopædia Britannica, with Notes by Prof. M. Vickar, of Columbia College, New-York.

Familiar Letters, by the Rev. John Newton, never before published. 1 vol. New-York. Wilder & Campbell.

Frederick De Algeroy, the Hero of Camden Plains. A Revolutionary Tale. By Giles Gazer, Esq. 12mo. New-York. J. & J. Harper.

Paris's Elements of Medical Chymistry, 8vo. with numerous Engravings. New-York.

Crabbe's English Synonymes, from the third London Edition, revised, corrected, and enlarged. 8vo. upwards of 800 pages. New-York.

Essay on Faith—By Lumen. Trenton. N. J. Francis S. Wiggins.

Memoirs of Joseph Fouché, Duke of Otranto, Minister of the General Police of France, translated from the French. Boston. Wells & Lilly.

Tales of the Crusaders, by the author of Waverley, Ivanhoe, etc. Philadelphia. Carey & Lea.

Published on the first and fifteenth day of every month, by CUMMINGS, HILLIARD, & Co., No. 134 Washington-Street, Boston, for the Proprietors. Terms, $5 per annum. Cambridge : Printed at the University Press, by Hilliard & Metcalf.

THE UNITED STATES

LITERARY GAZETTE.

Vol. II.   AUGUST 1, 1825.   No. 9.

REVIEWS.

A View of the Constitution of the United States of America.
By WILLIAM RAWLE. Philadelphia. 1825. 8vo. pp. 347.

THIS work is rather of the old school ; but this, considering its subject, is no objection to it. Sensible writings of the old school are safer than the more popular productions conceived in the spirit of the present day ; and certainly there is no subject, on which we want *safe* works more, than we do on this of the Constitution of the United States. The general design of the book is to teach the practical nature and operation of the Constitution of the United States of America, either as ascertained in its own clear text, or as settled by the authority of the organized bodies created by it, or existing under it. The following short preface, by indicating, in a prominent manner, the classes of the public, for whom the work is more immediately designed, will prepare the reader for the manner, in which it is conceived and executed.

If the following work shall prove useful, as an elementary treatise to the *American student*, the author will be gratified.

If *foreigners* are enabled, by the perusal of it, to obtain a general idea of the merits of the constitution, his satisfaction will be increased.

To the American *public in general*, its value may chiefly consist in the exhibition of those judicial decisions, which have settled the construction of some points that have been the subjects of controversy.

We feel no hesitation in pronouncing this work to be, what its author seems to have intended it should be—a treatise well calculated to give to the student an elementary view, to the foreigner a summary and connected view, to the reading public in general a popular and intelligible view of the most im-

41

portant written political system, which the world has ever seen, the Constitution of the United States of America.

We have said that it is a work of the old school. It broaches no startling questions upon ultimate principles, though there is no example in history so brilliant of a successful appeal to those principles, as that which is afforded by the dismemberment of the British empire, the erection of an independent government, and the peaceful formation of the Constitution of the United States.

The author does not touch, we believe, even by allusion, on the speculations which have so much exercised the bold spirits of the present day in Germany and France ; and which the philosophical statesmen of our own country have not wholly left unnoticed, respecting the *principle* of Constitutions ; the nature of the obligation they impose ; the nature and quality of *unconstitutional* popular acts. Mr Jefferson, in one of the letters with which his correspondents occasionally favour the public, without asking the permission of the venerable writer, with whose confidence they deal so unceremoniously, has said, in substance, that the world belongs to its inhabitants for the time being ; a proposition which it would not seem dangerous to grant, but which leads to perilous inferences, as to the validity of all acts, by which the inhabitants of the world in past ages claim to bind their successors. It is not probable, at least in any state of things now to be foreseen, that this scruple as to the abstract obligation of a constitution will ever become practically formidable. There is no danger, that the people of the United States will ever meet in convention to abolish the constitution ; if they did, however, the act of abolition, according to the *theory* of our institutions, would be valid, in our judgment. Others, we doubt not, entertain a different view on this subject, and conceive that such an act would be rebellion here, precisely as it would be in England, or in any other country where a hereditary government exists. But without intending any discussion of this question, we will only observe, that the theoretical views, which men entertain of the degree of power which one generation has constitutionally to bind another, will exert some influence on their opinions as to the great practical question of construction.

At the present day of united parties and forgotten feuds, when it has been found altogether impossible to keep up the ancient array of two opposed phalanxes in national politics, almost the only question of a general political nature which divides the minds of men regards the subject of *constructive powers.* It is true that, in reality, the parties are much nearer each other on this subject than they are willing to allow, as is commonly the case in controversy. The party in favor of constructions, does not mean that even by construction any power shall be assumed, by the national government, which is not fairly deducible from the instrument. They say indeed that the "general welfare" is one of the objects, which the constitution is to effect; but this object is to be effected, not by any and every measure, but by measures directly authorized by the text, or necessarily incident to what is directly authorized. Farther than this, we apprehend no advocate of constructive powers will go. On the other hand, the opponents of construction are obliged, every day, to sanction extremely liberal interpretations of the instrument; for the government could not be administered, if no function were performed beyond those which are expressed *totidem verbis* in the constitution. But the nominal difference between the two parties furnishes excellent ground for dispute; the topics are fruitful; the field for retort ample. In the progress of the discussion, the parties no doubt excite themselves to a higher pitch, than they could have reached by any course of private reasoning. The standing theme of discussion in Virginia—the theme not only of newspaper essays but of octavo volumes—is the total prostration of the rights of the several states by the constructive usurpations of Congress; although that Congress is a body returning periodically to the people, one branch of it the immediate representatives of the states, as such; and all their acts subject to the *veto* of a president, who hitherto has been, thirty years out of thirty-four, a Virginian. If, under these premises, the rights of the states in general and of Virginia in particular, have been *constructively* betrayed, they and she are most certainly *participes criminis.*

But we observed that the question of construction is a practical one; it is most highly and seriously so. The framers of the constitution were wise men, endued with foresight almost prophetical. We are the daily and the hourly witnesses of the sagacity, with which they were able to frame an instrument of government, whose operation is already most successful over a country, which can hardly be called the same, as that, for which they framed the constitution. Still, however, they were but men; they were not prophets: they were prudent, not inspired; they foresaw general results, they could not calculate for particular facts. The extent of the country is increasing, the number of important interests multiplying, the relations with other states assuming the most unlooked-for aspects. The constitution remains, and will, we trust, forever remain. But what shall we do with it? shall we, on every occasion when some new modification of measures, unforeseen in 1789, is called for, in the new state of things, shall we think it enough to set our foot down and say, "the framers of the constitution did not contemplate it, it is therefore unconstitutional?" The late distinguished senator from New York is understood, in the last session of Congress, to have declared, though in an unofficial way, that no such thing was dreamed of by the framers of the constitution, as the right of the national government to construct the Cumberland road. But was it dreamed of, that in less than thirty-five years after the date of that instrument, there would be not thirteen states, but twenty-four; and that for several branches of the public service a good road across the country was indispensable? But you say, "*amend* the constitution, if you find its powers inadequate to the present increased extent, relations, and wants of the country." But this is a most delicate point of political prudence. An amendment of the constitution is the very worst remedy that can be imagined. All the evils which imagination can conjure out of the abuses of *construction* are insignificant, compared with the disastrous consequences, that could not fail to flow from a habit of ready tampering with amendments. The power of amendment ought certainly to remain; as a kind of safety-valve to prevent a fatal accumulation of discontent, under the existence of what time might prove to be intolerable evils. But if this safety-valve is to be kept constantly opened, the power cannot be created to keep the heavy wheels of government in motion. A thousand, ten thousand times preferable is the practical over the theoretical remedy. With every branch of the government not only in name but in reality elective, what possibility is there of any organized and systematic encroachment of that government on the rights of the people. How much better to allow the people to proclaim their sense of the constitution in particular nice questions at the ballot boxes, than to be calling upon them constantly to take the constitution into their hands and alter it.

There is one remark only, which we will make in addition on this topic. The politicians of the Virginia school are very earnest in denouncing the constructive policy, as unconstitutional, in its tendency to aggrandize the national government and subvert state rights. They say nothing similar was contemplated by the glorious sages, who formed the constitution. But when we go back to the controversies, which arose on the question of adopting the constitution, we find that it was by this same class of politicians, with Patrick Henry at their head, objected to the instrument, that it had this effect ; to create a national, and to merge and consolidate the state governments. Whatever other objection then it may now be proper to make to the policy in question, it ought not to be objected that it is unconstitutional, when in 1789 it was objected to the constitution, that it was built on a consolidating policy. If this party are now in earnest, in the complaint of unconstitutionality, the language of Mr Gerry, of Mr Monroe, of Mr Henry in 1788 was mere cavil. If those distinguished patriots and statesmen were sincere (and who will doubt it?) then the present cry of unconstitutional and *constructive*, is unjust and inconsistent. That it is inconsistent we firmly believe. The constitution never had better friends than the men we have just named, from the moment they saw that its operation was salutary. They found that the power given the national government did not destroy the sovereignty of the states. And it is well known that Patrick Henry, the illustrious champion of the pure antifederalism of 1788, lived to hold the very language, which we have now held in a somewhat wider application ; and declared that after having made it an objection to the constitution, that it clothed the national government with strong powers, he could not and would not turn round and say, the exercise of those powers was unconstitutional. The last act of his public life was to offer himself for Congress, for the avowed purpose of maintaining on its floor those alien and sedition laws, which are still held up, by eminence, as unconstitutional.

With regard to Mr Rawle's work, we conceive that it will be very valuable as a text-book in our places of education. The Federalist has been hitherto used as a manual on the constitution of the country. But the Federalist is, in general, in style too diffuse for such an object : it is adapted rather for that, in view of which it was written—contemporary perusal in the newspapers. This however is not the only

exception, which may fairly be taken to the Federalist
as a text-book—it is avowedly a work designed to set
forth the bright side of the constitution, and is so far of
the nature of a panegyric, of which the object is to commend a favourite measure, against the assaults of active enemies.   Besides this, the Federalist was *prospectively* written.
Not a little of it is taken up in discussing objections, which
were started at that day, but which in practice never afterwards became important ; as for instance, the objection that
the constitution gives the national government the power of
controlling by law the times, places, and manner of holding
elections for representatives, and the times and manner of
holding elections for senators.   In our own state convention
for adopting the constitution, no provision was more anxiously
discussed than this ; no power granted to the general government was thought more dangerous ; none claimed, as more
important.   What could be more narcotic than such a debate
at the present day ! Finally, much has been settled, by experience in administering the constitution.   Mr Rawle's work
embraces every thing of this kind, and this alone would give
it a preference as a text-book.

, The most delicate questions under the constitution are those
which concern conflicting exercises of power on the part of
the national and state governments.   The following passage
will unfold Mr Rawle's views on the most serious conflict of
this kind that has occurred since the adoption of the constitution.

During the late war, a construction of this part of the constitution
was given in a highly respectable state, which excited no small uneasiness at the time, and ought not to be passed over in silence. The act of
congress declaring war took place on the 18th of June 1812, and the president was expressly authorized by the act to use the whole land and naval
forces to carry it into effect.   Orders were soon afterwards issued by
him for calling out certain portions of the militia from each state.   The
opinions of the judges of the Supreme Judicial Court of Massachusetts
were required by the governor, and three of them, in the absence of the
others, declared their sentiments, that the commander in chief of the
militia of a state had a right to decide whether or not the exigencies to
warrant the call existed.   Of course that whatever were the declara-
tions of congress, or the course pursued by the president, if the governor
of a state thought differently ; if he thought there was no war, no insurrection, no invasion, he was not obliged to obey such requisitions.   The
governor expressed the same opinion in a message to the legislature ;
and a line of conduct was adopted greatly tending to impair the energies of the country, and encourage the hopes of the enemy.

The apprehension professed was, that if congress, by determining that those special cases existed, could at any time call forth the whole of the militia and subject them to the command of the president, it might produce "a military consolidation of the states," without any constitutional remedy. And that under the act of February 28th, 1795, the militia of the several states would be in fact at his command at any time when he thought proper, whether the exigency existed or not.

But whatever weight might have been found in these objections against adopting the constitution, they ceased when it was adopted. It was then the choice of the people to repose this confidence in congress to enable them to provide for the common defence and general welfare. If it had been thought necessary to impose any check or control; if in opposition to the whole spirit of the instrument, it had been deemed expedient to disunite the system, by requiring the concurrence of the states, it could undoubtedly have been so expressed, and in this respect at least we should not have advanced a step beyond the imbecility of the old government. Nothing would be more likely to enfeeble the Union than to have subjected the right of exercising these powers to the governors, or even the legislatures of the different states, some of which might hold one opinion, and some insist upon another; and it is by no means clear that the people did not apprehend a greater danger of abuse of confidence from the governor and legislature of a state, than from the government of the United States.

There are several bad misprints in this work; one particularly in the paragraph at the bottom of the 311th page. In the appendix No IV, which purports to present "the entire constitution," we notice the extraordinary omission (also, we presume, a typographical error) of the whole of the preamble. ·

An Address, delivered at the Laying of the Corner Stone of the Bunker Hill Monument. By DANIEL WEBSTER. Boston. 8vo. pp. 40.

THE celebration which gave occasion to this address, considered in all its circumstances, is one of the most remarkable events of our time; and that is to say, of all times. It will be scarcely less famed, than the battle which it was intended to commemorate. History, poetry, and painting, will claim the one as much as the other; and fifty years hence, to have been a spectator of the scene of 1825, will be a distinction, as it now is to have been an actor in that of 1775. The ordinary epithets and images expressive and illustrative of moral grandeur are too tame, and too familiar, to be employed in describing the solemnities of this august and joyous jubilee. It was the result of so many causes, too high for human agency; it was dignified and graced by so many circumstances which time and Providence only could have created and combined, that no loftiness of language, no strength of conception, no liveliness of fancy, which we may bring to the task, can fitly represent it to our distant friends in this and in other lands. The time, the place, the purpose, the audience, the orator, " the guest," and the unclouded day, each in itself a separate source of sublime and pleasing emotions, ALL, ALL, united in happy confluence to swell the tide of universal joy ; without presumption may we say, that no ceremony of its kind ever equalled, none can surpass it.

" The Nation's Guest," having journeyed by land and water through every state in the union with incredible celerity, giving every where the purest pleasure, and receiving unexampled proofs of love and veneration, with a modesty and unpremeditated propriety, which form one of the most remarkable traits of his extraordinary character; having escaped, with characteristic good fortune, from a new danger, scarcely less threatening than those which had beset his previous and ever perilous career—arrived, and was again publicly and privately welcomed among us, with a less boisterous and eager gladness than at first, but with a steady affection, and chastened admiration, better suited to his character and to our own.

The survivors of Bunker Hill battle and of the revolutionary army,—none of them less than three score and ten, and many of them more than four score, one four score and fifteen,—assembled from different and distant quarters, and were gratefully welcomed, and hospitably entertained by the opulent gentlemen of the metropolis. Some of them had not revisited the neighbourhood since they fought the battle, whose fiftieth anniversary they were now called to celebrate. They had left Charlestown wrapt in flames, and the harassed inhabitants of this captive and beleaguered city, Boston, more wretched in retaining their homes, than those of Charlestown in losing them. How changed was the whole scene—themselves how changed! Charlestown, risen like Phœnix from her ashes, more beautiful than before—Boston, from a town of hovels and wooden houses, become a splendid city of brick and granite, exhibiting,—instead of here and there a solitary citizen with anxious and care-worn looks, scudding along the concealed alley, or cautiously emerging, fearful of an insulting and exasperated foe,—a countless multitude of happy and cultivated men and women, crowding her broad avenues with life, and motion, and joy, anxious only for improvement, and fearing no power but that which all must fear; instead of a wretched ferry-boat, propelled by the tardy and labouring oar, four *sublician* * bridges, so extended that their converging lights seem to deny the passenger an egress; and greater and better than these, that stupendous bulwark of the waves, which bids them, proud as they are, be stayed; steam-boats, which move with the power and rapidity of the levia-than, and the precision and safety of a stage-coach! Often did those aged and homebred heroes exclaim, " How every thing has changed; little did I think that I should live to see this day!" Verily the effects of time, and industry, and knowledge, and good government, are marvellous in our eyes.

About a week before the celebration, ground was broken on the summit of Breed's Hill, exactly on the site of the little redoubt which the yeomanry of New England threw up with so much vigour in half of a single brief night, and defended, all faint, fatigued, and unrefreshed, as they were, with so much valour on the following day. The digging was attended with the constant *exhumation* of the bones of those valiant men. These venerated remains were religiously collected and preserved. Stones of massive granite were hewn, to take the place of the earth and the relics thus removed, and to form the foundation of a suitable monument of ancestral glo-ry and filial gratitude. One of them was excavated to receive the records of history. A little below, towards the north, on the spot where our fathers gathered for the fight, and where a portion of them fell and lie buried, were erected under the open firmament extensive and successive rows of seats, rising in the manner of an amphitheatre to the summit of the hill. In the centre of the lower side, and near the foot of the de-clivity, was raised the rostrum, covered with an awning, re-sembling a triumphal arch, decorated with wreaths and roses, and surmounted by a colossal eagle. On the right and left of the rostrum, were two ranges of seats, also covered with an awning, extending on either hand about two hundred feet, and designed for the accommodation of ladies. On the top of Bunker Hill, about half a mile from the battle ground, was erected a spacious awning, larger than was ever beheld in this country, or perhaps in any country, decorated with flags and pendants; and tables were set beneath it for four thousand

* Ob commoditatem itineris, ponte *sublicio*, tum primum in Tiberim facto. Liv. i. 33.

guests. Twenty beautiful companies of militia, light troops, from Boston, Charlestown, Cambridge, Roxbury, Salem, and other towns from five to twenty miles distant, had volunteered, and were arriving and encamping on the Boston Common. Such and much more were the preparations on the evening of the sixteenth of June, which, after a moderate rain, shut in with a cloudless sky and a clear and temperate atmosphere, promising for the day following all that patriotism, eloquence, or curiosity could wish. And never was happy omen more happily fulfilled; never dawned a morning more fair and bright. The showers of the preceding day had imprisoned the dust, and enlivened the tints of the gay and variegated landscape. The bells of the metropolis, and the neighbouring towns rung an animating peal; the clamours of cannon were re-echoed from the wooded hills, whose shadows, an echo to the sight, were reflected from the mirrors of Mystic and Charles, and from the broad bay where their waters unite and wash the foot of the consecrated mount. As the day advanced, the different corps of citizen soldiers began to move to their assigned places, and to address themselves to their several duties. A well dressed, orderly, and delighted multitude gathered and spread over that superb park, for which we are so much indebted to the taste and forecast of our fathers, and thronged the streets from thence to the scene of the expected ceremonies. Glass windows were removed, and their places supplied by animated faces, as light and transparent as they.

At mid-day the procession began to move from the Capitol under a splendid escort of sixteen companies of infantry, and a corps of cavalry. First appeared the survivors of Bunker Hill battle, bearing badges on their breasts with this inscription, " Bunker Hill Battle, June 17th, 1775;" some of the most infirm in open carriages, but about one hundred on foot. Next followed the members of the association for building the monument. Then the Grand Lodge of Massachusetts, with deputations from the Grand Lodges of six states, a Grand Encampment of Knights Templars, a Grand Royal Arch Chapter, all arrayed in their appropriate and splendid " clothing," and bearing among other jewels a golden urn, containing a relic of Washington. Next advanced the Orator of the day, who was also President of the Association, accompanied by the other officers of that body; next to these the Chaplains of the day and the respected and beloved head of our oldest

University. Then came the "Nation's Guest," accompanied by his countryman, the gallant General Lallemand, his son, and secretary; next the survivors of the Revolutionary army, bearing badges expressive of that fact. Then advanced the Governor of Massachusetts, followed by the civil officers of this commonwealth; then the Governor of the state of Rhode Island, the Secretary of War and late Governor of Virginia, Senators and Representatives of the United States, Officers of the army and navy, Clergy, Officers of the militia, and, lastly, private citizens.

This procession formed a solid and continuous column, two miles in length, stretching from city to city, and from hill to hill; those twin and classic hills, hallowed by history and poetry, equal in height, but unequal in fame; for on one was erected a *beacon* to New England, but on the other a brighter one to the world! Numerous as was the procession, it formed but a slender stream, compared with the dense crowd of human and happy beings, who occupied the sides of the streets, the bridge, the public squares, the windows, and housetops, wherever it passed. After the ceremony of laying the corner stone by General Lafayette, the procession occupied the amphitheatre in front of the rostrum, the Bunker Hill survivors being on the right, and the Revolutionary on the left front; the side ranges having been already filled with ladies, whose faces added a bright charm to the severe solemnities of this precious day. Lafayette was at the head of the Revolutionary Survivors on a seat slightly raised. The amphitheatre was crowded to the summit and along the sides of the hill. The number within hearing distance was estimated at *fifteen thousand.* The Orator and Chaplains appeared upon the rostrum, which was a simple platform, raised five feet above the seats immediately round it. An appropriate prayer was offered by the Rev. Mr Thaxter, aged eighty-three, the Chaplain of Prescott's regiment,—the one which erected and defended the redoubt,—himself a brave and efficient soldier. This most venerable and interesting old gentleman deserves a particular description, but our limits will not admit of details so minute. No picture could be more patriarchal. His voice had nothing of childish treble, but was clear and sonorous. He was heard distinctly by many thousands. Then arose the Orator, a man emphatically made for the occasion, and realizing, if it ever is to be realized, our conception of the great Greek orator, pronouncing, before the

Athenians, the funeral oration of their countrymen slain at Chæronea.) An intense anxiety on the skirts of the crowd to approach nearer so as to hear, produced a slight disorder, which was soon quieted; and Mr Webster spake thus:

"This uncounted multitude before me, and around me, proves the feeling which the occasion has excited. These thousands of human faces, glowing with sympathy and joy, and, from the impulses of a common gratitude, turned reverently to heaven, in this spacious temple of the firmament, proclaim that the day, the place, and the purpose of our assembling have made a deep impression on our hearts.

"If, indeed, there be any thing in local association fit to affect the mind of man, we need not strive to repress the emotions which agitate us here. We are among the sepulchres of our fathers. We are on ground, distinguished by their valor, their constancy, and the shedding of their blood. We are here, not to fix an uncertain date in our annals, nor to draw into notice an obscure and unknown spot. If our humble purpose had never been conceived, if we ourselves had never been born, the 17th of June 1775 would have been a day on which all subsequent history would have poured its light, and the eminence where we stand, a point of attraction to the eyes of successive generations."

After slightly glancing at the first settlers of New England, he sets forth the origin and object of the Bunker Hill Monument Association. It is all sensible, some of it powerful; it concludes thus:

"We wish, finally, that the last object on the sight of him who leaves his native shore, and the first to gladden his who revisits it, may be something which shall remind him of the liberty and the glory of his country. Let it rise, till it meet the sun in his coming; let the earliest light of the morning gild it, and parting day linger and play on its summit."

Next follows a rapid enumeration of the great events which have taken place since the battle of Bunker Hill; the accomplishment of our own Revolution; the erection of " twenty-four sovereign states;" the forming of a general government over them all, " so safe, so wise, so free, so practical, that we might well wonder its establishment should have been accomplished so soon, were it not far the greater wonder that it should have been established at all;" the rapid augmentation of our population, revenues, and " navies, which take no law from superior force;" the " mighty revolution of Europe, which has dashed against one another thrones that had stood tranquil for centuries;" those of South America, and the annihilation of "European power from the place where he spoke to the south pole." These events, "so numerous and important that they might crowd and distinguish centuries," he said, were in our times "compressed within the compass of a single life"—the life of many of those who took part in the battle, from which they all took their date. By this easy and graceful transition Mr Webster comes to address the remnant of the men of '75; who spontaneously rose up and listened to these words:

"VENERABLE MEN! you have come down to us from a former generation. Heaven has bounteously lengthened out your lives, that you might behold this joyous day. You are now, where you stood, fifty years ago, this very hour, with your brothers, and your neighbours, shoulder to shoulder, in the strife for your country. Behold, how altered! The same heavens are indeed over your heads; the same ocean rolls at your feet; but all else, how changed! You hear now no roar of hostile cannon, you see no mixed volumes of smoke and flame rising from burning Charlestown. The ground strewed with the dead and the dying; the impetuous charge; the steady and successful repulse; the loud call to repeated assault; the summoning of all that is manly to repeated resistance; a thousand bosoms freely and fearlessly bared in an instant to whatever of terror there may be in war and death;— all these you have witnessed, but you witness them no more. All is peace. The heights of yonder metropolis, its towers and roofs, which you then saw filled with wives and children and countrymen in distress and terror, and looking with unutterable emotions for the issue of the combat, have presented you to-day with the sight of its whole happy population, come out to welcome and greet you with an universal jubilee. Yonder proud ships, by a felicity of position appropriately lying at the foot of this mount, and seeming fondly to cling around it, are not means of annoyance to you, but your country's own means of distinction and defence. All is peace; and God has granted you this sight of your country's happiness, ere you slumber in the grave forever. He has allowed you to behold and to partake the reward of your patriotic toils; and he has allowed us, your sons and countrymen, to meet you here, and in the name of the present generation, in the name of your country, in the name of liberty, to thank you!"

The succeeding part is addressed to the Revolutionary survivors, and is followed by a brief view of the causes which produced, the spirit which accompanied, and the immediate consequences which followed, this first battle of the Revolution.

The encomium passed upon the Revolutionary state papers gave us particular pleasure. With equal pleasure did we listen to the just tribute feelingly paid to the humanity and disinterestedness shown by the people of Salem, on the occasion of shutting the port of Boston. The plan of the British ministry was to punish Boston and seduce Salem; to distress some towns, to bribe others, and to terrify all; and certainly in itself the measure was well calculated to succeed.

"The temptation to profit by the punishment of Boston was strongest to our neighbours of Salem. Yet Salem was precisely the place, where this miserable proffer was spurned, in a tone of the most lofty self-respect, and the most indignant patriotism. ' We are deeply affected,' said its inhabitants, ' with the sense of our public calamities; but the miseries that are now rapidly hastening on our brethren in the capital of the Province, greatly excite our commiseration. By shutting up the port of Boston, some imagine that the course of trade might be turned hither and to our benefit; but we must be dead to every idea of justice, lost to all feelings of humanity, could we indulge a thought to seize on wealth, and raise our fortunes on the ruin of our suffering neighbours.' "

Among the other immediate consequences of the battle was the making of our cause and our character more generally known, and the producing of a conviction that America was in earnest, and if she fell would not fall without a struggle. This knowledge and this conviction reached the ears and the heart of a youthful and disinterested friend, who, by the signal favor of Heaven, was now again among us, and, rising from his seat, received the following just and noble tribute of respect and gratitude:

"Sir, we are assembled to commemorate the establishment of great public principles of liberty, and to do honor to the distinguished dead. The occasion is too severe for eulogy to the living. But, sir, your interesting relation to this country, the peculiar circumstances which surround you and surround us, call on me to express the happiness which we derive from your presence and aid in this solemn commemoration.

"Fortunate, fortunate man! with what measure of devotion will you not thank God for the circumstances of your extraordinary life! You are connected with both hemispheres and with two generations. Heaven saw fit to ordain, that the electric spark of Liberty should be conducted, through you, from the new world to the old; and we, who are now here to perform this duty of patriotism, have all of us long ago received it in charge from our fathers to cherish your name and your virtues. You will account it an instance of your good fortune, sir, that you crossed the seas to visit us at a time which enables you to be present at this solemnity. You now behold the field, the renown of which reached you in the heart of France, and caused a thrill in your ardent bosom. You see the lines of the little redoubt thrown up by the incredible diligence of Prescott; defended, to the last extremity, by his lion-hearted valor; and within which the corner stone of our monument has now taken its position. You see where Warren fell, and where Parker, Gardner, McCleary, Moore, and other early patriots fell with him. Those who survived that day, and whose lives have been prolonged to the present hour, are now around you. Some of them you have known in the trying scenes of the war. Behold! they now stretch forth their feeble arms to embrace you. Behold! they raise their trembling voices to invoke the blessing of God on you, and yours, forever.

" Sir, you have assisted us in laying the foundation of this edifice. You have heard us rehearse, with our feeble commendation, the names of departed patriots. Sir, monuments and eulogy belong to the dead. We give them, this day, to Warren and his associates. On other occasions they have been given to your more immediate companions in arms, to Washington, to Greene, to Gates, Sullivan, and Lincoln. Sir, we have become reluctant to grant these, our highest and last honors, further. We would gladly hold them yet back from the little remnant of that immortal band. *Serus in cælum redeas.* Illustrious as are your merits, yet far, oh, very far distant be the day, when any inscription shall bear your name, or any tongue pronounce its eulogy ! "

The remaining part of the address is taken up in describing the more remote consequences of this battle and of our Revolution,—the progress of knowledge and rational government,—the convulsions, the sufferings, and the improvement of society within these fifty years. The revolutions of France, South America, and Greece, form the leading topics of this part. The whole description of South American emancipation is beautiful and sublime, but too long for our limits. Several particular remarks have suggested themselves touching many portions of this address; but we must waive them for the present, and confine ourselves to one or two that are very general.

The first and most material one is, that this address contains, in some part or other, about all the prominent doctrines which should enter into the political creed of a citizen of this country. It appears to us, that the feelings expressed in this discourse are those which arise naturally out of the condition and institutions of our country; that the principles put forth in it are those in which all patriotic, enlightened, and high-minded Americans must cordially agree. They are not English nor French, federal nor democratic, but American. America, "our Country," is this great statesman's *Shibboleth.*

Our next remark goes to the style and manner. Mr Webster, as an orator, is decidedly of the Demosthenian school; and we have more than once, in other places, designated him as the Demosthenes of America, and we may add, of Greece also. It is extremely difficult to institute a comparison between illustrious orators of ancient and modern times, on account of the different states of science and general education, the very different manner of conducting the administration at home, and negotiations and wars abroad. What was eloquence then, is not necessarily so now; what was eloquence at Athens, may or may not be eloquence here. We well recollect a sensible and liberal remark, with which one of our cotemporaries at the university closed a successful prize dissertation on this subject. After a general view of the characteristics of ancient oratory, and of the manner and style of its two great ornaments, and after comparing them with some distinguished British orators, he concludes, that " Chatham and Burke, though different from both, were not inferior to either." If the structure and arrangement of Mr Webster's sentences were equal to the beauty and grandeur of his conceptions, he would be, in our times, *facile princeps,* clearly the first. We have heard most of the celebrated orators of this generation, and we have no hesitation in saying, that in native vigour and grasp of intellect, in the powers of comprehension and concentration, in that majestic movement of spirit, which bears onward the reason and the feelings of the hearer, he is without a rival on either side of the Atlantic. We however feel it due to our critical character to mention one fault, which occurs more or less in all this gentleman's performances; namely, dryness, jejuneness. The barrenness of his language often presents a strange contrast with the richness of his thoughts. We are aware that we expose ourselves to have a favourite poet cited against us. But we appeal to the decision of all nations, civilized and savage, to settle the point. Their decision is, that the most beautiful person should be dressed with some degree of art and ornament. To a truly beautiful and majestic person, all dress is deformity, and it belongs to art and taste to diminish that deformity as much as possible. So a man's thoughts, if they be just, dignified, and beautiful, cannot be conveyed to others through the medium of language (however they may be by painting, sculpture, and gesture) so strongly and so perfectly as he conceives them in his own mind; and he should endeavour to diminish the inconvenience arising from the imperfection of all language, as much as possible;—he should study, habitually, such a choice and arrangement of words and sentences, as will give the truest and most agreeable expression to the thoughts of his mind and the feelings of his heart. This is the business of labour and art; and it was precisely in this, that Demosthenes excelled all other men; and it is in this, that Mr Webster is deficient. We do not mean that he is greatly so, or that we had not rather err with him, than to be right with some other men; "Errare mehercule malo cum Platone, quàm cum istis vera sentire." We only mean to intimate that, in our opinion, there is, in this respect, room for improvement.

Some persons appear to have been disappointed, that none of those sudden and surprising effects, which we read of in the annals of ancient oratory, were produced on this occasion. We think this fact can be explained without the least disparagement of the speaker's general powers, or of the merits of this address. If we look into the history of the times to which those effects belong, we shall find that the minds both of the audience and of the orator were agitated by the strongest passions. The fears of invasion, defeat, captivity, and death; the hope of victory in a doubtful strife, and of salvation from these last of human calamities; the love of personal and national glory; the horror of contempt and infamy; the hatred of foreign foes, plunderers, and destroyers; the attachment to country, friends, wives, children, and home—these, or like passions, were heaving and struggling in the breasts of both the people and the speaker. Is it strange, that, under such circumstances, great and memorable effects should have been produced by accomplished masters of that living lyre, the human heart? At Bunker Hill, all was matter of calm retrospection and cool reflection. The events, which formed the appropriate topics of the occasion, were numbered with those before the flood. There was no present enemy to denounce, no pressing and imminent danger to guard against, no lives of

43

men, no sacrifices of substance, to be called for; no husband nor son to be torn from wife, parent, and home, to be devoted to country, to death, and to fame; no hostile hatred, ambition, and cruelty, to portray; nothing, in short, so far as regarded the subject, which in itself was calculated to produce any sudden and violent emotion, any more than the ordinary topics of a sacrament sermon. Yet uncommon effects were produced, and we think it fair to say, that those effects were more to be attributed to the talents of the speaker, than to the circumstances under which he spoke. In addition to these disadvantages, it may be remarked, that expectation was raised to the highest pitch both from the known and well tried talents of the orator, and from the singular and sublime, yet tranquil and pacific character of this sober celebration.

We would not have our readers suppose, that, in these remarks, we are answering objections of our own, and trying to work ourselves up, *invitâ minervâ*, into an intense and unnatural admiration of a performance to which our feelings are indifferent or repugnant. They are intended merely as a reply to those who demand, without regard to circumstances, not a production which should rival in its excellence, but one which should equal in its immediate effects, the most renowned efforts of ancient eloquence. Such an expectation was unnatural, unreasonable, unphilosophical, and ought to have been disappointed. This address, however, needs not our commendation or defence. It is already travelling to the four quarters of the world. It is transcribed on the hearts of the thousands who heard it, and will be on those of the millions who will read it.

Reform of Harvard College.

(For the Titles, see No. 6 of this Gazette.)

[CONTINUED.]

BESIDE the resident Professors already mentioned, there are two others, who are not concerned in the instruction of undergraduates, and whose salaries add nothing to the expense of instruction. On these, therefore, it is unnecessary to remark at present.

Having shown that the expense of the establishments of the resident Professors, may be partially diminished at present, and reduced still more in process of time, without injury or offence to any individual, we come next to the consideration of those of the non-resident Professors. Two of these are supported from the income of foundations, and add nothing, either directly or indirectly, to the expense of the instruction of undergraduates. They do not, therefore, come within the limits of our present intention. Of the remaining four, we notice first that of the Professor of the French and Spanish languages and literature. In the year 1816, the College received from the executors of Abiel Smith, Esq. of Boston, the nominal sum of $30,000, vested in the national stocks. The income of this was, by his will, to be appropriated to the " maintenance and support of a Teacher or Professor of the French and Spanish languages at said University." This income, according to the report now under consideration, is $1418.56. We think that the result to be expected from this very liberal donation was the appointment of some gentleman skilled in these languages, who should be resident in Cambridge, and ready to afford to the students the benefit of his instruction and conversation without any addition to their previous expenses. The college would thus have derived from this bequest an advantage wholly unincumbered.

Such a gentleman was appointed to reside in Cambridge with a salary of $1000; but of this sum only $418.56 is derived from the income of the foundation, the remainder is paid by the students. The remaining $1000 is given to a Professor of the French and Spanish languages and literature, who resides in Boston, and who may reside, for aught we know, at the Antipodes, provided he delivers a course of lectures, at a certain period of the year, in Cambridge. The course consists, according to the report, of fifty-five lectures. This arrangement strikes us as premature, to say the least of it. On this point, however, we desire to be clearly understood. We are very far from intending to depreciate the merit of these lectures, or of the accomplished individual who now fills the Professorial chair. The lectures we have understood to be highly valuable, learned, and beautiful. But we are of opinion, that they are a luxury which the funds of the College cannot well afford. Neither do we wish to give our opinion arrogantly, concerning the motive which influenced the Governors of the College in the formation of this establishment, as well as in other instances. This motive we suppose to be a desire to add to the celebrity, dignity, and usefulness, of the University, by attaching to it a numerous body of eminent individuals.   We are aware that, on this subject, wise and good men differ from us ; but as these are not the days when men pin their faith on any man's sleeve, we do not hesitate to give our opinion on this as well as on any other matter of public concernment which happens to come before us.

We think this notion of securing to the College the services of eminent persons may be carried too far, and that an institution, like an individual, may be extravagant.   We think it has been carried too far, and doubt the general soundness of the opinion implied by the gentlemen of the first committee of the Board of Overseers, " that the establishments in Cambridge are behind the spirit of our age and country."   We think that, in some instances, they are before it, and that the Professorship under consideration is an instance of it ; an annual course of lectures on French and Spanish literature is agreeable and useful ; a splendid work on botany, entomology, or any other natural science, is also agreeable and useful ; but either will hardly pay its own expense in this country ; and however we may regret the fact, we must quietly put up with it for the present.   The period will come, but it is not yet.   In this department, therefore, of French and Spanish instruction, we think about $600 per annum might have been saved.

The other non-residents are the medical Professors.   Two of them, the Professors of Physic and Anatomy, receive together $1200 ; of the income of funds appropriated by the donors to this purpose we find but $1031.03.   The balance, $168.97, it would seem, must be derived from the unappropriated funds, and of course goes to increase the assessments on the undergraduates.

An extensive building is provided for the Medical School in Boston, and the Professors derive an income from the fees from medical students.   The students are obliged to attend their lectures, before they can obtain a degree from the University.   A valuable collection of anatomical preparations is also provided for the Professor of Anatomy at the College. It seems to us, that under these circumstances it would not have been unreasonable to require these gentlemen to perform their duties at Cambridge gratuitously.   These duties are six lectures, biennally, from the Professor of Medicine, and from fifteen to twenty from the Professor of Anatomy, annually.

But as the income of the donations must be paid them, there is no more to be said, except that the addition of $168.97 to it, from the unappropriated funds, seems quite unnecessary.

The chemical Professor performs no duties at Cambridge. He receives $200 only from a specific appropriation. But since, as in the other cases, his title and office cause an income, we do not see why he should not be called on to deliver a course of lectures to the Students at Cambridge. If his time is too valuable to permit this, there seems no very strong reason why he should not appoint and pay a Lecturer, and thereby save to the College $800, or that part of it which is now paid from the unappropriated funds to such a Lecturer.

The salaries of the Tutors, we believe, are originally $666.

"In September 1811, it was 'voted by the Corporation, with the assent of the Overseers, that the annual salary of any Tutor who shall have been in office more than three years, and not exceeding six, shall be eight hundred dollars, to be paid to him quarter-yearly, so long as he shall remain Tutor; and that the annual salary of any Tutor who shall have been in office more than six years shall be one thousand dollars, to be paid to him quarter-yearly, so long as he shall remain Tutor. And be it further voted, that any Tutor who shall have been in office more than six years, shall have the style and rank of Professor of the department of which he is an Instructer, so long as he shall remain Tutor; provided, however, that said Professor be entitled to all the privileges, and subject to all the duties to which, as Tutor, he would be entitled and subject, and that the tenure of his office remain the same, he being bound to such further duties connected with his department and entitled to such exemptions as shall be determined by the Corporation, with the assent of the Overseers.' "

The intention of this vote was, as is evident, to induce gentlemen to remain in these offices long enough to become thoroughly acquainted with the business of instruction and government, and of course to be more useful than they could be by devoting only a portion of their time to the duties of an office, which would be regarded only as a temporary resource while the incumbent was preparing for some other business or profession. It was supposed, and it is the opinion of many now, that this arrangement was judicious, that the order and improvement of the students depended very much upon the skill and efficiency of their tutors, that this class of officers was a very important one, and that this progressive increase of salary was the best, if not the only way, of making it sufficiently useful and efficient.

The character of this office approaches to that of the school-master, and is highly important if it be true that a proportion of the students are, and will be sent to College, when they ought to be at school. And that this is the truth, we are very certain. This vote is now rescinded, except as it applies to the gentlemen now in office, who, in conformity with it, receive $800 each. If the opinion mentioned above is correct, the wisdom of the repeal admits of question.

We have thus gone over the various expenses of instruction, and have shown that a considerable part of these might have been saved. Whether they can be at present, we are unable to say, as this must depend upon the nature of the contract in individual cases. The savings to which there seems no objection are, first, by the promotion mentioned in our last number of two College Professors to the Eliot and Alford Professorships, $3145. By the cessation of the small addition of salary received by two professors, as mentioned in the former number, $300; in all, $3445, or about two ninths of the whole sum assessed on the undergraduates; but the average yearly assessment upon individuals we stated to be $55, from which take two ninths or $12, and there remains $43. This brings the yearly amount much nearer that at Yale, the next lowest in order of the New England Colleges.

The only remaining necessary expenses, included in the College bills are

Room Rent	.	.	.	$12
Library	.	.	.	3
Text Books	.	.	.	12 50
Expenses of public rooms, repairs, &c. 10			

Of these items we are unable to enter into so particular an examination as we could wish. We merely observe that they do not at first sight appear to us extravagant.

Other necessary expenses are wood, $7 per cord, and washing from $3 to 5 per quarter.

The expenses of clothing, pocket-money, &c. we shall not consider at present; they depend partly on the habits of the individual, and partly on the customs and habits of the University, and these will be noticed in another place.

We have dwelt at length on this part of the report, in this place, because it seemed as convenient as any, and because we have not observed that this subject has met with the attention which it seems to us to deserve, in any part of the public discussion now under review.

We proceed with the history of this discussion. In the winter session of 1824—5, the question of accepting these reports was discussed at length. Of the speeches on this occasion, we have nothing but unofficial newspaper reports, and can therefore give no account of them, except in a single instance, that of the speech of the Hon. John Pickering. This speech was published in a manner, which permits us to remark upon it without hesitation. This gentleman was a member of the first committee. His speech was made in defence of their report, and will be considered in our next number.

[*To be continued.*]

MISCELLANY.

ROMANCE IN THE HEROIC AND MIDDLE AGES.

" Magnanima menzogna, or quando è il vero
" Si bello, che si possa a te preporre ? "

We have lately been looking over some of the old Romances of chivalry, whose unsettled dialect savours much more strongly of their Norman genealogy, than does the ' English undefiled ' of father Chaucer, and we propose saying a few words concerning them. Our Journal, it is true, would seem to be more fitly occupied with the romances of our own day; but some notice of their ancient brethren may not be unwelcome to our readers, were it only by way of variety. In the midst of their chivalrous extravagancies, one may have many scenes of simplicity and nature; and the social habits of the unlettered ages which they represent, are sketched with a precision and apparent truth that would seem to entitle them to greater credit than they have generally obtained, as useful historical documents. Homer's poems were held in this kind of veneration by the ancients, and he is quoted by the most eminent Grecian writers, by the circumspect Thucydides even, as high authority. Yet his epics, the Odyssey in particular, are enveloped in fables quite as incredible as any of the wonders of romance. Works of fiction throw the best light upon manners. We learn more of the social relations of the ancients from the comedies of Aristophanes, of Plautus, and Terence, than from the philosophical pen of Thucydides, or the studied narratives of Sallust and Tacitus; and future ages will gather much more of this information from the novels of the author of Waverley, than from all the histories in the language. Yet the learned French antiquary, St Palaye, is almost the only scholar of eminence, who has systematically endeavoured to reflect light on the habits of the middle ages, from the fables of chivalry. And it is worthy of notice, that the conclusions to which he has been led, precisely correspond with the historical facts recorded in the chronicles of that period. Turner, in his "History of England," has cited from the latter many examples of predatory violence by the Norman barons, and even ecclesiastics. From their fortified castles and convents, they sallied out upon the unarmed traveller, who, in the absence of civil authority, could find redress only in the stronger arm of the knight-errant.

Not only the general condition of society depicted in these ancient romances, but many of the most extravagant circumstances appear to be countenanced by historical precedent. It is frequent in tales of chivalry, to find one knight maintaining against another, or against the whole world, the superior beauty, merit, &c. of his mistress; or to see him pledging himself by some valiant vow, not to eat, or drink, or see the face of his lady, until he has achieved a certain deed of emprise, taken some knight or monster captive, and sent him in chains to her feet. All which affords much reasonable merriment to Cervantes. That these *incredibilia* are not erroneous pictures of the age, however, the ancient chroniclers, and the circumstantial Froissart in particular, amply attest. Among instances of the latter kind, we remember one of a cavalier, who, in gratitude for some inconsiderable favour conferred upon him by Joanna, Queen of Naples, made a vow to pay her the tribute of two knights; which gallant feat he accomplished, after a perilous errantry through France, Germany, and Spain. Joanna graciously liberated her prisoners, acting much more magnanimously than the canons of St Peter's church in Rome, who, upon a knight being delivered to them in consequence of a similar vow, despoiled him of his horse and military equipments, and detained him a captive the rest of his life.

As to defiances and duels in honour of one's mistress, the gallant Froissart has related several with all the animated details of an amateur. Among other instances is a remarkable one that occurred at Cherbourg in 1379; where, in the midst of a hot rencontre between the French and English squadrons, an amatory challenge passed between two knights of the hostile nations, and both armies desisted from the engagement, until the duel was determined by the death of one of the parties. Froissart records another defiance equally extravagant, given in his time by three French knights to all Europe, and maintained at St Ingleverre, near Calais, for thirty days, against all comers, among whom were the flower of the English nobility. At Poictiers, the knights fought with the scarfs of their mistresses bound around their arms, challenging whoever might dispute their paramount beauty. The same Quixotic gallantry may be traced to a much later period; and as recently as the reign of Elizabeth, the accomplished Earl of Surry, a poet and a soldier, proclaimed a tournament at Florence, and in the true spirit of romance, broke a lance there, in honour of his mistress.

But although the ancient romances represented the manners of the age in which they were written, they sought for the *subject* of their fictions in a much earlier period of history ; and especially in the popular traditions respecting Arthur and Charlemagne. So little is known of the former of these worthies, that some learned antiquaries have doubted, others have denied his existence. Turner, in his "History of the Anglo-Saxons," has collected facts of sufficient authenticity, in his opinion, fully to establish it.   Among others he ascertains the place of his interment at Glastonbury, by means of an author who was present at the exhumation of the body, made by order of Henry II. six hundred years after the death of the Welch chieftain. That this was the real place of the sepulture of Arthur, he considers proved by their finding a leaden cross lying horizontally, at twelve feet distance above the coffin, with this inscription ;

" Hic jacet sepultus inclytus rex Arthurus, in insulâ Avalloniâ."

As Arthur, however, according to Mr Turner's own chronology, died some fifty years before the introduction of Christianity into the island,* the discovery of a *cross*, with the above inscription upon it, six centuries after his death, may be thought to furnish very doubtful evidence of the truth of his hypothesis.

All that is pretended to be ascertained of his history shows him to have been a rude, warlike, and sanguinary chief, who ruled over the southwestern parts of Britain in the beginning of the fifth century.   His life was spent in conflicts with neighbouring princes, and with the Saxon invaders of his country.   To these last wars, he is principally indebted for his celebrity in romance.   But however insignificant may have been his character, however doubtful even his actual existence, the illusions of poetry have conferred upon him an immortality, like that which Homer has given to some of his imaginary heroes.   His return was fondly expected, to a very late period, by the lower classes among the Welch, in the same manner as was Don Sebastian's by the Portuguese.   He has been the constant burthen of the songs of the minstrels ; his name has been inscribed on one of the most splendid monuments of human genius, in the ' Faery Queen ' of Spenser ;   and he is now recommended to our imaginations as the   earliest hero of Christianity, the patron of the Round Table, of chivalry and romance.

The other *cyclus* of Norman fictions is borrowed from Charlemagne.   A name of such notoriety might   naturally have suggest-

* Vide vol. I. p. 272, & p. 326,

44

ed them ; but it is a whimsical fact, that this long line of epics is derived from a circumstance in his history, which, in the opinion of many writers, never happened at all, and which, if it did, was certainly attended with no important consequence.   A spurious chronicle, of the 12th century, contains the particulars of this celebrated defeat of Charles by the Saracens, in the valley of Roncesvalles [Red Valley.]   The chronicle of the pseudo-Turpin is destitute of all historical probability, and is contemptible as a work of invention.   But notwithstanding this, it has been the fruitful source of fiction, not only in Normandy, but in the cultivated ages of Italian letters.

There has been much dispute between the French and English scholars, respecting the comparative merit of the romances of the Round Table, and those of Charlemagne.   These two classes, although, for the most part, originally written in the Norman language, exhibit each, in some measure, the peculiarities of their national literatures, and have very naturally found favour accordingly.   The Comte de Tressan is the only one of his countrymen, whom we recollect to have given it for the former class of fictions.   Perhaps the prejudices of education have led us to take greater satisfaction in the British romances.   They have less brilliancy of imagination than the French, but more tenderness and simplicity.   The latter are embellished with the elegant creations of oriental fable, and the reader finds himself transported into the same scenes of enchantment, with which he had early learned to be familiar in the " Arabian Nights."   The English, on the other hand, are very meagre in this way ; they have neither fairies nor genii, palaces glittering with diamonds, nor gardens breathing perfumes in the midst of the desert.   Giants, dwarfs, necromancers, a clumsy mythology, conceived in the cold brains of the North, constitute the bulk of their supernatural apparatus. But though inferior in artificial contrivance, they are much richer in pictures of natural scenery.   Scott, who has transferred much of the spirit of these old epics into his romantic poems, has shown a nice observation of their beauties in this particular.

The French may be said to display more fancy, the English more feeling.   Dante, in his affecting episode of Francesca da Rimini, makes her say, that the sympathy she manifests for Lancelot, one of the Round Table heroes, betrayed her own passion to her lover.   The French romances are generally vivacious and exhilarating.   The English are often plaintive, and the two best, " Tristrem " and " Sir Launcelot du Lac," have a most tragical conclusion.   The former class exhibit greater variety of incident, the latter greater depth and truth of character.   There is no portrait, that we recollect, in the French *cyclus* equal to that of Sir Lancelot du Lac.   This romance, which indicates most fully the frank and martial chivalry of the age, may be cited as the best of those of the Round Table, as "Ogier le Danois" affords, perhaps, the most perfect specimen of the other class.

[*To be continued.*]

ORIGINAL POETRY.

SONNET.

Earth holds no fairer, lovelier one than thou,
Maid of the laughing lip, and frolic eye.
Innocence sits upon thy open brow,
Like a pure spirit in its native sky.
If ever beauty stole the heart away,
Enchantress, it would fly to meet thy smile;
Moments would seem by thee a summer day,
And all around thee an Elysian isle.
Roses are nothing to the maiden blush
Sent o'er thy cheek's soft ivory, and night
Has nought so dazzling in its world of light,
As the dark rays that from thy lashes gush.
Love lurks amid thy silken curls, and lies
Like a keen archer in thy kindling eyes.

                                                  P.

TO L. M. B.

Oh! pass unto thy quiet grave!
But first thy holy blessing shed!
The last—sole boon our spirits crave
Ere thou thine angel wings shalt spread.

For thee the tomb no terrors hath,
Though thou art young and fair and blest;
Thou hast not stirr'd the chastener's wrath,
And gently wilt thou sink to rest.

Though early thou wert summoned hence,
While youth's fresh rose was on thy cheek,
And life was sweet to every sense,
The call grieves not thy spirit meek.

Thou hear'st it, like a seraph's sigh!
And darkness gathers round thee deep;
But hope sits brightening in thine eye,
To check us when we idly weep.

Yes! death has touched thy pure, pale cheek,
But life is in thy kindling eye!
And though thy failing frame grow weak,
We know thou canst not wholly die!

Then pass unto thy quiet rest !
As fade the tints of western skies !
As droops the ringdove in her nest !
As close the flowers when daylight dies !

                                        AGNES.

JECKOYVA.

The Indian chief, Jeckoyva, as tradition says, perished alone on the mountain which now bears his name. Night overtook him whilst hunting among the cliffs, and he was not heard of till after a long time, when his half-decayed corpse was found at the foot of a high rock, over which he must have fallen. Mount Jeckoyva is near the White Hills.

They made the warrior's grave beside
The dashing of his native tide :
And there was mourning in the glen—
The strong wail of a thousand men—
  O'er him thus fallen in his pride,
Ere mist of age—or blight or blast
Had o'er his mighty spirit past.

They made the warrior's grave beneath
The bending of the wild-elm's wreath,
When the dark hunter's piercing eye
Had found that mountain rest on high,
  Where, scattered by the sharp wind's breath,
Beneath the rugged cliff were thrown
The strong belt and the mouldering bone.

Where was the warrior's foot, when first
The red sun on the mountain burst ?—
Where—when the sultry noon-time came
On the green vales with scorching flame,
  And made the woodlands faint with thirst ?
'T was where the wind is keen and loud,
And the grey eagle breasts the cloud.

Where was the warrior's foot, when night
Veiled in thick cloud the mountain height ?
None heard the loud and sudden crash,—
None saw the fallen warrior dash
  Down the bare rock so high and white !—
But he that drooped not in the chase
Made on the hills his burial-place.

They found him there, when the long day
Of cold desertion passed away,
And traces on that barren cleft
Of struggling hard with death were left—
  Deep marks and foot-prints in the clay !
And they have laid this feathery helm
By the dark river and green elm.

                                        H. W. L.

TO FANCY.

In the bright mornin' o' my life,
Whan ilka day wi' joy was rife,
An' my young heart was free frae strife
       O' passion's storm,
An' music's sounds, the lute and fife,
       My bosom warmed;

There was a lassie bright an' fair,
In raven curlies waved her hair,
Her ilka motion light as air
       Whane'er she moved,
Nor do I blush whan I declare
       That her I loved.

For how could ane wi' een sae bright,
Wi' face sae fair, an' form sae dight,
Say, how could she be in ane's sight
       Frae day to day—
Withouten lovin' her outright?
       Ye canna say.

An' we did hae a bonny bower
Bedight wi' hue o' mony a flower,—
An' there we sat frae hour to hour,
       We twa alane,—
An' then on us nae een could glower,—
       We cared for nane.

There she did sketch, sae bright, sae fair,
Sweet sights which I shall see na mair,
Visions o' bliss, an' glories glare,
       Afore mine een,—
An' a' the leesome ways o' lair,
       In a' their sheen.

She drew the warld a' fu' o' glee,
A' bright wi' hope, frae passion free,
She said that joy should stap wi' me
       Whare'er I strayed,
An' my young heart should loupin' be
       Whare'er I gaed.

An' wad ye ken wha she is ca'd,
This lass, wha could wi' plaisance haud,
An' steal awa' a heart sae bauld
       A' in a blink?
Wha? Why, she is Fancy ca'd,
       I 'd hae ye think.

But she's a fausse deceitfu' hizzie,
Nae whare she should be aften busy,
The brains o' laddies makin dizzy
       Withouten drink;—
Degone, you fausse deceitfu' hizzie,
       Quick as a whuk!

I 'll hae nae mair to do wi' ye,
Ye, wi' your whigmaleries, flee
Far frae the ken o' human ee,
                    Brattlin' awa',
Or blaws as hard as mon can gie
                    Shall on ye fa' !

LONDOL.

CRITICAL NOTICES.

North American Review for July, 1825.
[Concluded.]

Here is a long, and to us a heavy, article of nearly forty pages on the "Common Law Jurisdiction." We presume those who understood the subject before, will be interested and instructed by it. But for ourselves, we will honestly confess that we read much and had only vague notions; indeed, we had well nigh read the article quite through without learning what the writer would prove or show, except particularly that he understood Latin and French and had read Governor Pownall, when we were fortunately informed that " agreeing with Mr Du Ponceau (the author under review) respecting the existence of an American Common Law, independent of that of England ; *we are induced to give it an origin somewhat beyond the breaking out of the revolution,*" whereas Mr Du Ponceau states its origin to be at that time. This opinion however, though it is most unquestionably correct, and is fairly deduced at the end of the forty pages, is so much qualified afterwards that we are not quite certain it was intended to be advanced ; and we are sure, if it was, that Mr Du Ponceau can take no offence after so many apologies. The writer of this article shows more patience in research, than power to reduce to form and clearly to state the results of his inquiries. He wants the acuteness and grasp of mind, which would enable him to seize upon the prominent facts of his subject only, to deduce from them the general principles to be inculcated, and then to set those principles forth in bold and strong relief, leaving his readers to reflect upon them. As to matter and arrangement, he says so much, and in such a confused manner, that he leaves no distinct and definite ideas upon his subject in the minds of his readers. As to style, he shows a playful imagination, and seems always to have an abundance of good words ; but the construction of his sentences somehow forcibly reminds us of a *nest of boxes.*

A short article on "European Politics" is very eloquent, but the writer must be a very intrepid political prophet, to foretell so much, and such speedy trouble for the different nations of Europe, and particularly England.

The next article, on Colombia, contains much valuable information upon the state of that country. "The present government of Colombia is founded on principles, nearly resembling those of our own constitution. It is a representative system, having a Congress of two Houses, and an elective President. It differs in two important respects from the fundamental principles of the constitution of the United States ;

the first is in regard to the mode of elections, and the second in the *departments*, or what we call the states. The right of suffrage is somewhat curtailed, by making it necessary for every voter to possess a small amount of property, or to exercise some trade or liberal profession. The people do not vote in the first instance for representatives, but for electors, by whom the senators and representatives are chosen.　By a law of Congress passed June 25th, 1824, the Republic is divided into 12 departments, embracing 37 provinces, and 230 cantons.　These cantons are further subdivided into parishes, each of which holds what is called a parochial assembly on a stated day, once in four years, and at these assemblies the electors are chosen by the persons duly qualified to be voters.　A representative to Congress is assigned to a population of 30,000, and also each *province* is entitled to another representative, when there is a fraction of more than 15,000.　The number of electors for each representative is 10, and if the population of the Republic be taken at 2,600,000, which is thought a fair estimate, the whole number of electors will not be less than 860.　The number of representatives would accordingly be 86.　But in fact both the electors and representatives exceed these numbers, because in case of an additional representative for a fraction, there is a full number of electors, for each fraction, although a less amount of population.　On this new division of the Republic, it is supposed the number of representatives will be 95.　The senate is established by the constitution to consist of 4 senators from each department, making 48 in the whole.　These electors meet once in four years, in the capitals of their respective provinces, and execute the very important duty of choosing on the same day, the President of the Republic, the Vice President, the Senators, and Representatives.　The votes are sent up to the Congress, where they are scrutinized in the manner pointed out by the Constitution.　The President and Vice President, are elected for four years, and no person can be chosen president more than twice in succession.　The representatives are chosen for four years, and the senators for eight.　The term of office for one half of the Senate expires at the end of every fourth year, so that only two senators from each department are chosen at the periodical elections."

Besides much such information as this, the article is enlivened—a strange sort of contrast—with many curious anecdotes and pretty stories, proper to be quoted into newspapers; one of which, an ingenious manner of catching ducks, taken principally from Buffon, we recommend as peculiarly appropriate for this purpose.

Upon the subject of "Major Long's Second Expedition," which constitutes the eighth article, we have expressed our opinions in the last volume of our work, and are glad to have our confidence in them strengthened by such good authority.

The next article, on "Da Ponte's Observations," is the last part of a controversy, and as we do not know what the other party has previously said upon the subject, we cannot say which has the best of it.　The article evinces a familiar acquaintance of the writer with the commentaries upon Italian literature, and is written in a chaste and elegant style.

The last article is a review of "Brainard's Poems," which we noticed in a late number of this Gazette.

Among the CRITICAL NOTICES, which by the way we consider as a sort of *stern chaser*, several pamphlets and small books are reprinted in a very interesting manner.   Some remarks are here made *about* Dr Jer. Van Rensselaer's Lectures on Geology, accompanied by a criticism upon its title page.   For an opinion of that work, we refer our readers to the second review in the last number of our Gazette.

We have now gone through with every article in the present number of this deservedly popular work.   We have remarked freely upon the different articles, because we think fair criticism is as wholesome when applied to this work as any other.   If there appears in the spirit of our remarks a captiousness and propensity to faultfinding, it certainly is not our habitual feeling towards this work, and has arisen probably in this instance from observing the extravagant praise (if praise of the N. A. can be extravagant) which is periodically lavished upon it, by some among us (we excuse all editors of course), whose zeal is greater than their judgment.   These unqualified *puffs* carry on their face something, which defeats their own object.   The most dignified—the most popular—and the most extensively circulated journal printed on this continent does not need such means to make its merits known.   However ingenious or well got up they may have been, they have done, and can do, no good. They only make those stare at the caricature, who do not understand them ; and make those chuckle at the joke who do.   To some even here they look silly, and strangely out of place in journals remarkable for good judgment, and we think they must look particularly so to reflecting people at a distance.

An Oration in Honour of General Lafayette, delivered in his Presence at Nashville, May 4, 1825.   At the Request of the Grand Lodge of Tennessee.   By William Gibbes Hunt.   Nashville.   1825.   8vo.   pp. 12.

Neither the size of this pamphlet, nor its literary merit merely, though that is far enough from being ordinary, would entitle it to a notice in this place.   But the addresses drawn out in times of popular excitement, indicate more accurately than any thing else the state of public opinion in those quarters from whence they proceed.   It is on this account as well as to express our cordial approbation of the liberal sentiments advanced in this oration, that we have determined to give our readers a few sentences of it.   The whole is full of good sense, and is written in a plain and perspicuous style, which we think is the more to be commended, as speakers on similar occasions, frequently consider themselves called upon to take such bold flights of imagination as to leave common sense quite confounded.

After the expression of a hearty welcome to the Guest before whom he spoke, and a just tribute to the philanthropic spirit of the institution, at the request of a branch of which he spoke, Mr Hunt observes ;

" Fortunately, the present occasion neither requires nor would permit the indulgence of any of those asperities of feeling, those hostile emotions, with which perhaps, in former times, the names of our revolutionary heroes were commonly associated.   We have outlived, I trust, this unpleasant association.   We wish now to call forth no sentiments but those of an enlarged, liberal, magnanimous character.   We come not here to indulge any little national jealousy, to revive any old, long-settled controversy, to cherish any narrow prejudice, or even to rehearse the catalogue of former injuries.   Our country is happily at peace with all the world, and would cultivate no other feelings towards any nation, than those of amity and good fellowship. As Americans indeed, we will ever maintain with firmness the principles of our government and the rights of our country; but we would exercise towards others the same candour and liberality, which we expect from them. With the land of our forefathers, the country of Shakspeare, and Milton, and Locke, and Sidney, and Hampden, we have many sympathies in common; and far be it from us to seek or create a cause of difference, or unnecessarily to interrupt the harmony, which now so happily prevails between us. Even our literary jealousies and commercial rivalships appear to be losing their asperity, and we have reason to hope they may soon be converted into a generous and honourable competition."

The following paragraph gives a fine picture of the happy and flourishing condition of the Western states, compared with the situation in which they were fifty years ago. " Even in these remote western regions where at the time of his (Lafayette's) first arrival on our continent, the voice of civilization had scarcely been heard; where the Indian warwhoop was then the only music that could greet the ear; where even the rudest form of agriculture had then scarcely commenced its inroads upon the native forest, and not a step could be taken by civilized man, except at the imminent risk of destruction by beasts of prey or merciless savages of the wilderness—he now finds richly cultivated fields, thriving villages, and even populous cities, adorned with art, and science, and taste, and all that can render life comfortable and delightful. Here, where not many years since the traveller could not reach us from abroad, except after a tedious journey from the Atlantic coast over roads scarcely passable, or by an inland voyage of nearly half a year's duration, he now pursues his way, by the aid of our widely-branching rivers and majestic steam-boats, with a rapidity scarcely to be surpassed in the oldest and most improved countries of Europe. Here, where half a century ago letters had scarcely found their way, and to read and write was the biggest object of literary ambition, he beholds not only schools of the most respectable character and academies in which the female mind is richly cultivated and adorned, but even colleges and universities proudly rearing their heads, vieing with each other in the march of usefulness and honour, and boldly claiming a rank, if not equal, at least not far below the oldest and most richly endowed institutions of our sisters on the Atlantic."

An Oration, delivered on Monday, Fourth of July, 1825, in commemoration of American Independence, before the Supreme Executive of the Commonwealth, and the City Council and Inhabitants of the City of Boston. By Charles Sprague. Printed by Order of the City Council. Boston. 1825. 8vo. pp. 34.

We think the public will hardly expect us often to notice productions so ephemeral and abundant as orations for the 4th of July. We remark upon the one before us, because it is of a nature somewhat different from those that have been usually delivered in Boston. One great end of these and other similar celebrations is to excite and enliven a national and American feeling throughout the Union; and an oration may produce much effect in this way, without possessing great claims on the score of literary execution or original thinking. We consider Mr Sprague's oration

45

as an eloquent performance, and one, that, if tolerably well delivered, would produce great effect ; and such, we are informed, was really the case. Now the effect at the time is the only proper test of the kind of merit required, and this oration must therefore be considered a good one, better indeed for the purpose, than many that have fewer faults. It indicates talent and imagination, and it is agreeable to perceive these, even though they are not sufficiently disciplined. The language is occasionally extravagant, and the metaphors sometimes scarcely in good taste. These matters however are easily corrected where the foundation is good. We repeat, that we were pleased with the performance, and felt some regret, on the perusal, that accident prevented us from hearing it, a sensation which has not often happened to us in regard to occasions of this kind.

INTELLIGENCE.

WORCESTER HISTORICAL SOCIETY.

An association, under this name, has been formed for the purpose of collecting and preserving materials for a complete and minute history of the county of Worcester, Mass. For the accomplishment of these objects, circulars have been addressed to gentlemen in different parts of the county, and to others, who are supposed to be capable of aiding in the advancement of the interests of the institution ; requesting communications upon various subjects, but particularly upon the six following :

1st. Such facts as relate to the Indians formerly inhabiting this part of the country.

2d. The settlement of the several towns.

3d. The ecclesiastical history of the several towns.

4th. Biographical notices and anecdotes of distinguished men.

5th. A view of the statistics of the county at different periods in its history.

6th. Descriptions of remarkable scenery ; of hills and caverns ; accounts of the sources and courses of streams, the divisions and boundaries of towns, and such other interesting particulars of topographical information as can be collected.

Under these general heads numerous specific topics are methodically arranged, with a view to direct the inquiries of gentlemen, and give order to the several communications, which would, probably, otherwise contain much confusion. The early history of our country, and of New England particularly, is in many respects peculiar. And although several have gone over the ground with a tolerable degree of accuracy, yet many important facts, illustrating the character of the natives, and of our ancestors and their institutions, still remain with the individuals who alone are acquainted with them, or among the records of private families. These facts should be collected, and then records or copies of them should be given up to the public, and preserved. They are a part, and an important part, of our history ; and if an effort is not soon made to rescue and preserve them, they will be beyond our reach. Societies, which, like the Worcester Historical Society, limit their inquiries to a small section of the country, will collect much that would escape more general inquirers. And these "minute" facts will not only be highly interesting and valuable to those who are more immediately connected with them, but perhaps still more valuable as authentic materials for a correct general history of our country.

BOOKS IN RUSSIA.

Previously to the year 1817, the number of works printed in Russia did not exceed 4000, about the same number as is annually contained in the catalogues of the fair at Leipsic. This number is now augmented to about 8000. There are, at Moscow, nine literary and ten printing establishments; at St Petersburg, nine of the former, and fifteen of the latter; and in various other towns, one of each. In the whole empire there are nine letter foundries. There are, at present, fifteen periodical papers in the four provinces of the Baltic.

MILTON.

By the persevering exertions of Mr Lemon, deputy keeper of state papers, (the gentleman to whom the learned world are indebted for the discovery of the work of Milton, about to appear,) several very curious and interesting papers have been rescued from oblivion. They make us acquainted with facts, hitherto unknown, relative to the official situation of the poet; and also communicate several particulars relative to his family affairs. They give some account of the property of his brother Christopher, and his father-in-law, Mr Richard Powell, of Forest Hill, Oxfordshire. The whole of these papers, communicated by Mr Lemon to his superiors in office, have by them been laid before Mr Todd; and a life of the poet by that eminent scholar, incorporating the documents, &c. may be expected in the course of the ensuing autumn, prefixed to a new edition of Milton's poetical works. Among these papers will be found the orders of Cromwell's council to Milton, addressed to him as Secretary for Foreign Languages, with notes of the salary paid to him, from time to time, for his services in that capacity.

UNIVERSITY IN LONDON.

Mr Campbell, in the London New Monthly Magazine, has been strenuously advocating the establishment of a University in London; and we perceive that Mr Brougham, who is always at hand when subjects of education are discussed, was about to submit to Parliament the proposition for incorporating the institution.

NEW EDITION OF THE WORKS OF LESSING.

Voss, a German bookseller, published at Berlin between the years 1771 and 1794 a complete collection of Lessing's writings, in 30 vols. 8vo. The same man, or one of the same name, is now about to publish another complete edition of the same author's works, on the plan of those of Wieland, Schiller and Klopstock, in 34 vols. Lessing is said, in a short biographical notice of him found in Joerden's Dictionary of German Authors, attached to the "Memoirs of Göthe," to be the real founder of the modern German language and literature, and the true model of the classic style in Germany. He was born at Kamenz in Lusitania, in January 1729, and died at Wolfenbüttel, February 15, 1791.

PRACTICABILITY OF JOINING THE ATLANTIC AND PACIFIC.

A succinct view and analysis of authentic information extant in original works on the practicability of joining the Atlantic and Pacific Oceans, by a ship-canal across the Isthmus of America (Darien); by Robert Birks Pitman. A work is in press in London with the above title. As it probably will contain much valuable information upon the subject, and as the question of *practicability*, seems to be preliminary in its nature, it might be well for those companies formed or forming for this great purpose to have the book before them, at least as soon as they begin to make excavations.

NEW PUBLICATIONS.

AGRICULTURE.

Memoirs of the Pennsylvania Agricultural Society ; with Selections from the most approved Authors, adapted to the Use of the Practical Farmers in the United States. Philadelphia. 8vo. pp. 322.

Although this volume has been some months before the public, we have never before had an opportunity to read it with that attention which was necessary, in order to give even a summary account of what it contains. The "Memoirs" are composed of original communications from scientific and intelligent practical farmers, residing in different parts of our country, chiefly upon topics exclusively interesting to agriculturists There are many descriptions of fine animals, accompanied with plates, exhibiting their forms and proportions. The communications also discuss the peculiar excellences and qualities of different breeds of sheep and cattle for different purposes—the best means of supporting and breeding them, &c. &c. Among these communications are some from distinguished gentlemen interested in agriculture in this vicinity. We notice one from His Excellency Gov. Lincoln " on the Breaking, Feeding, and Working of oxen," and " on the Cultivation of Indian corn." Besides these original communications, the volume contains extracts from various English authors upon the qualities of the different breeds of cattle, horses, sheep, &c. Many of these extracts, as well as the original communications, describe the adaptation of certain soils to the growing of certain vegetables, and the comparative degree of nourishment afforded by these same vegetables to certain classes of animals. The value of the volume is also enhanced by the addition of several plates, representing models of machines for different agricultural purposes. Many of the original pieces are from J. H. Powel, Esq. of Powelton, Philadelphia county, Pennsylvania. And most of the others seem to have been elicited from gentlemen in different parts of the country by his inquiries; and were chiefly addressed to him as Corresponding Secretary of the Pennsylvania Agricultural Society. This gentleman has devoted himself with great zeal to the improvement of the breeds of cattle of various kinds, and in short to whatever may be useful to the practical agriculturists throughout our country. No one, we believe, has done more, few have done so much. as Mr Powell, to improve our style of agriculture, and so far as that important branch of industry goes, to add to our national prosperity and resources.

BIOGRAPHY.

The Life and Character of the Chevalier John Paul Jones, a Captain in the Navy of the United States during their Revolutionary War. Dedicated to the Officers of the Navy of the United States. 1 vol. 8vo. with a Portrait. New York.

Memoirs of Keopuolani, late Queen of the Sandwich Islands. 12mo. pp. 48. Boston. Crocker & Brewster.

EDUCATION.

Visit of General Lafayette to the Lafayette Female Academy, in Lexington, Kentucky, May 16, 1825, and the Exercises in Honour of the Nation's Guest ; together with a Catalogue of the Instructers, Visiters, and Pupils of the Academy. Lexington, Ky. 1825. 8vo. pp. 32.

Gen. Lafayette visited the "Lexington Female Academy," which on the occasion took the name of the "Lafayette Female Academy," in the afternoon of the day on which he was received at Transylvania University. He was addressed by the Principal of the Academy,—by a committee of the pupils,—and by several individuals from among them. The performances, both in prose and poetry, are printed at length in a pamphlet under the above title. Some of them do credit to the good talents and good taste of the young ladies, and all of them are filled with expressions of gratitude to our country's benefactor, and evince a laudable patriotism.

This interesting and flourishing institution was established in 1821, under the care of Josiah Dunham, A. M. who, we believe, was formerly Principal of a similar establishment in Windsor, Vt. It has, since that time, received and given instruction to 343 different pupils, drawn to it from several of the Western states. The number of young ladies now at the institution is 135. Nine instructers and instructresses are engaged in the seminary, and pupils are taught all the branches which they are usually taught in our best female academies ; and those who desire it are instructed also in the accomplishments of Drawing, Music, and Dancing. It is interesting to observe with what zeal the Western states of the union are pressing on in the progress of improvement in their systems and means of education. We doubt very much if New England, the boasted land of schools, contains a "Female Academy" which surpasses that at Lexington, Ky. in the number of its pupils, or in the variety of branches taught. We know not to what degree of perfection the science of instruction has been carried there ; but whether it yet be in as good a state as it is here or not, it must soon be. The public attention is turned to the subject in good earnest, and that always ensures improvement, and as great a degree of perfection as the age requires.

Robert Fowle. Boston. 1825. 18mo. pp. 34.

Among the multitude of books which are almost daily issuing from the press, written professedly for children, we so rarely light upon one which, in our view, is adapted to their capacities, that it is with no small degree of pleasure, we recommend this to the notice of our readers. The making of children's books is one of the most difficult, as well as most useful employments, which can engage the best cultivated minds. It requires much more discrimination, and much more knowledge of the human mind and heart, to write a book perfectly suited to the capacities of children of six years old, than it does to make a treatise suited to their capacities at any future period. "Robert Fowle" is a story, the scene of which is laid in this city, and the characters are such as would probably occur only in a city. But the most difficult point is achieved. It is *suited to the capacities* of children at an early age ; and will leave none but the best impressions on their tender minds and hearts. Impressions made at this age frequently give a cast and direction to the developing character, which are more abiding than any that can afterwards be made. The author of "Robert Fowle" may confer obligations on the community, which few have the ability to do, if they had the disposition ; but it is to be hoped, if he attempts another child's book, he will describe scenes and events, with which a greater number of children can be fairly supposed familiar, as upon this its interest and usefulness will in a great degree depend.

LAW.

Reports of Cases Argued and Adjudged in the Supreme Court of the United States, February Term, 1825. By Henry Wheaton. Vol. X. New York. 1825. 8vo. pp. 504.

This volume contains, besides what is stated in its title, sixty-six pages filled with official documents relating principally to the slave-trade, and decisions of the English Courts upon several cases, and a Spanish Decree and Portuguese Edict touching the same subject. To these documents references are made in the course of the Reports. To the whole is annexed an index to the principal matters in the volume.

MEDICINE.

Contributions to Physiological and Pathological Anatomy. By John D. Godman, M. D. Lecturer on Anatomy and Physiology. Philadelphia.

The New-England Journal of Medicine and Surgery. Vol. XIV. No. 3. Boston.

MISCELLANEOUS.

The African Repository, and Colonial Journal. Vol. I. No. IV. Washington, D. C.

Philadelphia Magazine. No. 6.

An Oration, delivered on Monday, Fourth of July, 1825, in Commemoration of American Independence, before the Supreme Executive of the Commonwealth, and the City Council and Inhabitants of the City of Boston. By Charles Sprague. 8vo. pp. 31. Boston.

The New York Review, and Atheneum Magazine, No. 2, for July, 1825.

Boston Monthly Magazine. No. 2, for July, 1825. Boston.

An Oration, delivered in the Capitol in the City of Washington, on the Fourth of July, 1825. By Ashbury Dickens, Esq. Washington, D. C.

An Oration, delivered at Lexington, on the Fourth of July, 1825. By Caleb Stetson. Cambridge. 1825. 8vo. pp. 20

An Oration, delivered at Lancaster, Mass. in celebration of American Independence, July 4, 1825. By Joseph Willard. Boston. 8vo. pp. 24.

A Discourse, addressed to the New Hampshire Auxiliary Colonization Society, at their first annual meeting, Concord, June 2, 1825. By Daniel Dana, D. D. Minister of the Gospel in Londonderry. Published by the request of the Society. Concord. 1825. 8vo. pp. 24.

The Society, before whom this discourse was delivered, has been lately organized, by the choice of His Excellency Governor Morril for President, and several of the most distinguished men in New Hampshire for Vice Presidents and Managers. "The object to which its views shall be exclusively directed," as stated in the constitution, "is the colonization on the coast of Africa, with their own consent, of the free people of colour of the United States; and this Society will contribute its funds and efforts to the attainment of that object, in aid of the American Colonization Society." Dr Dana states the enormous and increasing evils of "Slavery" and the "Slave trade," and urges moral and religious motives for an effort, in conjunction with the efforts which are made by distinguished individuals in other parts of our country, to free ourselves from the greatest curse which rests upon us. The evils of slavery are not to be charged upon any part of our country, nor even upon this generation; they have been entailed upon us by others. Many of the most intelligent and largest slave-holders in our country are as anxious, and even more so, to free themselves from the evil, than any philanthropists can be, who have never felt it so directly. But innumerable difficulties present themselves in the way of any project for the purpose. Even the American Colonization Society, under the patronage and sanction of the government of the United States, together with all the Auxiliary Societies which have been organized to aid in accomplishing its object, though they combine the wealth, and are directed by the intelligence, of the most enlightened and philanthropic individuals in every part of our country, seem to us almost totally inadequate to the magnitude of their undertaking. The evil is too deep-rooted to be eradicated by any means which have been, or can well be brought to bear upon it. It is interwoven with the constitution of the United States, and is blended with all the institutions of many of the subordinate states. If no private and local interests were to be invaded, and no obstructions on this account to be encountered and overcome, it must take many generations to produce any very sensible diminution of its effects. It may be mitigated, by well directed efforts of the benevolent and philanthropic, but all human means (would to God it were otherwise!) seem, at present, too feeble to remove it.

NATURAL HISTORY.

Annals of the Lyceum of Natural History of New York. Vol. I. No. 9. for June, 1825.

POETRY.

A Defence of Col. William Lovetruth Bluster, in a Letter to William Wagtail, Esq. done into Verse, by Mr Aminidab Sledgehammer, Poet Laureate of Cataboola. 12mo. pp. 11. New-Orleans.

THEOLOGY.

Four Sermons on the Atonement. 1st. The Necessity of the Atonement. 2d. Its Nature. 3d. Its Nature. 4th. Its Extent. By Nathan S. S. Beman, Pastor of the Presbyterian Church in Troy. New-York.

The Missionary Herald. Vol. XXI. No. 7. for July, 1825.

Reply to the Review of Dr Beecher's Sermon (delivered at Worcester, Mass.) which appeared in the Christian Examiner for January, 1824. By the Author of the Sermon. Price 25 cents. Boston.

A Sermon, delivered in Newburyport. By the late Rev. Christopher Bridge Marsh, formerly Pastor of the North Congregational Church in this town. Second Edition. 8vo. pp. 20. Newburyport.

The Christian Spectator. Vol. VII. No. 7. for July, 1825.

A Funeral Sermon on the Death of the Rev. John Summerfield, preached in Light Street Church, June 26th, 1825. By the Rev. Samuel Merwin, containing a brief Account of his Life, Last Illness, and Death. 8vo. Baltimore.

A View of the Human Heart. By Barbara Allan Simon, Author of the "Evangelical Review of Modern Genius." Intended for the Instruction of Youth in the Fundamental Doctrines of Christianity, &c. Illustrated by numerous copperplate Engravings. New York.

Biblical Repertory. Vol. I. No. 3. for July, 1825. Princeton, N. J.

A Sermon, in two Parts, preached to the Church in Brattle Square, with Notes Historical and Biographical. By John G. Palfrey, Pastor of the Church. 8vo. pp. 81. Boston.

The Literary and Evangelical Magazine. Vol. VIII. No. 7. Richmond, Va.

TOPOGRAPHY.

The Fashionable Tour, in 1825. An Excursion to the Springs, Niagara, Quebec, and Boston. 18mo. pp. 169. Saratoga Springs.

This makes three little volumes, which we have seen within a few weeks, all of which have for their object to give short and instructive descriptions of the various places now become the resorts of those who travel for pleasure or for health. The title of this book is not very distinct, and gives us no idea of what we are to expect from a perusal of it. It would make all the difference in the world, whence a man started in his "excursion to the Springs, Niagara, Quebec, and Boston;" and he might have come from Canada, Ohio, or the Moon, for aught we are informed in the title of this volume. It is very important to have a clear, full, and honest title page to every book; as many have only time to read that part of most publications. It is the business of the author or the publishers, certainly not of reviewers, to supply this great defect in many of the books which are daily issuing from the press.

This Tour opens with a short description of Philadelphia, then passes to New York, describing the principal towns on the route. From New York the author takes us up the Hudson to Albany, giving short accounts of the villages and cities on both banks of the river. From Albany be proceeds to Saratoga, makes the usual excursion to Lake George, and then leaves Saratoga for Utica. All the principal places on the routes are sketched, and anecdotes and facts relating to them are stated. From Utica we are taken to Niagara, and thence by Lake Ontario to Montreal and Quebec, almost as soon as we can write a sentence. The return from Quebec is by way of Lake Champlain and Burlington, through Albany, to Boston. And another route, also more direct, from Burlington to Boston, is described. Those about to take this journey, or any part of it, will find the book full of interesting facts relating to the various places through which they must pass.

AMERICAN EDITIONS OF FOREIGN WORKS.

A Treatise on the Conduct of the Understanding. By John Locke, Gent. Boston. 1825. 18mo. pp. 132.

Locke's Essay on the Conduct of the Understanding is too well known and too highly appreciated to derive any advantage from our commendation. We will, therefore, only express the pleasure we feel at seeing this valuable tract printed in a form which gives every student access to it, without the expense of buying the whole " works " of the author. We know of no book of the same size with this, which will afford the student a better exercise for his mind, or give him a better knowledge of the common obstacles, which present themselves in the way of the inquiries which he must constantly make in a course of liberal studies. John Locke, Gent. is a patriarch, after all, in the science of Metaphysics, and we are sorry to see him thrust aside so unceremoniously, to give place to later writers. He may be wrong in some of his speculative opinions in metaphysics, but these a judicious instructer may correct. He undoubtedly has sometimes a homely manner of expressing himself. But his ideas are always clear, and he never attempted to adorn them at the expense of clearness. He will give more and a better discipline to the minds of his young readers (which is certainly one principal object in studying metaphysics) than all the round about and splendid vagaries of Stewart, or the eloquent talk of his successor Brown.

The History of the Emperors who have reigned in Europe and Part of Asia, from the Time of Julius Cæsar to Napoleon. Translated from the French, by Mrs Sarah Ann Harris. New York.

History of the Expedition to Russia, undertaken by the Emperor Napoleon, in the year 1812. By General Count Philip De Segur. With a Map. 8vo. pp. 546. Boston.

Operative Mechanic and British Machinist, being a practical Display of the Manufactories and Mechanic Arts of the United Kingdom. By John Nicholson, Esq. Civil Engineer. 2 vols. 8vo. One of Plates. New York.

The Lives of the Novelists. By Sir Walter Scott. Philadelphia.

The Forester. By the Author of " Lights and Shadows." 1 vol. 12mo. New York.

A Tour in Germany and some of the Southern Provinces of the Austrian Empire; in the Years 1820, 1821, and 1822. By John Russell, Esq. Reprinted from the second Edinburgh Edition. 8vo. pp. 469. Boston.

To CORRESPONDENTS.—The article on Italian Lyrical Poetry, though in type, is necessarily postponed, on account of the unusual length of the Reviews and the List of New Publications.

Published on the first and fifteenth day of every month, by CUMMINGS, HILLIARD, & Co., No. 134 Washington-Street, Boston, for the Proprietors. Terms, $5 per annum. Cambridge : Printed at the University Press, by Hilliard & Metcalf.

THE UNITED STATES

LITERARY GAZETTE.

| Vol. II. | AUGUST 15, 1825. | No. 10. |

REVIEWS.

1. *An Address to the Public from the Trustees of the Gardiner Lyceum.* Hallowell. 1822. 8vo. pp. 8.
2. *Catalogue of the Officers and Students of Gardiner Lyceum, with an Address to the Public.* Gardiner. 1824. 8vo. pp. 16.

As this is the first institution, on a liberal scale, which has been established in New England expressly for the benefit of farmers and mechanics, we suppose that some account of its plan, progress, and situation, cannot fail to be interesting to our readers. This account will be principally taken from the Addresses to the Public of the Trustees and Principal of the Lyceum, which have been published at various times since its incorporation in 1822.

It had its origin in the wants of the community,—wants similar to those which have led to the establishment of lectures for mechanics in many parts of Great Britain and in some of the cities of the United States,—and in the desire of useful, practical knowledge, which is more and more felt through all parts of a country, in proportion as it becomes more free. The greater part of our mechanics and farmers have little or no knowledge of the scientific principles of their arts. The eminent practical sagacity for which they are distinguished must often be exhausted in the discovery of methods, which would be deduced with perfect ease from simple principles in geometry and natural philosophy. But these sciences, together with chemistry and other analogous branches of knowledge, have been rarely taught, except at college,

46

and as a part of a course of studies for persons intended for the learned professions. The academies and high schools are almost universally preparatory and subordinate to the colleges. The instructers in them are selected with reference to this object; their attention is chiefly devoted to it; and even when they have the capacity and inclination to give instruction in the sciences, they are prevented by want of apparatus and of time. In the secondary schools, little else is taught but reading, writing, grammar, arithmetic, and geography. The Gardiner Lyceum was intended to supply this deficiency, for a portion of our country, and to furnish that kind of instruction which is not furnished elsewhere, and which is most necessary to many important classes in the community. Algebra, geometry, trigonometry, mensuration, book-keeping, surveying, navigation, mechanics, hydrostatics, pneumatics, and chemistry, together with the branches usually taught at schools, constitute the original course which was designed to occupy the space of two years. During the third year the learner was to proceed to other branches of natural philosophy and mathematics, and to natural history and the philosophy of the mind. These, with exercises in composition, instruction in natural and revealed religion, and lectures on several of the above branches, completed the original plan.

The Lyceum was opened in January, 1823, under the direction of Mr Benjamin Hale, as Principal. It began with only two or three students, but the number gradually increased until August, when a second class was admitted. In November there were twenty students, ten in each class. At this time a second Address of the Trustees was published, containing a more particular account of the studies to be pursued in the different years, than had before been given,—an outline of the lectures on chemistry and mechanics, and an intimation of the desire of the Trustees to have a farm and a professor of agriculture and the kindred arts, connected with the institution. The Address gives the following as " the principal objects, which the Trustees have in view, in establishing the professorship in connexion with a practical farm.

" 1st. To give to the future agriculturist the knowledge of those principles of science upon which his future success depends, and to let him see them reduced to practice.

" 2d. To furnish a beneficial employment, as recreation.

" 3d. To diminish the expenses of board.

" 4th. To try a series of agricultural experiments adapted to the soil and climate of Maine."

The trustees also express a hope, that they shall " be able to provide some suitable employment for those young men who may attend the institution with a view of becoming mechanics, by which they may be enabled to discharge their expenses." " Another object of the Trustees is to collect the best models of useful tools and machines."

The academical year begins in August; and the catalogue published in October 1824, states the whole number of students at the Lyceum, at that time, to be sixty-six,—a very large number for a school upon an entirely new plan, and drawn together within less than two years from its commencement. The address to the public, by the principal instructer, accompanying the catalogue of October 1824, gives an account of the adoption of three new and important measures.

I. For the benefit of those, who cannot attend throughout the year, winter classes are proposed for instruction in, 1. Surveying; 2. Navigation; 3. Carpentry and Civil Architecture; 4. Chemistry.

II. A boarding-house is established, at which the expenses for board, washing, and room are reduced to $1,50 a week, making only 65 dollars a year.

III. A new method of discipline and government is adopted, formed upon the model of the celebrated Hofwyl school, the constitution of which we have already laid before our readers at length. Some modifications have been made in that system of government, but we shall take no farther notice of them at this time; as a full account both of the method and its success will appear at some future period in this Gazette.

Arrangements are made to devise suitable courses of studies for mariners and merchants, as well as for those classes for which the institution seems to have been at first principally designed.

Two additional instructers are already employed,—a tutor in mathematics and an instructer in natural history.

The works used as text-books are, perhaps, as good as could be selected out of the miserable mass from which a selection must be made. Many of them, however, are too general and abstract for pupils, whose minds are so unaccustomed to study and close application, as the minds of those must be who form the generality of the school. Many of them are too voluminous for text-books, and some are radically and essentially wrong in principle. We mean in the principle of communicating knowledge. Unless, therefore, these inherent difficulties are overcome by more patience and devotedness in making oral and familiar explanations, than generally falls to the lot of teachers, the school must fail of accomplishing the utmost of which it is capable, until the experience of the instructers shall suggest plans for books more consonant with the principles and phenomena of the human mind, and of course better suited to the objects of this promising establishment.

Bézout's Arithmetic has been translated for the use of the school by one of the instructers. The original forms part of a course of pure and mixed mathematics, which has had for many years great popularity in France, has gone through numerous editions, and still holds its place in many of the best French schools. To the mathematician tolerably well acquainted with French scientific writers the name is familiar. Bézout devoted a great part of his life to instruction in mathematics, and it was with a perfect knowledge of the difficulties to be overcome, and of the simplest mode of presenting abstract ideas to the uncultivated mind, that he wrote his course for his own pupils and those in similar circumstances. The translator has made some considerable additions the better to meet the wants of American schools.

The increasing demand for scientific instruction in this country, must, as we before intimated, bring forward many new books adapted to our peculiar situation and wants. It is most sincerely to be hoped that something better will soon appear, than the miserable and disjointed copies of poor old English compends, which are now almost universally used. And while such works as Colburn's two Arithmetics, Woodbridge's Geography, and this Arithmetic of Bézout are becoming common, we may have confidence that when scholars and men of science will devote themselves to the humble task of making school-books, they will be rewarded by seeing darkness and error gradually giving place to truth and knowledge.

Mathematics may seem to occupy an undue space in the course of studies for the first two years; but when it is considered that they afford one of the sturdiest exercises for sobering the fickleness, and taming the waywardness of the youthful mind; and at the same time form the foundation of the arts of the mariner and the mechanic, and are of great use to the farmer and the merchant, it appears probable that it will be found necessary to increase the quantity rather than allow it to be diminished.

The Monday morning recitations are in Scripture History, Paley's Natural Theology, and Paley's Evidences of Christianity. It is impossible to speak too highly of an arrangement, which gives so conspicuous a place to a kind of knowledge essential to our social and political happiness.

There seems to be one defect in the course of study, which indeed is common to almost every school in New England. No effectual provision is made for instruction in *drawing ;* by which nothing more is here meant, than what is technically called right-line drawing. Without some knowledge of this, it is impossible that a correct draught or plan should be made of a bridge, a dam, or a house ; of a machine, a ship, a harbour, coast, or piece of land. It ought, therefore, to be one of the first objects of attention to the architect, the navigator, and the surveyor; all of whom are to be provided for in such a school as this. In most countries of Europe it is one of the first pursuits in the common schools, and it is so useful to all persons engaged in the manual arts, and would be so pleasing an acquisition to the scholar, that it strongly recommends itself to general notice. Some mention is made of it in a sketch of the studies for one of the winter classes, but it seems not to be thought of sufficient importance to be made a distinct study.

It could hardly be expected that an extensive apparatus should be collected within the short time this Lyceum has been established. Strong desires are expressed by the trustees of being able soon to procure the philosophical and mechanical instruments and models necessary for the more perfect instruction of the school. There is no doubt, considering the zeal and devotedness with which the interests of this school are prosecuted, both by the trustees and the teachers, that the best use would be made of them, and that they would not be suffered to fall to ruin from disuse and want of care, as philosophical instruments have been allowed to do in some parts of our country.* A small number they already have, and it is to be hoped that the munificence of those who may be induced to take an interest in the Lyceum, will enable them to make the collection complete.

The situation of the " Lyceum in the Town of Gardiner " is certainly "very fortunate, from its central position (with regard to Maine), on a navigable river, in a populous neigh-

---

* Most of the beautiful instruments purchased some time since by our government, have gone to ruin from neglect. This has happened even at West Point.

bourhood and fertile country, where commerce is continually extending; and in a town possessing uncommonly fine mill privileges; and which already offers to the student in mechanics the exhibition of a greater variety of machinery moved by water, than can be found in any other town in the state." These circumstances taken in connexion with the very low rate of board, and smallness of other expenses, render the situation extremely eligible, not only with reference to the inhabitants of Maine, but for those of other states, who may wish to send children to a good school of this kind.

In so favorable a situation, and under the management of persons so skillful and active as the instructer and directors have already shown themselves to be, it is very desirable that the experiment of a practical farm, superintended by a professor of agriculture, and carried on in a great degree by the students themselves, should be fairly tried. It is difficult to doubt of its utility as an instrument of instruction and agreeable recreation; but, whatever it may bring to the Lyceum, it can produce only good to the public. It is one of those great philosophical experiments, which the voice of the agricultural community has long called for, and the directors of the Lyceum at Gardiner are fortunate and wise in being the first to hear and understand the call. Philosophy has of late years enriched the arts of life with too many and too valuable gifts to leave it doubtful that a close union between enlightened theory and patient labour, on a great scale, will be productive of the most beneficial results.

It is with similar feelings and hopes, that the plan must be contemplated of building workshops, furnished with various instruments, for the recreation and exercise of those students, who may be destined to any of the mechanical arts.

There are several particulars relating to the Lyceum, which have been merely mentioned, though they are of a very interesting nature. Such are the new mode of government, the institution of winter classes, the places and modes of study and recitation. On these and many other points, experiments are making, in the true spirit, it strikes us, of philosophical induction, and they can lead only to the happiest results. We cannot conclude this brief notice of the plan and purposes of the Gardiner Lyceum, without expressing our admiration of the spirit with which the institution was projected, and with which its best interests have been guarded and fostered. From the different addresses of the trustees and the principal, as well as from personal observation, we are deeply interested, and shall watch the progress of this school with raised expectations. The instructers are zealously engaged in their profession, and neither bigotedly attached to old forms on the one hand, nor possessed of such a violent rage for improvement on the other, as will lead them much beyond the clear light of their own experience. That portion of our countrymen must be regarded as fortunate, who have in their neighbourhood an establishment so well adapted to their wants. We believe, and we cannot withhold the expression of our belief, that, although this school has less "pomp and circumstance"—the splendid quackery of education,—than many others, yet it will prove, in the end, to be more substantially useful than any institution for similar purposes within our knowledge.

---

1. *Memoirs of the Countess de Genlis, illustrative of the History of the Eighteenth and Nineteenth Centuries. Written by herself.* New York, and Philadelphia. 1825. 8vo. pp. 410.
2. *New Moral Tales, Selected and Translated from the French of Madame De Genlis. By an American.* New York. 1825. 12mo. pp. 233.

THE autobiography of a lady, and a French lady, and what is more an authoress of some celebrity, and one who has moved for half a century in the most literary and polished society of her country, may reasonably be expected to furnish much interesting matter. Such is the character of one of the books before us ; we accordingly formed high expectations from it, and if these have not been fully realized, they have been very nearly so. Of the literary history of the work we know nothing except what is to be gathered from the title page and some hints in the preface, that it was compiled from notes taken at various times in the course of the life of the authoress. The manner of the book is peculiar and characteristic, and accords well with the prevalent notions of the French character.

We shall begin our extracts as Madam de Genlis does her biography at the very beginning.

I was born [says she] on the 25th of January, 1746, on a little estate in Burgundy, near Autun, called Champcéri, by corruption, it is said, of

Champ de Cerès (the field of Ceres), the original name of the ground.
I was born so small and so weakly that they would not venture to put
me in swaddling-clothes, and in a few moments after my birth, I was on
the point of losing my life.   I had been placed in a down pillow, of
which, to keep me warm, the two sides were folded over me, and fastened with a pin ; and thus wrapped up, I was laid upon an arm-chair in
the room.   The judge of the district, who was almost blind, came to pay
his visit of compliment to my father : and as, in his country fashion,
he separated the huge flaps of his coat to sit down, some one saw that he
was going to place himself in the arm-chair where I was ; luckily he was
prevented from sitting down, and I escaped being crushed to death.

She escapes various other perils of life and limb, and arrives without material injury at the age of six years, when
she makes her first appearance at Paris and there undergoes
a kind of seasoning, which does not seem to have been particularly agreeable.

For the first few days of my stay at Paris I regretted St. Aubin bitterly.   I had two teeth pulled out ; I had whalebone stays which pinched
me terribly ; my feet were imprisoned in tight shoes, with which it was
impossible for me to walk ; I had three or four thousand curl-papers put
on my head ; and I wore, for the first time in my life, a hoop.   In order
to get rid of my country attitudes, I had an iron collar put on my
neck, and as I squinted a little at times, I was obliged to put on goggles
as soon as I awoke in the morning, and these I wore four hours.   I was,
moreover, not a little surprised, when they talked of giving me a master to teach me what I thought I knew well enough already—to *walk*.
Besides all this, I was forbidden to run, to leap, or to ask questions.

The following year she becomes a canoness.

After this trip, my mother, my aunt, my cousin, and myself, departed
together in an immense berline for Lyons, where my cousins and I were
to be received as canonesses of the noble chapter of Alix.   As it was
indispensible that the counts of Lyons should examine into the proofs of
nobility of the candidates, we were detained about a fortnight there.
Our proofs being found satisfactory, we departed for Alix, which is but a
few leagues from Lyons.   The chapter formed with its immense buildings
a singular appearance.   It was composed of a great number of pretty
little houses, all alike, and each having a little garden.   These houses
were so arranged, that they formed a half circle, of which the palace
of the abbess occupied the centre.   I was highly amused at Alix : the
abbess and all the ladies loaded me with caresses and sugar-plums, which
gave me a great taste for the vocation of canoness.

The day of my reception was a great day to me.   The evening which
preceded it was by no means so agreeable : I had my hair dressed, my
clothes tried on, I was catechised, &c.   At last the happy moment arrived ; my cousin and I were dressed in white, and conducted in pomp
to the church of the chapter.   All the ladies dressed in the fashion of
the day, but wearing black satin robes over their hoops, and large cloaks
lined with ermine, were in the choir.   A priest who officiated as Grand
Prior, catechised us, made us repeat the creed, and afterward kneel up-

on velvet cushions. His duty was next to cut out a small lock of our hair; but being very old and nearly blind, he cut my ear a little, but I supported the pain *heroically*, and the accident was only discovered by the bleeding of the ear. After this, he put on my finger a consecrated gold ring, and fastened on my head a piece of black and white stuff, about the length of one's finger, which the canonesses called *un mari* (a husband). I was then decorated with the signs of the order, a red ribbon with a beautiful enamelled cross, and a broad girdle of black-watered ribbon. After the ceremony he delivered a short exhortation; we then went and saluted all the canonesses before leaving the church; and afterwards we heard high mass. The remainder of the day after dinner, exepting the hour of church service, was spent in entertainments, in visits which we paid to all the ladies, and amusing little games. From this time I was called Madame la Comtesse de Lancy; my father being, as I have already said, lord of the manor of Bourbon-Lancy, was the cause of my receiving that name. The pleasure I had in hearing myself called *Madame* surpassed every other. In this chapter every one had the choice of taking the vows at the age prescribed, or later: but those who did not take them gained nothing by their reception into the order but the title of *lady* and *countess*, and the right of wearing its decorations. Those ladies who took the vows, got in time considerable prebends: those who did not, were not obliged to reside in the chapter; but those who did, were not only prevented from marrying but compelled to reside in the chapter two years out of three, passing the year of liberty, however, where they chose.

We continue our extracts with an account of a *fête* given by her mother, in honour of her father's return from Paris.

She [her mother] had a great natural talent for poetry; and though not very well acquainted with its rules, has written some very charming verses. She composed a kind of comic opera, in the pastoral style with a mythological prologue, in which I played Love. All the chambermaids, and my mother had four, all young and pretty, had parts to perform: besides this, there was to be a tragedy, and Iphigenia in Aulis was fixed upon: my mother played Clytemnestra, and I, Iphigenia. A physician of Bourbon-Lancy, called Doctor Pinot, took the part of Agamemnon; his eldest son, a youth of eighteen, was prodigiously applauded as the fiery Achilles, and he was in truth, fiery enough. His theatric genius had conceived all the contortions, the convulsions, the stampings of the foot, and the terrific cries, which have since been so much applauded on the Parisian stage; I hid myself in order to laugh, for, even at that age, false emphasis and all forced emotions appeared to me exceedingly ridiculous. Mademoiselle de Mars thought as I did, and we amused ourselves secretly in our own room, with imitating this great actor, whom we durst not ridicule at the rehearsals. My mother, to furnish our costume, sacrificed her handsomest dresses. I still recollect, that, in the prologue, my dress was rose colour, under point lace, ornamented with little artificial flowers of all colours; it reached only to my knee, and I had little boots, straw colour and silver, my long hair flowing, and azure wings. My dress, as Iphigenia, over a large hoop, was of China silk, cherry colour and silver, trimmed with sables. As my mother had no diamonds, she ordered from Moulins a prodigious

47

quantity of false stones, to complete our magnificent dresses. In the prologue, there was a passage which pleased me mightily, and of which the idea was certainly original. I represented Love, as I said before; a little boy of the village was Pleasure; and I sung a couplet, in which I was supposed to address myself to my father, which ended with—

> Au Plaisir j'arrache les ailes,
> Pour le mieux fixer près de vous.

As I finished, I was to run to little Pleasure, and to pluck off his wings; but it happened one day, at a grand dress-rehearsal, that his wings, being too firmly fastened, resisted: I shook Pleasure in vain—his wings refused to yield; I fell furiously upon Pleasure, and threw him down; he cried piteously, but I never quitted my hold, until I succeeded in plucking off the wings of *displeased* Pleasure, who roared with vexation.

Among other talents Madame de Genlis excelled as a musician.

Besides the harp, [says she] on which I played six or seven hours a day, I played on the harpsichord, the guitar, the mandolin, the viol, and the bagpipe, an instrument which was exceedingly graceful; the wind was produced (as I have said) not by the mouth, but through a small pair of bellows placed under the arm.

We remember to have seen an Italian lady playing gracefully on the Jew's-harp, and we believe that a French one may do the same with the bag-pipe; though the association of grace with the actual operation of "doudling the bag of wind," as Niel Blane expresses it, is a difficult one.

We intended at the commencement of this article to give some sketch of the life of the authoress. This however, we find would occupy considerable space, and we think those of our readers who may not be able to obtain the book will be better entertained with some of the numerous extracts which we have marked in its perusal, and the rather as the principal interest of the book consists in the smaller details of every-day business and amusement.

The following prank was played soon after her marriage:

I remained only a few days at Genlis; I was there entertained with pond-fishing. Unluckily I went with little white embroidered shoes, and when I got to the edge of the pond, I slipped into the mud: my brother-in-law came to my assistance, and remarking my shoes, called me *a fine lady from Paris*, which vexed me extremely; for, having been brought up in a country house, I had announced all the pretensions of a person to whom all sorts of rural amusements are familiar. I replied with some warmth to the pleasantries of my brother-in-law; but hearing all the neighbours assembled at the fishing, repeating that I was *a fine lady from Paris*, my vexation became extreme; so, stooping down, I picked up a small fish about the length of my finger, and swallowed it alive, saying, "This is to show that I am a fine lady from Paris." I have done many other foolish things in my life, but certainly nothing so whimsical as this.

Another still more remarkable happened many months after. She was then twenty years of age.

On quitting La Planchette, we all returned to Genlis. My brother passed the year at Genlis. He had just been received into the engineers, and undergone his examination in Bézout, with the utmost credit to himself; in fact, he showed a decided genius for the mathematics. I was transported with joy at seeing him again; he was handsome and ingenuous, and he had a sort of childish gayety which suited my humour exactly. One evening, when there was company at the château, and while my sister-in-law and Messieurs de Genlis were playing, after supper, at reversis, my brother proposed to me a walk in the court which was spacious, covered with sand, and planted all round with flowers, to which I consented. When we reached the court, he expressed a wish to take a walk in the village. I was as willing as he. It was ten o'clock; all the public houses were lighted; and we saw through the windows peasants drinking cider. I observed with surprise that they all wore a very grave air.

My brother was seized with a fit of frolicsome gayety, and he knocked at a window, crying out, " Good people, do you sell any *sacré chien*?" and after this exploit, he dragged me after him, as he ran into a little dark street, where we both hid ourselves, ready to die with laughter. Our delight was increased by hearing the tavern-keeper, at the door of his house, threatening, " to cudgel the little blackguards" who had knocked at his window. My brother explained to me that *sacré chien* meant brandy. I thought all this so pleasant, that I insisted on going to another little tavern adjoining, to make the same polite inquiry, which met with the same success; we repeated several times that agreeable pastime, trying which of us should say, " *sacré chien*," and ending by shouting it together, and every time running off to hide ourselves in the little street, where we burst into fits of laughter till we could hardly stand. Happy age! at which we are so easily transported with gayety; when nothing has yet exalted the imagination or troubled the heart!

The following is a specimen of the amusements at the château of the President Portal at Vaudreuil.

While in the drawing-room after dinner, the day after our return, the president received a letter which he read aloud, informing him that *pirates* had seen Madame de Merode and me at sea, and intended to carry us off to take us to the Grand Seigneur's seraglio. We were not greatly alarmed at this: however we asked him how we could preserve ourselves from so imminent a danger, and he replied that he saw no other way than to get ourselves received as vestals in the temple of the *petit bois.* This was a charming hut formed like a temple, and placed in a part of the garden near the castle; it was called the convent, was surrounded with walls, and completely secluded, for it was in the president's private garden which he carefully kept under lock and key, and which nobody entered but in his company. He had taken us thither several times to breakfast. It was settled that at eight o'clock next evening we should be received into the temple of Vesta. M. de Caraman led us thither, and immediately disappeared. We found the temple adorned with flowers, and all the ladies of the party dressed as vestals, with Madame de

Puisieux at their head as high priestess, and the president as high priest. He was the only man present within the enclosure. An harangue was delivered, and Madame de Vougny recited some very pretty verses. The ceremony of our reception was gone through. Daylight was fast disappearing, when we heard, all at once, very noisy music in the Turkish style, and messengers came round us on all hands to say that the Grand Seigneur was coming in person, with a great escort, to carry off all the vestals from the temple. Our high priest showed on this occasion a firmness worthy of his rank, for he declared that the gates should not be opened. Meanwhile the terrible music was approaching with alarming rapidity, and the Turks soon made thundering knocks at the gates. To avoid a scene that I disliked beforehand, I advised that the gates should be opened, and that we should surrender at discretion; but the president was firmly attached to his own plan, and fond of the pantomime, so that he reproached me with cowardice, and made the sultan be informed that the spot was consecrated ground. Thereupon, though the walls were pretty high, all the Turks jumped over immediately, several among them (who were servants or peasants) carrying torches; the gates were opened; more than three hundred Turks entered the garden, the gentlemen of the party carried off the ladies; the rest carried off about a dozen waiting maids, who had been mingled with us to increase our number. I always hated confusion and tumult, even in games, and this noisy party both displeased and frightened me, for I was afraid there might be some legs broken; and at seeing some Turks approach the vestals rather roughly, I thought the whole plan abominable. While in this bad humour, by the light of the torches I perceived M. de Caraman all glittering with gold and jewels (but who did not look well in his turban), and approaching me with an air of triumph, that roused my anger. I absolutely refused to be carried off, and this in such a rude way that he was greatly hurt. He laid hold of me, I resisted, pinched, scratched, and kicked his legs till he got into a passion, and then carried me off in spite of all my resistance. I was placed on a magnificent palanquin, while the sultan followed on foot, and reproached me bitterly. Seeing, however, that I ought not to spoil the fête by teasing him who really gave it, and who had become the hero only to make me queen, I endeavoured to laugh it off, and succeeded in appeasing him. All the ladies were placed in charming palanquins, and the Turks followed on foot with a band of music playing. In this manner we traversed throughout their whole length these immense and beautiful gardens, which were magnificently illuminated. The prospect was delightful. We found at the extremity of the park a splendid ball-room, with plenty of orange-trees, garlands of flowers, designs, and refreshments. The Grand Seigneur declared me his favourite sultana, and we danced all night. I have had many fêtes given me in the course of my life, but I never saw any so ingenious and delightful as this.

Compare the delight which Madame de Genlis expresses in what would appear to an English or American lady contemptibly childish, with the good and useful sense of her remarks a few pages farther.

I saw many snares and dangers scattered along my path, but I saw splendour, and I was carried away by vanity, curiosity, and presump-

tion.   We are seldom ruined by great passions, for their danger is too
clear, and when the disposition is naturally good, all its resources are
employed against them, and it triumphs over their allurements ; but we
never sufficiently distrust a crowd of little childish feelings, that seem
to us totally harmless, and which gradually influence our conduct and
lead us into danger.   Some adopt the dangerous practice of forming
their opinion, and regulating their conduct solely by what an action is
by itself, and of lulling their conscience by saying that it is altogether
innocent.   They ought to reflect on its consequences, and seriously consider whether their situation, temper, and private feelings do not render
it dangerous or improper for them, though it may be harmless to others.
But when we feel an inclination for any thing, we take good care not
to reckon thus, though it is the very thing that ought to be done. * * *
    Whenever claims are firmly and preservingly supported, though they
be not well-founded, they give the persons who make them a certain footing and consideration in society, when they are wealthy, clever, and
keep a good table.   Sharp-sighted people and keen observers may laugh at
them ; but the public yield, as the very obstinacy of their pretensions
seems to give them a just right.   Though the dandies are despised by the
ladies, yet they are reckoned *hommes à bonnes fortunes.*   Bustling and
self-important individuals without influence deceive no one ; yet they are
courted and flattered by the votaries of ambition and intrigue, who reckon it prudent to engage them in their interests.   Prudes obtain the external respect due to virtue ; pedants without real learning, enjoy in
conversation almost all the deference paid to the learned.   When we
reflect on the never-failing success of claims perseveringly supported,
who would attach much importance to the suffrages of society ?

The comparison is curious and worthy of the notice of
those who are ready to approve or condemn the character of
nations or individuals on no better foundation than a casual
consideration of manners and habits, and apt to consider an
action as evidence of frivolity, indelicacy, or something worse,
in France or Italy, because it would be so in Germany, England, or America.

Our extracts have hitherto related rather to remarkable
circumstances than persons ; from many of a different kind
which might be given, we select the following respecting the
Princess of Lamballe, a name indissolubly associated in the
recollections of the world with the brutal ferocities of the
revolution.

    Madame de Lamballe was extremely pretty, and though her shape
wanted elegance, and she had horrid hands, which contrasted strangely,
from their size, with the delicacy of her face, she was charming without
regularity ; her disposition was mild, obliging, equal, and gay, but was
totally destitute of talent ; her vivacity, her gayety, and her childish
air, concealed her insipidity in an agreeable manner ; she never held an
opinion of her own, but adopted in conversation the opinion of the person who passed for having the most wit, and this in a manner which was
altogether peculiar to herself.   When there was a serious discussion, she

never opened her lips, but affected absence of mind ; and then suddenly appearing to start from her reverie, she repeated, word for word, as from herself, what the speaker had said whose opinion she adopted, and affecting great astonishment when any one told her that the same thing had just been said, she assured every body that she had not heard it. She employed this little contrivance with great address, and it was a long time before I could discover it. She had, besides, a great many little failings, which were in fact nothing but childish affectation ; the sight of a bouquet of violets would make her faint—as would the sight of a craw-fish or a lobster, even in picture ; on these occasions she would close her eyes, and without changing colour, remain motionless for more than half an hour, in spite of all the assistance which was afforded her, though nobody believed in these pretended fainting fits. I saw her faint in this manner in Holland, in Mr Hope's cabinet, on casting her eyes on a small Flemish picture, representing a woman selling lobsters. A-nother time at Crécy at the Duke of Penthièvre's after supper, I was sitting by her on a sofa, while Mademoiselle Bagarotti was telling ghost stories ; suddenly she heard a domestic in the anti-room yawn aloud, as if waking. Madame de Lamballe affected so much emotion at this she fell *fainting* upon me, and remained so for such a length of time, that we sent to wake M. Guenault, the duke's surgeon, who came running down stairs in his dressing-gown. As the *fainting fit* continued, and I was very anxious to go to bed, I proposed aloud to M. Guenault who was a fool, to bleed the princess in the foot, being quite certain that she would recover from her fit before the bleeding. M. Guenault objected that it would be right to wait somewhat longer on account of supper ; but I told him I had remarked that the princess had scarcely eaten any thing. Upon this, without hesitation, M. Guenault ordered hot water, and with an air of triumph (for bleeding the princess was a glorious ex-ploit for him) he proposed to go and wake M. de Penthièvre, who al-ways went to bed before us : but this I opposed. At last the basin of hot water arrived : M. Guenault took out his lancet, when *suddenly* and *unexpectedly* the princess recovered her senses. I have seen her act a thousand times scenes of this kind. Afterward when periodic at-tacks of the nerves came into fashion, Madame de Lamballe never fail-ed to have two regularly every week, on the same days, and at the same hours, for a whole year. On these days according to the practice of other patients of the same kind, M. Saiffert, her physician, always came to her at the stated hours. He rubbed the hands and temples of the princess with spirituous liquid ; she was then put to bed where she lay two hours in *a fainting fit.* During this scene her intimate friends who came on these days formed a circle about her bed, and con-versed quietly until the princess rose from her lethargy. Such was the the person who exercised a supreme dominion over the mind of the queen, in the begining of her reign.

The work concludes rather abruptly about the period of the year 1780. We readily recommend it to the perusal of our readers, and hope we may see a continuation of it.

The other work noticed at the head of this article contains three tales, selected from the works of Madame de Genlis. On these short stories from the pen of an authoress so well known, it is scarcely necessary to make any remark. They are as entertaining as tales of this sort usually are. The spirit of these things depends much on the manner of telling them, and this is apt of course to be injured by translation. We should think that not much had been lost in this way in the present instance, and that the stories on the whole were well told and well translated.

Reform of Harvard College.

(For the Titles, see No. 6 of this Gazette.)

[CONTINUED.]

THE report of the first committee was criticised with considerable severity, and many weighty objections urged against its provisions in the pamphlet numbered 2, in our list of titles. No attempt to refute the reasoning in this pamphlet, nor any explanation or defence of the plan of reform, has ever been officially made public, so far as we know, except what may be found in the speech of Mr Pickering.

This gentleman does not seem inclined to be strenuous respecting that part of the report which regards the distribution of powers in the University, with respect to discipline. He seems to consider this arrangement as one not so urgently called for as those which relate to instruction. He does not attempt to defend it from the charge of utter absurdity and impracticability, which is pretty clearly implied in the " Remarks " on this Report. He refers, however, to the speech of the chairman of the committee, in which, perhaps, some such defence was made. But this speech has not been published. The following extract will show Mr Pickering's opinion respecting the Tutors.

In connexion with the administration of the government, there had been what he considered a radical error; it had been the practice to choose very young men for tutors, at moderate salaries, upon an understanding that their whole time would not be occupied with the duties of their office, and that they would have leisure to pursue professional studies; and although in the profession of the law no allowance would be made to a student for this portion of his studies, yet in divinity, as he had been informed, (he hoped the fact was not so) an allowance was made to students. It was evident, that, under such circumstances, a tutor would not give that undivided attention to the discharge of his duty, which the good of his pupils, and indeed his own reputation, demanded. So far, also, as respects the mere *police* of the University, it was understood, that tutors who were candidates for the ministry were allowed to be absent from their rooms on Sundays in order to preach; this indeed was a necessary consequence of the present system; but it was manifestly an inconvenience that any of the College buildings should be left without the instructers. It was much better to pay higher salaries to a few men who should be required to give their whole time to the students, than to employ, at low salaries, a larger number who should devote but a part of their time to them; there could be but little difference in the expenditure on this account, and the gain to the Institution would be incalculable.

We referred, in our last number, to an opinion of this kind, as one that existed among many, who had paid attention to the subject. Much may be said in defence of this opinion, though there appear to be some difficulties connected with the proposed amendment. It may be said that there are three classes of persons, likely to become Tutors in this Institution; first, young men who take this office for various reasons, previous to commencing the study of a profession; secondly, students in theology while actually engaged in their studies, or candidates for the ministry; thirdly, gentlemen who, from a taste for the business of instruction, ill success in their profession, dislike to it, or other reasons, conclude to devote themselves entirely to this business.

With respect to the first class, it may be questioned whether any salary, which it would be reasonable to give, would have the effect of long retaining one who is looking forward to the study and practice of a profession. In a country like ours, young men of talents are not often willing to delay many years the commencement of the business to which they intend to devote their lives. The second class would be excluded, on the ground taken by Mr Pickering. The actual officers, therefore, would, in most cases, be taken from the third class. But in this country men are very apt, when they have entered upon any business which they regard as permanent, to wish to marry, and in point of fact they usually do so. The consequence of this will be, that the Tutors will soon be without the walls, and their places within must be supplied with a set of temporary officers, with lower salaries. The permanent Tutors again must have salaries to support their families on a level with those of the other College officers; and thus the College will be, in the ordinary course of things, after a few years, just where it is now.

To keep up an establishment of permanent Tutors within the walls, like the Fellows of the English Universities, seems difficult, till we can attach to their offices the obligation of celibacy and the prospect of church preferment. The system of gradually increasing salaries, referred to in a former part of this article, appears best calculated to diminish the frequency of changes in this department of instruction. Mr Pickering next observes, that,

In the administration of the government, too, it was a manifest inconvenience, that the whole body of instructers must be convened in order to decide upon many offences of the smaller kinds, which might as well be committed to a part of them; and with the same view of preserving some gradation in the powers of the government, it appeared to be an improvement, that the President should have the authority and rank proposed in the Report.

It seems to us that this question may be resolved into another, which is, whether the President shall have the entire control and right of final decision in every case of misdemeanor. If we understand the Report, a sort of appeal lies, in every instance, from the inferior courts, if we may so speak, to the President. Now if this be the case, we can have no doubt, that such an appeal will be made in every instance, and very little concerning the authority likely to be retained by the inferior officers, after a single reversion of their decisions. We can not be quite so certain which, in such a state of things, would be the most disagreeable office, that of the President, or that of the inferior officers. The opinion of the author of the "Remarks," concerning the expediency of giving such powers to the President, is very decided.

The power given to the President is in its nature arbitrary and irresponsible, dependent merely on his own judgment and will, such as is not exercised by any other individual in the country, and such as I trust in the good providence of God, never will be.

With respect to the "inconvenience" of convening the whole body of instructers, it seems to us that it affects the resident officers only; and however considerable the inconvenience may be, we are very doubtful whether they would be gratified with the kind of relief proposed in this Report. Concerning the arrangement of powers, however, Mr Pickering professed himself not to be strenuous—he thought a change in the system of instruction more important. He then went into an examination of the duties of the instructers under the present system, and endeavoured to show, that they might reasonably be called

48

on to do much more. We think, from the examination of the table in the second report, that there is ground for this objection, although it seems to be stated in rather stronger terms than was quite candid, for, as it afterwards appears, much time is occupied in a manner which was not taken into consideration in forming the table. Moreover, it appears that the duties performed by some of the inferior officers, occupy more time (in the table at least) than those of some of the Professors. But this last circumstance does not strike us as evidence of an improper system. We think that the business of the Professors is not merely the instruction of the youth of the College, but also the instruction of the community; in other words, the advancement of science and literature. This is in itself a pleasant toil, and we before inferred, from this very circumstance, that their present salaries were too high.

A Professor's labours, in this way, cannot be estimated by tables, or any mechanical contrivance whatever. We would not have them, to be sure, relieved from every duty of instruction; but if they are to be tied down to an everlasting round of drilling, our previous reasoning respecting their salaries falls to the ground, and we cheerfully give it up. Admitting, however, that enough personal attention, in general, has not been paid to instruction, we agree with the committee, that this is the fault of the system rather than that of the officers, and wish we could perceive how this defect will be remedied by most of the provisions of the new one.

This system proposes to divide the officers of College, for the purposes of instruction, into departments, consisting of a head and members. On referring to the catalogue of officers, we perceive that there must be six or seven departments, of which two or three will contain but two individuals, and the others only one. But if Mr Pickering is correct in his notion, that the present officers have so little occupation, it would seem that they are rather too numerous, than otherwise. Their number does not call for increase, but diminution. Instead of having more members to each department, it would appear to follow, that it would be better to make one person do the whole duty. But it would be clearly impossible for individual heads of departments to arrange their lessons and lectures without consultation and combination, and thus this fiction of departments reduces itself to the simple proposition, that the Immediate Government (under a new name, the Faculty,) shall have the control, direction, and arrangement of the course of study, &c. in the University. This, as will appear in the consideration of the Memorial before mentioned, is the very point which the immediate government have long desired to obtain, and so far the views of the committee will probably be agreeable to them.

The next topic considered by Mr Pickering is the shortening of the vacations. In this particular we are happy to agree with him entirely. We think a quarter of the year too much to be taken up by vacations, and that the winter is not the most favourable period for the longest one. With respect to holidays and half holidays also, we think with him, that they are too numerous. One argument in favour of the winter vacation is thus satisfactorily opposed :

It had been urged in favour of a winter vacation, that it was beneficial to indigent students, who would thus have an opportunity of keeping country schools and earning something towards defraying their College expenses. This was certainly deserving of attention, and he was ready to go as far as any member of the board, in granting to meritorious scholars of that description, every reasonable indulgence. It would not be amiss, however, to look at the operation of the present practice upon the whole University. It appeared from the documents on the table, that, on an average, fifty-three students (about one fifth of the whole) annually were permitted to keep school, and were allowed a part of the winter term in addition to the vacation; and during that portion of the term the usual lectures were suspended, besides which, the government inform us, that those who remain at the University during that period, suffer a loss, and the standard of scholarship generally is lowered for a time. Thus four fifths of the students are sacrificed, to a certain extent, to one fifth; this was too great an inequality; it would be better to aid such indigent scholars by an assessment on the other four fifths, or by remitting their tuition fees, or in any other mode than the present. It should be considered, also, that the wealthier classes of citizens, who have contributed to endow the University, have some claims; they ought to have a fair portion (consistently with the just claims of others) of all the advantage of an institution which they have generously contributed to build up for the benefit of all.

Mr Pickering next remarks, that

With a view to preventing the frequent intercourse with the capital, and keeping the students under regular employment, within the College walls, the committee had recommended in the Report, that the room of every student should be visited by the instructers every evening at nine o'clock, and report made of every absence; but perhaps this object might be as effectually accomplished by requiring one of the regular recitations to be in the evening, and to continue at least as late as that hour. Some effectual regulation was indispensable, in the opinion of every parent.

The author of the " Remarks " observes, with respect to

the proposal, that the students' rooms should be visited at nine o'clock in the evening, that,

As a large portion of the students are scattered about in rooms in different dwellinghouses in the town, at the distance of at least half a mile from each other, the proposal seems hardly practicable. If the visitation should be confined to the rooms in the College buildings, its principal effect would be to lead those inclined to irregularity, to take rooms in the town. But it seems objectionable on other grounds. Such kind of inspection degrades the officers. It takes from them that influence with the students which is of more importance, as regards the true objects to be aimed at in the discipline of the College, than the enforcing of any amount of rules of such a character. It is treating the whole body of students as suspected persons; and tends to produce irritation and reaction on their part, and generally a state of feeling unfavourable to the operation of those motives, on which the main reliance must be placed as a security for their good conduct.

We shall take this opportunity of throwing together a few remarks on this very important subject of the discipline, habits, and manners of the students—observing, in the first place, that those of Cambridge have been much amended within the period to which our personal experience extends. We believe that the College has been improving rapidly within that period in many particulars; that the students learn more and better; that they are guilty of fewer irregularities and vices, and less wasteful dissipation of time, than they have been at any time within the last twenty years; and that customs and practices were formerly common which would not now be thought of; and that no other University in this country would better support, to say the least of it, the severe scrutiny to which that at Cambridge has lately been subjected. Still it must be conceded to the committee, that there is room for improvement, and admitted, that some objectionable customs have been gaining ground; such, for instance, as the employment of servants, which, ten years since, was a rare circumstance.

One distinction between a school and a University, we take to be, that, in the former, the pupil is compelled to learn, while in the latter, he may learn if he will. A University is therefore adapted to pupils of more advanced age and greater maturity of mind than a school. The students in the medical, law, and theological schools, want no coercion. But all the Universities in this country, as well as some in Europe, are of a mixed nature; and while some of the motives which influence the students in a pure University, exist with respect to the undergraduates in our own, and more might be made operative, the students

in most of them are too young to be entirely free from
the coercion which prevails in a school. We intimated that
some motives might be brought into action, which are now
dormant or feeble with a large proportion of the students.
A powerful one is public opinion,—the public opinion of the
students, without the co-operation of which every system of
checks and balances, short of the form, the birch, and the
master's eye, must be feeble. An indirect mode of influencing this is the removal of some objects of interest
foreign to literary improvement. One of these is the Military Company of the University, which we regard as a
preposterous incongruity in a literary institution. It occupies the time and thoughts, and excites the interest of the
students to an improper degree. Moreover it offers objects
of ambition, no way connected with literary excellence; and
a youth may console himself for deficiency in his class with
the splendour of an epaulet, or the glory of commanding a
squad. These things go to prevent the feeling, which ought
to prevail, that the only rank must be derived from literary
eminence. But it is urged, that the students need exercise,
and that this a good method. Do they need exercise more
now, than they did twenty years since? Or have they been
more healthy since the company was established? But this
is an idle plea. Of the four classes, only two can be members.
The officers are chosen from the senior class, and of course
few, if any, of them will probably be privates. A few, therefore, of one class, and not the whole of another, enjoy this
exercise; and what have the younger classes to do with it,
but to gaze, and long for the time, when they too may figure
in the ranks, or at the head of the array? Lastly, it is a
source of expense, and as good exercise may be had at a
cheaper rate.

[*To be continued.*]

MISCELLANY.

ITALIAN LYRICAL POETRY.

FILICAJA.

VINCENZO DA FILICAJA was born in Florence in 1642. His
parents were both of noble extraction, and fully indulged the taste
for study, which, mingled with strong feelings of piety, was
early exhibited by their son. He lived for many years a tranquil

and retired life, devoted to the cultivation of literature, and especially of poetry, until the time of the famous siege of Vienna by the Turks.   This event, and the subsequent raising of the siege by John Sobieski, acting at the same moment upon his piety and his poetical enthusiasm, drew from him several *Canzoni*, which, breathing a spirit of holy confidence in the protection of the true God, and of triumphant gratulation in the success of the Christians, instantly gave him a reputation completely European.   Complimentary letters were addressed to him by the Emperor Leopold, the King of Poland, and the Duke of Lorraine.   In addition to this, Christina, queen of Sweden, wrote him a complimentary letter to which Filicaja replied with a *canzone*; and the strictest friendship thenceforth subsisted between the poet and Christina until her death, which forms the subject of several of his poems.   Filicaja's fame as a poet introduced him also to the notice of the Grand Duke, who invested him with the rank of senator, and entrusted him from time to time with several conspicuous magistracies, of which he acquitted himself with great ability and integrity.   He was also made a member of the Academies of *La Crusca* and the *Arcadi*; and having become one of the most eminent poets of the day, he died in 1707, universally honoured and regretted.   He was married at the age of 31, and had two sons, one of whom survived him, and first collected his poems.

Filicaja wrote poems in the Latin, as well as in the Italian language.   High as the encomium may seem, it is not saying too much of him to affirm, that in comparison with the Italian poets of his age, perhaps with the Italian poets of any age, he is distinguished for the vivacity, vigour, and dignity of his style, and for sentiments which often rise to the height of sublimity, and always are strongly conceived, grave, and impressive.   The occasion which first inspired his muse, appears to have lifted him above the intolerably affected taste in poetical composition, which characterized most other Italian poets of the seventeenth century (the *seicentisti*).   Liberty and religion are his favourite themes, and they communicate their own animating and elevating character to his mind.   Many of his poems are purely devotional.   Many also are spirited exhortations to the Italian States to bury their petty jealousies in oblivion, and unite in the common cause of achieving the independence of Italy.   His countrymen have always dwelt upon these poems with melancholy pride, which, while it testified their sense of their own abject condition, sought consolation in the stirring recollection of their departed glory.

I begin my specimen of Filicaja with his memorable sonnet

TO ITALY.

Italia, oh Italia, hapless thou,
    Who didst the fatal gift of beauty gain,

A dowry fraught with never ending pain,—
A seal of sorrow stamped upon thy brow :—
Oh, were thy bravery more, or less thy charms !
Then should thy foes, they whom thy loveliness
Now lures afar to conquer and possess,—
Adore thy beauty less, or dread thine arms!
No longer then should hostile torrents pour
Adown the Alps ; and Gallic troops be laved
In the red waters of the Po no more ;
Nor longer then, by foreign courage saved,
Barbarian succour should thy sons implore,
Vanquished or victors still by Goths enslaved.

The following sonnet indicates the tendency to a religious train
of thought, which marks the poetry of Filicaja.

ON THE EARTHQUAKE OF SICILY.

Thou buried City, o'er thy site I muse :—
What ! Does no monumental stone remain,
To say, Here yawned the earthquake-riven plain,
Here stood Catania, and here Syracuse ?
Along thy sad and solitary sand,
I seek thee in thyself, yet find instead
Nought but the dreadful stillness of the dead ;
Startled and horror-struck I wond'ring stand,
And cry : Oh terrible, tremendous course
Of God's decrees ! I see it and I feel it here ;
Shall I not comprehend and dread its force ?
Rise, ye lost cities, let your ruins rear
Their massy forms on high, portentous corse,
That trembling ages may behold and fear !

Filicaja's best *Canzoni* are all of considerable length ; and
therefore my limits will not permit me to introduce more than one
here. It is the first in order in the common editions of his works,
the first in time of the odes upon the Turkish invasion, and second
to none in point of merit. In my translation, I have preserved
the succession of the rhymes, and have endeavoured to imitate
the lyrical movements, of the original ode.

THE SIEGE OF VIENNA.

How long, O Lord, shall vengeance sleep,
And impious pride defy thy rod ?
How long thy faithful servants weep,
Scourged by the fierce barbaric host ?
Where, where, of thine almighty arm, O God,
Where is the ancient boast ?
While Tartar brands are drawn to steep
Thy fairest plains in Christian gore,
Why slumbers thy devouring wrath,
Nor sweeps the offender from thy path ?

And wilt thou hear thy sons deplore
Thy temples rifled, shrines no more,
Nor burst their galling chains asunder,
And arm thee with avenging thunder?
See the black cloud on Austria lower,
Big with terror, death, and wo;
Behold the wild barbarians pour
In rushing torrents o'er the land!
Lo! host on host, the infidel foe
Sweep along the Danube's strand,
And darkly serried spears the light of day o'erpower!
There the innumerable swords,
The banners of the East unite;
All Asia girds her loins for fight;
The Don's barbaric lords,
Sarmatia's haughty hordes,
Warriors from Thrace, and many a swarthy file
Banded on Syria's plains, or by the Nile.
Mark the tide of blood, that flows
Within Vienna's proud imperial walls;
Beneath a thousand deadly blows,
Dismayed, enfeebled, sunk, subdued,
Austria's queen of cities falls;
Vain are her lofty ramparts to elude
The fatal triumph of her foes;
Lo! her earth-fast battlements
Quiver and shake; hark to the thrilling cry
Of war, that rends the sky,
The groans of death, the wild laments,
The sobs of trembling innocents,
Of wildered matrons. pressing to their breast
All which they feared for most and loved the best.
Thine everlasting hand
Exalt, O Lord, that impious men may learn
How frail their armour to withstand
Thy power, the power of God supreme.
Let thy consuming vengeance burn
The guilty nations with its beam.
Bind them in slavery's iron band,
Or, as the scattered dust in summer flies
Chased by the raging blast of heaven,
Before thee be the Thracians driven.
Let trophied columns by the Danube rise,
And bear the inscription to the skies:
Warring against the Christian Jove in vain,
Here was the Ottoman Typhœus slain.
*   *   *   *   *   *   *
If destiny decree,
If fate's eternal leaves declare,
That Germany shall bend the knee
Before a Turkish despot's nod,
And Italy the Moslem yoke shall bear,

I bow in meek humility,
And kiss the holy rod.
Conquer, if such thy will,
Conquer the Scythian, while he drains
The noblest blood from Europe's veins,
And Havoc drinks her fill;—
We yield thee trembling homage still,
We rest in thy command secure,
For thou alone art just and wise and pure.
But shall I live to see the day,
When Tartar ploughs Germanic soil divide,
And Arab herdsmen fearless stray
And watch their flocks along the Rhine,
Where princely cities now o'erlook his tide ?
The Danube's towers no longer shine,
For hostile flame has given them to decay ;
Shall devastation wider spread ?
Where the proud ramparts of Vienna swell,
Shall solitary Echo dwell,
And human footsteps cease to tread ?
O God, avert the omen dread :
If Heaven the sentence did record,
O let thy mercy blot the fatal word !
Hark to the votive hymn resounding
Through the temple's cloistered aisles ;
See, the sacred shrine surrounding,
Perfumed clouds of incense rise.
The Pontiff opes the stately piles
Where many a buried treasure lies,
With liberal hand, rich, full, abounding,
He pours abroad the gold of Rome.
He summons every christian king
Against the Moslemim to bring
Their forces leagued for Christendom;
The brave Teutonic nations come,
And warlike Poles like thunderbolts descend,
Moved by his voice their brethren to defend.
He stands upon the Esquiline,
And lifts to heaven his holy arm,
Like Moses, clothed in power divine,
While faith and hope his strength sustain.
Merciful God, has prayer no charm
Thy rage to sooth, thy love to gain ?
The pious king of Judah's line
Beneath thine anger lowly bended,
And thou didst give him added years ;
The Assyrian Nineveh shed tears
Of humbled pride, when death impended,
And thus the fatal curse forefended ;
And wilt thou turn away thy face,
When heaven's Vicegerent seeks thy grace ?

49

Sacred fury fires my breast,
　　And fills my labouring soul.
Ye, who hold the lance in rest,
　　And gird you for the holy wars,
On, on, like ocean waves to conquest roll,
Christ and the Cross your leading star:
Already he proclaims your prowess blest:
Sound the loud trump of victory,
Rush to the combat, Soldiers of the Cross;
High let your banners triumphantly toss;
For the heathen shall perish, and songs of the free
Ring through the heavens in jubilee.
Why delay ye?　Buckle on the sword and targe,
And charge, victorious champions, charge.

　　　　　　　　　　　　　　　　C. C.

ROMANCE IN THE HEROIC AND MIDDLE AGES.

" Magnanima menzogna, or quando è il vero
" Si bello, che si possa a te preporre?"

[CONCLUDED.]

It might be an interesting occupation, could we afford time and
space for it, to compare the actual condition of society, as well as
the mythological fables exhibited in these old Romances, with those
of Greek tradition, and particularly with those represented in the
poems of Homer.　We suspect that the Middle Ages would be
found to have much the advantage over the Heroic, in point of
refinement.　In the gloomiest period, Europe retained something
of the warmth which had been imparted to it by the genial ray
of science, in the days of polished antiquity.

The simplicity or rather rusticity of Homer's heroes is not in
perfect conformity with the lofty tone of knight-errantry.　The
Princess Nausicaa washing her own linen, Ulysses carpentering
his own bedstead, Achilles cooking a steak and spreading the
table for dinner, are certainly not in the taste of the lordly feudal times, of the Olivers, Rolands, and Percivals, who would sooner have fasted a month, than have condescended to such plebeian
operations.*　Indeed this fasting is characteristic of the modern
knight-errant, while Homer, with more honesty, makes his heroes
huge feeders on most occasions.　Ulysses floating on the wreck, in

---

* A most singular custom of the Heroic Age was that of females of rank attending a distinguished guest of the family to the bath.　Thus the Princess Polycaste, by
the command of her father, officiates as waiting maid to Telemachus, and after the
ablution perfumes the body of the young hero with fragrant oils.　We recollect no
parallel piece of courtesy in the ancient English romance, though we may find one
in the old epic of Boiardo, who somewhere represents Angelica as ministering to
Orlando, in this (as it would be considered in these degenerate times, at least,) somewhat embarassing situation.

his passage from the island of Calypso, to that of the Phæacians, furnishes the only example of superhuman abstinence, that we recollect. Hospitality, the virtue of a rude age, is common to both ; and we find the Grecian heroes enlivening their banquet by the song of the minstrel, in the same manner as the feudal baron called in the aid of the *trouveur* to dispel the ennui of a winter's evening. Thus Demodocus is represented as chanting the wars of Troy, at the table of Alcinous ; and thus the *rhapsodies* of Homer were repeated long after his decease by the wandering bards of Ionia. The difficulty of retaining in the memory such long poems as the epics of Homer, was once deemed a sufficient argument against their having been perpetuated by oral tradition. Yet the longer romances of chivalry were recited in the same manner by the bards of that day, and for the purpose of convenient pauses, were divided into *fyttes*, each of which may have occupied a single recitation.

Homer has paid a noble tribute to the sex, in his beautiful portraits of Andromache, Nausicaa, and Penelope. The feelings which they appear to have inspired, however, are not akin to the gallantry painted in romance. Chivalry,

> "Both Paynim and the peers of Charlemagne,"

fought for the beautiful Angelica at Albracca ; but Greek heroism was displayed, on the plains of Troy, in defence of an injured husband, not in devotion to a woman. The guilty Helen, readmitted into favour by her unfortunate spouse, may be a noble picture, but it is not at all after the fashion of the romantic. In the earlier ages of chivalry, however, the fierce character of the knight appears to have been much more under the influence of religion than of love. Turpin's fanatical chronicle contains no allusion to love.

In religion, the difference between the Greek and Norman fictions, is yet more apparent. The modern knight, slain in battle, was a christian martyr, and anticipated the highest joys of Paradise. Orlando was carried up to heaven in the presence of his army. The oath administered at the ceremony of dubbing a knight, devoted him to the service of "God and the ladies." The ruling impulse of the Greek is conveyed in the rebuke of Hector to Polydamas :

> "The best augury is to fight in defence of one's *country*." *

For the gods, stained with human impurities, they could have little respect. The frequent notices of the celestial dissensions in

---

* Εἷς οἰωνὸς ἄριστος, ἀμύνεσθαι περὶ πάτρης.
Iliad, xii, 243.

Homer's writings afforded a specious pretext to Plato for excluding them from his imaginary republic. The belief in a future state suggested no very animating hopes to the Heathen warrior ; and the remark made by the shade of Achilles, when visited by his old companion Ulysses in the Elysian fields, that " he had rather be the slave of the meanest living man, than rule a sovereign among the dead," presents no very cheering view of their expectations in this way. The Elysium of Homer can hardly be said to contain one contented inhabitant.

The mythological machinery of the old English romance certainly exhibits a strong affinity with the ancient Pagan traditions. Hercules, Theseus, Jason were the knights-errant of their day, and the " Gorgons, hydras, and chimæras dire," which they encountered at every step, have again been called up to assail the " chevalier preux " of modern times. The dragon of the Hesperides, the winged Pegasus and Bellerophon, have propagated a numerous posterity like themselves ; the invulnerable hide of Achilles has successively cloathed the bulky frames of Ferragus, Orlando, and Morgante ; and the enchantments of Circe and Calypso have been perpetuated in all their potency, from the grosser legerdemain of Merlin, to the seductive spells of Spenser's and Ariosto's sorceresses. Notwithstanding this, some scholars would refer the modern mythology to the Arabians, others to the Goths, and others again to both these sources. There is indeed a remarkable correspondence in the superstitions of the most remote nations, too widely diffused, and of too high antiquity, to allow them to be referred exclusively to Grecian fable. Those who are desirous of seeing these curious analogies assembled in one view, may consult the very learned preface by the editor of the late reprint of Warton's " English Poetry."

We have been led into an inconsiderate length of prosing, on a subject that can possess few attractions for those of our readers, who reasonably take a livelier interest in the " *nugæ canoræ* " of the present, than of past ages.* Such as may incline to dip into

---

* We admit that the novelties of the present age, and of our own extraordinary situation in particular, are sufficient to justify a preference for them over every other subject of investigation : and moreover that our own citizens have in general showed a liberal spirit in the pursuit of every subject connected with intellectual advancement. But we could wish, that when a work like Heeren's "Politics of Ancient Greece," the most profound disquisition that has yet appeared on the condition of that interesting people, has been translated by one of our own scholars, whose attainments have enabled him to do rare justice both to the subject and the language in which it was originally discussed; and which has moreover been recommended to the notice of the public in more than one able review,—we could wish, we say, for the credit of the "literary emporium," that a work of merit, like this, should, after eighteen month's publication, have obtained sufficient patronage to indemnify the enterprising publishers for the bare cost of the paper consumed in a moderate edition of it.

these antiquated tales of chivalry, will find a fair specimen of them in the metrical romance of "Sir Tristrem," published by Scott in the 4th vol. of his poetical works, Edin. 1821, accompanied by a rich collection of explanatory notes. His introduction endeavours to prove, that the English language was applied to poetry in Scotland, before it was so used in the sister kingdom. Whether the author may be thought to have established this startling conclusion, or not, the Essay is worth reading for its ingenious reasoning and antiquarian erudition. Among other accessible works, Ellis and Ritson have given extracts from several metrical romances. Southey has republished in two vols. 4to. Mallory's ancient compilation of the "Morte d' Arthur," which contains the series relating to the Welsh chieftain, done into most antiquated prose. Southey's elegant version of the Spanish or Portuguese Amadis, is however much more common. It has no connexion with the particular *cycli* of romances of which we have been speaking; but it may furnish some notion of the characteristics of the chivalrous ages; it is moreover well worth reading for its Arabic richness of invention; and the original, it may be remembered, was among the few of their race, which the Curate reprieved from the conflagration of Don Quixote's library.

ORIGINAL POETRY.

MORNING TWILIGHT.

The mountains are blue in the morning air,
And the woods are sparkling with dewy light;
The winds, as they wind through the hollows, bear
The breath of the blossoms that wake by night:
Wide o'er the bending meadows roll
The mists, like a lightly moving sea;
The sun is not risen — and over the whole
There hovers a silent mystery.

The pure blue sky is in calm repose;
The pillowy clouds are sleeping there;
So stilly the brook in its covert flows,
You would think its murmur a breath of air.
The water that floats in the glassy pool,
Half hid by the willows that line its brink,
In its deep recess has a look so cool,
One would worship its nymph, as he bent to drink.

Pure and beautiful thoughts, at this early hour,
Go off to the home of the bright and blessed;
They steal on the heart with an unseen power,
And its passionate throbbings are laid at rest:

O! who would not catch, from the quiet sky
And the mountains that soar in the hazy air,
When his harbinger tells that the sun is nigh,
The visions of bliss that are floating there.

                                                        P.

" The memory of joys that are past."
                                        Ossian.

Where are now the flowers that once detained me
Like a loiterer on my early way ?
Where the fragrant wreaths that softly chained me,
When young life was like an infant's play ?

Were they but the fancied dreams, that hover
Round the couch where tender hearts repose ?
Only pictured veils that brightly cover
With their skyey tints a world of woes?

They are gone—but Memory loves to cherish
All their sweetness in her deepest core.
Ah ! the recollection cannot perish,
Though the eye may never meet them more.

There are hopes, that like enchantment brighten ,
Gaily in the van of coming years ;
They are never met—and yet they lighten,
When we walk in sorrow and in tears.

When the present only tells of anguish,
Then we know their worth, and only then :
O ! the wasted heart will cease to languish,
When it thinks of joys that might have been.

Age, and suffering, and want, may sever
Every link, that bound to life, in twain :
Hope—even Hope may vanish, but forever
Memory with her visions will remain.

                                                        P.

THE SEA DIVER.

My way is on the bright blue sea,·
  My sleep upon its rocking tide ;
And many an eye has followed me
  Where billows clasp the worn sea-side.

My plumage bears the crimson blush,
  When ocean by the sun is kissed !
When fades the evening's purple flush,
  My dark wing cleaves the silver mist.

Full many a fathom down beneath
  The bright arch of the splendid deep
My ear has heard the sea-shell breathe
  O'er living myriads in their sleep.

They rested by the coral throne,
　And by the pearly diadem;
Where the pale sea-grape had o'ergrown
　The glorious dwellings made for them.

At night upon my storm-drenched wing,
　I poised above a helmless bark,
And soon I saw the shattered thing
　Had passed away and left no mark.

And when the wind and storm were done,
　A ship, that had rode out the gale,
Sunk down—without a signal gun,
　And none was left to tell the tale.

I saw the pomp of day depart,—
　The cloud resign its golden crown,
When to the ocean's beating heart,
　The sailor's wasted corse went down.

Peace be to those whose graves are made
　Beneath the bright and silver sea!—
Peace—that their relics there were laid
　With no vain pride and pageantry.

　　　　　　　　　　　　H. W. L.

THE SUMMER MORNING.

'T is rapture to hail the morning's birth,
When heaven seems bending to greet the earth,
And the fresh breeze, warm with life, sweeps by,
As a token of love from the crimson sky.
The moon has a mantle of silvery light,
When she walks with grace as the queen of night;
She's bright as the hopes of my youthful day—
She's cold as the friends who have passed away.
But thou, sweet daughter of beautiful spring,
O would I could chant the fit welcoming,
Or number the graces that round thee play,
From thy first soft glance of dawning day,
Till thy heaven-wrought robe is floating free,
And the sun has followed to gaze on thee.
The city may boast its gilded halls,
Where Fashion presides at her revels and balls;
And art may compel the air to fling
Such streams of light from its silver wing,
As rival the monarch of day's proud glare,
But the sweetness of morn is wanting there:
And happier far I deem my lot,
To muse at will in this lonely spot.
This fallen tree is my chosen seat,
Where the violets bloom beneath my feet;
Around me the flowery spray is shed,
And the young leaves flutter above my head.

As they joyed in the zephyr's breath to play,
And sun themselves in the eye of day.
Oh while on the glorious scene I gaze,
My heart is warmed with the morning rays;
And fancies bright as yon kindling sky,
Where gold is blending with purple dye;
And feelings pure as the pearly drop,
That trembles within the daisy's cup;
And thoughts as calm as the airs that pass,
Nor bend a blade of the tender grass;—
O morning, well may I deem thee divine,
When such fancies, feelings, and thoughts, are mine.

CORNELIA.

CRITICAL NOTICES.

Resignation, an American Novel. By a Lady, in 2 vols. 12mo. Boston. 1825. pp. 408 and 444.

THE story of this novel opens with the death of Mr Ellison, the father of the heroine of the work, upon Bunker Hill, on that memorable era, the 17th of June 1775,—a place singularly well chosen to kill a man in, now there is a monument erecting probably over his very grave. Elizabeth Ellison's mother soon dies, and she is taken to Virginia by Mr Harlington, her maternal uncle. This transfers the scene from Massachusetts to Virginia. While yet children, an attachment of peculiar interest arises between Elizabeth and Francis Onsville, whose father was a clergyman, educated in Scotland, and whose mother was a " highland lassie," of rich and respectable parentage. Francis receives a theological education in this country, but is obliged to remove to Aberdeen (Scotland) to comply with the dying request of his mother. Elizabeth is obliged by circumstances to remain in America, and the separation of the lovers necessarily causes a great deal of misery, which is heightened and aggravated by many other calamities. The scene is now partially transferred to Scotland. Francis, after having been a settled minister in Aberdeen, returns to New England, where Elizabeth is preparing to settle, just in time to interrupt an engagement between her and a boarding-school teacher. The first love prevails, and Francis and Elizabeth remove again to Virginia and are married. The scenes of the novel are laid, as our readers will perceive, in divers places. The characters are very numerous, so numerous indeed, that we cannot even call them up by name and tell where they were born, whom they married, and where they died.

Notwithstanding the very unnecessary number of characters, the complicated plan of the work, and our discouraging prepossessions, we have read it with considerable interest. The severity of criticism, which occasionally appears in our remarks upon the lighter works which come under our notice, is disarmed in this instance by the christian benevolence and the deep-toned piety with which our author's heart is imbued, and which pervades the whole work.

The story is one, which describes no magnificent achievements, nor convulsions of nations. There are in it no striking events,—no great catastrophe,—no plots and counterplots, to absorb the attention of the reader; and of course we have not felt in reading it that degree of interest which is excited by the rapid description of events and circumstances, important on account of their connexion with some great catastrophe. Perhaps it is well that it is so; for the author's design evidently was to recommend religion as it is exhibited in the quiet of domestic life. She has effectually guarded against one error—that of exhibiting human life brighter than it really is. Those, who complain of works of fiction, because they fill the youthful mind with the idea, that life is made up of chivalrous adventure, cannot utter the same complaint against the author of " Resignation." We think that she has erred on the other side, by representing life as a scene of sorrow too unmingled, and this world as a dwelling-place in which it is undesirable to live. For ourselves we believe, that God has made this world as happy as it could be, and be at the same time a state of probation; and that if man will serve him in sincerity, even on earth he shall be happy. Very rarely is it the case, that a family, and all connected with it by consanguinity or friendship, are involved in so many calamities as befell the heroes and heroines of " Resignation." There are many tender and affecting scenes in the course of the book; but we very much regret that they should be drawn out into the unnecessary length of two closely printed volumes. This diffuseness impairs the interest of the narration, and the reader's attention flags long before he finishes one volume. If our author's pen had been accustomed to more rapid and concise description, she would have interested her readers much more, and left more definite and vivid impressions on their minds. She needs more of that comprehensive activity of mind, which looks through a subject or a train of fictitious events, with a glance, giving prominence and definiteness to the most important views and circumstances, and sinking those which are unimportant into the shade. She needs a bolder hand, and an eye better disciplined in the rules of perspective. A good novelist, like a good painter, will make his scenes and heroes stand forth in an attitude of strength. One that is inferior may describe many personages and scenes in an interesting manner, but his paintings, like those of the Flemish schools, however beautiful may be the colouring, will wear an air of confusion, which will leave the mind of the reader in a dubious and unsatisfied state.

" Resignation " has other faults. We might mention the Irish and Negro gibberish, which the author has very unnecessarily introduced, as great blemishes to the work. Besides, we have to inform our author, and we can do it from actual and personal knowledge and observation, that she has not caught the negro dialect in Virginia at all. She has put into their mouths English far more horribly mangled than any which they are in the habit of using. Our author, too, should have been better acquainted with the diseases of Virginia. In her novel she has caused more to die of consumption in the neighbourhood of Richmond, than probably ever died of that disease in the whole state, from among its native inhabitants. If disposed, we could point out many other faults, but we do not wish to discourage. We like to see the daughters of America employing their pens, especially when they are enlisted on the side of piety

50

and virtue.   But let them not come before the public with too sanguine
expectations.   If they write novels, let them remember that small, thin
volumes, with wide margins and spaces, are much more acceptable generally, than those where the author is more prodigal of words; and that
one volume is far better than two.

1. The Christian Indian; or Times of the First Settlers.   (The First of a Series of
American Tales.)   1 vol. 12mo. New York. 1825. pp. 251.
2. Stranger of the Valley; or Louisa and Adelaide.   An American Tale.   By
a Lady. 2 vols. 12mo. New York. 1825.
3. Frederick de Algeroy, the Hero of Camden Plains.   A Revolutionary Tale.
By Giles Gazer, Esq. New York. 1825. pp. 235.

It is well known to many of our readers, that in the year 1614 the
celebrated Capt. Smith undertook a voyage of discovery and trade to
New-England, then called North Virginia. The author of the first of the
novels supposes that he took with him, on this occasion, a young Indian,
called Tantum, who had some years before been carried to England. The
voyage was on the whole unsuccessful, and accompanied as usual with occasional skirmishes with the natives.   In one of them, according to our
author, a young Englishman was wounded and left for dead.   He is recovered, however, and secreted by an old squaw.   In her wigwam he is
attended by a young Indian maiden, who falls in love with him, and conducts him, through many adventures, to a Dutch fort on the Hudson river.   Miona, the young woman, had been contracted to Tantum, who, in
some mysterious manner, assists her in guiding and protecting the white
man.   Miona finally kills herself to protect the Englishman from some
danger threatened by an Indian prophet; and the book ends with the
departure of the hero for Europe, and an explanatory letter from Tantum.   The object of the work is to set the Indian character in a better
light, than the author supposes it has yet appeared in, and to excite our
sympathy with the wrongs and sufferings of that devoted race.   It is
pretty well written, but we think it wants interest, and that the story
moves slowly and heavily, without sufficient variety of incident.   As it
is contained, however, in a single small volume, it is not " a great evil."
It is more important when considered as the first of a series.   It is so
announced on the title page; and we must confess, that we look forward
with some dread to the task of reading and noticing, however slightly,
a number of works, which, to judge from this specimen, will not be
likely to rise above mediocrity.
The second in order of these works reminded us of a chemical doctrine, to which, as that science has been so fashionable of late years, we
may venture to allude, without much risk of being charged with
pedantry.   The story is complicated, but the interest of it depends,
in the main, upon the adventures of several couples, who were contracted without any violent affection; united, as it were by quies-
cent affinity. They meet, however, in the course of the story, with
certain divellent affinities, and form new combinations, in some instances with detonation, and in others with slight effervescence.   In
plain English, the parties severally fall in love with other persons, and
marry them, with more or less difficulty to themselves and their friends.
It is an indifferent novel, with a plot and a set of *dramatis personæ*

which belong to another generation of novel-readers, and seem hackneyed, uninteresting, and tedious to the readers of the present day.

The third, "Frederick de Algeroy," we have read through with great difficulty. If it were not too despicable for serious notice, we should be tempted to treat parts of it with extreme severity. It is calculated to have a bad influence, if it has any; but we trust that the wretchedness of its execution will prevent its finding many readers.

With respect to works of this class, we desire to remark in general, that if we sometimes speak of them with bitterness, we ought not to be accused of unprovoked severity. It is expected of us to notice American publications. We must read the volumes which are deluging the community under the name of American novels,—we are mortal men, gifted with no more temper and patience than our fellows, and the authors must take the consequences.

A Brief Outline of the Evidences of the Christian Religion. By Archibald Alexander, Professor of Didactic and Polemic Theology in the Theological Seminary at Princeton, N. J. 1825. 18mo. pp. 299.

THE author of this book lays no claim to originality, either in regard to the several branches of evidence, or to the method of their arrangement. His object appears to have been, to present the evidences of our religion in a condensed and popular form, adapted rather to the common class of readers, than to those who wish to search deeply into the origin and progress of Christianity, or the grounds upon which our faith in it may be firmly established. This book, however, is well worth the perusal of the professed theologian. The author has touched upon almost every department of the evidences, and generally allotted to each its proper value. He has collected much important matter in a small compass, and expressed it in a clear and forcible manner. Thus he has effectually done all, which he proposed to himself to do. And they who feel desirous of renewing, or more firmly fixing, their impressions of the truths of revelation, cannot, perhaps, do it with less labour, than by reading with attention this little book.

INTELLIGENCE.

LAW SCHOOL AT NORTHAMPTON.

We extract from a circular letter of the gentlemen at the head of this establishment,* the following account of the advantages afforded to students.

"WE have an extensive law library, to which the students can at all times have access, and there are several rooms in the same building where the library is placed. A lecture of an hour is given three days in a week, when we are not occupied in court, and will probably be given every day after the present year. Recitations are also attended to three times a week; and the discussion of a legal question, by the

---

* Hon. E. H. Mills and Samuel Howe.

students, takes place once a week. To give our pupils an acquaintance with the practical details of the profession, and in some measure to supply to them the advantages of experience, in addition to the professional business done in the office, great pains are taken to state to them the cases which occur on the circuits, and the various questions raised in the trial, the arguments urged in the discussion, and the disposition finally made of them. * * *

"We are situated in one of the most delightful and healthy villages in New England. Its scenery is almost unequalled in our country. Its population is moral and intelligent—and comprises many gentlemen of literary, scientific, and professional eminence. Our communications with every part of the country are easy and frequent, and no day passes without being able to receive and communicate intelligence in every direction. Our establishment is at present in the centre of the village, but we have it in contemplation shortly to remove it to a more retired part of the town, in the immediate neighbourhood of the justly celebrated school of Messrs Cogswell and Bancroft, on Round hill. Our terms are one hundred dollars a year, including rooms, fuel, and candles."

ADDITIONAL VOLUMES OF THE ARABIAN NIGHTS' ENTERTAINMENTS.

Two or three additional volumes of these Tales, translated by the Rev. Dr Wait, from the Arabic manuscripts in the public library of the University of Cambridge, are about to be published in England.

VARIATION OF BOILING POINTS AND INCREASED PRODUCTION OF VAPOUR.

It has been known, for some time, that when certain kinds of extraneous substances are introduced into boiling fluids, considerable effect is produced upon the boiling point, vapour being formed either at lower points, or with much increased facility. Thus, Gay-Lussac has shown, that metal filings thrown into water, heated in a glass vessel, lower the boiling point of the water $2°$ or $3°$; and Mr South pointed out the effect produced by putting platina wire, or slips of platina foil, into hot sulphuric acid, causing it to boil readily, quietly, and at lower points in glass vessels, than it otherwise would do, the difference here being several degrees. Dr Bostock has observed a remarkable fact of this kind in the extent to which the boiling point of ether may be changed by the introduction of a small chip of wood, or a portion of quill or feather of any kind. Ether in a glass vessel, boiled freely at $112°$, and with difficulty at $110°$. On employing another glass vessel, it would not boil till the temperature had attained $150°$, and the latter point was retained in other vessels. Repeating the experiment in a new vessel, it boiled earlier than before, but the vapour was observed to come off from one point where some substance had adhered to the glass. This led to the introduction of a small cedar chip, when the wood was quickly covered with bubbles, and the ether brought rapidly into ebullition. In this way ether boiled at $102°$, which, without the wood, required $150°$. The wood was not so effectual after some time as at first. When completely soaked with the ether, it sunk to the bottom, and the ebullition nearly ceased; a fresh piece renewed it. Fragments of broken glass lowered the boiling point considerably. A small piece of metallic wire or copper filing, put into ether at 145°, caused a sudden and copious explosion of gas and vapour, and lowered the boiling point many degrees. Plunging a thermometer into the hot ether, caused the production of bubbles at a temperature many degrees below the boiling point when no thermometer was present; after a time the effect ceased, but a removal of the thermometer from the ether, and a re-immersion of it, produced a repetition of the effect. The cedar wood acted best when perfectly dry. Alcohol of specific gravity 848, boiled in a glass vessel at 182°, but by dropping in successive pieces of cedar wood, the boiling point was reduced as much as 30 or 40°. The boiling point of water Dr Bostock found, was altered 4° or 5° by chips of cedar wood, requiring a temperature of about 217° when heated in a glass tube, by means of hot brine, but being brought down to the usual boiling point by the chips.

CRIMES IN SWEDEN.

THE state of crime in Sweden is less distressing than in most other countries. The whole number of persons committed to prison for offences does not exceed 1500, viz. about 800 convicted of various crimes, and 700 imprisoned for vagrancy and other offences of police. A royal commissioner has been appointed to superintend all the prisons and houses of correction, so as to place their discipline and administration on a common footing. A house of correction is building at Stockholm, in which the prisoners will be allowed part of the gains made by their work, and may lay it up to form a sum against the time of their liberation. Similar measures are also in progress at Christiana in Norway.

NEW PUBLICATIONS.

AGRICULTURE AND CHEMISTRY.

Introductory Discourse to a few Lectures on the Application of Chemistry to Agriculture, delivered before the New York Atheneum. By William James Mac Neven, M. D. 8vo. pp. 40. New York. G. & C. Carvill.

HISTORY.

History of Boston, No. 12. Boston.

Annals of the American Revolution; or a Record of the Causes and Events, which produced and terminated in the Establishment and Independence of the American Republic, &c. To which is prefixed a summary Account of the Settlement of the Country, and some of the principal Indian Wars, which have, at successive periods, afflicted its Inhabitants. To which are added Remarks on the Principles and Comparative Advantages of the Constitution of our National Government, and an Appendix, containing a Biography of the principal Military Officers, who were instrumental in achieving our Independence, compiled from a Mass of authentic Documents, and arranged in Chronological and Historical Order. By Jedidiah Morse, D. D. Author of the American Universal Gazeteer. 8vo. pp. 450. Hartford.

This title is sufficiently full and explicit, and requires no commentary from us.

LAW.

Laws of the State of New-York, in relation to the Erie and Champlain Canals, together with the Annual Reports of the Canal Commissioners, and other Documents requisite for a complete official History of these Works. With Surveys, and other Engravings. Containing a detailed Account of the Dimensions and Cost of the Canal and the several Locks. 2 vols. royal 8vo. Albany. Published by the Authority of the State.

MATHEMATICS.

A Treatise on Surveying, &c. By the Rev. Abel Flint. Fifth Edition. With Additions and Illustrations. By George Gillett, Surveyor-General of the State of Connecticut. 8vo. Hartford.

Walsh's Mercantile Arithmetic. Fifth Edition. Salem. J. R. Buffum.

MISCELLANEOUS.

Christian Patriotism: An Address delivered at Concord, July the Fourth, 1825. By the Rev. Nathaniel Bouton. 8vo. pp. 24. Concord.

A Plea for Africa, delivered July the Fourth. By the Rev. Leonard Bacon. 8vo. pp. 22. New Haven. T. G. Woodward & Co.

The New York Review and Atheneum Magazine. No. 3, for August 1825.

Boston Monthly Magazine. No. 3. for August, 1825.

A Sermon preached to the Church in Brattle Street, with Notes Historical and Biographical. By John G. Palfrey, Pastor of the Church. 8vo. pp. 81. Boston.

The Long Island Journal of Philosophy and Cabinet of Variety, No. 3, for July. Huntington, L. I.

NOVELS.

Frederick De Algeroy, the Hero of Camden Plains. A Revolutionary Tale. By Giles Gazer, Esq. 1 vol. 12mo. pp. 235. New York. Collins & Co. and others.

Tadeuskund, the Last King of the Lenape. An Historical Tale. 12mo. pp. 276. Boston. Cummings, Hilliard, & Co.

Tales of the Crusaders. By the Author of Waverley, Quentin Durward, &c. 12mo. 4 vols in 2. [The Betrothed. pp. 163, 177. The Talisman. pp. 168, 180.] Philadelphia.

ORNITHOLOGY.

American Ornithology; or the Natural History of Birds inhabiting the United States, not given by Wilson; with Figures drawn, engraved, and coloured. By Charles Lucien Bonaparte. Vol. 1st. Imperial 4to. Philadelphia. Samuel Augustus Mitchell.

This work, which is to be comprised in three volumes, is intended as a Supplement to Wilson, and is the most splendidly executed book that has ever issued from the American Press.

POETRY.

The Garland, or New General Repository of Fugitive Poetry. Edited by G. A. Gamage. No. 1, June, 1825. 8vo. pp. 16.

The design of this publication is good, and this first number promises well for the execution, as it contains several beautiful pieces. The price, four dollars per annum, for such a volume of selections as will be composed of twelve numbers of

16 pages each, seems to us rather high. We suppose that it is by a typographical error, that the titles of the pieces, in the list of contents, stand in a different order from that of the pieces themselves in the number.

POLITICAL ECONOMY.

Outlines of Political Economy ; being a Republication of the Article upon that subject, contained in the Edinburgh Supplement to the Encyclopædia Britannica. Together with Notes explanatory and critical, and a Summary of the Science. By Rev. John M'Vickar, A. M. of Columbia College. 8vo. pp. 188. New York. Wilder & Campbell.

THEOLOGY.

Missionary Herald. Vol. XXI. No. 8, for August. Boston. Crocker & Brewster.

A Sermon on Human Depravity. By Edmund Q. Sewall. 8vo. pp. 34. Amherst, N. H.

The American Baptist Magazine. Vol. V. No. 8, for August. Boston.

The Gospel Advocate, for August. Vol. V. No. 8. Boston.

AMERICAN EDITIONS OF FOREIGN WORKS.

Quarterly Review. No. 63, for June. Boston.

Memoirs and Reflections of Count Segur, written by himself. 1 vol. 8vo. pp. 359. Boston and New York.

Stories, selected from the History of England, for Children. Hartford.

A Compend of History from the Earliest Times ; comprehending a general View of the Present State of the World, with respect to Civilization, Religion, and Government, and a brief Dissertation on the Importance of Historical Knowledge. By Samuel Whelpley, D. D. Principal of the Newark Academy. Eighth Edition, with Corrections and important Additions and Improvements, by Rev. Joseph Emerson, Principal of the Female Seminary in Wethersfield. 2 vols. in 1. Boston.

The Surgical and Physiological Works of John Abernethy, F. R. S. &c. &c. From the Sixth London Edition. Embracing Reflections of Gall and Spurzheim's System of Physiology and Phrenology. 2 vols. 8vo. Hartford.

The Memoirs of Joseph Fouché, Duke of Otranto, Minister of the General Police of France. Translated from the French. 1 vol. 8vo. pp. 474. Boston.

Letters on the Importance, Duty, and Advantage of Early Rising ; addressed to the Heads of Families, the Man of Business, the Lover of Nature, the Student, and the Christian. By A. C. Buckland. From the Fifth London Edition, with an additional Letter and a Preface. 18mo. pp. 237. Boston.

Village Dialogues, between Farmer Littleworth, Thomas Newman, Rev. Mr. Lovegood and others. By the Rev. Rowland Hill, A. M. From the Eighteenth London Edition, with additional Dialogues. 3 vols. 12mo. New York.

LIST OF WORKS IN PRESS.

The Christian Father's Present to his Children. By the Rev. J. A. James. 2 vols. 18mo. Boston.

Elements of Phrenology. By George Combe, with two Engravings. Philadelphia. E. Littell.

Pharmacologia. 2 vols. 8vo. Sixth Edition. By John Ayrton Paris, M D.

A Dictionary of Pathology and the Practice of Medicine. 1 royal 8vo. vol.

Blackall on Dropsy. From the Fourth London Edition.

Sir Astley Cooper's Lectures. Complete Edition.

Potter's Grecian Antiquities. By Charles Anthon. 1 vol. 8vo. New York.

Essays on Education. By the Rev. William Barrow, Philadelphia. Harrison Hall.

Biographical Memoirs of Eminent Men, with Portraits, Autographs, &c. Philadelphia.

The Commercial Chart and Universal Traveller. Containing general al Information respecting Roads, Steam-Boats, Stages, Packets, Hotels, &c. in the United States. By D. Hewitt.

Merivale's Reports. 3 vols. O. Halsted. New York.

Shaw's Manual for the Student of Anatomy. Revised, and with Notes. By William Anderson, D. D. Troy, N. York.

Atkins' Reports, third London Edition, revised and corrected, with Notes and References. By Francis W. Sanders. 3 vols. royal 8vo. New York.

History of the United States. 1 vol. 12mo. New York. C. Wiley.

Seventeenth and Eighteenth Cantos of Don Juan. C. Wiley.

Law of Actions and Trials at Nisi Prius. By Isaac Espinasse. New York.

Lévizac's Grammar. 1 vol. 12mo. New York.

Questions to Adam's Roman Antiquities, for the use of Colleges, &c.

The Precepts of Jesus, the Guide to Peace and Happiness, extracted from the Books of the New Testament ascribed to the Four Evangelists. To which are added, the First and Second Appeal to the Christian Public, in reply to the Observations of Dr Marshman, of Serampore. By Rammohun Roy, of Calcutta. From the London Edition. New York. B. Bates.

An Elementary System of Physiology. By John Bostock, M. D. Boston.

A Practical Treatise on the Law of Evidence, and Digest of Proofs, in Civil and Criminal Proceedings. By Thomas Starkie, Esq. of the Inner Temple, Barrister at Law. With Notes and References to American Decisions. By Theron Metcalf. 3 vols. 8vo. Boston.

The Works of the Right Hon. Edmund Burke. Complete from the last London Edition. Boston.

The "Practical Reader," in five books. By M. R. Bartlett. Utica N. Y.

A Planisphere or Map of the Sensible Heavens in two Hemispheres one N. and the other S. divided at the Equinoxial Circle. By M. R. Bartlett.

Published on the first and fifteenth day of every month, by CUMMINGS, HILLIARD, & Co., No. 134 Washington-Street, Boston, for the Proprietors. Terms, $5 per annum. Cambridge : Printed at the University Press, by Hilliard & Metcalf.

THE UNITED STATES

LITERARY GAZETTE.

| Vol. II. | SEPTEMBER 1, 1825. | No. 11. |

REVIEWS.

1. *Tales of the Crusaders.* By the author of "*Waverley*," "*Quentin Durward*," &c. 4 vols in 2. [The Betrothed. pp. 163, 177. The Talisman. pp. 168, 130.] Philadelphia. 1825.
2. *Lives of the Novelists.* By Sir WALTER SCOTT. Philadelphia. 1825. 2 vols. 12mo.

It is now a twelvemonth precisely since we had the opportunity of reviewing a Waverley novel, and we have been compelled in the interim to peruse so many unhappy imitations, that the very contrast may incline us to hold a more favourable opinion of the " Tales of the Crusaders," than they really merit ; as meat of an indifferent quality and carelessly prepared may have the *haut gout* for a palate just escaped from the nauseousness of draughts and the insipidity of ptisans.

The events of the first tale, entitled " The Betrothed," are supposed to have happened on the borders or marches of Wales, in the latter part of the twelfth century and during the reign of Henry the Second. Gwenwyn, a Welsh Prince, is so far forgetful of prudence and good policy, as to ask the hand of Eveline, daughter of Raymond Berenger, the Norman castellane of a fortress in his neighbourhood, and of course a formidable enemy to his name and nation. Raymond refuses on two grounds ; first, that such matches are unequal, ill-assorted, and impolitic ; and secondly, that his daughter is already promised to Hugo de Lacy, a Noble Norman and the Constable of Chester. Either of these reasons was enough to rouse the fury of the Camorian, who advances to the attack of the

51

fortress at such short warning, that the Norman has not time to receive the succours of the neighbouring barons. This would have been a matter of little consequence to Raymond, and the Welsh might have knocked their heads against the walls, to as little purpose as they had often done before, but for an unfortunate promise which, during the short preceding interval of tranquillity, he had made to Gwenwyn, to meet him on any future occasion in fair fight and without the protection of ditches and engines. The chivalrous notions of the times compelled him to march out with a part of his slender garrison to certain destruction, leaving the castle and his daughter to the protection of a small band of Flemish feudatories. The knight is of course slain, and the victorious Gwenwyn attacks the castle, which, after being defended a single day with difficulty, is relieved by the advance of Hugo de Lacy, by whom the Welsh Prince is slain and his followers cut to pieces. In return for this service, and in consequence of certain previous arrangements with her father, he seeks the hand of Eveline, and after a reasonable time is solemnly affianced to her. This conduct excites the indignation of Baldwin, archbishop of Canterbury, by whose preaching the Constable had lately been induced to assume the ensigns of a Crusader. He insists on the immediate performance of his vow, and De Lacy is obliged to leave his betrothed bride under the care of his nephew Damian. The result of this arrangement every reader will anticipate. The Constable, on his return, finds his affairs at home on the point of utter ruin, and Damian charged with breach of trust to him and his sovereign. Though these charges prove to be in the main false, De Lacy is wise enough to perceive that Eveline will be a more suitable bride for his nephew, and the work closes with their marriage.

Our limits will not permit more than this meagre abstract of the story, of which the interest is increased by much connecting action, and many subordinate characters. Of these last, Wilkin Flammock, the leader of the Flemings, and his daughter Rose, are evidently the favourites of the author and of course the most interesting to the reader. We find in this Tale a degree of a fault common to many imitations of this class of novels :—the characters are too numerous and the interest divided among too many. The consequence of this is, that the author has not space to make any one sufficiently interesting. Thus the character of De Lacy is a grand conception, but he does not appear long enough to make a full impression.

We want to see more of him and to have him shown in various circumstances and in different lights, and regret that the author leaves him just when he is beginning to enter into the spirit of the delineation. Moreover the novelist is evidently shackled in this work as in some others, by the circumstances of time and place. The reader of Shakspeare seldom considers any more than the author seems to have done, whether his persons are French or English, Greeks or Romans, or even human or supernatural; they have an intellectual identity, which is but slightly dependent upon outward circumstances. Macbeth is Macbeth, though dressed in a full-bottomed wig and Louis-Quatorze boots. The sentiments, affections, and passions are what strikes us in Ariel and Caliban, not the wings of the one or the claws of the other. But we cannot but feel occasionally that the Scottish author is labouring to make Normans of the twelfth century, or Frenchmen of the fifteenth. It may be that he has succeeded; few of us have antiquarian lore sufficient to detect his mistakes if any exist. But it requires only observation of our fellow-creatures to perceive, when an author mingles in the same character traits inconsistent with themselves, or foreign to humanity. Our limits will not permit us to pursue this subject farther, and with one extract from this tale, we shall pass on to the second. Certain proceedings of Wilkin which seemed dubious in the eyes of the confessor of the castle, give rise to the following dialogue. Our readers will perceive that the author is not able entirely to forget Friar Tuck.

At this place, which was rather the weakest point of the Garde Doloureuse, the good father found Wilkin Flammock anxiously superintending the necessary measures of defence. He greeted him courteously, congratulated him on the stock of provisions with which the castle had been supplied during the night, and was inquiring how they had been so happily introduced through the Welch besiegers, when Wilkin took the first occasion to interrupt him.

"Of all this another time, good father; but I wish at present, and before other discourse, to consult thee on a matter which presses my conscience, and moreover deeply concerns my worldly estate."

"Speak on, my excellent son," said the father, conceiving that he should thus gain the key to Wilkin's real intentions. "O, a tender conscience is a jewel! and he that will not listen when it saith, 'Pour out thy doubts into the ear of the priest,' shall one day have his own dolorous outcries choaked with fire and brimstone. Thou wert ever of a tender conscience, son Wilkin, though thou hast but a rough and borrel bearing."

"Well, then," said Wilkin, "you are to know, good father, that I have some dealings with my neighbour, Jan Vanwelt, concerning my daughter Rose, and that he has paid me certain guilders on condition that I will match her to him."

"Pshaw, pshaw! my good son," said the disappointed confessor, "this gear can lie over—this is no time for marrying or giving in marriage, when we are all like to be murdered."

"Nay, but hear me, good father," said the Fleming, "for this point of conscience concerns the present case more nearly than you wot of. You must know I have no will to bestow Rose on this same Jan Vanwelt, who is old, and of ill conditions; and I would know of you whether I may, in conscience, refuse him my consent."

"Truly," said Aldrovand, "Rose is a pretty lass, though somewhat hasty; and I think you may honestly withdraw your consent, always on paying back the guilders you have received."

"But there lies the pinch, good father," said the Fleming—"the refunding this money will reduce me to utter poverty. The Welsh have destroyed my substance; and this handful of money is all, God help me! on which I must begin the world again."

"Nevertheless, son Wilkin," said Aldrovand, "thou must keep thy word, or pay the forfeit; for what saith the text? *Quis habitabit in tabernaculo, quis requiescet in monte sancto?*—Who shall ascend to the tabernacle, and dwell in the holy mountain? Is it not answered again, *Qui jurat proximo et non decepit?*—Go to, my son—break not thy plighted word for a little filthy lucre—better is an empty stomach and a hungry heart with a clear conscience, than a fatted ox with iniquity and word-breaking.—Sawest thou not our late noble lord, who (may his soul be happy!) chose rather to die in unequal battle, like a true knight, than live a perjured man, though he had but spoken a rash word to a Welchman over a wine flask?"

"Alas! then," said the Fleming, "this is even what I feared! We must e'en render up the castle, or restore to the Welchman Jorworth, the cattle, by means of which I had schemed to victual and defend it."

"How—wherefore—what doest thou mean?" said the monk in astonishment. "I speak to thee of Rose Flammock, and Jan Van-devil, or whatever you call him, and you reply with talk about cattle and castles, and I wot not what!"

"So please you, holy father, I did but speak in parables. This castle was the daughter I had promised to deliver over—the Welchman Jan Vanwelt, and the guilders were the cattle he has sent in, as a part-payment beforehand of my guerdon."

"Parables!" said the monk, colouring with anger at the trick put upon him; "what has a boor like thee to do with parables?—But I forgive thee—I forgive thee."

"I am therefore to yield the castle to the Welchman or restore him his cattle?" said the impenetrable Dutchman.

"Sooner yield thy soul to Satan!" replied the monk.

"I fear me it must be the alternative," said the Fleming; "for the example of thy honourable lord ————"

"The example of an honourable fool——" answered the monk; then presently subjoined, "Our Lady be with her servant!—this Belgic-brained boor makes me forget what I would say."

"Nay, but the holy text which your reverence cited to me even now," continued the Fleming.

" Go to," said the monk ; "what hast thou to do to presume to think
of texts?—knowest thou not that the letter of the Scripture slayeth, and
that it is the exposition which maketh to live ?   Art thou not like one
who, coming to a physician, conceals from him half the symptoms of the
disease ?—I tell thee, thou foolish Fleming, the text speaketh but of
promises made unto Christians, and there is in the Rubric a special exception of such as are made to Welchmen."   At this commentary the
Fleming grinned so broadly as to show his whole case of broad strong
white teeth.   Father Aldrovand himself grinned in sympathy, and then
proceeded to say,—" Come, come, I see how it is.   Thou hast studied
some small revenge on me for doubting of thy truth ; and, in verity, I
think thou hast taken it wittily enough.   But wherefore didst thou not
let me into the secret from the beginning ? I promise thee I had foul
suspicions of thee."

" What !" said the Fleming, " is it possible I could ever think of involving your reverence in a little matter of deceit ?   Surely Heaven
hath sent me more grace and manners."

The second tale, entitled " The Talisman," forms a connecting link between the one already noticed and the novel of
Ivanhoe.   In " The Betrothed," Richard Cœur de Lion appears for a few moments as the heir apparent to the throne.
The reader of " The Talisman " finds him in Palestine, having
left his kingdom, not long after his accession to its throne, to
the miseries and distractions described in Ivanhoe.   The story
is principally occupied with the sickness of Richard and his
contests with his fellow-crusaders, Austria and France.   An important character is the Prince Royal of Scotland, who serves
incognito in the English army, and finally marries the sister of
the English monarch.   Saladin appears in various disguises,
not always probable or consistent, in one of which he cures
Richard with a Talisman.   This tale is the more interesting
of the two.   The author enters into the character of Richard
with spirit, and it occupies a large part of the work.   The persons in whom the reader is expected to take any interest are
fewer and the attention is not so much distracted as in the
first tale.   The last of course will be likely to make the most
enduring impression upon the mind and to acquire the strongest hold on the public estimation.   The story of this last seems
to have been carelessly patched together, and we doubt much
whether the author originally intended that Sheerkohf should
turn out to be Saladin.   Our limits will permit but one short
extract from this tale.   This we are induced to select on account of a religious sentiment, delivered in the author's own
person, and standing as the expression of his own feeling, the
like of which we do not recollect to have seen, in any former

novel, though all have been remarkable for their general respect for religion and morality. The respect however has seemed to be rather that of the philosopher and philanthropist, than the Christian.

The act of devotion, however, [says he] though rendered in such strange society, burst purely from his natural feelings of religious duty, and had its usual effect in composing the spirits, which had been long harassed by so rapid a succession of calamities. The sincere and earnest approach of the Christian to the throne of the Almighty, teaches the best lesson of patience under affliction ; since wherefore should we mock the Deity with supplications, when we insult him by murmuring under his decrees ?—or how, while our prayers have in every word admitted the vanity and nothingness of the things of time in comparison to those of eternity, should we hope to deceive the Searcher of Hearts, by permitting the world and worldly passions to reassume their turbulent empire over our bosoms, the instant when our devotions are ended ? There have been, and perhaps are now, persons so inconsistent, as to suffer earthly passion to reassume the reins even immediately after a solemn address to Heaven; but Sir Kenneth was not of these. He felt himself comforted and strengthened, and better prepared to execute or submit to whatever his destiny might call upon him to do or to suffer.

The Introduction to these tales we consider on the whole a failure, though some smart sayings pass between the persons of the interlude. It contains the following singular paragraph.

"I intend to write the most wonderful book which the world ever read—a book in which every incident shall be incredible, yet strictly true—a work recalling recollections with which the ears of this generation once tingled, and which shall be read by our children with an admiration approaching to incredulity. Such shall be the LIFE of NAPOLEON BUONAPARTE by the AUTHOR of WAVERLEY ! "

Whether this be a part of the joke, or a real advertisement of such a work, we know not, but we sincerely hope the latter.

The curious in these matters will probably be interested in the comparison between this Talisman and the Saracen of Madame Cottin, a crusade romance of great reputation in its day. The time, the place, and the principal characters in both are the same. It is evident that the writers have drawn in many instances from the same sources, but with what comparative effect we have not leisure or space to decide.

We have placed at the head of this article the titles of two works, partly because they are the work of the same author, of which fact (if evidence were wanting, there is abundance in the Lives of the Novelists,) and partly from the natural connexion of the subjects.

An edition of the works of the principal British novelists has lately been published in Edinburgh, accompanied by a biographical notice of each author and a short criticism on his works, by Sir Walter Scott.   These notices and criticisms, printed in a separate form, make the volumes before us.   Beside the interest arising from the smoothness and beauty of the style, and the general soundness of the author's criticisms upon works so widely known as those of Fielding, Smollett, Richardson, &c. there is one of another kind, when we consider many of these criticisms in the light of explanation or defence of the principles which have governed him in constructing his own novels.   That the author is often thinking of his own works, as well as those under his examination might be shown at great length.   We shall notice only his opinions respecting the supernatural machinery of novels.

The following extract is from the remarks on Walpole's " Castle of Otranto."

It is doing injustice to Mr Walpole's memory to allege, that all which he aimed at in *The Castle of Otranto*, was "the art of exciting surprise and horror;" or, in other words, the appeal to that secret and reserved feeling of love for the marvellous and supernatural, which occupies a hidden corner in almost every one's bosom. * * * * It was his object to draw such a picture of domestic life and manners, during the feudal times, as might actually have existed, and to paint it chequered and agitated by the action of supernatural machinery, such as the superstition of the period received as matter of devout credulity. The natural parts of the narrative are so contrived, that they associate themselves with the marvellous occurrences ; and, by the force of that association, render those *speciosa miracula* striking and impressive, though our cooler reason admits their impossibility.   Indeed, to produce, in a well cultivated mind, any portion of that surprise and fear which are founded on supernatural events, the frame and tenor of the whole story must be adjusted in perfect harmony with this main-spring of the interest.   He who, in early youth, has happened to pass a solitary night in one of the few ancient mansions which the fashion of more modern times has left undespoiled of their original furniture, has probably experienced, that the gigantic and preposterous figures dimly visible in the defaced tapestry—the remote clang of the distant doors which divide him from living society*—the deep darkness which involves the high and fretted roof of the apartment—the dimly seen pictures of ancient knights, renowned for their valour, and perhaps for their crimes—the varied and indistinct sounds which disturb the silent desolation of a half-deserted mansion—and, to crown all, the feeling that carries us back to ages of feudal power and papal superstition, join together to excite a corresponding sensation of supernatural awe, if not of terror.   It is in such situations, when superstition becomes contagious, that we listen with

* See the Antiquary, vol. I. chap. x.

respect, and even with dread, to the legends which are our sport in the garish light of sunshine, and amid the dissipating sights and sounds of every day life. Now, it seems to have been Walpole's object to attain, by the minute accuracy of a fable, sketched with singular attention to the costume of the period in which the scene was laid, that same association which might prepare his reader's mind for the reception of prodigies congenial to the creed and feelings of the actors. His feudal tyrant, his distressed damsel, his resigned yet dignified churchman—the castle itself, with its feudal arrangements of dungeons, trap-doors, oratories, and galleries*—the incidents of the trial, the chivalrous procession, and the combat;—in short, the scene, the performers, and action, so far as it is natural, form the accompaniments of his spectres and his miracles, and have the same effect on the mind of the reader, that the appearance and drapery of such a chamber as we have described may produce upon that of a temporary inmate. This was a task which required no little learning, no ordinary degree of fancy, no common portion of genius, to execute. The association of which we have spoken is of a nature peculiarly delicate, and subject to be broken and disarranged. It is, for instance, almost impossible to build such a modern gothic structure as shall impress us with the feelings we have endeavoured to describe. It may be grand, or it may be gloomy; it may excite magnificent or melancholy ideas; but it must fail in bringing forth the sensation of supernatural awe, connected with halls that have echoed to the sounds of remote generations, and have been pressed by the footsteps of those who have long since passed away. Yet Horace Walpole has attained, in composition, what, as an architect, he must have felt beyond the power of his art. The remote and superstitious period in which his scene is laid—the art with which he has furnished forth its gothic decorations—the sustained, and, in general, the dignified tone of feudal manners—prepare us gradually for the favourable reception of prodigies which, though they could not really have happened at any period, were consistent with the belief of all mankind at that in which the action is placed. It was therefore the author's object, not merely to excite surprise and terror, by the introduction of supernatural agency, but to wind up the feelings of his reader till they became for a moment identified with those of a ruder age, which

> "Held each strange tale devoutly true."

The difficulty of attaining this nice accuracy of delineation may be best estimated by comparing *The Castle of Otranto* with the less successful efforts of later writers; where, amid all their attempts to assume the tone of antique chivalry, something occurs in every chapter so decidedly incongruous, as at once reminds us of an ill-sustained masquerade, in which ghosts, knights-errant, magicians, and damsels gent, are all equipped in hired dresses from the same warehouse in Tavistock-street.*

There is a remarkable particular in which Mr Walpole's steps have been departed from by the most distinguished of his followers.

Romantic narrative is of two kinds—that which, being in itself possible, may be matter of belief at any period: and that which, though held

---

* See Waverley, chap. i.

impossible by more enlightened ages, was yet consonant with the faith of earlier times. The subject of *The Castle of Otranto* is of the latter class. Mrs Radcliffe, a name not to be mentioned without the high respect due to genius, has endeavoured to effect a compromise between those different styles of narrative, by referring her prodigies to an explanation founded on natural causes, in the latter chapters of her romances. To this improvement upon the gothic romance there are so many objections, that we own ourselves inclined to prefer, as more simple and impressive, the narrative of Walpole, which details supernatural incidents as they would have been readily believed and received in the eleventh or twelfth century. In the first place, the reader feels indignant at discovering that he has been cheated into sympathy with terrors, which are finally explained as having proceeded from some very simple cause ; and the interest of a second reading is entirely destroyed by his having been admitted behind the scenes at the conclusion of the first. Secondly, the precaution of relieving our spirits from the influence of supposed supernatural terror, seems as unnecessary in a work of professed fiction, as that of the prudent Bottom, who proposed that the human face of the representative of his lion should appear from under his mask, and acquaint the audience plainly that he was a man as other men, and nothing more than Snug the joiner. Lastly, these substitutes for supernatural agency are frequently to the full as improbable as the machinery, which they are introduced to explain away and to supplant. The reader who is required to admit the belief of supernatural interference, understands precisely what is demanded of him ; and, if he be a gentle reader, throws his mind into the attitude best adapted to humour the deceit which is presented for his entertainment, and grants, for the time of perusal, the premises on which the fable depends. But if the author voluntarily binds himself to account for all the wondrous occurrences which he introduces, we are entitled to exact that the explanation shall be natural, easy, ingenious, and complete. Every reader of such works must remember instances, in which the explanation of mysterious circumstances in the narrative has proved equally, nay, even more incredible, than if they had been accounted for by the agency of supernatural beings ; for the most incredulous must allow, that the interference of such agency is more possible than that an effect resembling it should be produced by an inadequate cause. But it is unnecessary to enlarge further on a part of the subject, which we have only mentioned to exculpate our author from the charge of using machinery more clumsy than his tale from its nature required. The bold assertion of the actual existence of phantoms and apparations seems to us to harmonize much more naturally with the manners of feudal times, and to produce a more powerful effect upon the reader's mind, than any attempt to reconcile the superstitious credulity of feudal ages with the philosophic scepticism of our own, by referring those prodigies to the operation of fulminating powder, combined mirrors, magic lanterns, trap-doors, speaking trumpets, and such like apparatus of German phantasmagoria.*

Again he observes in his account of the novels of Mrs Radcliffe.

---

* See again Waverley, chap. i.

Curiosity and a lurking love of mystery, together with a germ of superstition, are more generally ingredients in the human mind, and more widely diffused through the mass of humanity, than either taste or feeling. * * * *

The present public deal as rigidly, and compel an explanation from the story-teller; and he must either at once consider the knot as worthy of being severed by supernatural aid, and bring on the stage his actual fiend or ghost, or, like Mrs Radcliffe, refer to natural agency the whole materials of his story.

We have already, in some brief remarks on *The Castle of Otranto*, avowed some preference for the mode of boldly avowing the use of supernatural machinery. Ghosts and witches, and the whole tenets of superstition having once, and at no late period, been matter of universal belief, warranted by legal authority, it would seem no great stretch upon the reader's credulity to require him, while reading of what his ancestors did, to credit for the time what those ancestors devoutly believed in. And yet, notwithstanding the success of Walpole and Maturin, (to whom we may add the author of *Forman*), the management of such machinery must be ackowledged a task of a most delicate nature. "There is but one step," said Buonaparte, "betwixt the sublime and the ridiculous;" and in an age of universal incredulity, we must own it would require, at the present day, the support of the highest powers, to save the supernatural from slipping into the ludicrous. The *incredulus odi* is a formidable objection.

There are some modern authors, indeed, who have endeavoured, ingeniously enough, to compound betwixt ancient faith and modern incredulity. They have exhibited phantoms, and narrated prophecies strangely accomplished, without giving a defined or absolute opinion, whether these are to be referred to supernatural agency, or whether the apparitions were produced (no uncommon case) by an overheated imagination, and the accompanying presages by a casual, though singular, coincidence of circumstances. This is however an evasion of the difficulty, not a solution; and besides, it would be leading us too far from the present subject, to consider to what point the author of fictitious narrative is bound by his charter to gratify the curiosity of the public, and whether, as a painter of actual life, he is not entitled to leave something in the shade, when the natural course of events conceals so many incidents in total darkness. Perhaps, upon the whole, this is the most artful mode of terminating such a tale of wonder, as it forms the means of compounding with the taste of two different classes of readers; those who, like children, demand that each particular circumstance and incident of the narrative shall be fully accounted for: and the more imaginative class, who, resembling men that walk for pleasure through a moonlight landscape, are more teased than edified by the intrusive minuteness with which some well-meaning companion disturbs their reveries, divesting stock and stone of the shadowy semblances in which fancy had dressed them, and pertinaciously restoring to them the ordinary forms and common-place meanness of reality.

These are the rules; the application of them may be seen without mentioning slighter instances, in the Bodach Glas of Vich Ian Vohr, the astrological prediction and its accomplishment in **Guy Mannering ;**—the ominous traditions respecting the Kelpie's Flow and the Mermaiden's Well in the **Bride of Lammermoor ;** the **White Lady** of the Monastery and the **Abbot ; Horse-shoe** of Redgauntlet ; and the apparition of Vanda in the first of the tales now before us. In his person of critic, our author has decided on the best course ; in his capacity of author, he has uniformly followed it. We could fill pages with evidence from this work that the author of both is one and the same, but they cannot fail to suggest themselves to every diligent reader of the Waverley novels.

Of the critical notices in these Lives, though all are highly entertaining, we think those on the works of Richardson and Mrs Radcliffe the most so. From the latter we shall make the following extract for the benefit of novel-readers.

One [tribute] might still be found of a different and higher description, in the dwelling of the lonely invalid, or the neglected votary of celibacy, who was bewitched away from a sense of solitude, of indisposition, of the neglect of the world, or of secret sorrow, by the potent charms of this mighty enchantress. Perhaps the perusal of such works may, without injustice, be compared with the use of opiates, baneful, when habitually and constantly resorted to, but of a most blessed power in those moments of pain and languor, when the whole head is sore, and the whole heart sick. If those who rail indiscriminately at this species of composition were to consider the quantity of actual pleasure which it produces, and the much greater proportion of real sorrow and distress which it alleviates, their philanthropy ought to moderate their critical pride, or religious intolerance.

While we acknowledge that there is some foundation for this, we may reply in our author's own figure and with a parody of the words of one of his own characters, the learned Counsellor Pleydell, " *a novel* is like laudanum, it is easier to use it as a quack does, than to learn to apply it like a physician."

The doctrine of our author on the effects of novels in another place is as follows.

Excluding from consideration those infamous works which address themselves directly to awakening the grosser passions of our nature, we are inclined to think the worst evil to be apprehended from the perusal of novels is, that the habit is apt to generate an indisposition to real history and useful literature ; and that the best which can be hoped is, that they may sometimes instruct the youthful mind by real pictures of life, and sometimes awaken their better feelings and sympathies by strains of generous sentiment, and tales of fictious wo. Beyond this point they are a mere elegance, a luxury contrived for the amusement of polished life, and the gratification of that half love of literature which pervades all ranks in an advanced stage of society, and are read much more for amusement than with the least hope of deriving instruction from them.

This opinion he backs with an apophthegm of Doctor Johnson. A somewhat similar one, if we rightly recollect, is expressed in a very pleasant, spirited, and judicious article on the subject of novels in a late number of the Christian Spectator;—an article by the way, which is another testimony to the astonishing popularity of the Waverley novels, which have worked their way, in a few years, from the ladies' work-table and the lounger's parlour window, to a temporary fellowship at least with the dusty corpuses of the civilian, and the ponderous polyglotts of the divine.

We cannot leave the consideration of these works without a passing notice, at least, of the mechanical execution of this American edition. That of the Tales is bad enough, but that of the Lives would disgrace any press, and is indeed an insult to the public.

Reform of Harvard College.

(For the Titles, see No. 6 of this Gazette.)

[CONTINUED.]

ANOTHER pursuit which seems to us to need discouragement is that of music. Except in a few individuals, even a low degree of musical excellence requires a vast deal of time and attention; and, supposing that this occupation does not intrude upon the hours allotted to study, it is expedient that the leisure hours of a student should be employed in some more healthful amusement, than bending over a music book, or straining at a clarionett. But it is impossible to prevent even the hours of study from encroachment, so long as the musical performances of the students make a part of the entertainment at the exhibitions, and so long as the detestable practice of serenading shall be permitted. We use strong language, for of the ill effects of this practice and its necessary accompaniments upon the health and sometimes the morals of the students, there can be no question. If we take into consideration the time spent in learning to play upon some instrument and the necessary annoyance to all the neighbours of the learner, we think it cannot be denied that College is no place for music. If a student must learn this art, let him learn it in the vacations.

But neither this practice nor the objections to it are very novel. More than one hundred and fifty years ago, Dr Hoar, afterwards president of the University, wrote in these words to his cousin Flint, who was then a freshman. "Music I had almost forgot; I suspect you seek it both too soon and too much. This be assured of, that if you be not excellent at it, it is nothing at all; and if you be excellent, it will take up so much of your time and mind, that you will be worth little else. And when all that excellence is attained, your acquest will prove little or nothing of real profit to you, unless you intend to take up the trade of fiddling."

Another method of influencing public opinion will supply another motive for exertion, the consideration of the effect of one's conduct at College upon after life. A degree is valuable now, and it is to be wished that it were possible to make it more so, by making it more necessary in the professions. It may be made somewhat more so by difficulty of attainment. Many of our readers will perceive that we are about to propose an examination for a degree. The practice which, as we are informed, prevails at Oxford seems excellent. The time occupied by the students there, as here, is four years; but at the end of the second year the student undergoes a severe examination, and if deficient, is turned back to remain another year. At the end of the fourth year, if he has passed his first examination, he is admitted to that for a degree, in which, if he fail, he is, as before, turned back. For the attainment of a degree, an examination in certain branches is necessary, but there are other honours to be attained by the candidate's offering himself for examination in other branches. A degree obtained in this way would be a public and lasting testimony of industry, while failure would subject the candidate to bitter mortification. The effect of this upon the opinions and conduct of the students may be supposed *a priori*, but we may illustrate it by some examples. The medical students of all schools within our knowledge are subjected to severe examinations, and we believe it will be admitted, that, as a body, these students are the most persevering in their application and acquire the strongest professional *esprit du corps* and zeal for improvement in their science. At Cambridge in England, there is no examination for a degree; or at most a mere form. We are informed from most respectable authority that the difference in the degree of application in these Universities is very great. The severe examinations at Oxford are a comparatively late innovation, and the effect is stated to have been great and immediate. We have heard that an eminent

wine-seller in Bristol, on inquiring why so few pipes of wine
had of late years been ordered at Oxford, was informed
that the examination for degrees had nearly ruined the trade.
There is one College at Oxford, the New, or Winchester College, where no examination for a degree takes place, and the
consequence is said to be, that though the students are all beneficiaries and admitted after a severe examination, being of
course among the best prepared in the University, the standard of diligence in this College is lower than in any other.
Lastly how often do we see a youth labouring with unabat-
ing diligence to prepare for the examination which precedes
his admission to the College, and then becoming idle and
indifferent to the studies that follow it? Now what process
is more simple and likely to be more effectual than the application of a stimulus, which has been found so powerful with
the candidates for the freshman class, to those for the sopho-
more, junior, and senior classes, and finally to those who
aspire to a degree? We ought to observe in justice to the
Governors of Cambridge College, that we believe that by the
arrangements of late years public opinion among the students
has been much and favourably influenced, and that industry is
more fashionable than it used to be.

But the College must after all partake of the character of
a school; the students are generally too young to be left entirely to their own discretion. Of the various checks and punishments now in operation, we are of opinion, that most are
theoretically judicious and practically useful. One of them,
that of fines, seem not to be so, and the report, upon which we
have been remarking, recommends, very judiciously,

That the punishment by fines be abolished; and tasks, or some other
equivalents, which shall operate directly on the students themselves, be
substituted in their stead.

This is the practice at Oxford; tasks, technically termed
" *impositions*," are imposed at the pleasure of the Proctor. It
seems to us that it would be well that the officers within the
walls should have the power of imposing these for the smaller
offences, nor does any check upon this power seem necessary,
except a periodical report to the meetings of the Faculty.

There is a mechanical contrivance, which we have heard
recommended, which strikes us favourably. It is, that the
College and grounds should be surrounded by a wall of moderate height surmounted by an iron rail and having only a
single entrance. This would be ornamental, and, with the as-

sistance of the belt of trees now existing, would have the effect of giving the Colleges a quiet and secluded appearance. This in itself is favourable to habits of study. Every one knows the power of external circumstances and appliances upon intellectual habits. If the gate were regularly closed at nine in the evening and every one reported who demanded admission after that hour, the effect would be increased. At present the bell rings for study hours at nine o'clock; but what student thinks of making that an excuse for leaving an evening party in town? The law that they shall be in their rooms at that hour is felt to be obsolete. It may be said that any such contrivance would only excite the ingenuity of the students to evade or surmount the obstacles. Doubtless some would prefer climbing the wall to reporting themselves, but we believe it would not be common. The trouble, difficulty, and risk of detection would prevent many from acquiring habits of negligence. The difficulty would balance slight temptations, and this is all the effect to be expected. No wall, bar, or gate would be of much use with those who come to College with strong habits of self-indulgence, dissipation, and impatience of restraint, and such had better be dismissed altogether. Parents who are unable to govern their own children must not expect them to be always well governed in a public institution. And yet, from our experience, we should judge, that children of this class are those who are most offensively irregular, and parents of this class those who are loudest in their complaints of the mis-government of the College. It was very weakly and hastily said, that the officers of the College stand with regard to the students in *loco parentis*, and that they should act as such—and it was well replied, that the officers were as ready to be parents as the students were to be children. It is plain that no contrivance can give the officers a power, which depends upon opinion, and a real relation, which in their case does not exist; moreover it is equally undeniable that if they had all the power and influence which is possessed and exerted by some parents, it would not answer the purpose. Some of the students must be better governed at College than they ever were at home, or they will not do for the situation. It would be a bold opinion to express, though we are not sure that it would be an incorrect one, that this is often the case. To render this arrangement more effectual, the practice of living out of the College walls, except in the house of an officer of government or that of the student's own family, should be utterly prohibited. The College buildings contain in all 120 rooms; allow one room in each entry for an officer and there remain 111, or enough to accommodate 222 students, the exact number now in College, according to the annual catalogue; but some live with their families and some with the officers of government. Between 40 and 50 now have rooms in private houses, where they must be in a great measure beyond the control of the government in regard to many small matters, which tend to foster habits of inattention and irregularity.

The remaining part, and nearly half, of Mr Pickering's speech was devoted to the consideration of the advantages of classical learning and the state of the University in this particular.

[To be continued.]

Helon's Pilgrimage to Jerusalem. A Picture of Judaism, in the Century which preceded the Advent of our Saviour. Translated from the German of FREDERICK STRAUSS. Boston. 1825. 2 vols. 12mo. pp. 236 and 252.

THIS novel is exactly what one would expect from the object which its author had in view, and the plan upon which it was written. Its object is to illustrate Jewish antiquities, by a representation of the customs, manners, religious observances, &c. of the Jewish nation, as they existed about a hundred years before the advent of our Saviour; the plan, to connect this representation with the fortunes and adventures of a few individuals. Now with regard to the writers of most of the historical novels which have been so popular within the last few years, their main purpose has been to write popular novels; and, as incidentally contributing to this, they have introduced historical characters and incidents to assist in filling up. In the present case, on the other hand, the novel has been the secondary object and the illustration of Judaism the principal; for although we have a hero and heroine compounded of the usual ingredients; a murder, a trial, a slander, &c. to make out the plot, yet it is clear that, in the opinion of the author, the story is merely the string to his pearls, valuable only as it brings them together, and the more completely covered by the glittering treasures, the better.

But although a very indifferent novel, this is a valuable and indeed interesting book, considered in its proper character, as presenting a view of the Jewish manners, customs, and religion, as existing in the Holy Land. Since this remarkable people has been an exiled nation, wandering over the face of the earth, far from the favoured spot assigned to them by the Deity himself, and endeared to them by a thousand of the holiest and highest, as well as tenderest associations, we have lost sight of them in their primitive elevated character, and have permitted ourselves to confine our views to the state in which we at present find them, outcast and degraded. If we analyze our feelings, we shall find that we do not regard them as of the same race with that great monarch whose temple to the true God was the wonder of his age, and whose power, riches, and wisdom have been the boast of his countrymen and the admiration of mankind in all succeeding ages. Our associations with the Jews are mostly of a degrading character, and to acquire juster notions, we must go back to old times, and consider them at home, in their own country, governed by their own laws, and enjoying their own institutions. To enable us to do this is precisely the object of Helon's Pilgrimage; and little skill as its author has exhibited as a novelist, he has communicated a great mass of information in a very agreeable and occasionally in a lively manner. Of the correctness of his representations we do not pretend to be competent judges; few persons are so. But there is an air of complete familiarity with the subject, an appearance of truth, and a correspondence with what we know about the matter, which gives us a confidence in his accounts of those things of which we know nothing. There is no reason to doubt that he has studied the antiquities of the Jews very thoroughly; and there can be no reason for believing that he would misrepresent or misjudge.

He has chosen for the period of his story that in which the Jewish people were suffered, for the last time, to enjoy, in independence and security, their own laws, their own religion, and their own political institutions. This period existed immediately after the successful resistance by the family of the Maccabees to the tyrannical sway of the king of Syria, and whilst John Hyrcanus, one of the family, exercised the double office of prince and high priest. The hero is a Jew of Egypt, residing and educated in Alexandria; who

53

has been deeply imbued with the schemes of philosophy of the day; has tried them all, but finds nothing to satisfy him till he returns to the law and the observances of his fathers. In those days, as indeed with the true Jews in all ages, the Holy Land, and more particularly Jerusalem, was the spot towards which the eyes of an Israelite indeed were always turned. Wherever over the face of the earth he was carried or driven,—in exile, in poverty, in death,—his heart yearned towards Jerusalem. There only could God be acceptably worshipped. There was the temple and the mount of God. There were the bones of his fathers and of a line of kings consecrated and anointed by the Deity himself. There was the Messiah to appear. Returning to the primitive faith of Israel, Helon's first and strongest desire is to visit this seat of his faith. He makes accordingly a pilgrimage to Jerusalem at the Passover, in the year 109 before the birth of Christ. He remains there during the half year which includes the principal religious festivals; becomes a priest, marries,—and, in the interval between the feasts of his religion and his duties as a priest, travels into the most interesting parts of the territory of Palestine, and is finally drowned, very unceremoniously, with nearly all the other *dramatis personæ*, on his return to Alexandria. His adventures are so contrived as to embrace a description of almost every thing which is curious and important in the customs and manners of the Jews, and even of the privacy of their domestic life.

The individuals who principally figure in the management of the plot, beside the hero, are Elisama, an uncle of Helon, advanced in life, a Jew bigoted to every thing Jewish, narrow-minded, and with a full share of that spiritual pride which the institutions of his nation were calculated to produce. He is contrasted with Myron, a young Greek, a companion and fellow student of Helon, lively and volatile, full of the Platonic philosophy, and listening with a philosophical scepticism to the enthusiastic encomiums bestowed on their religion, by his friends, the Jews.

The pilgrimage to Jerusalem is undertaken by Elisama and Helon; and they are accompanied part of the way by Myron. They travel from Alexandria as far as Gaza with a caravan; the night being principally occupied with their journey, whilst the heat of the day was devoted to repose. This journey occupies no less than an hundred and forty pages, and embraces no one single incident of importance.   To relieve the dullness of the time during which they halted each day, Elisama undertakes to relate to Myron the history of the Jewish nation.   The narrative is taken almost entirely from Scripture, and if it were not more entertaining to Myron than it was to us, the tediousness of his hours must have been but little relieved.   It is in fact a bare detail of a history familiar to us from infancy; and although it might be perfectly civil in Elisama to relate it to Myron, to whom doubtless it was quite novel and instructive, yet it was certainly an error of judgment to retail it to us good Christians who have it all by heart.

Many passages of a descriptive nature in this account of the journey of the caravan, have considerable merit, and are interesting as conveying some idea of the ancient manner of travelling.   The following passage presents a well combined picture.

The caravan still lay buried in profound slumber.   By the time that the camels were loaded and themselves ready to depart, the morning began to dawn, and a singular spectacle was unfolded by it.   The camels were crouching in a wide circle around the baggage, the horses, and the merchandise; and their long necks and little heads rose like towers above a wall.   The men had encamped round fires or in tents. Most of the fires had burnt out, only here and there dying embers occasionally shot a flame, which feebly illuminated the singular groups around.   Within the great circle all was still, save that the watchmen with their long staves were going their rounds, and calling their watchword in the stillness of the hour.   In the distance were heard the hoarse sounds of the waves, breaking on the shore.   On the other side of the camp was Gaza with its towers and ruins; and the fiery glow of morning was lightening up the scene of the fearful accomplishment of the word of prophecy.   Gaza, once so populous, magnificent, and strong, when she committed the shameful outrage on Samson, had no longer any gates at the spot where the mighty hero once lifted them up, and placed them on the hill opposite to Hebron.

There is nothing perhaps better done in this work than the representation given of the national pride and enthusiasm of the Jews.   It is displayed in a variety of ways, and it is every where apparent, either relating to their country or their political and religious institutions.   They look down upon the heathen, not with the compassion and pity which their delusion would seem calculated to inspire, but rather with horror, and something like scorn and hatred.   This we take to be perfectly natural and characteristic.   No nation, perhaps, ever experienced these feelings so strongly as the Jews. With them Palestine was the garden of the earth, Jerusalem the queen of cities, and their temple the only seat of the Deity. We quote a passage in which Elisama reproves Myron, who had been reflecting upon his nation for its comparative ignorance and want of taste in the fine arts.

"A nation," said Myron, "which, in its most flourishing period, is obliged to engage artists from foreign kings, and can do nothing by its own ingenuity and dexterity, is surely a poor and helpless race. How different from the great Hellenic people! Poetry in abundance I have indeed heard from you, but this is the only branch of art in which you have done any thing. No painting, no statuary, no drama!"

"Thou speakest," said Elisama, interposing angrily, "like a blind heathen, and what I have so often intimated seems to have been lost upon thee. Israel was not designed, nor ever aimed, to excel in such worldly arts. It was to be a kingdom of priests and a holy people, to receive and to preserve the law of Jehovah; and on this account he calls it his people, his Jeshurun, his beloved Israel. The time which other nations might devote to the culture of the elegant arts, Israel was to spend in the observance of the law. You have omitted all mention too of our music. This and our poetry are alone worthy to accompany the people before the presence of Jehovah; his temple must be splendid, but it was of no consequence that it was made so by foreign hands. Besides, the present temple, which yields little if at all to the former, was built by native artists; and supposing that in Solomon's time architecture was unknown among us, could this skill be reasonably expected in a nation, which had struggled for five hundred years for the possession of the soil, which even then had not been completely united for more than half a century, and had passed a considerable portion even of that short time in internal commotion.!"

From Hebron, Helon and Elisama travel in company with the Jews who are going to the Holy City to celebrate the Passover, filled with zeal and enthusiasm. This journey is described with much spirit and effect. When they had arrived near the object and termination of their pilgrimage,

The eager haste of the multitudes now increased with every step, and their impatience for the first sight of Jerusalem was expressed in the following psalm:

Great is the Lord; and greatly to be praised
The mountain of his holiness in the city of our God.
Beautiful for situation, the joy of the whole land
Is mount Zion, on the north of the city of the great King.
God is known in her palaces for a refuge,
We think of thy loving-kindness, O God,
In the midst of thy temple.
As thy name, so thy praise reacheth to the ends of the earth.
Thy right hand is full of righteousness.
Let the hill of Zion rejoice,
Let the daughters of Judah be glad
Because of thy judgments!

Walk about Zion, go round about her !
Tell her Towers !
Mark well her bulwarks !
Consider her palaces !
That ye may tell it to the generation following.
For this God is our God, for ever and ever.
He will be our guide, as in our youth.—Ps. xlviii.

Expectation had reached the highest pitch. The last strophes were not completely sung ; many were already silent, eagerly watching for the first sight of Jerusalem. All eyes were turned towards the north ; a faint murmur spread from rank to rank among the people, only those who had been at the festival before continued the psalm, and these solitary scattered voices formed a solemn contrast with the silence of the rest of the multitude. Helon's heart was in his eye, and he could scarcely draw his breath. When the psalm was concluded, the instruments prolonged the sound for a moment, and then all that mighty multitude, so lately jubilant, was still as death.

All at once the foremost ranks exclaimed, Jerusalem, Jerusalem ! Jerusalem, Jerusalem ! resounded through the valley of Rephaim.* " Jerusalem, thou city built on high, we wish thee peace ! " The children dragged their parents forward with them, and all hands were lifted up to bless.

The high white walls of the Holy City cast a gleam along the valley : Zion, rose with its palaces, and from Moriah the smoke of the offering was ascending to heaven. It was the hour of the evening sacrifice. Scarcely had the multitude recovered a little, when they began to greet the temple and the priests :

Bless ye the Lord, all ye servants of the Lord,
Who stand by night in the house of the Lord !
Lift up your hands towards the sanctuary,
And bless the Lord.
So will Jehovah bless thee out of Zion ;
He who made heaven and earth.—Ps. cxxxiv.

We omit some passages, which we had marked for quotation, containing a description of the ceremonies at the feast of the Passover, and retain one only which relates to the temper of mind in which the Jews were accustomed to celebrate their religious rites.

Festivity and cheerful conversation now reigned among the whole assemblage. Whether it be that a people, which had suffered so much calamity and oppression, naturally enjoys the more keenly a temporary interval of pleasure, or that every approach to God is to the pure mind a source of joy and peace, certain it is, that no nation has ever more carefully studied to remove all trace of sorrow from religious services than the Jews. If the service of the law was a heavy burthen, the

---

* Ecco apparir Gerusalem si vede,
Ecco additar Gerusalem si scorge,
Ecco da mille voci unitamente
Gerusalemme salutar si sente.
Gerusalemme Liberata, Canto III.

service of God was freedom and happiness. All the regulations enjoin
this, all the customs of Israel proceed from this principle, that the
marks of mourning should be carefully removed from their worship.
To praise, to give thanks and sing, to make a joyful noise unto the
Lord, to be glad on the day which he had made, to rejoice in him, are
all expressions by which their religious services are described. * * * *
How earnestly do Ezra and Nehemiah exhort the people to lay aside
their mourning, when the law was read at the feast of tabernacles, and
the curse on its violation made known! "This day is holy unto the
Lord your God: mourn not nor weep; neither be ye sorry, for the joy
of the Lord is your strength. Go your way, eat the fat and drink the
sweet; for this day is holy unto the Lord."

This is certainly a delightful feature in the Jewish religion; and it is one which belongs equally to the Christian.

Helon, discovering that he has a hereditary descent from
the first priest, Aaron, and of course a right to the sacerdotal
office, is admitted to that holy calling, and thus affords an
opportunity for describing at length the services of the priests
in the temple during their turn of ministration, which came
but for two weeks in the year to each individual.

He travels to Jericho, and selects and is bethrothed to a
wife. This affair is conducted by our author in the most
business-like manner possible. He to be sure represents his
hero as desperately in love, but that is a thing with which he
has very little to do, and he makes no use of it for the purpose of exciting an interest in his characters and his story.
His sole and simple object in this match is that he may have
an opportunity of describing the forms and ceremonies of a
betrothment and marriage. Nothing can really have less of
the sentimental or romantic in it than this event. It is brought
about in the most awkward manner imaginable, and the parties are engaged to each other in a very summary way, and
with as little demur as if they had been a widow and widow-
er in the third week of their bereavement.

One of the greatest defects in this work is the clumsiness
with which those parts which are fictitious and those which
relate to the history and customs of the Jews, are jointed
together. It is all "turned the seamy side without"—we
can see the piecing and patching a great deal too plainly.
Almost every important incident in the book is not only
really, but very apparently, introduced for the sole purpose
of furnishing an opportunity for the description of some
ceremony, some custom, or some place, and for the exhibition
of a fund of antiquarian knowledge. One might almost suppose
that the author had taken his common-place book of Jewish

antiquities as a text-book, and worked in all the various items of information, just as they rose, as best he might, without being very scrupulous with regard to any interruption of the important parts of his plot which they would occasion.

Thus our hero is sent upon various excursions to different parts of Palestine, that the reader may be benefited by a political, historical, and topographical description of the towns, cities, &c. through which he passes, and in consequence some parts of the book are made to appear too much like the pages of a gazetteer. He is made to lose his way in the desert in order that he may fall in with some lepers, of whose condition and treatment by the Jews, in conformity with the ordinances of their religion, an account becomes necessary. His wife is rendered liable to the imputation of unfaithfulness, for no other purpose but that we may be regaled with a description of the severe trial, through which she is made to pass, before her innocence can be fully made out ; and finally, his venerable friend and preceptor, Elisama, becomes a homicide, that we may be edified with a detail of the powers and duties of the avenger of blood, and the nature of the protection afforded by cities of refuge. This piece of information also costs a quiet and unoffending citizen of Jericho his life.

In general we have no objection to this mode of management, but in the present case there is a great want of neatness and dexterity of manner ; too much is attempted; the illustration of the greater part of the religious and political institutions of a people, and of their domestic life and manners ; a description of their country, and an epitome of their national history, is almost too much to crowd into a single work which it is intended shall have the form and possess the interest of a novel.

But with all the faults we have indicated, Helon's Pilgrimage may be read with a great deal of pleasure and instruction. Defective as it is as a work of fancy, still its form and some very considerable excellencies of execution give an air of reality to many things of which from Scripture alone we are never able to form any adequate conception. We do not know whether it is so with others, but we always associate with the idea of the Jewish nation in Palestine, a rudeness, plainness, and primitive simplicity of manners and mode of living which probably did not belong to them. Such impressions the perusal of Helon's Pilgrimage will do much to remove. Wealth, commerce, and intercourse with foreign nations produced the same changes in the Jews as they will in all people.

The manner in which the Jews made use of quotations from their sacred writings is well illustrated. These, it may be remarked, probably formed the great body of their literature, and were familiar to the memories of the people. When they wished to express themselves with unusual strength and energy, to give vent to their devotional feelings, or in short upon any occasion of excitement, they had recourse to that language which was to them the most forcible as well as the most holy, the language of Scripture. The introduction of these quotations is somewhat too frequent in the work before us, but they are selected with great taste, and are given in a translation which preserves their poetical form, as far probably as it is capable of being preserved.

MISCELLANY.

DESCRIPTION OF MADRID.

PALACE ROYAL.——PALACE OF THE RETIRO——EQUESTRIAN STATUE OF PHILIP IV—MUSEUM OF THE PRADO—PUBLIC HOSPITALS—CHAPEL OF THE CONVENT OF LAS SALESAS.

Madrid, 10th March, 1825.

THE Spanish capital, I believe, is less frequently visited by our countrymen than any other in Europe; and this, not so much from its being destitute of interest, as from causes peculiar to its situation,—to the inattention paid to the comforts of travellers,—and particularly, at the present day, to the great insecurity of their persons and property. I will, therefore, in compliance with your desire, give you such a sketch of this capital as my hasty and busy visit will enable me to do.

In approaching Madrid from the north (and I am told it is the same from the other quarters) there is nothing which indicates the approach to a great and ancient city. No flourishing villages; no perceptible increase of travellers; no city equipages in pursuit of air and exercise; no trees, and but a scanty and imperfect cultivation of the soil. The city is not perceived from the road by which I came, till within half a mile of it; when it is suddenly, and for nearly its whole extent, presented to the view. Its first appearance is by no means prepossessing; indeed it was rather that of an Asiatic than of a European city, and reminded me of the panorama I had seen of Grand Cairo. Nor does its interior correspond at all with its renown. One would expect to see, in a city which had been the residence of a Charles V, and of a Philip II, into whose coffers the Americas had been so long emptying their inexhaustible supplies of gold and silver,—a city, within whose walls a king of France had been kept as a prisoner, and whose monarchs had given law to Europe,—something corresponding with such power and such riches ; but whoever expects this will be disappointed. The troops, who are garrisoned here for the preservation of the precious life of Ferdinand, give some life and animation to the scene ; but excepting these every thing wears the appearance of the poverty and distress inevitably resulting from the late repeated revolutions, not less than from present misrule.

Of the palaces, that in which the royal family now reside was intended to have been one of the most magnificent in the world, but a want of means has prevented its completion. As it is, however, it presents the most beautiful and chaste piece of architecture to be seen here. It is situated advantageously, on an eminence, with abundant space on every side. It forms a square, each side of which is four hundred and seventy feet, and is built of handsome grey stone. The workmanship of the interior, the paintings, tapestry, furniture, &c. are said to be of the richest and most costly kind, and worthy the observation of strangers ; but strangers are not admitted while the royal family inhabit it, which is the case during winter.

The palace of the Retiro, without the walls of the city, is likewise situated on an eminence, and with its gardens, woods, pond, &c. is enclosed within a high wall. This was the favourite residence of Philip IV, who was at great expense in ornamenting it ; and of whom there is an equestrian statue of great beauty, which is so elevated as to be seen to advantage from without the wall. This statue is curious from the ingenuity and skill exhibited by the artist, in giving to such an enormous weight an equilibrium which enables it to be supported, on its hind feet only, in the attitude of rearing up. It is of four times the natural size, and weighs eighteen thousand pounds. This royal residence was much defaced by the French during the time of Napoleon.

Near to this, and fronting the Prado, is a magnificent building, in an unfinished state, of about four hundred feet front, called the Museum of the Prado. Its vast halls are used for the royal collection of paintings ; and there is an academy held here for instruction in that art. It is open two days in the week for visitors, when any well-dressed people are admitted gratis. The custom-house, the post-office, the house containing the cabinet of natural history, &c. are among the most splendid buildings of the

54

city ; the two former, in particular, are on a gigantic scale. There are also many of the houses of the nobles which are worthy of observation, rather however for extent and size than for beauty of material or chasteness of style ;—such as those of the duke of Medina Celi, of the duke of Villahermosa, of the duke of Liria, of the Prince of Peace, and others.

The three great hospitals are on a scale of magnitude corresponding with the former rich state of the country, to which they · were an honour. They are said to receive, one year with another, from twenty to twenty-five thousand sick ; but this must have been before the great decline of the population of the city. There are, besides, a number of hospitals of less magnitude ; and, moreover, a number of houses for charitable purposes, such as a foundling and a lying-in house, and one for the reception of the old and infirm, one for orphan boys, and another for girls who are to be taken care of till they can earn their living, &c. And yet, with all these benevolent establishments, the streets are thronged with beggars. The houses generally, belonging to the commonalty of this city, make a very ordinary appearance without ; and, owing to the economy necessary to be observed with regard to fuel, are, at this season of the year, very uncomfortable within. They are from two to four and a few of them five stories high, built of half-baked bricks, and plastered ; and the plaster, occasionally falling off, gives them a ruinous appearance. The windows of the lower story have a barricado of heavy iron bars the whole length, which give them the resemblance of prisons. The entrance is by great, unwieldy doors, which are left open during the day, and the entry or court seems to be considered as much for the use of the public as the streets, and generally are much more offensive to the *olfactories*. To get at a family, who are up one flight of stairs, some preliminary steps are required. On ringing at the door, a servant comes, and before opening it, asks, " Who's there ? " If the answer is not satisfactory, a slide is removed, which covers a hole cut in the door, about five inches square, across which are nailed pieces of iron. Here a parley takes place, and the person is admitted or not, as is judged proper. The rooms are generally lofty and finished with some taste, though roughly. Some few, inhabited by the most wealthy, have fire-places, which appear to have been constructed in the earliest period of the invention of those conveniences, being built square, and from three to four feet deep, so that those only who sit directly in front of the fire can see it or feel its effects. But, generally, families use the *brazero*, which is a great pan of coals set in a wooden frame in the centre of the room, and during dinner, under the table. Fuel is very dear here. Wood is now at about forty cents the hundred pounds, for it is sold by weight ; and yet, notwithstanding this scarcity, and the vacant lands' in the vicinity of the city adapted to its cultivation, there is not sufficient enterprise in the community for its accomplishment. The poorer class can afford to keep no more fire than is barely sufficient for the purposes of cooking ; and in the sunshiny days they are seen,—men, women, and children,—performing their domestic labours under the sunny side of their houses and walls.

I feel that I ought to beg pardon of the church for having neglected to notice her temples before the buildings already enumerated. This omission may have been caused by the circumstance of there being no churches here which are remarkable for beauty or magnificence—none corresponding either with the pomp of the national religion or with those which are common in most of the provincial towns of this kingdom. Churches and monasteries, however, abound here ; and some of the latter are upon a scale sufficiently extensive to hasten the ruin of a state whose affairs are managed with more wisdom than are those of Spain. The only convent I visited was that of Las Salesas, built by Don Fernando VI, in the year 1749, for the education of noble females. It is a square of great extent, and for this reason only its exterior is remarkable. But its chapel, the finest in Madrid, is worthy the attention of strangers. It is, as usual, in the form of a cross. Over the centre of which is a spacious dome, surmounted by a cupola, from whence it is lighted. The view from below up to this cupola of about two hundred feet, is uninterrupted. The ceiling of the dome is ornamented with beautiful paintings by some of the best Spanish masters. The great altar is ornamented with four solid columns of beautiful green marble, of one piece, each seventeen feet in height. The capitals and bases are of bronze gilt. A great painting in the centre, painted by Murillo, in Naples, representing the Visitation ; and the statues in white marble on either side of the altar, of San Fernando VI and his queen Barbara, are all very beautiful. Behind an immense iron grating (gilt) and on one side of the great altar, I heard the nuns repeating their prayers, which resembled the responses, excepting that there was no pause, of the congregation of an Episcopal church.

[*To be continued.*]

ITALIAN LYRICAL POETRY.

TOLOMMEI.

CLAUDIO TOLOMMEI occupied too large a space in the public eye, among the lyrical poets of the sixteenth century, to be entirely neglected, in an attempt to give a full idea of the secondary

Italian poetry.   He was born at Siena in 1492.   In 1526 he was banished from his native city for some sin against that state, which, in the obscurity of its petty politics, is unknown to posterity.   In 1529, he entered the service of Cardinal Ippolito de' Medici, and was employed by him in a mission to Vienna; and afterwards he became attached to Luigi Farnese, duke of Parma, who gave him the appointment of minister of justice in Placentia. In 1549 he was made bishop of Corsola.   Besides his occasional residences elsewhere, he lived a considerable part of his life at Rome, where he died in 1554.

Tolommei was a very meritorious scholar; but as a poet he is most remarkable for a fantastic plan of introducing the Latin prosody into Italian verse.   He composed stanzas to be scanned with dactyls and spondees; and was followed, at first, by a numerous school of imitators.   But criticism, good sense, and experience, soon convinced the literary world of the absurdity of the attempt.   In fact, the genius of the two languages, in the structure of verse, is so unlike, that this circumstance is only mentioned as a curious fact in literary history.   English readers well know the success of a similar experiment on English verse, made first in the age of Elizabeth, and recently by Mr Southey, whose "Vision of Judgment" is so unsparingly but justly dealt with, by the Edinburgh Review (vol. xxxv. p. 422.)

ROTA.

BERNARDINO ROTA, a Neapolitan gentleman, born in 1509, and deceased in 1575, was a successful and polished writer of both Italian and Latin poetry.   His *Piscatory Eclogues* enjoyed some reputation in their day; but his sonnets are most remembered. He closely imitated Petrarca, and in his verses mourned the death of his wife Porzia Capece, as Petrarca did that of Laura. A single sonnet is selected from his pieces upon this subject.

> My breast, my mind, my bursting heart shall be
>   Thy sepulchre, and not this marble tomb,
>   Which I prepare for thee in grief and gloom;
>   No meaner grave, my wife, is fitting thee.
> Oh! ever cherished be thy memory;
>   And may thine image dear my path illume,
>   And leave my heart for other hopes no room,
>   While sad I sail o'er sorrow's troubled sea.
> Sweet gentle soul, where thou wert used to reign,
>   My spirit's queen, when wrapt in mortal clay,
>   There, when immortal, shalt thou rule again.
> Let death, then, tear my love from earth away;
>   Urned in my bosom, she will still remain,
>   Alive or dead, untarnished by decay.

C. C.

ORIGINAL POETRY.

THE MYTHOLOGY OF GREECE.

There was a time, when the o'erhanging sky,
And the fair earth with its variety,
Mountain and valley, continent and sea,
Were not alone the unmoving things that lie
Slumbering beneath the sun's unclouded eye;
But every fountain had its spirit then,
That held communion oft with holy men,
And frequent from the heavenward mountain came
Bright creatures, hovering round on wings of flame,
And some mysterious sybil darkly gave
Responses from the dim and hidden cave:——
Voices were heard waking the silent air,
A solemn music echoed from the wood,
And often from the bosom of the flood
Came forth a sportive Naiad passing fair,
The clear drops twinkling in her braided hair;
And as the hunter through the forest strayed,
Quick-glancing beauty shot across the glade,
Her polished arrow levelled on her bow
Ready to meet the fawn or bounding roe;
And often on the mountain tops the horn
Rang round the rocky pinnacles, and played
In lighter echoes from the chequered shade,
Where through the silvery leaves at early morn
Stole the slant sunbeams, shedding on the grass
Brightness, that quivered with the quivering mass
Of thickly arching foliage;——often there
Dian and all her troop of girls were seen
Dancing by moonlight on the dewy green,
When the cool night wind through the forest blew,
And every leaf in tremulous glances flew;
And in the cloudless fields of upper air,
With coldly pale and melancholy smile
The moon looked down on that bright spot, the while,
Which in the depth of darkness shone as fair,
As in lone southern seas a palmy isle;
And when a hunter-boy, who far away
Had wandered through the wild-wood from his home,
Led by the eagerness of youth to roam,
Buried in deep unbroken slumber lay,——
Then as the full moon poured her mellow light
Full on the mossy pillow where he slept,
One more than nymph, in sylvan armour dight,
Bent fondly over him, and smiled, and wept.
Each lonely spot was hallowed then—the oak
That o'er the village altar hung, would tell

Strange hidden things ;—the old remembered well,
How from its gloom a spirit often spoke.
There was not then a fountain or a cave,
But had its reverend oracle, and gave
Responses to the fearful crowd, who came
And called the indwelling Deity by name ;
Then every snowy peak, that lifted high
Its shadowy cone to meet the bending sky,
Stood like a heaven of loveliness and light ;—
And as the gilt cloud rolled its glory by,
Chariots and steeds of flame stood harnessed there,
And gods came forth and seized the golden reins,
Shook the bright scourge, and through the boundless air
Rode over starry fields and azure plains.
It was a beautiful and glorious dream,
Such as would kindle high the soul of song ;
The bard, who struck his harp to such a theme,
Gathered new beauty as he moved along—
His way was now through wilds and beds of flowers ;
Rough mountains met him now, and then again
Gay valleys hung with vines in woven bowers
Led to the bright waves of the purple main.
All seemed one deep enchantment then ;—but now,
Since the long sought for goal of truth is won,
Nature stands forth unveiled, with cloudless brow,
On earth ONE SPIRIT OF LIFE, in heaven ONE SUN.

P.

DREAM OF THE SEA.

I dreamt that I went down into the sea
Unpained amid the waters—and a world
Of splendid wrecks, formless and numberless,
Broke on my vision. It did seem the skies
Were o'er me pure as infancy—yet waves
Did rattle round my head, and fill mine ears
Like the measureless roar of the far fight
When battle has set up her trumpet shout !
I seemed to breathe the air ; and yet the sea
Kept dallying with my life as I sunk down.
'T was in the fitful fashion of a dream—
Water and air—walking, and yet no earth.
The deep seemed bare and dry—and yet I went
With a rude dashing round my reeking face,
Until my outstretched and trembling feet
Stood still upon a bed of glittering pearls !
The hot sun was right over me, at noon—
Sudden it withered up the ocean—till
I seemed amidst a waste of shapeless clay.
A thousand bones were whitening in his rays,
Mass upon mass,—confused and without end.

I walked on the parched wilderness, and saw
The hopeless beauty of a lifeless world!
Wealth that once made some poor vain heart grow light
And leap with it into the flood, was there
Clutched in the last mad agony.   And gold
That makes of life a happiness and curse—
That vaunts on earth its brilliancy, lay here
(An outcast tyrant in his loneliness)
Beggared by jewels that ne'er shone through blood
Upon the brow of kings!   Here there were all
The bright beginnings and the costly ends,
Which envied man enjoys and expiates,—
Splendour and death—silence, and human hopes,—
Gems, and smooth bones—life's pageantry! the cross
That thought to save some wretch in his late need
Hugged in its last idolatry—all, all
Lay here in deathly brotherhood—no breath—
No sympathy—no sound—no motion—and no hope!
I stood and listened,—
The eternal flood rushed to its desolate grave!
And I could hear above me all the waves
Go bellowing to their bounds!   Still I strode on,
Journeying amid the brightest of earth's things
Where yet was never life, nor hope, nor joy!
My eye could not but look, and my ear hear;
For now strange sights and beautiful and rare
Seemed ordered from the deep through the rich prism
Above me—and sounds undulated through
The surges, till my soul grew mad with visions!
Beneath the canopy of waters I could see
Palaces and cities crumbled—and the ships
Sunk in the engorging whirlpool, while the laugh
Of revelry went wild along their decks—and ere
The oath was strangled in their swollen throats;—
For there they lay, just hurried to one grave
With horrible contortions and fixed eyes
Waving among the cannon, as the surge
Would slowly lift them—and their streaming hair
Twining around the blades that were their pride.

And there were two locked in each others arms,
And they were lovers!
Oh God, how beautiful! cheek to cheek
And heart to heart upon that splendid deep,
A bridal bed of pearls!   A burial
Worthy of two so young and innocent.
And they did seem to lie there, like two gems
The fairest in the halls of ocean—both
Sepulchred in love—a tearless death—one look,
One wish, one smile, one mantle for their shroud,
One hope, one kiss—and that not yet quite cold!
How beautiful to die in such fidelity!
E'er yet the curse has ripened, or the heart

Begins to hope for death as for a joy,
And feels its streams grow thicker, till they cloy
With wishes that have sickened and grown old.
I saw their cheeks were pure and passionless,
And all their love had passed into a smile,
And in that smile they died!

Sudden a battle rolled above my head,
And there came down a flash into the deep
Illumining its dim chambers—and it past;
The waters shuddered—and a thousand sounds
Sung hellish echoes through the caverned waster
The blast was screaming on the upper wave,
And as I looked above me I could see
The ships go booming through the murky storm,
Sails rent—masts staggering—and a spectre crew.
Blood mingled with the foam bathing their bows,
And I could hear their shrieks as they went on
Crying of murder to their bloody foes!

A form shot downward close at my feet;
His hand still grasped the steel—and his red eye
Was full of curses even in his death,
And he had been flung into the abyss
By fellow men! before his heart was cold.

Again I stood beside the lovely pair—
The storm and conflict were as they 'd not been.
I stood and shrieked and laughed and yet no voice
That I could hear came in my madness—
It hardly seemed as they were dead—so calm,
So beautiful! the sea-stars round them shone,
Like emblems of their souls so cold and pure!
The bending grass wept silent over them,
Truer than any friend on earth—their tomb
The jewelry of the ocean—and their dirge
The everlasting music of its roar.

I seemed to stand wretched in dreamy thought,
Cursing the constancy of human hearts
And vanity of human hopes—and felt
As I have felt on earth in my sick hours.
How thankless was this legacy of breath
To those who knew the woe of a scathed brain!
Oh ocean—ocean! if thou coverest up
The ruins of a proud and broken soul
And giv'st such peace and solitude as this,
Thy depths are heaven to man's ingratitude!

I seemed to struggle in an agony;
My streaming tears gushed out to meet the wave;
I woke in terror, and the beaded sweat
Coursed down my temples like a very rain—
As though I had just issued from the sea!

G. M.

CRITICAL NOTICES.

The Sixty-third Number of the Quarterly Review.

WE have taken up this Number of the Quarterly with a peculiar interest, growing out of our desire to learn what character the new editor intends to give to this journal.   A very general dissatisfaction was expressed at the temper which appeared to actuate the former editor. His intimate friends said of him, that though mild and gentle in personal intercourse, he was a tiger the moment he took pen in hand. Though we Americans were naturally led to notice this spirit more in the scandalous articles relative to this country, yet liberal readers could not but be disgusted with a vein of fierce bigotry running through the whole work.

It would be quite premature to speak of the spirit, which this widely spread journal is to breathe under its new editor, from the specimens which we have yet seen.   The present number contains among its articles some that are plainly—but not very offensively—marked by the religious and political tone that has ever characterized the Quarterly Review; but the number is principally made up of matter which bears no such stamp,—which is simply learned or miscellaneous in its nature; and if we may pronounce a judgment without intending to bear it out by a minute analysis of the number, it contains nothing of very brilliant character.

The article on " Church of England Missions," reads to us like the Laureate's.   There is some information in it;—a good deal of narrow jealousy of the fame of Roman Catholic missions ;—and a considerable blindness on the subject of the peculiar excellence of the Church of England.   How can a fair man, of large reading in history of all ages and literature of all subjects, say, " that the plain sincerity of the Protestant accounts [of missions] and the elaborate machinery in those of the Catholics, would go far towards satisfying any sane mind upon the question, which is the true church ?"   In this article a long and curious extract is made from Mather's Magnalia.

The article on " Palladian Architecture," with a great deal of learning on the history of architecture in modern Italy, contains views not less sound than bold, on the merits of particular works.   We refer especially to those on St Peter's.

A very long article on the " Origin of Equitable Jurisdiction" we reverently eschew.   We have read to the end of the second sentence, which is to this purport ; " Blackstone has observed, that ' nothing was extant in his day, which would give a stranger a *tolerable idea* of our courts of equity ;' and his own chapter on the subject, elegant and ingenious as it is, cannot be said to supply the deficiency."   If all that the learned Commentator has said on the subject does not afford a "*tolerable idea*" of it, we think it not worth while to plunge into an article of about forty pages, written probably by one no more a Solomon than his neighbours.

The article on " South America " is entertaining, but not otherwise of note.   It is a good compilation from the late travellers.

Mr " Dibdin's Literary Companion " is handled with a severity, just

55

indeed, except as not deserved by the importance of the miserable work in question.

"Past and Present State of the Country," well drawn up and entertaining, without pretensions to vigour. It winds up with a cut at the reformers.

"Irish Fairy Tales" consists of amusing extracts from a book of similar title. "Sacred Poetry" discusses the susceptibility of sacred subjects of a poetical treatment, in opposition to Dr Johnson's dogma to the contrary ; and also sketches the history of English sacred poetry ;— a sensible article. "Ancient and Modern Wines" appears to be a clever abstract of Dr Henderson's work on the subject, with free criticisms upon that work, and some original speculations.

The article on "Early Roman History," which is the third in order, is in some respects particularly worthy of notice. It purports to be a notice of the Roman History of Baron Niebuhr ; an essay on the same subject, by Professor Wachsmuth of Halle ; and a sketch of Roman antiquities by Professor Creuzer of Heidelberg. The Roman History of Niebuhr was reviewed in the North American Review above two years ago. The present Quarterly reviewer says of it, " The history of Niebuhr has thrown new light upon our knowledge of Roman affairs, to a degree of which those who are unacquainted with it can scarcely form an adequate notion. *Yet we are not aware, that it has been so much as noticed in this country* [England], except by ourselves in a former Number of this journal (Quarterly Review No. XXVII. p. 280), and more recently within the last few months by a writer in another periodical publication."

Considering the contemptuous opinion, which has hitherto been inculcated in the Quarterly Review of the state of literature in America, it would not have been amiss for the reviewer to hint, that the American public had two years before the English been put in possession of some of the new and important views contained in Niebuhr's work, in a formal review of it.

This present article in the Quarterly is principally compiled from Niebuhr's account of the Roman military system and the great and inconceivably misunderstood subject of *the Agrarian laws*. Niebuhr's views on this subject were explained in the North American, in the article just alluded to. In the former article in the Quarterly, though its writer professed to have read and admired Niebuhr, he used the old language about "equalization of property," "levelling laws," and "destroying the motives to industry," and plainly showed that he had not read even the prominent chapters of the work he undertook to commend. The writer of this present article (apparently the same individual) has discovered the nature of the Agrarian laws, and calls them wise : but he does not hint at the leading views of Niebuhr as to the peculiar origin of the Roman state, and we strongly suspect had only had a chapter or two of Niebuhr's translated for him. If he will wait a little longer before he writes on Niebuhr again, he will have the work entire (as far as it is written) in an English version from a gentleman of South Carolina College ; a translation is also announced in England.

In the same article it is said, " In this country [England] even professed scholars know in general very little of the works of the Roman lawyers ; in proof of which we may remark, that the recent discovery of the Institutes of Gaius has been scarcely noticed, and not half a dozen copies sold in England, while an entire edition has been disposed of on the continent, and the work either is or was a very short time since out of print." Of this recent discovery (made in 1816) a particular account was given to the American public more than four years ago, and might have been given four years earlier by several American scholars.

There is, however, in this article, towards its close, a train of very liberal reflection, particularly toward the Germans; and a moderate estimate of the merit of the English, in certain departments, where they have been wont most undeservedly to claim a superiority; and which we are disposed to put on record, as a strong testimony against the prejudices of certain of our citizens. " But our inferiority " —it is the Quarterly that speaks—" is still more striking and less excusable, in *every branch of study* connected with the history, antiquities, and literature of Greece and Rome. We believe that there are many writers of those nations, whose works have never been edited in England at all; but it is more to the purpose to inquire, in how many instances the editions of any of them, generally received as the best, have been executed by Englishmen. If we except certain portions of the Greek dramatists and poets, *we really cannot remember a single one*, and if this be spoken too universally (as through forgetfulness it may be), we are sure at least that the exceptions will not be more than sufficient to prove the rule. In lexicography our list contains scarcely a name of high reputation; *and the many defects and errors of the Greek grammar which is most commonly used in our schools, may well excite a foreigner's astonishment.*"

In a note to this passage it is observed, " It will be seen at once, that we refer to the Eton Greek Grammar; by whom it was first written, and what character it deserved to bear in relation to the then existing state of knowledge, we know not—*but it is decidedly behind the present age*, AND DOES NOT TEND TO GIVE BOYS AN ACCURATE KNOWLEDGE OF THE PARTS OF SPEECH OR THE PRINCIPLES OF SYNTAX."

Walladmor, a Romance, freely translated from the English of Walter Scott, and now freely translated from the German into English. London. 1825. 2 vols. 12mo.

Most of our readers have heard of this production, which was offered to the German trade, at the fair of Leipsic, as a genuine translation. The circumstances of the fraud gave it a temporary interest in England, and we procured a copy with the intention of giving our readers a particular account of it, with large extracts, but on examination it seems to us to be unworthy of it. It has little claim to be considered even as an imitation of the Waverley novels, being altogether German in its character. It is sometimes flippant, but generally heavy and dull.

INTELLIGENCE.

NORTH AMERICAN TRADITION OF THE FLOOD.

Mr WEST, in his very interesting journal of his residence at the Red River Colony, lately published, relates the following tradition, current among the North American Indians. It seems, however, to bear marks of modern interpretation. "They spake of an univeral deluge, which, they said, was commonly believed by all Indians. When the flood came and destroyed the world, they say, that a very great man, called Waesackoochack, made a large raft, and embarked, with otters, beavers, deer, and other kinds of animals. After it had floated upon the waters for some time, he put out an otter with a long piece of shagganappy or leathern cord, tied to his leg ; and it dived very deep without finding any bottom, and was drowned. He then put out a beaver, which was equally unsuccessful, and shared the same fate. At length he threw out a muskrat, that dived and brought up a little mud in its mouth, which Waesackoochack took, and, placing it in the palm of his hand, he blew upon it till it greatly enlarged itself, and formed a good piece of earth. He then turned out a deer, that soon returned, which led him to suppose, that the earth was not large enough ; and, blowing upon it again, its size was greatly increased, so that a loon, which he then sent out, never returned. The new earth being now of a sufficient size, he turned adrift all the animals that he had reserved."

FOSSIL ELEPHANT.

The Journal of Lyons gives an interesting account of the discovery of a Fossil Elephant on the hill which separates the Rhone and Saone, to the east of the city of Lyons. Some workmen, digging a pit on clayey marle, found, at a depth of seven and a half feet, some fragments of bones, which were white and rather friable. They were surprised to see these animal remains in what the gardeners call a virgin earth. "I went to the place," says the writer of the notice, "and soon recognised some of the bones of an elephant. Among the persons present, some pretended they were bones of a giant ; others, not so ignorant, said they were the skeleton of a mammoth. Those who agreed with me, that these large bones had belonged to an elephant, took it into their heads, they were the remains of one of those belonging to the army of Hannibal."

RICE PAPER.

The substance, commonly known by the name of rice paper, is brought from China, and although it has a general resemblance to a substance formed by art, yet a slight examination of it with the microscope is sufficient to indicate a vegetable organization. A series of experiments to ascertain its structure have shown, that it consists of long hexagonal cells, whose length is parallel to the surface of the film. These cells are filled with air, when the film is exposed in its usual state, and from this circumstance it derives its peculiar softness. It is a membrane of the bread-fruit tree, the *artocarpus incissifolia* of naturalists, and when the film is exposed to polarized light, the longitudinal *septa* of the cells polarize it like other vegetable membranes.

MR POINSETT'S NOTES ON MEXICO.

This work, which has been some time before the American public, and has received from all quarters the commendation due to its distinguished merits, has just been re-published in London.

NEW PUBLICATIONS.

BIOGRAPHY.

Memoir of Catharine Brown, a Christian Indian, of the Cherokee Nation. By Rufus Anderson, A. M. Assistant Secretary of the American Board of Foreign Missions. Second edition. 18mo. pp. 144. Boston. Crocker & Brewster.

GEOGRAPHY.

Geographical Questions for the use of Schools, adapted to the Maps and Charts in most common use. 18mo. pp. 54. Middletown, Ct. E. & H. Clark.

The author has formed his questions without reference to any particular system of geography or maps, with a view to enable pupils to use different systems, and still to recite in the same class, without confusion to themselves or to their instructer.

HISTORY.

View and Description of the City of New Orange (now New York), as it was in the year 1673; with Explanatory Notes. By Joseph W. Moulton, Esq. with an Engraved View of the City at that Period. New York.

LAW.

Trial of Moses Parker, James Buckland, Joseph Wade, William Walker, Cornelius Holley, Abraham Potts, and Noah Doremus, on an Indictment for the Murder of David R. Lambert, on the 3d of June, 1825, at a Court of Oyer and Terminer, held in and for the City and County of New York, on the third Monday of June, 1825, before the Hon. Ogden Edwards, Judge of the First Circuit. 8vo. New York. H. Spear.

Strictures upon the Constitutional Powers of the Congress and Courts of the United States over the Execution Laws of the several States, in their Application to the Federal Courts. By a Citizen of Ohio. 8vo. pp. 17. Cincinnati. Morgan, Lodge, & Fisher.

" At their last term, the Supreme Court of the United States decided, that the Execution Laws of the several States, enacted since 1789, do not apply to proceedings upon judgments in the United States Circuit Courts. This decision, though principally founded upon acts of Congress, nevertheless assumes a construction of the Constitution of vital importance to the States and to the people. It is this:—In all cases to which the judicial power is extended by the Constitution, Congress is empowered to enact laws for enforcing by execution the judgments of the courts. And this, whether such law prescribe only a rule of practice to the courts, or, in addition, a rule of property to the citizen." The author of the pamphlet, whose title we have printed above, thus states the proposition, which it his is object to controvert. His " Strictures" are written in a good temper, and with a degree of candour which has not always characterized the writings of our Western brethren, when investigating the conflicting claims of the State governments and the government of the United States. We may take occasion, at some future time, to examine these " Strictures" more at length in another department of our work.

The Maryland Justice; containing Approved Forms for the use of Justices of the Peace of the State of Maryland; with a Compilation of the Acts of the General Assembly relating to their Office and Jurisdiction, and to the Office and Duties of Constable. Compiled by Ebenezer H. Cummings, Esq. Baltimore. Cushing & Jewett.

MATHEMATICS.

The Mathematical Diary.   No. III.   New York.   S. Ryan.

MEDICINE.

The Philadelphia Journal of the Medical and Physical Sciences. No. XX.

MISCELLANEOUS.

The Boston Directory; containing Names of the Inhabitants; their Occupations, Places of Business, and Dwelling Houses; with Lists of the Streets, Lanes, and Wharves, the City Officers, Public Offices, and Banks, and other useful information. 18mo. pp. 324. Boston. J. H. A. Frost.

On the Aim of the Order of the Freemasons. Translated from the German, by ——. 12mo. Albany. E. & E. Hosford.

Memoir read before the Historical Society of the State of New York, December 31, 1816. By E. Benson. Second edition, with Notes. New York. Wilder & Campbell.

An Address delivered at the Opening of the Tenth Exhibition of the American Academy of the Fine Arts. By Gulian C. Verplanck. Second edition. 8vo. pp. 52. New York. G. & C. Carvill.

Journal of the Academy of Natural Sciences of Philadelphia. Vol. V. No. II.

An Address in Commemoration of the Battle at Fryeburg, delivered May 19, 1825. By Charles S. Daveis. 8vo. pp. 64. Portland. James Adams, jr.

An Oration, pronounced at Cambridge, before the Society of Phi Beta Kappa, August 26th, 1824. By Edward Everett. Fourth Edition. 8vo. pp. 67. Boston. Cummings, Hilliard, & Co.

The Worcester Magazine and Historical Journal. No. I. Vol. I. June, 1825. pp. 32.

An Address pronounced at Worcester, Mass. on the 4th of July, 1825, being the Forty-ninth Anniversary of the Independence of the United States, before an Assembly convened for the purpose of celebrating this event religiously. By Samuel Austin, D. D. 8vo. Worcester. William Manning.

Ninth Report of the Directors of the American Asylum, at Hartford, for the Education of the Deaf and Dumb, exhibited to the Asylum, May 14, 1825. 8vo. pp. 36. Hartford.

We learn from this report, that provisions have been made for the instruction of the pupils at the Asylum in several of the "Mechanic trades;" with a view to preserve habits of industry as well as to enable them, or such of them as are indigent, to support themselves by labour when they shall leave the institution. The expenses for the present year for each pupil, placed at the Asylum, are one hundred and fifteen dollars, including the usual instruction, board, washing, and lodging; stationary for school rooms, and instruction in mechanic trades. As the funds of the institution increase, this annual expense will probably be diminished, and of course a greater number of pupils will have access to the advantages which are here offered to them. Since the opening of the institution in April, 1817, one hundred and forty three different pupils have been admitted and have received instruction in it. Of this number, seventy one are still members of the establishment. From personal observation, as well as from the specimens of composition annexed to this report, we could say much of the philosophical principles of education reduced to practice in the instruction of the deaf and dumb, and of the corresponding improvement of the pupils; but the character of the instructers and the results of their devoted labours are too well known to the community to require any farther testimony from us.

First Annual Report of the Albany Institute. Presented July 1, 1825. 8vo. pp. 8.

The Albany Institute was organized in May, 1824. It is composed of three branches or departments; 1st. The department of Mathematics and Physical Science and the Arts;—2d. The department of Natural History;—and 3d. The department of History and General Literature. The Hon. Stephen Van Rensselaer is President of the Institute. Each department has its president, who is *ex officio* a vice-president of the Institute; and each has also its corresponding and recording secretaries. We think the institution promises interest to its members, and usefulness to the public. The society have already a considerable Library, and many Mineralogical, Geological, and Zoological specimens; besides some specimens of organic remains. The members meet every fortnight during the four first months of the year, and read original essays or dissertations upon the various topics relating to the objects of the association.

Addresses delivered at Oxford, Ohio, on the 30th of March, 1825, at the Inauguration of the Rev. Robert H. Bishop as President of the Miami University. Published by order of the Board of Trustees. Hamilton, Ohio. James B. Camron.

Address delivered before the Citizens of North Yarmouth, on the Anniversary of American Independence, July 4, 1825. By Grenville Mellen. 8vo. pp. 20. Portland. D. & S. Paine.

Remarks on the Disorders of Literary Men, or an Inquiry into the Means of Preventing the Evils usually incident to Sedentary and Studious Habits. 12mo. pp. 92. Boston. Cummings, Hilliard, & Co.

Plan of a Seminary for the Education of Instructers of Youth. By Thomas H. Gallaudet, Principal of the American Asylum for the Education of the Deaf and Dumb. Boston. Cummings, Hilliard, & Co.

THEOLOGY.

Familiar Sermons. By Asa Rand, Editor of the Christian Mirror, and lately Pastor of the Church in Gorham, Me. 12mo. pp. 393. Portland, Me.

A Century Sermon, delivered at Hopkinton, Mass. on Lord's Day, December 24th, 1815. By Nathaniel Howe, A. M. Pastor of the Church. Third edition, with Notes, revised and corrected. 8vo. pp. 82. Boston. Crocker & Brewster.

A Treatise concerning Heaven and its Wonders, also concerning Hell, being a relation of Things seen and heard. Translated from the Latin of Emanuel Swedenborg. Second American from the sixth English edition. 1 vol. 8vo. Boston. Cummings, Hilliard, & Co.

AMERICAN EDITIONS OF FOREIGN WORKS.

Elements of Physiology. By A. Richerand. Translated from the French, by G. I. M. De Sys, M. D. With Notes, and a Copious Appendix, by James Copland, M. D. 8vo. New York. W. E. Dean.

The Last Days of Lord Byron; with his Lordship's Opinions on Various Subjects, particularly on the State and Prospects of Greece. By William Parry, Major of Lord Byron's Brigade, and Engineer in the Service of the Greeks. 12mo.

Patience; A Tale. By Mrs Hofland, author of Decision, &c. &c. 18mo. pp. 309. New York. W. B. Gilley.

LIST OF WORKS IN PRESS.

A practical Treatise on Rail Roads, showing the Principles of estimating their Proportions, Strength, and Expense; with the Theory,

Effect, and Expense of Steam Carriages, Stationary Engines, and Gas Machines. By Thomas Fredgold. From a late London copy. New York. E. Bliss & E. White.

Thompson's Conspectus of the London and Edinburgh Pharmacopœias, together with Magendie's Formulary. New York. E. Bliss & E. White.

Good's Study of Medicine. 5 vols. 8vo. A New Edition from the second London edition, with numerous Additions and Corrections. Boston. Wells & Lilly.

Life of R. S. Sheridan. By Thomas Moore, Esq. Philadelphia.

Zophiel; a Poem. By an American Lady. Boston.

Mason on Self-Knowledge, with Questions adapted for Schools and Academies. Fourth edition. Boston. James Loring.

Blair's Catechism of Common Things in Use. Fifth edition. Boston. James Loring.

Murray's Exercises. Twelfth edition. Boston. James Loring.

A View of South America and Mexico, comprising the History, Political Condition, Commerce, &c. of the two Countries; with two Maps and a Portrait of Bolivar. Hartford. H. Huntington, jr.

Miss Hamilton's Letters on Education. 2 vols. 12mo. Boston. S. H. Parker.

Gramática Completa de la Lengua Inglesa, para Uso de los Españoles; con un Suplemento, que contiene las Frases mas precisas para romper in una Conversacion, Formas de Documentos Comerciales, y Descripciones de las Cuidades de Filadelfia y de Washington. Por Stephen M. L. Staples, A. M. Filadelfia. H. C. Carey y I. Lea: y E. Bliss y E. White, Nueva York.

The Last of the Mohians. A Novel. By the Author of the Spy, Pioneers, &c. New York. Charles Wiley.

The Universal Historical Dictionary, or an Explanation of the Names of Persons and Places, in the departments of Biblical, Political, and Ecclesiastical History, Mythology, Heraldry, Biography, Geography, Numismatics. Illustrated with nearly 800 portraits, and a vast number of wood cuts from medals, coins, &c. By George Crabb, A. M. New York, W. B. Gilley.

Reciprocal Duties of Parents and Children. By Mrs. Taylor. Second edition. 18mo. Boston. James Loring.

Lectures. By Sir Ashley Cooper. From the first London edition. 8vo. Boston. Wells & Lilly.

The Biblical Reader, consisting of copious Selections from the Sacred Scriptures, with Questions, Practical Observations, &c. &c. for the Use of Schools. By the Rev. J. L. Blake. Ornamented with numerous Engravings. 1 vol. 12mo. Boston. Lincoln & Edmands.

Pronouncing Bible. Second stereotype edition. Boston. Lincoln & Edmands.

Journal of a Tour around Hawaii, one of the Sandwich Islands. By a Deputation of the Mission on those Islands. 12mo. Boston. Crocker & Brewster.

Published on the first and fifteenth day of every month, by CUMMINGS, HILLIARD, & Co., No. 134 Washington-Street, Boston, for the Proprietors. Terms, $5 per annum. Cambridge: Printed at the University Press, by Hilliard & Metcalf

THE UNITED STATES
LITERARY GAZETTE.

| VOL. II. | SEPTEMBER 15, 1825. | No. 12. |

REVIEWS.

Reform of Harvard College.

(For the Titles, see No. 6 of this Gazette.)

[CONTINUED.]

THE great object [said Mr Pickering] of a liberal education is to qualify young persons for the three liberal professions ; the few exceptions of those who are not designed for them need not be taken into the account in a general view. Now of the three professions, two, it was obvious, required a deep and solid foundation of *literature* as distinguished from the *sciences*, particularly the *exact sciences;* which last are useful, rather as a discipline for the intellectual powers, than as the positive acquisition of so much knowledge which is to be brought into actual use in those professions ; the remaining profession, it was true, required a portion of science, yet this, again, was not of the exact sciences (except as they are subsidiary to the rest), but only of the subdivision usually denominated *physical science.* It seemed an obvious conclusion, then, that the most useful course of instruction should be that which should with the greatest certainty effect the most extensive and thorough acquisitions in literature (to use the term in its full extent) within the period of time usually allotted to a university education. Now, by the common consent of the nations of Europe, the basis of these solid acquisitions is what is called *classical learning.* * * *

We had, like some others, been carried away by the very vague and deceptive name of *useful knowledge ;* as if no knowledge was to be considered as useful, except such as was used in obtaining national or private wealth and in providing for the *physical* wants of man ; but the eminent statesmen of the most enlightened nations had assigned the first rank to that kind of knowledge, which most directly promoted the development of the *intellectual powers*, and furnished the greatest stock of intellectual wealth, to enable men to comprehend their moral and political relations, and, practically, to discharge their duties

56

towards each other and towards the community or state of which they are members; and this object was best attained by that course of thorough classical education, which had been long established in the celebrated institutions of the old world.   It was needless to support these opinions by the weight of individual authority; but the whole argument was so strikingly presented in a few words by the great English moralist, that it could not be deemed out of place to refer gentlemen to the sentiments of that great man upon the subject of education.   [Mr Pickering here read the following extract from Johnson's Life of Milton :—" The truth is, that the knowledge of external nature, and the sciences which that knowledge requires or includes, are not the great or the frequent business of the human mind.   Whether we provide for action or conversation, whether we wish to be useful or pleasing, the first requisite is the religious and moral knowledge of right and wrong; the next is an acquaintance with the history of mankind, and with those examples which may be said to embody truth and prove by events the reasonableness of opinions.   Prudence and justice are virtues and excellencies of all places; we are perpetually moralists, but we are geometricians only by chance.   Our intercourse with intellectual nature is necessary; our speculations upon matter are voluntary and at leisure.   Physiological learning is of such rare emergence, that one may know another half his life without being able to estimate his skill in hydrostatics or astronomy; but his moral and prudential character immediately appears.   *Those authors, therefore, are to be read at schools, that supply most axioms of prudence, most principles of moral truth, and most materials for conversation;* and these purposes are best served by poets, orators, and historians."]

If any thing could be added to the consideration here urged with so much force, it would be the sentiments of an eminent British statesman [Sir James Mackintosh], who has said, in a speech distinguished by his usual eloquence, that we ought to have a perfect familiarity with the classic authors, who were the models of thought, the masters of moral teaching, and of civil wisdom, and above all things of *civil liberty.*

We have made these long extracts in order to give a distinct view of Mr Pickering's opinion on this subject, and supposing that this would be better exhibited in his words than in our own; besides that, by this course, we at least avoid the risk of misrepresentation.

On this subject opinions very different from those of Mr Pickering have been held and publicly defended, with some ingenuity at least; and we have ourselves been accused, in some periodical publication, of favouring this literary heresy. It may not be amiss on this occasion, therefore, to deliver our creed, and we gladly seize the opportunity to express a part of it in the language of one, whose name and whose memory will long be dear to the friends of American literature.

" At that early period of life," says Mr Frisbie, " when the languages of these nations [the Greeks and Romans] are usually learned, their study affords a useful discipline to the mind, which could not perhaps, at that age, be so well derived from any other source. In discovering the meaning of a passage, there is not only a vigorous exercise of the powers of invention and comprehension; but in that grammatical analysis of each sentence, which is necessary for this purpose, a constant process of reasoning is carried on. By translation, a youth, while he acquires that copiousness of expression, so much insisted on by Quintilian, forms, at the same time, the habit of nicely discriminating the import of words, and perceiving their minutest shades of difference; and this much more from the dead, than living languages, because their idiom and modes of combination vary more from our own. The importance of the early formation of this habit will be obvious to those, who consider, that language is not only the vehicle of our thoughts, when we impart them to others, but the very body in which they appear to ourselves. We think in propositions, and in proportion to the propriety and definiteness of our words, will be those of our ideas. It is true, that during the period we have mentioned, many facts in geography, civil, and even natural history, might be stored in the memory. But, not to mention that, especially with the children of the wealthy, there is time enough for all these; we hold it to be a maxim, that discipline, rather than knowledge, should be the object of education. We do not consider that youth as best taught, who has read or knows the most; but him, who carries into the world an understanding, formed successfully to grapple with whatever subject may be proposed, and most able, in whatever situation he may be placed, to think and act with sagacity, with truth and effect." * We may add, that the early study of these languages, especially the Latin, for we think the Greek less necessary, is the best method of promoting the object proposed by some of the opposers of this study. The time spent, say they, in learning this dead language, might be more usefully employed in acquiring one or more of the modern ones. But this is a narrow view of the subject. It is not that the student is merely acquiring the power of reading a single language; he is acquiring the power of learning every language with facility,—he is fixing in his mind the principles and rules of universal grammar, by the study of a model

---

* North American Review, March, 1818, p. 325.

now settled and unchangeable. The youth who is well in-structed in Latin grammar wants neither that of English, French, Spanish, nor indeed that of any other language, ex-cept for the explanation of an occasional exception to his general rule. The study of Latin, in short, is a labour-sav-ing invention, if it is nothing better, and this is a sufficient an-swer to the demand of *cui bono?*

The arguments in favour of this study, however, apply to an age earlier than that at which young men are usually ad-mitted to the university;—the acquiring of a competent knowledge of the Latin certainly, and perhaps of the Greek, should be prior to their admission. This is to be effected by making it necessary for this purpose. The governors of the College have been, for some years, gradually advancing in this particular, by increasing their demands upon the can-didates, and we know no better way. Whether they have advanced fast enough our knowledge of the subject does not enable us to say; it is evident this must depend in some de-gree upon the state of schools.

But we infer from his language that Mr Pickering means by "classical learning" something more than the mere knowledge of the ancient languages and the power of read-ing them with tolerable facility; he would have the stu-dents acquainted with the works of most of the celebrated ancient authors and the peculiarities of their style. He would have them acquire a taste for their perusal and a relish for their beauties. He would have them prepared and enabled to find amusement for a leisure hour, or solace for an anxious one, in the pages of Pindar, Homer, and Horace, as readily as in those of Milton, Childe Harold, or Waver-ley; and he implies, if we understand him, that this result had better be obtained at the expense of much scientific knowledge—that it is even necessary for professional men. But in this we differ from him. That a highly cultivated taste of this sort is a source of happiness, and innocent hap-piness, we admit; but so is a taste for the fine arts, for paint-ing, sculpture, and the like; and the general cultivation of taste in all these things is advantageous to society.

> *Has* didicisse fideliter artes
> Emollit mores, nec sinit esse feros.

But any degree of cultivation of this sort requires time, leis-ure, and application to a degree that is not permitted to many individuals in a young nation like our own. It is a luxury, while scientific and professional acquirements are necessaries; and we contend that those important years which are usually spent in College must not be wholly, nor indeed in a great degree, employed in cultivating tastes no way connected with commercial, manufacturing, agricultural, political, or professional excellence. We deny that classical learning, in the sense in which it seems to be understood by Mr Pickering and of which he himself is well known to be a brilliant illustration, is any more necessary to either of the professions than it is to any gentleman in any situation. We look upon it in the light of the "burnish of a complete man," and in no other. As to the quotations from Dr Johnson and Sir James Mackintosh, they have no weight with us in our view of the question; every moral and every political question, every argument in favour of civil liberty, all the history and all the reasoning of the ancients may be obtained without a knowledge of their language. The world is filled with translations, imitations, and plagiarisms; their sentiments have been borrowed and repeated and mixed and compounded in our own language, till nothing is left to be discovered in the original. To know all that the ancients said or thought, we want no language but our own; the knowledge of the exact manner in which they have said it, is all that is to be gained by the first degree of classical learning; and this we contend is a luxury, and not a necessary.

But there are occasionally, individual students, with whom the principal object of a liberal education is to become accomplished scholars, and this class is likely to increase with the wealth and population of the country. It would seem desirable that the College should afford facilities for this purpose, while it seems incompatible with the routine, which confines all to the same course of study. The recommendation of the committee, that there should be a certain liberty of choice, seems judicious, though there appear to be some objections on the score of practicability, which, however, our limits will not enable us to discuss.

In what we have said above we do not mean to imply that no attention ought to be paid to classical learning in the University; we think the accomplishment is worth much, though we do not consider it the sole, nor even the most important, object of a liberal education. But, in any point of view, is sufficient attention paid to classical learning in Harvard University?

Mr Pickering thinks not ; but from the difference of our views on the general subject, it is not easy to decide whether we should, on the whole, agree with him. One evidence of the fact, in his view, is the difference between the attention now given, and that which was fashionable a century or more ago. But this weighs not at all with us ; a sort of pedantic and useless erudition was then often encouraged to the neglect of more important knowledge. The graduates of the present day cannot indeed boast the scholastic lore, which addled the brains of Cotton Mather, and enabled him to "write himself down an ass " in Greek and Latin as well as in English ; but besides a tolerable general knowledge of the ancient tongues, they have a store of that scientific information, in which he was so wofully deficient. Another evidence is the general inability to speak Latin. The students are no longer able to speak " suo ut aiunt Marte ;" one of our professors, on going abroad, was compelled to learn to speak Latin ; another professor was unable to reply in that language to the address of a foreign officer of engineers, &c. But this again weighs lightly with us. We know numberless instances in which an inability to speak a language, either living or dead, is perfectly compatible with the power of reading and understanding it with the greatest facility, with an acquaintance with the fine writings in it, and a high relish of its beauties. Moreover, the power of conversing in Latin is a cheap accomplishment, easily acquired and easily lost ; it is taught in almost every petty conventual school in Europe, and in many where little else can be learned that is worth learning ; and thus it becomes, in Catholic countries at least, a common acquirement with many who possibly never heard of Tully or Quintilian. We have known a whole hive of contemptible monks, in a convent where Latin composition was taught with great diligence, who regarded the belief of the earth's motion as an heretical blasphemy, to whom such a map of the world as every urchin can draw in a New England school was a prodigy, a brown paper armillary sphere, a month's wonder, and a Greek testament, a sealed book ; yet had one of these wretched dealers in the dead languages wandered by any accident to America, he might, by this principle, have triumphed over our classical professors ; and with no more reading than the Fasti of Ovid, or the " Vocalem breviant aliâ subeunte Latini," might have put to the blush many a one to whom Virgil and Horace and Juvenal and Persius were familiar names and cherished companions. In short, though they are not taught to speak Latin at Cambridge, we believe that the acquirement would be as easy as it would be useless. Another evidence is, that on the occasion of a public examination at Cambridge several errors in the pronunciation of the students were detected. We can believe this, without supposing any remarkable inattention of the instructers. The truth is, that pronunciation is learned early and changed with difficulty, and that formerly many of our schools were exceedingly deficient in this particular, and very probably some of them are so still. The consequence was, as we suppose it now is, that some students were admitted to College with a good knowledge of Latin and with an indifferent pronunciation. Any person, who has observed the offences against Walker, which are not uncommon among gentlemen otherwise well educated and accomplished, and that too in spite of considerable watchfulness on their own part, may suspect that the errors noticed by Mr Pickering did not necessarily imply a blameable want of diligence on the part of the instructers. Those who have some experience in this matter, and recollect the almost unintermitting and apparently hopeless endeavour at the *Cæsăris* and *Consŭlis*, which within our memory characterized the Latin recitation room, will think this charge upon the instructers a hard one.

After all, we admit that the students in Harvard College generally do not make so much proficiency in classical or in any other branch of learning as might be wished; but this, we think, arises rather from their own want of diligence than from any defect of opportunities; and of the modes of remedying the habits of the University in this particular we have already spoken. While on this subject of classical learning, we cannot avoid remarking upon a note appended to this speech. It relates to the practice of employing foreign professors, and is as follows:

The practice of employing foreign professors is common all over the continent of Europe; and even in England, where there has been less inclination than elsewhere to adopt it, there are instances of professorships founded upon the express condition, that they shall be open to all nations. As, for instance, in the Savilian professorship of geometry and astronomy, at Oxford, the electors and visitors "are *solemnly conjured* by the founder to seek the ablest mathematicians in other countries as well as our own; and without regard to particular universities or nations, to elect those whom they shall deem best qualified for the office."

But we are not told the founder's reason for this earnestness. It is, as he informs us in the preamble to this deed of gift, " that geometry was wholly abandoned and unknown in England, and that the best learning of the age was the study of the ancients." This is the state of things from which the English colleges, and more particularly our own, have *degenerated*, and we trust that the restoration of the *ancien regime* in the literature of the country, is no nearer at hand than it is in its politics.

We may observe here that one of the best methods of acquiring an accurate knowledge of the dead languages, and indeed of every language, living or dead, is the practice of composing in them, and that this practice is too much neglected, not in Cambridge only, but in every American school or college, one only excepted, of which we have ever had any knowledge.

We do not exactly take the force of the following anecdote in relation to this subject.

Mr Pickering said he was permitted (by the honourable chairman of the Committee) to mention a little occurrence in the life of that late distinguished man, Mr Pinkney (not long since our minister in Great Britain), who used to relate it to his young friends as a warning to them. While that gentleman was at the court of St James's, it happened, at a social party, that some little question in classical literature became the subject of conversation at table, and the guests, in turn, gave their opinions upon it; Mr Pinkney being silent for some time, an appeal was at length made to him for his opinion, when (as he used to relate with much feeling) he had the mortification of being compelled to avow his incompetency to give any opinion upon the subject; and what was the consequence? This distinguished man, brilliant and commanding as were his native talents, confessed that he felt constrained, in his mature years, to take his grammar and dictionary, and actually to put himself under the instruction of a master in the ancient languages.

Certainly this can have little to do with the state of our colleges, since the eminent statesman alluded to never enjoyed any regular collegiate education; and as to the advantages of classical learning, it would appear to prove that a man may attain to high fame, usefulness, and honour without it.

The result of the debate concerning the reports of the two committees was the reference of both to the corporation. This body, after consideration of the whole subject, presented to the board of overseers, at their next meeting, a new code of laws for the future regulation of the University; which, having been ratified by them, will be in force the present college year.   We shall offer some remarks on this code, after bringing down to the same period the history of another important document, the memorial of the resident officers.*

[To be continued.]

Outlines of Political Economy, being a Republication of the Article upon that Subject, contained in the Edinburgh Supplement to the Encyclopædia Britannica. Together with Notes, Explanatory and Critical, and a Summary of the Science.   By the Rev. JOHN M' VICKAR, A. M. Professor of Moral Philosophy and Political Economy in Columbia College, New York. New York. 1825. 8vo. pp. 183.

THE author of this work is Mr M'Culloch, late of Edinburgh, who has been honoured by being selected as the first lecturer, on the foundation established by the late Mr Ricardo.   Professor M'Vickar has caused its republication, for the purpose of " diffusing in a more popular form a valuable essay on a most important subject."   This enterprise is worthy of all praise.   In no country ought the knowledge of political economy to be more widely diffused than in this, at this moment ; not merely on account of the popular frame of our legislative institutions, in consequence of which great power is thrown into the hands of active and able men of every class in society ; but still more, because the country is not yet tied down to any system ; it is not yet necessary to persevere in any course, merely because it has been for time immemorial established ;—and because, also, the country is unfolding itself so rapidly, that there is no time to be lost.   We must every day take steps of vast moment, in the national march ; and it deserves all attention, that they be taken with

---

* In an early number of this article, when comparing the price of board at Cambridge with the same at other Colleges, we stated the latter in some instances too high.   That at Yale, for example, as we have since been informed, being $1 75, instead of $2 25, we take this opportunity of observing that we were not then aware that any change had taken place in this particular at Yale since the publication of our authority, Worcester's Gazetteer. We had no intention of misrepresenting the state of that, or any other College, but were only attempting to show that this charge at Cambridge was not, considering the local circumstances of the College, an extravagant one ; and this position we do not think affected materially by the correction now made.   We regret the error however, and the rather if it has given the impression in any quarter, that we intended to bring Harvard College and other institutions into comparison, to the prejudice of the latter, as to the subject of expenses.

57

such care, that hereafter we may be spared the odious and almost desperate task of applying the remedy to inveterate evils.

Mr M'Culloch's Essay can hardly be called classical; that is, a treatise perfect in all its parts, containing nothing superfluous, omitting nothing essential. Being written for the Encyclopædia, it passes over several topics, as already disposed of, or to be treated in subsequent articles. For popular use, the Notes of Professor M'Vickar, though we cannot join him in all his criticisms, enhance considerably the value of the book. He supplies some of the omitted topics, explains some things stated over briefly in the original Essay, and especially refers to various authorities still farther illustrative of the important subjects successively brought up. He has performed a valuable service to the science in the preparation of these Notes, which display a full acquaintance with a subject, many of whose topics are exceedingly subtile and abstract.

It is not designed to detract from this commendation nor to qualify it, when we add our impression, that Mr M'Culloch's Essay is not *so* well adapted to the object, which Professor M'Vickar had in view, as it would have been in his power to render an essay of equal compass, which should have been entirely of his own composing. The science of political economy is at a lamentably low ebb in this country. Of the only considerable treatise which has been produced in it, Mr Raymond's, almost every proposition in any degree peculiar to that gentleman, is wholly false; and the newspaper political economy which is bestowed upon the country in some of the widest circulated journals is wholly exploded in every other region. We venture to say, that if a work should appear in London or Paris, in which much was said about " the drain of specie " or " the balance of trade," the price of hellebore would advance perceptibly. Far different is the case here. Though among those conversant with the subject, we have reason to believe a very great majority entertain sound general views upon it, a far greater zeal has been employed in propagating the antiquated prejudices. The battle against these is not yet fought out; nor are we quite ripe for the exquisite analysis of the school of Ricardo.

It is very desirable that a popular manual treatise of political economy should be composed for the use of this country. The strong peculiarity of the state of things here existing requires a different selection of topics from that which would be made for an European community. The slight burden of taxation—the abundance and cheapness of good land—the absence of a class of tenantry—the infancy of the manufacturing system, are so many features of the state of society in America, requiring topics to be pressed, wholly different from those which are of leading importance in England. The doctrines of rent and wages are here of scarce any importance ; at the same time that the exquisite subtilty of the speculations, on which they are founded, by the writers of the school of Ricardo, must prevent their gaining access to the minds of those, whom it is of most importance to illuminate. The great doctrine of political economy, which ought to be inculcated in this country, not merely as a truth in science and as a doctrine essential to the accumulation of national wealth, but as a part of our grand system of liberty, is, the greatest possible freedom of trade. The community ought to bear inculcated, with the same perseverance that the reverse has been inculcated,—that the wealth of the citizens is the wealth of the republic—that the will of the citizen should be his guide in the choice of a pursuit—that commerce is an exchange of values—and that protecting duties are a tax levied on all the community for the benefit of the manufacturer. While it is conceded (as Adam Smith concedes, and every judicious man must not so much concede as assert) that manufactures are a source of wealth, a step in the national progress, a means of enhancing the value of land and its products—of calling into valuable exercise the power of natural agents ; it ought to be at the same time taught, that all these desirable objects ought to be attained, *in the course of nature :* that it by no means follows from the fact that a thing is good, that it is good to tax the people to enable the manufacturer to produce it ; in a word, that any manufacture, which *permanently* yields the article at a dearer rate than it could (without duties) be imported, is and must be,— however profitable to the undertaker—though villages rise around his factories as by enchantment, though the voice of the water wheel be heard out of the deepest glen of the mountains,—a waste of national wealth.

We have observed, that though we admire the acuteness of many of Professor M'Vickar's Notes, and the good sense of most, we cannot agree with him in all. We do not join him in his exception to Mr M'Culloch's doctrine, that capital is but labour accumulated; or rather, we should say, since Professor M'Vickar grants the abstract justice of this maxim and himself repeatedly asserts it, we do not join him in condemning the use of the phraseology founded on that doctrine. He tells us indeed that the practical economist will be perplexed by finding things, so different as capital and labour, confounded. But the practical economist, who can digest the principle that rent forms no part of price (indubitable as the principle is), will not be disturbed at any thing else in this treatise.

Considering the object of the work, we think it would have been desirable to have it printed in a rather more cheerful form. The type is too small, even in the text; and the editor's valuable Notes cannot be studied, without endangering a treasure, which all the wealth of all the nations could not compensate,—a healthy eyesight. We have sometimes been inclined to think, that the reason why Smith's immortal work has not more circulated among us is, that the American edition of it is so villanously printed.

MISCELLANY.

DESCRIPTION OF MADRID.

[CONCLUDED.]

ROYAL ACADEMIES—PUBLIC LIBRARIES—SCHOOL FOR THE DEAF AND DUMB—CIRCUS FOR BULL-FIGHTS—THE PRADO AND DELICIAS CABINET OF NATURAL HISTORY—THE ROYAL COLLECTION OF PAINTINGS—THE ROYAL ARMORY—MUSEUM OF THE PARK OF ARTILLERY—POLICE OF THE CITY.

There are royal academies here, of history, of natural philosophy, of medicine, of jurisprudence, of the fine arts, of economy, of the sacred canons and ecclesiastical discipline, &c. There are also royal colleges and schools for instruction in all the branches of education. The botanical school possesses advantages surpassing those of most other countries, inasmuch as the royal botanical garden, where it is situated, possesses probably a greater abundance and variety of rare plants, than any other garden in Europe. Botany and agriculture is here publicly taught. The course of lectures begins in May, and is continued till September or October. The schools for children, I am told, are on a very miserable footing. The time of the pupils is mostly employed in learning to repeat Latin prayers, not one word of which do they understand. But this exercise, they are taught to believe, is most useful to them. The education of women here seems to be considered of as little importance as it is in Turkey, it being confined to their prayers and books of devotion; and it is not improbable, that hence might be traced one of the principal causes of the present degraded state of the kingdom; for the difference between these and the sensible, well educated mothers of England, for instance, is as great, as is the difference in the political and moral condition of the two countries.

The public libraries of this city are creditable to the monarchs of Spain. The royal library, founded by Philip V. in 1712, has been enlarged by succeeding monarchs, and now consists of more than 200,000 volumes, besides a great number of valuable Arabic manuscripts. This library is open to the public at stated hours, every day in the week. The library of San Isidro, containing 60,000 volumes, is open to the public every day, excepting holydays. The library of San Fernando is open to the public three days in the week. There are besides these, two or three others of minor importance. When on the subject of schools, I forgot to mention one for the instruction of the deaf and dumb. The Spaniards boast of being the first, who conceived the idea, and gave rules for reducing to an art, the mode of teaching this unfortunate class of human beings. The first attempt was made by Juan Pablo Bonet, in the time of Philip III. This system was afterwards improved by Father Bernardino Ponce, from whom the Abbé l'Epie took the idea, and succeeded in bringing it to a high degree of perfection.

Of theatres, there were formerly four in this city—but at present there are only two, neither of which is now open, as it is the season of Lent. The favourite amusement of the Spaniards, and, much to the honour of human nature, I believe it is peculiar to them, is bull-fighting. The great circus for these exhibitions is situated a little without the gate of Alcalá, and it is said will contain from 12 to 14,000 persons. It is of two stories, built of brick and plastered. This amusement is confined to fifteen or sixteen days in the autumn, and here it is that a stranger has the best opportunity of seeing the beauty and fashion of Madrid. Much has been said and written, on the inhumanity of this amusement. The Pope, Pius V., in the year 1567, issued a bull against it, and those who were engaged in it; but his successor, Clement VIII. in 1576, revoked it; since which, the Popes have not meddled with it, and the Spaniards will probably always possess the exclusive enjoyment of this barbarous and disgraceful diversion.

There are fifteen entrances to the city, through gates, some of which resemble the Roman triumphal arches, and constitute some of its best ornaments. The streets of the city, excepting those of Alcalá and Atocha, are narrow and dark ; there is a flagging, of only about two feet from the walls of the houses ; across which are stretched, in various parts, groups of blind beggars, singing, and playing the guitar ; women with sick or deformed children ; old men, who seem as if the exposure must hasten their relief by death, some without legs, others without arms, and all crying out, in the most piteous tones, to those passing, to give them something for the love of God. To avoid treading on these people, you must go off the flagging ; from whence, in the spaces not thus occupied, you are constantly subjected to be jostled off by other pedestrians, who are regardless of our rule of taking the right. Nor is it a matter of trifling importance to be thus jostled off, as the streets, being paved with the flint stone, are exceedingly rough, and the walking on them is difficult and painful. To make amends for this defect in the streets, Madrid possesses some of the finest public walks in the world. The Prado, within the walls, and the Delicias, without, are those most frequented. The former is ornamented with several beautiful fountains ; one of which is a colossal figure of Cybele, seated on a chariot of four wheels, and drawn by two lions, all of white marble ; another is the figure of Apollo, on a square pedestal, supported by four figures representing the seasons, of marble ; another, and the finest, is a colossal figure of Neptune, standing on a conch shell as a car, and drawn by two sea horses. In front of the horses, are seen the heads of four tritons, spouting water from their mouths ; and from a pipe in the conch shell, the water is thrown in a horizontal direction, as far as the heads of the horses. These fountains, as well as others not named, are enclosed in large basons of stone work. The walk between the fountains of Cybele and Neptune, which for distinction is termed the Saloon, is the most frequented and favourite walk of the fashionables of the city. Here on sundays and holydays are collected all the beaux and belles of Madrid, to the amount of some thousands, passing to and fro on the saloon, of about one third of a mile, and leaving the rest of the walk to the contemplative, if there are any such ; or to those whose object is not that solely of seeing and being seen. I passed and repassed among the multitude several times, with the view of observing the beauties of the city, but, certainly, I have no recollection of ever having seen so many of the fairer part of creation together before, without observing one pretty face ; not one that would be termed, with us, *tolerably* pretty ; but many *intolerably* ugly. On each side of this walk there are carriage roads, where the nobles and rich display their fine carriages and equipages ; the young men, their dexterity in riding. There is always a squadron of cavalry distributed along the road, at certain distances, to see that the coachmen observe the regulations prescribed by the police, and to prevent disorderly behaviour. The walk on one side is bounded by the palaces of Medina Celi, Villahermosa, a chapel, and other buildings; and on the opposite, by the palace in which are the paintings, the open fence of the botanical garden, which, even at this season, makes a pretty appearance, and the collateral walks leading to the Retiro.

The north view from the city is bounded by the mountains of Guadarrama, whose tops are at this season of the year covered with snow. And when the wind blows from that quarter it is as cold as are our clear northwesters in April and November. The river Manzanares, which encircles about one half of the city on the N. W., has its source in those mountains, and emptying into the Xarama, finds its way to the Tagus. This river, however, during the greater part of the year, is nothing but a rivulet, fordable every where. There are, notwithstanding, two superb and very expensive stone bridges thrown across it, the Toledo and the Segovia, which are not surpassed in beauty, magnitude, and solidity, by those crossing the Thames at London. It was observed by a wag, that, " never were seen more beautiful bridges ; there was wanting only a river." Various attempts have been made to procure a water communication with the Tagus by means of a canal, for which purpose a privilege was granted to a company by Charles III. in the year 1770. It was begun near the bridge of Toledo ; but with all the encouragement given to it by the monarch, and all the advantages that, it was apparent, would result from its execution, it was abandoned, after about one half of it was completed, by cutting a distance of six or seven miles. If one fourth of the amount of property, which has been squandered in the royal residences, had been expended in the accomplishment of such useful works at this canal, it is highly probable the royal exchequer would not have been at the low ebb it now is ; and that many in the middling class, among other luxuries, would have been able to keep better fires than they now can. The last consideration, probably, does not much disturb the royal breast.

I hardly know how to begin, in order to convey to you an idea of the contents of the cabinet of natural history. An imperfect one only can be gained by a transient view of it ; still more imperfect must that be, received from my description. There are two large rooms, on the same floor, where the minerals, gems, and crystals are exhibited in glass cases. In two others adjoining, are the beasts, birds, and reptiles ; in a third are fishes and shells ; in the fourth, a collection of Grecian vases ; in the fifth, a great variety of *guaqueros* and other curiosities from South America ; and in the sixth, an elephant's skin stuffed, and the skeleton of a non-descript animal. The minerals occupy the four sides of a large room; and the great variety and brilliancy of the specimens make a display, equalled only by the collection at Paris. There is one lump of pure silver which weighs two hundred and eighty-five pounds;—a large piece of virgin gold of great value;—a large collection of stones, exceedingly curious for the variety and beauty of the natural landscapes seen on them; but taken together the collection is less striking for its intrinsic value, though this is great, than for its brilliancy, variety, and beauty, and the taste displayed in the distribution. The gems are also displayed so as to be seen to the greatest advantage, and the eyes of the observer are almost dazzled with the view of the rich diamonds, rubies, emeralds, amethysts, topazes, &c. which this case contains. There is also a great number of beautiful pearls, some of which are seen as originally attached to their shells; also a case of very valuable and beautiful cameos, another of agates, jaspers, cornelians, &c. Along the centre of the room are long tables, on which, and under glasses, are exhibited a most beautifully varied collection of crystals; also a meteoric stone weighing ten pounds, which has a volcanic appearance. The halls containing the beasts and birds are sufficiently spacious for that purpose, and the animals are tastefully arranged; but I saw none among them of a kind which I had not seen before, excepting the non-descript skeleton. This was found in making an excavation at Paraguay. It is nearly as large as the elephant, but bears no resemblance to that animal. The celebrated Cuvier has given it the name of Megatherium. The shells are an extensive and most beautiful collection; and among those most rare, are many, exhibiting in wax the form of the fish attached to them. The Grecian vases, if not the most curious, are among the most beautiful objects to be seen here. They are made, some of the clearest and most beautiful crystals, and some, of precious stones. All, for variety and gracefulness of form, beauty of colours, brilliancy of polish, and exquisite taste, surpass any thing of the kind I have ever seen. Their value I could not ascertain, but presume it to be such that monarchs only can own them. The room containing the Indian curiosities, Chinese dresses, a mandarin in full dress, &c. is less than the Asiatic Marine Hall in Salem; and the variety is much less, being principally confined to curiosities from their possessions in South America.

The royal collection of paintings are deposited in the palace, near the Prado. They are exhibited in three immensely long halls, two of which contain exclusively those of the Spanish school, and the other those of the Italian. The paintings are all numbered, and for twenty cents the visitor is furnished with a little book which contains a description of each.　With this book in hand I went the round of the three rooms in about as many hours ; consequently, as you will imagine, I could take no more than a glance at each ; indeed it would require a month to give them the examination they merit.　My knowledge of the art, I confess, is not sufficient to enable me to distinguish the superiority, which is said to exist, of the Italian over the Spanish pictures. The latter appear to me to be quite equal to the former ; and I am induced to believe that the value of *these* over *those* is established, rather by the circumstance of the impossibility of any more being produced by those authors, than by their intrinsic merit.　I will name only a few of the most striking ;—a large picture by Murillo ; a Spaniard, the subject, the infant Jesus holding up a bird to prevent its being seized by a little dog, who is eager for it, and while the infant is retreating, he is received into the arms of Joseph ; the Virgin appears to suspend her work, and to be viewing with great interest the movements of her son.　It is one of those which were selected to ornament the Louvre, and have since been returned to Madrid.—The martyrdom, by stoning to death, of Stephen, by Velasquez ; this is very fine.—The subject of Jesus interrogated by the Pharisees, whether it was proper to pay tribute to Cæsar ; a fine picture by Arias ; the figures are as large as life.—A very large painting, representing the monks, sent by Charles IV. to Algiers to redeem the prisoners, in the act of paying the ransom and receiving them ; by Aparacio, a Spaniard.—A scene, by the same author, of the Famine in Madrid in 1811 and 1812 ; a picture as large as Peele's " Court of Death."　In the foreground are represented a woman and child, both dead ; a man lies near them, to the left, on the floor, with only sufficient strength remaining to enable him to wave his hand in refusal of a loaf of bread presented by a French officer.　Two grenadiers accompany this officer, who appear to be horror-struck with the scene of misery before them ; near, and a little back of the dead and dying, is an old man, whose daughter is leaning on his shoulder, both presenting the picture of despair ; in the back-ground are men and women upbraiding the French as the authors of such calamities.　This is a picture terribly true to nature.—A much celebrated painting, by Titian, of the emperor Charles V. on horseback.—A picture, by Raphael, of Jesus oppressed under the weight of the cross, and Simon, the Cyrenian, applying to the chief of the soldiers to succour him.　This painting is of great celebrity, and ranks next to that of the Transfiguration, by the same author, which is at Rome.　The catalogue amounts to five hundred and twelve ; but I will not try your patience by particularizing any more.

The royal armory, or hall of ancient arms, is contiguous to the royal residence. It is about two hundred feet by sixty. On either side, the walls are hung with coats of mail, helmets, bucklers, shields, crossbows, lances, long match-locks used before the invention of artillery, and several flags preserved as trophies, among which are those taken by Don Juan of Austria at the battle of Lepanto. These are all very tastefully distributed. On entering the hall you are desired to notice the vehicle in which the emperor Charles V. used to travel. It is a clumsy box, of about five feet by two. Over the end of it, where the seat is placed, there is a covering like a chaise top, with canvass to roll up at the sides, and an apron or boot to cover the front part. This awkward machine was suspended lengthwise between two mules, and in this way did the arbiter of Europe travel over a large portion of its surface. Near to this, is the first coach that was ever seen in Spain. It belonged to the time of Doña Urraca, and is a heavy, clumsy thing, with much carved work on the exterior. Passing along, we observed the coats of mail and arms of Fernando and Isabel, of Charles V., of the little Moor the last king of Grenada, of Henry IV. of France when a boy, of Don Juan of Austria, of Cortes, Pizarro, and others. In handsome glass cases, are exhibited arms ornamented with diamonds and rubies, saddles ornamented with the same materials ; gold stirrups, and spurs ; all presents from the Grand Seignior, probably at a period, when to be in the good graces of Spain was more important than it is at the present day. · There are also some beautiful specimens of rich arms, made in France and Spain ; several air-guns ; a number of shields, studded with precious stones ; the spear of Don Pedro the cruel ; the turban of the bashaw, taken at the battle of Lepanto ; two waistcoats of Charles V. lined with steel, and pliable. In the centre of the room are several equestrian statues, all clad in polished steel, horses as well as riders ; they are of Charles V., Philip II., and others. There are several pieces of artillery ; a great number of saddles covered with silk, which were used at the tournaments, &c. After having gone the rounds of this hall, the conductor takes you to the upper end, where, drawing up a velvet curtain, within a glass case, by strings without, you are presented with a sitting figure, as large as life, of St Ferdinand the Catholic, with the same gold crown on his head, which is used for the coronation of the kings of Spain. An advertisement within, recommends your kneeling before this saint (for which purpose there is a velvet cushion) and praying for the prosperity and happiness of the kingdom, and of the reigning family. Although aware that no country ever stood more in need of assistance from above, I nevertheless declined. It seemed to me that it would hardly be in the power of St. Ferdinand soon to restore order and happiness, where confusion and misery seem so firmly to have established their empire.

The museum of the park of artillery (St Joseph Street) is said to be well worthy the attention of a stranger, but to see this, it is necessary to obtain the permission of the commandant of the park ; and having failed in a first attempt, in consequence of his absence, I had not time to make a second.

The squares of Madrid are not remarkable for their size or beauty ; indeed, excepting what is called the Great square, there are none of any importance. This is 434 feet long by 334 broad. The houses forming the sides of this square, are uniform as to height, but are not handsome ; the upper stories are used as dwellings, the lower ones as shops. The former projecting over the latter about fifteen feet, form a shelter, which secures the pedestrian from the heat of the sun, or the annoyance of the rain. This square is the Smithfield of Madrid, and *here,* as *there,* unfortunate beings have been burnt to death, for differing in opinion from their spiritual fathers. For the interior police of the city, it is divided into eight parts, and each is under the charge of an alcalde of the court. These again are subdivided into eight wards, each having its alcalde, or magistrate. The superintendance of these magistrates is sufficient, in ordinary times, to preserve tranquillity ; but in times of excitement, like the present, it is considered necessary to keep a considerable military force within the walls.

Notwithstanding the dearness of fuel ; the tax upon all kinds of provisions brought in from the country, which is levied at the gates ; and the restrictions, rigidly enforced, which do not allow the man who sells beef, to sell mutton also, and so of every thing else ; I do not find that the living in Madrid is more expensive, than it is in the other European capitals. For two dollars a day, a man will find such lodging and food, as will be satisfactory to all who are not very fastidious.

Adieu.

ORIGINAL POETRY.

MORNING AMONG THE HILLS.

A night had passed away among the hills,
And now the first faint tokens of the dawn
Showed in the east. The bright and dewy star,
Whose mission is to usher in the morn,
Looked through the cool air, like a blessed thing
In a far purer world. Below there lay
Wrapped round a woody mountain tranquilly

A misty cloud.　Its edges caught the light,
That now came up from out the unseen depth
Of the full fount of day, and they were laced
With colours ever brightening.　I had waked
From a long sleep of many-changing dreams,
And now in the fresh forest air I stood
Nerved to another day of wandering.
Before me rose a pinnacle of rock,
Lifted above the wood that hemmed it in,
And now already glowing.　There the beams
Came from the far horizon, and they wrapped it
In light and glory.　Round its vapoury cone
A crown of far-diverging rays shot out,
And gave to it the semblance of an altar
Lit for the worship of the undying flame,
That centred in the circle of the sun,
Now coming from the ocean's fathomless caves,
Anon would stand in solitary pomp
Above the loftiest peaks, and cover them
With splendour as a garment.　Thitherward
I bent my eager steps; and through the grove
Now dark as deepest night, and thickets hung
With a rich harvest of unnumbered gems,
Waiting the clearer dawn to catch the hues
Shed from the starry fringes of its veil
On cloud and mist and dew, and backward thrown
With undiminished beauty, on I went
Mounting with hasty foot, and thence emerging.
I scaled that rocky steep, and there awaited
Silent the full appearing of the sun.
　Below there lay a far extended sea
Rolling in feathery waves.　The wind blew o'er it,
And tossed it round the high ascending rocks,
And swept it through the half hidden forest tops,
Till, like an ocean waking into storm,
It heaved and weltered.　Gloriously the light
Crested its billows, and those craggy islands
Shone on it like to palaces of spar
Built on a sea of pearl.　Far overhead
The sky without a vapour or a stain,
Intensely blue, even deepened into purple,
Where nearer the horizon it received
A tincture from the mist that there dissolved
Into the viewless air,—the sky bent round
The awful dome of a most mighty temple
Built by omnipotent hands for nothing less
Than infinite worship.　There I stood in silence—
I had no words to tell the mingled thoughts
Of wonder and of joy, that then came o'er me,
Even with a whirlwind's rush.　So beautiful,
So bright, so glorious!　Such a majesty
In yon pure vault!　So many dazzling tints
In yonder waste of waves,—so like the ocean

ORIGINAL POETRY.

With its unnumbered islands there encircled
By foaming surges, that the mounting eagle,
Lifting his fearless pinion through the clouds
To bathe in purest sunbeams, seemed an ospray
Hovering above his prey, and yon tall pines,
Their tops half mantled in a snowy veil,
A frigate with full canvass, bearing on
To conquest and to glory.   But even these,
Had round them something of the lofty air
In which they moved ;——not like to things of earth,
But heightened and made glorious, as became
Such pomp and splendour.
                Who can tell the brightness,
That every moment caught a newer glow;
That circle, with its centre like the heart
Of elemental fire, and spreading out
In floods of liquid gold on the blue sky
And on the opaline waves, crowned with a rainbow
Bright as the arch that bent above the throne
Seen in a vision by the holy man
In Patmos ! Who can tell how it ascended,
And flowed more widely o'er that lifted ocean,
Till instantly the unobstructed sun
Rolled up his sphere of fire, floating away—
Away in a pure ether, far from earth,
And all its clouds,—and pouring forth unbounded
His arrowy brightness!   From that burning centre
At once there ran along the level line
Of that imagined sea, a stream of gold—
Liquid and flowing gold, that seemed to tremble
Even with a furnace heat, on to the point,
Whereon I stood.   At once that sea of vapour
Parted away, and melting into air
Rose round me, and I stood involved in light,
As if a flame had kindled up, and wrapped me
In its innocuous blaze.   Away it rolled,
Wave after wave.   They climbed the highest rocks,
Poured over them in surges, and then rushed
Down glens and valleys, like a wintery torrent
Dashed instant to the plain.   It seemed a moment,
And they were gone, as if the touch of fire
At once dissolved them.   Then I found myself
Midway in air ;——ridge after ridge below,
Descended with their opulence of woods
Even to the dim seen level, where a lake
Flashed in the sun, and from it wound a line,
Now silvery bright, even to the farthest verge
Of the encircling hills.   A waste of rocks
Was round me—but below how beautiful,
How rich the plain—a wilderness of groves
And ripening harvests ; while the sky of June—
The soft blue sky of June, and the cool air,
That makes it then a luxury to live,

Only to breathe it, and the busy echo
Of cascades, and the voice of mountain brooks,
Stole with such gentle meanings to my heart,
That where I stood seemed Heaven.

                                                P.

DREAMS.

Oh that dreams were not dreams, for mine have been
The shadows of my hopes.   Thence have I grown
In love with ideal forms.   In youth I saw
Most beauteous beings in mine hours of sleep—
Fair maidens with their bright and sunny locks
Falling o'er necks whose hue was of the snow,
O'er bosoms whose soft throbbings not the veil
Of gossamer could hide from the tranced eye.
I saw, when that my cheek had lost its down,
And I wrote MAN, a world of glittering words
Writ by the hand of health upon that leaf
Of human life.   I saw bright swords, brave plumes,
And staves of office—robes of honour—all
That speak of high employment, and awards
Of national emprises.   Other thoughts
That were, by day, *hopes*, and in slumber, *dreams*,
Came to me, of my line continued in
Illustrious heirs.   The boy upon my knee
Became a Socrates, and he who played
With the dark ringlets on his mother's brow,
The saviour of a realm.   The little maid
Who, lost in mimic tenderness, caressed
A pasteboard emblem of our helpless state,
I wedded to a warrior, sworn and pledged
To die as had his fathers, at the call
Of liberty.
        Time flew, and I am now
An aged man with hoary hair, and step
All trembling ; yet I entertain a crowd
Of dreams, but they are of the world whereto
Age, and hopes crushed, are hurrying me.   I see
In slumber an offended God, begirt
With Cherubim around his hidden throne,—
And angels of his attributes, the guards
Of his dominions.   They who represent
Truth, Peace, and Justice ask the darker doom
Upon my head, for I had wildly erred ;
But Mercy, darling child of the Most High,
Pleads for me, and prevails.   I hear a voice
Ring through the spheres of heaven—a voice of love
Pronouncing pardon, and I join the choir
That worships, and shall worship him eternally.

                                                J.

CRITICAL NOTICES.

Reports of Cases, argued and determined in the Supreme Judicial Court of the State of Maine. By Simon Greenleaf, Counsellor at Law. Vol. II. containing the Cases of the Years 1822 and 1823. Hallowell. 1824. 8vo.

It is matter of no small credit at this day, to win the reputation of a good reporter. The books of decisions have increased, and are increasing with such a fearful rapidity, that there is a serious duty upon the good sense and ingenuity of the author to render his work sufficiently compendious for readers who have so much on their hands, as well as a serious affair for gentlemen of the profession to peruse and digest them as they come from our publishers. And yet we know not that this can be helped, and for the good of the cause, perhaps we ought not to mourn about it. Added to all this, the frequency of these volumes is little more than what we have reason to expect. Besides the disposition of the present age to fix and perpetuate legal decisions, under every form of record, there appears to be in our country, a sectional pride and ambition, professed by a majority of the states, to preserve the decisions of their tribunals, in the shape of a book of authorities. It is not enough in this nation, or in England that the great principles of the law should be well circulated in society, and matter of common learning amongst the people; but learned and industrious minds have thought it better that their various applications should be seen *in extenso* in order to be better understood and better appreciated. Hence books of reports, as well as treatises in which leading cases are cited and commented upon, have literally poured from the press in latter times; and compared with the days even of Lord Mansfield, our own may be said to be an age of peculiar advantages in the learning of jurisprudence.

In this country, the modern English reports are of doubtful value. Upon the whole we would rather have our own. In some of the states where the technical severities of the English law are but little departed from, there may be some love left for their books of decisions; but we believe they are going out of date.

The peculiar situation of this country, as an Union, consisting of so many independent parts, will readily suggest the necessity of a multitude of reports: and it is surely as much our duty, and should be as much our pleasure, to examine the judicial features of our *own* country expressed in these books, as to contemplate those of another that possess, each day, less and less interest for us.

We are pleased with Mr Greenleaf's book as well for the *lucidus ordo* that distinguishes it, as for the brief but comprehensive manner in which he arranges the arguments of counsel. There is nothing laboured in the style of his reporting, and yet there is nothing omitted which is relevant to the case, so far as he is concerned in setting it down. This, certainly, is a great excellence in these book-bearing days—and will operate as an essential aid to those whose ambition or professional practice may lead them to a long, and sometimes, of necessity, a rapid examination of cases through the multitude of authorities. It is, in fact, making a digest of the volume itself, and yet doing perfect justice to the logic and learning of the bar.

The decisions, which, for the most part, are delivered by Chief Justice Mellen, form a valuable addition to the book and the jurisprudence of the state. It is almost needless to say they are lucid, direct, and learned expositions of the law, and will give new weight and respectability to the mass of high legal authorities with which our country abounds.

We think the profession of his state, as well as of others, will have particular reason to thank Mr Greenleaf for the " aid and comfort " of this volume; and though this is not the first time he has come honourably and successfully before the public as a law author, still we will not withhold from him our testimony to his merit, nor the expression of our belief that a continuation of his labours will be highly acceptable to his brethren.

Fauna Americana. Being a Description of the Mammiferous Animals inhabiting North America. By Richard Harlan, M. D. &c. &c. Philadelphia. 1825. pp. 318.

THE great and increasing attention paid to the cultivation of American natural history, is highly gratifying, and no where has there been more zeal displayed, and no where has it been more successfully exerted than at Philadelphia. "The manor of living nature,"—this is the motto to Dr Harlan's book,—is so ample, that all may be allowed to sport on it freely; the most jealous proprietor cannot entertain any apprehension that the game will be exhausted or even perceptibly thinned. This is more especially true of our own country than of any other. There is no department of natural history which does not afford ample scope for the exertion of all the zeal and talents which may be devoted to its service. The author of this work fills the office of Professor of Comparative Anatomy to the Philadelphia Museum, and both from his situation and his pursuits has had many opportunities for acquiring a knowledge of this subject. There is every evidence that he is well grounded in the principles of the science to which he is devoted, and the present publication we believe upon the whole a very useful and important one; but we are constrained to say that there are marks of haste and a want of finish about it which we should have rejoiced not to see. There is nothing in it, perhaps, to mislead or confound an adept in the science; but it is to be recollected that there are few besides beginners among American students of natural history; and the work should have been more carefully adapted to their wants than it appears to have been.

Dr Harlan describes one hundred and forty-seven species as inhabitants of North America, of which several are new and described for the first time by him, and eleven are fossil and extinct.

To the order Primates belong	1	species
Carnivora	60	
Glires	37	
Edentata	6	
Pachydermata	2	
Ruminantia	13	
Cetacea	28	
	147	

The Improvisatrice, and other Poems. By L. E. L. Boston. 1825. 18mo. pp. 287.

We cannot find place for a long and complete review of Miss Landon's Improvisatrice, though the reputation of a noble name, and the merit of a young writer might seem to demand it of us. It may give interest to this work, to know that the writer is of a noble family : but in the literary world there is no aristocracy, nor pride, nor power, but that of genius ; and whatever influence the high rank of an author may have with English critics, it can have none with us. The Improvisatrice is a beautiful poem, but it has great defects. It is written in that free and careless way in which we are led to think an *improvisatrice* would sing. It is a romance of a maid of Florence, who recites the story of her own life, and a tale of her love, " fond, faithful, and unhappy."

The story of the Improvisatrice is as follows. She was singing to her lute in a calm evening by the Arno's side, and among her listeners was one, Lorenzo, who became loved by her and her lover. The tale she sung was " A Moorish Romance," from which we shall make one extract, as this will serve for a fair specimen of those characteristic features of the style of the poem, which we wish to exhibit to our readers.

> Day fades apace : another day,
> That maiden will be far away,
> A wanderer o'er the dark-blue sea,
> And bound for lovely Italy,
> Her mother's land ! Hence on her breast
> The cross beneath a Moorish vest ;
> And hence those sweetest sounds, that seem
> Like music murmuring in a dream,
> When in our sleeping ear is ringing
> The song the nightingale is singing ;
> When by that white and funeral stone,
>   Half-hidden by the cypress gloom,
> The hymn the mother taught her child
>   Is sung each evening at her tomb.
> But quick the twilight time has past,
> Like one of those sweet calms that last
> A moment and no more, to cheer
> The turmoil of our pathway here.
>   The bark is waiting in the bay,
> Night darkens round :—Leila, away !
> Far, ere to-morrow, o'er the tide,
> Or wait and be—Abdalla's bride !

Lorenzo and the Improvisatrice met afterwards in the Florentine galleries and at a masquerade, but not as lovers meet. Lorenzo was already betrothed to another, to whom he was soon married. The Improvisatrice was one night passing the cathedral of St Mark. It was lighted up, and she entered the old walls, where preparations had been made for a marriage ceremony. Lamps were burning at the altar, and sweet flowers were strown in the aisles ; and when the bridal train came in she recognised, in the face of the bridegroom, the pale, features of Lorenzo. From that time her life became one of desertion and sorrow. Ere long, however, the bride of Lorenzo died, and he returned to his Improvisatrice with all the fervour of a first love. But it was too late ; she was dying and wasted away. The narrative closes with the prophecy of her own death.

The tale exhibits all the enthusiasm and fine feeling which belong to an Improvisatrice ; and in reference to this assumed character, the very carelessness of the composition renders it more true to nature, by bringing it nearer to the free style of extemporaneous recitation.

The Miscellaneous Poems occupy the greater part of the volume, and are of very various merit. We consider the following as the most beautiful of those, whose length would permit their being quoted.

THE SOLDIER'S FUNERAL.

And the muffled drum rolled on the air,
Warriors with stately step were there ;
On every arm was the black crape bound,
Every carbine was turned to the ground :
Solemn the sound of their measured tread,
As silent and slow they followed the dead.
The riderless horse was led in the rear,
There were white plumes waving over the bier ;
Helmet and sword were laid on the pall,
For it was a soldier's funeral.

That soldier had stood on the battle-plain,
Where every step was over the slain ;
But the brand and the ball had passed him by,
And he came to his native land to die.
'T was hard to come to that native land,
And not clasp one familiar hand !
'T was hard to be numbered amid the dead,
Or ere he could hear his welcome said !
But 't was something to see its cliffs once more,
And to lay his bones on his own loved shore ;
To think that the friends of his youth might weep
O'er the green grass turf of the soldier's sleep.

The bugles ceased their wailing sound
As the coffin was lowered into the ground ;
A volley was fired, a blessing said,
One moment's pause—and they left the dead !—
I saw a poor and an aged man,
His step was feeble, his lip was wan :
He knelt him down on the new-raised mound,
His face was bowed on the cold damp ground,
He raised his head, his tears were done,—
The father had prayed o'er his only son !

INTELLIGENCE.

OPINION OF LIONEL LINCOLN, FROM BLACKWOOD'S MAGAZINE.

It is an agreeable book, written in a pleasant style, with a light, sketchy manner. The novel part of the story is puzzled and not very clever. There is an attempt at a sort of Davie Gellatly, in the person of an idiot of the name of Job Pray, which cannot be commended after remembering its original. An eating, drinking, good-hearted, good-humoured English officer is pretty well done—but after Dalgetty he is not wanted. One great absurdity pervades the book : A man escaped from an English mad-house is in fact the hero—he manages the private meetings of the discontented colonists—he takes a great share in the military actions of Lexington and Bunker's bill—he passes in and out of the beleaguered city of Boston, as easily as fairies are said to get through key-holes, is present in the councils of the military officers opposed to the colonists, and in the very inmost mysteries of their antagonists. Now this is more revolting, critically speaking, more improbable, than a ghost

Let me turn to something better. The whole account of the battle of Bunker's or rather Breed's hill, is capitally done. There are some sketches of country American manners too, so well executed, that I could wish for more of the same kind, and on the same key. I allude to the little episode of the old man, who drives Lionel and his wife on the cart, and that of the woman whose sons were named after the old king. There is a newness about these, which to me at least is very agreeable. On the whole Lionel Lincoln is a pleasant graphic novel. It is, I perceive, translated into French,—very poorly, I understand—as badly I suppose, as the Waverley novels; it could not be worse. I remember among other specimens of the French translator's acquaintance with our tongue, that one of them rendered the verse of " Bessy Bell and Mary Gray," (quoted in the Pirate)

"They bigged a bower on yon burn-brae,
And theekit it ower wi' RASHES,"

into—" Elles se sont baties un maison sur la colline, *et elles en ont chassé* LES IMPRUDENS."—" L'homme verd et tranquille," for " the green man and still "—was nothing to this."

DEAF AND DUMB.

Dr Dulan has lately read before the royal academy of sciences of Paris, a memoir on the operations by means of which he has succeeded in restoring the faculties of hearing and of speech to a child born deaf and dumb. Having seen only the account of the conclusion of this memoir, we are not informed what the nature of the operation is, but we give an analysis of that part which we have met with. " The principal object of the author was to fix the attention upon the singular sympathy that exists between the sense of hearing and the organs of speech. An intermediate intellectual operation is, according to him, indispensable for the existence of this sympathy, and it is from this cause that children understand our language long before they can themselves pronounce any words. The principal observations that have struck his attention in the case of the present young patient are, first, that the child was able to read before he was able to speak ; second, that even at this moment he pronounces much better what he reads than what he hears ; third, that he hears perfectly distinct every noise made within a certain distance, which enables him, when in the street, to avoid being run over by the carriages ; fourth, that he can distinguish the difference between the times in music, and that he takes great pleasure in the airs that he hears sung." The Doctor added, that although it is not more than a year since he commenced the education of his young pupil, he can already understand and explain the words composing four hundred phrases, but that he is not yet sufficiently advanced to answer all those who may question him.

The child himself was present and recited some verses. His pronunciation is so distinct as to allow every word he said to be heard ; but his voice has not the least degree of harmony, and produces the disagreeable effect caused by that of deaf and dumb persons, who have been taught to pronounce some words in their harsh and unintelligible manner.

MINUTE ENGRAVING.

A very curious specimen of minute engraving has been recently published by Mr Williamson of Lambeth. This is a plate on steel representing the crucifixion. Immediately over the head of the Redeemer, a small circle appears, the eighth of an inch in diameter, in which the whole of the Lord's prayer is accurately and even elegantly engraved. This would seem almost impossible, and at first the eye glances incredulously at the space said to be so occupied, but a magnifying glass shows the statement to be perfectly true. Every word may be distinctly read. The letters t e m p t a, in the word temptation, are rather darker than the rest, but the whole is very legible ; and the letter A in the word amen, has a bold flourish. The surrounding ornaments are in good taste. The Lord's Supper group is peculiarly happy. The scroll on the cross contains in letters, even smaller than those of the circle, the name of the artist.

MAMMOTH STEAM BOAT.

The Dutch are making preparations to surpass all other nations in vessels navigable by steam. There is now building at Rotterdam a vessel, which, when completed, will be of the burden of 1100 tons, to be propelled by an engine of 300 horse power. She is intended to carry troops to Batavia, and will be commanded by a lieutenant in the Dutch navy.

THE LONDON UNIVERSITY

Through the politeness of a friend, now in England, we have just received a Prospectus of the London University. The institution it appears has received the approbation and support of some of the most distinguished men in the kingdom. Its advantages have been developed by several gentlemen of the first respectability, and among them, by Sir James Mackintosh, Mr Brougham, and Mr Thomas Campbell—by the latter in several able essays upon the subject in the magazine which he conducts. We are assured that there is no doubt but the scheme will go into execution. The capital of the institution is to be £300,000. This sum is to be raised by 3000 shares of £100 each; or donations of £50, which will entitle the donor to the same privileges for life as a shareholder for £100. We quote the Prospectus entire, believing that it may afford not only interesting intelligence, but many useful hints for an establishment for somewhat similar purposes in our own country.

"The primary object of this Institution is to bring the means of a complete scientific and literary education home to the inhabitants of the metropolis, who may thus be enabled to educate their sons at a moderate expense, and under their own immediate superintendence. Under existing circumstances a young man cannot be maintained and instructed at Oxford or Cambridge at a less charge than 200*l.* or 250*l.* per annum: while the expenses of most, exceed this sum, and nearly five months in the year are allowed for vacations.

The whole expense for each student's instruction at the London University, will not exceed 25*l.* or 30*l.* per annum,* with not more than ten weeks of vacation.

A treaty is now in progress for a suitable peice of ground, in a central situation, for the building and walks; and it is expected that the structure will be completed in August 1826, and the classes opened in October following.

The vacations will comprise a fortnight at Easter, about six weeks from the middle of August to the end of September, and a fortnight at Christmas.

Each holder of a 100*l.* share will receive interest at a rate not exceeding *four per cent.* per annum, payable half-yearly, and be entitled to present one student for each share. The shares will be transferable by sale and by bequest, and descend to the holder's representatives in cases of intestacy. The money will be called for by instalments, as wanted; but it is calculated that not more than two thirds of the amount will be required, and the remaining third will thus be in reserve, to provide for an extension of the plan, or any unforeseen contingency.

No person to hold more than ten shares; and a donor of 50*l.* to have all the privileges of a shareholder during life, except the receipt of interest and transfer of his rights.

The interest on the shares will be paid out of the surplus revenue of the institution, after defraying all expenses of conducting the same, and arising from the annual payment of five guineas by each student to the General Fund, exclusive of one guinea per annum to the library, museum, and collection of maps, charts, drawings, and models.

The rules for the establishment will be submitted to a general meeting of shareholders and donors; who, it is anticipated, will be induced to vest its government in a chancellor, vice-chancellor, and nineteen ordinary members of council (a proportion of which will go out of office annually), to be elected by the shareholders and donors, voting either in person or by proxy. The professors will have moderate salaries, but their emoluments will principally depend on the fees received from students.

_____

* This supposes a Student to attend five or six of the general classes; but the medical education will be necessarily more expensive, from the costs of the anatomical department.

NEW PUBLICATIONS.

ARTS, SCIENCES, AND PHILOSOPHY.

The Boston Journal of Philosophy and the Arts. No. 12.

Transactions of the American Philosophical Society, held at Philadelphia, for promoting useful knowledge. Vol ii. New Series. Philadelphia.

AGRICULTURE.

Original Communications, made to the Agricultural Society of South Carolina ; and Extracts from select Authors on Agriculture. Published by Order of the Society. Price $1,25. Charleston, S. C.

DRAMA.

Phelles, King of Tyre ; A Tragedy. New York.

EDUCATION.

Adam's Latin Grammar, with some Improvements, and the following Additions : Rules for the right Pronunciation of the Latin Language; A Metrical Key to the Odes of Horace ; A List of Latin Authors arranged according to the different Ages of Roman Literature ; Tables showing the value of the different Coins, Weights, and Measures used among the Romans. By Benjamin A. Gould, Master of the Public Latin School in Boston. 12mo. pp. 284. Boston. Cummings, Hilliard, & Co.

The Institutes of English Grammar, methodically arranged ; with examples for Parsing, Questions for Examination, False Syntax for Correction, Exercises, &c. to which are added four Appendixes. Designed for the Use of Schools, Academies, and Private Learners. By Goold Brown. Baltimore. S. S. Wood & Co.

Comly's Grammar considerably enlarged and improved, fourteenth Edition. Philadelphia. Kimber & Sharpless.

HISTORY.

A History of the Political and Military Events of the late War between the United States and Great Britain. By Samuel Perkins, Esq. 8vo. pp. 512. New Haven. S. Converse.

LAW.

The Office of Surrogate, and Executors' and Administrators' Guide, with Precedents and Forms suited to all Cases in relation to the Duties of Executors, and Administrators. By T. Attwood Bridgen, Esq. Surrogate of Albany. 8vo. Price $1,50. Albany. William Gould & Co.

Wheeler's Criminal Cases. 8vo. vol. 3d. Albany. W. Gould & Co.

METAPHYSICS.

The Alphabet of Thought, or Elements of Metaphysical Science. By a Lady. Price 63 cts. Harrisburg, Pa. Hugh Hamilton.

MISCELLANEOUS.

The Eighth Annual Report of the American Society for the Colonizing of the free People of Colour of the United States. With an Appendix. 8vo. pp. 71. Washington, D. C.

An Examination of Commodore Porter's Exposition, in which some of the Errors and Inaccuracies of that Publication are rectified, and some of its Deficiencies supplied. By Richard S. Coxe, Judge Advocate of the Court of Inquiry. 8vo. Washington. Davis & Force.

An Address delivered at the Laying of the Corner Stone of the Bunker Hill Monument. By Daniel Webster. Translated into the Spanish Language. New York. Wilder & Campbell.

An Account of the Asylum for the Insane, established by the Society of Friends, near Frankford in the vicinity of Philadelphia. By Robert Waln, Jr. Philadelphia. B. & T. Kite.

Soliloquy of Napoleon Bonaparte, in his Exile at St Helena, written and translated By P. Menard. Price 25 cts.

An Address delivered in the Chapel of Dartmouth College, upon the Induction of the Author into the Professorship of Moral and Intellectual Philosophy, May 19, 1825. By Daniel Oliver, M. D.

Moral Education. An Address, delivered at China, Me. June 25th, 1825, at the Installation of Central Lodge. By Stephen Chapin. Waterville, 1825. 8vo. pp. 32.

We are far from yielding our assent to some of the speculative opinions pretty clearly implied in this address ; but we agree with the author entirely in the cheerful views he entertains of the continual progress of moral improvement. And while such opinions as the following, advanced by Professor Chapin, are advocated in different parts of the country with the zeal and enthusiasm which he brings to his subject ; we are confident, that the cause of education, both moral and intellectual, will continue to occupy the public attention ; and that its happy influences will continue to be more and more widely and deeply felt through the whole community. "It [education] is distinctly acknowledged as a subject entitled to the first place among the tenets of our order, and as one, which involves the highest personal and public welfare. In no way can we do so much to strengthen the foundation of our happy republic, to promote the prosperity of our country, and the good of mankind, as to take care to leave behind us a truly enlightened and well educated posterity. A great bulwark of our national security ' is to be formed in education ; the culture of the heart and the head ; the diffusion of knowledge, piety, and morality. A virtuous and enlightened man can never submit to degradation, and a virtuous and enlightened people will never breathe in the atmosphere of slavery. Upon education, then, we must rely for the purity, the preservation, and the perpetuation of Republican government. In this sacred cause, we cannot exercise too much liberality. It is identified with our best interests in this world, and with our best destinies in the world to come.' "

POLITICS.

Extracts of a Letter on the Mode of Choosing the President and Vice President of the United States, from Wm. C. Somerville, Esq. of Westmoreland, Va. to the Hon. Robert S. Garnett, in Congress. 12mo. pp. 12. Baltimore. J. D. Toy.

THEOLOGY.

The Christian Repository. Vol. vi. No. 2. Hartland, Vt.

An Enquiry into the Consistency of Popular Amusements, with a Profession of Christianity. By T. Charlton Henry, D. D. Price 75 cts. Charleston, S. C. W. Riley.

The Doctrine of Friends, or Principles of the Christian Religion, as held by the Society of Friends, commonly called Quakers. By Elisha Bates. Baltimore.

A Discourse delivered at Princeton, August 23, 1825, before the Princeton Female Society for the Education of Female Children in India. By Ashbel Green, D. D. Philadelphia. A. Finley.

Prayer and Sermon, by John Potts, Pastor of the Methodist Episcopal Church, Trenton, New Jersey; July 10, 1825. Taken in short hand. By Marcus T. C. Gould, Stenographer. Philadelphia. 8vo. pp. 22.

AMERICAN EDITIONS OF FOREIGN WORKS.

Reports of Cases argued and determined in the English Courts of Common Law. Edited By Thomas Sergeant and John C. Lowber, Esqrs. of the Philadelphia Bar. Vols. 4 & 9. 8vo. Philadelphia. P. H. Nicklin.

A Letter addressed to the King, by Thomas Thrush, on resigning his Commission as a Captain in the Royal Navy, on the Ground of the Unlawfulness of War. From the London Edition. 8vo. pp. 24. Cambridge. Hilliard & Metcalf.

This pamphlet is sensible without any pretension to being able. It contains, too, a superabundance of apologies to the King, for the liberty assumed in addressing him. These are very proper in their place, but they are certainly less interesting to us, and we think less calculated to subserve the cause of peace, than would have been a clearer statement of the argument which induced this worthy captain to resign.

Diccionario Filosofico de Voltaire, traduccion al Español, en la que se han refundido las Cuestiones sobre la Enciclopedia, la Opinion en Alfabeto, los Articulos insertos en la Enciclopedia y otros muchos; por C. Lanuza. In 10 vols. 18mo. New York.

Stories selected from the History of England, from the Conquest to the Revolution. For Children. Hartford. J. Huntington Jr. 1825. 18mo. pp. 144.

In the preface to the American edition of this valuable little volume, it is stated that its author is JOHN WILSON CROCKER, ESQ. secretary to the Admiralty Board in England. We state this fact merely to show, that a gentleman of distinguished attainments has thought it worth while to prepare a child's book; and we would express in this connexion the hope, that others may be induced to do the same in our own country. Speaking of the difficulty of supplying suitable stories for children, at the age when they begin to be most inquisitive, the author observes, "I have found that *fictions* lead to inquires, which it is not easy to satisfy. *Supernatural* fictions, such as fairy tales, vitiate the young taste, and disgust it from its more substantial nourishment; while the fictions of common life, such as histories of *Jenny* and *Tommy*, dolls and tops, &c. though very useful lessons, have not enough of the marvellous to arrest the attention to a degree necessary for amusement." In order to make his stories attractive and yet to avoid the evils above named, the author has selected some of the most interesting persons, facts, and events in the history of England, and described them in the most simple manner possible; indeed his language seldom rises above the " mere nursery style." While the stories, therefore, are adapted to the comprehension of children, and have all the interest of highly wrought fictions, they are nevertheless literal facts; and we have no doubt, simple as they are, that the child, who has his feelings interested by the perusal of them, will, at any future period of his life. read the history of England with some of that peculiar satisfaction, which we always feel, when we find facts and the experience of age agreeing with and confirming the impressions of childhood and youth.

Published on the first and fifteenth day of every month, by CUMMINGS, HILLIARD, & Co., No. 134 Washington-Street, Boston, for the Proprietors. Terms. $5 per annum. Cambridge: Printed at the University Press, by Hilliard & Metcalf.

INDEX TO VOL. II.

𝕷𝖎𝖙𝖊𝖗𝖆𝖗𝖞 𝕬𝖉𝖛𝖊𝖗𝖙𝖎𝖘𝖊𝖗.

MAY 1, 1825.

An additional half sheet will hereafter be annexed to our work, to be called the LITERARY ADVERTISER. This will enhance the value of the work to our subscribers without any additional expense to them—and enable publishers and booksellers throughout the country to advertise the works, in which they are interested, at a moderate price. The Advertiser is not paged, and forms no part of the Gazette. Our numbers, at the close of the year, may be bound in two volumes, of 480 pages each; and the Advertiser may be thrown out, as having answered all the purposes for which it was designed.

*** Advertisements of books of all kinds, stationary, maps, globes, mathematical and astronomical instruments, &c. are solicited.

The whole forming a complete system of Geography and History. By M. LAVOISNE. From the last London edition, improved by C. GROS, of the University of Paris, and J. ASPIN, Professor of History, &c. Carefully revised and corrected. Enlarged by the addition of several Charts and Maps of American History and Geography. Completed to the year 1821. In folio.

Historical, Chronological, Geographical, and Statistical Atlas of North and South America and the West Indies, with all their divisions into States, Kingdoms, &c. on the plan of LE SAGE, and intended as a companion to LAVOISNE'S ATLAS. In one volume, folio, containing the following Maps :—

1. America—historical, geographical, and statistical map.

2. Pautography of American history : exhibiting, at one view, the relative situation of the various States, &c. of America, from their first settlement to the present time. With a list of eminent characters, and the periods at which they lived.

3. North America—historical, geographical, and statistical map.

4. Historical, geograpical, and statistical map of Upper and Lower Canada, and the other British Possessions.

5. Geographical map of the United States.

6. Geographical and statistical map of the United States.

7. Historical map of the United States from their settlement to the present time.

8. Charts of the Constitutions of the United States and different States, showing all the provisions relative to the Legislative, Executive, and Judicial departments of the goverment.

9. Chronological map of the United States from their settlement to the Declaration of Independence.

10. Chronological map of the United States, from the Revolution to the present time.

Historical, Geographical, and Statistical Maps of

11. Maine.	22. District of Columbia.
12. New Hampshire.	23. Virginia.
13. Massachusetts.	24. North Carolina.
14. Rhode Island.	25. South Carolina.
15. Connecticut.	26. Georgia.
16. Vermont.	27. Ohio.
17. New York.	28. Kentucky.
18. New Jersey.	29. Tennessee.
19. Pennsylvania.	30. Mississippi.
20. Delaware.	31. Alabama.
21. Maryland.	32. Louisiana.

33. Indiana.	44. Porto Rico and the Virgin Isles.
34. Illinois.	45. Windward Islands.
35. Missouri.	46. Leeward Islands.
36. Arkansas Territory.	47. South America.
37. Michigan Territory.	48. Republic of Colombia.
38. Florida.	49. Brazil.
39. Mexico.	50. Buenos Ayres.
40. West Indies.	51. Peru.
41. Cuba and the Bahama	52. Chili.
Islands.	53. Map and description of the most
42. Jamaica.	important Rivers in the World.
43. Hispaniola.	54. Map and description of the most important Mountains in the World.

This work has been prepared by a number of gentlemen from the latest and most accurate information that could be obtained. The very liberal patronage bestowed upon the Atlas of Lavoisne induced the publishers to this attempt to reduce to the same system all the information that could be obtained relative to this Continent and the adjacent Islands. Arduous as has been this undertaking, they have been much gratified to find the result has been such as to receive great praise from numerous persons fully competent to judge of it.

The two volumes now form the most complete system of Geography and History that has ever been published ; and when it is considered that the whole (125 maps) is furnished for forty-five dollars (exactly the price of the London edition of Lavoisne's Atlas, containing 67 maps), they believe it will be admitted that it is the cheapest work that has ever appeared in this country.

Illustrations of the Sketch Book, finely engraved on steel, by Charles Heath, from designs by Westall.

ENGLISH AND AMERICAN LAW BOOKS.

PHILIP H. NICKLIN, Law Bookseller, No. 75 Chesnut-street, Philadelphia, has always on hand a very extensive assortment of English and American Law Books, which he will sell on liberal terms. Catalogues to be had at the store. Large discounts are allowed from the Catalogue prices ; and, having the largest stock of Law Books in this country, he is enabled to supply orders at the shortest notice.

VALUABLE BOOKS.

R. H. SMALL, Chesnut street, Philadelphia, has lately published,

A Practical Treatise on the Law of Partnership, by "Niel Gow, Esq. of Lincoln's Inn, Barrister of Law." First American from the last London edition, with Notes and References to American Cases, by Edward W. Ingraham, Esq. 1 vol. 8vo.

Prior's Life of Burke.

Private Journal of Madam Campan.

IN PRESS.

Blackstone's Commentaries, with Notes by Christian and Archbald, 4 vols. 8vo.

Booder's Life of Kemble, comprising a complete History of the English Stage since the time of Garrick.

HORNE'S INTRODUCTION.

E. LITTLE, No. 88 Chesnut street, Philadelphia, has in press,

An Introduction to the Critical Study and Knowledge of the Holy Scriptures. By Thomas Hartwell Horne, M. A.

It will be printed from the London edition of 1823, in four large octavo volumes; it will contain numerous Maps and Fac Similes of Biblical Manuscripts, and in short, every thing that is contained in that edition, and will be very neatly printed on good paper.

The first London edition of this work was published in 1818—the second in 1821—the third in 1822—the fourth in 1823. So great a sale of so large a work, on such a subject, is the best evidence that can be offered of its value. There has yet been no American edition.

Vol. I. contains a Critical Inquiry into the genuineness, Authenticity, uncorrupted Preservation, and Inspiration of the Holy Scriptures.

Vol. II. In Two Parts, treats, first on Sacred Criticism; including an Historical and Critical Account of the Original Languages of Scripture, and of the Cognate or kindred Dialects; an Account, with numerous Fac Similes, of the principal Manuscripts of the Old and New Testaments, &c. &c. In this part of the work, the History of the authorized English version of the Bible is particularly considered. The various **Readings**, the Quotations from the Old Testament in the New, the Poetry of the Hebrews and Harmonies of the Scriptures, form a portion of this Part.

Second Part. *Of the Interpretation of the Scriptures. Subsidiary Means for ascertaining the Sense of Scripture*, viz.——Anthology of Languages ; Anthology of Scripture : Scholia and Glossaries ; Subject-matter, Context, Scope, Historical Circumstances, and Christian Writers.

These discussions are followed by the application of the preceding principles——to the Historical Interpretation of the Sacred Writings ; the Interpretation of the Figurative Language of Scripture ; the Spiritual Interpretation of the Scriptures ; the Interpretation of Prophecy, of Types, of the Doctrinal and Moral parts of Scripture, of Threatenings therein contained ; and of the Inferential and Practical Reading of the Sacred Writings.

Vol. III. contains an Outline of the Historical and Physical Geography of the Holy Land. The Political and Military Affairs of the Jewish and other Nations incidently mentioned in the Scriptures. Sacred Antiquities of the Jews. The Domestic Antiquities, or the Private Life, Manners, Customs, Amusements, &c. of the Jews and other Nations incidently mentioned in the Scriptures.

Vol. IV. is appropriated to the Analysis of Scripture.

PRICE TWELVE DOLLARS.

After publication the price will be *sixteen dollars.*

MECHANICS' MAGAZINE,

Containing selections from the most valuable Foreign Journals, as well as useful original matter. Conducted by Associated Mechanics.

" *The most valuable gift which the hand of Science has ever yet offered to the artisan.*"

The object of this publication is one of incalculable importance ; and, at the same time, of entire novelty. A numerous and valuable portion of the community, including all who are manually employed in our different trades and manufactures, had begun to feel strongly the want of a periodical work, which, at a price suited to their means, would diffuse among them a better acquaintance with the history and principles of the arts they practise ; convey them to earlier information than they had hitherto been able to procure, of new discoveries, inventions, and improvements ; and furnish also a medium through which they could themselves commit their thoughts and observations to writing for public benefit.

THE MECHANICS' MAGAZINE, besides containing a greater quantity of original contributions on matters of arts and science, from practical men, than any other publication, supplies its readers regularly with the essence of all that is valuable in other journals, foreign and domestic.

This work will be published every Saturday, in a pamphlet of sixteen octavo pages, containing several fine wood engravings. Subscriptions $4 per annum, half payable on delivery of the 4th number, the remainder on delivery of the 26th number.

No. 221 *Broadway, New York.*   J. V. SEAMAN.

☞ Subscriptions to the above work are received at the Library, No. 98 Washington street, where subscribers can receive it, either in weekly or monthly numbers, as they prefer.

S. H. PARKER, *Agent to the Publisher.*

MALTE-BRUN'S GEOGRAPHY.

WELLS & LILLY, No. 98 Court street, Boston, have just published,

Universal Geography, or a Description of all Parts of the World, on a New Plan, according to the great natural Divisions of the Globe ; accompanied with analytical, synoptical, and elementary Tables. By M. Malte-Brun. Improved by the addition of the most recent information, derived from various sources, —Part 2 of vol. 2—forming No. 4 of the work.

This celebrated work is to be completed in fourteen parts, forming seven volumes 8vo. Price, to subscribers, $1,50 a part. Persons who are disposed to patronize it, are requested to send in their names, and those who have subscribed will please send for the numbers published.

" M. Malte-Brun is probably known to most of our readers as the author of a Systematic Work on Geography ; he is besides the editor of Nouvelles Annales des Voyages ; the first is as much superior to the compilations of our Guthries and Pinkertons, as the other is to the garbled productions of our Truslers and Mavors."—*Quarterly Review, No.* 52.

" Its design is to bring together the whole of ancient and modern geography.—But immense and difficult as the undertaking is, the author has done and is doing it ample justice. It is at once a system of geography for every day use, and at the same time an example of enlarged philosophical views. It is alike calculated to gratify those who read merely from curiosity, and those who seek its pages for the more definite purposes of education and scientific intelligence. It is admirable in its original form, it is well translated, it is printed in a fair style, and in fine, it is a work that neither library, nor family, nor school, should be without.—*Literary Gazette.*

LAW BOOKS.

HARRISON GRAY, No. 74 Washington street, Boston, has for sale,

Complete sets of Massachusetts Reports, 17 vols. and any volume that may be wanted to complete sets,—continuation of the same work, by Octavius Pickering, Esq.; Bigelow's old Digest of the 12 first vols. of Massachusetts Reports; Metcalf's Continuation, containing a Digest of the 5 last vols. of Tyng's and the 1st vol. of Pickering's Reports; Bigelow's new Digest of Massachusetts Reports, complete, in one vol.; Gow on Partnership, first American edition, with American Decisions; Rawle's View of the Constitution of the United States; Norris' edition of Peake on Evidence; Stearns on Real Actions; Phillips on Insurance; Dane's Abridgment of American Law; Davis' Justice; Gallison's Reports; 2d. vol. Maine Reports by Greenleaf; Russell on Crimes; Montague on Partnership; Stephen on Pleading; Sargeant on Constitutional Law; Chitty's Pleadings, a new edition, with corrections and additions by Dunlap, and additional Notes and References by Ingraham; and a large stock of other Law Books, recently received,—among which are the 3 first volumes of the new edition of Comyn's Digest, with American Decisions, by Thomas Day, Esq. The price of this work will be six dollars per vol. to those who engage it before the 8th and last vol. is printed, after which time the price will be raised to eight dollars. Those who wish for this work at subscription price, will please apply soon, as above, or to Gray, Childs, & Co. Portsmouth, N. H.

PINNOCK'S CATECHISMS.

MUNROE & FRANCIS, No. 137 Washington street, Boston, have for sale,

Pinnock's Catechisms for Children, viz. First Catechism; Catechisms of the Christian Religion; Drawing; Electricity; General Knowledge; History of Greece; History of America, 2 parts; Mental Philosophy; Morality; Natural

History; Poetry; Religious Denominations; Universal History, &c.

The following notice of the above Works is from the London Literary Gazette.

"We have merely selected the above from a long list of Catechisms, for which the rising generations are indebted to Messrs. Pinnock & Maunder, in order to bring them, with our honest commendations, more distinctly than by advertisement, under public consideration. It may be, that the circumstance of Messrs. P. & M. being the publishers of the Literary Gazette, may have led to our examining these little volumes with greater attention than we might otherwise have bestowed upon them; but sure we are that no circumstance would tempt us to stake our credit by laying a fallacious report upon them before parties so jealously interested in the education of youth as teachers and parents. But in truth, being led to look into these works, we have been pleasingly surprised at the variety and accuracy of the information they contain, within so small a compass and in so excellent a form; and we feel that we are only discharging an useful duty in communicating the result of our remarks to the public.

"The antiquity and universal adoption of the catechetical manner of conveying instruction, is perhaps the best proof of its value. The memory is aided by the question, and the mind impressed by the answer; the former is the help which infant years need, and the latter is the essence of all intellectual acquirement. The skill necessary to balance the two qualities, so as neither to assist so much as to weaken the reasoning powers, nor to expect so much as to overpower the capacity of childhood, does appear to us to be happily displayed in these Catechisms. And we would say, that more convenient, accurate, well arranged, and proper publications for the purposes they embrace, were never submitted to general approbation."

FLORULA BOSTONIENSIS.

CUMMINGS, HILLIARD, & CO. 134 Washington street, Boston, have lately published

Florula Bostoniensis :—A Collection of Plants of Boston and its Vicinity, with their generic and specific characters, principal synonymes, descriptions, places of growth, and time of flowering, and occasional remarks. By Jacob Bigelow, M. D. Second edition greatly enlarged. To which is added, a Glossary of the Botanical terms used in the work.

𝕷𝖎𝖙𝖊𝖗𝖆𝖗𝖞 𝕬𝖉𝖛𝖊𝖗𝖙𝖎𝖘𝖊𝖗.

MAY 15, 1825.

An additional half sheet will hereafter be annexed to our work, to be called the LITERARY ADVERTISER. This will enhance the value of the work to our subscribers without any additional expense to them—and enable publishers and booksellers throughout the country to advertise the works in which they are interested, at a moderate price. The Advertiser is not paged, and forms no part of the Gazette. Our numbers, at the close of the year, may be bound in two volumes, of 480 pages each; and the Advertiser may be thrown out, as having answered all the purposes for which it was designed.

*** Advertisements of books of all kinds, stationary, maps, globes, mathematical and astronomical instruments, &c. are solicited.

---

the Last Edinburgh Edition. With a continuation of the History of Greece, from the Mahometan Conquest to the present year, and other additions, by Charles Anthon, Adjunct Professor of Languages in Columbia College, New York.

——— Antiquam exquirite Matrem.   *Virgil.*

——— Vos exemplaria Græca
Nocturna versate manu, versate diurna.   *Horat.*

The above work will be comprised in one thick octavo volume, and will contain, besides additions to the main work, a continuation of the History of Greece from the period of the Mahometan conquest to the present time, and remarks on the history of Grecian Literature. It will be edited by Professor Anthon of Columbia College.

Potter's Grecian Antiquities is a book of so much value, both to the student and the more advanced scholar, that it is a matter of regret that no edition of it has hitherto appeared in this country. The principal obstacle to its republication here has been the expense of the plates which accompany the English copy. This, however, will be removed in the present instance, by making a selection of such of the plates as are of importance in elucidating points of antiquity, while others, answering the purpose of mere ornament, will be omitted. The work will be presented to the public on good paper, in a neat type, and at a moderate price.

HORNE'S INTRODUCTION.

E. LITTELL, No. 88 Chesnut street, Philadelphia, has in press,

An Introduction to the Critical Study and Knowledge of the Holy Scriptures. By Thomas Hartwell Horne, M. A.

It will be printed from the London edition of 1823, in four large octavo volumes; it will contain numerous Maps and Fac-Similes of Biblical Manuscripts, and in short, every thing that is contained in that edition, and will be very neatly printed on good paper.

The first London edition of this work was published in 1818—the second in 1821—the third in 1822—the fourth in 1828. So great a sale of so large a work, on such a subject, is the best evidence that can be offered of its value. There has yet been no American edition.

Vol. I. contains a Critical Inquiry into the genuineness, Authenticity, uncorrupted Preservation, and Inspiration of the Holy Scriptures.

Vol. II. in Two Parts, treats, first on Sacred Criticism ; including an Historical and Critical Account of the Original Languages of Scripture, and of the Cognate or kindred Dialects ; an Account, with numerous Fac-Similes, of the principal Manuscripts of the Old and New Testaments, &c. &c. In this part of the work, the History of the authorized English version of the Bible is particularly considered. The various Readings, the Quotations from the Old Testament in the New, the Poetry of the Hebrews, and Harmonies of the Scriptures, form a portion of this Part.

Second Part. *Of the Interpretation of the Scriptures. Subsidiary Means for ascertaining the Sense of Scripture*, viz.—Anthology of Languages ; Anthology of Scripture : Scholia and Glossaries ; Subject-matter, Context, Scope, Historical Circumstances, and Christian Writers.

These discussions are followed by the application of the preceding principles—to the Historical Interpretation of the Sacred Writings ; the Interpretation of the Figurative Language of Scripture ; the Spiritual Interpretation of the Scriptures; the Interpretation of Prophecy, of Types, of the Doctrinal and Moral parts of Scripture, of Threatenings therein contained ; and of the Inferential and Practical Reading of the Sacred Writings.

Vol. III. contains an Outline of the Historical and Physical Geography of the Holy Land. The Political and Military Affairs of the Jewish and other Nations incidentally mentioned in the Scriptures. Sacred Antiquities of the Jews. The Domestic Antiquities, or the Private Life, Manners, Customs, Amusements, &c. of the Jews and other Nations incidentally mentioned in the Scriptures.

Vol. IV. is appropriated to the Analysis of Scripture.

PRICE TWELVE DOLLARS.

After publication the price will be *sixteen dollars*.

ENGLISH AND AMERICAN LAW BOOKS.

PHILIP H. NICKLIN, Law Bookseller, No. 75 Chesnut-street, Philadelphia, has always on hand a very extensive assortment of English and American Law Books, which he will sell on liberal terms. Catalogues to be had at the store. Large discounts are allowed from the Catalogue prices ; and, having the largest stock of Law Books in this country, he is enabled to supply orders at the shortest notice.

VALUABLE SCHOOL BOOKS,

Published and sold by LINCOLN & EDMANDS, No. 59 Washton street.

Walker's School Dictionary, printed on fine paper, and handsome stereotype plates. The great inconvenience in the common editions, arising from the intermixture of the I and J and U and V, is remedied in this edition. $1 25.

The Elements of Arithmetic, an appropriate work for the young classes in schools, by question and answer. By James Robinson, Jr. 12 1-2 cents.

" Boston, March 25, 1824.

" At a legal meeting of the School Committee this day :— Ordered, That Robinson's Elements of Arithmetic, by Question and Answer, be hereafter used by the third and fourth classes, in the writing department of the public Grammar and Writing Schools in this city."

E. CLAPP, *Sec. of the School Committee.*

The American Arithmetic, a new and admirable work for schools, combining the various improvements in modern works on this subject, by James Robinson, Jr. intended as a Sequel to the Elements. The work contains all the rules necessary to adapt it to Schools in cities and in the country, embracing Commission, Discount, Duties, Annuities, Barter, Gauging, Mechanical Powers, &c. &c. Although the work is put at a low price, it will be found to contain a greater quantity of matter than most of the School Arithmetics in general use. 75 cents.

The Child's Assistant in the Art of Reading, containing a pleasing selection of Easy Readings for young children. Price 12 1-2 cents.

The Pronouncing Introduction, being Murray's Introduction, with accents, calculated to lead to a correct pronunciation, agreeably to Walker's System. 37 1-2 cents.

The Pronouncing English Reader, being Murray's Reader accented, divided into paragraphs, enriched with a frontispiece exhibiting Walker's illustration of the Inflections of the voice. The work is printed on fine paper, with stereotype plates.

Dr Adams's Geography, a work highly approved, having passed through numerous editions, and obtained a general circulation in the United States. Accompanying the work is a neat and correct Atlas.

Richardson's American Reader, consisting of Pieces selected wholly from American Authors. 37 1-2 cents.

Temple's Arithmetic, with additions and improvements, printed on fine paper. Ninth edition. To this edition are added about 150 questions for mental exercise, and questions on Arithmetic. 37 1-2 cents.

The Pronouncing Testament, in which all the proper names, and numerous other words, are divided and accented, agreeably to Walker's Dictionary and Key. By Israel Alger, Jr.

The Pronouncing Testament has probably contributed more to produce a uniform and correct pronunciation, than any other work extant. It has received numerous testimonials of approbation, and should obtain a place in every school and family.

Conversations on Natural Philosophy, with Questions for examination, additional notes and illustrations, a frontispiece representing the Solar System, &c. &c. being a greatly improved edition. By the Rev. J. L. Blake. $1 50.

It is believed that Mrs Bryan, the author of this work, has done more by its publication to promote the study of Natural Philosophy, among young people, than has been accomplished by all other works on the subject. Her familiar comparisons and illustrations interest and gain the attention of every reader.

Alger's Murray, a new and greatly improved edition of Murray's Grammar abridged, in which large additions of notes and rules are inserted from the larger work. 25 cents.

The English Teacher, in which Murray's Exercises and Key, are placed in opposite columns, with Rules and Observations from Murray's Grammar, furnishing a work of much value to teachers and private learners. By I. Alger, Jr. $1.

Murray's Exercises, a new and much improved stereotype edition, by Israel Alger, Jr. 50 cents.

Lincoln's Scripture Questions, with the answers from Scripture annexed, a very appropriate work for Sabbath Schools and families. 12 cts.

Also for sale the School Books in general use.

The Pronouncing Bible, in which all the proper names, and many other words, are accented as they ought to be pronounced, has just been issued from the press of Lincoln & Edmands, and is recommended by numerous literary gentlemen, as most happily adapted to promote a uniform and correct pronunciation agreeable to Walker's System.

In issuing the above works, it has been the object of the Publishers to elevate the style of School Books in typographical execution; and they cherish the expectation that Instructers and School Committees will, on examination, be disposed to patronise them.

LARGE COLLECTION OF BOOKS.

HARRISON GRAY, No. 74 Washington street, Boston, has
for sale,

An extensive assortment of Law, School, and Miscellaneous
Books, comprising whole editions of many valuable works.

American Books furnished to booksellers at publishers' prices.

Foreign Books at a small advance upon cost of importation.

Libraries supplied with new publications on liberal terms.

Complete sets of Massachusetts Reports, 17 vols. and any
volume that may be wanted to complete sets,—continuation of
the same work, by Octavius Pickering, Esq. ; Bigelow's old Digest
of the 12 first vols. of Massachusetts Reports ; Metcalf's Continuation, containing a Digest of the 5 last vols. of Tyng's and the
1st vol. of Pickering's Reports ; Bigelow's new Digest of Massachusetts Reports, complete, in one vol. ; Gow on Partnership,
first American edition, with American Decisions ; Rawle's View
of the Constitution of the United States ; Norris' edition of
Peake on Evidence ; Stearns on Real Actions ; Phillips on Insurance ; Dane's Abridgment of American Law ; Davis' Justice ;
Gallison's Reports ; 2d. vol. Maine Reports by Greenleaf ;
Russell on Crimes ; Montague on Partnership ; Stephen on
Pleading ; Sargeant on Constitutional Law ; Chitty's Pleadings,
a new edition, with corrections and additions by Dunlap, and additional Notes and References by Ingraham ; and a large stock
of other Law Books, recently received. Among these are the
3 first volumes of the new edition of Comyn's Digest, with American Decisions, by Thomas Day, Esq. The price of this work
will be six dollars per vol. to those who engage it before the 8th
and last vol. is printed, after which time the price will be raised
to eight dollars. Those who wish for this work at subscription
price, will please to apply soon, as above, or to Gray, Childs, &
Co. Portsmouth, N. H.

MUNROE AND FRANCIS,

128 Washington street, have lately published,

The Improvisatrice and other Poems, by L. E. L., copied from
the English edition, with many more pieces selected from the
Literary Gazette.

"It lies not in our power to love or hate,
For will in us is overruled by Fate."

Conversations on Common Things ; or, a Guide to Knowledge.
By a Teacher. Three hundred topics, more or less interesting,

are here conversed on in a very intelligent manner, and it forms a very useful volume for a family of children.

Hymns for Children, selected and altered : with appropriate texts of Scripture. By the Author of " Conversations on Common Things."

Patronage, being the seventh volume of the complete Works of Miss Edgeworth ; which are to be comprised in thirteen octavo volumes, taking in her last new work about being published in England. Volume XI. is now in press.

A great variety of Books for Children are constantly for sale.

MECHANICS' MAGAZINE,

Containing selections from the most valuable Foreign Journals, as well as useful original matter. Conducted by Associated Mechanics.

" The most valuable gift which the hand of Science has ever yet offered to the artisan."

The object of this publication is one of incalculable importance ; and, at the same time, of entire novelty. A numerous and valuable portion of the community, including all who are manually employed in our different trades and manufactures, had begun to feel strongly the want of a periodical work, which, at a price suited to their means, would diffuse among them a better acquaintance with the history and principles of the arts they practise ; convey to them earlier information than they had hitherto been able to procure, of new discoveries, inventions, and improvements ; and furnish also a medium through which they could themselves commit their thoughts and observations to writing for public benefit.

THE MECHANICS' MAGAZINE, besides containing a greater quantity of original contributions on matters of arts and science, from practical men, than any other publication, supplies its readers regularly with the essence of all that is valuable in other journals, foreign and domestic.

This work will be published every Saturday, in a pamphlet of sixteen octavo pages, containing several fine wood engravings. Subscriptions $4 per annum, half payable on delivery of the 4th number, the remainder on delivery of the 26th number.

No. 221 Broadway, New York.　　　　　J. V. SEAMAN.

☞ Subscriptions to the above work are received at the Library, No. 98 Washington street, where subscribers can receive it, either in weekly or monthly numbers, as they prefer.

S. H. PARKER, *Agent to the Publisher.*

𝕷𝖎𝖙𝖊𝖗𝖆𝖗𝖞 𝕬𝖉𝖛𝖊𝖗𝖙𝖎𝖘𝖊𝖗.

JUNE 1, 1825.

AN additional half sheet will hereafter be annexed to our work, to be called the LITERARY ADVERTISER. This will enhance the value of the work to our subscribers without any additional expense to them—and enable publishers and booksellers throughout the country to advertise the works in which they are interested, at a moderate price. The Advertiser is not paged, and forms no part of the Gazette. Our numbers, at the close of the year, may be bound in two volumes, of 480 pages each; and the Advertiser may be thrown out, as having answered all the purposes for which it was designed.

*** Advertisements of books of all kinds, stationary, maps, globes, mathematical and astronomical instruments, &c. are solicited.

EVERETT'S ORATIONS.

JUST PUBLISHED,

AN ORATION DELIVERED AT CONCORD, April the Nineteenth, 1825. By Edward Everett.

Also, lately published, a second and cheap edition of

AN ORATION DELIVERED AT PLYMOUTH, December 22, 1824. By Edward Everett.

CUMMINGS, HILLIARD & CO.

MEMOIR OF JOSIAH QUINCY, JUN.

JUST PUBLISHED,

MEMOIR OF THE LIFE OF JOSIAH QUINCY, JUN. of Massachusetts, by his Son, Josiah Quincy.

CUMMINGS, HILLIARD & CO.

DANE'S ABRIDGMENT OF AMERICAN LAW.

Cummings, Hilliard, & Co.

No. 134 Washington-street, Boston, have just published,

The Eighth and last Volume of A General Abridgment and Digest of American Law, with Notes and Comments. By Nathan Dane, LL. D. Counsellor at Law.

Subscription price for the work, complete in 8 vols. bound, $45.

The design of this work is to furnish the profession with a complete body of American Law, in so cheap and compendious a form, and at the same time so comprehensive, that it cannot fail to be practically useful, especially to those lawyers and students, who cannot afford to purchase many books.

In November, 1819, the work was submitted to Judge Story, to be examined by him as far as his duties would allow. The parts he had to inspect were the general plan and the parts deemed the most difficult to be executed well; as divisions 8, 9, 10, 23, 24, 25, 26, and 28, and some other parts, in all about one third of the work. The result of his examination was the opinion subjoined.

Salem, May, 1821.

The Hon. Nathan Dane, of Beverly, has prepared for publication a new Digest, or Abridgment of the Law. I am entirely satisfied with the plan, which proposes to separate that portion of the Common Law, which is applicable to and in use in our country, from that which exclusively concerns England. The decisions and doctrines of the most important American Reports are also incorporated into the work. I have examined, with as much care and attention, as my other duties would allow, several leading titles of the work, and can without hesitation declare, that they exhibit a far more complete and methodical view of the law, than the corresponding titles of any abridgment now in general use. To those who are acquainted with the great learning, diligence, and high professional character of the author, who has expended the leisure of more than thirty years on the enterprise, it might be useless to say more; but to those, who are not in this predicament, I beg to state, that from my knowledge of the author and the work, I hazard nothing in stating that it will be found of great utility to American Lawyers, and will peculiarly facilitate the labours of students in the profession.

JOSEPH STORY.

that they exhibit a far more complete and methodical view of the law, than the corresponding titles of any abridgment now in general use. To those who are acquainted with the great learning, diligence, and high professional character of the author, who has expended the leisure of more than thirty years on the enterprise, it might be useless to say more ; but to those, who are not in this predicament, I beg to state, that from my knowledge of the author and the work, I hazard nothing in stating that it will be found of great utility to American Lawyers, and will peculiarly facilitate the labours of students in the profession.

JOSEPH STORY.

FROM THE HON. WILLIAM PRESCOTT.

I have examined, with some care, the chapter on Insurance in the new Digest and Abridgment of the Law compiled by the Hon. Nathan Dane. His division and arrangement of the different subjects appear to me methodical and perspicuous. Principles, upon which the cases in the several points depend, are concisely and clearly stated, and I believe all the cases of any importance, which have been decided by the Courts in England and the United States, are quoted, and most of them either judiciously abridged, or the points stated.

I know of no digest of the Law of Insurance, equally compendious with this chapter, so useful as I think this will prove to the profession.

I have not had leisure to peruse the other parts of the work, but from this chapter, and from the plan of the work exhibited in the concise view of it, which the author has published, as well as from my long and intimate knowledge of his talents, industry, and great learning, I have no doubt that to American Lawyers and Students it will prove a more useful and valuable Digest and Abridgment of the Law, than any now in use.

WILLIAM PRESCOTT

Boston, June 5, 1822.

EVERETT'S ORATIONS.

JUST PUBLISHED,

AN ORATION DELIVERED AT CONCORD, April the Nineteenth, 1825. By Edward Everett.

Also, lately published, a second and cheap edition of

AN ORATION DELIVERED AT PLYMOUTH, December 22, 1824. By Edward Everett.

CUMMINGS, HILLIARD & CO.

SPANISH GRAMMAR.

Munroe & Francis,

128 Washington-street, have just published,

The second edition of JOSSE'S SPANISH GRAMMAR, with Practical Exercises. Revised, improved, and adapted to the English language, by F. SALES, Instructer of French and Spanish at Harvard University, Cambridge.

NOTICE.

Grateful for the approbation that our labours have met with in the rapid diffusion of a large edition of this Grammar, and encouraged by the favourable judgment passed on the theoretical and practical method observed in this elementary work, by the most distinguished philologists and eminent scholars in our country; we now present to the American nation a second edition, carefully revised, considerably altered, and improved throughout; particularly in the arrangement of the Conjugation of the Irregular Verbs; in giving the English signification of the Table of Prepositions published by the Royal Academy; in prefixing an article to every word in the Vocabulary to denote its gender; and in assimilating as far as possible the English phraseology to the Spanish, in the Familiar Phrases and Dialogues.

We have enlarged this new edition by the addition of interesting extracts from some of the best Spanish writers; with specimens of critical, familiar, and commercial Letters; Mercantile Documents; a Treatise on Spanish Versification, translated from the latest Paris edition of Josse's Grammar; and a copious Table of Contents;—the whole corrected in conformity to the most recent decisions on orthography of the Spanish Academy.

Our earnest purpose having been to render this publication entensively useful and acceptable to all classes and ages of learners, the public may rest assured that no pains have been spared to attain so desirable an object.

Boston, May, 1825.

BOOK OF COMMON PRAYER.

R. P. & C. Williams,

Cornhill-Square, have for sale,

A Rational Illustration of the Book of Common Prayer of the Church of England, being the substance of every thing liturgical in Bishop Sparrow, M. L'Estrange, Dr Comber, Dr Nichols, and all former Ritualits, Commentators, or others, upon the same subject; collected and reduced into one combined and regular method, and interspersed all along with new Observations. By Charles Wheatley, A. M. Vicar of Brent and Furneaux Pelham, in Hertfordshire. Improved by Additions and Notes drawn from a comparison with Shepherd and other writers on the Liturgy, adapting this edition to the present state of the Protestant Episcopal Church in America, without any alteration of the Original Text.

Ostendas Ceremonias et Rituum volendi.

LAWYERS' COMMON-PLACE BOOK.

Cummings, Hilliard, & Co.—Boston,

HAVE JUST PUBLISHED

The Lawyers' Common-Place Book, with an Alphabetical Index of the heads which occur in general reading and practice.

EXTRACT FROM THE PREFACE.

The utility of Common-Place Books has rarely been controverted since the decided testimony of Mr Locke in their favour. His opinion was given after many years' experience, and has been sanctioned by all those who have made trial of the plan proposed by him. His method, although exceedingly useful to the general reader, has been less so to the professional student, on account of the difficulty of arranging and dividing the subjects in a proper manner.

Few lawyers however have attained to any considerable eminence in the profession, without a Common-Place Book of some sort. To facilitate the use of them so as to induce their adoption by every individual engaged in professional pursuits is the object of the present publication.

The student will here find a title prepared for him for nearly every thing he can take an interest in preserving. Should any of the heads be found too general, they can easily be subdivided. Should the student at any time feel at a loss under which of two or more heads a particular article ought to be placed, he will find it useful to refer to it under each of them. Many of the titles may never be used; but the want of them might prove an inconvenience, while their insertion can do no harm.

We are far from recommending to the student to transcribe all that he reads; yet we feel confident he will find great benefit from the free use of the book now offered. As a reference to cases and principles, it cannot be too freely used. Copious extracts of sentiments and opinions which appear to possess any striking merit or peculiarity will also be found highly convenient.

The price of the book is little beyond the value of the paper and binding; and its size will render it more convenient for use than if it were larger. When one volume is filled, another can be taken, and any improvement in the arrangement, which experience may suggest, can easily be adopted in the second. The work will be found equally adapted to every portion of our country. Price 3,25.

BOSTON TYPE AND STEREOTYPE FOUNDRY.

The subscribers inform their friends and printers generally, that they are extensively engaged in the business of manufacturing

Printing Types and Stereotype Plates,

and can furnish, at short notice, all the variety of Types cast in this country, warranted to be made of the best materials, and in the best manner; their letter has been newly cut, is very handsome and well adapted to the critical taste of the times. Orders are respectfully solicited.

T. H. CARTER & CO,

Salem-Street, near the North Church.

NEW YORK PAPER AND ACCOUNT BOOK WAREHOUSE.

The subscriber has taken, in addition to his store at No. 82 State-street, Boston, that large, convenient, fire-proof building, No. 245 Pearl-street, New-York, where he proposes opening, on a very extensive scale, a Wholesale Stationary, Paper, and Account Book Warehouse, and solicits consignments of every kind of Foreign and Domestic Stationary, Paper, Charts, Nautical Works, School Books and Bibles, or other articles in any way relating thereto. The strictest personal attention will be paid to the interest of the consigner, and the terms as favourable as at any house in the United States.

The advantages of such an establishment, where the manufacturer can deposit his goods and receive a liberal advance; and the purchaser obtain articles of the best qualities at the very lowest prices, and in larger quantities than in any other store in the United States, must be obvious to every person.

All communications previous to the first of August, to be addressed to Boston, after that date to New-York. DAVID FELT.

Refer to

Messrs. Cummings, Hilliard & Co. ⎫
 " William Parker & Co. ⎬ Boston.
 " James Vila & Co. ⎭
 " Valentine, Pettingell & Co. ⎫
 " E. Bliss & E. White, ⎬ N. York.
 " Goddard, Gillet & Co. ⎭

CONVERSATIONS ON NATURAL PHILOSOPHY.

Lincoln & Edmands,—59 Washington Street,

Have published a beautiful edition of Conversations on Natural Philosophy, with Questions for examination, additional Illustrations, a Dictionary of Philosophical Terms, and an elegant Frontespiece, exhibiting a View of the Solar System. By Rev. J. L. Blake.

This valuable work is obtaining an extensive circulation in schools, and the present greatly improved edition cannot fail to receive the patronage of instructers.

☞ The above work is stereotyping by Lincoln and Edmands, and will shortly be completed, from the foundry of Messrs. T. H. Carter & Co.

BICHAT'S GENERAL ANATOMY,

FOUR VOLUMES IN THREE,

Lately published

By Richardson & Lord,—Boston.

From the New England Medical Journal.

"We congratulate the medical profession in America, upon the appearance of this work. We are happy in being able to state, that the Government of the Massachusetts Medical Society, with that laudable ardour for the advancement of professional science, for which they have always been highly distinguished, have already added it to the list of those books which candidates are required to have studied before being admitted to an examination for license. In the lectures of our University it had always been recommended with a due regard for its extraordinary merit, but being confined to a foreign language, has been hitherto inaccessible to a large majority of our students. We trust, however, now that it has at length appeared, accurately and faithfully translated, it will become as extensively circulated and read as it deserves to be, and exercise an influence upon medical studies which will not fail to be salutary and beneficial."

From the North American Review.

"We are happy to see this work in an English dress, and especially so, that the labour of translating it has been performed by one of our own countrymen, and by one so well qualified in every point of view, to do justice to it, as Dr Hayward." "The translation of it is every way worthy of confidence, as a faithful picture of the original. We have carefully examined the greater part of this volume in comparison with the French, and have been able to detect scarcely any instances in which there appears to be a deviation from the meaning of the author. It will form certainly a most valuable addition to our medical literature, and will, we trust, be extensively circulated. It has even higher claims upon the attention, than the former works of Bichat, which have been published in this country ; it will richly repay the physician for a careful and diligent study of it, and is not unworthy the perusal of even the general reader." "There is, we think, no medical author so well calculated as Bichat, by the character of his writings, to excite the interest and fix the attention of extra professional readers. He contrives to throw a charm over the most dry and forbidden details, of which no other writer has been capable."

From a Review of Professor Beclard's Additions to Bichat's Anatomy in the Quarterly Journal of Foreign Medicine and Surgery.

"The admirable work of Bichat [his ' *General Anatomy* '] is now, we presume, in the hands of every one who makes any pretension to a philosophical study of his profession. The strongest proof of its great merit is, that it has passed through, almost untouched, the severest of all ordeals, the test of time."

RICHARDSON AND LORD

Have also lately published, in one volume octavo,

ADDITIONS TO BICHAT'S GENERAL ANATOMY, By Professor Beclard, of Paris.

Journal of Foreign Medicine and Surgery.

"The additions of M. Beclard, whose accurate research and extensive knowledge we cannot too highly praise, are almost as many and as varied as the subjects of the original work." "Such are a few of the interesting details furnished in this able continuation of the Anatomie Generale. We should have been much more particular in our analysis, had we not foreseen that all who possess the original work, and who are interested in the progress of science, will add those additions of M. Beclard to their libraries."

☞ This volume is accompanied with a correct likeness of BICHAT.

BONAPARTE'S AMERICAN ORNITHOLOGY.

S. A. Mitchell,—Philadelphia,

Is now publishing by subscription, The American Ornithology, or History of the Birds inhabiting the United States, with Coloured Figures from Original Drawings, executed from Nature. By Charles Lucien Bonaparte. In 3 vols. imperial 4to.

The first volume of this work is now published, and as a specimen of the arts is unrivalled, the mechanical execution of it being acknowledged to surpass that of any work ever before published in this country.

Mr UNDERWOOD, who has taken the agency of the work for Boston and the vicinity, will shortly take the liberty of calling on gentlemen, to show them a copy of the 1st volume, and to receive the subscriptions of any who may choose to give their names;—and he flatters himself that the prejudice, existing against subscriptions generally, will not extend to this, as from the nature of the work, it will be seen to be necessary that the publisher should know about what number of copies are wanted, which number in striking off the work will not be far exceeded. Mr U. can be seen in regard to the work at No. 6 Hanover Street. Letters addressed to him or to the publisher by mail will receive attention.

Boston, August 15, 1825.

MISS EDGEWORTH'S WORKS.

Munroe & Francis, 128 Washington-street—Boston,

Inform the public, and the present subscribers to their edition of *Edgeworth's Works*, in 13 vols. octavo, that *Eight Volumes* are ready for delivery; that the *Ninth* will be published on September 1st ; and the remaining four volumes on the first days of the succeeding four months.

M. & F. solicit subscribers to these useful works. Great pains have been taken to have them well done, and it is not probable another edition will ever be attempted, as the expense is so great; and patronage can never be better bestowed.

To put the subject in a clear point of view, and to show the economy of the present subscription, the publishers annex a schedule of the price of the different editions of this lady's writings, to excite the liberal to come forward and aid in accomplishing the Boston edition.

	English Editions, as usually sold in this country.	Ordinary American Editions.	Boston Edition.
VOL. I.			
Practical Education - -	7 50	4 50	1 50
VOL. II.			
Letters to Literary Ladies -	1 50	75	
Castle Rackrent - - -	1 25	75	} 1 50
Leonora - - - -	3 00	1 00	
Essay on Irish Bulls - -	1 50	75	
VOL. III.			
Belinda - - -	4 00	2 00	1 50
VOL. IV.			
Popular Tales - - -	3 50	2 00	1 50
VOL. V.			
Tales of Fashionable Life - -	5 00	2 25	1 50
VOL. VI.			
Vivian, and Emilie de Coulanges -	3 00	1 00	} 1 50
Absentee - - - -	2 00	1 75	
VOL. VII.			
Patronage - - -	7 50	3 00	1 50
VOL. VIII.			
Harrington and Ormond - -	4 00	2 00	1 50
VOL. IX.			
Griselda - - - -	1 12	75	} 1 50
Moral Tales - - -	3 00	1 50	
VOL. X.			
Parents' Assistant - -	5 00	2 50	1 50
VOL. XI.			
Early Lessons, Rosamond - -	5 00	4 50	1 50
VOL XII.			
Ealy Lessons, Frank - -	5 00	4 50	1 50
VOL. XIII.			
Readings on Poetry - -	1 25	75	} 1 50
Comic Dramas - - -	1 50	1 00	
Sequel to Harry and Lucy - -	2 00	1 50	
	67 62	37 00	19 50

The English Editions have never been afforded cheaper than as put down above. There has been no uniform American edition previous to ours, and we have given the selling price of those printed. The public have now an opportunity of getting the best of books at *half price.*

COLLECTANEA GRAECA MINORA.

JUST PUBLISHED

An improved edition of Collectanea Graeca Minora with explanatory Notes collected or written by Andrew Dalzel, A. M. F. R. S. E. Professor of Greek in the University of Edinburgh. Sixth Cambridge edition, in which the Notes and Lexicon are translated from the Latin into English.

EXTRACT FROM THE PREFACE.

It has long been a complaint, that the Notes of Collectanea Graeca Minora, being written in Latin, were not so useful as they might be to beginners, for whose use they were prepared. In this edition therefore the Notes and Lexicon have been translated into English; so that the work may be used without any previous knowledge of the Latin language. In this edition also a few notes have been added, particularly upon the most difficult part—the Extracts from Tyrtaeus.

The text also has been diligently compared with the latest and best editions of the works, from which the extracts were made, belonging to the Library of Harvard University, and a few new readings have been introduced which throw light on obscure passages. It is hoped, therefore, that those who have heretofore used and approved the work, will be still better satisfied with it, now that it is more free from errors, and more easy and instructive to young students.

CELESTIAL PLANISPHERE.

PROPOSALS,

By M. R. Bartlett,—Utica, N. Y.

FOR PUBLISHING, BY SUBSCRIPTION,

A CELESTIAL PLANISPHERE, or MAP OF THE HEAVENS.

This map presents a view of the Sensible Heavens in two hemispheres, about *four feet two inches, by two feet four inches*, divided at, and projected upon, the plane of the Equinoctial Circle, the secondaries of which are all accurately drawn. It also exhibits all the Constellations of the Heavens, both Ancient and Modern, carefully and elegantly drafted, and correctly located, each bearing its Classical and English names; with its right ascension and declination, and its number of visible stars (to the most prominent of which the right ascension and declination are also added) expressed in figures.

The great and small Circles of the Heavens are likewise carefully drawn, and the Equinoctial, the Ecliptic, and the Colures, with an Analamma, properly graduated, and an additional Circle for the Equation of time. The Zodiac, the Great Belt of the Heavens, crossed transversely by the Milky Way, exhibits the twelve months of the year, with divisions for the days, and the twelve corresponding signs, with their appropriate emblems, properly graduated to the days of the months;—by all of which, with a few marginal directions, most of the Astronomical

Problems, usually solved on the Celestial Globe, may be easily, correctly, and expeditiously performed and clearly illustrated.

A pamphlet of about thirty pages will accompany the Map, containing a collection of amusing problems, and the history, so far as it can be traced, of the several Constellations, with a table of the Fixed Stars.

CONDITIONS.

The Plates for the Celestial Planisphere, are now in the hands of the first artists in the state, who are pledged to execute them in a superior style of workmanship; and the various figures of the Constellations most happily furnish very appropriate subjects for a full display of taste and talent. The Map shall be printed upon the first quality of Elephant Paper. Colored, varnished, mounted on rollers, and finished throughout in a style strictly corresponding with the execution of the artists, and shall be furnished to subscribers at $5 per copy, payable on delivery, while to non-subscribers it shall at no time be sold for less than $6.

This work will be ready for delivery in the course of 1825.

INSTRUCTION IN DECLAMATION.

MR RUSSELL

has commenced giving lessons in Declamation at the Hall, on the south side of Winter Street, near the corner of Winter and Washington Streets. *Entrance as to Mr Labasse's Academy.* The lessons are as follows.

FIRST COURSE.

ELOCUTION.

Lesson 1st. Utterance.—2d. Articulation.—3d. Orthoepy, or the pronunciation of Letters and Syllables.—4th. Inflections of Words.—5th. Emphasis.—6th. Inflections of Clauses.—7th. Pauses.—8th. Cadence.—9th. Modulation.—10th. Rate.—11th. 12th. Tones.

GESTURE.

13th. Position and Movement of the Colloquial style.—14th. of the Epic.—15th. of the Rhetorical.—16th. 17th. 18th. Recapitulation and practice, accompanied by explanatory analysis.

The subsequent courses of lessons consist chiefly of practice on the principles and rules contained in the first course. The hours of attendance are such as do not interfere with the business of other schools.

The system of instruction has the following recommendations.

Mr Russell's system of instruction in Declamation, as explained and illustrated in his introductory lecture, seems likely to form a useful course of practical lessons for young learners, and is, in my opinion, deserving of public patronage.

EDWARD T. CHANNING.

Cambridge, July, 1824.

I have attended Mr Russell's explanatory lectures, and taken some pains to inform myself of the principles of his system, and his mode of instruction, and am persuaded that his lessons are calculated to be highly useful in forming a correct and easy style of delivery.

HENRY WARE, Jr.

Boston, July 15, 1825.

I have, for some years, known Mr William Russell, as a very successful teacher of the Latin and Greek Languages, Elocution, Composition, &c. He has devoted much of his time to the theory and practice of Elocution; and, though I have not witnessed any performance of his own in this art, I am satisfied from the proficiency of his pupils that he is well qualified to succeed in this branch of instruction.

CHAUNCEY A. GOODRICH,
(Professor of Rhetoric and Oratory, Yale College.)

New Haven, July 21, 1825.

A Second class will be formed, as soon as a sufficient number of applications is made. Mr R. may be seen at the Hall on Tuesday, Thursday, or Saturday, from 7 till half past 7 in the morning.
Boston, July 22, 1825.

THE NOTHERN TRAVELLER.

Wilder & Campbell—New York,

HAVE LATELY PUBLISHED

THE NOTHERN TRAVELLER, containing the routes to Niagara, Quebec, and the Springs; with descriptions of the principal scenes, and useful hints to strangers. To which is added an Appendix, containing a list of Steam-Boats and Coach Roads in different parts of the country, the arrangements of the Erie Canal Packet Boats, and the Routes from Boston to Winnipisiogee Lake and the White Mountains,—also from Boston to Albany. With numerous Maps and Copperplates. Price $2.

HISTORY OF THE EXPEDITION TO RUSSIA, undertaken by the Emperor Napoleon in the year 1812. By General Count Philip De Segur.

> Quamquam animus meminisse horret, luctuque refugit,
> Incipiam.————
> VIRGIL.

In one vol. octavo, with a Map. Price $2,75.

THE FORESTERS; by the author of "Lights and Shadows of Scottish Life," and the "Trials of Margaret Lyndsay."

These works are for sale by Booksellers generally.

Literary Advertiser.

SEPTEMBER 1, 1825.

The LITERARY ADVERTISER will enhance the value of our work to subscribers without any additional expense to them—and enable publishers and booksellers throughout the country to advertise the works in which they are interested, at a moderate price. The Advertiser is not paged, and forms no part of the Gazette. Our numbers, at the close of the year, may be bound in two volumes, of 480 pages each; and the Advertiser may be thrown out, as having answered all the purposes for which it was designed.

* Advertisements of books of all kinds, stationary, maps, globes, mathematical and astronomical instruments, &c. are solicited.

Literary Advertiser.

S. H. PARKER,

AT HIS

Piano-Forte, Music, and Book Store,

NO. 164 WASHINGTON STREET (LATE MARLBORO')

WILL publish in a few days, Miss Hamilton's Letters on Education, in 2 vols. 12mo. on fine paper.

SOLICITS subscriptions to the *second* edition of the Waverly Novels, now publishing in 8vo. and 12mo as above, at the "Waverley Press," where specimens of the Paper, Type, and Plates may be seen.

BOOKS of all discriptions furnished to order, as low as they can be purchased at any other store—where also

A Circulating Library, already consisting of 8000 vols. is liberally supplied with the *new* publications of the day, affording accommodation to the generality of readers.

STATIONARY and Fancy Articles constantly for sale as above, together with a general assortment of

PRINTED MUSIC, and various Instruments and Articles in the Musical line.

PIANO-FORTES bought, sold, and loaned.

VALUABLE MEDICAL WORK.

For sale by Cummings, Hilliard, & Co.—Boston,

A TREATISE ON VERMINOUS DISEASES, preceded by the Natural History of Intestinal Worms, &c. By *Valerian Lewis Brera*, Professor of Clinical Medicine in the University of Padua. Translated from a French edition of the work, with Additions, by J. G. Coffin, M. D. of Boston.

Extract from a review of the work in the Medico-Chirurgical Review, pulished in London.

"It is somewhat remarkable, that in these days, when every the most trivial disease has one or more monographers, the important subject of Worms should have led to no *ex professo* treatise, so far as we know, in our language. Dr Coffin has ably supplied this defect, by giving to his countrymen a translation of Professor Brera's excellent work; and all we can do for such of our brethren as cannot import either the original or translation, is to lay before them as comprehensive an analysis of Dr Coffin's translation as our limits will permit, and as concentrated a record as literary labour can accomplish."

After copious extracts from the work, the reviewer concludes thus:—

"We have now presented the prominent features of our learned author's work, and that of his able and intelligent translator. We have concentrated into a small space a great mass of useful information, which we hope may prove acceptable to the profession." Those who may wish to be more particularly acquainted with the practical value of this work are referred to a review of it in the 6th volume of the New England Journal of Medicine.

come as extensively circulated and read as it deserves to be, and exercise an influence upon medical studies which will not fail to be salutary and beneficial." *New England Medical Journal.*

" We are happy to see this work in an English dress, and especially so, that the labour of translating it has been performed by one of our own countrymen, and by one so well qualified in every point of view, to do justice to it, as Dr Hayward." " The translation of it is every way worthy of confidence, as a faithful picture of the original. We have carefully examined the greater part of this volume in comparison with the French, and have been able to detect scarcely any instances in which there appears to be a deviation from the meaning of the author. It will form certainly a most valuable addition to our medical literature, and will, we trust, be extensively circulated. It has even higher claims upon the attention, than the former works of Bichat, which have been published in this country ; it will richly repay the physician for a careful and diligent study of it, and is not unworthy the perusal of even the general reader." " There is, we think, no medical author so well calculated as Bichat, by the character of his writings, to excite the interest and fix the attention of extra professional readers. He contrives to throw a charm over the most dry and forbidden details, of which no other writer has been capable." *N. A. Review.*

" This admirable work of Bichat is now, we presume, in the hands of every one who makes any pretension to a philosophical study of his profession. The strongest proof of its great merit is, that it has passed through, almost untouched, the severest of all ordeals, the test of time." *Quarterly Journal of Foreign Medicine and Science.*

Also, lately published, in one volume octavo,
ADDITIONS TO BICHAT'S GENERAL ANATOMY, By Professor Beclard, of Paris.

" The additions of M. Beclard, whose accurate research and extensive knowledge we cannot too highly praise, are almost as many and as varied as the subjects of the original work." " Such are a few of the interesting details furnished in this able continuation of the Anatomie Generale. We should have been much more particular in our analysis, had we not foreseen that all who possess the original work, and who are interested in the progress of science, will add those additions of M. Beclard to their libraries."—*Journal of Foreign Medicine and Science.*

☞This volume is accompanied with a correct likeness of BICHAT.

BONAPARTE'S AMERICAN ORNITHOLOGY.

S. A. Mitchell,—Philadelphia,

Is now publishing by subscription, The American Ornithology, or History of the Birds inhabiting the United States, with Coloured Figures from Original Drawings, executed from Nature. By Charles Lucien Bonaparte. In 3 vols. imperial 4to.

The first volume of this work is now published, and as a specimen of the arts is unrivalled, the mechanical execution of it being acknowledged to surpass that of any work ever before published in this country.

Mr UNDERWOOD, who has taken the agency of the work for Boston and the vicinity, will shortly take the liberty of calling on gentlemen,

to show them a copy of the 1st volume, and to receive the subscriptions of any who may choose to give their names ;—and he flatters himself that the prejudice, generally existing against subscriptions, will not extend to this, as from the nature of the work, it will be seen to be necessary that the publisher should know about what number of copies are wanted ; which number in striking off the work will not be far exceeded. Mr U. can be seen at No. 6 Hanover Street. Letters addressed to him or to the publisher by mail will receive attention.
Boston, August 15, 1825.

MISS EDGEWORTH'S WORKS.

Munroe & Francis, 128 Washington-street—Boston,

Inform the public, and the present subscribers to their edition of *Edgeworth's Works*, in 13 vols. octavo, that the *ninth volume* is this day ready for delivery; and that the remaining four volumes will be published on the first days of the next four months.

M. & F. solicit subscribers to these useful works. Great pains have been taken to have them well done, and it is not probable another edition will ever be attempted, as the expense is so great ; and patronage can never be better bestowed. Price $1,50 per volume.

THE NOTHERN TRAVELLER.

Wilder & Campbell—New York,

HAVE LATELY PUBLISHED

THE NOTHERN TRAVELLER, containing the routes to Niagara, Quebec, and the Springs ; with descriptions of the principal scenes, and useful hints to strangers. To which is added an Appendix, containing a list of Steam-Boats and Coach Roads in different parts of the country, the arrangements of the Erie Canal Packet Boats, and the Routes from Boston to Winnipisiogee Lake and the White Mountains,—also from Boston to Albany. With numerous Maps and Copperplates. Price $2.

HISTORY OF THE EXPEDITION TO RUSSIA, undertaken by the Emperor Napoleon in the year 1812. By General Count Philip De Segur.

> Quamquam animus meminisse horret, luctuque refugit,
> Incipiam.————————   VIRGIL.

In one vol. octavo, with a Map. Price $2,75.

THE FORESTERS; by the author of "Lights and Shadows of Scottish Life," and the "Trials of Margaret Lyndsay."

These works are for sale by Booksellers generally.

COLBURN'S ALGEBRA.

Cummings, Hilliard, & Co.—Boston,

HAVE JUST PUBLISHED

AN INTRODUCTION TO ALGEBRA UPON THE INDUCTIVE METHOD OF INSTRUCTION. By Warren Colburn, author of First Lessons in Arithmetic &c. 1 vol. 12mo. Price $1,25.

COLLECTANEA GRAECA MINORA.
JUST PUBLISHED

By Cummings, Hilliard, & Co.—Boston,

An improved edition of Collectanea Græca Minora with explanatory Notes collected or written by Andrew Dalzel, A. M. F. R. S. E. Professor of Greek in the University of Edinburgh. Sixth Cambridge edition, in which the Notes and Lexicon are translated from the Latin into English.

EXTRACT FROM THE PREFACE.

It has long been a complaint, that the Notes of Collectanea Græca Minora, being written in Latin, were not so useful as they might be to beginners, for whose use they were prepared. In this edition therefore the Notes and Lexicon have been translated into English; so that the work may be used without any previous knowledge of the Latin language. In this edition also a few notes have been added, particularly upon the most difficult part—the Extracts from Tyrtæus.

The text also has been diligently compared with the latest and best editions of the works, from which the extracts were made, belonging to the Library of Harvard University, and a few new readings have been introduced which throw light on obscure passages. It is hoped, therefore, that those who have heretofore used and approved the work, will be still better satisfied with it, now that it is more free from errors, and more easy and instructive to young students.

CELESTIAL PLANISPHERE.

PROPOSALS,

By M. R. Bartlett,—Utica, N. Y.

FOR PUBLISHING, BY SUBSCRIPTION,

A CELESTIAL PLANISPHERE, or MAP OF THE HEAVENS.

This map presents a view of the Sensible Heavens in two hemispheres, about *four feet two inches, by two feet four inches*; divided at, and projected upon, the plane of the Equinoctial Circle, the secondaries of which are all accurately drawn. It also exhibits all the Constellations of the Heavens, both Ancient and Modern, carefully and elegantly drafted, and correctly located, each bearing its Classical and English names; with its right ascension and declination, and its number of visible stars (to the most prominent of which the right ascension and declination are also added) expressed in figures.

The great and small Circles of the Heavens are likewise carefully drawn, and the Equinoctial, the Ecliptic, and the Colures, with an Analamma, properly graduated, and an additional Circle for the Equation of time. The Zodiac, the Great Belt of the Heavens, crossed transversely by the Milky Way, exhibits the twelve months of the year, with divisions for the days, and the twelve corresponding signs, with their appropriate emblems, properly graduated to the days of the months;—by all of which, with a few marginal directions, most of the Astronomical Problems, usually solved on the Celestial Globe, may be easily, correctly, and expeditiously performed and clearly illustrated.

A pamphlet of about thirty pages will accompany the Map, containing a collection of amusing problems, and the history, so far as it can be traced, of the several Constellations, with a table of the Fixed Stars.

CONDITIONS.

The Plates for the Celestial Planisphere, are now in the hands of the first artists in the state, who are pledged to execute them in a superior style of workmanship; and the various figures of the Constellations most happily furnish very appropriate subjects for a full display of taste and talent. The Map shall be printed upon the first quality of Elephant Paper. Colored, varnished, mounted on rollers, and finished throughout in a style strictly corresponding with the execution of the artists, and shall be furnished to subscribers at $5 per copy, payable on delivery, while to non-subscribers it shall at no time be sold for less than $6.

This work will be ready for delivery in the course of 1825.

EVIDENCES OF CHRISTIANITY.

JUST PUBLISHED

By D. A. Borrenstein,—Princeton, N. J.

A BRIEF OUTLINE OF THE EVIDENCES OF THE CHRISTIAN RELIGION ; By Archibald Alexander, Professor of Didactic and Polemic Theology, in the Theological Seminary. at Princeton, N. J.

☞The publisher of the above work has the gratification of informing the public, that the favourable sale of the present edition has induced him to put a Second Edition to press. It will be printed on a *Superfine Royal Paper*, duodecimo, with a larger type. Price to subscribers, in boards, 87½ Cents. Non-subscribers will have to pay $1,25.

Individuals subscribing for six copies, will be entitled to a seventh *gratis.*

All orders (*postage paid*) will be duly attended to.

Subscriptions will also be received by Messrs. G. & C. Carvill, and John P. Haven, New York; Mr A. Finley, Philadelphia; Mr D. Fenton, Trenton, N. J.; and through the medium of Booksellers generally.

May 20, 1825.

STATIONARY.

Cummings, Hilliard, & Co.—Washington-Street, Boston,

HAVE CONSTANTLY ON HAND

A general assortment of the best LONDON STATIONARY. They have now for sale an extensive assortment of *ENGLISH LETTER* and *BILLET PAPER*, both plain and gilt.

— ALSO —

Quills, (Miller's manufacture).	Pencil Cases with Penknives.
Penknives, (Rogers' and Simpson's manufacture).	Durable Ink.
Scissors, Ink, and Sand.	Sealing Wax and Wafers.
Ebony and bronze Inkstands.	Razor Strops.
Chessmen.	Pocket Books and Wallets (elegant).
Writing Desks, (mahogany and rose-wood).	Dissected Maps.
	Ink Powder, Ink, &c.

𝕷𝖎𝖙𝖊𝖗𝖆𝖗𝖞 𝕬𝖉𝖛𝖊𝖗𝖙𝖎𝖘𝖊𝖗.

SEPTEMBER 15, 1825.

The LITERARY ADVERTISER will enhance the value of our work to subscribers without any additional expense to them—and enable publishers and booksellers throughout the country to advertise the works in which they are interested, at a moderate price. The Advertiser is not paged, and forms no part of the Gazette. Our numbers, at the close of the year, may be bound in two volumes, of 480 pages each ; and the Advertiser may be thrown out, as having answered all the purposes for which it was designed.

*** Advertisements of books of all kinds, stationary, maps, globes, mathematical and astronomical in struments, &c. are solicited.

that has yet appeared. to the state of society as it is in this country; and less obnoxious to complaint, on the ground of its national or political character, than it is reasonable to expect that any English compilation would be, among a people whose manners, opinions, literary institutions, and civil government, are so strictly republican as our own.

EXTRACT FROM THE RECORDS OF THE SCHOOL COMMITTEE, BOSTON.

"At a meeting of the School Committee, held July 18, 1823, it was ordered, that the American First Class Book be hereafter used in the public reading schools instead of Scott's Lessons.

Attest, WILLIAM WELLS, *Secretary.*

NEW BOOKS.

Cummings, Hilliard, & Co.—Boston.

HAVE FOR SALE

NARRATIVE of an Expedition to the Source of St Peter's River, Lake Winnepeek, Lake of the Woods, &c. &c. performed in the year 1823, by order of the Hon. J. C. Calhoun, Secretary of War; under the command of Stephen H. Long, Major U. S. T. E. Compiled from the notes of Major Long, and Messrs. Say, Keating, and Colhoun, by William H. Keating, A. M. &c. Professor of Mineralogy and Chemistry, as applied to the Arts, in the University of Pennsylvania; Geologist and Historiographer to the expedition. In 2 vols.

MEMOIRS OF THE COUNTESS DE GENLIS; illustrative of the History of the 18th and 19th centuries. Written by herself.

HISTORY OF MASSACHUSETTS, from July 1775, when Gen. Washington took command of the American army, at Cambridge, to the year 1789 (inclusive), when the federal government was established under the present constitution. By Alden Bradford, author of the volume of the History of Massachusetts, published 1822.

DISCOURSES AND DISSERTATIONS on the scriptural doctrines of Atonement and Sacrifice; and on the principal arguments advanced, and the mode of reasoning employed, by the opponent of those doctrines, as held by the established church; with an appendix. containing some strictures on Mr Belsham's account of the Unitarian scheme, in his review of Mr Wilberforce's treatise; together with Remarks on the version of the New Testament, lately published by the Unitarians. By William Magee, D. D. F. R. S. M. R. I. A. Dean of Cork, Chaplain to his Excellency the Lord Lieutenant of Ireland, late S. F. T. C. and Professor of Mathematics in the university of Dublin. From the London edition, with considerable additions.

TADEUSKUND, the last King of the Lenape.—An Historical Tale.

LUCAS' CABINET ATLAS.

Cummings, Hilliard, & Co.—Boston,

HAVE JUST RECEIVED

A new supply of this very elegant and extensive Atlas, which contains ninety eight maps, besides a plate representing the comparative heights of the principle mountains, and another exhibiting the comparative lengths and magnitudes of the chief rivers of the world.

In every respect this Atlas answers the purpose for which it was intended; it is an excellent compend of maps for practical purposes, being sufficiently copious and minute for all the ordinary inquiries in geography and history. Mr Lucas, we understand, has for several years devoted much of his time to the work, and his well known ability as a geographer and skilful draftsman would be enough to insure its accuracy, were this less evident than it is from internal testimony. As far as his work relates to America, both North and South, and the West Indies, it is particularly valuable; and if we were to select a *single Atlas.* in which our purpose would be to obtain the greatest amount of matter within the smallest space, presented in a commodious form, and at a comparatively moderate expense, we should not hesitate to choose this in preference to any we have seen —*North American Review.*

NEW LAW BOOKS.

Harrison Gray,—No. 72 Washington Street,

HAS FOR SALE,

A Treatise on the Law of Descents, in the several United States of America. By Tapping Reeves, late Chief Justice of Connecticut.

A new edition of Blackstone's Commentaries, in 4 vols. with Archibold and Christian's notes.

Fell on Guarantees, with notes and references to American decisions.

Dane's Abridgment of American Law, complete in 8 vols.

White's View of the jurisdiction and proceedings of the Courts of Probate in Massachusetts.

All the volumes now published of the new American edition of Comyns' Digest,—and a large stock of good editions of old standard works—terms liberal.

ADAM'S LATIN GRAMMAR.

JUST PUBLISHED BY

Cumming's, Hilliard, & Co. and Richardson & Lord.

Adam's Latin Grammar, with some improvements and the following additions; Rules for the right Pronunciation of the Latin Language; a Metrical Key to the Odes of Horace; a list of Latin Authors, arranged according to the different ages of Roman Literature; Tables showing the Value of the various Coins, Weights, and Measures used among the Romans. By B A. Gould, Master of the Public Latin School in Boston. This Edition is adopted by the University at Cambridge, Mass. and is recommended to the use of those preparing for that Seminary.

Extract from the Preface.

The experience of twenty six years, and the united approbation of the most judicious instructers in our country, give ample testimony to the excellence of Adam's Latin Grammar. And it is worthy of remark, that amidst the changes of almost every thing connected with education, this work has maintained its popularity throughout the country since the year 1799, when it was recommended by the University of Cambridge. But several typographical errors, which were adopted from that Edinburgh edition, from which the first American edition was copied, have been transmitted through subsequent editions to the present time with such scrupulous exactness, that they have now become canonized and are received as authority. Besides these, other errors have been creeping in, till a thorough revision of the work has become necessary. At the time this book was first compiled, the state of education in Scotland may have been such as to render the connexion of the Latin with the English necessary, in the manner they were blended by Dr Adam; but that necessity does not exist in this country where English Grammar is separately taught from the more complete systems of Lowth and Murry. For this reason, and because what is not used in a manual becomes a hindrance, the portion pertaining exclusively to English Grammar has been omitted in this edition; and some few additions and alterations have been made which were deemed important. But in all cases where it was practicable, the words of the original grammar have been preserved.

our language. Dr Coffin has ably supplied this defect, by giving to his countrymen a translation of Professor Brera's excellent work; and all we can do for such of our brethren as cannot import either the original or translation, is to lay before them as comprehensive an analysis of Dr Coffin's translation as our limits will permit, and as concentrated a record as literary labour can accomplish."

After copious extracts from the work, the reviewer concludes thus:—

"We have now presented the prominent features of our learned author's work, and that of his able and intelligent translator. We have concentrated into a small space a great mass of useful information, which we hope may prove acceptable to the profession." Those who may wish to be more particularly acquainted with the practical value of this work are referred to a review of it in the 6th volume of the New England Journal of Medicine.

NEW YORK PAPER AND ACCOUNT BOOK WAREHOUSE.

The subscriber has taken, in addition to his store at No. 82 State-street, Boston, that large, convenient, fire-proof building, No. 245 Pearl-street, New-York, where he proposes opening, on a very extensive scale, a Wholesale Stationary, Paper, and Account Book Warehouse, and solicits consignments of every kind of Foreign and Domestic Stationary, Paper, Charts, Nautical Works, School Books and Bibles, or other articles in any way relating thereto. The strictest personal attention will be paid to the interest of the consigner, and the terms as favourable as at any house in the United States.

The advantages of such an establishment, where the manufacturer can deposit his goods and receive a liberal advance; and the purchaser obtain articles of the best qualities at the very lowest prices, and in larger quantities than in any other store in the United States, must be obvious to every person.

All communications to be addressed to the subscriber, at New York.
DAVID FELT.

Refer to Messrs

Cummings, Hilliard & Co.	Bos-	Valentine, Pettingell & Co.	New
William Parker & Co.	ton.	E. Bliss & E. White,	York.
James Vila & Co.		Goddard, Gillet & Co.	

BICHAT'S GENERAL ANATOMY,
FOUR VOLUMES IN THREE,
Lately published

By Richardson & Lord,—Boston.

"We congratulate the medical profession in America, upon the appearance of this work. We are happy in being able to state, that the Government of the Massachusetts Medical Society, with that laudable ardour for the advancement of professional science, for which they have always been highly distinguished, have already added it to the list of those books which candidates are required to have studied before being admitted to an examination for license. In the lectures of our University it had always been recommended with a due regard for its extraordinary merit, but being confined to a foreign language, has been hitherto inaccessible to a large majority of our students. We trust, however, now that it has at length appeared, accurately and faithfully translated, it will become as extensively circulated and read as it deserves to be, and exercise an influence upon medical studies which will not fail to be salutary and beneficial." *New England Medical Journal.*

" We are happy to see this work in an English dress, and especially so, that the labour of translating it has been performed by one of our own countrymen, and by one so well qualified in every point of view, to do justice to it, as Dr Hayward." " The translation of it is every way worthy of confidence, as a faithful picture of the original. We have carefully examined the greater part of this volume in comparison with the French, and have been able to detect scarcely any instances in which there appears to be a deviation from the meaning of the author. It will form certainly a most valuable addition to our medical literature, and will, we trust, be extensively circulated. It has even higher claims upon the attention, than the former works of Bichat, which have been published in this country ; it will richly repay the physician for a careful and diligent study of it, and is not unworthy the perusal of even the general reader." " There is, we think, no medical author so well calculated as Bichat, by the character of his writings, to excite the interest and fix the attention of extra professional readers. He contrives to throw a charm over the most dry and forbidden details, of which no other writer has been capable." *N. A. Review.*

" This admirable work of Bichat is now, we presume, in the hands of every one who makes any pretension to a philosophical study of his profession. The strongest proof of its great merit is, that it has passed through, almost untouched, the severest of all ordeals, the test of time." *Quarterly Journal of Foreign Medicine and Science.*

Also, lately published, in one volume octavo, ADDITIONS TO BICHAT'S GENERAL ANATOMY, By Professor Beclard, of Paris.

" The additions of M. Beclard, whose accurate research and extensive knowledge we cannot too highly praise, are almost as many and as varied as the subjects of the original work." " Such are a few of the interesting details furnished in this able continuation of the Anatomie Generale. We should have been much more particular in our analysis, had we not foreseen that all who possess the original work, and who are interested in the progress of science, will add those additions of M. Beclard to their libraries."—*Journal of Foreign Medicine and Science.*

☞This volume is accompanied with a correct likeness of BICHAT.

COLBURN'S ALGEBRA.

Cummings, Hilliard, & Co.—Boston,

HAVE JUST PUBLISHED

AN INTRODUCTION TO ALGEBRA UPON THE INDUCTIVE METHOD OF INSTRUCTION. By Warren Colburn, author of First Lessons in Arithmetic &c. 1 vol. 12mo. Price $1,25.

Check Out More Titles From HardPress Classics Series In this collection we are offering thousands of classic and hard to find books. This series spans a vast array of subjects – so you are bound to find something of interest to enjoy reading and learning about.

Subjects:
Architecture
Art
Biography & Autobiography
Body, Mind &Spirit
Children & Young Adult
Dramas
Education
Fiction
History
Language Arts & Disciplines
Law
Literary Collections
Music
Poetry
Psychology
Science
…and many more.

Visit us at www.hardpress.net